SEVENTH EDITION

HOW
HUMANS
EVOLVED

SEVENTH EDITION

HOW HUMANS EVOLVED

Robert Boyd and Joan B. Silk

Arizona State University

W. W. NORTON & COMPANY

NEW YORK · LONDON

W. W. Norton & Company has been independent since its founding in 1923, when William Warder Norton and Mary D. Herter Norton first published lectures delivered at the People's Institute, the adult education division of New York City's Cooper Union. The firm soon expanded its program beyond the Institute, publishing books by celebrated academics from America and abroad. By midcentury, the two major pillars of Norton's publishing program—trade books and college texts—were firmly established. In the 1950s, the Norton family transferred control of the company to its employees, and today—with a staff of four hundred and a comparable number of trade, college, and professional titles published each year—W. W. Norton & Company stands as the largest and oldest publishing house owned wholly by its employees.

Editor: Eric Svendsen
Project Editor: Rachel Mayer
Editorial Assistant: Lindsey Thomas
Manuscript Editor: Candace Levy
Managing Editor, College: Marian Johnson
Managing Editor, College Digital Media: Kim Yi
Production Manager: Eric Pier-Hocking
Media Editors: Toni Magyar and Taci Quinn
Marketing Manager, Anthropology: Meredith Leo
Design Director: Rubina Yeh
Designer: Alexandra Charitan
Photo Editor: Evan Luberger
Photo Researcher: Ted Szczepanski
Permissions Manager: Megan Jackson
Permissions Clearing: Bethany Salminen
Composition: Brad Walrod/Kenoza Type, Inc.
Illustrations: Imagineering Art
Manufacturing: Transcontinental Interglobe, Inc.

The text of this book is composed in Century Schoolbook with the display set in Gotham and Trade Gothic.

Permission to use copyrighted material is included in the credits section of this book, which begins on page A15.

Library of Congress Cataloging-in-Publication Data

Boyd, Robert, Ph. D.
    How humans evolved/Robert Boyd, Joan B. Silk, Arizona State University.—Seventh edition.
      pages cm
    Includes bibliographical references and index.
    ISBN 978-0-393-93677-3 (pbk. : alk. paper)
1. Human evolution.   I. Silk, Joan B.   II. Title.
    GN281.B66 2015
    599.93'8—dc23   2014027463

W. W. Norton & Company, Inc., 500 Fifth Avenue, New York, NY 10110-0017

wwnorton.com

W. W. Norton & Company Ltd., Castle House, 75/76 Wells Street, London W1T 3QT

2 3 4 5 6 7 8 9 0

ABOUT THE AUTHORS

ROBERT BOYD

has written widely on evolutionary theory, focusing especially on the evolution of cooperation and the role of culture in human evolution. His book *Culture and the Evolutionary Process* received the J. I. Staley Prize. He is the coauthor of *Not by Genes Alone* and several edited volumes. He has also published numerous articles in scientific journals and edited volumes. He is currently a professor in the School of Human Evolution and Social Change at Arizona State University.

JOAN B. SILK

has conducted extensive research on the social lives of monkeys and apes, including extended fieldwork on chimpanzees at Gombe Stream Reserve in Tanzania and on baboons in Kenya and Botswana. She is also interested in the application of evolutionary thinking to human behavior. She is the coeditor of *The Evolution of Primate Societies* and has published numerous articles in scientific journals and edited volumes. She is currently a professor in the School of Human Evolution and Social Change at Arizona State University.

CONTENTS

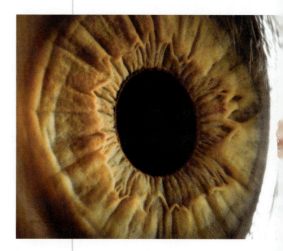

Part Two: Primate Ecology and Behavior

Part Three: The History of the Human Lineage

PREFACE

How Humans Evolved focuses on the processes that have shaped human evolution. This approach reflects our training and research interests. As anthropologists, we are interested in the evolutionary history of our own species, *Homo sapiens*, and the diversity of contemporary human societies. As evolutionary biologists, we study how evolution works to shape the natural world. In this book, we integrate these two perspectives. We use current theoretical and empirical work in evolutionary theory, population genetics, and behavioral ecology to interpret human evolutionary history. We describe the changes that have occurred as the human lineage has evolved, and we consider why these changes may have happened. We try to give life to the creatures that left the bones and made the artifacts that paleontologists and archaeologists painstakingly excavate by focusing on the processes that generate change, create adaptations, and shape bodies and behavior. We also pay serious attention to the role of evolution in shaping contemporary human behavior. There is considerable controversy over evolutionary approaches to human behavior within the social sciences, but we think it is essential to confront these issues openly and clearly. Positive responses to the first six editions of *How Humans Evolved* tell us that many of our colleagues endorse this approach.

One of the problems in writing a textbook about human evolution is that there is considerable debate on many topics. Evolutionary biologists disagree about how new species are formed and how they should be classified; primatologists argue about whether large primate brains are adaptations to social or ecological challenges and whether reciprocity plays an important role in primate societies; paleontologists disagree about the taxonomic relationships among early hominin species and the emergence of modern humans; and those who study modern humans disagree about the meaning and significance of race, the role of culture in shaping human behavior and psychology, the adaptive significance of many aspects of modern human behavior, and a number of other things. Sometimes multiple interpretations of the same data can be defended; in other cases, the facts seem contradictory. Textbook writers can confront this kind of uncertainty in two different ways. They can weigh the evidence, present the ideas that best fit the available evidence, and ignore the alternatives. Or they can present opposing ideas, evaluate the logic underlying each idea, and explain how existing data support each of the positions. We chose the second alternative, at the risk of complicating the text and frustrating readers looking for simple answers. We made this choice because we believe that this approach is essential for understanding how science works. Students need to see how theories are developed, how data are accumulated, and how theory and data interact to shape our ideas about how the world works. We hope that students remember this long after they have forgotten many of the facts that they will learn in this book.

New in the Seventh Edition

The study of human evolution is a dynamic field. No sooner do we complete one edition of this book than researchers make new discoveries that fundamentally change our view of human evolution. New developments in human evolutionary studies require regular updates of the textbook. Although we have made a number of changes throughout the book to reflect new findings, clarify concepts, and improve the flow of the text, readers familiar with prior editions will find the most substantive changes in Part Three, "The History of the Human Lineage" and Part Four, "Evolution and Modern Humans."

As usual, new fossil finds have been incorporated into Part Three. For example, Chapter 10 includes a more extensive description of the morphology and diet of *Australopithecus sediba*, and Chapter 12 includes a description of a very small brained hominin from Dmanisi. Chapter 13 has been extensively revised to reflect new insights from genetic analyses of modern peoples and extinct hominin species. We now have high-resolution genomes for Neanderthals and for Denisovans, and these data provide rich information about human evolution in the later Pleistocene. Rapidly accumulating archaeological evidence indicates that modern human behavior appeared in Africa more than 70,000 years ago and then spread across southern Asia, and finally arrived in Europe about 40,000 years ago. Chapter 13 now reflects this temporal sequence; it begins with Africa, and then moves across Asia and Europe.

In Part Four, we have made a number of important changes. In Chapter 14, we draw on findings emerging from comparative studies of the genomes of humans and great apes that measure the magnitude of genetic differences between modern humans and great apes and give us some insight about the functional signficance of these differences. Then, this edition includes an entirely new Chapter 16, which focuses on the question of how humans have come to be so different from all other organisms in the planet. We argue that human uniqueness is the joint product of the fact that our cognitive abilities exceed those of other organisms, we are able to orchestrate cooperation with nonrelatives on a much larger scale than other organisms, and we rely more heavily on culturally acquired information than other organisms do. Users will find that most of the material that appeared in the previous edition's Chapter 16 has been condensed into Chapter 15.

We wrote this book with undergraduates in mind and have designed a number of features to help students use the book effectively. We have retained the "key idea" statements (now printed in blue-green type), and we recommend that students use these key ideas to keep track of important concepts and facts and to structure their review of the material. Important terms that may be unfamiliar are set in boldface type when they first appear. Readers can find definitions for these terms in the Glossary. Discussion questions appear at the end of each chapter. These questions are meant to help students synthesize material presented in the text. Some of the questions are designed to help students review factual material, but most are intended to help students to think about the processes or theoretical principles they have learned. Some questions are open-ended and meant to encourage students to apply their own values and judgment to the material presented in the text. Students tell us that they find these questions useful as they attempt to master the material and prepare for exams. The list of references for further reading at the end of each chapter provides a starting point for students who want to delve more deeply into the material covered in that chapter.

The book is richly illustrated with photographs, diagrams, figures, and graphs. These illustrations provide visual information to complement the text. For some subjects, a picture is clearly worth a thousand words—no amount of description can enable students to conjure up an image of an aye-aye or appreciate how much more similar the australopith pelvis is to the modern human pelvis than to the chimpanee pelvis. The diagrams of evolutionary processes that appear in Part One are designed to help students visualize how natural selection works. The figures depicting the hominin fossils are drawn to scale, so each is presented in the same orientation and to the same scale. This should help students compare one hominin specimen with another. We have often been advised that you cannot put graphs in an undergraduate textbook, but we think that the graphs help students understand the evidence more fully. For us, it is easier to remember data that are portrayed graphically than to recall verbal descriptions of results.

Ancillary Materials for Teaching and Learning

Visit wwnorton.com/instructors to download resources.

InQuizitive

InQuizitive is a formative, adaptive learning tool that improves student understanding of important learning objectives by personalizing quiz questions for each student. Engaging, game-like elements built into InQuizitive motivate students as they learn.

InQuizitive includes a variety of question types that test student knowledge in different ways and enrich the user experience. Performance-specific feedback creates teaching moments that help students understand their mistakes and get back on the right track. Animations, videos, and other resources built into InQuizitive allow students to review core concepts as they answer questions.

InQuizitive is easy to use. Instructors can assign InQuizitive out of the box or use intuitive tools to customize the learning objectives they want students to work on. Students can access InQuizitive on computers, tablets, and smartphones, making it easy to study on the go.

Student access codes to InQuizitive can be packaged with your text or purchased as a standalone. Contact your W. W. Norton sales rep, or visit www.wwnorton.com to learn more.

Student Access Codes

If students need to purchase an access code for InQuizitive, they can purchase or order an access card at their local college bookstore. Or, immediate online access can be purchased at http://inquizitive.wwnorton.com/evolve7.

Coursepacks

Available at no cost to professors or students, Norton Coursepacks for online or hybrid courses are available in a variety of formats, including Blackboard, WebCT, Moodle, Canvas, Angel, and D2L. With just a simple download from our instructor's website, instructors can bring high-quality Norton digital media into a new or existing online course (no extra student passwords required). Content includes new and engaging visual questions especially designed for the distance or blended learning environment. Norton animations and streaming videos are also made available to integrate in your classes. Of course, test banks, quizzes, and student study questions are all available for your use. All visual materials in our Coursepacks are ADA compliant.

Physical Anthropology in Action Videos

This new streaming videos service is available through Norton Coursepacks and the Norton instructor website. A selection of one- to seven-minute film clips come from across the discipline but with an emphasis on paleoanthropology and primatology, making it easy for instructors to illustrate key concepts and spark classroom discussion. Links are provided for easy cutting and pasting into your online course, campus LMS, syllabus, handouts, or in-class presentation. All videos stream from Norton servers, so are ad free and reliable. All videos are ADA compliant

Physical Anthropology in Action Animations

New animations of key concepts are available through Norton Coursepacks or are available to download or stream from the Norton instructor website. Animations are brief and easy to use and great for explaining concepts either in class or in a distance learning environment. All animations are ADA compliant.

PowerPoint Package and PowerPoint Update Service

Prepared by Jeremy DeSilva of Boston University.

The PowerPoint slides for this edition retain their richly illustrated format and extensive lecture notes. Designed to cover the core material in a highly visual way

Videos with teaching resources are available streaming from W. W. Norton for use in your classes (either in person or online) or through your campus LMS.

A selection of animations was created for this text. They are available either streaming from W. W. Norton or on our instructor DVD.

using photography and art from the text, these PowerPoint slides bring the concepts in each chapter to life with additional photography and design. These slides also include a lecture script in the notes field. And to help cover what is new in the discipline, each semester we will provide an additional set of updated lectures, notes, and assessment material covering current and breaking research. This material is available for download at the instructor's resource site.

JPEGs of Art

To help you improve your class, JPEGs of all the art and photographs are available for download from the Norton instructor website.

Instructor's Manual

Prepared by Kathleen Droesch, Suffolk County Community College; Ashley Hurst, University of Texas at San Antonio; Greg Laden, Century College; Mary Kelaita, University of Texas at San Antonio; and LeAndra Bridgeman.

The Instructor's Manual provides an overview of each chapter's key concepts with additional explanation for topics that students may find more challenging as well as answers to the end-of-chapter Study Questions found in the text. Available for download at the Norton instructor website.

Test Bank

Prepared by Kathleen Droesch, Suffolk County Community College; Ashley Hurst, University of Texas at San Antonio; Greg Laden, Century College; Mary Kelaita, University of Texas at San Antonio; and LeAndra Bridgeman.

The Test Bank offers teachers approximately 60 multiple-choice and essay questions (organized by difficulty level and topic) for each chapter. New to the this edition are updated questions in every chapter, Bloom's knowledge types, and learning objectives keyed to the textbook for every question. Available in downloadable formats in the Exam View Assessment Suite, as a PDF, and in formats compatible with MS Word and other word processors.

Ebook: Same Great Book, a Fraction of the Price

An affordable and convenient alternative, Norton ebooks retain the content and design of the print book and allow students to highlight and take notes with ease, print chapters as needed, and search the text.

Acknowledgments

Over the last 15 years, many of our colleagues have provided new information, helpful comments, and critical perspectives that have enriched this book. We are grateful for all those who have responded to our requests for photographs, clarifications, references, and opinions. For the Seventh Edition we thank Curtis Merean for reviewing Chapter 13 and Kim Hill for reading Chapter 16. For the Sixth Edition, we thank Christopher Kirk for reviewing Chapter 5, Leanne Nash for reviewing Chapters 4 and 8, Roberto Delgano for reviewing Chapters 6 and 7, and Carol Ward and Jeremy DeSilva for help with Chapter 9. For the Fourth Edition, Laura MacLatchy provided help with the Miocene apes in Chapter 10, Dan Fessler and David Schmitt gave us access to material for Chapter 16, and Kermyt Anderson dug up original data for figures in Chapter 17. Steven Reznik reviewed our discussion of the rapid evolution of placentas in the minnows he studies and kindly provided an image. Leslie Aiello helped with our discussion of hominin developmental rates. For help with the Third Edition, we thank Carola Borries, Colin Chapman, Richard Klein, Cheryl Knott, Sally McBrearty, Ryne Palombit, Steve Pinker, Karin Stronswold, and Bernard Wood. For help with the Second Edition, we also thank Tom Plummer, Daniel Povinelli, Beverly Strassman, and Patricia Wright. We remain grateful for the help we received for the First Edition from Leslie Aiello, Monique Borgerhoff Mulder, Scott Carroll, Dorothy Cheney, Glenn Conroy, Martin Daly, Robin Dunbar, Lynn Fairbanks, Sandy Harcourt, Kristin Hawkes, Richard Klein, Phyllis Lee, Nancy Levine, Jeff Long, Joseph Manson,

Henry McHenry, John Mitani, Jocelyn Peccei, Susan Perry, Steve Pinker, Tom Plummer, Tab Rasmussen, Mark Ridley, Alan Rogers, Robert Seyfarth, Frank Sulloway, Don Symons, Alan Walker, Tim White, and Margo Wilson.

A number of people reviewed all or parts of previous editions of this text. We thank the following: Stephanie Anestis, Thad Bartlett, AnnMarie Beasley, Rene Bobe, Barry Bogin, Doug Broadfield, Bryce Carlson, Joyce Chan, Margaret Clarke, Julie Cormack, Douglas Crews, Roberto Delgado, Arthur Durband, Charles Edwards, Donald Gaff, Renee Garcia, Susan Gibson, Peter Gray, Mark Griffin, Corinna Guenther, Sharon Gursky, Kim Hill, Andrew Irvine, Trine Johansen, Andrea Jones, Barbara King, Richard Klein, Kristin Krueger, Darrell La Lone, Clark Larsen, Lynette Leidy, Joseph Lorenz, Laura MacLatchy, Lara McCormick, Elizabeth Miller, Shannon Mills, John Mitani, Peer Moore-Jansen, M. J. Mosher, Martin Muller, Marilyn Norconk, Ann Palkovich, Amanda Wolcott Paskey, James Paterson, Michael Pietrusewsky, Barbara Quimby, Ulrich Reichard, Michael Robertson, Michael Schillaci, Liza Shapiro, Eric Smith, Craig Stanford, Horst Steklis, Joan Stevenson, Mark Stoneking, Rebecca Storey, Rebecca Stumpf, Roger Sullivan, Yanina Valdos, Timothy Weaver, Elizabeth Weiss, Jill Wenrick, and Patricia Wright. Several anonymous reviewers also read previous editions and provided suggestions. Although we are certain that we have not satisfied all those who read and commented on parts of the book, we found all of the comments to be very helpful as we revised the text.

Richard Klein provided us with many exceptional drawings of fossils that appear in Part Three—an act of generosity that we continue to appreciate. We also give special thanks to Neville Agnew and the Getty Conservation Institute for granting us permission to use images of the Laetoli conservation project for the cover of the Second Edition.

Many users of the book have commented on the quality of the illustrations. For this we must thank the many friends and colleagues who allowed us to use their photographs: Bob Bailey, Carola Borries, Colin Chapman, Nick Blurton Jones, Sue Boinski, Monique Borgerhoff Mulder, Richard Byrne, Scott Carroll, Marina Cords, Diane Doran, Robert Gibson, Peter Grant, Kim Hill, Kevin Hunt, Lynne Isbell, Charles Janson, Alex Kacelnik and the Behavioral Ecology Research Group, Nancy Levine, Carlão Limeira, Joe Manson, Frank Marlowe, Laura MacLatchy, Bill McGrew, John Mitani, Claudio Nogueira, Ryne Palombit, Susan Perry, Craig Stanford, Karen Strier, Alan Walker, Katherine West, and John Yellen. The National Museums of Kenya kindly allowed us to reprint a number of photographs.

We also acknowledge the thousands of students and dozens of teaching assistants at our previous university UCLA who have used various versions of this material over the years. Student evaluations of the original lecture notes, the first draft of the text, and the first six editions were helpful as we revised and rewrote various parts of the book. The teaching assistants helped us identify many parts of the text that needed to be clarified, corrected, or reconsidered.

We thank all the people at Norton who helped us produce this book, particularly our outstanding editors Leo Wiegman, Pete Lesser, Aaron Javsicas, and Eric Svendsen. We are also grateful to our excellent editorial assistant, Lindsey Thomas. We would also like to thank all of those who saw the book through the production process, including Eric Pier-Hocking, Rachel Mayer, Evan Luberger, Ted Szczepanki, and Laura Musich. And special thanks to Kathleen Droesch, Ashley Hurst, Greg Laden, Mary Kelaita, Elizabeth Erhart, Christina Grassi, Tracy Betsinger, Jeremy DeSilva, LeAndra Bridgeman, Heather Worne, Renee Garcia, Timothy Weaver, and Lauri Reitsema for helping create and test the instructor support package in this and recent editions.

WHY STUDY HUMAN EVOLUTION?

Origin of man now proved—Metaphysics must flourish—He who understand baboon would do more toward metaphysics than Locke.

—*Charles Darwin, M Notebook, August 1838*

In 1838, Charles Darwin discovered the principle of evolution by natural selection and revolutionized our understanding of the living world. Darwin was 28 years old, and it was just two years since he had returned from a five-year voyage around the world as a naturalist on the HMS *Beagle* (**Figure 1**). Darwin's observations and experiences during the journey had convinced him that biological species change through time and that new species arise by the transformation of existing ones, and he was avidly searching for an explanation of how these processes worked.

In late September of the same year, Darwin read Thomas Malthus's *Essay on the Principle of Population*, in which Malthus (**Figure 2**) argued that human populations invariably grow until they are limited by starvation, poverty, and disease. Darwin realized that Malthus's logic also applied to the natural world, and this intuition inspired the conception of his theory of evolution by natural selection. In the intervening century and a half, Darwin's theory has been augmented by discoveries in genetics and amplified by studies of the evolution of many types of organisms. It is now the foundation of our understanding of life on Earth.

This book is about human evolution, and we will spend a lot of time explaining how natural selection and other evolutionary processes have shaped the human species. Before we begin, it is important to consider why you should care about this topic. Many of you will be working through this book as a requirement for an undergraduate class in biological anthropology and will read the book in order to earn a good grade. As instructors of a class like this ourselves, we approve of this motive. However, there is a much better reason to care about the processes that have shaped human evolution: understanding how humans evolved is the key to understanding why people look and behave the way they do.

The profound implications of evolution for our understanding of humankind were apparent to Darwin from the beginning. We know this today because he kept notebooks in which he recorded his private thoughts about various topics. The quotation that begins this prologue is from the *M Notebook*, begun in July 1838, in which Darwin jotted down his ideas about humans, psychology, and the philosophy of science. In the nineteenth century, metaphysics involved the study of the human mind. Thus Darwin was saying that because he believed humans evolved from a creature something like a baboon, it followed that an understanding of the mind of a baboon would contribute more to an understanding of the human mind than would all of the works of the great English philosopher John Locke.

Darwin's reasoning was simple. Every species on this planet has arisen through the same evolutionary processes. These processes determine why organisms are the way they are by shaping their morphology, physiology, and behavior. The traits that characterize the human species are the result of the same evolutionary processes that created all other species. If we understand these processes and the conditions under which the human species evolved, then we will have the basis for a scientific understanding of human nature. Trying to comprehend the human mind without an understanding of human evolution is, as Darwin wrote in another notebook that October, "like puzzling at astronomy without mechanics." By this, Darwin meant that his theory of evolution could play the same role in biology and psychology that Isaac Newton's laws of motion had played in astronomy. For thousands of years, stargazers, priests, philosophers, and mathematicians had struggled to understand the motions of the planets without success. Then, in the late 1600s, Newton discovered the laws of mechanics and showed how all of the intricacies in the dance of the planets could be explained by the action of a few simple processes (**Figure 3**).

In the same way, understanding the processes of evolution enables us to account for the stunning sophistication of organic design and the diversity of life and to understand why people are the way they are. As a consequence, understanding how natural selection and other evolutionary processes shaped the human species is relevant to all of the academic disciplines that are concerned with human beings. This vast intellectual domain includes medicine, psychology, the social sciences, and even the humanities. Beyond academia, understanding our own evolutionary history can help us answer many questions that confront us in everyday life. Some of these questions are relatively trivial: Why do we sweat when hot or nervous? Why do we crave salt, sugar, and fat, even though large amounts of these substances cause disease (**Figure 4**)? Why are we better marathon runners than mountain climbers? Other questions are more profound: Why do only women nurse their babies? Why do we grow old and eventually die? Why do people look so different around the world? As you will see, evolutionary theory provides answers or insights about all of these questions. Aging, which eventually leads to death, is an evolved characteristic of humans and most other creatures. Understanding how natural selection shapes the life histories of organisms tells us why we are mortal, why our life span is about 70 years, and why other species live shorter lives. In an age of horrific ethnic conflicts and growing respect for multicultural diversity, we are constantly reminded of the variation within the human species. Evolutionary analyses tell us that genetic differences between human groups are relatively minor and that our notions of race and ethnicity are culturally constructed categories, not biological realities.

FIGURE 1

When this portrait of Charles Darwin was painted, he was about 30 years old. He had just returned from his voyage on the HMS *Beagle* and was still busy organizing his notes, drawings, and vast collections of plants and animals.

FIGURE 2

Thomas Malthus was the author of *An Essay on the Principle of Population*, a book Charles Darwin read in 1838 that profoundly influenced the development of his theory of evolution by natural selection.

FIGURE 3

Sir Isaac Newton discovered the laws of celestial mechanics, a body of theory that resolved age-old mysteries about the movements of the planets.

FIGURE 4

A strong appetite for sugar, fat, and salt may have been adaptive for our ancestors, who had little access to these foods. We have inherited these appetites and now have easy access to sugar, fat, and salt. As a consequence, many of us suffer from obesity, high blood pressure, diabetes, and heart disease.

FIGURE 5

One of the great debates in Western thought focuses on the essential elements of human nature. Are people basically moral beings corrupted by society or fundamentally amoral creatures socialized by cultural conventions, social strictures, and religious beliefs?

All of these questions deal with the evolution of the human body. However, understanding evolution is also an important part of our understanding of human behavior and the human mind. The claim that understanding evolution will help us understand contemporary human behavior is much more controversial than the claim that it will help us understand how human bodies work. But it should not be. The human brain is an evolved organ of great complexity, just like the endocrine system, the nervous system, and all of the other components of the human body that regulate our behavior. Understanding evolution helps us understand our mind and behavior because evolutionary processes forged the brain that controls human behavior, just as they forged the brain of the chimpanzee and the salamander.

One of the great debates in Western thought centers on the essence of human nature. One view is that people are basically honest, generous, and cooperative creatures who are corrupted by an immoral economic and social order. The opposing view is that we are fundamentally amoral, egocentric beings whose antisocial impulses are held in check by social pressures. This question turns up everywhere. Some people believe that children are little barbarians who are civilized only through sustained parental effort; others think that children are gentle beings who are socialized into competitiveness and violence by exposure to negative influences like toy guns and violent TV programs (**Figure 5**). The same dichotomy underpins much political and economic thought. Economists believe that people are rational and selfish, but other social scientists, particularly anthropologists and sociologists, question and sometimes reject this assumption. We can raise an endless list of interesting questions about human nature: Does the fact that, in most societies, women rear children and men make war mean that men and women differ in their innate predispositions? Why do men typically find younger women attractive? Why do some people neglect and abuse their children, while others adopt and lovingly raise children who are not their own?

Understanding human evolution does not reveal the answers to all of these questions or even provide a complete answer to any one of them. As we will see, however, it can provide useful insights about all of them. An evolutionary approach does not imply that behavior is genetically determined or that learning and culture are unimportant. In fact, we will argue that learning and culture play crucial roles in human behavior. Behavioral differences among peoples living in different times and places result mainly from flexible adjustments to different social and environmental conditions. Understanding evolution is useful precisely because it helps us understand why humans respond in different ways to different conditions.

Overview of the Book

Humans are the product of organic evolution. By this we mean that there is an unbroken chain of descent that connects every living human being to a bipedal, apelike creature that walked through the tall grasses of the African savanna 3 million years ago (mya); to a monkeylike animal that clambered through the canopy of great tropical forests covering much of the world 35 mya; and, finally, to a small, egg-laying, insect-eating mammal that scurried about at night during the age of the dinosaurs, 100 mya. To understand what we are now, you have to understand how this transformation took place. We tell this story in four parts.

Part One: How Evolution Works

More than a century of hard work has given us a good understanding of how evolution works. The transformation of apes into humans involved the assembly of many new, complex adaptations. For example, in order for early humans to walk upright on two legs, there had to be coordinated changes in many parts of their bodies, including their feet, legs, pelvis, backbone, and inner ear. Understanding how natural selection gives rise to such complex structures and why the genetic system plays a crucial role in this process is essential for understanding how new species arise. Understanding these processes also allows us to reconstruct the history of life from the characteristics of contemporary organisms.

Part Two: Primate Ecology and Behavior

In the second part of the book, we consider how evolution has shaped the behavior of nonhuman primates—an exercise that helps us understand human evolution in two ways. First, humans are members of the primate order: we are more similar to other primates, particularly the great apes, than we are to wolves, raccoons, or other mammals. Studying how primate morphology and behavior are affected by ecological conditions helps us determine what our ancestors might have been like and how they may have been transformed by natural selection. Second, we study primates because they are an extremely diverse order and are particularly variable in their social behavior. Some are solitary, others live in pair-bonded groups, and some live in large groups that contain many adult females and males. Data derived from studies of these species help us understand how social behavior is molded by natural selection. We can then use these insights to interpret the hominin fossil record and the behavior of contemporary people (**Figure 6**).

Part Three: The History of the Human Lineage

General theoretical principles are not sufficient to understand the history of any lineage, including our own. The transformation of a shrewlike creature into the human species involved many small steps, and each step was affected by specific environmental and biological circumstances. To understand human evolution, we have to reconstruct the actual history of the human lineage and the environmental context in which these events occurred. Much of this history is chronicled in the fossil record. These bits of mineralized bone, painstakingly collected and reassembled by paleontologists, document the sequence of organisms that link early mammals to modern humans. Complementary work by geologists, biologists, and archaeologists allows us to reconstruct the environments in which the human lineage evolved (**Figure 7**).

Part Four: Evolution and Modern Humans

Finally, we turn our attention to modern humans and ask why we are the way we are. Why is the human species so variable? How do we acquire our behavior? How has evolution shaped human psychology and behavior? How do we choose our mates? Why do people commit infanticide? Why have humans succeeded in inhabiting every corner of the Earth when other species have more limited ranges? We will explain how an understanding of evolutionary theory and a knowledge of human evolutionary history provide a basis for addressing questions like these.

The history of the human lineage is a great story, but it is not a simple one. The relevant knowledge is drawn from many disciplines in the natural sciences, such as physics, chemistry, biology, and geology, and from the social sciences, mainly anthropology, psychology, and economics. Learning this material is an ambitious task, but it offers a very satisfying reward. The better you understand the processes that have shaped human evolution and the historical events that took place in the human lineage, the better you will understand how we came to be and why we are the way we are.

FIGURE 6

We will draw on information about the behavior of living primates, such as this chimpanzee, to understand how behavior is molded by evolutionary processes, to interpret the hominin fossil record, and to draw insights about the behavior of contemporary humans.

FIGURE 7

Fossils painstakingly excavated from many sites in Africa, Europe, and Asia provide us with a record of our history as a species. Two million years ago in Africa, there were a number of apelike species that walked bipedally but still had ape-size brains and apelike developmental patterns. These are the fossilized remains of *Homo habilis,* a species that some think is ancestral to modern humans.

1

HOW EVOLUTION WORKS

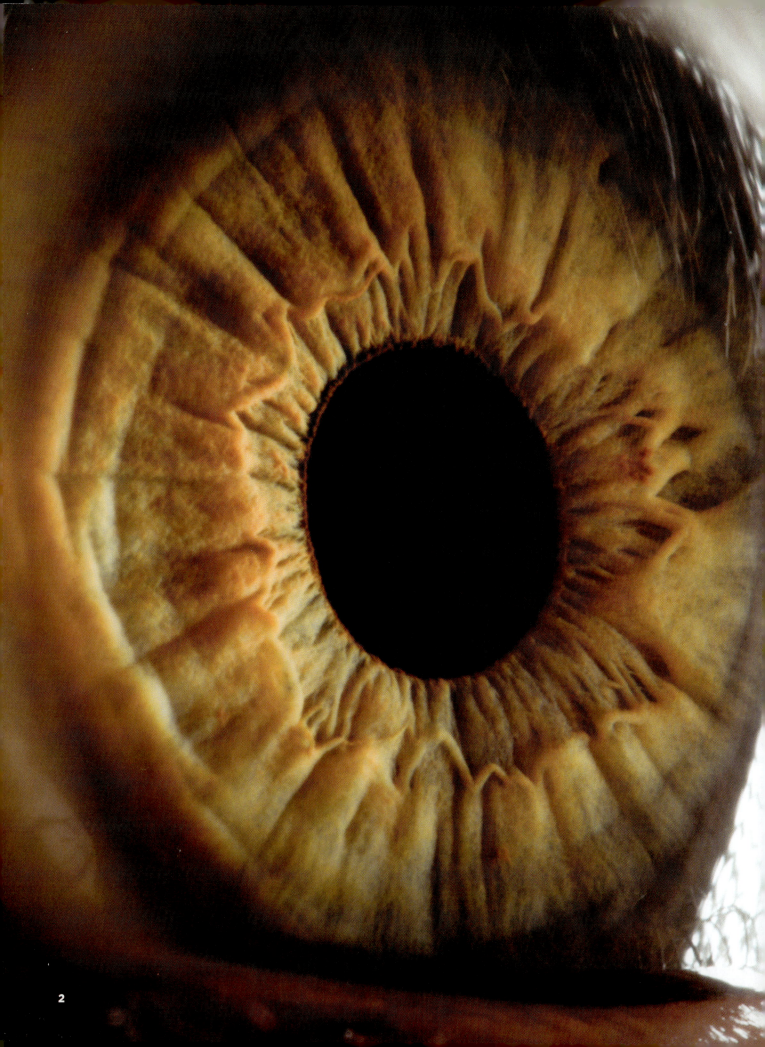

CHAPTER OBJECTIVES

By the end of this chapter you should be able to

- Describe why our modern understanding of the diversity of life is based on the ideas of Charles Darwin.

- Explain how competition, variation, and heritability lead to evolution by natural selection.

- See why natural selection sometimes causes species to become better adapted to their environments.

- Understand why natural selection can produce change or cause species to remain the same over time.

- Explain how natural selection can produce very complex adaptations like the human eye.

- See why natural selection usually works at the level of the individual, not the level of the group or species.

ADAPTATION BY NATURAL SELECTION

Explaining Adaptation before Darwin

Darwin's Theory of Adaptation

The Evolution of Complex Adaptations

Rates of Evolutionary Change

Darwin's Difficulties Explaining Variation

Explaining Adaptation before Darwin

Animals and plants are adapted to their conditions in subtle and marvelous ways. Even the casual observer can see that organisms are well suited to their circumstances. For example, fish are clearly designed for life under water, and certain flowers are designed to be pollinated by particular species of insects. More careful study reveals that organisms are more than just suited to their environments: They are complex machines, made up of many exquisitely constructed components, or **adaptations**, that interact to help the organism survive and reproduce.

The human eye provides a good example of an adaptation. Eyes are amazingly useful: They allow us to move confidently through the environment, to locate critical resources like food and mates, and to avoid dangers like predators and cliffs. Eyes are extremely complex structures made up of many interdependent parts (**Figure 1.1**). Light enters the eye through a transparent opening, then passes through a diaphragm called the iris, which regulates the amount of light

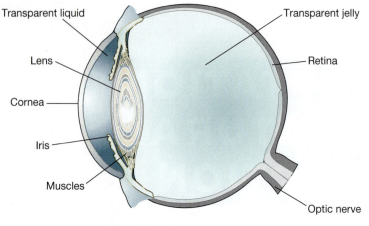

FIGURE 1.1

A cross section of the human eye.

Transparent liquid
Lens
Cornea
Iris
Muscles
Transparent jelly
Retina
Optic nerve

entering the eye and allows the eye to function in a wide range of lighting conditions. The light then passes through a lens that projects a focused image on the retina on the back surface of the eye. Several different kinds of light-sensitive cells then convert the image into nerve impulses that encode information about spatial patterns of color and intensity. These cells are more sensitive to light than the best photographic film. The detailed construction of each of these parts of the eye makes sense in terms of the eye's function: seeing. If we probed into any of these parts, we would see that they, too, are made of complicated, interacting components whose structure is understandable in terms of their function.

Differences between human eyes and the eyes of other animals make sense in terms of the types of problems each creature faces. Consider, for example, the eyes of fish and humans (**Figure 1.2**). The lens in the eyes of humans and other terrestrial mammals is much like a camera lens; it is shaped like a squashed football and has the same index of refraction (a measure of light-bending capacity) throughout. In contrast, the lens in fish eyes is a sphere located at the center of the curvature of the retina, and the index of refraction of the lens increases smoothly from the surface of the lens to the center. It turns out that this kind of lens, called a spherical gradient lens, provides a sharp image over a full 180° visual field, a very short focal length, and high light-gathering power—all desirable properties. Terrestrial creatures like us cannot use this design because light is bent when it passes from the air through the cornea (the transparent cover of the pupil), and this fact constrains the design of the remaining lens elements. In contrast, light is not bent when it passes from water through the cornea of aquatic animals, and the design of their eyes takes advantage of this fact.

Before Darwin there was no scientific explanation for the fact that organisms are well adapted to their circumstances.

As many nineteenth-century thinkers were keenly aware, complex adaptations like the eye demand a different kind of explanation than other natural objects. This is not simply because adaptations are complex, since many other complicated objects exist in nature. Adaptations require a special kind of explanation because they are complex in a particular, highly improbable way. For example, the Grand Canyon, with its maze of delicate towers intricately painted in shades of pink and gold, is byzantine in its complexity (**Figure 1.3**). Given a different geological history, however, the Grand Canyon might be quite different—different towers in different hues—yet we would still recognize

FIGURE 1.2

(a) Like those of other terrestrial mammals, human eyes have more than one light-bending element. A ray of light entering the eye (*dashed lines*) is bent first as it moves from the air to the cornea and then again as it enters and leaves the lens. (b) In contrast, fish eyes have a single lens that bends the light throughout its volume. As a result, fish eyes have a short focal length and high light-gathering power.

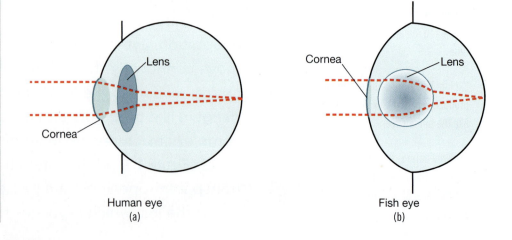

Lens
Cornea
Human eye
(a)

Cornea
Lens
Fish eye
(b)

it as a canyon. The particular arrangement of painted towers of the Grand Canyon is improbable, but the existence of a spectacular canyon with a complex array of colorful cliffs in the dry sandstone country of the American Southwest is not unexpected at all; and in fact, wind and water produced many such canyons in this region. In contrast, any substantial changes in the structure of the eye would prevent the eye from functioning, and then we would no longer recognize it as an eye. If the cornea were opaque or the lens on the wrong side of the retina, then the eye would not transmit visual images to the brain. It is highly improbable that natural processes would randomly bring together bits of matter having the detailed structure of the eye because only an infinitesimal fraction of all arrangements of matter would be recognizable as a functioning eye.

In Darwin's day, most people were not troubled by this problem because they believed that adaptations were the result of divine creation. In fact, the theologian William Paley used a discussion of the human eye to argue for the existence of God in his book *Natural Theology,* published in 1802. Paley argued that the eye is clearly *designed* for seeing; and where there is design in the natural world, there certainly must be a heavenly designer.

Although most scientists of the day were satisfied with this reasoning, a few, including Charles Darwin, sought other explanations.

Darwin's Theory of Adaptation

Charles Darwin was expected to become a doctor or clergyman, but instead he revolutionized science.

Charles Darwin was born into a well-to-do, intellectual, and politically liberal family in England. Like many prosperous men of his time, Darwin's father wanted his son to become a doctor. But after failing at the prestigious medical school at the University of Edinburgh, Charles went on to Cambridge University, resigned to becoming a country parson. He was, for the most part, an undistinguished student—much more interested in tramping through the fields around Cambridge in search of beetles than in studying Greek and mathematics. After graduation, one of Darwin's botany professors, John Stevens Henslow, provided him with a chance to pursue his passion for natural history as a naturalist on the HMS *Beagle.*

The *Beagle* was a Royal Navy vessel whose charter was to spend two to three years mapping the coast of South America and then to return to London, perhaps by circling the globe (**Figure 1.4**). Darwin's father forbade him to go, preferring that he get serious about his career in the church, but Darwin's uncle (and future father-in-law) Josiah Wedgwood II intervened. The voyage turned out to be the turning point in Darwin's life. His work during the voyage established his reputation as a skilled naturalist. His observations of living and fossil animals ultimately convinced him that plants and animals sometimes change slowly through time and that such evolutionary change is the key to understanding how new species come into existence. This view was rejected by most scientists of the time and was considered heretical by the general public.

Darwin's Postulates

Darwin's theory of adaptation follows from three postulates: (1) the struggle for existence, (2) variation in fitness, and (3) the inheritance of variation.

In 1838, shortly after the *Beagle* returned to London, Darwin formulated a simple mechanistic explanation for *how* species change through time. His theory follows from three postulates:

FIGURE 1.3

Although an impressive geological feature, the Grand Canyon is much less remarkable in its complexity than the eye.

FIGURE 1.4

The HMS *Beagle* in Beagle Channel on the southern coast of Tierra del Fuego.

(a)

(b)

FIGURE 1.5

(a) The islands of the Galápagos, which are located off the coast of Ecuador, house a variety of unique species of plants and animals. (b) Cactus finches from Charles Darwin's *The Zoology of the Voyage of H.M.S. Beagle* (1840).

1. The ability of a population to expand is infinite, but the ability of any environment to support populations is always finite.

2. Organisms within populations vary, and this variation affects the ability of individuals to survive and reproduce.

3. This variation is transmitted from parents to offspring.

Darwin's first postulate means that populations grow until they are checked by the dwindling supply of resources in the environment. Darwin referred to the resulting competition for resources as "the struggle for existence." For example, animals require food to grow and reproduce. When food is plentiful, animal populations grow until their numbers exceed the local food supply. Because resources are always finite, it follows that not all individuals in a population will be able to survive and reproduce. According to the second postulate, some individuals will possess traits that enable them to survive and reproduce more successfully (producing more offspring) than others in the same environment. The third postulate holds that if the advantageous traits are inherited by offspring, then these traits will become more common in succeeding generations. Thus traits that confer advantages in survival and reproduction are retained in the population, and traits that are disadvantageous disappear. When Darwin coined the term **natural selection** for this process, he was making a deliberate analogy to the artificial selection practiced by animal and plant breeders of his day. A much more apt term would be "evolution by variation and selective retention."

An Example of Adaptation by Natural Selection

Contemporary observations of Darwin's finches provide a particularly good example of how natural selection produces adaptations.

In his autobiography, first published in 1887, Darwin claimed that the curious pattern of adaptations he observed among the several species of finches that live on the Galápagos Islands off the coast of Ecuador—now referred to as "Darwin's finches"—was crucial in the development of his ideas about evolution (**Figure 1.5**). Some evidence suggests that Darwin was actually confused about the Galápagos finches during his visit, and they played little role in his discovery of natural selection. Nonetheless, Darwin's finches hold a special place in the minds of most biologists.

Peter and Rosemary Grant, biologists at Princeton University, conducted a landmark study of the ecology and evolution of one particular species of Darwin's finches

FIGURE 1.6

The medium ground finch, *Geospiza fortis,* uses its beak to crack open seeds.

(a)   (b)

FIGURE 1.7

Daphne Major (a) in March 1976, after a year of good rains, and (b) in March 1977, after a year of very little rain.

on one of the Galápagos Islands. The study is remarkable because the Grants were able to directly document how Darwin's three postulates led to evolutionary change. The island, Daphne Major, is home to the medium ground finch (*Geospiza fortis*), a small bird that subsists mainly by eating seeds (**Figure 1.6**). The Grants and their colleagues caught, measured, weighed, and banded nearly every finch on the island each year of their study—some 1,500 birds in all. They also kept track of critical features of the birds' environment, such as the distribution of seeds of various sizes, and they observed the birds' behavior.

A few years into the Grants' study, a severe drought struck Daphne Major (**Figure 1.7**). During the drought, plants produced many fewer seeds, and the finches soon depleted the stock of small, soft, easily processed seeds, leaving only large, hard, difficult-to-process seeds (**Figure 1.8**). The bands on the birds' legs enabled the Grants to track the fate of individual birds during the drought, and the regular measurements that they had made of the birds allowed them to compare the traits of birds that survived the drought with the traits of those that perished. The Grants also kept detailed records of the environmental conditions, which allowed them to determine how the drought affected the finch's habitat. It was this vast body of data that enabled the Grants to document the action of natural selection among the finches of Daphne Major.

The Grants' data show how the processes identified in Darwin's postulates lead to adaptation.

The events on Daphne Major embodied all three of Darwin's postulates. First, the supply of food on the island was not sufficient to feed the entire population, and many finches did not survive the drought. From the beginning of the drought in 1976 until the rains came nearly two years later, the population of medium ground finches on Daphne Major declined from 1,200 birds to only 180.

Second, beak depth (the top-to-bottom dimension of the beak) varied among the birds on the island, and this variation affected the birds' survival. Before the drought began, the Grants and their colleagues had observed that birds with deeper beaks were able to process large, hard seeds more easily than birds with shallower beaks. Deep-beaked birds usually concentrated on large seeds, while shallow-beaked birds normally focused their efforts on small seeds. The open bars in the histogram in **Figure 1.9a** show what the distribution of beak sizes in the population was like before the drought. The height of each open bar represents the number of birds with beaks in a given range of depths—for example, 8.8 to 9.0 mm, or 9.0 to 9.2 mm. During the drought, the relative abundance of small seeds decreased, forcing shallow-beaked birds to shift to larger and harder seeds. Shallow-beaked birds were then at a distinct disadvantage because it was harder for them to crack the seeds. The

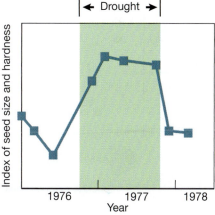

FIGURE 1.8

During the two-year drought, the size and hardness of seeds available on Daphne Major increased because birds consumed all of the desirable small, soft seeds, leaving mainly larger and harder seeds. Each point on this plot represents an index of seed size and hardness at a given time.

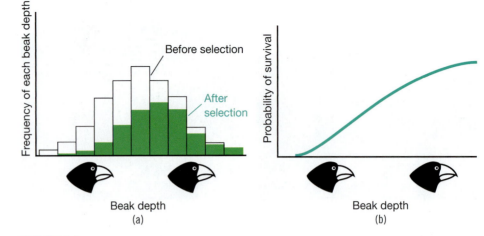

FIGURE 1.9

How directional selection increased mean beak depth among medium ground finches on Daphne Major. (a) The heights of the bars represent the numbers of birds whose beak depths fall within each of the intervals plotted on the *x* axis, with beak depth increasing to the right. The open bars show the distribution of beak depths before the drought began. The shaded bars show the distribution of beak depths after a year of drought. Notice that the number of birds in each category has decreased. Because birds with deep beaks were less likely to die than birds with shallow beaks, the peak of the distribution shifted to the right, indicating that the mean beak depth had increased. (b) The probability of survival for birds of different beak depths is plotted. Birds with shallow beaks are less likely to survive than are birds with deep beaks.

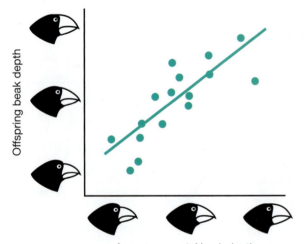

FIGURE 1.10

Parents with deeper-than-average beaks tend to have offspring with deeper-than-average beaks. Each point represents one offspring. Offspring beak depth is plotted on the vertical axis (deeper beaks farther up the axis), and the average of the two parents' beak depths is plotted on the horizontal axis (deeper beaks farther to the right).

distribution of individuals within the population changed during the drought because finches with deeper beaks were more likely to survive than were finches with shallow beaks (**Figure 1.9b**). The shaded portion of the histogram in Figure 1.9a shows what the distribution of beak depths would have been like among the survivors. Because many birds died, there were fewer remaining in each category. However, mortality was not random. The proportion of shallow-beaked birds that died greatly exceeded the proportion of deep-beaked birds that died. As a result, the shaded portion of the histogram shows a shift to the right, which means that the average beak depth in the population increased. Thus, the average beak depth among the survivors of the drought was greater than the average beak depth in the same population before the drought.

Third, parents and offspring had similar beak depths. The Grants discovered this by capturing and banding nestlings and recording the identity of the nestlings' parents. When the nestlings became adults, the Grants recaptured and measured them. The Grants found that, on average, parents with deep beaks produced offspring with deep beaks (**Figure 1.10**). Because parents were drawn from the pool of individuals who survived the drought, their beaks were, on average, deeper than those of the original residents of the island, and because offspring resemble their parents, the average beak depth of the survivors' offspring was greater than the average beak depth before the drought. This means that, through natural selection, the average **morphology** (an organism's size, shape, and composition) of the bird population changed so that birds became better adapted to their environment. This process, operating over approximately two years, led to a 4% increase in the mean beak depth in this population (**Figure 1.11**).

Selection preserves the status quo when the most common type is the best adapted.

So far, we have seen how natural selection led to adaptation as the population of finches on Daphne Major evolved in response to changes in their environment. Will this process continue forever? If it did, eventually all the finches would have deep enough beaks to efficiently process the largest seeds available. However, large beaks have disadvantages as well as benefits. The Grants showed, for instance, that birds with large beaks are less likely to survive the juvenile period than are birds with small beaks, probably because large-beaked birds require more food (**Figure 1.12**). Evolutionary theory predicts that, over time, selection will increase the average beak depth in the population until the costs of larger-than-average beak size exceed the benefits. At this point, finches with the average beak size in the population will be the most likely to survive and reproduce, and finches with deeper or shallower beaks than the new average will be at a disadvantage. When this is true, beak size does not change, and we say that an **equilibrium** exists in the population in regard to beak size. The process that produces this equilibrium state is called **stabilizing selection**. Notice that even though the average characteristics of the beak in the population will not change in this situation, selection is still going on. Selection is required to change a population, and selection is also required to keep a population the same.

It might seem that beak depth would also remain unchanged if this trait had no effect on survival (or put another way, if there were no selection favoring one type of beak over another). Then all types of birds would be equally likely to survive from one generation to the next, and beak depth would remain constant. This logic would be valid if selection were the only process affecting beak size. However, real populations

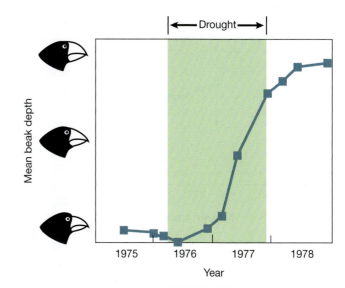

FIGURE 1.11

The average beak depth in the population of medium ground finches on Daphne Major increased during the drought of 1975–1978. Each point plots an index of average beak depth of the population in a particular year. Deeper beaks are plotted higher on the *y* axis.

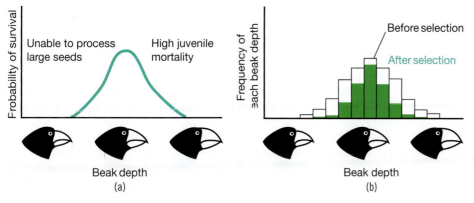

FIGURE 1.12

When birds with the most common beak depth are most likely to survive and reproduce, natural selection keeps the mean beak depth constant. (a) Birds with deep or shallow beaks are less likely to survive than are birds with average beaks. Birds with shallow beaks cannot process large, hard seeds, and birds with deep beaks are less likely to survive to adulthood. (b) The open bars represent the distribution of beak depths before selection, and the shaded bars represent the distribution after selection. As in Figure 1.9, notice that there are fewer birds in the population after selection. Because birds with average beaks are most likely to survive, however, the peak of the distribution of beak depths does not shift and mean beak depth remains unchanged.

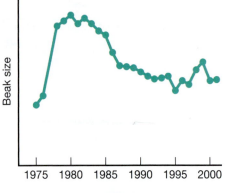

FIGURE 1.13

An index of mean beak size on Daphne Major for the period 1975–2001.

are also affected by other processes that cause **traits**, or **characters**, to change in unpredictable ways. We will discuss these processes further in Chapter 3. The point to remember here is that populations do not remain static over the long run unless selection is operating.

Evolution need not always lead to change in the same direction.

Natural selection has no foresight; it simply causes organisms to change so that they are better adapted to their current environment. Often environments fluctuate over time; and when they do, selection may track these fluctuations. We see this kind of pattern in the finches on the Galápagos over the last 25 years. During this time there have been dry periods (1976–1978), but there have also been wet periods (1983–1985), when small, soft, easy-to-process seeds were exceedingly abundant. During wet years, selection favors smaller beaks, reversing the changes in beak size and shape wrought by natural selection during the drought years. As **Figure 1.13** shows, beak size has wobbled up and down during the Grants' long study of the medium ground finch on Daphne Island.

Species are populations of varied individuals that may or may not change through time.

As the Grants' work on Daphne Major makes clear, a species is not a fixed type or entity. Species change in their general characteristics from generation to generation according to the postulates Darwin described. Before Darwin, however, people thought of species as unchanging categories, much the same way that we think of geometrical figures: a finch could no more change its properties than a triangle could. If a triangle acquired another side, it would not be a modified triangle, but rather a rectangle. In much the same way, to biologists before Darwin, a changed finch was not a finch at all. The late Ernst Mayr, a distinguished evolutionary biologist, called this pre-Darwinian view of immutable species "essentialism." According to Darwin's theory, a **species** is a dynamic *population* of individuals. The characteristics of a particular species will be static over a long period of time only if the most common type of individual is consistently favored by stabilizing selection. Both stasis (staying the same) and change result from natural selection, and both require explanation in terms of natural selection. Stasis is not the natural state of species.

Individual Selection

Adaptation results from the competition among individuals, not between entire populations or species.

It is important to note that selection produces adaptations that benefit *individuals*. Such adaptation may or may not benefit the population or species. In the case of simple morphological characters such as beak depth, selection probably does allow the population of finches to compete more effectively with other populations of seed predators. However, this need not be the case. Selection often leads to changes in behavior or morphology that increase the reproductive success of individuals but decrease the average reproductive success of the group, population, and species.

The fact that almost all organisms produce many more offspring than are necessary to maintain the species provides an example of the conflict between individual and group interests. Suppose that a female monkey, on average, produces 10 offspring during her lifetime (**Figure 1.14**). In a stable population, only two of these offspring will survive and reproduce on average. From the point of view of the species, the other eight are a waste of resources. They compete with other members of their species

FIGURE 1.14

A female blue monkey holds her infant.

for food, water, and sleeping sites. The demands of a growing population can lead to serious overexploitation of the environment, and the species as a whole might be more likely to survive if all females produced fewer offspring. This does not happen, however, because natural selection among individuals favors females who produce many offspring.

To see why selection on individuals will lead to this result, let's consider a simple hypothetical case. Suppose the females of a particular species of monkey are maximizing individual reproductive success when they produce 10 offspring. Females that produce more than or less than 10 offspring will tend to leave fewer descendants in the next generation. Further suppose that the likelihood of the species becoming extinct would be lowest if females produced only two offspring apiece. Now suppose that there are two kinds of females. Most of the population is composed of low-fecundity females that produce just two offspring each, but a few high-fecundity females produce 10 offspring each. (**Fecundity** is the term demographers use for the ability to produce offspring.) High-fecundity females have high-fecundity daughters, and low-fecundity females have low-fecundity daughters. The proportion of high-fecundity females will increase in the next generation because such females produce more offspring than do low-fecundity females. Over time, the proportion of high-fecundity females in the population will increase rapidly. As fecundity increases, the population will grow rapidly and may deplete available resources. The depletion of resources, in turn, will increase the chance that the species becomes extinct. However, this fact is irrelevant to the evolution of fecundity before the extinction, because natural selection results from competition among individuals, not competition among species.

The idea that natural selection operates at the level of the individual is a key element in understanding adaptation. In discussing the evolution of social behavior in Chapter 7, we will encounter several additional examples of situations in which selection increases individual success but decreases the competitive ability of the population.

The Evolution of Complex Adaptations

The example of the evolution of beak depth in the medium ground finch illustrates how natural selection can cause adaptive change to occur rapidly in a population. Deeper beaks enabled the birds to survive better, and deeper beaks soon came to predominate in the population. Beak depth is a fairly simple character, lacking the intricate complexity of an eye. As we will see, however, the accumulation of small variations by natural selection can also give rise to complex adaptations.

Why Small Variations Are Important

There are two categories of variation: continuous and discontinuous.

It was known in Darwin's day that most variation is continuous. An example of **continuous variation** is the distribution of heights in people. Humans grade smoothly from one extreme to the other (short to tall), with all the intermediate types (in this case, heights) represented. However, Darwin's contemporaries also knew about **discontinuous variation**, in which a number of distinct types exist with no intermediates. In humans, height is also subject to discontinuous variation. For example, there is a genetic condition, called achondroplasia, that causes affected individuals to be much shorter than other people, have proportionately shorter arms and legs, and bear a variety of other distinctive features (Peter Dinklage, who plays Tyrion Lannister in *Game of Thrones*, has this condition). Discontinuous variants are usually quite rare in nature. Nonetheless, many of Darwin's contemporaries who were convinced of the reality of evolution believed that new species arise as discontinuous variants.

Discontinuous variation is not important for the evolution of complex adaptations because complex adaptations are extremely unlikely to arise in a single jump.

Unlike most of his contemporaries, Darwin thought that discontinuous variation did not play an important role in evolution. A hypothetical example, described by the Oxford University biologist Richard Dawkins in his book *The Blind Watchmaker*, illustrates Darwin's reasoning. Dawkins recalls an old story in which an imaginary collection of monkeys sits at typewriters happily typing away. Lacking the ability to read or write, the monkeys strike keys at random. Given enough time, the story goes, the monkeys will reproduce all the great works of Shakespeare. Dawkins points out that this is not likely to happen in the lifetime of the universe, let alone the lifetime of one of the monkey typists. To illustrate why it would take so long, Dawkins presents these illiterate monkeys with a much simpler problem: reproducing a single line from *Hamlet*, "Methinks it is like a weasel" (III.ii). To make the problem even simpler for the monkeys, Dawkins ignores the difference between uppercase and lowercase letters and omits all punctuation except spaces. There are 28 characters (including spaces) in the phrase. Because there are 26 characters in the alphabet and Dawkins is keeping track of spaces, each time a monkey types a character, there is only a 1-in-27 chance that it will type the right character. There is also only a 1-in-27 chance that the second character will be correct. Again, there is a 1-in-27 chance that the third character will be right, and so on up to the twenty-eighth character. Thus the chance that a monkey will type the correct sequence at random is $1/27$ multiplied by itself 28 times, or

$$\underbrace{\frac{1}{27} \times \frac{1}{27} \times \frac{1}{27} \times \cdots \times \frac{1}{27}}_{28 \text{ times}} \approx 10^{-40}$$

This is a *very* small number. To get a feeling for how small a chance there is of the monkeys typing the sentence correctly, suppose a very fast computer could generate 100 billion (10^{11}) characters per second and run for the lifetime of the earth—about 4 billion years, or 10^{17} seconds. Then the chance of randomly typing the line "Methinks it is like a weasel" even once during the whole of Earth's history would be about 1 in 1 trillion! Typing the whole play is obviously astronomically less likely, and although *Hamlet* is a very complicated thing, it is much less complicated than a human eye. There's no chance that a structure like the human eye would arise by chance in a single trial. If it did, it would be, as the astrophysicist Sir Frederick Hoyle is reported to have said, like a hurricane blowing through a junkyard and chancing to assemble a Boeing 747.

Complex adaptations can arise through the accumulation of small random variations by natural selection.

Darwin argued that continuous variation is essential for the evolution of complex adaptations. Once again, Richard Dawkins provides an example that makes Darwin's reasoning clear. Again imagine a room full of monkeys and typewriters, but now the rules of the game are different. The monkeys type the first 28 characters at random, and then during the next round they attempt to copy the same initial string of letters and spaces. Most of the sentences are just copies of the previous string, but because monkeys sometimes make mistakes, some strings have small variations, usually in only a single letter. During each trial, the monkey trainer selects the string that most resembles Shakespeare's phrase "Methinks it is like a weasel" as the string to be copied by all the monkeys in the next trial. This process is repeated until the monkeys come up with the correct string. Calculating the exact number of trials required to generate the correct sequence of characters is quite difficult, but it is easy to simulate the process on a computer. Here's what happened when Dawkins performed the simulation. The initial random string was

```
WDLMNLT DTJBKWIRZREZLMQCO P
```

After one trial Dawkins got

```
WDLMNLT DTJBSWIRZREZLMQCO P
```

After 10 trials:

```
MDLDMNLS ITJISWHRZREZ MECS P
```

After 20 trials:

```
MELDINLS IT ISWPRKE Z WECSEL
```

After 30 trials:

```
METHINGS IT ISWLIKE B WECSEL
```

After 40 trials:

```
METHINKS IT IS LIKE I WEASEL
```

The exact phrase was reached after 43 trials. Dawkins reports that it took his 1985-vintage Macintosh only 11 seconds to complete this task.

Selection can give rise to great complexity starting with small random variations because it is a *cumulative* process. As the typing monkeys show us, it is spectacularly unlikely that a single random combination of keystrokes will produce the correct sentence. However, there is a much greater chance that some of the many *small* random changes will be advantageous. The combination of reproduction and selection allows the typing monkeys to accumulate these small changes until the desired sentence is reached.

Why Intermediate Steps Are Favored by Selection

The evolution of complex adaptations requires all of the intermediate steps to be favored by selection.

There is a potent objection to the example of the typing monkeys. Natural selection, acting over time, can lead to complex adaptations, but it can do so only if each small change along the way is itself adaptive. Although it is easy to assume that this is true in a hypothetical example of character strings, many people have argued that it is unlikely for every one of the changes necessary to assemble a complex organ like the eye to be adaptive. An eye is useful, it is claimed, only after all parts of the complexity have been assembled; until then, it is worse than no eye at all. After all, what good is 5% of an eye?

Darwin's answer, based on the many adaptations for seeing or sensing light that exist in the natural world, was that 5% of an eye *is* often better than no eye at all. It is quite possible to imagine that a very large number of small changes—each favored by selection—led cumulatively to the wonderful complexity of the eye. Living mollusks, which display a broad range of light-sensitive organs, provide examples of many of the likely stages in this process:

1. Many invertebrates have a simple light-sensitive spot (**Figure 1.15a**). Photoreceptors of this kind have evolved many times from ordinary epidermal (surface) cells—usually ciliated cells whose biochemical machinery is light sensitive. Those individuals whose cells are more sensitive to light are favored when information about changes in light intensity is useful. For example, a drop in light intensity may often indicate that a predator is in the vicinity.

2. By having the light-sensitive cells in a depression (Figure 1.15a), the organism will get some additional information about the direction of the change in light intensity. The surface of organisms is variable, and those individuals whose photoreceptors are in depressions will be favored by selection in environments in which such information is useful. For example, mobile organisms may need better information about what is happening in front of them than do immobile ones.

3. Through a series of small steps, the depression could deepen (**Figure 1.15b**), and each step could be favored by selection because better directional information would be available.

4. If the depression got deep enough (**Figure 1.15c**), it could form images on the light-sensitive tissue, much the way pinhole cameras form images on photographic film. In settings in which detailed images are useful, selection could then favor the elaboration of the neural machinery necessary to interpret the image.

5. The next step is the formation of a transparent cover (**Figure 1.15d**). This might be favored because it protects the interior of the eye from parasites and mechanical damage.

6. A lens could evolve through gradual modification of either the transparent cover or the internal structures within the eye (**Figure 1.15e and f**).

Notice that evolution produces adaptations like a tinkerer, not an engineer. New organisms are created by small modifications of existing organisms, not by starting with a clean slate. Clearly many beneficial adaptations will not arise because they are blocked at some step along the way when a particular variation is not favored by selection. Darwin's theory explains how complex adaptations can arise through natural processes, but it does not predict that every possible adaptation, or even most, will occur. This is not the best of all possible worlds; it is just one of many possible worlds.

Sometimes unrelated species have independently evolved the same complex adaptation, suggesting that the evolution of complex adaptations by natural selection is not a matter of mere chance.

The fact that natural selection constructs complex adaptations like a tinkerer might lead you to think that the assembly of complex adaptations is a chancy business. If even a single step were not favored by selection, the adaptation could not arise. Such reasoning suggests that complex adaptations are mere coincidence. Although chance does play a very important role in evolution, the power of cumulative natural selection should not be underestimated. The best evidence that selection is a powerful process for generating complex adaptations comes from a phenomenon called **convergence**, the evolution of similar adaptations in unrelated groups of animals.

The similarity between the marsupial faunas of Australia and South America and the placental faunas of the rest of the world provides a good example of convergence.

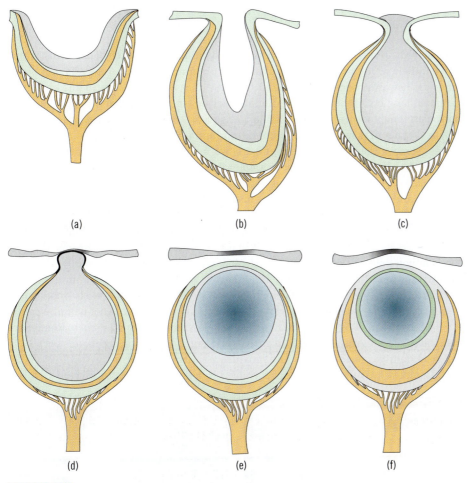

(a) (b) (c)

(d) (e) (f)

FIGURE 1.15

Living gastropod mollusks illustrate all of the intermediate steps between a simple eye cup and a camera-type eye. (a) The eye pit of a limpet, *Patella* sp.; (b) the eye cup of Beyrich's slit shell, *Pleurotomaria beyrichii;* (c) the pinhole eye of a California abalone, *Haliotis* sp.; (d) the closed eye of a turban shell, *Turbo creniferus;* (e) the lens eye of the spiny dye-murex, *Murex brandaris;* (f) the lens eye of the Atlantic dog whelk, *Nucella lapillus.* (Lens is shaded in e and f.)

FIGURE 1.16

The marsupial wolf that lived in Tasmania until early in the twentieth century (drawn from a photograph of one of the last living animals). Similarities with placental wolves of North America and Eurasia illustrate the power of natural selection to create complex adaptations. Their last common ancestor was probably a small insectivorous shrew-like creature.

In most of the world, the mammalian fauna is dominated by **placental mammals**, which nourish their young in the uterus during long pregnancies. Both Australia and South America, however, became separated from an ancestral supercontinent, known as Pangaea, long before placental mammals evolved. In Australia and South America, **marsupials** (nonplacental mammals, like kangaroos, that rear their young in external pouches) came to dominate the mammalian fauna, filling all available mammalian niches. Some of these marsupial mammals were quite similar to the placental mammals on the other continents. For example, there was a marsupial wolf in Australia that looked very much like placental wolves of Eurasia, even sharing subtle features of their feet and teeth (**Figure 1.16**). These marsupial wolves became extinct in the 1930s. Similarly, in South America a marsupial saber-toothed cat independently evolved many of the same adaptations as the placental saber-toothed cat that stalked North America 10,000 years ago. These similarities are more impressive when you consider that the last common ancestor of marsupial and placental mammals was a small, nocturnal insectivorous creature, something like a shrew, that lived about 120 million years ago (mya). Thus selection transformed a shrew step by small step, each step favored by selection, into a saber-toothed cat—and it did it twice. This cannot be coincidence.

The evolution of eyes provides another good example of convergence. Remember that the spherical gradient lens is a good lens design for aquatic organisms because it has good light-gathering ability and provides a sharp image over the full 180° visual field. Complex eyes with lenses have evolved independently eight different times in

FIGURE 1.17

Complex eyes with lenses have evolved independently in a number of different kinds of aquatic animals, including the (a) slingjaw wrasse and (b) squid.

(a)

(b)

distantly related aquatic organisms: once in fish, once in cephalopod mollusks like squid, several times among gastropod mollusks like the Atlantic dog whelk, once in annelid worms, and once in crustaceans (**Figure 1.17**). These are very diverse creatures whose last common ancestor was a simple creature that did not have a complex eye. Nonetheless, in every case they have evolved very similar spherical gradient lenses. Moreover, no other lens design is found in aquatic animals. Despite the seeming chanciness of assembling complex adaptations, natural selection has achieved the same design in every case.

Rates of Evolutionary Change

Natural selection can cause evolutionary change that is much more rapid than we commonly observe in the fossil record.

In Darwin's day, the idea that natural selection could change a chimpanzee into a human, much less that it might do so in just a few million years, was unthinkable. Even though people are generally more accepting of evolution today, many still think of evolution by natural selection as a glacially slow process that requires millions of years to accomplish noticeable change. Such people often doubt that there has been enough time for selection to accomplish the evolutionary changes observed in the fossil record. And yet, as we will see in subsequent chapters, most scientists now believe that humans evolved from an apelike creature in only 5 million to 10 million years. In fact, some of the rates of selective change observed in contemporary populations are far faster than necessary for such a transition. The puzzle is not whether there has been enough time for natural selection to produce the adaptations that we observe. The real puzzle is why the change observed in the fossil record was so slow.

The Grants' observation of the evolution of beak morphology in Darwin's finches provides one example of rapid evolutionary change. The medium ground finch of Daphne Major is one of 14 species of finches that live in the Galápagos. Evidence suggests that all 14 are descended from a single South American species that migrated to the newly emerged islands about half a million years ago (**Figure 1.18**). This doesn't seem like a very long time. Is it possible that natural selection created 14 species in only half a million years?

To start to answer the question, let's calculate how long it would take for the medium ground finch (*Geospiza fortis*) to come to resemble its closest relative, the large ground finch (*Geospiza magnirostris*), in beak size and weight (**Figure 1.19**). The large ground finch is 75% heavier than the medium ground finch, and its beak is about 20% deeper. Remember that beak size increased about 4% in two years during the 1977 drought. The Grants' data indicate that body size also increased by a similar amount. At this rate, Peter Grant calculated that it would take between 30 and 46 years for selection to increase the beak size and body weight of the medium ground finch to match those of the large ground finch. But these changes occurred in response to an extraordinary environmental crisis. The data suggest that selection doesn't generally push consistently in one direction. Instead, in the Galápagos, evolutionary change seems to go in fits and starts, moving traits one way and then another. So let's suppose that a net change in beak size like the one that occurred during 1977 occurs only once every century. Then it would take about 2,000 years to transform the medium ground finch into the large ground finch—still a very rapid process.

Similar rates of evolutionary change have been observed elsewhere when species invade new habitats. For example, about 100,000 years ago a population of elk (called "red deer" in Great Britain) colonized the island of Jersey, off the French coast, and then became isolated, presumably by rising sea levels. By the time the island was reconnected with the mainland approximately 6,000 years later, the red deer

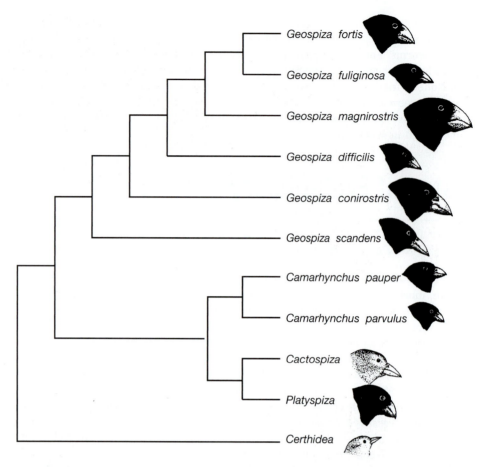

FIGURE 1.18

We can trace the relationship among various species of Darwin's finches by analyzing their protein polymorphisms. Species that are closely linked in the phylogenetic tree are more similar to one another genetically than to other species because they share a more recent common ancestor. The tree does not include 3 of the 14 species of Darwin's finches.

FIGURE 1.19

The large ground finch (*Geospiza magnirostris*) has a beak that is nearly 20% deeper than the beak of its close relative, the medium ground finch (*Geospiza fortis*). At the rate of evolution observed during the drought of 1977, Peter Grant calculated that selection could transform the medium ground finch into the large ground finch in less than 46 years.

had shrunk to about the size of a large dog. The University of Michigan paleontologist Philip Gingerich compiled data on the rate of evolutionary change in 104 cases in which species invaded new habitats. These rates ranged from a low of zero (that is, no change) to a high of about 22% per year, with an average of about 0.1% per year.

The changes the Grants observed in the medium ground finch are relatively simple: the birds and their beaks just got bigger. More complex changes usually take longer to evolve, but several kinds of evidence suggest that selection can produce big changes in remarkably short periods of time.

One line of evidence comes from artificial selection. Humans have performed selection on domesticated plants and animals for thousands of years, and for most of this period this selection was not deliberate. There are many familiar examples. All domesticated dogs, for instance, are believed to be descendants of wolves. Scientists are not sure when dogs were domesticated, but 15,000 years ago is a good guess, which means that in a few thousand generations, selection changed wolves into Pekingese, beagles, greyhounds, and Saint Bernards. In reality, most of these breeds were created fairly recently, and most were the products of directed breeding. Darwin's favorite example of artificial selection was the domestication of pigeons. In the nineteenth century, pigeon breeding was a popular hobby, especially among working people who competed to produce showy birds (**Figure 1.20**). They created a menagerie of wildly different forms, all descended from the rather plain-looking rock pigeon. Darwin pointed

(a)

(b)

(c)

(d)

FIGURE 1.20

In Darwin's day, pigeon fanciers created many new breeds of pigeons, including (a) pouters, (b) fantails, and (c) carriers, all from (d) the common rock pigeon.

out that these breeds are so different that if they were discovered in nature, biologists would surely classify them as members of different species. Yet they were produced by artificial selection within a few hundred years.

Rapid evolution of a complex feature has also been documented in a recent study of a group of very closely related species of fish from the genus *Poeciliopsis* (**Figure 1.21**). These small minnows can be found in tropical lowland streams, high-altitude lakes, and desert springs and streams in Mexico and Central America. All the species in this genus bear live young, but the sequence of events between fertilization and birth varies. In most species, females endow the eggs with nutrients before fertilization. As the young develop, they consume this endowment. As a consequence, the emerging offspring are smaller than the egg they came from. In a few species, however, females continue to provide nutrients to their unborn offspring throughout development using highly differentiated tissues that are analogous to mammalian placentas. When they are born, these offspring can be more than 100 times the mass of the egg at fertilization. Biologist David Reznick of the University of California, Riverside, and his colleagues have shown that these placental tissues evolved independently in three different groups of species within the genus *Poeciliopsis*. Genetic data indicate that one of these species groups diverged from ancestors lacking placental tissue only 0.75 mya, and the other two diverged less than 2.4 mya.

FIGURE 1.21

Fish in the genus *Poeciliopsis* include small minnows like *Poeciliopsis occidentalis,* shown here.

176 steps

362 steps

270 steps

225 steps

192 steps

308 steps

296 steps

FIGURE 1.22

A computer simulation of the evolution of the eye generates this sequence of forms. Between each pair of forms is the number of 1% changes (steps) necessary to transform the upper form into the lower one. The eye begins as a flat patch of light-sensitive tissue (*red*) that lies between a transparent layer (*light blue*) and a layer of dark pigmented tissue (*black*). After 176 steps that each increase resolving power, a shallow eye cup is formed. After 362 additional steps, the eye cup deepens. Eventually, a spherical gradient lens evolves, leading to a camera-type eye. The entire process involves about 1,800 changes of 1%.

These time estimates actually represent the time since these species shared a common ancestor, and they set an upper bound on the amount of time required for the placenta to evolve. The generation time for these fish ranges from six months to a year, so this complex adaptation evolved in fewer than a million generations.

A third line of evidence comes from theoretical studies of the evolution of complex characters. Dan-Eric Nilsson and Susanne Pelger of Lund University, in Sweden, have built a mathematical model of the evolution of the eye in an aquatic organism. They start with a population of organisms, each with a simple eyespot, a flat patch of light-sensitive tissue sandwiched between a transparent protective layer and a layer of dark pigment. They then consider the effect of every possible small (1%) deformation of the shape of the eyespot on the resolving power of the eye. They determine which 1% change has the greatest positive effect on the eye's resolving power and then repeat the process again and again, deforming the new structure by 1% in every possible way at each step. The results are shown in **Figure 1.22.** After 538 changes of 1% each, a simple concave eye cup evolves; after 1,033 changes of 1%, crude pinhole eyes emerge; after 1,225 changes of 1%, an eye with an elliptical lens is created; and after 1,829 steps, the process finally comes to a halt because no small changes increase resolving power. The end result is an eye with a spherical gradient lens just like those in fish and other aquatic organisms. As Nilsson and Pelger point out, 1,829 changes of 1% add up to a substantial amount of change. For instance, 1,829 changes of 1% would lengthen a 10-cm (4-in.) human finger to a length of 8,000 km (5,500 miles)—about the distance from Los Angeles to New York and back. Nonetheless, making very conservative assumptions about the strength of selection, Nilsson and Pelger calculate that this would take only about 364,000 generations. For organisms with short generations, the complete structure of the eye can evolve from a simple eyespot in less than a million years, a brief moment in evolutionary time.

By comparison, most changes observed in the fossil record are much slower. Human brain size has roughly doubled in the last 2 million years—a rate of change of 0.00005% per year. This is 10,000 times slower than the rate of change that the Grants observed in the Galápagos. Moreover, such slow rates of change typify what can be observed from the fossil record. As we will see, however, the fossil record is incomplete. It is quite likely that some evolutionary changes in the past were rapid, but the sparseness of the fossil record prevents us from detecting them.

Darwin's Difficulties Explaining Variation

Darwin's *On the Origin of Species,* published in 1859, was a best seller during his day, but his proposal that new species and other major evolutionary changes arise by the accumulation of small variations through natural selection was not widely embraced. Most educated people accepted the idea that new species arise through the transformation of existing species, and many scientists accepted the idea that natural selection is the most important cause of organic change (although by the turn of the twentieth century even this consensus had broken down, particularly in the United States). But only a minority endorsed Darwin's view that major changes occur through the accumulation of small variations.

Darwin couldn't convince his contemporaries that evolution occurred through the accumulation of small variations because he couldn't explain how variation is maintained.

Darwin's critics raised a telling objection to his theory: The actions of blending inheritance (described in the next paragraph) and selection would both inevitably deplete variation in populations and make it impossible for natural selection to continue. These were potent objections that Darwin was unable to resolve in his lifetime because he and his contemporaries did not yet understand the mechanics of inheritance.

Everyone could readily observe that many of the characteristics of offspring are an average of the characteristics of their parents. Most people, including Darwin, believed this phenomenon to be caused by the action of **blending inheritance**, a model of inheritance that assumes the mother and father each contribute a hereditary substance that mixes, or "blends," to determine the characteristics of the offspring. Shortly after publication of *On the Origin of Species*, a Scottish engineer named Fleeming Jenkin published a paper in which he clearly showed that, with blending inheritance, there could be little or no variation available for selection to act on. The following example shows why Jenkin's argument was so compelling. Suppose a population of one species of Darwin's finches displays two forms: tall and short. Further suppose that a biologist controls mating so that every mating is between a tall individual and a short individual. Then, with blending inheritance, all of the offspring will be the same intermediate height, and their offspring will be the same height as they are. All of the variation for height in the population will disappear in a single generation. With random mating, the same thing will occur, though it will take longer. If inheritance were purely a matter of blending parental traits, then Jenkin would have been right about its effect on variation. However, as we will see in Chapter 3, genetics accounts for the fact that offspring are intermediate between their parents and does not assume any kind of blending.

Another problem arose because selection works by removing variants from populations. For example, if finches with small beaks are more likely to die than finches with larger beaks over the course of many generations, eventually all that will be left are birds with large beaks. There will be no variation for beak size, and Darwin's second postulate holds that without variation there can be no evolution by natural selection. For example, suppose the environment changes so that individuals with small beaks are less likely to die than those with large beaks. The average beak size in the population will not decrease because there are no small-beaked individuals. Natural selection destroys the variation required to create adaptations.

Even worse, as Jenkin also pointed out, there was no explanation of how a population might evolve beyond its original range of variation. The cumulative evolution of complex adaptations requires populations to move far outside their original range of variation. Selection can cull away some characters from a population, but how can it lead to new types not present in the original population? This apparent contradiction was a serious impediment to explaining the logic of evolution. How could elephants, moles, bats, and whales all descend from an ancient shrewlike insectivore unless there were a mechanism for creating new variants not present at the beginning? For that matter, how could all the different breeds of dogs have descended from their one common ancestor, the wolf (**Figure 1.23**)?

Remember that Darwin and his contemporaries knew there were two kinds of variation: continuous and discontinuous. Because Darwin believed that complex adaptations could arise only through the accumulation of small variations, he thought discontinuous variants were unimportant. However, many biologists thought that

(a)

(b)

(c)

FIGURE 1.23

(a) The wolf is the ancestor of all domestic dogs, including (b) the poodle and (c) the Saint Bernard. These transformations were accomplished in several thousand generations of artificial selection.

the discontinuous variants, called "sports" by nineteenth-century animal breeders, were the key to evolution because they solved the problem of the blending effect. The following hypothetical example illustrates why. Suppose that a population of green birds has entered a new environment in which red birds are better adapted. Some of Darwin's critics believed that any new variant that was slightly more red would have only a small advantage and would be rapidly swamped by blending. In contrast, an all-red bird would have a large enough selective advantage to overcome the effects of blending and could increase its frequency in the population.

Darwin's letters show that these criticisms worried him greatly; and although he tried a variety of counterarguments, he never found one that was satisfactory. The solution to these problems required an understanding of genetics, which was not available for another half century. As we will see, it was not until well into the twentieth century that geneticists came to understand how variation is maintained and Darwin's theory of evolution was generally accepted.

Key Terms

adaptations
natural selection
morphology
equilibrium
stabilizing selection
traits
characters
species
fecundity
continuous variation
discontinuous variation
convergence
placental mammals
marsupials
blending inheritance

Study Questions

1. It is sometimes observed that offspring do not resemble their parents for a particular character, even though the character varies in the population. Suppose this were the case for beak depth in the medium ground finch.
   (a) What would the plot of offspring beak depth against parental beak depth look like?
   (b) Plot the mean depth in the population among (i) adults before a drought, (ii) the adults that survived a year of drought, and (iii) the offspring of the survivors.

2. Many species of animals engage in cannibalism. This practice certainly reduces the ability of the species to survive. Is it possible that cannibalism could arise by natural selection? If so, with what adaptive advantage?

3. Some insects mimic dung. Ever since Darwin, biologists have explained this behavior as a form of camouflage: Selection favors individuals who most resemble dung because they are less likely to be eaten. The late Harvard paleontologist Stephen Jay Gould objected to this explanation. He argued

CHAPTER 1: ADAPTATION BY NATURAL SELECTION

that although selection could perfect such mimicry once it evolved, it could not cause the resemblance to arise in the first place. "Can there be any edge," Gould asked, "to looking 5% like a turd?" (R. Dawkins, 1996, *The Blind Watchmaker,* New York: Norton, p. 81). Can you think of a reason why looking 5% like a turd would be better than not looking at all like a turd?

4. In the late 1800s an American biologist named Hermon Bumpus collected a large number of sparrows that had been killed in a severe ice storm. He found that birds whose wings were about average in length were rare among the dead birds. What kind of selection is this? What effect would this episode of selection have on the mean wing length in the population?

Further Reading

Browne, J. 1995. *Charles Darwin: A Biography,* vol. I: *Voyaging.* New York: Knopf.

Dawkins, R. 1996. *The Blind Watchmaker: Why the Evidence of Evolution Reveals a Universe without Design.* New York: Norton.

Dennett, D. C. 1995. *Darwin's Dangerous Idea: Evolution and the Meanings of Life.* New York: Simon & Schuster.

Ridley, M. 1996. *Evolution.* 2nd ed. Cambridge, Mass.: Blackwell Science.

Weiner, J. 1994. *The Beak of the Finch: A Story of Evolution in Our Time.* New York: Knopf.

CHAPTER OBJECTIVES

By the end of this chapter you should be able to

- Describe how experiments by Gregor Mendel revealed the logic of inheritance.

- Explain how Mendel's laws follow from the machinery of cell replication.

- Understand why genes affecting different traits are sometimes linked.

- Explain how the properties of DNA are consistent with the role of genes in inheritance.

- Describe how genes control the structure of proteins and influence the properties of organisms.

- Explain how gene regulation allows the same genes to control the development and function of many different parts of the body.

GENETICS

Mendelian Genetics

Cell Division and the Role of Chromosomes in Inheritance

Molecular Genetics

Mendelian Genetics

Although none of the main participants in the nineteenth-century debate about evolution knew it, the key experiments necessary to understand how genetic inheritance really worked had already been performed by an obscure monk, Gregor Mendel, living in what is now Slovakia (**Figure 2.1**). The son of peasant farmers, Mendel was recognized by his teachers as an extremely bright student, and he enrolled in the University of Vienna to study the natural sciences. While he was there, Mendel received a first-class education from some of the scientific luminaries of Europe. Unfortunately, Mendel had an extremely nervous disposition: every time he was faced with an examination, he became physically ill, taking months to recover. As a result, he was forced to leave the university, and then he joined a monastery in the city of Brno, more or less because he needed a job. Once there, Mendel continued to study inheritance, an interest he had developed in Vienna.

By conducting careful experiments with plants, Mendel discovered how inheritance works. Between 1856 and 1863, using the common edible garden pea plant (**Figure 2.2**), Mendel isolated a number of traits with only two forms, or **variants**. For example, one of the traits he studied was pea color. This trait had

FIGURE 2.1

Gregor Mendel, about 1884, 15 years after abandoning his botanical experiments.

two variants: yellow and green. He also studied pea texture, a trait that also had two variants: wrinkled and smooth. Mendel cultivated populations of plants in which these traits bred true, meaning that the traits did not change from one generation to the next. For example, **crosses** (matings) between plants that bore green peas always produced offspring with green peas, and crosses between plants that bore yellow peas consistently produced offspring with yellow peas. Mendel performed a large number of crosses between these different kinds of true-breeding peas.

Before going further, we need to establish a way to keep track of the results of the matings. Geneticists refer to the original founding population as the F_0 **generation**, the offspring of the original founders as the F_1 **generation**, and so on. In this case, the original true-breeding plants constitute the F_0 generation, and the plants created by crossing true-breeding parents constitute the F_1 generation. The offspring of the F_1 generation will be the F_2 **generation**.

In one set of Mendel's experiments with garden peas, a series of crosses between green and yellow variants yielded offspring that all bore yellow peas, matching only one of the parent plants (**Figure 2.3**). Mendel's next step was to perform crosses among the offspring of these crosses. When members of the F_1 generation (all of which bore yellow peas) were crossed, some of the offspring produced yellow seeds and some produced green seeds. Unlike most of the people who had experimented with plant crosses before, Mendel performed many of these kinds of crosses and kept careful count of the numbers of each kind of individual that resulted. These data showed that, in the F_2 generation, there were three individuals with yellow seeds for every one with green seeds.

Mendel was able to formulate two principles that accounted for his experimental results.

Mendel derived two insightful conclusions from his experimental results:

1. The observed characteristics of organisms are determined jointly by two particles, one inherited from the mother and one from the father. The American geneticist T. H. Morgan later named these particles **genes**.

2. Each of these two particles, or genes, is equally likely to be transmitted when **gametes** (eggs and sperm) are formed. Modern scientists call this **independent assortment**.

These two principles account for the pattern of results in Mendel's breeding experiments, and as we shall see, they are the key to understanding how variation is preserved.

Cell Division and the Role of Chromosomes in Inheritance

Nobody paid any attention to Mendel's results for almost 40 years.

Mendel thought that his findings were important, so he published them in 1866 and sent a copy of the paper to Karl Wilhelm von Nägeli, a very prominent botanist. Nägeli was studying inheritance and should have understood the importance of Mendel's experiments. Instead, Nägeli dismissed Mendel's work, perhaps because it contradicted his own results or because Mendel was an obscure monk. Soon after this, Mendel was elected abbot of his monastery and was forced to give up his experiments. His ideas did not resurface until the turn of the twentieth century, when several botanists independently replicated Mendel's experiments and rediscovered the laws of inheritance.

FIGURE 2.2

Mendel's genetic experiments were conducted on the common garden pea.

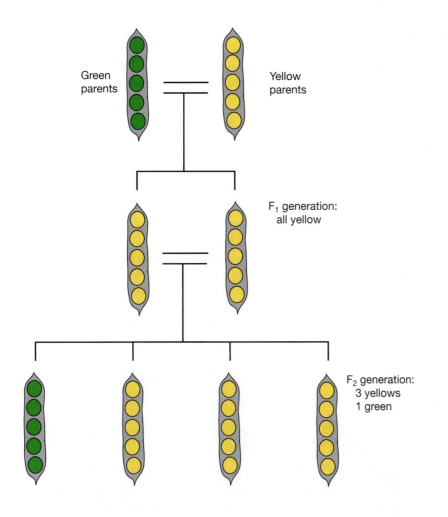

Green parents

Yellow parents

F₁ generation: all yellow

F₂ generation: 3 yellows 1 green

FIGURE 2.3

In one of Mendel's experiments, crossing true-breeding lines of green and yellow peas led to all yellow offspring. Crossing these F_1 individuals led to an F_2 generation with a 3:1 ratio of yellow to green individuals.

In 1896, the Dutch botanist Hugo de Vries unknowingly repeated Mendel's experiments with poppies. Instead of publishing his results immediately, however, he cautiously waited until he had replicated his results with more than 30 plant species. Then in 1900, just as de Vries was ready to send off a manuscript describing his experiments, a colleague sent him a copy of Mendel's paper. Poor de Vries; his hot new results were already 30 years old! About the same time, two other European botanists, Carl Correns and Erich Tschermak, also duplicated Mendel's breeding experiments, derived similar conclusions, and discovered that they too had been scooped. Correns and Tschermak graciously acknowledged Mendel's primacy in discovering the laws of inheritance, but de Vries was less magnanimous. He did not cite Mendel in his treatise on plant genetics and refused to sign a petition advocating the construction of a memorial in Brno commemorating Mendel's achievements.

When Mendel's results were rediscovered, they were widely accepted because scientists now understood the role of chromosomes in the formation of gametes.

By the time Mendel's experiments were rediscovered in 1900, it was well known that virtually all living organisms are built out of cells. Moreover, careful embryological work had shown that all the cells in complex organisms arise from a single cell through the process of cell division. Between the time of Mendel's initial discovery of the nature of inheritance and its rediscovery at the turn of the twentieth century, a crucial feature of cellular anatomy was discovered: the **chromosome**. Chromosomes are small linear bodies contained in every cell and replicated during cell division (**Figure 2.4**).

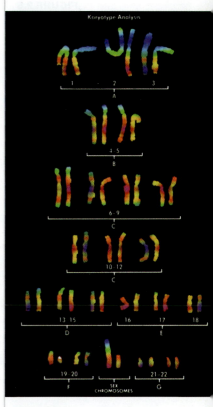

Karyotype Analysis

FIGURE 2.4

When a human cell divides, 23 pairs of chromosomes appear in its nucleus, including a pair of sex chromosomes (X and Y for a male, as shown here). Different chromosomes can be distinguished by their shape and by the banding patterns created by dyes that stain the chromosomes.

Moreover, scientists had also learned that chromosomes are replicated in a special kind of cell division that creates gametes. As we will see in subsequent sections, this research provides a simple material explanation for Mendel's results. Our current model of cell division, which was developed in small steps by a number of different scientists, is summarized in the sections that follow.

Mitosis and Meiosis

Ordinary cell division, called mitosis, creates two copies of the chromosomes present in the nucleus.

When plants and animals grow, their cells divide. Every cell contains within it a body called the **nucleus** (plural *nuclei*; **Figure 2.5**); when cells divide, their nuclei also divide. This process of ordinary cell division is called **mitosis**. As mitosis begins, a cloud of material begins to form in the nucleus, and gradually this cloud condenses into a number of linear chromosomes. The chromosomes can be distinguished under the microscope by their shape and by how they stain. (Stains are dyes added to cells in the laboratory that allow researchers to distinguish different parts of a cell.) Different

FIGURE 2.5

In all plants and animals, every cell contains a body called the nucleus (the solid red circle in the center of this magnified image). The nucleus contains the chromosomes.

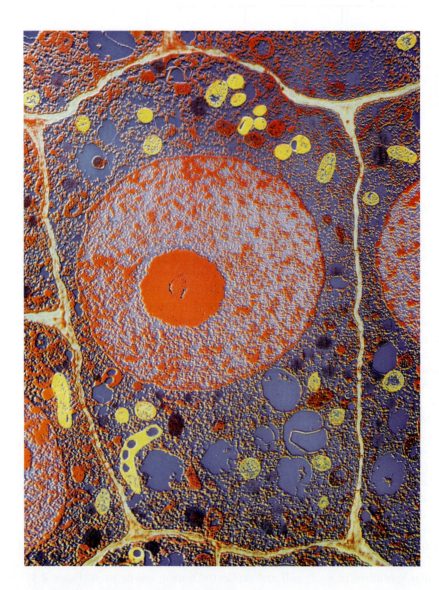

organisms have different numbers of chromosomes, but in **diploid** organisms, chromosomes come in **homologous pairs** (pairs whose members have similar shapes and staining patterns). All primates are diploid, but other organisms have a variety of arrangements. Diploid organisms also vary in the number of chromosome pairs their cells have. The fruit fly *Drosophila* has 4 pairs of chromosomes, humans have 23, and some organisms have many more.

Two features of mitosis suggest that the chromosomes play an important role in determining the properties of organisms. First, the original set of chromosomes is duplicated so that each new daughter cell has an exact copy of the chromosomes present in its parent. This means that, as an organism grows and develops through a sequence of mitotic divisions, every cell will have the same chromosomes that were present when the egg and sperm united. Second, the material that makes up the chromosome is present even when cells are not dividing. Cells spend little of their time dividing; most of the time they are in a "resting" period, doing what they are supposed to do as liver cells, muscle cells, bone cells, and so on. During the resting period, chromosomes are not visible. However, the material that makes up the chromosomes is always present in the cell.

> In meiosis, the special cell division process that produces gametes, only half of the chromosomes are transmitted from the parent cell to the gamete.

The sequence of events that occurs during mitosis is quite different from the sequence of events during **meiosis**, the special form of cell division leading to the production of gametes. The key feature of meiosis is that each gamete contains only *one* copy of each chromosome, whereas cells that undergo mitosis contain a *pair* of homologous chromosomes. Cells that contain only one copy of each chromosome are said to be **haploid** (**Figure 2.6**). When a new individual is conceived, a haploid sperm from the father unites with a haploid egg from the mother to produce a diploid **zygote**. The zygote is a single cell that then divides mitotically over and over to produce the millions and millions of cells that make up an individual's body.

Chromosomes and Mendel's Experimental Results

> Mendel's two principles can be deduced from the assumption that genes are carried on chromosomes.

In 1902, less than two years after the rediscovery of Mendel's findings, Walter Sutton, a young graduate student at Columbia University, made the connection between chromosomes and the properties of inheritance revealed by Mendel's principles. Recall that the first of Mendel's two principles states that an organism's observed characteristics are determined by particles acquired from each of the parents. This concept fits with the idea that genes reside on chromosomes, because individuals inherit one copy of each chromosome from each parent. The idea that observed characteristics are determined by genes from both parents is consistent with the observation that mitosis transmits a copy of both chromosomes to every daughter cell, so every cell contains copies of both the maternal and the paternal chromosomes. Mendel's second principle states that genes segregate independently. The observation that meiosis involves the creation of gametes with only one of the two possible chromosomes from each homologous pair is consistent with two notions: (1) that one gene is inherited from each parent and (2) that each of these genes is equally likely to be transmitted to gametes. Not everyone agreed with Sutton, but over the next 15 years, Morgan and his colleagues at Columbia performed many experiments that proved Sutton right.

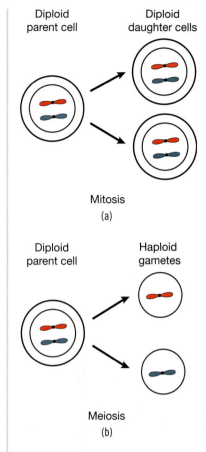

Diploid parent cell → **Diploid daughter cells**

Mitosis
(a)

Diploid parent cell → **Haploid gametes**

Meiosis
(b)

FIGURE 2.6

Diploid cells have *n* pairs of homologous chromosomes; *n* varies widely among species, but here *n* = 1. Members of homologous pairs may differ in the alleles they carry at specific sites along the chromosome. (a) Mitosis duplicates the chromosomes. (b) Meiosis creates gametes that carry only one member of each homologous pair of chromosomes.

> Different varieties of a particular gene are called alleles. Individuals with two copies of the same allele are homozygous; individuals with different alleles are heterozygous.

To see more clearly the connection between chromosomes and the results of Mendel's experiments with the peas, we need to introduce some new terms. The word *gene* is used to refer to the material particles carried on chromosomes. Later you will learn that genes are made of a molecule called DNA. **Alleles** are different varieties of a single gene. Individuals with two copies of the same allele are **homozygous** for that allele and are called homozygotes. When individuals carry copies of two different alleles, they are said to be **heterozygous** for those alleles and are called heterozygotes.

Consider the case in which all the yellow individuals in the parental generation carry two genes for yellow pea color, one on each chromosome. We will use the symbol *A* for this allele. Thus these plants are homozygous (*AA*) for yellow pea color. All of the individual plants with green peas are homozygous for a different allele, which we denote *a*, so green-pea plants are *aa*. As we will see, this is the only pattern that is consistent with Mendel's model. What happens if we cross two yellow-pea plants with each other, or two green-pea plants with each other? Because they are homozygous, all of the gametes produced by the yellow parents will carry the *A* allele. This means that all of the offspring produced by the crossing of two *AA* parents will also be homozygous for that *A* allele and therefore will also produce yellow peas. Similarly, all of the gametes produced by parents that are homozygous for the *a* allele will carry the *a* allele; when the gametes of two *aa* parents unite, they will produce only *aa* individuals with green peas. Thus we can explain why each type breeds true.

> A cross between a homozygous dominant parent and a homozygous recessive parent produces all heterozygotes in the F_1 generation.

Next let's consider the offspring of a mating between a true-breeding green parent and a true-breeding yellow parent (**Figure 2.7**). The green parent produces only

FIGURE 2.7

In Mendel's experiments, crosses of two true-breeding lines of the garden pea produced offspring that all had yellow peas. All of the gametes produced by homozygous *AA* parents carry the *A* allele. Similarly, all of the gametes produced by homozygous *aa* parents carry the *a* allele. All of the zygotes from an *AA* × *aa* mating get an *A* from one parent and an *a* from the other parent. Thus all F_1 offspring are *Aa*, and because *A* is dominant, they all produce yellow seeds.

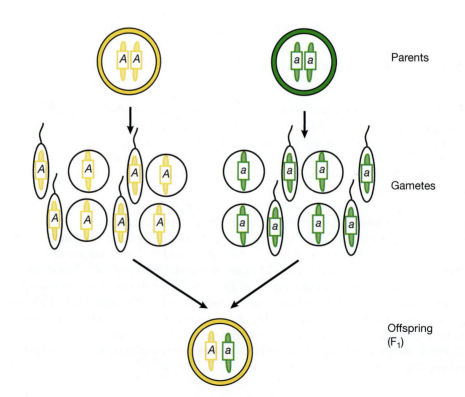

Parents

Gametes

Offspring
(F_1)

a gametes, and the yellow parent produces only *A* gametes. Thus every one of their offspring inherits an *a* gamete from one parent and an *A* gamete from the other parent. According to Mendel's model, all the individuals in the F₁ generation will be *Aa*. Given that Mendel discovered that all offspring of such crosses have yellow peas, it must be that heterozygotes bear yellow peas. To describe these effects, geneticists use the following four terms:

1. **Genotype** refers to the particular combination of genes or alleles that an individual carries.

2. **Phenotype** refers to the observable characteristics of the organism, such as the color of the peas in Mendel's experiments.

3. The *A* allele is **dominant** because individuals with only one copy of the dominant allele have the same phenotype, yellow peas, that individuals with two copies of that allele have.

4. The *a* allele is **recessive** because it has *no* effect on phenotype in heterozygotes.

As you can see in **Table 2.1**, *AA* and *Aa* individuals have the same phenotype but different genotypes; knowing an individual's observable characteristics, or phenotype, does not necessarily tell you its genetic composition, or genotype.

A cross between heterozygous parents produces a predictable mixture of all three genotypes.

Now consider the second stage of Mendel's experiment: crossing members of the F₁ generation with each other to create an F₂ generation (**Figure 2.8**). We have seen that

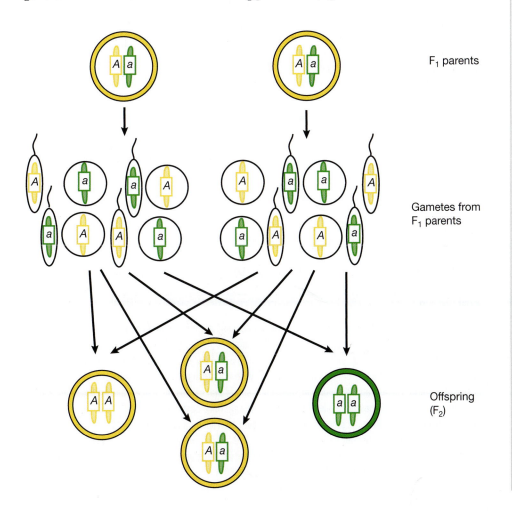

TABLE 2.1

Genotype	Phenotype
AA	Yellow
Aa	Yellow
aa	Green

The relationship between genotype and phenotype in Mendel's experiment on pea color.

FIGURE 2.8

Crosses of the F₁ heterozygotes yielded a 3:1 ratio of phenotypes in Mendel's experiments. All the parents are heterozygous, or *Aa*. This means that half of the gametes produced by each parent carry the *A* allele, and the other half produce the *a* allele. Thus one-quarter of the zygotes will be *AA*, half will be *Aa*, and the remaining quarter will be *aa*. Because *A* is dominant, three-quarters of the offspring (¼ *AA* + ½ *Aa*) will produce yellow seeds.

F₁ parents

Gametes from F₁ parents

Offspring (F₂)

every individual in the F_1 generation is heterozygous, Aa. This means that half of their gametes contain a chromosome with an A allele and half with an a allele. (Remember, meiosis produces haploid gametes.) On average, if we draw pairs of gametes at random from the gametes produced by the F_1 generation, one-quarter of the individuals will be AA, half will be Aa, and one-quarter will be aa.

To see why there is a 1:2:1 ratio in the F_2 generation, it is helpful to construct an event tree, like the one shown in **Figure 2.9.** First pick the paternal gamete. Every male in the F_1 generation is heterozygous: he has one chromosome with an A allele and one with an a allele. Thus, there is a probability of $\frac{1}{2}$ of getting a sperm that carries an A, and a probability of $\frac{1}{2}$ of getting a sperm that carries an a. Suppose you select an A by chance. Now pick the maternal gamete. Once again you have a $\frac{1}{2}$ chance of getting an A and a $\frac{1}{2}$ chance of getting an a. The probability of getting two As, one from the father and one from the mother, is

$$Pr(AA) = Pr(A \text{ from Dad}) \times Pr(A \text{ from Mom}) = \frac{1}{2} \times \frac{1}{2} = \frac{1}{4}$$

If you repeated this process a large number of times—first picking male gametes and then picking female gametes—roughly a quarter of the F_2 individuals produced would be AA. Similar reasoning shows that a quarter would be aa. Half would be Aa because there are two ways of combining the A and a alleles: the A could come from the mother and the a from the father or vice versa. Because both AA and Aa individuals

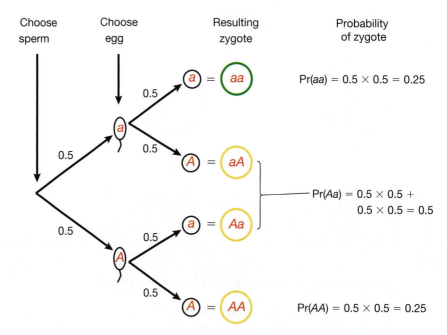

FIGURE 2.9

This event tree shows why there is a 1:2:1 genotypic ratio among offspring in the F_2 generation. Imagine forming a zygote by first choosing a sperm and then an egg. The numbers along each branch give the probability that a choice at the previous node ends on that branch. The circles at the end of each branch represent the resulting zygote, and the color of the ring denotes the phenotype: yellow or green peas. The first node represents the choice of a sperm. There is a 50% chance of selecting a sperm that carries the A allele and a 50% chance of selecting a sperm that carries the a allele. Now choose an egg. Once again, there is a 50% chance of selecting an egg with each allele. Thus the probability of getting both an A sperm and an A egg is $0.5 \times 0.5 = 0.25$. Similarly, the chance of getting an a egg and an a sperm is $0.5 \times 0.5 = 0.25$. The same kind of calculation shows that there is a 25% chance of getting an a sperm and an A egg and a 25% chance of getting an A sperm and an a egg. Thus the probability of getting an Aa zygote is 50%.

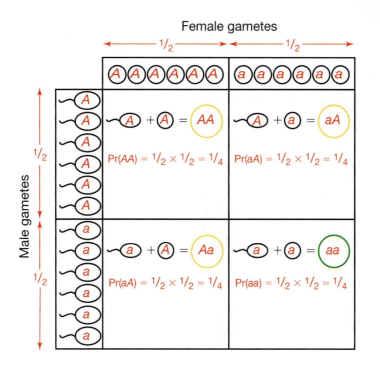

Female gametes

Male gametes

$\Pr(AA) = \frac{1}{2} \times \frac{1}{2} = \frac{1}{4}$ $\Pr(aA) = \frac{1}{2} \times \frac{1}{2} = \frac{1}{4}$

$\Pr(aA) = \frac{1}{2} \times \frac{1}{2} = \frac{1}{4}$ $\Pr(aa) = \frac{1}{2} \times \frac{1}{2} = \frac{1}{4}$

FIGURE 2.10

This diagram, called a Punnett square, provides another way to see why there is a 1:2:1 genotypic ratio among offspring in the F_2 generation. The horizontal axis is divided in half to reflect the equal proportion of *A* and *a* eggs. The vertical axis is divided according to the proportion of sperm carrying each allele, and again it is divided in half. The areas of squares formed by the intersection of the vertical and horizontal dividing lines give the proportion of zygotes that result from each of the four possible fertilization events: *AA* = 0.25 (one of the four squares), *Aa* = 0.25 + 0.25 = 0.50 (two of the four squares), and *aa* = 0.25 (one of the four squares). Thus zygotes will have genotypes in the ratio 1:2:1.

have yellow peas, there will be three yellow individuals for every green one among the offspring of the F_1 parents. Another way to visualize this result is to construct a diagram called a **Punnett square**, like the one shown in **Figure 2.10.**

Linkage and Recombination

Mendel also performed experiments involving two traits he believed showed that separate characters segregate independently.

Mendel also performed experiments that involved two characters. For example, he crossed individuals that bred true for two different traits: pea color and seed texture. He crossed plants with smooth, yellow seeds and plants with wrinkled, green seeds. All of the F_1 individuals were smooth and yellow, but the F_2 individuals occurred in the following ratio:

9 smooth yellow:3 smooth green:3 wrinkled yellow:1 wrinkled green

This experiment is important because it demonstrates that sexual reproduction shuffles genes that affect different traits, thereby producing new combinations of traits—a phenomenon called **recombination**. This process is extremely important for maintaining variation in natural populations. We will return to this issue in Chapter 3.

To understand Mendel's experiment, recall that each of the parental characters (pea color and seed texture) breeds true, which means that each is homozygous for a different allele controlling seed color: the yellow line is *AA*, and the green line is *aa*. Because seed texture is also a true-breeding character, the parental lines must also be homozygous for genes affecting seed texture. Let's suppose that the parents with smooth seeds are *BB* and the parents with wrinkled seeds are *bb*. Then in the parental generation there are only two genotypes: *AABB* and *aabb*. By the F_2 generation, sexual reproduction has generated all 16 possible genotypes and two new phenotypes: smooth green and wrinkled yellow. The details are given in Closer Look 2.1.

2.1 More on Recombination

The first step to a deeper understanding of recombination is to see the connections among Mendel's two-trait experiment, independent segregation, and chromosomes. Mendel crossed a smooth-yellow (*AABB*) parent and a wrinkled-green (*aabb*) parent to produce members of an F₁ generation. Smooth-yellow parents produce only *AB* gametes, and wrinkled-green parents produce only *ab* gametes; all members of the F₁ generation are, therefore, *AaBb*. If we assume that the genes for seed color and seed texture enter gametes independently, then each of the four possible types—*AB, Ab, aB,* and *ab*—will be represented by one-quarter of the gametes produced by members of the F₁ generation (**Figure 2.11**).

With this information, we can construct a Punnett square predicting the proportions of each genotype in the F₂ generation (**Figure 2.12**). Once again, we divide the vertical and horizontal axes in proportion to the frequency of each type of gamete, in this case dividing each axis into four equal parts. The areas of the rectangles formed by the intersection of the vertical and horizontal dividing lines give the

proportions of zygotes that result from each of the 16 possible fertilization events. Because the area of each cell in this matrix is the same, we can determine the phenotypic ratios of zygotes that result from each of the 16 possible fertilization events in this example by simply counting the number of squares that contain each phenotype. There are nine smooth-yellow squares, three wrinkled-yellow squares, three smooth-green squares, and one wrinkled-green square. Thus the 9:3:3:1 ratio of phenotypes that Mendel observed was consistent with the assumption that genes on different chromosomes segregate independently. If the genes controlling these traits did not segregate independently, the ratio of phenotypes would be different, as we will see next.

During meiosis, chromosomes frequently become damaged, break, and recombine. This process, called crossing over, creates chromosomes with combinations of genes not present in the parent (see text). In the preceding example, remember that all members of the F₁ generation were *AaBb*. Now suppose that the locus controlling seed color and the locus controlling seed texture are

carried on the same chromosome. Further assume that when the chromosomes are duplicated during meiosis, a fraction *r* of the time there is crossing over (**Figure 2.13**) and a fraction $1 - r$ of the time there is no crossing over. Next, chromosomes segregate independently into gametes. The types of chromosomes present in the parental generation, *Ab* and *ab*, each occur in a fraction $(1 - r)/2$ of the gametes; the novel, recombinant types *Ab* and *aB* each occur in a fraction $r/2$ of the gametes (**Figure 2.14**).

Now we can use a Punnett square to calculate the frequency of each of the 16 possible genotypes in the F₂ generation (**Figure 2.15**). As before, we divide the vertical and horizontal axes in proportion to the relative frequency of each type of gamete, and the area of the rectangles formed by the intersection of these grid lines gives the frequency of each genotype. If recombination rates are low, most members of the F₂ generation will be of three genotypes—*AABB, AaBb,* and *aabb*—just as if there were only two alleles, *AB* and *ab*. If the recombination rate is higher, however, more of the novel recombinant genotypes will be produced.

FIGURE 2.11

This event tree shows why an F₁ parent is equally likely to produce all four possible gametes when genes for two traits are carried on different chromosomes. The first node represents the choice of the chromosome carrying the gene for seed color (*A* or *a*), and the second node represents the choice of the chromosome that carries the gene for seed texture (*B* or *b*). The number along each branch gives the probability that the choice at the previous node ends on that branch. The circles at the end of each branch represent the resulting gametes.

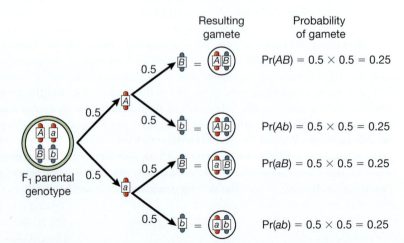

Resulting gamete | Probability of gamete

Pr(*AB*) = 0.5 × 0.5 = 0.25

Pr(*Ab*) = 0.5 × 0.5 = 0.25

Pr(*aB*) = 0.5 × 0.5 = 0.25

Pr(*ab*) = 0.5 × 0.5 = 0.25

F₁ parental genotype

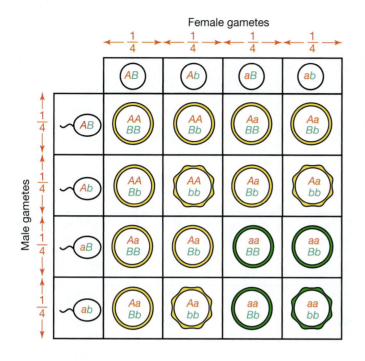

Female gametes

FIGURE 2.12

This Punnett square shows why there is a 9:3:3:1 phenotypic ratio among offspring of the F₂ generation when the genes for the two traits, seed color and seed texture, are carried on different chromosomes. The rings in each square show the color (green or yellow) and seed texture (wrinkled or smooth) of the phenotype associated with each genotype.

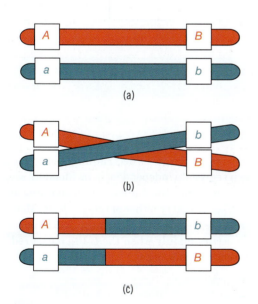

FIGURE 2.13

Crossing over during meiosis sometimes leads to recombination and produces novel combinations of traits. Suppose that the A allele leads to yellow seeds and the a allele to green seeds, while the B allele leads to smooth seeds and the b allele to wrinkled seeds. (a) Here an individual carries one AB chromosome and one ab chromosome. (b) During meiosis, the chromosomes are damaged and crossing over occurs. (c) Now the A allele is paired with b, and the a allele is paired with B.

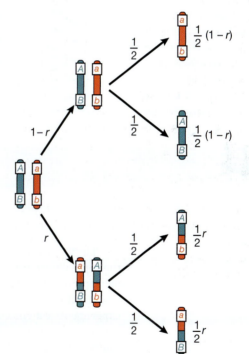

FIGURE 2.14

This event tree shows how to calculate the fraction of each type of gamete that will be produced when genes are carried on the same chromosome. The first node represents whether or not crossing over takes place. There is a probability r that crossing over takes place and produces novel trait combinations and a probability 1 − r that there is no crossing over. At the second node, chromosomes are randomly assigned to gametes. The value given above each branch represents the probability of reaching that branch from the previous node. The likelihood of forming each type of genotype is the product of the probabilities along each pathway.

FIGURE 2.15

This Punnett square shows how to calculate the frequency of each phenotype among offspring in the F$_2$ generation if the genes for seed color and seed texture are carried on the same chromosome. The horizontal axis is divided according to the proportion of each type of egg: *AB*, *Ab*, *aB*, and *ab*. When genes are carried on the same chromosome, the frequency of each type of gamete is calculated as shown in Figure 2.14. The vertical axis is divided according to the proportion of each type of sperm, and the horizontal axis is divided according to the proportion of each type of egg. The areas of the rectangles formed by the intersection of the vertical and horizontal dividing lines give the proportions of zygotes that result from each of the 16 possible fertilization events.

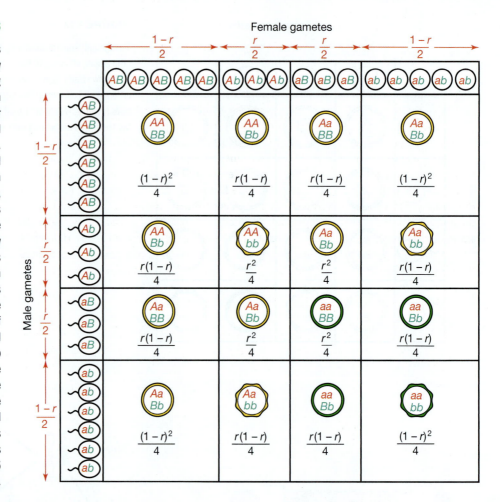

The 9:3:3:1 ratio of phenotypes tells us that the genes determining seed color and the genes determining seed texture each segregate independently, as Mendel's second principle predicts. Thus knowing that a gamete has the *A* allele tells us nothing about whether it will have *B* or *b;* it is equally likely to carry either of these alleles. Mendel's experiments convinced him that all traits segregate independently. Today, however, we know that independent segregation occurs mainly when the traits measured are controlled by genes that reside on different chromosomes.

Genes are arranged on chromosomes like beads on a string.

It turns out that the genes for a particular character occur at a particular site on a particular chromosome. Such a site is called a **locus** (plural *loci*). Loci are arranged on the chromosomes in a line, like beads on a string. A particular locus may hold any of several alleles. The gene for seed color is always in the same position on a particular chromosome, whether it codes for green or for yellow seeds. Keep in mind that the locus for seed color may be located on one chromosome and the locus for seed texture located on another chromosome. All of the genes carried on all of the chromosomes are referred to as the **genome**.

Traits may not segregate independently if they are affected by genes on the same chromosome.

Mendel's conclusion that traits segregate independently is true only if the loci that affect the traits are on different chromosomes because links between loci on the same chromosome alter the patterns of segregation. When loci for different traits occur on the same chromosome, they are said to be **linked**; loci on different chromosomes are said to be **unlinked**. You might think that genes at two loci on the same chromosome would always segregate together as if they were a single gene. If this were true, then a gamete receiving a particular chromosome from one of its parents would get all of the same genes that occurred on that chromosome in its parent. There would be no recombination. However, chromosomes frequently tangle and break as they are replicated during meiosis. Thus chromosomes are not always preserved intact, and genes on one chromosome are sometimes shifted from one member of a homologous pair to the other (see Figure 2.13). We call this process **crossing over**. Linkage reduces the rate of recombination but does not eliminate it altogether. The rate at which recombination generates novel combinations of genes at two loci on the same chromosome depends on the likelihood that a crossing-over event will occur. If two loci are located close together on the chromosome, crossing over will be rare and the rate of recombination will be low. If the two loci are located far apart, then crossing over will be common and the rate of recombination will approach the rate for genes on different chromosomes. This process is discussed more fully in Closer Look 2.1.

Molecular Genetics

Genes are segments of a long molecule called DNA, which is contained in chromosomes.

In the first half of the twentieth century, biologists learned a lot about the cellular events that take place during meiosis and mitosis and began to understand the chemistry of reproduction. For instance, by 1950 it was known that chromosomes contain two structurally complex molecules: protein and **deoxyribonucleic acid**, or **DNA**. It had also been determined that the particle of heredity postulated by Mendel was DNA, not protein, though exactly how DNA might contain and convey the information essential to life was still a mystery. Then in 1953, two young biologists at Cambridge University, Francis Crick and James Watson, made a discovery that revolutionized biology: they deduced the structure of DNA. Watson and Crick's elucidation of the structure of DNA was the wellspring of a great flood of research that continues to provide a deep and powerful understanding of how life works at the molecular level. We now know how DNA stores information and how this information controls the chemistry of life, and this knowledge explains why heredity leads to the patterns Mendel described in pea plants and why there are sometimes new variations.

Understanding the chemical nature of the gene is critical to the study of human evolution: (1) molecular genetics links biology to chemistry and physics and (2) molecular methods help us reconstruct the evolutionary history of the human lineage.

Modern molecular genetics, the product of Watson and Crick's discovery, is a field of great intellectual excitement. Every year yields new discoveries about how living things work at the molecular level. This knowledge is deeply important because it links biology to chemistry and physics. One of the grandest goals of science is to provide a single consistent explanatory framework for the way the world works. We want to place evolution in this grand scheme of scientific explanation. It is important to be able to explain not only how new species of plants and animals arise but also how a wide range of phenomena—from the origin of stars and galaxies to the rise of complex societies—have evolved. Modern molecular biology is profoundly important because it connects physical and geochemical evolution to Darwinian processes.

Molecular genetics also provides data that help biologists and anthropologists reconstruct evolutionary history. As we will see in Chapter 4, comparing the DNA sequences of different species allows us to reconstruct their evolutionary histories. For example, this kind of analysis tells us that humans share a more recent common ancestor with chimpanzees than members of either species share with gorillas. The same data tell us that the last common ancestor of chimpanzees and humans lived between 5 and 7 million years ago (mya). Patterns of variation in DNA sequences within species are also informative. In Chapter 13, we will see that patterns of genetic variation within the human species allow anthropologists to figure out when the first modern humans left Africa and where they went. In Chapter 14, we will see that the patterns of genetic variation also provide important clues about how natural selection has shaped adaptation within the human species.

In this section, we provide a very brief and highly selective introduction to molecular genetics. Our aim is to give enough background to allow students to understand the molecular evidence about human evolution. Students who want a richer understanding of the science of molecular genetics and its important implications for human societies should consult the Further Readings section at the end of this chapter.

Genes Are DNA

DNA is unusually well suited to be the chemical basis of inheritance.

The discovery of the structure of DNA was fundamental to genetics because the structure itself implied how inheritance must work. Each chromosome contains a single DNA molecule roughly 2 m (about 6 ft.) long that is folded up to fit in the nucleus. DNA molecules consist of two long strands, and each strand has a "backbone" of alternating sequences of sugar and phosphate molecules. Attached to each sugar is one of four molecules, collectively called **bases: adenine**, **guanine**, **cytosine**, or **thymine**. The two strands of DNA are held together by very weak chemical bonds, called "hydrogen bonds," which connect some of the bases on different strands. Thymine bonds only with adenine, and guanine bonds only with cytosine (**Figure 2.16**).

The repeating four-base structure of DNA allows the molecule to assume a vast number of distinct forms. Each DNA configuration is exactly like a message written in an alphabet with letters that stand for each of the four bases (T for thymine, A for adenine, G for guanine, and C for cytosine). Thus

TCGGTAGTAGTTACGG

is one message and

ATCCGGATGCAATCCA

is another message. Because the DNA in a single chromosome is millions of bases long, there is room for a nearly infinite variety of messages.

These messages would be of no consequence if they were not preserved over time and transmitted faithfully; DNA is uniquely suited to this task. Each of the staggering

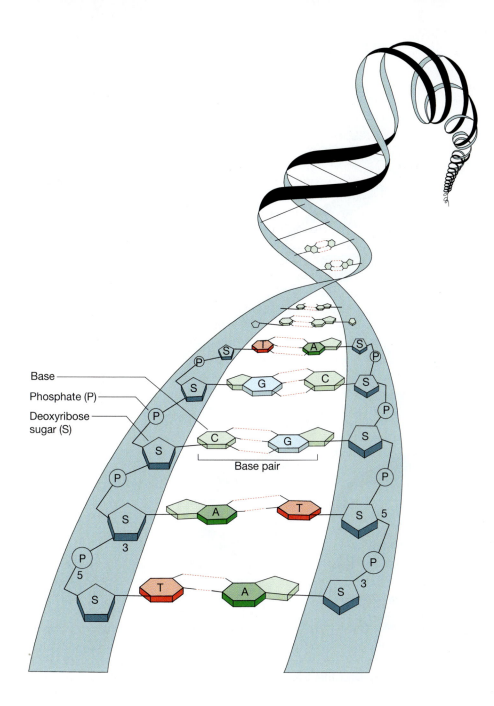

FIGURE 2.16

The chemical structure of DNA consists of two long backbones made of alternating sugar and phosphate molecules. One of four bases—adenine (A), guanine (G), cytosine (C), or thymine (T)—is attached to each of the sugars. The two strands are connected to each other by hydrogen bonds (*dotted lines*) between certain pairs of bases. Thymine bonds only to adenine, and guanine bonds only to cytosine.

Base

Phosphate (P)

Deoxyribose sugar (S)

Base pair

number of DNA molecules that could exist in nature are equally stable chemically. DNA is not the only complex molecule with many alternative forms, but other molecules have some forms that are less stable than others. Such molecules would be unsuitable for carrying information because the messages would become garbled as the molecules changed toward a more stable form. What makes DNA unusual is that all of its nearly infinite number of forms are equally stable.

In addition to preserving a message faithfully, hereditary material must be replicable. Without the ability to make copies of itself, the genetic message could not be spread to offspring, and natural selection would be impossible. DNA is replicated within cells by a highly efficient cellular machinery: it first unzips the two strands, and then, with the help of other specialized molecular machinery, it adds complementary bases to each of the strands until two identical sugar and phosphate backbones are

FIGURE 2.17

When DNA is replicated, the two strands of the parent DNA are separated and two daughter DNA strands are formed.

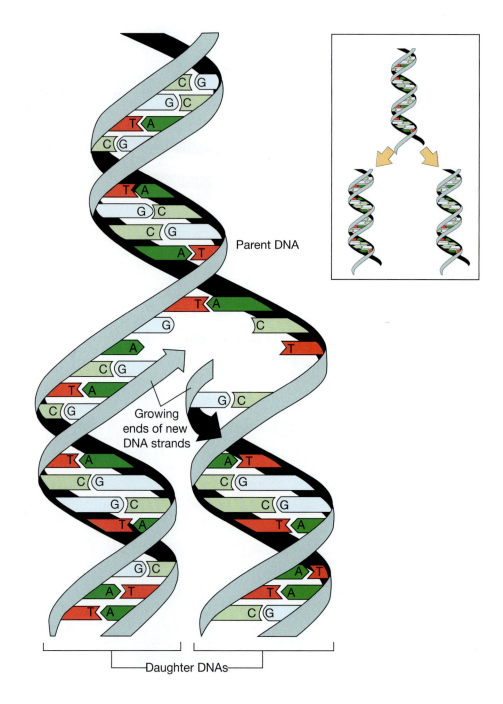

Parent DNA

Growing ends of new DNA strands

Daughter DNAs

built (**Figure 2.17**). There are also mechanisms that "proofread" the copies and correct errors that crop up. These proofreading mechanisms are astoundingly good; they miss only one error in every *billion* bases replicated.

The message encoded in DNA affects phenotypes in several different ways.

For DNA to play an important role in evolution, different DNA messages must lead to different phenotypes. Here the story gets more complicated because DNA affects phenotypes in a number of different ways. The three most important ways that DNA affects phenotypes are the following:

1. DNA in **protein coding genes** (or protein coding sequences) specifies the structure of proteins. Proteins play many important roles in the machinery of life. In

particular, many proteins are **enzymes**, which regulate much of the biochemical machinery of organisms.

2. DNA in **regulatory genes** (or regulatory sequences) determines the conditions under which the message encoded in a protein coding gene will be expressed. Regulatory genes play a crucial role in shaping the differentiation of cells during development.

3. DNA specifies the structure of several different kinds of ribonucleic acid (RNA) molecules that perform important cellular functions. These include RNA molecules that play a crucial role in the machinery of protein synthesis and other RNA molecules that help regulate the expression of other genes.

Some Genes Code for Proteins

Proteins called enzymes influence an organism's biochemistry.

The cells and organs of living things are made up of a very large number of chemical compounds, and it is this combination of compounds that gives each organism its characteristic form and structure. All organisms use the same raw materials, but they achieve different end results. How does this happen?

The answer is that enzymes present in the cell determine what the raw materials are transformed into when cells are built (**Figure 2.18**). The best way to understand how enzymes determine the characteristics of organisms is to think of an organism's biochemical machinery as a branching tree. Enzymes act as switches to determine what will happen at each node and thus what chemicals will be present in the cell. For example, glucose serves as a food source for many cells, meaning that it provides energy and a source of raw materials for the construction of cellular structures. Glucose might initially undergo any one of an extremely large number of slow-moving reactions. The presence of particular catalytic enzymes will determine which reactions occur rapidly enough to alter the chemistry of the cell. For example, some enzymes

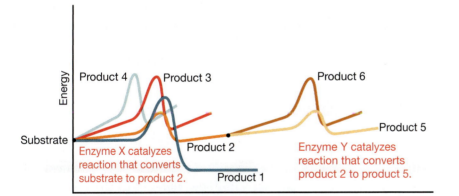

FIGURE 2.18

Enzymes control the chemical composition of cells by catalyzing some chemical reactions but not others. In this hypothetical example, the molecules that provide the initial raw material (called a substrate) of the pathway could undergo four different reactions yielding different molecules, labeled products 1 through 4. However, because enzyme X is present, the reaction that yields product 2 proceeds much more rapidly than the other reactions (note that this reaction has the lowest activation energy), and all of the substrate is converted to that product. Product 2 could then undergo two different reactions yielding products 5 and 6. When enzyme Y is present, it lowers the activation energy, thus causing the reaction yielding product 5 to proceed much more rapidly, and only product 5 is produced. In this way, enzymes link products and reactants into pathways that satisfy particular chemical functions, such as the extraction of energy from glucose.

lead to the metabolism of glucose and the release of its stored energy. At the end of the first branch, there is another node representing all of the reactions that could involve the product(s) of the first branch. Again, one or more enzymes will determine what happens next.

This picture has been greatly simplified. Real organisms take in many different kinds of compounds, and each compound is involved in a complicated tangle of branches that biochemists call pathways. Real **biochemical pathways** are very complex. One set of enzymes causes glucose to be shunted to a pathway that yields energy. A different set of enzymes causes the glucose to be shunted to a pathway that binds glucose molecules together to form glycogen, a starch that functions as energy storage. The presence of a different set of enzymes would lead to the synthesis of cellulose, a complex molecule that provides the structural material in plants. Enzymes play roles in virtually all cellular processes—from the replication of DNA and division of cells to the contraction and movement of muscles.

FIGURE 2.19

All amino acids share the same chemical backbone, here colored *blue*. They differ according to the chemical structure of the side group attached to the backbone, here colored *tan*.

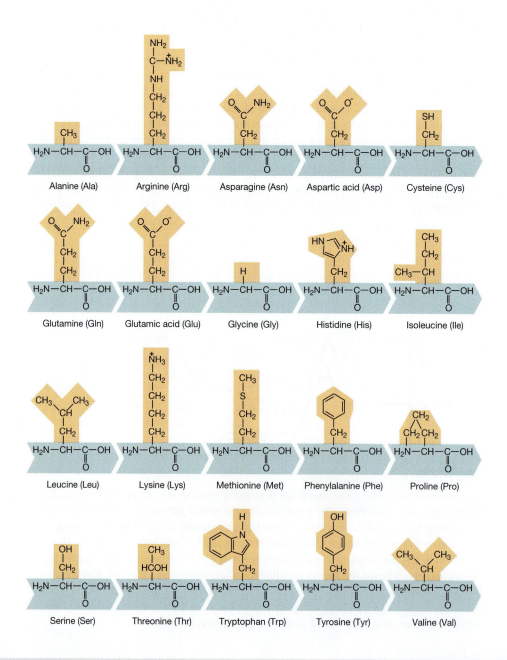

Proteins play a number of other important roles in the machinery of life.

Some proteins have crucial structural functions in living things. For example, your hair is made up mainly of a protein called keratin, and your ligaments and tendons are strengthened by another protein, called collagen. Other proteins act as tiny mechanical contraptions that accomplish many important functions. Some are tiny valves for regulating what goes into and out of cells. Still others, like insulin, convey chemical signals from one part of the body to another or act as receptors that respond to these messages.

The sequence of amino acids in proteins determines their properties.

Proteins are constructed of amino acids. There are 20 different amino acid molecules. All **amino acids** have the same chemical backbone, but they differ in the chemical composition of the side chain connected to this backbone (**Figure 2.19**). The sequence of amino acid side chains, called the **primary structure** of the protein, is what makes one protein different from others. You can think of a protein as a very long railroad train in which there are 20 different kinds of cars, each representing a different amino acid. The primary structure is a list of the types of cars in the order that they occur.

When proteins are actually doing their business, they are folded in complex ways. The three-dimensional shape of the folded protein, called the **tertiary structure**, is crucial to its catalytic function. The way the protein folds depends on the sequence of amino acid molecules that make up its primary sequence. This means that the function of enzymes depends on the sequence of the amino acids that make them up. (Proteins also have secondary structure and sometimes quaternary structure; but to keep things simple, we will ignore those levels here.)

These ideas are illustrated in **Figure 2.20**, which shows the folded shape of part of a **hemoglobin** molecule, a protein that transports oxygen from the lungs to the tissues via red blood cells. As you can see, the protein folds into a roughly spherical glob, and oxygen is bound to the protein near the center of the glob. **Sickle-cell anemia**, a condition common among people in West Africa and among African Americans, is caused by a single change in the primary sequence of amino acids in the hemoglobin molecule. Glutamic acid is the sixth amino acid in normal hemoglobin molecules, but in people afflicted with sickle-cell anemia, valine is substituted for glutamic acid. This single substitution changes the way that the molecule folds and reduces its ability to bind oxygen.

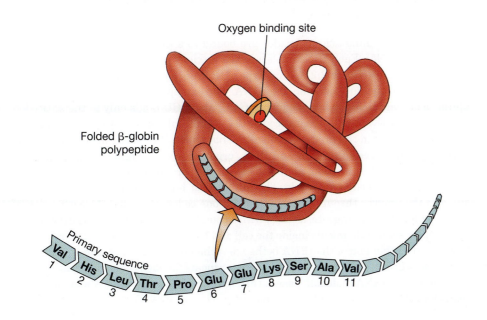

Oxygen binding site

Folded β-globin polypeptide

Primary sequence

Val 1 · His 2 · Leu 3 · Thr 4 · Pro 5 · Glu 6 · Glu 7 · Lys 8 · Ser 9 · Ala 10 · Val 11

FIGURE 2.20

The primary and tertiary structures of hemoglobin, a protein that transports oxygen on red blood cells. The primary structure is the sequence of amino acids making up the protein. The tertiary structure is the way the protein folds into three dimensions.

DNA specifies the primary structure of protein.

Now we return to our original question: how does the information contained in DNA—its sequence of bases—determine the structure of proteins? Remember that DNA encodes messages in a four-letter alphabet. Researchers determined that these letters are combined into three-letter "words" called **codons**, each of which specifies a particular amino acid. Because there are four bases, there are 64 possible three-letter combinations for codons (4 possibilities for the first base times 4 for the second times 4 for the third, or $4 \times 4 \times 4 = 64$). Of these codons, 61 are used to code for the 20 amino acids that make up proteins. For example, the codons GCT, GCC, GCA, and GCG all code for alanine; GAT and GAC code for asparagine; and so on. The remaining three codons are "punctuation marks" that mean either "start, this is the beginning of the protein" or "stop, this is the end of the protein." Thus if you can identify the base pairs, it is a simple matter to determine what proteins are encoded on the DNA.

You might be wondering why several different codons code for the same amino acid. This redundancy serves an important function. Because a number of processes can damage DNA and cause one base to be substituted for another, redundancy decreases the chance that a random change will alter the primary sequence of the protein produced. Proteins represent complex adaptations, so we would expect most changes to be deleterious (harmful). But because the code is redundant, many substitutions have no effect on the message of a particular stretch of DNA. The importance of this redundancy is underscored by the fact that the most common amino acids are the ones with the greatest number of codon variants.

Before DNA is translated into proteins, its message is first transcribed into messenger RNA.

DNA can be thought of as a set of instructions for building proteins, but the real work of synthesizing proteins is performed by other molecules. The first step in the translation of DNA into protein occurs when a facsimile of one of the strands of DNA, which will serve as a messenger or chemical intermediary, is made, usually in the cell's nucleus. This copy is **ribonucleic acid**, or **RNA**. RNA is similar to DNA, except that it has a slightly different chemical backbone, and the base **uracil** (denoted U) is substituted for thymine. RNA comes in several forms, many of which aid in protein synthesis. The form of RNA used in this first step is **messenger RNA (mRNA)**.

The ribosome then synthesizes a particular protein by reading the mRNA copy of the gene.

Meanwhile, amino acid molecules are bound to a different kind of RNA, called **transfer RNA (tRNA)**. Each tRNA molecule has a triplet of bases, called an **anticodon**, at a particular site (**Figure 2.21**). Each type of tRNA is bound to the amino acid whose codon binds to the anticodon on the tRNA. For example, one of the codons for the amino acid alanine is the base sequence GCU, and GCU binds only to the anticodon CGA. Thus the tRNA with the anticodon CGA binds only to the amino acid alanine.

The next step in the process involves the **ribosomes**. Ribosomes are small cellular **organelles**. Composed of protein and RNA, organelles are cellular components that perform a particular function, analogous to the way organs such as the liver perform a function for the body as a whole. The mRNA first binds to ribosomes at a binding site and then moves through the binding site one codon at a time. As each codon of mRNA enters the binding site, a tRNA with a complementary anticodon is drawn from the complex soup of chemicals inside the cell and bound to the mRNA. The amino acid bound to the other end of the tRNA is then detached from the tRNA and added to one end of the growing protein chain. The process repeats for each codon, continuing until the end of the mRNA molecule passes through the ribosome. Voilà! A new protein is ready for action.

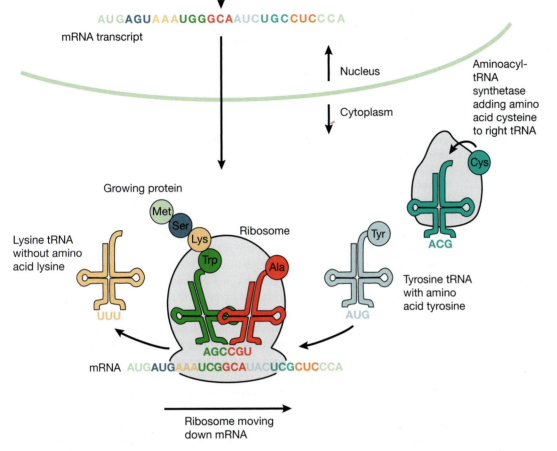

DNA template

TACTCATTTACCCGTAGTACGGAGGGT
||||||||||||||||||||||||||
ATGAGTAAATGGGCATACTGCCTCCCA

AUGAGUAAAUGGGCAAUCUGCCUCCCA

mRNA transcript

Nucleus

Cytoplasm

Aminoacyl-tRNA synthetase adding amino acid cysteine to right tRNA

Cys

ACG

Growing protein

Met
Ser
Lys
Trp

Ribosome

Ala

Tyr

Lysine tRNA without amino acid lysine

UUU

AUG

Tyrosine tRNA with amino acid tyrosine

AGCCGU

mRNA AUGAUGAAAUCGGCAUACUCGCUCCCA

Ribosome moving down mRNA

FIGURE 2.21

The information encoded in DNA determines the structure of proteins in the following way. Inside the nucleus, an mRNA copy is made of the original DNA template. The mRNA is coded in three-base codons. Here each codon is given a different color. For example, the sequence AUG codes for the start of a protein and the amino acid methionine, the sequence AGU codes for serine, and the sequence AAA codes for lysine. The mRNA then migrates to the cytoplasm. In the cytoplasm, special enzymes called aminoacyl-tRNA synthetases locate a specific kind of tRNA and attach the amino acid whose mRNA codon will bind to the anticodon on the tRNA. For example, the mRNA codon for cysteine is UGG, and the appropriate anticodon is ACC because U binds to A and C binds to G. In this diagram, matching mRNA codons and tRNA anticodons are given the same color. The initiation of protein assembly is complicated and involves specialized enzymes. Once the process is started, each codon of the mRNA binds to the ribosome. Then the matching tRNA is bound to the mRNA, the amino acid is transferred to the growing protein, the tRNA is released, the ribosome shifts to the next codon, and the process is repeated.

In eukaryotes, the DNA that codes for proteins is interrupted by noncoding sequences called introns.

So far, our description of protein synthesis applies to almost all organisms. However, most of this information was learned through the study of *Escherichia coli,* a bacterium that lives in the human gut. Like other bacteria, *E. coli* belongs to a group of organisms called the **prokaryotes** because it does not have a chromosome or a cell nucleus. In prokaryotes, the DNA sequence that codes for a particular protein is uninterrupted. A stretch of DNA is copied to RNA and then translated into a protein. For many years, biologists thought that the same would be true of **eukaryotes** (organisms like plants, birds, and humans that have chromosomes and a cell nucleus).

Beginning in the 1970s, new recombinant DNA technology allowed molecular geneticists to study eukaryotes. These studies revealed that in eukaryotes, the segment of DNA that codes for a protein is almost always interrupted by at least one—and sometimes many—noncoding sequences called **introns**. (The protein coding sequences are called **exons**.) Protein synthesis in eukaryotes includes one additional step not mentioned in our discussion so far: after the entire DNA sequence is copied to make an mRNA molecule in the nucleus, the intron-based parts of the mRNA are snipped out and the mRNA molecule is spliced back together. Then, the mRNA is exported out of the nucleus, and protein synthesis takes place.

Alternative splicing allows the same DNA sequence to code for more than one protein.

When the introns are snipped out and the RNA is spliced back together, not all of the exons are necessarily included. This means that the same sequence of DNA can yield many different mRNAs and code for many different proteins. **Figure 2.22** shows how this can work. A hypothetical protein has four exons (in colors) and three introns (in gray). The entire DNA sequence is transcribed into RNA, and the introns are removed. The exons are always spliced back together in their original order, but not all of the exons are included in every new RNA molecule. By including different exons in the final RNA, different proteins can be produced.

Alternative splicing seems to be important. It has been estimated that more than half of the protein coding sequences in the human genome yield more than one protein, and some yield as many as 10. Some biologists think that this flexibility is important in multicellular organisms in which different types of proteins are required for the function of diverse cell types. Adherents of this hypothesis think that introns proliferated at the origin of eukaryotes. Other biologists think that introns are weakly deleterious bits of DNA that are maintained in eukaryotes because their population sizes are much smaller than prokaryotes. As we will see in Chapter 3, small populations are subject to a random nonadaptive evolutionary process called genetic drift that usually works against natural selection. In bacterial populations numbering in the hundreds of millions, drift is weak and selection eliminates the introns. In the much smaller eukaryotic populations, drift is strong enough to maintain introns.

Regulatory Sequences Control Gene Expression

The DNA sequence in regulatory genes determines when protein coding genes are expressed.

Gene regulation in the bacterium *Escherichia coli* provides a good example of how the DNA sequence in regulatory genes controls gene expression. *E. coli* uses the sugar glucose as its primary source of energy. When glucose runs short, *E. coli* can switch to other sugars, such as lactose, but this switch requires a number of enzymes that allow lactose to be metabolized. The genes for these lactose-specific enzymes are always present, but they are not expressed when there is plenty of glucose available. This is efficient because it would be wasteful to produce these enzymes if they were not needed. The genes for making enzymes that allow the metabolism of lactose to glucose are expressed only when glucose is in short supply *and* sufficient lactose is present. Two regulatory sequences are located near the protein coding genes that encode the amino acid sequence for three enzymes necessary for lactose metabolism. When there

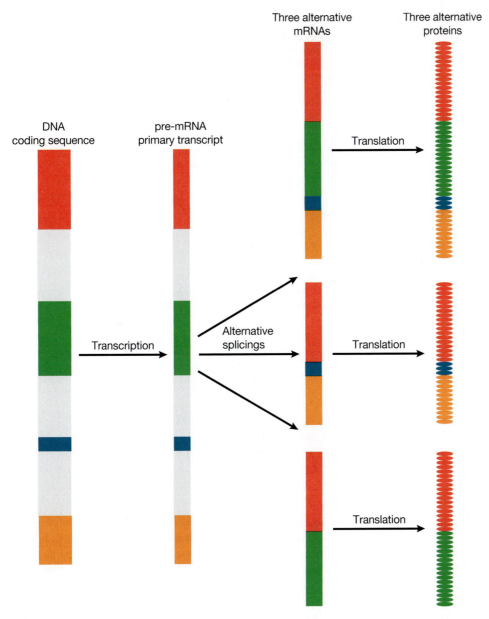

DNA coding sequence   **pre-mRNA primary transcript**   Three alternative mRNAs   Three alternative proteins

Transcription   Alternative splicings   Translation

FIGURE 2.22

A hypothetical protein has four exons (*red*, *green*, *blue*, and *brown*) and three introns (*gray*). The entire DNA sequence is transcribed into a pre-mRNA molecule. After introns are snipped out, the exons are spliced back together to yield three different mRNAs, and these are translated into three different proteins.

is glucose in the environment, a **repressor** protein binds to one of the two regulatory sequences, thereby preventing the protein coding genes from being transcribed (**Figure 2.23a**). When glucose is absent, the repressor protein changes shape and does not bind to the DNA in the regulatory sequence (**Figure 2.23b**). The second regulatory sequence is an **activator**. In the presence of lactose, an activator protein binds to this DNA sequence, greatly increasing the rate at which the protein coding genes are transcribed (**Figure 2.23c**). The specific DNA sequences of the regulatory genes control whether or not the repressor and activator proteins that control DNA transcription bind to the DNA. This means that the sequence of DNA in regulatory genes affects the phenotype and creates variation. Therefore, regulatory genes are subject to natural selection, just as protein coding genes are.

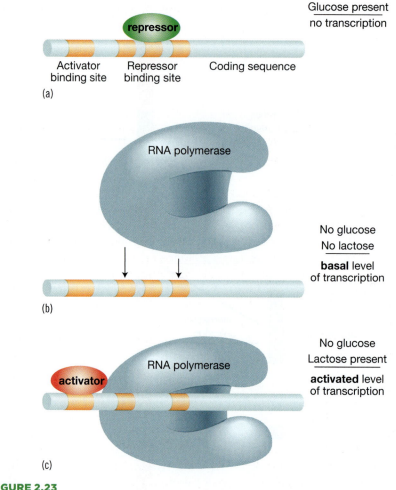

Glucose present
no transcription

Activator binding site   Repressor binding site   Coding sequence

(a)

RNA polymerase

No glucose
No lactose

basal level of transcription

(b)

activator   RNA polymerase

No glucose
Lactose present

activated level of transcription

(c)

FIGURE 2.23

This diagram shows how regulatory sequences binding activator and repressor proteins control the expression of the enzymes necessary to digest lactose in *E. coli*. (a) When glucose is present, the repressor protein binds to the regulatory sequence, thus preventing the enzyme RNA polymerase from creating an mRNA from the DNA template. (b) When glucose is absent and there is no lactose that the RNA polymerase can bind, the genes necessary for metabolism of lactose are expressed but at a low (basal) level. (c) When lactose is present, the activator protein can bind to its regulatory sequence, thereby greatly increasing the rate at which the RNA polymerase binds and increasing the level of gene expression.

In humans and other eukaryotes, the expression of a given protein coding gene is often affected by many regulatory sequences, which are sometimes located quite far from the coding sequence that they regulate. The proteins that bind to these regulatory genes can interact in complex ways, so that multiple proteins bound to sequences of DNA at widely separate sites may act to activate or repress a particular protein coding gene. However, the basic principle is usually the same: Under some circumstances the DNA sequence in the regulatory gene binds to a protein that in turn affects the expression of a particular protein coding gene.

The existence of multiple regulatory sequences allows for **combinatorial control** of gene expression. In *E. coli,* the combination of a repressor and an activator means that the genes necessary to metabolize lactose are synthesized in a particular combination of circumstances: the presence of lactose *and* the absence of glucose. This is a simple example. Combinatorial control of gene expression is often more complex in eukaryotes: there may be dozens of activators and multiple different combinations that influence gene expression.

Gene regulation allows cell differentiation in complex multicellular organisms like humans.

Complex, multicellular organisms are made of many different kinds of cells, each with its own specific chemical machinery: cells in the liver and pancreas secrete digestive enzymes, nerve cells carry electrical signals throughout the body, muscle cells respond to these signals by performing mechanical work, and so on. Nonetheless, in a single individual, all cells have exactly the same genetic composition. The cells differ in their function because different genes are activated in different cell types.

The development of the vertebrate nervous system provides an example of how this works. At a certain point in the development of all vertebrate embryos, cells that are going to give rise to the spinal cord differentiate to form the neural tube. Special cells at one end of this structure secrete a molecule called "Sonic Hedgehog" (after the video game character of the same name). Cells close to the source of this signaling molecule experience a high concentration of Sonic Hedgehog; those more distant experience a lower concentration. The concentrations of Sonic Hedgehog affect the expression of genes in these future nerve cells. Low concentrations lead to the expression of genes that destine the cells to become motor neurons, which control muscles; higher concentrations lead to the expression of genes that cause cells to become the neurons of the brain and spinal cord.

A single signal can trigger the complex series of events that transform a cell into a liver cell or a nerve cell because the expression of one gene causes a different set of genes to be expressed, and this in turn causes additional sets of genes to be expressed. For example, a gene called PAX6 codes for a regulatory protein that is important in the differentiation of the cells in the developing eye. Artificially activating this gene in one cell in a fruit fly antenna leads to the synthesis of a regulatory protein that sets off a cascade of gene expression, which eventually involves the expression of about 2,500 other genes and the development of an extra eye on the fly's antenna.

Not All DNA Codes for Protein

Some DNA sequences code for functional RNA molecules.

Messenger RNA is not the only important form of RNA. Some RNA molecules bind together with proteins to perform a variety of cellular functions. Ribosomes are an example, as are **spliceosomes**, the organelles that splice the mRNA in eukaryotes after the introns have been snipped out. It has long been known that some DNA codes for these RNAs, but it was thought that the bulk of the 98% of the genome that lies outside of exons was just "junk DNA" with no real function. However, at least half of the DNA that lies in introns and between genes seems to be expressed as **noncoding RNA (ncRNA)**. One form of ncRNA, short RNA segments called **microRNAs (miRNAs)**, plays an important role in regulating the translation of mRNA into protein. These sequences are transcribed, and the resulting miRNAs move outside the nucleus, where, after much processing, they bind to complementary mRNA molecules and affect the rate at which the mRNA is translated into protein, providing an alternative mechanism for regulation of gene expression. Much like regulatory sequences, some miRNAs play an important role in regulating development and cell differentiation in complex organisms like humans. Longer RNA segments called **long noncoding RNAs (lncRNAs)** have a wide variety of functions and may be especially important in regulating the expression of genes during development.

Chromosomes also contain long strings of simple repeated sequences.

Introns are not the only kind of DNA that is not involved in the synthesis of proteins. Chromosomes also contain a lot of DNA that is composed of simple repeated patterns. For example, in fruit flies there are long segments of DNA composed of adenine and thymine in the following monotonous five-base pattern:

...ATAATATAATATAATATAATATAATATAATATAATATAAT...

In all eukaryotes, simple repeated sequences of DNA are found in particular sites on particular chromosomes.

At this point, there is some danger of losing sight of the genes amid the discussion of introns, exons, and repeat sequences. A brief reprise may be helpful.

In summary, chromosomes contain an enormously long molecule of DNA. Genes are short segments of this DNA. After suitable editing, a gene's DNA is transcribed into mRNA, which in turn is translated into a protein whose structure is determined by the gene's DNA sequence. Proteins determine the properties of living organisms by selectively catalyzing some chemical reactions and not others and by forming some of the structural components of cells, organs, and tissues. Genes with different DNA sequences lead to the synthesis of proteins with different catalytic behavior and structural characteristics. Many changes in the morphology or behavior of organisms can be traced back to variations in the proteins and genes that build them. It is important to remember that evolution has a molecular basis. The changes in the genetic constitution of populations that we will explore in Chapter 3 are grounded in the physical and chemical properties of molecules and genes discussed here.

Key Terms

variants
crosses
F_0 generation
F_1 generation
F_2 generation
genes
gametes
independent assortment
chromosome
nucleus
mitosis
diploid
homologous pairs
meiosis
haploid
zygote
alleles
homozygous
heterozygous

genotype
phenotype
dominant
recessive
Punnett square
recombination
locus
genome
linked
unlinked
crossing over
deoxyribonucleic acid (DNA)
bases:
  adenine
  guanine
  cytosine
  thymine
protein coding genes
enzymes

regulatory genes
biochemical pathways
proteins
amino acids
primary structure
tertiary structure
hemoglobin
sickle-cell anemia
codons
ribonucleic acid (RNA)
uracil
messenger RNA (mRNA)
transfer RNA (tRNA)
anticodon
ribosomes
organelles
prokaryotes
eukaryotes
introns

exons
repressor
activator

combinatorial control
spliceosome
noncoding RNA (ncRNA)

microRNA (miRNA)
long noncoding RNA (lncRNA)

Study Questions

1. Explain why Mendel's principles follow from the mechanics of meiosis.

2. Mendel did experiments in which he kept track of the inheritance of seed texture (wrinkled or smooth). First he created true-breeding lines: parents with smooth seeds produced offspring with smooth seeds, and parents with wrinkled seeds produced offspring with wrinkled seeds. When he crossed wrinkled and smooth peas from these true-breeding lines, all of the offspring were smooth. Which trait is dominant? What happened when he crossed members of the F_1 generation? What would have happened had he backcrossed members of the F_1 generation with individuals from a true-breeding line (like their parents) with smooth seeds? What about crosses between the F_1 generation and the wrinkled-seed true-breeding line?

3. Mendel also did experiments in which he kept track of two traits. For example, he created true-breeding lines of smooth-green and wrinkled-yellow peas, and then crossed these lines to produce an F_1 generation. What were the F_1 individuals like? He then crossed the members of the F_1 generation to form an F_2 generation. Assuming that the seed color locus and the seed texture locus are on different chromosomes, calculate the ratio of each of the four phenotypes in the F_2 generation. Calculate the ratios (approximately), assuming that the two loci are very close together on the same chromosome.

4. Many animals, such as birds and mammals, have physiological mechanisms that enable them to maintain their body temperature well above the air temperature. They are called "homeotherms." "Poikilotherms," like snakes and other reptiles, regulate body temperature by moving closer to or farther away from sources of heat. Use what you have learned about chemical reactions to develop a hypothesis that explains why animals have mechanisms for controlling body temperature.

5. Why is DNA so well suited for carrying information?

6. Recall the discussion about crossing over, and try to explain why introns might increase the rate of recombination between surrounding exons.

Further Reading

Barton, N. H., D. E. G. Briggs, J. A. Eisen, D. B. Goldstein, and N. H. Patelet. 2007. *Evolution*. Woodbury, N.Y.: Cold Spring Harbor Press.

Maynard Smith, J. 1998. *Evolutionary Genetics*. 2nd ed. New York: Oxford University Press.

Olby, R. C. 1985. *Origins of Mendelism*. 2nd ed. Chicago: University of Chicago Press.

Snustad, D. P. and M. J. Simmons. 2011. *Principles of Genetics*. 6th ed. Hoboken, N.J.: Wiley.

Watson, J. D., T. A. Baker, S. P. Bell, A. Gann, M. Levine, and R. Losicket. 2013. *Molecular Biology of the Gene*. 7th ed. San Francisco: Pearson/Benjamin Cummings.

3

CHAPTER OBJECTIVES

By the end of this chapter you should be able to

- Describe the genetic composition of populations in terms of the frequencies of genes and genotypes.

- Explain how sexual reproduction changes genotypic frequencies, sometimes leading to the Hardy–Weinberg equilibrium.

- Understand how natural selection changes gene frequencies in populations.

- Explain how population genetics explains the maintenance of variation, which is necessary for evolution to occur.

- Explain how natural selection shapes learned behavior.

- Understand why evolution does not always produce adaptations.

THE MODERN SYNTHESIS

Population Genetics | Natural Selection and Behavior
The Modern Synthesis | Constraints on Adaptation

Population Genetics

Evolutionary change in a phenotype reflects change in the underlying genetic composition of the population. When we discussed Mendel's experiments in Chapter 2, we briefly introduced the distinction between genotype and phenotype: phenotypes are the observable characteristics of organisms, and genotypes are the underlying genetic compositions. There need not be a one-to-one correspondence between genotype and phenotype. For example, there were only two seed-color phenotypes in Mendel's pea populations (yellow and green), but there were three genotypes (*AA, Aa,* and *aa*; **Figure 3.1**).

From what we now know about the genetic nature of inheritance, it is also clear that evolutionary processes must entail changes in the genetic composition of populations. When evolution alters the morphology of a character like the finch's beak, there must be a corresponding change in the distribution of genes that control beak development within the population. To understand how Mendelian genetics solves each of Darwin's difficulties, we need to look more closely at what happens to genes in populations that are undergoing natural selection. This is the domain of **population genetics**.

FIGURE 3.1

Peas were a useful subject for Mendel's botanical experiments because they have a number of dichotomous traits. For example, pea seeds are either yellow or green, but not an intermediate color.

Genes in Populations

Biologists describe the genetic composition of a population by specifying the frequency of alternative genotypes.

It's easiest to see what happens to genes in populations if we consider a trait that is controlled by one gene operating at a single locus on a chromosome. Phenylketonuria (PKU), a potentially debilitating, genetically inherited disease in humans, is determined by the substitution of one allele for another at a single locus. Individuals who are homozygous for the PKU allele are missing a crucial enzyme in the biochemical pathway that allows people to metabolize the amino acid phenylalanine. If the disease is not treated, phenylalanine builds up in the bloodstream of children with PKU and leads to severe mental retardation. Fortunately, treatment is possible: people with PKU raised on a special low-phenylalanine diet can develop normally and lead normal lives as adults.

How do evolutionary processes control the distribution of the PKU allele in a population? The first step in answering this question is to characterize the distribution of the harmful allele. Population geneticists do this by specifying the **genotypic frequency**, which is simply the fraction of the population that carries that genotype. Let's label the normal allele A and the deleterious PKU allele a. Suppose we perform a census of a population of 10,000 individuals and determine the number of individuals with each genotype. Geneticists can do this using established biochemical methods for determining an individual's genotype for a specific genetic locus. **Table 3.1** shows the number of individuals with each genotype and the frequencies of each genotype in this hypothetical population. (In most real populations, the frequency of individuals homozygous for the PKU allele is only about 1 in 10,000. We have used larger numbers here to make the calculations simpler.)

Genotypic frequencies must add up to 1.0 because every individual in the population has to have a genotype. We keep track of the frequencies of genotypes, rather than the numbers of individuals with each genotype, because the frequencies provide a description of the genetic composition of populations that is independent of population size. This makes it easy to compare populations of different sizes.

One goal of evolutionary theory is to determine how genotypic frequencies change through time.

A variety of events in the lives of plants and animals act to change the frequency of alternative genotypes in populations from generation to generation. Population geneticists categorize these processes into a number of evolutionary mechanisms, or forces. The most important mechanisms are sexual reproduction, natural selection, mutation, and genetic drift. In the remainder of this section we will see how

TABLE 3.1

Genotype	Number of Individuals	Frequency of Genotype
aa	2,000	freq(*aa*) = 2,000/10,000 = 0.2
Aa	4,000	freq(*Aa*) = 4,000/10,000 = 0.4
AA	4,000	freq(*AA*) = 4,000/10,000 = 0.4

The distribution of individuals with each of the three genotypes in a population of 10,000.

sexual reproduction and natural selection alter the frequencies of genes and genotypes, and later in the chapter we will return to consider the effects of mutation and genetic drift.

How Random Mating and Sexual Reproduction Change Genotypic Frequencies

The events that occur during sexual reproduction can lead to changes in genotypic frequencies in a population.

First, let's consider the effects of the patterns of inheritance that Mendel observed. Imagine that men and women do not choose their mates according to whether they are afflicted with PKU, but mate randomly with respect to the individual's genotype for PKU. It is important to study the effects of random mating because, for most genetic loci, mating is random. Even though humans may choose their mates with care and might even avoid mates with particular genetic characteristics, such as PKU, they cannot choose mates with a particular allele at each locus because there are more than 22,000 genetic loci in humans. Random mating between individuals is equivalent to the random union of gametes. In this sense, it's not really different from oysters shedding their eggs and sperm into the ocean, where chance dictates which gametes will form zygotes.

The first step in determining the effects of sexual reproduction on genotypic frequencies is to calculate the frequency of the PKU allele in the pool of gametes.

We can best understand how segregation affects genotypic frequencies by breaking the process into two steps. In the first step, we determine the frequency of the PKU allele among all the gametes in the mating population. Remember that the a allele is the PKU allele and the A allele is the "normal" allele. Table 3.1 gives the frequency of each of the three genotypes among the parental generation. We want to use this information to determine the genotypic frequencies among the F_1 generation. First, we calculate the frequencies of the two types of alleles in the pool of gametes. (The frequency of an allele is also referred to as its **gene frequency**.) Let's label the frequency of A as p and the frequency of a as q. (Because there are only two alleles, $p + q = 1$.) If all individuals produce the same number of gametes, then we can calculate q as follows:

$$q = \frac{\text{no. of } a \text{ gametes}}{\text{total no. of gametes}}$$

Note that this is simply the definition of a frequency. We can calculate the values of the numerator and denominator of this fraction from information we already know. Because a gametes can be produced only by aa and Aa individuals, the total number of a gametes is simply the sum of the number of Aa and aa parents multiplied by the number of a gametes that each parent produces. The denominator is the number of gametes per parent multiplied by the total number of parents. Hence

$$q = \frac{\left(\begin{array}{c}\text{no. of } a \\ \text{gametes per} \\ aa \text{ parent}\end{array}\right)\left(\begin{array}{c}\text{no. of } aa \\ \text{parents}\end{array}\right) + \left(\begin{array}{c}\text{no. of } a \\ \text{gametes per} \\ Aa \text{ parent}\end{array}\right)\left(\begin{array}{c}\text{no. of } Aa \\ \text{parents}\end{array}\right)}{(\text{no. of gametes per parent})(\text{total no. of parents})} \tag{3.1}$$

To simplify this equation, let's first examine the terms that involve numbers of individuals. Remember that the population size is 10,000 individuals. This means that the number of *aa* parents is equal to the frequency of *aa* parents multiplied by 10,000. Similarly, the number of *Aa* parents is equal to the frequency of *Aa* parents multiplied by 10,000. Now we examine the terms that involve numbers of gametes. Suppose each parent produces two gametes. For *aa* individuals, both gametes contain the *a* allele, so the number of *a* gametes per *aa* parent is 2. For *Aa* individuals, half of the gametes will carry the *a* allele and half will carry the *A* allele, so here the number of *a* gametes per *Aa* parent is 0.5 × 2. Now we substitute all these values into Equation (3.1) to get

$$q = \frac{2[\text{freq}(aa) \times 10{,}000] + (0.5 \times 2)[\text{freq}(Aa) \times 10{,}000]}{2 \times 10{,}000}$$

We can reduce this fraction by dividing the top and bottom by 2 × 10,000, which yields the following formula for the frequency of the *a* allele in the pool of gametes:

$$q = \text{freq}(aa) + 0.5 \times \text{freq}(Aa) \tag{3.2}$$

Notice that this form of the formula contains neither the population size nor the average number of gametes per individual in the population. Under normal circumstances, the population size and the average number of gametes per individual do not matter. This means that you can use this expression as a general formula for calculating gene frequencies among the gametes produced by any population of individuals, as long as the genetic locus of interest has only two alleles. It is important to keep in mind that the formula results from applying Mendel's laws and from counting the number of *a* gametes produced.

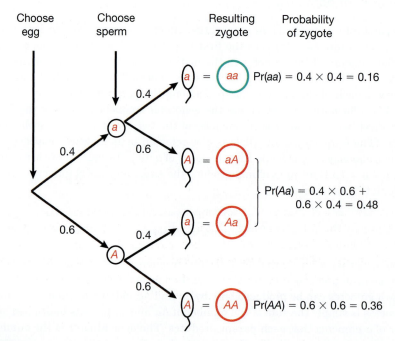

FIGURE 3.2

This event tree shows how to calculate the frequency of each genotype among the zygotes created by the random union of gametes. In this pool of gametes, the frequency of *a* is 0.4 and the frequency of *A* is 0.6. The first node represents the choice of an egg. There is a 40% chance that the egg will carry the *a* allele and a 60% chance it will carry the *A* allele. The second node represents the choice of the sperm. Once again, there is a 40% chance of drawing an *a*-bearing sperm and a 60% chance of drawing an *A*-bearing sperm. We can calculate the probability of each genotype by computing the probability of taking a path through the tree. For example, the probability of getting an *aa* zygote is 0.4 × 0.4 = 0.16.

By using Equation (3.2) and values from Table 3.1, for this particular population we get $q = 0.2 + (0.5 \times 0.4) = 0.4$. Because $p + q$ must sum to 1.0, p (the frequency of the A gametes) must be 0.6. Notice that the frequency of each allele in the pool of gametes is the same as the frequency of the same allele among parents.

The next step is to calculate the frequencies of all the genotypes among the zygotes.

Now that we have calculated the frequency of the PKU allele among the pool of gametes, we can determine the frequencies of the genotypes among the zygotes. If each zygote is the product of the random union of two gametes, the process of zygote formation can be schematically represented in an event tree (**Figure 3.2**) similar to the one we used to represent Mendel's crosses (for example, Figure 2.9). First we select a gamete—say, an egg. The probability of selecting an egg carrying the a allele is 0.4 because this is the frequency of the a allele in the population. Now we randomly draw a second gamete, the sperm. Again, the probability of getting a sperm carrying an a allele is 0.4. The chance that these two randomly chosen gametes are both a is 0.4×0.4, or 0.16. Figure 3.2 also shows how to compute the probabilities of the other two genotypes. Note that the sum of the three genotypes always equals 1.0, because all individuals must have a genotype.

If we form a large number of zygotes by randomly drawing gametes from the gamete pool, we will obtain the genotypic frequencies shown in **Table 3.2**. Compare the frequencies of each genotype in the parental population (Table 3.1) with the frequencies of each genotype in the F_1 generation: the genotypic frequencies have changed because the processes of independent segregation of alleles into gametes and random mating alter the distribution of alleles in zygotes. As a result, genotypic frequencies between the F_0 generation and the F_1 generation are altered. [Note, however, that the frequencies of the two *alleles*, a and A, have not changed; you can check this out using Equation (3.2).]

When no other forces (such as natural selection) are operating, genotypic frequencies reach stable proportions in just one generation. These proportions are called the Hardy–Weinberg equilibrium.

If no other processes act to change the distribution of genotypes, the set of genotypic frequencies in Table 3.2 will remain unchanged in subsequent generations. That is, if members of the F_1 generation mate at random, the distribution of genotypes in the F_2 generation will be exactly the same as the distribution of genotypes in the F_1 generation. The fact that genotypic frequencies remain constant was recognized independently by the British mathematician Godfrey Harold Hardy and the German physician Wilhelm Weinberg in 1908, and these constant frequencies are now called the **Hardy–Weinberg equilibrium**. As we will see later in this chapter, the realization that it's not just sexual reproduction alone that alters phenotypic and genotypic frequencies was the key to understanding how variation is maintained.

TABLE 3.2

freq(*aa*)	=	0.4×0.4	=	0.16
freq(*Aa*)	=	$(0.4 \times 0.6) + (0.4 \times 0.6)$	=	0.48
freq(*AA*)	=	0.6×0.6	=	0.36

The distribution of genotypes in the population of zygotes in the F_1 generation.

In general, the Hardy–Weinberg proportions for a genetic locus with two alleles are

$$\text{freq}(aa) = q^2$$
$$\text{freq}(Aa) = 2pq$$
$$\text{freq}(AA) = p^2 \qquad (3.3)$$

where q is the frequency of allele a, and p is the frequency of allele A. Using a Punnett square, **Figure 3.3** shows how to calculate these frequencies.

If no other processes act to change genotypic frequencies, the Hardy–Weinberg equilibrium frequencies will be reached after only one generation and will remain unchanged thereafter. Moreover, if the Hardy–Weinberg proportions are altered by chance, the population will return to Hardy–Weinberg proportions in one generation. If this seems like an unlikely conclusion, work through the calculations in Closer Look 3.1, which shows how to calculate the genotypic frequencies after a second episode of segregation and random mating. As you can see, genotypic frequencies remain constant.

We have seen that sexual reproduction and random mating can change the distribution of genotypes, which will reach equilibrium after one generation. We have also seen that neither process changes the frequencies of alleles. Clearly, sexual reproduction and random mating alone cannot lead to evolution over the long run. We now turn to a process that can produce changes in the frequencies of alleles: natural selection.

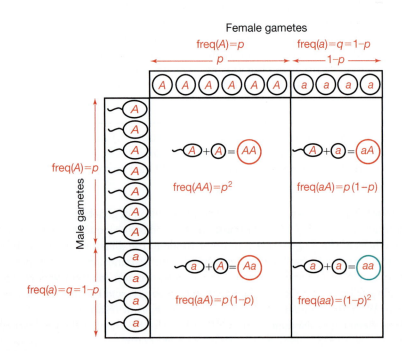

FIGURE 3.3

This Punnett square shows a second way to calculate the frequency of each type of zygote when there is random mating. The horizontal axis represents the proportion of *A* and *a* eggs and is thus divided into fractions p and q, where $q = 1 - p$. The vertical axis is divided according to the proportion of sperm carrying each allele, and again it is divided into fractions p and q. The areas of the rectangles formed by the intersection of the vertical and horizontal dividing lines give the proportion of zygotes that results from each of the four possible fertilization events. The area of the square containing *aa* zygotes is q^2, the area of the square containing *AA* zygotes is p^2, and the total area of the two rectangles containing *Aa* zygotes is $2pq$.

3.1 Genotypic Frequencies after Two Generations of Random Mating

From Equation (3.2) given in the text, we know that the frequency of the gametes produced by adults in the second generation carrying the a allele will be

$$q = \text{freq}(aa) + 0.5 \times \text{freq}(Aa)$$
$$= 0.16 + 0.5 \times 0.48$$
$$= 0.16 + 0.24 = 0.4$$

Because there are only two alleles, the frequency of A is 0.6. As we asserted in the text, the frequency of the two alleles remains unchanged and the frequencies of the gametes produced by random mating among members of this generation are the same as in the previous generation. The calculations for these frequencies are the same as those shown in Table 3.2.

How Natural Selection Changes Gene Frequencies

If different genotypes are associated with different phenotypes and those phenotypes differ in their ability to reproduce, then the alleles that lead to the development of the favored phenotype will increase in frequency.

Genotypic frequencies in the population will remain at the Hardy–Weinberg proportions [Equation (3.3)] as long as all genotypes are equally likely to survive and produce gametes. For PKU, this is approximately correct in wealthy countries where the disease can be treated. However, this assumption will not be valid in environments in which PKU is not treated. Suppose a catastrophe interrupted the supply of modern medical care to our hypothetical population just after a new generation of zygotes was formed. In this case, virtually none of the PKU individuals (genotype aa) would survive to reproduce. Suppose the frequency of the PKU allele was 0.4 among zygotes and the population was in Hardy–Weinberg equilibrium. Let's compute q', the frequency of the PKU allele among adults, which is given by

$$q' = \frac{\text{no. of } a \text{ gametes produced by adults in the next generation}}{\text{total no. of gametes produced by adults in the next generation}} \qquad (3.4)$$

We have already calculated the frequency of each of the genotypes among zygotes just after conception (see Table 3.2), but if PKU is a lethal disease without treatment, not all of these individuals will survive. Now we need to calculate the frequency of a gametes after selection, which we can do by expanding Equation (3.4) as follows:

$$q' = \frac{\begin{pmatrix}\text{no. of } a \\ \text{gametes per} \\ aa \text{ parent after} \\ \text{selection}\end{pmatrix}\begin{pmatrix}\text{no. of } aa \\ \text{parents} \\ \text{after} \\ \text{selection}\end{pmatrix} + \begin{pmatrix}\text{no. of } a \\ \text{gametes per} \\ Aa \text{ parent after} \\ \text{selection}\end{pmatrix}\begin{pmatrix}\text{no. of } Aa \\ \text{parents} \\ \text{after} \\ \text{selection}\end{pmatrix}}{(\text{no. of gametes per parent})(\text{total no. of parents after selection})} \tag{3.5}$$

Because none of the aa individuals will survive, the first term in the numerator will be equal to zero. If we assume that all of the AA and Aa parents survive, then the number of parents after selection is $10,000 \times [\text{freq}(AA) + \text{freq}(Aa)]$ and thus Equation (3.5) can be simplified to

$$q' = \frac{(0.5 \times 2)(0.48 \times 10,000)}{2 \times (0.36 + 0.48) \times 10,000} = 0.2857$$

This calculation shows that the frequency of the PKU allele in adults is 0.2857, a big decrease from 0.4.

Several important lessons can be drawn from this example:

- Selection cannot produce change unless there is variation in the population. If all the individuals were homozygous for the normal allele, gene frequencies would not change from one generation to the next.

- Selection does not operate directly on genes and does not change gene frequencies directly. Instead, natural selection changes the frequency of different phenotypes. In this case, individuals with PKU cannot survive without treatment. Selection decreases the frequency of the PKU allele because it is more likely to be associated with the lethal phenotype.

- The strength and direction of selection depend on the environment. In an environment with medical care, the strength of selection against the PKU allele is negligible.

It is also important to see that although this example shows how selection can change gene frequencies, it does not yet show how selection can lead to the evolution of new adaptations. Here, all phenotypes were present at the outset; all selection did was change their relative frequency.

The Modern Synthesis

The Genetics of Continuous Variation

When Mendelian genetics was rediscovered, biologists at first thought it was incompatible with Darwin's theory of evolution by natural selection.

Darwin believed that evolution proceeded by the gradual accumulation of small changes. But Mendel and the biologists who elucidated the structure of the genetic system around the turn of the twentieth century were dealing with genes that had a noticeable effect on the phenotype. The substitution of one allele for another in Mendel's peas changed pea color. Genetic substitutions at other loci had visible effects on the shape of the pea seeds and the height of the pea plants. Genetics seemed to prove that inheritance was fundamentally discontinuous, and early-twentieth-century geneticists like Hugo de Vries and William Bateson argued that this fact could not be reconciled with Darwin's idea that adaptation occurs through the accumulation of small variations. If one genotype produces short plants and the other two genotypes produce tall

(a)

(b)

(c)

FIGURE 3.4

Shown here are the three architects of the modern synthesis, which showed how Mendelian genetics could be used to account for continuous variation: (a) Ronald A. Fisher, (b) J. B. S. Haldane, and (c) Sewall Wright.

plants, then there will be no intermediate types, and the size of pea plants cannot change in small steps. In a population of short plants, tall ones must be created all at once by mutation, not gradually lengthened over time by selection. Most biologists of the time found these arguments convincing, and consequently Darwinism was in decline during the early part of the twentieth century.

Mendelian genetics and Darwinism were eventually reconciled, resulting in a body of theory that solved the problem of explaining how variation is maintained.

In the early 1930s, the British biologists Ronald A. Fisher and J. B. S. Haldane and the American biologist Sewall Wright showed how Mendelian genetics could be used to explain continuous variation (**Figure 3.4**). We will see how their insights led to the resolution of the two main objections to Darwin's theory: (1) the absence of a theory of inheritance and (2) the problem of accounting for how variation is maintained in populations. When the theory of Wright, Fisher, and Haldane was combined with Darwin's theory of natural selection and with modern field studies by biologists such as Theodosius Dobzhansky, Ernst Mayr, and George Gaylord Simpson, a powerful explanation of organic evolution emerged. This body of theory, and the supporting empirical evidence, is now called the **modern synthesis**.

Continuously varying characters are affected by genes at many loci, each locus having only a small effect on phenotype.

To see how the theory of Wright, Fisher, and Haldane works, let's start with an unrealistic, but instructive, case. Suppose that there is a measurable, continuously varying character such as beak depth, and suppose that two alleles, + and −, operating at a single genetic locus control the character. We'll assume that the gene at this locus influences the production of a hormone that stimulates beak growth, and that each allele leads to production of a different amount of the growth hormone. Let's say that each "dose" of the + allele increases the beak depth, while a − dose decreases it. Thus + + individuals have the deepest beaks, − − individuals have the shallowest beaks, and + − individuals have intermediate beaks. In addition, suppose the frequency of the + allele in the population is 0.5. Now we use the Hardy–Weinberg rule [Equation (3.3)] to calculate the frequencies of different beak depths in the population. A quarter of the population will have deep beaks (+ +), half will have intermediate beaks (+ −), and the remaining quarter will have shallow beaks (− −; **Figure 3.5**).

This does not look like the smooth, bell-shaped distribution of beak depths that the Grants observed on Daphne Major (see Chapter 1). If beak depth were controlled by a single locus, natural selection could not increase beak depth in small increments. But it turns out that the beak morphology is actually affected by genes at more than one locus. Arkhat Abzhanov, a Harvard molecular biologist, and the Grants have identified several genes that affect beak morphology in Darwin's finches. The level of expression of one of these genes, BMP4, affects beak depth, and the level of expression of two other genes, BMP2 and BMP7, influences overall beak size. Scientists do not yet know whether the levels of expression in these genes are due to mutations in associated regulatory sequences or mutations that affect other genes that regulate their expression. But imagine what would happen if other genes at a second locus on a different chromosome also affected beak depth, perhaps because they controlled the synthesis of the receptors for the growth hormone. As before, we assume there is a + allele that leads to larger beaks and a − allele that leads to smaller beaks. Using the Hardy–Weinberg proportions and assuming the independent segregation of chromosomes, we can show that there are now more types of genotypes, and the distribution of phenotypes begins to look somewhat

FIGURE 3.5

The hypothetical distribution of beak depth, assuming that beak depth is controlled by a single genetic locus with two alleles that occur at equal frequency. The height of each bar represents the fraction of birds in the population with a given beak depth. The heights of the bars are computed by means of the Hardy–Weinberg formula. The birds with the smallest beaks are homozygous for the − allele and have a frequency of 0.5 × 0.5 = 0.25. The birds with intermediate beaks are heterozygotes and have a frequency of 2(0.5 × 0.5) = 0.5. The birds with the deepest beaks are homozygous for the + allele and thus have a frequency of 0.5 × 0.5 = 0.25.

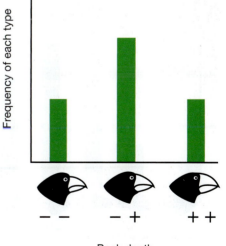

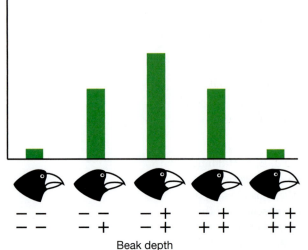

Frequency of each type

Beak depth

FIGURE 3.6

When beak depth is controlled by two loci, each locus having two alleles that occur with equal frequency, intermediate types are observed. The frequencies are calculated by means of a more advanced form of the Hardy–Weinberg formula, on the assumption that the genotypes at each locus are independent.

FIGURE 3.7

When beak depth is controlled by three loci, each locus having two alleles that occur with equal frequency, the distribution of phenotypes begins to resemble a bell-shaped curve.

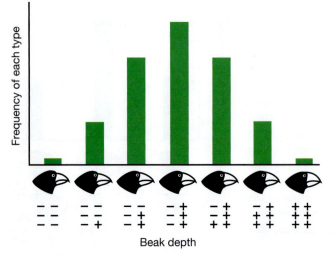

Frequency of each type

Beak depth

smoother (**Figure 3.6**). Now imagine that a third locus controls the calcium supply to the growing beak, and that once again there is a + allele leading to larger beaks and a – allele leading to smaller beaks. As **Figure 3.7** shows, the distribution of beak depths is now even more like the bell-shaped distribution seen in nature. However, small gaps still exist in this distribution of beaks. If genes were the only influence on beak depth, we might expect to see a more broken distribution than the Grants actually observed in the Galápagos.

The observed distribution of phenotypic values is a smooth, bell-shaped curve for two reasons. First, the phenotypic expression of all characters, whether affected by one locus or by many loci, depends on the environment in which the organism develops, leading to **environmental variation**. For example, the size of a bird's beak will depend on how well the bird is nourished during its development. When there is only one locus and the effect of an allelic substitution at that locus is large, environmental variation is not important; it is easy to distinguish the phenotypes associated with different genotypes. This was the case for seed color in Mendel's peas. But when there are many loci and each has a small effect on the phenotype, environmental variation tends to blur together the phenotypes associated with different genotypes. You can't be sure whether you are measuring a + + + − − − bird that matured in a good environment or a + + + + − − bird that grew up in a poor environment. Second, it is likely that complex characters like beak depth are affected by genes at many more than three loci. As we will see in Chapter 14, new tools have allowed geneticists to identify the loci that affect human height. So far 50 different loci have been implicated, and it is likely that many more are involved. The locus with the largest effect leads to a 4-mm change in height. Such a large number of loci would lead to a very smooth, bell-shaped distribution of phenotypes.

Darwin's view of natural selection is easily incorporated into the genetic view that evolution typically results from changes in gene frequencies.

Darwin knew nothing about genetics, and his theory of adaptation by natural selection was framed in purely phenotypic terms: there is a struggle for existence, there is phenotypic variation that affects survival and reproduction, and this phenotypic variation is heritable. In Chapter 1, we saw how this theory could explain the adaptive changes in beak depth in a population of Darwin's finches on the Galápagos Islands. As we saw earlier in this chapter, however, population geneticists take the seemingly different view that evolution means changes in allelic frequencies by natural selection. But these two views of evolution are easily reconciled. Suppose that Figure 3.7 gave the distribution of beak depths before the drought on Daphne Major. Remember that individuals with deep beaks were more likely to survive the drought and reproduce than individuals with smaller beaks. Figure 3.7 illustrates that individuals with deep beaks are more likely to have + alleles at the three loci assumed to affect beak depth. Thus at each locus, + + individuals have deeper beaks on average than + − individuals, which in turn have deeper beaks on average than − − individuals. Because individuals with deeper beaks had higher fitness, natural selection would favor the + alleles at each of the three loci affecting beak depth, and the + alleles would increase in frequency.

How Variation Is Maintained

Genetics provides a ready explanation for why the phenotypes of offspring tend to be intermediate between those of their parents.

Recall from Chapter 1 that the blending model of inheritance appealed to nineteenth-century thinkers because it explained the fact that for most continuously varying characters, offspring are intermediate between their parents. However, the genetic model developed by Fisher, Wright, and Haldane is also consistent with this fact. To see why, consider a cross between the individuals with the biggest and smallest beaks: $(+ + + + + +) \times (- - - - - -)$. All of the offspring will be $(+ - + - + -)$, intermediate between the parents because during development the effects of + and − alleles are averaged. Other matings will produce a distribution of different kinds of offspring, but intermediate types will tend to be the most common.

There is no blending of genes during sexual reproduction.

We know from population genetics that, in the absence of selection (and other factors to be discussed later in this chapter), genotypic frequencies reach equilibrium after one generation and the distribution of phenotypes does not change. Furthermore, we know that sexual reproduction produces no blending in the genes, even though offspring may appear to be intermediate between their parents. This is because genetic transmission involves faithful copying of the genes themselves and their reassembly in different combinations in zygotes. The only blending that occurs takes place at the level of the expression of genes in phenotypes. The genes themselves remain distinct physical entities (**Figure 3.8**).

These facts do not completely solve the problem of the maintenance of variation, because selection tends to deplete variation. When selection favors birds with deeper beaks, we might expect − alleles to be replaced at all three loci affecting the trait, leaving a population in which every individual has the genotype + + + + + +. There would still be phenotypic variation due to environmental effects, but without genetic variation there can be no further adaptation.

Mutation slowly adds new variation.

Genes are copied with amazing fidelity, and their messages are protected from random degradation by a number of molecular repair mechanisms. Every once in a while, however, a mistake in copying is made and goes unrepaired, and a new allele is introduced into the population. In Chapter 2, we learned that genes are pieces of DNA. Certain forms of ionizing radiation (such as X-rays) and certain kinds of chemicals damage the DNA and alter the message that it carries. These changes are called **mutations**, and they add variation to a population by continuously introducing new alleles, some of which may produce novel phenotypic effects that selection can assemble into adaptations. Although rates of mutation are very low—ranging from 1 in 100,000 to 1 in 10 million per locus per gamete in each generation—this process plays an important role in generating variation.

Low mutation rates can maintain variation because a lot of variation is protected from selection.

For characters that are affected by genes at many different loci, low rates of mutation can maintain variation in populations. This is possible because many different

FIGURE 3.8

The blending model of inheritance assumes that the hereditary material is changed by mating. When red and white parents are crossed to produce a pink offspring, the blending model posits that the hereditary material has mixed, so that when two pink individuals mate, they produce only pink offspring. According to Mendelian genetics, however, the effects of genes are blended in their *expression* to produce a pink phenotype, but the genes themselves remain unchanged. Thus when two pink parents mate, they can produce white, pink, or red offspring.

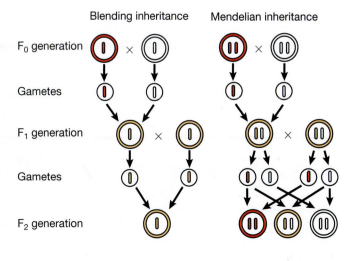

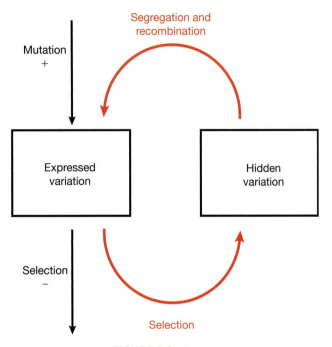

Mutation
+

Segregation and
recombination

Expressed
variation

Hidden
variation

Selection
−

Selection

FIGURE 3.9

There are two pools of genetic variation: hidden and expressed. Mutation adds new genetic variation to the pool of expressed variation, and selection removes it. Segregation and recombination shuffle variation back and forth between the two pools within each generation.

genotypes generate intermediate phenotypes that are favored by stabilizing selection. If individuals with a variety of genotypes are equally likely to survive and reproduce, a considerable amount of variation is protected (or hidden) from selection. To make this concept clearer, let's consider the action of stabilizing selection on beak depth in the medium ground finch. Remember that stabilizing selection occurs when birds with intermediate-size beaks have higher fitness than birds with deeper or shallower beaks. If beak depth is affected by genes at three loci, as shown in Figure 3.7, individuals with several different genotypes may develop very similar, intermediate-size beaks. For example, individuals that are + + at one locus affecting the trait may be − − at another locus and thus may have the same phenotype as an individual that is + − at both loci. Thus when a large number of loci affect a single trait, only a small fraction of the genetic variability present in the population is expressed phenotypically. As a result, selection removes variation from the population very slowly. The processes of segregation and recombination slowly shuffle and reshuffle the genome and expose the hidden variation to natural selection in subsequent generations (**Figure 3.9**). This process provides the solution to Darwin's other dilemma; because a considerable amount of variation is protected from selection, a very low mutation rate can maintain variation despite the depleting action of selection.

Hidden variation explains why selection can move populations far beyond their initial range of variation.

Remember from Chapter 1 Fleeming Jenkin's argument that Darwin's theory could not explain cumulative evolutionary change because it provided no account of how a population could evolve beyond the initial range of variation present. Selection would cull away all of the small-beaked finches, he would have argued, but it could never make the average beak bigger than the biggest beak initially present. If this argument were correct, then selection could never lead to cumulative, long-term change.

Jenkin's argument was wrong because it failed to take hidden variation into account. Hidden variation is always present in continuously varying traits. Let's suppose that environmental conditions favor larger beaks. When beak depth is affected by genes at many loci, the birds in a population with the deepest beaks do not carry all + alleles. They carry a lot of + alleles and some − alleles. When the finches with the shallowest beaks die, alleles leading to small beaks are removed from the breeding population. As a result, the frequency of + alleles at every locus increases. But because even the deepest-beaked individuals had some − alleles, a huge amount of variation remains. This variation is shuffled through the process of sexual reproduction. Because + alleles become more common, more of these alleles are likely to be combined in the genotype of a single individual. The greater the proportion of + alleles in an individual, the larger the beak will be. Thus the biggest beak will be larger than the biggest beak in the previous generation. In the next generation, the same thing happens again: the deepest-beaked individuals still carry − alleles, but fewer than before. As a result, the biggest beaks can be bigger than any beaks in the previous generation.

This process can go on for many generations. An experiment on oil content in corn begun at the University of Illinois Agricultural Experiment Station in 1896 provides a good example. Researchers selected for high and low oil content in corn, and, as **Figure 3.10** shows, each generation showed significant change. In the initial population of 163 ears of corn, oil content ranged from 4% to 6%. After nearly 80 generations of selection, both the high and low values for oil content far exceeded the initial range of variation. Researchers were then even able to reverse the direction of adaptation by taking plants from the high oil line and selecting for low oil content.

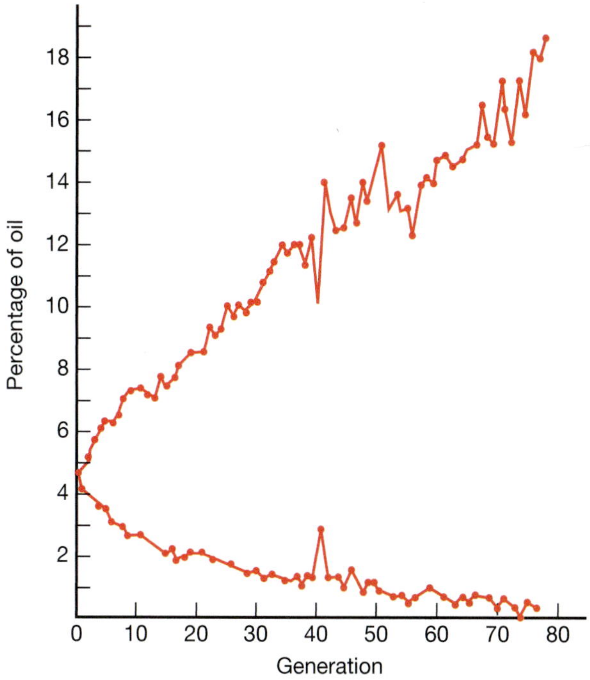

Natural Selection and Behavior

The evolution of mate guarding in the soapberry bug illustrates how flexible behavior can evolve.

So far we have considered the evolution of morphological characters, like beak depth and eye morphology, that do not change once an individual has reached adulthood. In much of this book, we will be interested in the evolution of the behavior of humans and other primates. Behavior is different from morphology in an important way: it is flexible, and individuals adjust their behavior in response to their circumstances. Some people think natural selection cannot account for flexible responses to environmental contingencies because natural selection acts only on phenotypic variation that results from genetic differences. Although this view is very common (particularly among social scientists), it is incorrect. To see why, let's consider an elegant empirical study that illustrates exactly how natural selection can shape flexible behavioral responses.

The soapberry bug (*Jadera haematoloma*), a seed-eating insect found in the southeastern United States, has been studied by biologist Scott Carroll of the Institute for Contemporary Evolution. (It's OK to call them "bugs" because they are members of the insect order Hemiptera, the true bugs.) Adult soapberry bugs are bright red and black and 1 to 1.5 cm (0.5 in.) long (**Figure 3.11**). They gather in huge groups near the plants they eat. During mating, males mount females and copulate. The transfer of sperm typically takes about 10 minutes. However, males remain in the copulatory position, sometimes for hours, securely anchored to females by large genital hooks. This behavior is called **mate guarding**. Biologists believe that the function of mate guarding is to prevent other males from copulating with the female before she lays her eggs. When a female mates with several males, they share in the paternity of the eggs that she lays. By guarding his mate and preventing her from mating with other males, a male can increase his reproductive success. However, mate guarding also has a cost: a male cannot find and copulate with other females while guarding a mate. The relative magnitude of the costs and benefits of mate guarding depends on the **sex ratio** (the relative numbers of males and females). When the ratio of males to females is high, males have little chance of finding another female, and guarding is the best strategy. When females are more common than males, the chance of finding an unguarded female increases, so males may benefit more from looking for additional mates than from guarding.

Behavioral plasticity allows male soapberry bugs to vary their mate-guarding behavior adaptively in response to variation in the local abundance of females.

In populations of soapberry bugs in western Oklahoma, the sex ratio is quite variable. In some places, there are equal numbers of males and females; in others, there are twice as many males as females. Males guard their mates more often where females are

FIGURE 3.10

Selection can carry a population far beyond the original range of variation because at any given time a lot of genetic variation is not expressed as phenotypic variation. The range of variation in the oil content of corn at the beginning of this experiment was 4% to 6%. After about 80 generations, oil content in the line selected for high oil content had increased to 19%, and oil content in the low oil line had decreased to less than 1%.

FIGURE 3.11

The male soapberry bug on the left is guarding the (larger) female to his right. Biologist Scott Carroll painted numbers on the bugs in order to identify individuals.

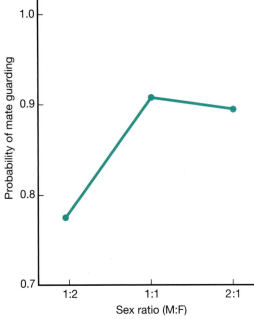

FIGURE 3.12

The probability of mate guarding is a function of sex ratio in this population of the soapberry bug. Males are less likely to guard their mates when females are relatively more common than when they are relatively rare.

rare than where they are common (**Figure 3.12**). Two possible mechanisms might produce this pattern: (1) males in populations with high sex ratios might differ genetically from males in populations with low sex ratios or (2) males might adjust their behavior in response to the local sex ratio. To distinguish between these two possibilities, Carroll brought soapberry bugs into the laboratory and created populations with different sex ratios. Then he watched males mate in each of these populations. If the mate-guarding trait were **canalized** (that is, showed the same phenotype in a wide range of environments), then a male would behave the same way in each population; if the trait were **plastic**, then a male would adjust his behavior in relation to the local sex ratio. Carroll's data confirmed that soapberry bug males in Oklahoma have a plastic behavioral strategy that causes them to modify their mating behavior in response to current social conditions.

Evidence suggests that the soapberry bug's plasticity has evolved in response to the variability in conditions in Oklahoma.

Most soapberry bugs live south of Oklahoma, in warmer, more stable habitats like the Florida Keys, and the sex ratio in these areas is always close to even. (Hence females are relatively rare.) Carroll subjected male soapberry bugs from the Florida Keys to the same experimental protocol as the bugs from Oklahoma. As **Figure 3.13** shows, the Florida males did not change their behavior in response to changes in sex ratio. They guarded their mates about 90% of the time, regardless of the abundance of females. In a stable environment like the Florida Keys, sex ratios do not vary much from time to time, and the ability to adjust mate-guarding behavior provides no advantage. Behavioral flexibility is costly in a number of ways. For example, flexible males must spend time and energy assessing the sex ratio before they mate, males sometimes make mistakes about the local sex ratio and behave inappropriately, and flexibility probably requires a more complex nervous system. Thus a simple fixed behavioral rule is likely to be best in stable environments. In the variable climate of Oklahoma, however, the ability to adjust mate-guarding behavior provides enough fitness benefits to compensate for the costs of maintaining behavioral flexibility.

Behavioral plasticity evolves when the nature of the behavioral response to the environment is genetically variable.

How did behavioral flexibility evolve in the Oklahoma bugs? It evolved like any other adaptation: by the selective retention of beneficial genetic variants. For any character to evolve, (1) the character must vary, (2) the variation must affect reproductive success, and (3) the variation must be heritable. Mate guarding in soapberry bugs satisfies each of these conditions: First, there is variation, and this variation affects fitness. By bringing individual bugs into the laboratory and observing their behavior at different sex ratios, Carroll showed that individual males in Oklahoma have different behavioral strategies. **Figure 3.14** plots the probability of mate guarding for four representative individuals numbered 1 to 4. Males 1 and 4 both have fixed behavioral strategies. Male 1 guards about 90% of the time, and male 4 guards about 80% of the time. Males 2 and 3 have variable behavioral strategies. Male 2 is very sensitive to changes in sex ratio; male 3 is less sensitive. Notice that both the amount of mate guarding and the amount of flexibility vary among the bugs in Oklahoma.

Second, it seems likely that this variation would affect male reproductive success. In Oklahoma, males would experience a range of sex ratios, so it seems likely that males with flexible strategies, like male 2, would tend to have the most offspring. In Florida, males with inflexible strategies, like male 1, would have the most offspring.

Third, the character is heritable. By controlling matings in the laboratory, Carroll was able to show that males tended to have the same strategies as their fathers.

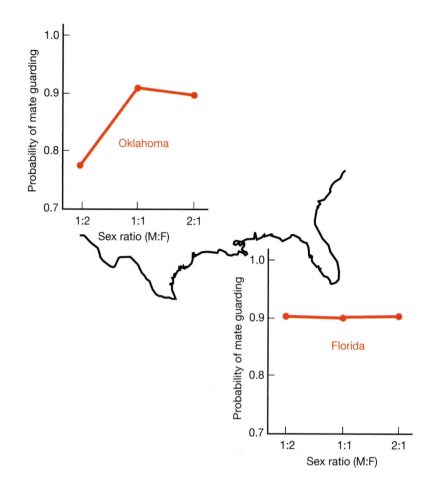

FIGURE 3.13

The average probability of mate guarding varies between populations of soapberry bugs in Oklahoma and Florida. In Oklahoma, males are more likely to guard when females are relatively rare; in Florida, males do not vary their mate-guarding behavior in relation to the local sex ratio.

Bugs like male 1 had sons with fixed strategies, and bugs like male 2 had sons with flexible strategies. Thus the Oklahoma bugs would come to have a variable strategy, while the Florida bugs would come to have a fixed strategy.

Behavior in the soapberry bug is relatively simple. Mate guarding depends on the sex ratio in the local population. The behavior of humans and other primates is much more complex, but the principles that govern the evolution of complex forms of behavior are the same as the principles that govern the evolution of simpler forms of behavior. That is, individuals must differ in the ways they respond to the environment, these differences must affect their ability to survive and reproduce, and at least some of these differences must be heritable. Then individual responses to

FIGURE 3.14

There is genetic variation in the behavioral rules of individual soapberry bugs, illustrated here by four representative males. There is variation in both the level of mate guarding (for example, male 1 spends more time guarding mates than male 4 does for all sex ratios) and in the amount of plasticity (for example, the behavior of males 1 and 4 does not change, the behavior of male 3 changes a bit, and the behavior of male 2 changes a lot). If this variation is heritable, the rule that works best, averaged over all of the environments of the population, will tend to increase.

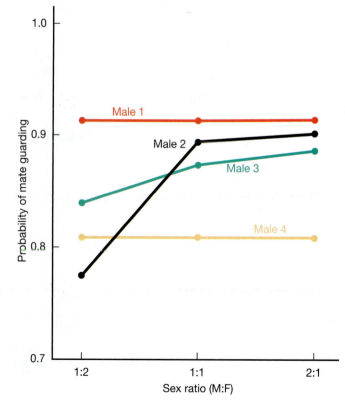

environmental circumstances will evolve in much the same way that finch beaks and male soapberry bugs' mate-guarding behavior evolve.

Constraints on Adaptation

Natural selection plays a central role in our understanding of evolution because it is the only mechanism that can explain adaptation. However, evolution does not always lead to the best possible phenotype. In this section, we consider five reasons this is the case.

Correlated Characters

When individuals that have particular variants of one character also tend to have particular variants of a second character, the two characters are said to be correlated.

So far, we have considered the action of natural selection on only one character at a time. This approach is misleading if natural selection acts on more than one character simultaneously and the characters are nonrandomly associated, or correlated. It's easiest to grasp the meaning and importance of correlated characters in the context of a now familiar example: Darwin's finches. When the Grants and their colleagues captured medium ground finches on Daphne Major, they measured beak depth, beak width, and a number of other morphological characters. Beak depth is measured as the top-to-bottom dimension of the beak; beak width is the side-to-side dimension. As is common for morphological characters like these, the Grants found that beak depth and beak width are positively correlated: birds with deep beaks also have wide beaks (**Figure 3.15**). Each point in Figure 3.15 represents one individual. Beak width is plotted on the vertical axis, and beak depth is plotted along the horizontal axis. If the cloud of points were round or the points were randomly scattered in the graph, it would mean these characters were uncorrelated. Then information about an individual's beak depth would tell us nothing about its beak width. However, the cloud of points forms an ellipse with the long axis oriented from the lower left to the upper right, so we know that the two characters are **positively correlated**: deep beaks also tend to be wide. If birds with deep beaks tended to have narrow beaks, and birds

FIGURE 3.15

Beak depth and beak width are correlated in the medium ground finch on Daphne Major. The vertical axis gives the difference between the individual's beak width and the mean width in the population, and the horizontal axis gives the difference between the individual's beak depth and the population mean. Each point represents one individual. The data show that birds with deep beaks are likely to have wide beaks, and birds with shallow beaks generally have narrow beaks.

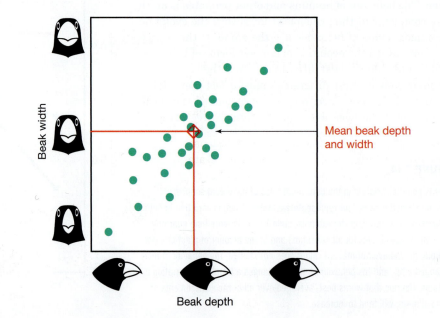

Mean beak depth and width

Beak width

Beak depth

with shallow beaks tended to have wide beaks, the two characters would be **negatively correlated**, and the long axis of the cloud of points would run from the upper left to the lower right.

Correlated characters occur because some genes affect more than one character.

Genes that affect more than one character are said to have **pleiotropic effects**, and probably most genes fall into this category. Often genes that are expressed early in development and affect overall size also influence a number of other discrete morphological traits. This means that individuals carrying mutations that lead to increased expression in the genes that influence overall beak size, BMP2 and BMP7, will have deeper and wider beaks than individuals who don't carry these mutations. The PKU locus provides another good example of pleiotropy. Untreated PKU homozygotes are phenotypically different from heterozygotes or normal homozygotes in several ways. For example, they have lower IQs and different hair color from individuals with other genotypes. Thus the substitution of another PKU allele for the normal allele in a heterozygote would affect a wide variety of phenotypic characters.

When two characters are correlated, selection that changes the mean value of one character in the population also changes the mean value of the correlated character.

Returning to the finches, suppose that there is selection for individuals with deep beaks, and that beak width has no effect on survival (**Figure 3.16**). As we would expect, the mean value of beak depth increases. Notice, however, that the mean value of beak width also increases, even though beak width has no effect on the probability that an individual will survive. Selection on beak depth affects the mean value of beak width because the two traits are correlated. This effect is called the **correlated response** to selection. It results from the fact that selection increases the frequency of genes that increase beak depth and individuals who carry those genes also tend to have genes that lead to the development of wider beaks.

A correlated response to selection can cause other characters to change in a maladaptive direction.

To understand how selection on one character can cause other characters to change in a **maladaptive** (less fit) direction, let's continue with our example. It turns out that beak width did affect survival during the Galápagos drought. By holding beak depth constant, the Grants showed that individuals with *thinner* beaks were more likely to survive during the drought, probably because birds with thinner beaks were able to generate more pressure on the tough seeds that predominated during the drought. If selection were acting only on beak width, then we would expect the mean beak width in the population to decrease. However, the correlated response to selection on beak depth also acts to increase mean beak width. If the correlated response to selection on beak depth were stronger than the effect of selection directly on beak width, mean beak width would increase,

FIGURE 3.16

Selection on one character affects the mean value of correlated characters, even if the other characters have no effect on fitness. The distribution of beak depth and beak width in the population is plotted here, assuming that only birds whose beaks are greater than a threshold depth survive. Beak width is assumed to have no effect on survival. Selection leads to an increase in both average beak depth and average beak width. Mean beak width is increased by the correlated response of selection on beak depth.

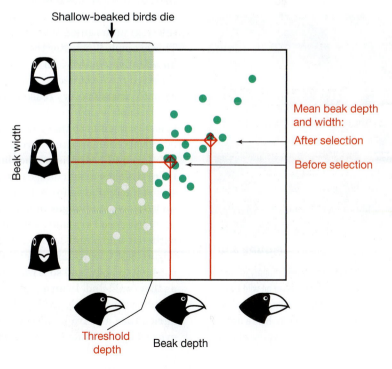

Shallow-beaked birds die

Beak width

Mean beak depth and width:

After selection

Before selection

Threshold depth

Beak depth

FIGURE 3.17

The correlated response to selection can cause less fit phenotypes to become more common. The distribution of beak depth and beak width in the population is plotted here, assuming that all birds whose beaks are less than a threshold depth or greater than a threshold width die. All others survive. Even though there is selection favoring narrower beaks, beak width increases as a result of the correlated response to selection on beak depth.

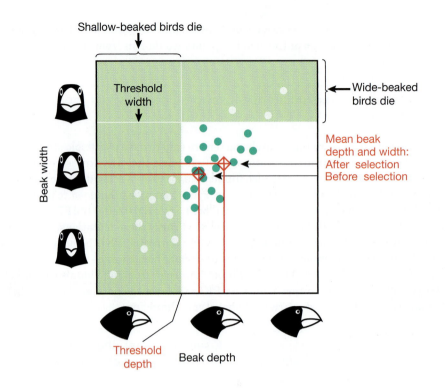

even though selection favors thinner beaks. This is exactly what happened on Daphne Major (**Figure 3.17**).

Disequilibrium

Selection produces optimal adaptations only at equilibrium.

In Chapter 1, we saw how natural selection could gradually increase beak depth, generation by generation, until an equilibrium was reached—a point where stabilizing selection maintained the average beak depth in the population at the optimum size. This example illustrates the principle that selection keeps changing a population until an adaptive equilibrium is reached. It is easy to forget that the populations being observed have not necessarily reached equilibrium. If the environment has changed recently, there is every reason to suspect that the morphology or behavior of residents is not adaptive under current conditions. How long does it take for populations to adapt to environmental change? This depends on how quickly selection acts. As we have seen, enormous changes can be created by artificial selection in a few dozen generations.

Disequilibrium is particularly important for some human characters because there have been big changes in the lives of humans during the last 10,000 years. It seems likely that many aspects of the human phenotype have not had time to catch up with recent changes in our subsistence strategies and living conditions. Our diet provides a good example. Ten thousand years ago, most people hunted wild game and gathered wild plants for food. Typically, people had little access to sugar, fat, and salt (**Figure 3.18**), which are essential dietary requirements for the proper functioning of the human body, and so it was probably good for people to eat as much of these things as they could find. In an adaptive response to human dietary needs, evolution equipped people with a nearly insatiable appetite for fat, salt, and sugar. With the advent of agriculture and trade, however, these substances became readily available and our evolved appetites for them became problematic. Today, eating too much fat, salt, and

FIGURE 3.18

For most of our evolutionary history, humans have subsisted on wild game and plant foods. Sugar, salt, and fat were in short supply. Here a Hadza woman digs up a tuber.

sugar is associated with a variety of health problems, including bad teeth, obesity, diabetes, and high blood pressure.

Genetic Drift

When populations are small, genetic drift may cause random changes in gene frequencies.

So far, we have assumed that evolving populations are always very large. When populations are small, however, random effects caused by sampling variation can be important. To see what this means, consider a statistical analogy. Suppose that we have a huge urn like the one in **Figure 3.19**. The urn contains 10,000 balls—half of them black and half of them red. Suppose we also have a collection of small urns, each of which holds 10 balls. We draw 10 balls at random from the big urn to put in each small urn. Not all of the little urns will have five red balls and five black balls. Some will have four red balls, some three red balls, and a few may even have no red balls. The fact that the distribution of black and red balls among the small urns varies is called **sampling variation**.

The same thing happens during genetic transmission in small populations (**Figure 3.20**). Suppose there is an organism that has only one pair of chromosomes with two possible alleles, *A* and *a*, at a particular locus and that selection does not act on this trait. In addition, a population of five individuals of this species is newly isolated from the rest. In this small population (generation 1), each allele has a frequency of 0.5, so five chromosomes carry *A* and five carry *a*. These five individuals mate at random and produce five surviving offspring (generation 2). To keep things simple, assume that the gamete pool is large, so there is no sampling variation. This means that half of the gametes produced by generation 1 will carry *A* and half will carry *a*. However, only 10 gametes will be drawn from this gamete pool to form the next generation of five individuals. These gametes will be sampled in the same way the balls were sampled from the urn (see Figure 3.19). The most likely result is that there are five *A* alleles and five *a* alleles in generation 2, as there were in generation 1. However, just as there is some chance of drawing three, four, six, seven, or even zero black balls from the urn, there is some chance that generation 2 will not carry equal numbers of *A* and *a* alleles. Suppose the five individuals in generation 2 have six *A* alleles and four *a* alleles. Because the frequency of the *A* allele is now 0.6, when these individuals mate, the frequency of the *A* allele in the pool of gametes will be 0.6 as well. This means the frequency of the allele in the population has changed by chance alone. In the third generation the gene frequencies change again, this time in the opposite direction. This phenomenon is called **genetic drift**. In small populations, genetic drift causes random fluctuations in genetic frequencies.

The way alleles are sampled in real populations depends on the biology of the evolving species and the nature of the selective forces that the species faces. For instance, population size in some bird species might be limited by nesting sites, and success in obtaining nesting sites might be related to body size: perhaps the larger the bird, the more chance there would be that it would have success in battling others for a prime

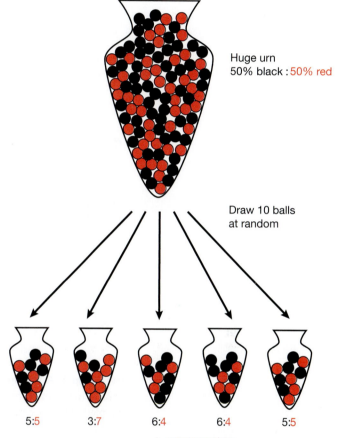

Huge urn
50% black : 50% red

Draw 10 balls
at random

5:5   3:7   6:4   6:4   5:5

FIGURE 3.19

A huge urn contains 10,000 balls, half of them black and half red. Suppose 10 balls are drawn from the large urn at random and placed in each of five small urns. Not all of the small urns will contain 5 red balls and 5 black balls. This phenomenon is called sampling variation.

FIGURE 3.20

Sampling variation leads to changes in gene frequency in small populations. Suppose that a population produces half *A* gametes (*black*) and half *a* gametes (*white*), and the next generation consists of just five individuals. It is not unlikely that, by chance, these individuals will carry six *A* gametes and four *a* gametes. This new population will produce 60% *A* gametes. Thus sampling variation can change gene frequencies. Notice here that gene frequencies change again in generation 3, this time in the reverse direction, to 30% *A*.

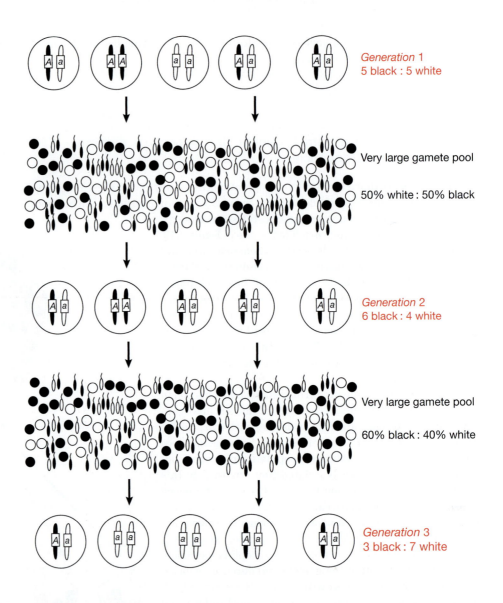

Generation 1
5 black : 5 white

Very large gamete pool

50% white : 50% black

Generation 2
6 black : 4 white

Very large gamete pool

60% black : 40% white

Generation 3
3 black : 7 white

nesting spot. Although body size is influenced partly by genes, and selection would favor genes for large body size, many genes don't affect body size, and they may be sampled randomly in this particular population.

The rate of genetic drift depends on population size.

Genetic drift causes more rapid change in small populations than in large ones because sampling variation is more pronounced in small samples. To see why this is true, consider a simple example. Suppose a company is trying to predict whether a new product—say, low-fat peanut butter—will succeed in the marketplace. The company commissions two different survey firms to find out how many peanut butter fans would switch to the new product. One firm conducts interviews with five people, four of whom say that they would switch immediately to the low-fat variety. The other company polls 1,000 people, and 50% of them say they would prefer low-fat peanut butter. Which survey should the company trust? Clearly, the second survey is more credible than the first one. It is easy to imagine that by chance we might find four fans of low-fat peanut butter in a sample of five people, even if the actual frequency of such preferences in the population were only 50%. In contrast, in a sample of 1,000 people, we would be very unlikely to find such a large discrepancy between our sample and the population.

The same principle applies to genetic drift. In a population of five individuals (with 10 chromosomes) in which two alleles are equally common (frequency = 0.5), there is a good chance that in the next generation the frequency of one of the alleles will be greater than or equal to 0.8. But in a population of 1,000 individuals, there is virtually no chance that such a large deviation from the initial frequency will occur.

Genetic drift causes isolated populations to become genetically different from each other.

Genetic drift leads to unpredictable evolution because the changes in gene frequency caused by sampling variation are random. As a result, drift causes isolated populations to become genetically different from one another over time. Results from a computer simulation illustrate how this works for a single genetic locus with two alleles (**Figure 3.21**). Initially, there is a large population in which each allele has a frequency of 0.5. Then four separate populations of 20 individuals (each individual carrying two sets of chromosomes) are created. These four populations are maintained at a constant size and remain isolated from each other during all subsequent generations. During the first generation, the frequency of *A* in the gamete pool is 0.5 in each population. However, the unpredictable effects of sampling variation alter the frequencies of *A* among adults in each population. From the first generation, we sample 40 gametes from each of the four populations. In population 1 (indicated by red solid circles), the frequency of *A* increases dramatically; in populations 2 (blue open triangles) and 3 (blue solid triangles), it increases a little; and in population 4 (red open circles), it decreases. In each case, the change is created by chance alone.

During the next generation, the same process is repeated, except that the gamete pools of each of the four populations now differ. Once again, 40 gametes are sampled from each population. This time the frequency of *A* in populations 2, 3, and 4 increases, while the frequency of *A* in population 1 decreases substantially. As these random and unpredictable changes continue, the four populations become more and more different from one another. Eventually, one of the alleles is lost entirely in two of our populations (*A* in population 2 and *a* in population 4), making all individuals in these populations identical at the locus in question. Such populations are said to have reached **fixation**. In general, the smaller the population, the sooner it reaches fixation. Theoretically, if genetic drift goes on long enough, all populations eventually reach fixation. When populations are large, however, this may take such a long time that

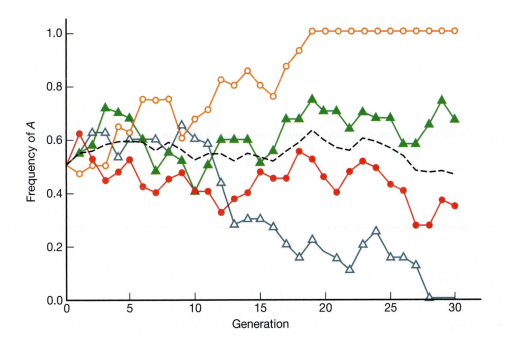

FIGURE 3.21

This computer simulation demonstrates that genetic drift causes isolated populations to become genetically different from one another. Four populations are initially formed by 20 individuals' being drawn from a single large population. In the original population, one gene has two alleles that each have a frequency of 0.5. The graph tracks the frequency of one of these alleles in each of these populations over time. Population 1 is in red (*solid circles*), population 2 in blue (*open triangles*), population 3 in green (*solid triangles*), and population 4 in orange (*open circles*). The dotted line shows the global frequency of the *A* allele. In each population, the frequency of the allele fluctuates randomly under the influence of genetic drift. Notice that populations 2 and 4 eventually reach fixation, meaning that one of the two alleles is lost.

the species becomes extinct before fixation occurs. Populations remain at fixation until mutation introduces a new allele.

As you might expect, the rate at which populations become genetically different is strongly affected by their size: small populations differentiate rapidly; larger populations differentiate more slowly. We will see in Chapter 13 that the relationship between population size and the rate of genetic drift allows us to make interesting and important inferences about the size of human populations tens of thousands of years ago.

Populations must be quite small for drift to lead to significant maladaptation.

Random changes produced by genetic drift will create adaptations only by chance, and we have seen that the probability of assembling complex adaptations in this way is small indeed. This means that genetic drift usually leads to maladaptation. The importance of genetic drift in evolution is a controversial topic. Nearly everyone agrees that populations must be fairly small (say, less than 100 individuals) for drift to have an important effect when it is opposed by strong natural selection. There is a lot of debate about whether populations in nature are usually that small. Most scientists agree, however, that genetic drift is not likely to generate significant maladaptation in traits that vary continuously and are affected by many genetic loci. Thus a trait such as beak size in Darwin's finches is unlikely to be influenced much by genetic drift.

Local versus Optimal Adaptations

Natural selection may lead to an evolutionary equilibrium at which the most common phenotype is not the best possible phenotype.

Natural selection acts to increase the adaptedness of populations, but it does not necessarily lead to the best possible phenotypes. The reason is that natural selection is myopic: it favors small improvements to the existing phenotype, but it does not take into account the long-run consequences of these alterations. Selection is like a mountaineer who tries to climb a peak cloaked in dense cloud; she cannot see the surrounding country, but she figures she will reach her goal if she keeps climbing uphill. The mountain climber will eventually reach the top of something if she continues climbing, but if the topography is the least bit complicated, she won't necessarily reach the summit. Instead, when the fog clears, she is likely to find herself on the top of a lower, subsidiary peak. In the same way, natural selection keeps changing the population until no more small improvements are possible, but there is no reason to believe that the end product is the optimal phenotype. The phenotype arrived at in such cases is called a "local adaptation"; it is analogous to the subsidiary peak reached by the mountaineer.

As an example of this effect, let's consider the evolution of eyes (**Figure 3.22**). Humans, other vertebrates, and some invertebrates such as octopi have **camera-type eyes**. In this type of eye, there is a single opening in front of a lens, which projects an image on photoreceptive tissue. Insects, by contrast, have **compound eyes**, in which many very small separate photoreceptors build up an image composed of a grid of dots, something like a television image. Compound eyes are inferior to camera-type eyes in most ways. For example, they have lower resolution and less light-gathering power than similarly sized camera-type eyes have. If this is so, why haven't insects evolved camera-type eyes?

The most likely answer is that once a species has evolved complex, compound eyes, selection cannot favor intermediate types, even though this might eventually allow superior camera-type eyes to evolve. Consider the early lineages in which eyes were first evolving. There may have come a time when selection favored greater light sensitivity. In the vertebrates and mollusks, greater light sensitivity was achieved by increases in the area of sensitive tissue within each eye. In insects, it seems likely that

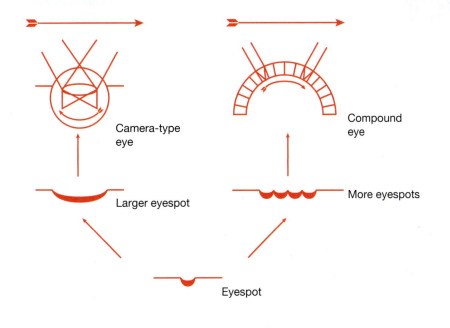

FIGURE 3.22

Researchers believe that different evolutionary pathways led to the development of camera-type and compound eyes. Selection for greater light sensitivity in a simple organism could favor the development of a larger eyespot or of multiple eyespots. The first pathway could lead to camera-type eyes and the second to compound eyes. Images are formed very differently in compound and camera-type eyes, making it virtually impossible for compound eyes to evolve into camera-type eyes.

increased sensitivity was achieved by multiplication of the number of small photorecep-tors, each in its own cup. At this early stage, these alternatives yielded equally useful eyes. Once the insect lineage had evolved a visual system based on many small eyes, however, images could not be formed the same way as in camera-type eyes because the camera-type eye inverts images, but the compound eye does not. It does not seem structurally possible to evolve from a compound eye to a camera-type eye in a series of small steps, each favored by selection.

Some local adaptations are called developmental constraints.

Most kinds of organisms begin life as a single fertilized cell, a zygote. As an organ-ism grows, this cell divides many times, giving rise to specialized nerve cells, liver cells, and so on. This process of growth and differentiation is called **development**, and the development of complex structures like eyes involves many different interdepen-dent processes. Developmental changes that would produce desirable modifications are often selected against because these alterations have many other negative effects. For example, as we will see later in the text, there is good reason to believe that it would be adaptive for males in some primate species to be able to **lactate** (produce milk for their young). However, no primate males can lactate, and most biologists believe that the developmental changes that would allow males to lactate would also make them sterile. Thus developmental processes constrain evolution, but such constraints are not absolute. They result from the particular phylogenetic history of the lineage. If primate reproductive biology had evolved along a different pathway so that the develop-ment of mammary glands and other elements of the primate reproductive system were independent, then there would be no constraints on the evolution of male lactation.

Other Constraints on Evolution

Evolutionary processes are also constrained by the laws of physics and chemistry.

The laws of physics and chemistry place additional constraints on the kinds of adapta-tions that are possible. For example, the laws of mechanics predict that the strength of bones is proportional to their cross-sectional area. This fact constrains the evolution of

3.2 The Geometry of Area/Volume Ratios

When an animal becomes larger without otherwise changing shape, the ratio of any fixed area measurement to its volume decreases. This is easiest to understand if we compute how the ratio of an animal's entire surface area to its volume changes as the animal becomes larger. To see why, suppose that the animal is a cube x centimeters on a side. Then its volume is x^3 and its surface area is $6x^2$. Thus the ratio of its surface area to its volume is

$$\frac{\text{surface area}}{\text{volume}} = \frac{6x^2}{x^3} = \frac{6}{x}$$

This means that an animal measuring 1 cm on a side has 6 cm^2 of surface area for each cubic centimeter of volume. An animal 2 cm on a side has only 3 cm^2 of surface area for each cubic centimeter of volume. Of course, there aren't any cubic animals, but it turns out that the shape doesn't alter this relationship. When an animal's linear dimension is doubled without a change in shape, the ratio of surface area to volume is halved. We will see later that this fact has consequences for how temperature affects the size of animals.

The same geometric principle governs the relationship between any area measure and volume. Suppose the cubic animal has a vertical bone running through its center that supports the weight of the rest of the animal. For simplicity, we make the bone square in cross section and assume that it has the dimensions $\frac{1}{2}x$ by $\frac{1}{2}x$, as shown in **Figure 3.23**. The cross-sectional area of this bone, then, is $\frac{1}{2}x \times \frac{1}{2}x^2$. Thus the ratio of the cross-sectional area of the bone to the volume of the animal is

$$\frac{\frac{1}{4}x^2}{x^3} = \frac{1}{4x}$$

So if the linear dimensions of an animal are doubled, its weight will increase eightfold, but the cross-sectional area of its bones—and therefore their strength—will increase only fourfold.

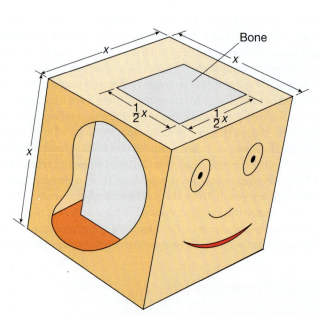

FIGURE 3.23

A cutaway diagram of the cubic animal discussed here.

morphology. To see why, suppose that an animal's size (that is, its *linear* dimensions) doubles as the result of natural selection. This means that the animal's weight (which is proportional to its *volume*) will increase by a factor of 8 (see Closer Look 3.2). The strength to bear an animal's weight comes from its muscles and bones and is determined largely by their cross-sectional areas. If the linear dimensions of bones and muscles double, however, their cross-sectional areas will increase by a factor of only 4. This means that the bones and muscles will be only half as strong relative to the animal's weight as they were before. Thus if the bones are to be as strong as they were before, they must be more than four times greater in cross section, which means that they must become proportionally thicker. Of course, thicker bones are heavier, and this greater weight imposes other constraints on the animal. If it is heavier, it may not be able to move as fast or suspend itself from branches. This constraint (and a closely related one that governs the strength of muscles) explains why big animals like elephants are typically slow and ponderous, whereas smaller animals like squirrels move quickly and are often agile leapers. It also explains why all flying animals are relatively light. Natural selection might well favor an elephant that could run like a cheetah, vault obstacles like an impala, and climb like a monkey. But because of the trade-offs imposed by the laws of physics, there are no mutant pachyderms whose bones are both light and strong enough to permit these behaviors (**Figure 3.24**).

Such constraints are closely related to genetic correlations. Selection eliminates mutants with heavier, weaker bones; and the trade-offs inherent in the design of structures mean that mutant animals that have lighter, stronger bones are also not possible. The genotypes that remain in the population lead to the development of either lighter bones or stronger bones, but not both. Thus bone weight and bone strength typically show a positive genetic correlation.

FIGURE 3.24

It might be advantageous for animals to be large enough to be relatively invulnerable to predators but agile enough to leap considerable distances. But physical constraints limit evolution; not all things are possible.

Key Terms

population genetics
genotypic frequency
gene frequency
Hardy–Weinberg equilibrium
modern synthesis
environmental variation
mutations
mate guarding

sex ratio
canalized
plastic
positively correlated
negatively correlated
pleiotropic effects
correlated response
maladaptive

sampling variation
genetic drift
fixation
camera-type eyes
compound eyes
development
lactate

Study Questions

1. In human populations in Africa, two common alleles affect the structure of hemoglobin, the protein that carries oxygen on red blood cells. What is regarded as the normal allele (the allele common in European populations) is usually labeled *A,* and the sickle-cell allele is designated *S*. There are three hemoglobin genotypes, and the phenotypes associated with these genotypes can be distinguished in a variety of ways. In one African population of 10,000 adults, for example, there are 3,000 *AS* individuals, 7,000 *AA* individuals, and 0 *SS* individuals.

   (a) Suppose that these individuals were to mate at random. What would be the frequency of the

A and *S* alleles among the gametes that they produced?

(b) What would be the frequency of the three genotypes that resulted from random mating?

(c) Is the original population of adults in Hardy–Weinberg equilibrium?

2. The three common genotypes at the hemoglobin locus have very different phenotypes: *SS* individuals suffer from severe anemia, *AS* individuals have a relatively mild form of anemia but are resistant to malaria, and *AA* individuals have no anemia but are susceptible to malaria. The frequency of the *S* allele among the gametes produced by the first generation of a central African population is 0.2.

(a) Assuming that mating occurs at random, what are the frequencies of the three genotypes among zygotes produced by this population?

(b) In this area, no *SS* individuals survive to adulthood, 70% of the *AA* individuals survive, and all of the *AS* individuals survive. What is the frequency of each of the three genotypes among the second generation of adults?

(c) What is the frequency of the *S* allele among gametes produced by these adults?

3. Tay-Sachs disease is a lethal genetic disease controlled by two alleles: the Tay-Sachs allele *T* and the normal allele *N*. Children who have the *TT* genotype suffer from mental deterioration, blindness, paralysis, and convulsions, and they die sometime between the ages of three and five years. The proportion of infants afflicted with Tay-Sachs disease varies in different ethnic groups. The frequency of the Tay-Sachs allele is highest among descendants of central European Jews. Suppose that in a population of 5,000 people descended from central European Jews the frequency of the Tay-Sachs allele is 0.02.

(a) Assuming that members of this population mate at random and each adult has four children on average, how many gametes from each person are successful at being included in a zygote?

(b) Calculate the frequency of each of the three genotypes among the population of zygotes.

(c) Assume that no *TT* zygotes survive to become adults, and that 50% of the *TN* and *NN* individuals survive to become adults. What is the frequency of the *TT* and *TN* genotypes among these adults?

(d) When the adult individuals resulting from zygotes in (b) produce gametes, what is the frequency of the *T* allele among their gametes? Compare your answer to the frequency of the *T* allele among gametes produced by their parents. Think about your result, given that these numbers are roughly realistic and that there have been no substantial medical breakthroughs in the treatment of Tay-Sachs disease. What is the paradox here?

4. Consider a hypothetical allele that is lethal, like the Tay-Sachs allele, but is dominant rather than recessive. Assume that this allele has a frequency of 0.02, like the Tay-Sachs allele. Recalculate the answers to 3a, 3b, and 3c. Is selection stronger against the recessive allele or the dominant one? Why? Assuming that mutation to the deleterious allele occurs at the same rate at both loci, which allele will occur at a higher frequency? Why?

5. Consider the Rh blood group. For this example we will assume that there are only two alleles, *R* and *r,* of which *r* is recessive. Homozygous *rr* individuals produce certain nonfunctional proteins and are said to be Rh-negative (Rh⁻), while *Rr* and *RR* individuals are Rh-positive (Rh⁺). When an Rh⁻ female mates with an Rh⁺ male, their offspring may suffer serious anemia while still in the uterus. The frequency of the *r* allele in a hypothetical population is 0.25. Assuming that the population is in Hardy–Weinberg equilibrium, what fraction of the offspring in each generation will be at risk for this form of anemia?

6. The blending model of inheritance was attractive to nineteenth-century biologists because it explained why offspring tend to be intermediate in appearance between their parents. This model fails, however, because even though it predicts a loss in variation, variation is maintained. How does Mendelian genetics explain the intermediate appearance of offspring without the loss of variation? Be sure to explain why the properties of the Hardy–Weinberg equilibrium are an important part of this explanation.

7. In a particular species of fish, egg size and egg number are negatively correlated. Draw a graph that illustrates this fact. What will happen to egg size if selection favors larger numbers of eggs?

8. A plant breeder trying to increase the yield of wheat selects plants with larger kernels. After several generations of selection, the size of kernels produced has increased substantially. However, the number of kernels per plant has decreased, so the total yield remains constant. What two sources of maladaptation best explain this result?

9. The compound eyes of insects provide poor image clarity compared with the images produced by the camera-type eyes of vertebrates. Explain why insects don't evolve camera-type eyes.

10. Explain why genetic drift has no effect on genetic loci that are not variable. (When all individuals in the population are homozygous for the same allele, that genetic locus is not variable.) What does this mean about the long-term outcome of genetic drift?

11. Why does natural selection produce adaptations only at equilibrium?

12. Two dog breeders are using artificial selection to create new breeds. Both begin with dachshunds. One breeder wants to create a breed with longer forelimbs and hindlimbs. The second breeder wants to create a breed with shorter forelimbs and longer hindlimbs. Which breeder will make more rapid progress? Why?

13. When selection makes animals larger overall, their bones also get thicker. The increase in bone thickness could be due to the correlated response to selection or to independent selection for thicker bones or to some combination of the two factors. How could you determine the relative importance of these two processes?

Further Reading

Barton, N. H., D. E. G. Briggs, J. A. Eisen, D. B. Goldstein, and N. H. Patelet. 2007. *Evolution.* Woodbury, N.Y.: Cold Spring Harbor Press.

Dawkins, M. S. 1995. *Unraveling Animal Behavior.* 2nd ed. New York: Wiley.

Dawkins, R. 1996. *The Blind Watchmaker: Why the Evidence of Evolution Reveals a Universe without Design.* New York: Norton.

Falconer, D. S. and T. F. C. Mackay. 1996. *Introduction to Quantitative Genetics.* 4th ed. Essex, UK: Longman.

Hedrick, P. W. 2009. *Genetics of Populations.* 4th ed. Boston: Jones & Bartlett.

Maynard Smith, J. 1998. *Evolutionary Genetics.* 2nd ed. New York: Oxford University Press.

Ridley, M. 2004. *Evolution.* 3rd ed. Malden, Mass.: Blackwell.

_____. 1985. *The Problems of Evolution.* New York: Oxford University Press.

4

CHAPTER OBJECTIVES

By the end of this chapter you should be able to

- Describe how species are defined.

- Understand how new species arise through the process of evolution.

- Explain why speciation causes organisms to be organized hierarchically and how this pattern can be described with a phylogenetic tree.

- Understand why reconstructing phylogenies is important.

- Reconstruct phylogenies using patterns of variation in living species.

SPECIATION AND PHYLOGENY

What Are Species?

Microevolution refers to how populations change under the influence of natural selection and other evolutionary forces; macroevolution refers to how new species and higher taxa are created. So far, we have focused on how natural selection, mutation, and genetic drift cause populations to change through time. These are mechanisms of **microevolution**, and they affect the morphology, physiology, and behavior of particular species in particular environments. For example, microevolutionary processes are responsible for variation in the size and shape of the beaks of medium ground finches on Daphne Major.

However, this is not all there is to the process of evolution. Darwin's major work was titled *On the Origin of Species* because he was interested in how new species are created as well as how natural selection operates within populations. Evolutionary theory tells us how new species, genera, families, and higher groupings come into existence.

These processes are mechanisms of **macroevolution**. Macroevolutionary processes play an important role in the story of human evolution. To properly interpret the fossil record and reconstruct the history of the human lineage, we need to understand how new species and higher groupings are created and transformed over time.

Species can usually be distinguished by their behavior and morphology.

(a)

(b)

FIGURE 4.1

(a) Chimpanzees and (b) gorillas sometimes occupy the same forests and share certain traits. However, these two species are readily distinguished because no animals are intermediate between them.

Organisms cluster into distinct types called species. The individual organisms that belong to a species are similar to each other and are usually quite distinct from the members of other species. For example, in Africa some tropical forests house two species of apes: chimpanzees and gorillas. These two species are similar in many ways: both are tailless, both bear weight on their knuckles when they walk, and both defend territories. Nonetheless, these two species can easily be distinguished on the basis of their morphology: chimpanzees are smaller than gorillas; male gorillas have tiny **testes** (singular *testis;* the organs that produce sperm), while male chimpanzees have quite large ones; and gorillas have a fin of bone on their skull, while chimpanzees have more rounded skulls. Gorillas and chimpanzees also differ in their behavior: chimpanzees make and use tools in foraging, while gorillas do not; male gorillas beat their chests when they perform displays, while male chimpanzees flail branches and charge about; and gorillas live in smaller groups than chimpanzees do. These two species are easy to distinguish because no animals are intermediate between them; there are no "gimps" or "chorillas" (**Figure 4.1**).

Species are not abstractions created by scientists; they are real biological categories. People all over the world name the plants and animals around them, and biologists use the same kinds of phenotypic characteristics to sort animals into species that other people use. For the most part, there is little problem in identifying any particular specimen from its phenotype.

Although nearly everyone agrees that species exist and can recognize species in nature, biologists are much less certain about how species should be defined. This uncertainty arises from the fact that evolutionary biologists do not agree about *why* species exist. There is now a considerable amount of controversy about the processes that give rise to new species and the processes that maintain established ones. Although there are many different views on these topics, we will concentrate on two of the most widely held points of view: the biological species concept and the ecological species concept.

The Biological Species Concept

The biological species concept defines a species as a group of interbreeding organisms that are reproductively isolated from other organisms.

Most zoologists believe in the **biological species concept**, which defines a biological species as a group of organisms that interbreed in nature and are reproductively isolated. **Reproductive isolation** means that members of a given group of organisms do not mate successfully with organisms outside the group. For example, there is just one species of gorilla, *Gorilla gorilla*, and this means that all gorillas are capable of mating with one another and they do not breed with any other kinds of animals in nature. According to adherents of the biological species concept, reproductive isolation is the reason that there are no gimps or chorillas.

The biological species concept defines a species in terms of the ability to interbreed because successful mating leads to **gene flow**, the movement of genetic material within parts of a population or from one population to another. Gene flow tends to maintain similarities among members of the same species. To see how gene flow preserves homogeneity within species, consider the hypothetical situation diagrammed in **Figure 4.2a**. Imagine a population of finches living on a small island in which there are two habitats: wet and dry. Natural selection favors different sizes of beaks in each habitat. Large beaks are favored in the dry habitat, and small beaks are favored in the wet habitat. Because the island is small, however, birds fly back and forth between the two environments and mate at random, so there is a lot of gene flow between habitats. Unless selection is very strong, gene flow will swamp its effects. On average, birds in both habitats will have medium-size beaks, a compromise between the optimal phenotypes for each habitat. In this way, gene flow tends to make the members of a species evolve as a unit.

Now suppose that there are finches living on two different islands, one wet and one dry, and that the islands are far enough apart that the birds are unable to fly from one island to the other (**Figure 4.2b**). This means that there will be no interbreeding and no gene flow will occur. With no genetic exchange between the two independent groups to counter the effects of selection, the two populations will diverge genetically and become less similar phenotypically. Birds on the dry island will develop large beaks, and birds on the wet island will develop small beaks.

Reproductive isolation prevents species from genetically blending.

Reproductive isolation is the flip side of interbreeding. Suppose chimpanzees and gorillas could and did interbreed successfully in nature. The result would be gene

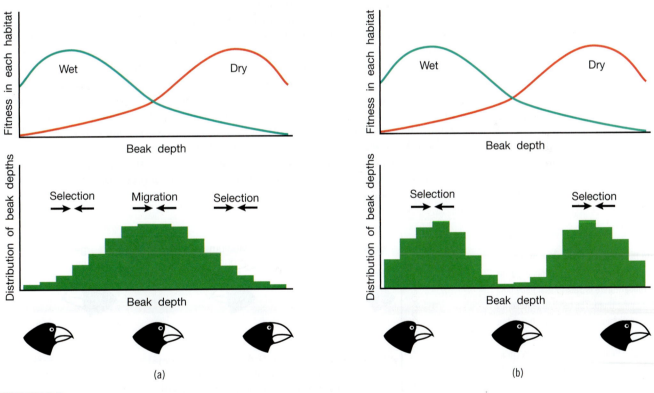

(a)   (b)

FIGURE 4.2

Gene flow among populations destroys differences between them. (a) Suppose a population of finches lives on an island with both wet and dry habitats. In the dry habitat, selection favors deep beaks, but selection in the wet habitat favors shallow beaks. Because interbreeding leads to extensive gene flow between populations in the two habitats, the population beak size responds to an average of the two environments. (b) Now suppose two populations of finches live on different islands, one wet and one dry, with no gene flow between the two islands. In this scenario, deep beaks are common on the dry island, and shallow beaks are common on the wet island.

flow between the two kinds of apes, and this phenomenon would produce animals that were genetically intermediate between chimpanzees and gorillas. Eventually, the two species would merge into one. There are no chorillas or gimps in nature because chimpanzees and gorillas are reproductively isolated.

Reproduction is a complicated process, and anything that alters the process can act as an isolating mechanism. Even subtle differences in activity patterns, courtship behavior, or appearance may prevent individuals of different types from mating. Moreover, even if a mating among individuals of different types does take place, the egg may not be fertilized or the zygote may not survive.

The Ecological Species Concept

The ecological species concept emphasizes the role of selection in maintaining species boundaries.

Critics of the biological species concept point out that gene flow is neither necessary nor sufficient to maintain species boundaries in every case, and they argue that selection plays an important role in preserving the boundaries between species. The view that emphasizes the role of natural selection in creating and maintaining species is called the **ecological species concept**.

In nature, species boundaries are often maintained even when there are substantial amounts of gene flow between species. For example, the medium ground finch readily breeds with the large ground finch on islands where they co-exist. Peter Grant and his colleagues have estimated that approximately 10% of the time, medium ground finches mate with large ground finches, leading to considerable gene flow between these two species. Yet they have not merged into a single species. Grant and his colleagues have concluded that the medium ground finch and the large ground finch have remained distinct because these two species represent two of the three optimal beak sizes for ground finches (**Figure 4.3**). These three optimal sizes are based on the availability of seeds of different size and hardness and the ability of birds with different-size beaks to harvest these seeds. According to the calculations of Grant's group, the three optimal beak sizes for ground finches correspond to the average beak sizes of the small (*Geospiza fuliginosa*), medium (*G. fortis*), and large (*G. magnirostris*) ground finch species (**Figure 4.4**). These researchers suggest that hybrids are selected against because their beaks fall in the "valleys" between these selective "peaks." The

FIGURE 4.3

In the Galápagos, selection maintains three species of ground finches, even though there is substantial gene flow among them. The red line represents the amount of food available in the environment for birds with different-size beaks. Each peak in this curve represents a different species.

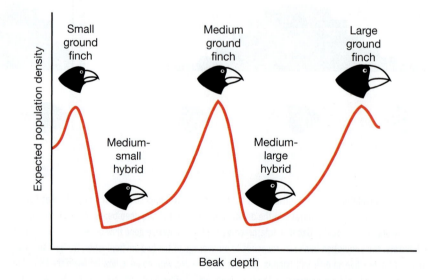

CHAPTER 4: SPECIATION AND PHYLOGENY

(a)

(b)

(c)

FIGURE 4.4

(a) The small ground finch, *Geospiza fuliginosa*; (b) the medium ground finch, *G. fortis*; (c) the large ground finch, *G. magnirostris*.

kind of interbreeding seen in the Galápagos finches is not particularly unusual. A survey of 114 plant species and 170 animal species by Loren Rieseberg and his collaborators at Indiana University indicates that a substantial fraction of species are not reproductively isolated (**Figure 4.5**).

In addition, a number of species have maintained their coherence with no gene flow between isolated subpopulations. For example, the checkerspot butterfly (**Figure 4.6**) is found in scattered populations throughout California. Members of different populations are very similar morphologically and are all classified as members of the species *Euphydryas editha*. However, careful studies by Stanford University biologist Paul Ehrlich have shown that these butterflies rarely disperse more than 100 m (about 110 yd.) from their place of birth. Given that populations are often separated by several

FIGURE 4.5

About half of a broad sample of plant and animal species are reproductively isolated, and about half are not. Members of species that are reproductively isolated do not produce viable offspring when mated to other species.

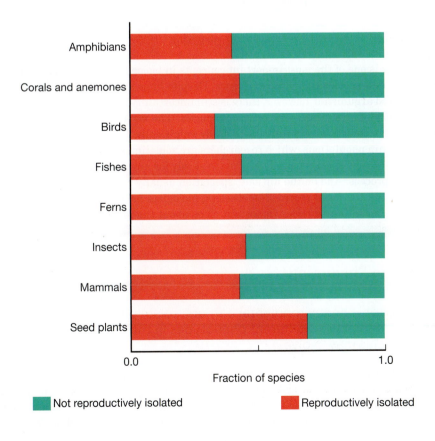

FIGURE 4.6

Checkerspot butterflies living in localized populations throughout California are all members of the same species, but there is probably very little gene flow among different populations.

kilometers and sometimes by as much as 200 km (about 124 mi.), it seems unlikely that there is enough gene flow to unify the species.

The existence of strictly asexual organisms provides additional evidence that species can be maintained without gene flow. Asexual species, which reproduce by budding or fission, simply replicate their own genetic material and produce exact copies of themselves. Thus gene flow cannot occur in asexual organisms, and it does not make sense to think of them as being reproductively isolated. Nonetheless, many biologists who study purely asexual organisms contend that it is just as easy to classify them into species as to classify organisms that reproduce sexually.

What maintains the coherence of species in these cases? Most biologists think the answer is natural selection. To see why, let's return to the Galápagos once more. Imagine a situation in which selection favored finches with small beaks in one habitat and finches with large beaks in another habitat but did not favor birds with medium beaks in either habitat. If birds with medium-size beaks consistently failed to survive or reproduce successfully, natural selection could maintain the difference between the two bird species even if they interbred freely. In the case of the checkerspot butterflies and asexual species, we can imagine the opposite scenario: selection favors organisms with the same morphology and physiology and thus maintains their similarity even in the absence of gene flow.

Today most biologists concede that selection maintains species boundaries in a few odd cases like Darwin's finches, but they generally insist that reproductive isolation plays the major role in most instances. However, a growing minority of researchers contends that selection plays an important role in maintaining virtually all species boundaries.

The Origin of Species

Speciation is difficult to study empirically.

The species is one of the most important concepts in biology, so it would be helpful to know how new species come into existence. Despite huge amounts of hard work and many heated arguments, however, there is still uncertainty about what Darwin called the "mystery of mysteries"—the origin of species. The mystery persists because the process of speciation is very difficult to study empirically. Unlike microevolutionary change within populations, which researchers are sometimes able to study in the field or laboratory, new species usually evolve too slowly for any single individual to study the entire process. And on the flip side, speciation usually occurs much too rapidly to be detected in the fossil record. Nonetheless, biologists have compiled a substantial body of evidence that provides important clues about the processes that give rise to new species.

Allopatric Speciation

If geographic or environmental barriers isolate part of a population, and selection favors different phenotypes in these regions, then a new species may evolve.

Allopatric speciation occurs when a population is divided by some type of barrier and different parts of the population adapt to different environments. The following hypothetical scenario captures the essential elements of this process. Mountainous islands in the Galápagos contain dry habitats at low elevations and wet habitats at higher elevations.

Suppose that a finch species that lives on mountainous islands has a medium-size beak, which represents a compromise between the best beak for survival in the wet areas and the best beak for survival in the dry areas. Further suppose that a number of birds are carried on the winds of a severe storm to another island that is uniformly dry, like the small, low-lying islands in the Galápagos archipelago. On this new dry island, only large-beaked birds are favored because large beaks are best for processing the large, hard seeds that predominate there. As long as there is no competition from some other small bird adapted to the dry habitat and there is very little movement between the two islands, the population of finches on the dry island will rapidly adapt to their new habitat and the birds' average beak size will increase (**Figure 4.7**).

Now let's suppose that after some time, finches from the small, dry island are blown back to the large island from which their ancestors came. If the large-beaked newcomers successfully mate with the medium-beaked residents, then gene flow between the two populations will rapidly eliminate the differences in beak size between them, and the recently created large-beaked variety will disappear. If, on the other hand, large-beaked immigrants and small-beaked residents cannot successfully interbreed, then the differences between the two populations will persist. As we noted earlier, a variety of mechanisms can prevent successful interbreeding, but it seems that the most common obstacle to interbreeding is that hybrid progeny are less viable than other offspring. In this case, we might imagine that when the two populations of finches became isolated, they diverged genetically because of natural selection and genetic drift. The longer they remain isolated, the greater the genetic difference between the populations becomes. When the two distinct types then come into contact, hybrids may have reduced viability, either because genetic incompatibilities have arisen during their

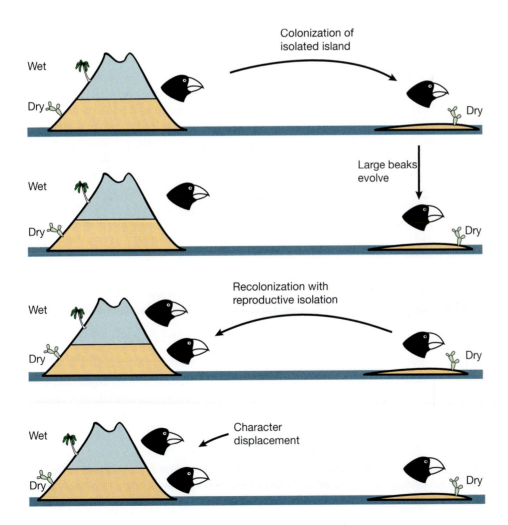

FIGURE 4.7

A likely sequence of events in a hypothetical allopatric speciation event in the Galápagos. Initially, one population of finches occupies an island with both wet and dry habitats. Because there is extensive gene flow between habitats, these finches have intermediate-size beaks. By chance, some finches disperse to a dry island, where they evolve larger beaks. Then, again by chance, some of these birds are reintroduced to the original island. If the two populations are reproductively isolated, then a new species has been formed. Even if there is some gene flow, competition between the two populations may cause the beaks of the residents and immigrants to diverge further, a process called character displacement.

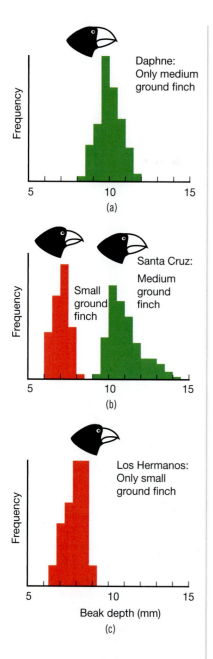

Daphne:
Only medium
ground finch

(a)

Santa Cruz:

Small
ground
finch

Medium
ground
finch

(b)

Los Hermanos:
Only small
ground finch

Beak depth (mm)

(c)

FIGURE 4.8

The distribution of beak sizes of the small ground finch (*G. fuliginosa*) and the medium ground finch (*G. fortis*) on three of the Galápagos Islands illustrates the effects of character displacement. (b) The distribution of beak depth for each species on Santa Cruz Island, where the two species compete. (a, c) The distributions of beak depth for the small and medium ground finches on islands where they do not compete with each other (*G. fortis* on Daphne Major and *G. fuliginosa* on Los Hermanos). The beaks of the two species are the most different where there is direct competition. Careful measurements of seed density and other environmental conditions suggest that competition, not environmental differences, is responsible for the difference between the populations.

isolation or because hybrid birds are unable to compete successfully for food. If these processes cause complete reproductive isolation, then a new species has been formed.

Even if there is some gene flow after the members of the two populations initially come back into contact, two additional processes may increase the degree of reproductive isolation and facilitate the formation of a new species. The first process, **character displacement**, may occur if competition over food, mates, or other resources increases the morphological differences between the immigrants and the residents. In our example, the large-beaked immigrants will be better suited to the dry parts of the large island and will be able to outcompete the original residents of these areas. Resident birds will be better off in the wet habitats, where they face less competition from the immigrants. Because small beaks are advantageous in wet habitats, residents with smaller-than-average beaks will be favored by selection. At the same time, because large beaks are advantageous in dry habitats, natural selection will favor increased beak size among the immigrants. This process will cause the beaks of the competing populations to diverge. There is good evidence that character displacement has played an important role in shaping the morphology of Darwin's finches (**Figure 4.8**).

A second process, called **reinforcement**, may act to reduce the extent of gene flow between the populations. Because hybrids have reduced viability, selection will favor behavioral or morphological adaptations that prevent matings between members of the two populations. This process will further increase the reproductive isolation between the two populations (**Figure 4.9**). Thus character displacement and reinforcement may amplify the initial differences between the populations and lead to two new species.

Allopatric speciation requires a physical barrier that initially isolates part of a population, interrupts gene flow, and allows the isolated subpopulation to diverge from the original population under the influence of natural selection. In our example, the physical barrier is the sea, but mountains, rivers, and deserts can also restrict movement and interrupt gene flow. Character displacement and reinforcement may work to increase differences when members of the two populations renew contact. However, these processes are not necessary elements in allopatric speciation. Many species become completely isolated while they are separated by a physical barrier.

Parapatric and Sympatric Speciation

New species may also form if there is strong selection that favors two different phenotypes.

Biologists who endorse the biological species concept usually argue that allopatric speciation is the most important mechanism for creating new species

FIGURE 4.9

Finch courtship displays can be quite elaborate. Here a male finch displays to attract the female's attention. Subtle variations in courtship behavior among members of different populations may prevent mating and increase reproductive isolation.

in nature. For these scientists, gene flow "welds" a species together, and species can be split only if gene flow is interrupted. Biologists who think that natural selection plays an important role in maintaining species often contend that selection can lead to speciation even when there is interbreeding. There are strong and weak versions of this hypothesis. The weak version, called **parapatric speciation**, holds that selection alone is not sufficient to produce a new species, but new species can be formed if selection is combined with partial genetic isolation. For example, baboons range from Saudi Arabia to the Cape of Good Hope and occupy an extremely broad range of environments. Some baboons live in moist tropical forests, some live in arid deserts, and some live in high-altitude grasslands (**Figure 4.10**). Different behaviors and morphological traits may be favored in each of these environments, and this variation may cause baboons in different regions to vary. At habitat boundaries, animals that come from different

(a)

(b)

(c)

(d)

FIGURE 4.10

Baboons are distributed all over Africa and occupy a very diverse range of habitats. (a) In the Drakensberg Mountains in South Africa, winter temperatures drop below freezing, and snow sometimes falls. (b) In the Matopo Hills of Zimbabwe, woodlands are interspersed with open savanna areas. (c) Amboseli National Park lies at the foot of Mount Kilimanjaro just inside the Kenyan border. (d) Gombe Stream National Park lies on the hilly shores of Lake Tanganyika in Tanzania.

FIGURE 4.11

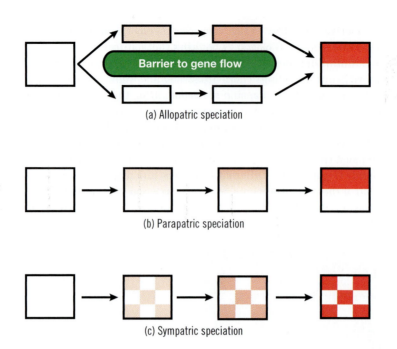

(a) Allopatric speciation

(b) Parapatric speciation

(c) Sympatric speciation

There are three different mechanisms of speciation. (a) Allopatric speciation occurs when a species is divided into two reproductively isolated populations that subsequently diverge. If the divergent populations regain contact, they cannot interbreed and two new species exist. (b) Parapatric speciation occurs when a species experiences different environments in different parts of its geographic range. Natural selection causes different populations of the species to diverge while adapting to these different surroundings, and eventually reproductive isolation is achieved. (c) Sympatric speciation occurs when selection strongly favors different adaptations to a similar environment within a single species.

habitats and have different characteristics may mate and create a **hybrid zone**. Study of hybrid zones in a wide variety of species suggests that hybrids are usually less fit than nonhybrids. When this is the case, selection should favor behavior or morphology that prevents mating between members of individuals from different habitats. If such reinforcement does occur, gene flow will be reduced, and eventually two new, reproductively isolated species will evolve.

The strong version of the hypothesis, called **sympatric speciation**, contends that strong selection favoring different phenotypes can lead to speciation even when there is no geographic separation, and therefore initially there is extensive gene flow among individuals in the population. Sympatric speciation is theoretically possible, and this form of speciation has been induced in laboratory populations, but it is uncertain how often it occurs in nature. The three speciation mechanisms are diagrammed in **Figure 4.11**.

Adaptive radiation occurs when there are many empty niches.

Ecologists use the term **niche** to refer to a particular way of "making a living," which includes the kinds of food eaten as well as when, how, and where the food is acquired. One consequence of all three models of speciation is that the rate of speciation depends on the number of available ecological niches. Once again, Darwin's finches provide a good example. When the first finches migrated to the Galápagos from the

FIGURE 4.12

When the first finches arrived in the Galápagos 500,000 years ago, there were many empty niches. (a) Some finches became cactus eaters, (b) others became seed eaters, and (c) some became predators on insects and other arthropods.

(a)

(b)

(c)

mainland of South America (or perhaps from the Cocos Islands) about half a million years ago, all of the niches for small birds in the Galápagos were empty. There were opportunities to make a living as a seed eater, a cactus eater, and so on. The finches' ancestors diversified to fill all of these ecological niches, and eventually they became 14 distinct species (**Figure 4.12**). An even more spectacular example of this process occurred at the end of the Cretaceous era. Dinosaurs dominated the earth during the Cretaceous era but disappeared suddenly 65 mya. The mammals that co-existed with the dinosaurs were mostly small, nocturnal, and insectivorous. But when the dinosaurs became extinct, these small creatures diversified to fill a broad range of ecological niches, evolving into elephants, killer whales, buffalo, wolves, bats, gorillas, humans, and other kinds of mammals. When a single kind of animal or plant diversifies to fill many available niches, the process is called **adaptive radiation** (**Figure 4.13**).

The Tree of Life

Organisms can be classified hierarchically on the basis of similarities. Many such similarities are unrelated to adaptation.

In Chapter 1, we saw how Darwin's theory of evolution explains the existence of adaptation. Now we can show how the same theory explains why organisms can be classified into a hierarchy on the basis of their similarities, a fact that puzzled nineteenth-century biologists much more than the existence of adaptations did. Richard Owen, a nineteenth-century anatomist who was one of Darwin's principal opponents in the debates following the publication of *On the Origin of Species*, used dugongs (aquatic mammals much like manatees), bats, and moles as an example of this phenomenon. All three of these creatures have the same kind and number of bones in their forelimbs, even though the shapes of these bones are quite different (**Figure 4.14**). The forelimb of the bat is adapted

FIGURE 4.13

Darwin's finches are not the only example of adaptive radiations that occur when immigrants encounter a range of empty ecological niches. In the Hawaiian archipelago, the adaptive radiation of honeycreeper finches, shown here, produced an even greater diversity of species.

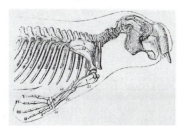
(a)

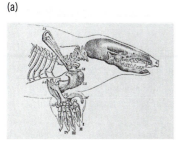
(b)

(c)

FIGURE 4.14

Organisms show patterns of similarity that have nothing to do with adaptation. Richard Owen's drawings of the forelimbs of three mammalian species illustrate this fact. (a) The dugong, (b) the mole, and (c) the bat all have the same basic bone structure in their forelimbs; dugongs use their forelimbs to swim in the sea, moles use their forelimbs to burrow into the earth, and bats use their forelimbs to fly.

FIGURE 4.15

The dugong is an aquatic animal. Its forelimb is adapted for paddling through the water.

to flying, and that of the dugong to paddling (**Figure 4.15**). Nonetheless, the basic structure of a bat's forelimb is much more similar to that of a dugong than to the forelimb of a swift, even though the swift's forelimb is also designed for flight.

Such patterns of similarity make it possible to cluster species hierarchically—like a series of nested boxes (**Figure 4.16**). This remarkable property of life is the basis of the system for classifying plants and animals devised by the eighteenth-century Swedish biologist Carolus Linnaeus. All species of bats share many similarities and are grouped together in one box. Bats can be clustered with dugongs and moles in a larger box that contains all of the mammals. Mammals in turn are classified together with birds, reptiles, and amphibians in an even larger box. Sometimes the similarities that lead us to classify animals together are functional similarities. Many of the features shared by different species of bats are related to the fact that they fly at night. However, many shared features bear little relation to adaptation; bats, tiny aerial acrobats, for example, are grouped with the enormous placid dugong, and not with the small acrobatic swift.

Speciation explains why organisms can be classified hierarchically.

The fact that new species derive from existing species accounts for the existence of the patterns of nonadaptive similarity that allow organisms to be classified hierarchically. Clearly, new species originate by splitting off from older ones, and we can arrange a group of species that share a common ancestor into a family tree, or **phylogeny**. **Figure 4.17** shows the family tree of the **hominoids**—the superfamily that includes apes and humans—and **Figure 4.18** shows what some of these present-day apes look like. At the root of the tree is an unknown ancestral species from which all hominoids

Vertebrates

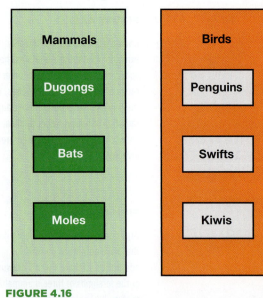

FIGURE 4.16

Patterns of similarity allow organisms to be classified hierarchically into a series of nested boxes. All mammals share more similarities with each other than they do with birds, even though some mammals, such as bats, must solve the same adaptive problems that birds face.

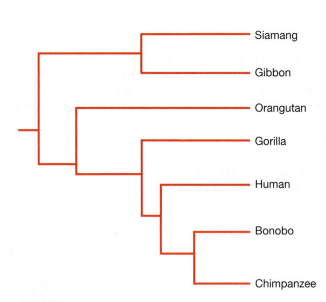

FIGURE 4.17

A phylogeny for the hominoids. The names of living species are given at the ends of the branches. The branching pattern of the phylogenetic tree reflects the ancestry of extant (still-living) lineages. For example, chimpanzees and bonobos have a more recent common ancestor than chimpanzees and orangutans do.

(a)

(b)

(c)

(d)

evolved. Each branch represents a speciation event in which one species split into two daughter species, and one or both of the new daughter species diverged in morphology or behavior from the parent species.

It is important to realize that when two daughter species diverge from each other, they don't differ in all phenotypic details. A few traits may differ while most others retain their original form. For example, the hominoids share many common features, including an unspecialized digestive system, five toes on each foot, and no tail. At the same time, these animals have diverged in a number of ways. Gorillas usually live in groups that contain one adult male and several adult females; orangutans are mainly solitary. Male and female gibbons are about the same size, but among the other apes, males are larger than females. In general, we expect to see the greatest divergence in those traits that are related to making a living in different habitats and to choosing mates.

Now let's return to the family tree. Each time one species splits to become two new species, the new daughter species will differ in some way. They will continue to diverge through time because once speciation has occurred, the two lineages evolve independently. Some differences will arise because the two species adapt to different habitats; other differences may result from random processes like genetic drift. In general, species that have recently diverged will have more characteristics in common with one another than with species that diverged in the more distant past. For example, chimpanzees and gorillas share more traits with one another than they do with orangutans or gibbons because they share a more recent common ancestor. This pattern of sharing traits is the source of the hierarchical nature of life.

Why Reconstruct Phylogenies?

Phylogenetic reconstruction plays three important roles in the study of organic evolution.

We have seen that descent with modification explains the hierarchical structure of the living world. Because new species always evolve from existing species and species are reproductively isolated, all living organisms can be placed on a single phylogenetic tree, which we can then use to trace the ancestry of all living species. In the remainder of this chapter, we will see how the pattern of similarities and differences

(a)

(b)

FIGURE 4.19

Knuckle walking among the great apes. (a) Chimpanzees and gorillas are knuckle walkers; this means that when they walk, they bend their fingers under their palms and bear weight on their knuckles. (b) In contrast, orangutans are not knuckle walkers; when they walk, they bear their weight on their palms.

observed in living things can be used to construct phylogenies and to help establish the evolutionary history of life.

Reconstructing phylogenies plays an important role in the study of evolution for three reasons:

1. *Phylogeny is the basis for the identification and classification of organisms.* In the latter part of this chapter we will see how scientists use phylogenetic relationships to name organisms and arrange them into hierarchies. This endeavor is called **taxonomy**.

2. *Knowing phylogenetic relationships often helps explain why a species evolved certain adaptations and not others.* Natural selection creates new species by modifying existing body structures to perform new functions. To understand why a new organism evolved a particular trait, it helps to know what kind of organism it evolved from, and this is what phylogenetic trees tell us. The phylogenetic relationships among the apes provide a good example of this point. Most scientists used to believe that chimpanzees and gorillas shared a more recent common ancestor than either of them shared with humans. This view influenced their interpretation of the evolution of locomotion, or forms of movement, among the apes. All of the great apes are **quadrupedal**, which means that they walk on their hands and feet. However, gorillas and chimpanzees curl their fingers over their palms and bear weight on their knuckles, a form of locomotion called **knuckle walking**, whereas orangutans bear weight on their palms (**Figure 4.19**). Humans, of course, stand upright on two legs. Knuckle walking involves distinctive modifications of the anatomy of the hand, and because human hands show none of these anatomical features, most scientists believed that humans did not evolve from a knuckle-walking species. Because both chimpanzees and gorillas are knuckle walkers, it was generally assumed that this trait evolved in their common ancestor (**Figure 4.20**). However, more recent measurements of genetic similarity have now convinced most scientists that humans and chimpanzees are more closely related to one another than either species is to the gorilla. If this is correct, then the old account of the evolution of locomotion in apes must be wrong. Two accounts are consistent with the new phylogeny. It is possible that the common ancestor of humans, chimpanzees, and gorillas was a knuckle walker and that knuckle walking was retained in the common ancestor of humans and chimpanzees. This would mean that knuckle walking evolved only once and that humans are descended from a knuckle-walking species (**Figure 4.21a**). Alternatively, the common ancestor of humans, chimpanzees, and other apes may not have been a knuckle walker. If this was the case, then knuckle walking evolved independently in chimpanzees and gorillas (**Figure 4.21b**). Each of these scenarios raises interesting questions about the evolution of locomotion in humans and apes. If chimpanzees and gorillas evolved knuckle walking independently, then a close examination should reveal subtle differences in their morphology. If humans evolved from a knuckle walker, then perhaps more careful study will reveal the traces of our former mode of locomotion. As we will see in Chapter 10, such traces can be found in the wrists of one of our putative ancestors.

3. *We can deduce the function of morphological features or behaviors by comparing the traits of different species.* This technique is called the **comparative method**. As we will see in Part Two, most primates live in groups. Some scientists have argued that **terrestrial** (ground-dwelling) primates live in larger groups than **arboreal** (tree-dwelling) primates because terrestrial species are more vulnerable to predators and animals are safer in larger groups. To test the relationship between group size and terrestriality using the comparative method, we would collect data on group size and lifestyle (arboreal/terrestrial) for many different primate species. However, most biologists believe that only independently evolved cases should be counted in comparative analyses, so we must take the phylogenetic relationships among species into account. Closer Look 4.1 provides a hypothetical example of how phylogenetic information can alter our interpretations of comparative data.

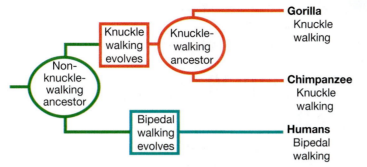

Knuckle walking evolved in the common ancestor of chimpanzees and gorillas

FIGURE 4.20

If chimpanzees are more closely related to gorillas than to humans, as morphological evidence suggests, then this is the most plausible scenario for the evolution of locomotion in gorillas, chimpanzees, and humans. The fossil record suggests that the ancestor of chimpanzees, gorillas, and humans was neither knuckle-walking nor bipedal. The simplest account of the current distribution of locomotion is that knuckle walking evolved once in the common ancestor of chimpanzees and gorillas.

For many years, scientists constructed phylogenies only for the purpose of classification. The terms *taxonomy* and *systematics* were used interchangeably to refer to the construction of phylogenies and to the use of such phylogenies for naming and classifying organisms. With the recent realization that phylogenies have other important uses like the ones just described, there is a need for terms that distinguish phylogenetic construction from classification. Here we adopt the suggestion of the Field Museum of Natural History anthropologist Robert Martin to employ the term **systematics** to refer

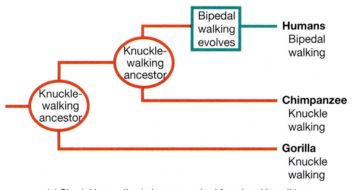

(a) Bipedal locomotion in humans evolved from knuckle walking

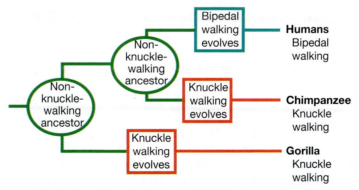

(b) Knuckle walking evolved indepently in chimpanzees and gorillas

FIGURE 4.21

If humans are more closely related to chimpanzees than to gorillas, as the genetic data suggest, then there are two possible scenarios for the evolution of locomotion in these three species. (a) If the common ancestor of chimpanzees and gorillas was a knuckle walker, then it follows that human bipedal locomotion evolved from knuckle walking. (b) If the common ancestor of all three species was not a knuckle walker, then knuckle walking must have evolved independently in chimpanzees and gorillas.

4.1 The Role of Phylogeny in the Comparative Method

To understand why it is important to take phylogeny into account when using the comparative method, consider the phylogeny illustrated in **Figure 4.22**, which shows the pattern of relationships for eight hypothetical primate species.

As you can see, three terrestrial species live in large groups and three arboreal species live in small groups. Only one terrestrial species lives in small groups, and only one arboreal species lives in large groups. Thus, if we based our determinations on living species, we would conclude that there is a statistical relationship between group size and lifestyle. If we count independent evolutionary events, however, we get a very different answer. Large group size and terrestriality are found together only in species B and its descendants: B1, B2, and B3. This combination evolved only once, although we now observe this combination in three living species. There is also only one case of selection creating an arboreal species that lives in small groups (species C and its descendants: C1, C2, and C3). Note that each of the other possible combinations has also evolved once. When we tabulate independent evolutionary events, we find no consistent relationship between lifestyle and group size. Clearly, phylogenetic information is crucial to making sense of the patterns we see in nature.

FIGURE 4.22

The phylogenetic relationships among eight hypothetical primate species are shown here. Living species lie at the ends of branches, and their ancestors are identified at the branching points of the tree. These species vary in group size (small or large) and lifestyle (arboreal or terrestrial). The lineages in which novel associations between group size and lifestyle first evolved are marked with a double red bar. The left-hand matrix below tallies the association between group size and lifestyle among living species, and suggests that whereas arboreal species live in small groups, terrestrial species live in large ones. The right-hand matrix tallies the number of times the association between group size and lifestyle changed in the course of the evolution of these species.

In this case, no relationship between group size and lifestyle is evident. This example demonstrates why it is important to keep track of independent evolutionary events in comparative analyses.

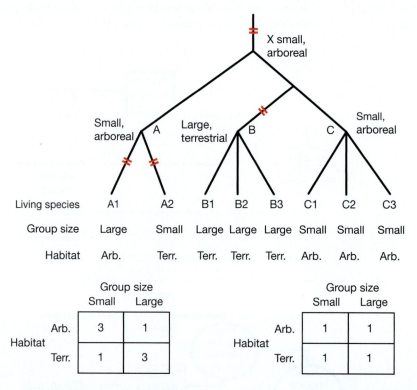

Living species	A1	A2	B1	B2	B3	C1	C2	C3
Group size	Large	Small	Large	Large	Large	Small	Small	Small
Habitat	Arb.	Terr.	Terr.	Terr.	Terr.	Arb.	Arb.	Arb.

	Group size	
	Small	Large
Arb.	3	1
Terr.	1	3

Habitat

Counting living species implies that habitat predicts group size.

	Group size	
	Small	Large
Arb.	1	1
Terr.	1	1

Habitat

Counting evolutionary events implies that habitat does *not* predict group size.

to the construction of phylogenies, and the term *taxonomy* to mean the use of phylogenies in naming and classification. Although this distinction may not seem important now, it will become more relevant as we proceed.

How to Reconstruct Phylogenies

We reconstruct phylogenies on the assumption that species with many phenotypic similarities are more closely related than species with fewer phenotypic similarities are.

To see how systematists reconstruct a phylogeny, consider the following example. We begin with three species—named for the moment A, B, and C—whose myoglobin (a cellular protein involved in oxygen metabolism) differs in the ways shown in **Table 4.1**. Remember from Chapter 2 that proteins are long chains of amino acids; the letters in Table 4.1 stand for the amino acids present at various positions along the protein chain.

A systematist wants to find the pattern of descent that is most likely to have produced these data. The first thing she would notice is that all three types of myoglobin have the same amino acid at many positions, exemplified here by the positions 1 (all G), 2 (all L), and 3 (all S). At positions 5, 9, 13, 30, and 34, species A and B have the same amino acids, but species C has a different set. At position 48, species B and C have the same amino acid; and at position 59, A and C have the same amino acid. At position 66, all three species have different amino acids. The systematist would see that there are fewer differences between species A and B than between A and C or between B and C. She would infer that fewer genetic changes have accumulated since A and B shared a common ancestor sometime in the past than since A and C, or B and C, shared a common ancestor. Because fewer evolutionary changes are necessary to convert A to B than A to C or B to C, A and B are assumed to have a more recent common ancestor than either species shares with C (**Figure 4.23**). In other words, species that are more similar are assumed to be more closely related.

Let's end the suspense and reveal the identities of the three species. Species A is our own species, *Homo sapiens*; species B is the duck-billed platypus (**Figure 4.24**); and species C is the domestic chicken. The phylogeny shown in Figure 4.23 suggests that humans and duck-billed platypuses (A and B) are more closely related to each other than either of them is to chickens (C). However, this phylogeny is not based on nearly enough data to be conclusive. To be convinced of the relationships among these

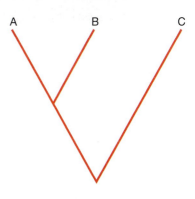

FIGURE 4.23

The phylogenetic tree for species A, B, and C derived from their myoglobin amino acid sequences, portions of which are shown in Table 4.1.

FIGURE 4.24

Duck-billed platypuses illustrate the importance of distinguishing between derived and ancestral traits. These creatures lay eggs and have horny bills like birds, but they lactate like mammals.

TABLE 4.1

	Amino Acid Number										
Species	1	2	3	5	9	13	30	34	48	59	66
A	G	L	S	G	L	V	I	K	H	E	A
B	G	L	S	G	L	V	I	K	G	A	I
C	G	L	S	Q	Q	I	M	H	G	E	Q

The amino acid sequence for the protein myoglobin is shown for three different species. The numbers refer to positions on the myoglobin chain, and the letter in each cell stands for the particular amino acid found at that position in each kind of myoglobin. All three species have the same amino acids at all of the positions not shown here, as well as at positions 1 to 3. At eight positions, however, there is at least one discrepancy among the three species (shaded).

three organisms, we would need to gather and analyze data on many more characters and generate the same tree each time. In fact, many other characters show the same pattern as myoglobin. Humans and duck-billed platypuses, for example, have hair and mammary glands, but chickens lack these structures. The phylogeny in Figure 4.23 is the currently accepted tree for these three species.

Problems Due to Convergence

In constructing phylogenies, we must avoid basing decisions on characters that are similar because of convergent evolution.

Despite the evidence just discussed, not everything about the phylogeny for humans, platypuses, and chickens is hunky-dory. Two amino acid positions, 48 and 59 (see Table 4.1), are not consistent with the phylogeny shown in Figure 4.23. Moreover, certain other characters don't fit this tree. For example, both platypuses and humans lactate, but chickens don't (**Figure 4.25a**); both humans and chickens are bipedal, but platypuses are not (**Figure 4.25b**); and both platypuses and chickens lay eggs (**Figure 4.25c**), have a feature of the gut called a cloaca, and sport horny bills, but humans don't. Why don't these characters fit neatly into our phylogeny?

One reason for these anomalies is convergent evolution. Sometimes traits shared by two species are not the result of common ancestry. Instead, they are separate adaptations independently produced by natural selection. Chickens and humans are bipedal *not* because they are descended from the same bipedal ancestor, but rather because they *each* evolved this mode of locomotion independently. Similarly, the horny bills of chickens and platypuses are not similarities due to descent; they are independently derived characters. Systematists say that characters similar because of convergence are **analogous**, while characters whose similarity is due to descent from a common ancestor are **homologous**. It is important to avoid using convergent traits in reconstructing phylogenetic relationships. Although it is fairly obvious that bipedal locomotion in humans and chickens is not homologous, convergence is sometimes very difficult to detect.

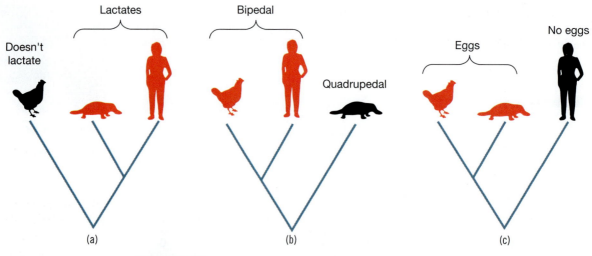

FIGURE 4.25

(a) Many traits, such as lactation, generate the same pattern of relationships among humans, chickens, and platypuses that myoglobin does (see Figure 4.23). (b) Other characters, such as bipedal locomotion, suggest a closer relationship between humans and chickens than between humans and platypuses or between platypuses and chickens. (c) Some traits, like egg laying, suggest a closer relationship between chickens and platypuses than between chickens and humans or between platypuses and humans.

Problems Due to Ancestral Characters

It is also important to ignore similarity based on ancestral characters, traits that also characterized the common ancestor of the species being classified.

There are also homologous traits that do not fit neatly into correct phylogenies. For example, chickens and platypuses reproduce by laying eggs, while humans do not. It seems likely that both chickens and platypuses lay eggs because they are descended from a common egg-laying ancestor. But if these characters are homologous, why don't they allow us to generate the correct phylogeny (see Figure 4.25c)?

Egg laying is an example of what systematists call an **ancestral trait**, one that characterized the common ancestor of chickens, platypuses, and humans. Egg laying has been retained in the chicken and the platypus but lost in humans. It is important to avoid using ancestral characters when constructing phylogenies. Only **derived traits**—features that have evolved since the time of the last common ancestor of the species under consideration—can be used in constructing phylogenies.

To see why we need to distinguish between ancestral and derived traits, consider the three hypothetical species of "cooties" pictured in **Figure 4.26**. At first glance the red-eyed cootie and the blue-necked cootie seem more similar to one another than either is to the orange-spotted cootie, and a careful count of characters will show that they do share more traits with one another than with the orange-spotted variety. But consider **Figure 4.27**, which shows the phylogeny for the three species. You can see that the blue-necked cootie is actually more closely related to the orange-spotted cootie

Red-eyed cootie   Blue-necked cootie   Orange-spotted cootie

FIGURE 4.26

The red-eyed cootie and the blue-necked cootie share more traits with one another (such as green legs, blue body, and green antennae) than either of them shares with the orange-spotted cootie. If phylogenetic reconstruction were based on overall similarity, we would conclude that the blue-necked cootie and the red-eyed cootie are more closely related to each other than either is to the orange-spotted cootie.

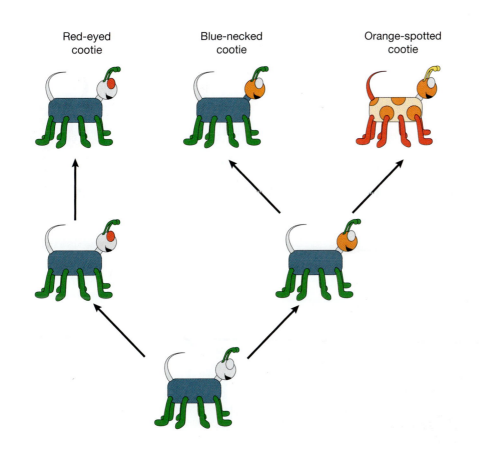

Red-eyed cootie   Blue-necked cootie   Orange-spotted cootie

FIGURE 4.27

The phylogenetic history of the three cootie species shown in Figure 4.26 indicates that the blue-necked cootie is actually more closely related to the orange-spotted cootie than to the red-eyed cootie. This is because the blue-necked cootie and the orange-spotted cootie have a more recent common ancestor with each other than with the red-eyed cootie.

because they share a more recent common ancestor. The blue-necked cootie seems more similar to the red-eyed cootie because they share many ancestral characters, but the orange-spotted cootie has undergone a period of rapid evolution that has eliminated most ancestral characters. Looking at ancestral traits will not generate the correct phylogeny if rates of evolution differ among species.

If we base our assessment of similarity only on the number of derived characters that each species displays (as shown in **Figure 4.28**), then the most similar species are the ones most closely related. The blue-necked cootie and orange-spotted cootie share one derived character (an orange face) with each other, but they share no derived characters with the red-eyed cootie. Thus if we avoid ancestral characters, we can construct the correct phylogeny.

Systematists distinguish between ancestral and derived characters using the following criteria: ancestral characters (1) appear earlier in organismal development, (2) appear earlier in the fossil record, and (3) are seen in out-groups.

It is easy to see that distinguishing ancestral characters from derived characters is important but hard to see how to do it in practice. If you can observe only living organisms, how can you tell whether a particular character in two species is ancestral or derived? There is no surefire solution to this problem, but biologists use three rules of thumb:

1. The development of a multicellular organism is a complex process, and it seems logical that modifications occurring early in the process are likely to be more disruptive than modifications occurring later. As a result, evolution often (but not always) proceeds by modifying the ends of existing developmental pathways. To the extent that this generalization is true, characters that occur early in development are ancestral. For example, humans and other apes do not have tails, but

FIGURE 4.28

In this phylogeny, only derived characters are shown: red eyes in the red-eyed cootie; orange face in the last common ancestor blue-necked and orange-spotted cooties; blue neck and orange face in the blue-necked cootie; and red legs and tail, yellow antennae, orange face, gray body, and orange spots in the orange-spotted species. The correct phylogeny is based on similarity in shared, derived characters.

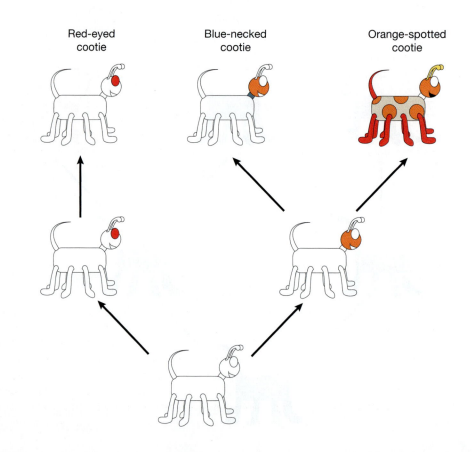

Red-eyed cootie   Blue-necked cootie   Orange-spotted cootie

the fact that a tail appears in the development of the human embryo and then disappears is evidence that the tail is an ancestral character (**Figure 4.29**). We conclude from this that the absence of a tail in humans is derived. This reasoning will not be helpful if ancestral traits have been completely lost during development or if traits (like egg laying) are expressed only in adults.

2. In many cases, fossils provide information about the ancestors of modern species. If we see in the fossil record that all of the earliest likely ancestors of apes had tails, and that primates without tails appear only later in the fossil record, then it is reasonable to infer that having a tail is an ancestral character. This criterion may fail if the fossil record is incomplete and, therefore, a derived character appears in the fossil record before an ancestral one. As we will see in Chapter 10, new fossil finds can sometimes lead to radical revisions of existing phylogenies.

3. Finally, we can determine which characters are ancestral in a particular group by looking at neighboring groups, or **out-groups**. Suppose we are trying to determine whether having a tail is ancestral in the primates. We know that monkeys have tails and that apes do not, but we don't know which state is ancestral. To find out, we look at neighboring mammalian groups, such as insectivores or carnivores. Because the members of these out-groups typically have tails, it is reasonable to infer that the common ancestor of all primates also had a tail.

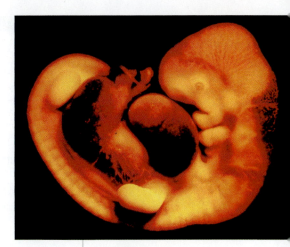

Using Genetic-Distance Data to Date Phylogenetic Events

Genetic distance measures the overall genetic similarity of two species.

Biologists and anthropologists often find it useful to compute a measure of overall genetic similarity, called **genetic distance**, between pairs of species. There are a number of different ways to measure genetic distance, but here we will focus on genetic-distance estimates based on DNA sequence data. For example, to compute the genetic distance between humans and chimpanzees, the biologist first identifies homologous DNA segments in the two species. This means that the segments are descended from the same DNA sequence in the common ancestor of humans and chimpanzees. These DNA segments are then sequenced. The number of nucleotide sites at which the two sequences differ is used to compute the genetic distance between the two species. The mathematical formulas used for these calculations are beyond the scope of this book, but suffice it to say that the larger the number of nucleotide differences, the bigger the genetic distance.

Genetic-distance data are often consistent with the hypothesis that genetic distance changes at an approximately constant rate.

The genetic distances among noncoding sequences of the DNA of humans, chimpanzees, gorillas, and orangutans are shown in **Table 4.2.** Notice that gorillas, humans, and chimpanzees are essentially the same genetic distance from orangutans. This close similarity is evidence that genetic distance changes at an approximately constant rate. To see why, think of genetic distance accumulating along the path leading from the last common ancestor of all of the hominoids to each living species. The total distance between any pair of living species is the sum of their paths from the last common ancestor. For example, the genetic distance between humans and orangutans is the accumulated distance between the last common ancestor of all four of these species and orangutans plus the accumulated distance between the last common ancestor and humans. Now notice that the distance between orangutans and humans is the same

TABLE 4.2

	Human	Chimpanzee	Gorilla	Orangutan
Human	—	1.24	1.62	3.08
Chimpanzee		—	1.63	3.12
Gorilla			—	3.09
Orangutan				—

Genetic distances among humans and the three great ape species, based on sequence divergence in noncoding regions of DNA.

as the distance between chimpanzees and orangutans. This means that the genetic distance between the last common ancestor of orangutans and humans is the same as the distance between the last common ancestor of chimpanzees and orangutans. Because the time that elapsed since the branching off from the last common ancestor is the same for all these species, it follows that the rate of change of genetic distance along both of these paths through the phylogeny must be approximately the same and that the genetic distance between two species is a measure of the time elapsed since both had a common ancestor. Evolutionists refer to genetic distances with a constant rate of change as **molecular clocks** because genetic change acts like a clock that measures the time since two species shared a common ancestor. Data from many other groups of organisms suggest that genetic distances often have this clocklike property, but there are also important exceptions.

A majority of biologists agree that as long as genetic distances are not too big or too small, the molecular-clock assumption is a useful approximation. However, there is some controversy about *why* genetic distance changes in a clocklike way. Advocates of the **neutral theory** believe that most changes in DNA sequences have little or no effect on fitness, so the evolution of this neutral DNA must be controlled by drift and mutation. The neutral theory suggests that under the right circumstances, mutation and drift will produce clocklike change. Other biologists argue that the molecular clock is the product of natural selection in variable environments.

If the molecular-clock hypothesis is correct, then knowing the genetic distance between two living species allows us to estimate how long ago the two lineages diverged.

The data from contemporary species indicate that genetic distance changes at a constant rate, but the data don't provide a clue as to what that rate might be. However, dated fossils allow us to estimate when the splits between lineages occurred. By dividing the known genetic distance between a pair of species by the time since the last common ancestor, we can estimate the rate at which genetic distance changes through time. For example, fossil evidence (see Chapter 9) indicates that the last common ancestor of orangutans and humans lived about 14 mya and the genetic distance between these two species is 3.1. Dividing the genetic distance between humans and orangutans by the time since their last common ancestor indicates that genetic distance accumulates at a rate of 0.22 units per million years.

Once we have an estimate of the rate at which genetic distance changes through time, the molecular-clock hypothesis can be used to date the divergence times for lineages, even when we don't have any fossils. For example, to estimate the last common ancestor of humans and chimpanzees, we divide the genetic distance, 1.24, by the estimated rate, 0.22. This calculation indicates that the last common ancestor of these two species lived about 5.6 mya.

In practice, scientists use a number of different divergence dates to calibrate the rate at which genetic distance changes through time. Each divergence date produces a slightly different estimate of the rate of change of genetic distance, and this estimate in turn generates different estimates of the divergence times. Thus divergence dates for humans and chimpanzees range from 7 to 5 mya.

Taxonomy: Naming Names

The hierarchical pattern of similarity created by evolution provides the basis for the way science classifies and names organisms.

Putting names on things is, to some extent, arbitrary. We could give species names like Sam or Ruby, or perhaps use numbers like the Social Security system does. This is, in fact, the way common names work. The word *lion* is an arbitrary label, as is "Charles" or "550-72-9928." The problem for scientists is that the number of animals and plants is very large, encompassing far too many species for any individual to keep track of. One way to cope with this massive complexity is to devise a system in which organisms are grouped together in a hierarchical system of classification. Once again, there are many possible systems. For example, we could categorize organisms alphabetically, grouping alligators and apricots with the *A*s, barnacles and baboons with the *B*s, and so on. This approach has little to recommend it, because knowing how an animal is classified tells us nothing about the organism besides its location in the alphabet. An alternative approach would be to adopt a system of classification that groups together organisms with similar characteristics, analogous to the Library of Congress system used by libraries to classify books. The *Q*s might be predators, the *QH*s aquatic predators, the *QP*s aerial predators, and so on. Thus knowing that the scientific name of the red-tailed hawk is QP604.4 might tell you that the hawk is a small aerial predator that lives in North America. The problem with such a system is that not all organisms would fall into a single category. Where would you classify animals that eat both animals and plants, such as bears, or amphibious predators, such as frogs?

The scientific system for naming animals is based on the hierarchy of descent: species that are closely related are classified together. Closely related species are grouped together in the same **genus** (plural *genera;* **Figure 4.30**). For example, the genus *Pan* contains two closely related species of chimpanzees: the common chimpanzee, *Pan troglodytes;* and the bonobo, *Pan paniscus.* Closely related genera are usually grouped together in a higher unit, often the **family**. Chimpanzees are in the family Hominidae along with orangutans (*Pongo pygmaeus*), gorillas (*Gorilla gorilla*), and humans (*Homo sapiens*). Closely related families are then grouped together in a more inclusive unit, often a **superfamily**.

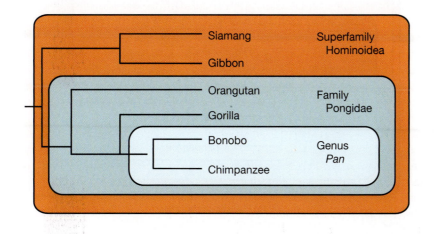

FIGURE 4.30

Bonobos and chimpanzees are classified together in the genus *Pan,* both of these species are classified with gorillas and orangutans in the family Pongidae, and all of the apes are grouped together in the superfamily Hominoidea. Note that humans are missing from this phylogenetic tree.

Taxonomists disagree about whether overall similarity should also be used in classifying organisms.

The majority of taxonomists agree that descent should play a major role in classifying organisms. However, they vehemently disagree about whether descent should be the *only* factor used to classify organisms. The members of a relatively new school of thought, called **cladistic taxonomy** (or sometimes "cladistic systematics"), argue that only descent should matter. Adherents to an older school of taxonomy, called **evolutionary taxonomy** (or "evolutionary systematics"), believe that classification should be based both on descent *and* on overall similarity. To understand the difference between these two philosophies, consider **Figure 4.31**, in which humans have been added to the phylogeny of the apes shown in Figure 4.30. Evolutionary taxonomists would say that humans are qualitatively different from other apes and so deserve to be distinguished at a higher taxonomic level (**Figure 4.31a**). Accordingly, these taxonomists classify humans in a family of their own, the Hominidae. For a cladist, this is unacceptable because humans are descended from the same common ancestor as other members of the family. This means that humans *must* be classified in the same family as chimpanzees, bonobos, and gorillas (**Figure 4.31b**). It is not just chauvinism about our own place in the primate phylogeny that causes discrepancies between these classification

FIGURE 4.31

Cladistic and evolutionary taxonomic schemes generate two different phylogenies for the hominoids. (a) The evolutionary classification classifies humans in a different family from other apes because apes are more similar to each other than they are to humans. (b) According to the cladistic classification, humans must be classified in the same family as the other great apes because they share a common ancestor with these creatures.

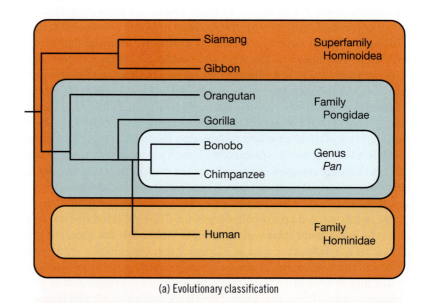

(a) Evolutionary classification

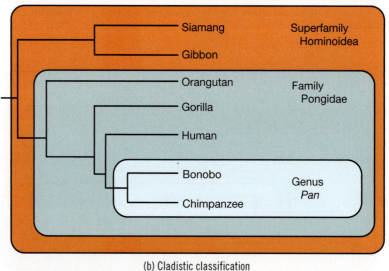

(b) Cladistic classification

schemes. The same problem arises in many other taxa. For example, it turns out that crocodiles and birds share a more recent common ancestor than either does with lizards. For a cladist, this means that birds and crocodiles must be classified together, and lizards must be classified separately. Evolutionary taxonomists argue that birds are obviously distinctive and deserve a separate taxonomic grouping.

In theory, cladistic taxonomy is both informative and unambiguous. It is informative because knowing an organism's name and its position in the hierarchy of life tells us how it is related to other organisms. It is unambiguous because the position of each organism is given by the actual pattern of descent. Once you are confident that you understand the phylogenetic relationships within a group, there is no doubt about how any organism in that group should be classified. Cladists believe that evolutionary taxonomy is ambiguous because judgments of overall similarity are necessarily subjective. On the other hand, evolutionary taxonomists complain that the advantages of cladistics are mainly theoretical. In real life, they argue, uncertainty about phylogenetic relationships introduces far more ambiguity and instability in classification than do judgments about overall similarity. For example, we are not completely certain whether chimpanzees are more closely related to humans or to gorillas. Morphological data suggest that chimpanzees are more closely related to gorillas. Although most measures of genetic distance indicate that chimpanzees are more closely related to humans, some genetic-distance data suggest the opposite. Given such uncertainty, how would cladists name and classify these species?

It is important to keep in mind that this controversy is not about what the world is like, or even about how evolution works. Instead it is a debate about how we should name and classify organisms. Thus no experiment or observation can prove either school right or wrong. Instead, scientists must determine which system is more useful in practice.

Key Terms

microevolution

macroevolution

testes

biological species concept

reproductive isolation

gene flow

ecological species concept

allopatric speciation

character displacement

reinforcement

parapatric speciation

hybrid zone

sympatric speciation

niche

adaptive radiation

phylogeny

hominoids

taxonomy

quadrupedal

knuckle walking

comparative method

terrestrial

arboreal

systematics

analogous

homologous

ancestral trait

derived trait

out-groups

genetic distance

molecular clocks

neutral theory

genus

family

superfamily

cladistic taxonomy

evolutionary taxonomy

Study Questions

1. There are two large plants in the authors' yard: a yucca tree and an enormous prickly pear cactus. Both have rough, scaly bark, but it is known that these plants are not closely related.
   (a) What are two different explanations for the similarity of the bark?
   (b) It is also known that yuccas are descended from a grass species instead of a tree species. Which of the two explanations given in part a is consistent with this fact?

2. Chimpanzees and gorillas more closely resemble each other anatomically than either resembles humans. For example, the hands of chimpanzees and gorillas are structurally similar and quite different from human hands. Genetic-distance data suggest, however, that humans and chimpanzees are more closely related to each other than either is to gorillas. Assuming that the genetic-distance data are correct, give two different explanations for the observed anatomical similarity between chimpanzees and gorillas.

3. Use the genetic-distance matrix that follows to establish the taxonomic relationships between the species listed. (*Hint:* Draw a phylogenetic tree to illustrate these taxonomic relationships.)

	A	B	C	D
B	4.8	—		
C	0.7	5.0	—	
D	3.6	4.7	3.6	—

4. According to the biological species concept, what is a species? Why do some biologists define species in this way?

5. What is the ecological species concept? Why have some biologists questioned the biological species concept?

6. Molecular methods allow biologists to measure the amount of gene flow among populations that make up a species. When such methods first became available, systematists were surprised to find that many morphologically indistinguishable populations seem to be reproductively isolated from each other and thus, according to the biological species concept, are considered entirely different species. Is it possible to account for the existence of such cryptic species by allopatric speciation? by parapatric speciation? by sympatric speciation?

7. New plant species are sometimes formed by the hybridization of existing species. A new species retains all of the genes of each parent. For example, the variety of wheat used to make bread is a hybrid of three different grass species. Explain how such hybridization affects the family tree of these plants.

Further Reading

Barton, N. H., D. E. G. Briggs, J. A. Eisen, D. B. Goldstein, and N. H. Patelet. 2007. *Evolution*. Woodbury, N.Y.: Cold Spring Harbor Press.

Dawkins, R. 1996. *The Blind Watchmaker: Why the Evidence of Evolution Reveals a Universe without Design*. New York: Norton, ch. 11.

Ridley, M. 2004. *Evolution*. 3rd ed. Malden, Mass.: Blackwell.

_____. 1986. *Evolution and Classification: The Reformation of Cladism*. New York: Longman.

2

PART TWO

PRIMATE ECOLOGY AND BEHAVIOR

5

CHAPTER OBJECTIVES

By the end of this chapter you should be able to

- Identify the complex of traits that define the primate order.

- Show where primates live in the world.

- Describe the major characteristics that differentiate one kind of primate from another.

- Understand how primates cope with primary ecological challenges: finding food and avoiding predation.

- Identify what kinds of groups primates form.

- Discuss major factors that threaten the status of wild primate populations.

PRIMATE DIVERSITY AND ECOLOGY

Two Reasons to Study Primates

Features That Define the Primates

Primate Biogeography

A Taxonomy of Living Primates

Primate Diversity

Primate Ecology

Primate Sociality

Primate Conservation

Two Reasons to Study Primates

The chapters in Part Two focus on the behavior of living nonhuman primates. Studies of nonhuman primates help us understand human evolution for two complementary but distinct reasons. First, closely related species tend to be similar morphologically because, as we saw in Chapter 4, they share traits acquired through descent from a common ancestor. For example, **viviparity** (bearing live young) and lactation are traits that all placental and marsupial mammals share, and these traits distinguish mammals from other taxa, such as reptiles. The existence of such similarities means that studies of living primates often give us more insight into the behavior of our ancestors than do studies of other organisms. This approach is called "reasoning by homology." The second reason we study primates is based on the idea that natural selection favors similar adaptations in similar environments. By assessing the patterns of diversity in the behavior and morphology of organisms in relation to their environments, we can see how evolution shapes adaptation in response to different selective pressures. This approach is called "reasoning by analogy."

Primates Are Our Closest Relatives

Because humans and other primates share many characteristics, other primates provide valuable insights about early humans.

Humans are more closely related to nonhuman primates than to any other animal species. The anatomical similarities among monkeys, apes, and humans led the Swedish naturalist Carolus Linnaeus to place us in the order Primates in the first scientific taxonomy, *Systema Naturae*, published in 1735. Later, naturalists such as Georges Cuvier and Johann Blumenbach placed us in our own order because of our distinctive mental capacities and upright posture. In *The Descent of Man*, however, Charles Darwin firmly advocated reinstating humans in the order Primates; he cited the biologist Thomas Henry Huxley's essay enumerating the many anatomical similarities between us and apes, and he mused that "if man had not been his own classifier, he would never have thought of founding a separate order for his own reception." Modern systematics unambiguously confirms that humans are more closely related to other primates than to any other living creatures.

Because we are closely related to other primates, we share with them many aspects of morphology, physiology, and development. For example, like other primates, we have well-developed vision and grasping hands and feet. We share features of our life history with other primates as well, including an extended period of juvenile development and larger brains in relation to body size than the members of other taxonomic groups. Homologies between humans and other primates also extend to behavior because the physiological and cognitive structures that underlie human behavior are more similar to those of other primates than to members of other taxonomic groups. The existence of this extensive array of homologous traits, the product of the common evolutionary history of the primates, means that nonhuman primates provide useful models for understanding the evolutionary roots of human morphology and for unraveling the origins of human nature.

Primates Are a Diverse Order

Diversity within the primate order helps us understand how natural selection shapes behavior.

During the last 30 years, hundreds of researchers from a variety of academic disciplines have spent thousands of hours observing many different species of nonhuman primates in the wild, in captive colonies, and in laboratories. All primate species have evolved adaptations that enable them to meet the basic challenges of life, such as finding food, avoiding predators, obtaining mates, rearing young, and coping with competitors. At the same time, there is great morphological, ecological, and behavioral diversity among species within the primate order. For example, primates range in size from the pygmy mouse lemur, who weighs about 30 g (about 1 oz.), to the male gorilla, who weighs about 260 times more—160 kg (350 lb.). Some species live in dense tropical forests; others are at home in open woodlands and savannas. Some subsist almost entirely on leaves; others rely on an omnivorous diet of fruits, leaves, flowers, seeds, gum, nectar, insects, and small animal prey. Some species are solitary, and others are highly gregarious. Some are active at night (**nocturnal**); others are active during daylight hours (**diurnal**). One primate, the fat-tailed dwarf lemur, enters a torpid state and sleeps for six months each year. Some species actively defend territories from incursions by other members of their own species (**conspecifics**); others do not.

In some species, only females provide care of their young; in others, males participate actively in this process.

This variety is inherently interesting. However, evidence of diversity among closely related organisms living under somewhat different ecological and social conditions also helps researchers understand how evolution shapes behavior. Animals that are closely related to one another phylogenetically tend to be very similar in morphology, physiology, life history, and behavior. Thus differences observed among closely related species are likely to represent adaptive responses to specific ecological conditions. At the same time, similarities among more distantly related creatures living under similar ecological conditions are likely to be the product of convergence.

This approach, sometimes called the "comparative method," has become an important form of analysis as researchers attempt to explain the patterns of variation in morphology and behavior observed in nature. The same principles have been borrowed to reconstruct the behavior of extinct hominins, early members of the human lineage. Because behavior leaves little trace in the fossil record, the comparative method provides one of our only objective means of testing hypotheses about the lives of our hominin ancestors. For example, the observation that there are substantial differences in male and female body size, a phenomenon called **sexual dimorphism**, in species that form non-pair-bonded groups suggests that highly dimorphic hominins in the past were not pair bonded. In Part Three, we will see how the data and theories about behavior produced by primatologists have played an important role in reshaping our ideas about human origins.

Features That Define the Primates

Members of the primate order are characterized by a number of shared, derived characters, but not all primates share all of these traits.

The animals pictured in **Figure 5.1** are all members of the primate order. These animals are similar in many ways: they are covered with a thick coat of hair, they have four limbs, and they have five fingers on each hand. They give birth to live young, and mothers suckle their offspring. However, they share these ancestral features with all mammals. Beyond these ancestral features, it is hard to see what the members of this group of animals have in common that makes them distinct from other mammals. What distinguishes a ring-tailed lemur from a mongoose or a raccoon? What features link the elegant langur and the bizarre aye-aye?

In fact, primates are a rather nondescript mammalian order that cannot be unambiguously characterized by a single derived feature shared by all members. In his extensive treatise on primate evolution, however, biologist Robert Martin of the Field Museum of Natural History in Chicago defines the primate order in terms of the derived features listed in **Table 5.1.**

The first three traits in Table 5.1 are related to the flexible movement of hands and feet. Primates can grasp with their hands and feet (**Figure 5.2a**), and most monkeys and apes can oppose their thumb and forefinger in a precision grip (**Figure 5.2b**). The flat nails, distinct from the claws of many animals, and the tactile pads on the tips of primate fingers and toes further enhance their dexterity (**Figure 5.2c**). These traits enable primates to use their hands and feet differently from the ways most other animals do. Primates are able to grasp fruit, squirming insects, and other small items in their hands and feet, and they can grip branches with their fingers and toes. During grooming sessions, they delicately part their partner's hair and use their thumb and forefinger to remove small bits of debris from the skin.

Traits 4 and 5 in Table 5.1 are related to a shift in emphasis among the sense organs. Most primates are characterized by a greater reliance on visual stimuli and less reliance on olfactory stimuli than other mammals. Many primate species can perceive color, and their eyes are set forward in the head, providing them with binocular,

(a)

(b)

(c)

FIGURE 5.1

All of these animals are primates: (a) aye-aye, (b) ring-tailed lemur, (c) leaf monkey, (d) howler, (e) gelada baboon. Primates are a diverse order and do not possess a suite of traits that unambiguously distinguish them from other animals.

stereoscopic vision (**Figure 5.3**). **Binocular vision** means that the fields of vision of the two eyes overlap so that both eyes perceive the same image. **Stereoscopic vision** means that each eye sends a signal of the visual image to both hemispheres in the brain to create an image with depth. These trends are not uniformly expressed within the primate order; for example, olfactory cues play a more important role in the lives of **strepsirrhine** primates than in the lives of **haplorrhine** primates. As we will explain shortly, the strepsirrhine primates include the lorises and lemurs, and the haplorrhine primates include tarsiers, monkeys, and apes.

Features 6 and 7 in Table 5.1 result from the distinctive life history of primates. As a group, primates have longer pregnancies, mature at later ages, live longer, and have larger brains than other animals of similar body size. These features reflect a progressive trend toward increased dependence on complex behavior, learning, and

TABLE 5.1

1. The big toe on the foot is **opposable**, and hands are **prehensile**. This means that primates can use their feet and hands for grasping. The opposable big toe has been lost in humans.

2. There are flat nails on the hands and feet in most species, instead of claws, and there are sensitive tactile pads with "fingerprints" on the fingers and toes.

3. Locomotion is **hind-limb dominated**, meaning that the hind limbs do most of the work, and the center of gravity is nearer the hind limbs than the forelimbs.

4. There is an unspecialized **olfactory** (smelling) apparatus that is reduced in diurnal primates.

5. The visual sense is highly developed. The eyes are large and moved forward in the head, providing stereoscopic vision.

6. Females have small litters, and gestation and juvenile periods are longer than in other mammals of similar size.

7. The brain is large compared with the brains of similarly sized mammals, and it has a number of unique anatomical features.

8. The **molars** are relatively unspecialized, and there is a maximum of two **incisors**, one **canine**, three **premolars**, and three molars on each half of the upper and lower jaw.

9. There are a number of other subtle anatomical characteristics that are useful to systematists but are hard to interpret functionally.

Definition of the primate order. See the text for more complete descriptions of these features.

(a)

(b)

(c)

FIGURE 5.2

(a) Primates have grasping feet, which they use to climb, cling to branches, hold food, and scratch themselves. (b) Primates can oppose the thumb and forefinger in a precision grip—a feature that enables them to hold food in one hand while they are feeding, to pick small ticks and bits of debris from their hair while grooming, and (in some species) to use tools. (c) Most primates have flat nails on their hands and sensitive tactile pads on the tips of their fingers.

FIGURE 5.3

In most primates, the eyes are moved forward in the head. The field of vision of the two eyes overlaps, creating binocular, stereoscopic vision.

FIGURE 5.4

A high degree of intelligence characterizes some animals besides primates. Dolphins, for example, have very large brains in relation to their body size, and their behavior is quite complex.

FIGURE 5.5

The distribution of living and fossil nonhuman primates. Primates are now found in Central America, South America, Africa, and Asia. They are found mainly in tropical regions of the world. Primates were formerly found in southern Europe and northern Africa. There have never been indigenous populations of primates in Australia or Antarctica.

behavioral flexibility within the primate order. As the noted primatologist Alison Jolly points out, "If there is an essence of being a primate, it is the progressive evolution of intelligence as a way of life." As we will see in the chapters that follow, these traits have a profound impact on mating and parenting strategies and the patterns of social interaction within primate groups.

The eighth feature in Table 5.1 concerns primate dentition. Teeth play a very important role in the lives of primates and in our understanding of their evolution. The utility of teeth to primates themselves is straightforward: Teeth are necessary for processing food and are also used as weapons in conflicts with other animals. Teeth are also useful features for those who study living and fossil primates. Primatologists sometimes rely on tooth wear to gauge the age of individuals, and they use features of the teeth to assess the phylogenetic relationships among species. As we will see, paleontologists often rely on teeth, which are hard and preserve well, to identify the phylogenetic relationships of extinct creatures and to make inferences about their developmental patterns, their dietary preferences, and their social structure. Closer Look 5.1 describes primate dentition in greater detail.

Although these traits are generally characteristic of primates, you should keep two points in mind. First, none of them makes primates unique. Dolphins, for example, have large brains and extended periods of juvenile development, and their social behavior may be just as complicated and flexible as that of any nonhuman primate (**Figure 5.4**). Second, not every primate possesses all of these traits. Humans have lost the grasping big toe that characterizes other primates, some strepsirrhine primates have claws on some of their fingers and toes, and not all monkeys have color vision.

Primate Biogeography

Primates are mainly restricted to tropical regions of the world.

The continents of Asia, Africa, and South America and the islands that lie near their coasts are home to most of the world's nonhuman primates (**Figure 5.5**). A few species remain in Mexico and Central America. Nonhuman primates were once found in southern Europe, but no natural population survives there now. There are no natural populations in Australia or Antarctica, and none occupied these continents in the past.

Nonhuman primates are found mainly in tropical regions, where the fluctuations

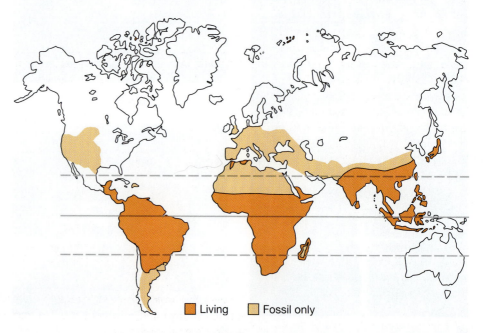

Living

Fossil only

5.1 Teeth and Guts: You Are What You Can Chew

For various reasons, biological anthropologists spend a lot of time thinking about teeth. Teeth are useful markers for taxonomic identity because various kinds of primates have different numbers of teeth. Teeth are also useful because they tell us things about what kinds of food primates eat. If we can detect a relationship between dental morphology and diet, we can apply these insights to the fossil record. This is particularly handy because teeth are the most commonly preserved parts of the body. Finally, teeth and gut morphology provide examples of how natural selection has created adaptations that enable animals to cope with their environments more effectively.

Dental Formula

To appreciate the basic features of primate dentition, you can consult **Figure 5.6**, or you can simply look in a mirror because your teeth are much like those of other primates. Teeth are rooted in the jaw. The jaw holds four different kinds of teeth: in order, they are, first, the incisors at the front; then come the canines, premolars, and the molars in the rear. All primates have the same kinds of teeth, but species vary in how many of each kind of tooth they have. For convenience, these combinations are expressed in a standard format called the **dental formula**, which is commonly written in the following form:

$$\frac{2.1.3.3}{2.1.3.3}$$

Reading from left to right, the numerals tell us how many incisors, canines, premolars, and molars a particular species has (or had) on one side of its jaw. The top line of numbers represents the teeth on one side of the upper jaw (**maxilla**),

and the bottom line represents the teeth on the corresponding side of the lower jaw (**mandible**). Usually, but not always, the formula is the same for both upper and lower jaws. Like most other parts of the body, our dentition is **bilaterally symmetrical**, which means that the left side is identical to the right side. The ancestral pattern shown here has been modified in various primate taxa, as the total number of teeth has been reduced.

The dental formulas among living primates vary (**Table 5.2**). The lorises, pottos, galagos, and a number of lemurids have retained the primitive mammalian dental formula, but other strepsirrhine taxa have lost incisors, canines, or premolars. Tarsiers have lost one incisor on the mandible but have retained two on the maxilla. All of the New World monkeys, except the marmosets and tamarins, have retained the primitive dental formula; the marmosets and tamarins

have lost one molar. The Old World monkeys, apes, and humans have only two premolars.

Dental Morphology

Primates who rely heavily on gum tend to have large and prominent incisors, which they use to gouge holes in the bark of trees (**Figure 5.7**). In some strepsirrhine species, the incisors and canines are projected forward in the jaw and are used to scrape hardened gum off the surface of branches and tree trunks. Dietary specializations are also reflected in the size and shape of the molars. Primates who feed mainly on insects and leaves have molars with well-developed shearing crests that permit them to cut their food into small pieces when they chew. Insectivores tend to have higher and more pointed cusps on their molars, which are useful for puncturing and crushing the bodies of their prey. The molars of frugivores tend to

---

TABLE 5.2

Primate taxa		Dental Formula
Strepsirrhines	Lorises, pottos, galagos, dwarf lemurs, mouse lemurs, true lemurs	$\frac{2.1.3.3}{2.1.3.3}$
	Indris	$\frac{2.1.2.3}{2.0.3.3}$
	Aye-ayes	$\frac{1.0.1.3}{1.0.0.3}$
Haplorrhines	Tarsiers	$\frac{2.1.3.3}{1.1.3.3}$
	New World monkeys (most species)	$\frac{2.1.3.3}{2.1.3.3}$
	Marmosets, tamarins	$\frac{2.1.3.2}{2.1.3.2}$
	Old World monkeys, apes, humans	$\frac{2.1.2.3}{2.1.2.3}$

Primates vary in the numbers of each type of tooth that they have. The dental formulas listed here give the number of incisors, canines, premolars, and molars on each side of the upper jaw (maxilla) and lower jaw.

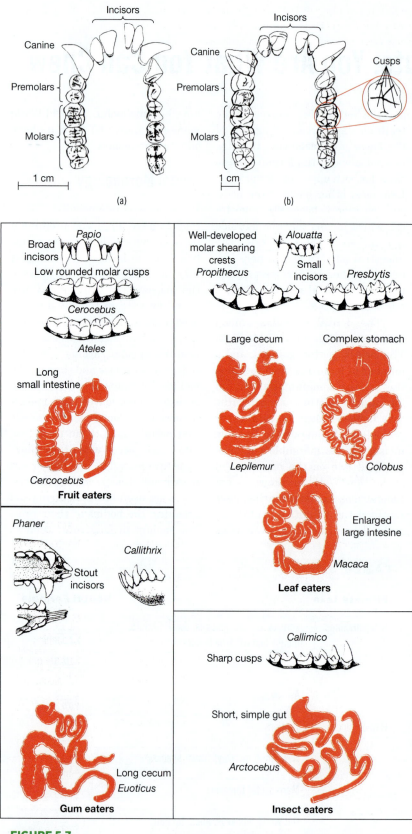

Incisors

Canine

Premolars

Molars

1 cm

(a)

Incisors

Canine

Premolars

Molars

Cusps

1 cm

(b)

FIGURE 5.6

The upper jaw (left) and lower jaw (right) are shown here for a male colobus monkey (a) and a male gorilla (b). In Old World monkeys, the prominent anterior and posterior cusps of the lower molars form two parallel ridges. In apes, the five cusps of the lower molar form a Y-shaped pattern.

have flatter, more rounded cusps, with broad and flat areas used to crush their food. Primates who rely on hard seeds and nuts have molars with very thick enamel that can withstand the heavy chewing forces needed to process these types of food.

Guts

Primates who feed principally on insects or animal prey have relatively simple digestive systems that are specialized for absorption. They generally have a simple small stomach, a small cecum (a pouch located at the upper end of the large intestine), and a small colon relative to the rest of the small intestine. Frugivores also tend to have simple digestive systems, but frugivorous species with large bodies have capacious stomachs to hold large quantities of the leaves they consume along with the fruit in their diet. Folivores have the most specialized digestive systems because they must deal with large quantities of cellulose and secondary plant compounds. Because primates cannot digest cellulose or other structural carbohydrates directly, folivores maintain colonies of microorganisms in their digestive systems that break down these substances. In some species, these colonies of microorganisms are housed in an enlarged cecum; in other species, the colon is enlarged for this purpose. Colobines, for example, have an enlarged and complex stomach divided into a number of different sections where microorganisms help process cellulose.

Fruit eaters

Papio

Broad incisors

Low rounded molar cusps

Cercocebus

Ateles

Long small intestine

Cercocebus

Fruit eaters

Gum eaters

Phaner

Stout incisors

Callithrix

Long cecum
Euoticus

Gum eaters

Leaf eaters

Well-developed molar shearing crests
Propithecus

Alouatta

Small incisors

Presbytis

Large cecum

Complex stomach

Lepilemur

Colobus

Enlarged large intesine

Macaca

Leaf eaters

Insect eaters

Callimico

Sharp cusps

Short, simple gut

Arctocebus

Insect eaters

FIGURE 5.7

The dentition and digestive tracts of fruit-eating (frugivorous), leaf-eating (folivorous), gum-eating (gummivorous), and insect-eating (insectivorous) primates typically differ.

in temperature from day to night greatly exceed fluctuations in temperature over the course of the year. In the tropics, the distribution of resources that primates rely on for subsistence is affected more strongly by seasonal changes in rainfall than by seasonal changes in temperature. Some species extend their ranges into temperate areas of Africa and Asia, where they manage to cope with substantial seasonal fluctuations in environmental conditions.

Within their ranges, nonhuman primates occupy an extremely diverse set of habitats, including all types of tropical forests, savanna woodlands, mangrove swamps, grasslands, high-altitude plateaus, and deserts. The vast majority, however, are found in forested areas, where they travel, feed, socialize, and sleep in a largely arboreal world.

A Taxonomy of Living Primates

Scientists classify primates into two suborders: Strepsirrhini and Haplorrhini (**Table 5.3**). Many of the primates included in the suborder Strepsirrhini are nocturnal, and,

TABLE 5.3 Taxonomy of the living primates

Suborder	Infraorder	Superfamily	Family	Subfamily	Examples
Strepsirrhini	Lemuriformes	Lemuroidea	Cheirogaleidae		Dwarf lemurs, mouse lemurs
			Daubentoniidae		Aye-ayes
			Indriidae		Indris, sifakas
			Lemuridae		Lemurs
			Lepilemuridae		Sportive lemurs
	Lorisiformes	Lorisoidea	Galagidae	Galaginae	Galagos
			Lorisidae	Lorisinae	Lorises
				Perodicticinae	Pottos
Haplorrhini	Tarsiiformes	Tarsiodea	Tarsiidae	Tarsinae	Tarsiers
	Platyrrhini	Ceboidea (New World monkeys)	Atelidae	Alouattinae	Howler monkeys
				Atelinae	Spider monkeys
			Cebidae	Aotinae	Owl monkeys
				Callitrichinae	Marmosets, tamarins
				Cebinae	Capuchins
				Saimirinae	Squirrel monkeys
			Pitheciidae	Callicebinae	Titi monkeys
				Pitheciinae	Sakis, uakaris
	Catarrhini	Cercopithecoidea (Old World monkeys)	Cercopithecidae	Cercopithecinae	Mangabeys, macaques, vervets, baboons
				Colobinae	Langurs, colobus, leaf monkeys
		Hominoidea (apes, humans)	Hylobatidae		Gibbons, siamang
			Hominidae	Ponginae	Orangutans
				Homininae	Gorillas, chimpanzees, humans

like some of the earliest primates that lived 50 mya, they have many adaptations to living in darkness, including a well-developed sense of smell, large eyes, and independently movable ears. By contrast, monkeys, apes, and humans, which make up the suborder Haplorrhini, evolved adaptations more suited to a diurnal lifestyle early in their evolutionary history. In the Haplorrhini, traits related to increased complexity of behavior, including large brains and longer life spans, are most fully developed. Haplorrhine monkeys are generally larger than strepsirrhines, are active during the day, are more fully dependent on vision than smell, and live in bigger and more complex social groups.

The classification of the primates that we have adopted here reflects the pattern of descent within the order. Tarsiers are included in the haplorrhines because genetic and morphological data indicate that they are more closely related to monkeys and apes than to the strepsirrhines. However, like many of the strepsirrhines, they are small-bodied and nocturnal. A cladistic classification places tarsiers within the haplorrhini, but an evolutionary taxonomy would group tarsiers with strepsirrhines because of their overall similarity in morphology, genetics, and behavior.

Primate Diversity

The Strepsirrhines

The strepsirrhine primates are divided into two infraorders: Lemuriformes and Lorisiformes

The **infraorder** Lemuriformes includes lemurs, which are found only on Madagascar and the Comoro Islands, off the southeastern coast of Africa. These islands have been separated from Africa for 120 million years. The primitive primates that reached Madagascar evolved in total isolation from primates elsewhere in the world as well as from many of the predators and competitors that primates confront in other places. Faced with a diverse set of available ecological niches, the lemurs underwent a spectacular adaptive radiation. When humans first colonized Madagascar about 2,000 years ago, there were approximately 44 species of lemurs, some as small as mouse lemurs and others as big as gorillas. In the next few centuries, all of the larger lemur species became extinct, probably the victims of human hunters or habitat loss. The extant lemurs are mainly small- or medium-size arboreal residents of forested areas (**Figure 5.8a**). They travel quadrupedally or by jumping in an upright posture from one tree to another, a form of locomotion known as vertical clinging and leaping (**Figure 5.8b**). Activity patterns of lemurs are quite variable: About half are primarily diurnal, others are nocturnal, and some are active during both day and night. One of the most interesting aspects of lemur behavior is that females routinely dominate males. In most lemur species, females are able to supplant males from desirable feeding sites; and in some lemur species, females regularly defeat males in aggressive encounters. Although such behavior may seem unremarkable in our own liberated times, female dominance is very rare in other primate species.

The infraorder Lorisiformes is composed of small, nocturnal, arboreal residents of the forests of Africa and Asia. These animals include two subfamilies with different types of locomotion and activity patterns. Galagos are active and agile, leaping through the trees and running quickly along the tops of branches (**Figure 5.8c**). The lorises move with ponderous deliberation, and their wrists and ankles have a specialized network of blood vessels that allows them to remain immobile for long periods of time. These traits may be adaptations that help them avoid detection by predators. Traveling alone, the Lorisiformes generally feed on fruit, gum, and insect prey. The Lorisiformes leave their dependent offspring in nests built in the hollows of trees or hidden in masses

(a)

(b)

(c)

FIGURE 5.8

(a) Ring-tailed lemurs, with their distinctive striped tails, live in social groups and are active during daylight hours. In a number of lemur species, females are dominant over males. (b) Sifakas use their powerful legs to jump in an upright posture, a form of locomotion known as vertical clinging and leaping. (c) Galagos are small, arboreal, nocturnal animals that can leap great distances. They are mainly solitary, though residents of neighboring territories sometimes rest together during the day.

of tangled vegetation. During the day, females sleep, nurse their young, and groom, sometimes in the company of mature offspring or familiar neighbors.

The Haplorrhines

The suborder Haplorrhini contains three infraorders: Tarsiiformes, Platyrrhini, and Catarrhini.

The infraorder Tarsiiformes includes tarsiers, which are enigmatic primates that live in the rain forests of Borneo, Sulawesi, and the Philippines (**Figure 5.9**). Like many of the strepsirrhine primates, tarsiers are small, nocturnal, and arboreal, and they move by vertical clinging and leaping. Some tarsiers live in pair-bonded family groups, but many groups have more than one breeding female. Female tarsiers give birth to infants who weigh 25% of their own weight; mothers leave their bulky infants behind in safe hiding places when they forage for insects. Tarsiers are unique among primates because they are the only primates that rely exclusively on animal matter, feeding on insects and small vertebrate prey.

The two infraorders Platyrrhini and Catarrhini are commonly referred to as the New World monkeys and the Old World monkeys and apes, respectively, because platyrrhine monkeys are found in South and Central America, while catarrhine

FIGURE 5.9

Tarsiers are small, insectivorous primates that live in Asia. Some tarsiers form pair bonds.

monkeys and apes are found in Africa and Asia. This geographic dichotomy breaks down with humans, however: We are catarrhine primates, but we are spread over the globe.

The infraorder Platyrrhini (New World monkeys) is divided into three separate families: Atelidae, Cebidae, and Pitheciidae. Although the New World monkeys encompass considerable diversity in size, diet, and social organization, they do share some basic features. All but those in one genus are diurnal, all live in forested areas, and all are mainly arboreal. The New World monkeys range in size from the 600-g (21-oz.) squirrel monkey to the 9.5-kg (21-lb.) muriqui (**Figure 5.10**). Most New World monkeys are quadrupedal, moving along the tops of branches and jumping between adjacent trees. Some species in the family Atelidae can suspend themselves by their hands, feet,

(a)

(b)

(c)

(d)

FIGURE 5.10

Portraits of some New World monkeys. (a) Muriquis, or woolly spider monkeys, are large bodied and arboreal. They are extremely peaceful creatures, rarely fighting or competing over access to resources. (b) Spider monkeys rely heavily on ripe fruit and travel in small parties. They have prehensile tails that they can use much like an extra hand or foot. (c) Capuchin monkeys have a larger brain in relation to their body size than any of the other nonhuman primates. (d) Squirrel monkeys form large multimale, multifemale groups. In the mating season, males gain weight and become "fatted" and then compete actively for access to receptive females.

or tail and can move by swinging by their arms beneath branches. Although many people think that all monkeys can swing by their tails, prehensile tails are actually restricted to the largest species of platyrrhine monkeys.

The family Atelidae is composed of howler monkeys, spider monkeys, woolly monkeys, and muriquis. Howler monkeys are named for their long-distance roars in intergroup interactions. They live in small one-male or multimale groups, defend their home ranges, and feed mainly on leaves. Spider monkeys, woolly monkeys, and muriquis subsist mainly on fruit and leaves, and they live in multimale, multifemale groups of 15 to 25. Spider monkeys, which rely heavily on ripe fruit, typically break up into small parties for feeding (**Figure 5.10b**). Spider monkeys and muriquis (**Figure 5.10a**) are unusual among primates because females disperse from their natal (birth) groups when they reach sexual maturity, while males remain in their natal groups for life.

The family Cebidae includes capuchins, owl monkeys, squirrel monkeys, marmosets, and tamarins. Capuchin monkeys (**Figure 5.10c**) are notable, in part, because they have very large brains in relation to their body size (see Chapter 9). They display a number of behavioral traits that play an important role in thinking about human origins, including tool use, social learning, and the development of behavioral traditions. Capuchins and squirrel monkeys (**Figure 5.10d**) live in multimale, multifemale groups of 10 to 50 individuals and forage for fruit, leaves, and insects (Figure 5.10d). Owl monkeys, which form pair bonds and defend territories, are the only nocturnal haplorrhine primates.

The marmosets and tamarins, which belong to the subfamily Callitrichinae, share several morphological features that distinguish them from other haplorrhine primate species: they are extremely small, the largest weighing less than 1 kg (2.2 lb.); they have claws instead of nails; they have only two molars, whereas all other monkeys have three; and they frequently give birth to twins and sometimes triplets (**Figure 5.11**). Marmosets and tamarins are also notable for their domestic arrangements: In most groups there is a single breeding pair, and other group members help the parents rear the offspring.

The family Pitheciidae includes the diurnal titi monkey, which lives in pair-bonded family groups. This family also includes the uakaris and sakis, which are not yet very well studied in the wild. While most primates that eat fruit swallow or spit out the seeds, which are rich in lipids, the sakis are specialized seed eaters.

FIGURE 5.11

Marmosets are small-bodied South American monkeys that form pair-bonded or polyandrous social groups. Males and older offspring actively participate in the care of infants.

The infraorder Catarrhini contains the monkeys and apes of the Old World and humans.

As a group, the catarrhine primates share a number of anatomical and behavioral features that distinguish them from the New World primates. For example, most Old World monkeys and apes have narrow nostrils that face downward, while New World monkeys have round nostrils. Old World monkeys have two premolars on each side of the upper and lower jaws; New World monkeys have three. Most Old World primates are larger than most New World species, and Old World monkeys and apes occupy a wider range of habitats than New World species do.

The catarrhine primates are divided into two superfamilies: Cercopithecoidea (Old World monkeys) and Hominoidea (apes and humans). Cercopithecoidea contains one extant (still living) family, which is further divided into two subfamilies of monkeys: Cercopithecinae and Colobinae.

The superfamily Cercopithecoidea encompasses great diversity in social organization, ecological specializations, and biogeography.

Members of the subfamily Colobinae, which includes the colobus monkeys of Africa and the langurs and leaf monkeys of Asia, may be the most elegant of the primates

FIGURE 5.12

(a) African colobines, like this guereza colobus monkey, are arboreal and feed mainly on leaves. These animals are sometimes hunted for their spectacular coats. (b) Gray langurs, also known as Hanuman langurs, are native to India and have been the subject of extensive study during the last four decades. In some areas, gray langurs form one-male, multifemale groups, and males engage in fierce fights over membership in bisexual groups. In these groups, infanticide often follows when a new male takes over the group.

(a)   (b)

(**Figure 5.12**). They have slender bodies, long legs, long tails, and often beautifully colored coats. The guereza colobus monkey, for example, has a white ring around its black face, a striking white cape on its black back, and a bushy white tail that flies out behind as it leaps from tree to tree. These monkeys are mainly leaf and seed eaters, and most species spend the majority of their time in trees. They have complex stomachs, almost like the chambered stomachs of cows, which allow them to maintain bacterial colonies that facilitate the digestion of cellulose. Colobines, langurs, and leaf monkeys are most often found in groups composed of one adult male and a number of adult females. As in many other vertebrate taxa, the replacement of resident males in one-male groups is often accompanied by lethal attacks on infants by new males. Infanticide under such circumstances is believed to be favored by selection because it improves the relative reproductive success of infanticidal males. This issue is discussed more fully in Chapter 7.

Most cercopithecine monkeys are found in Africa, though one particularly adaptable genus (*Macaca*) is widely distributed through Asia and part of northern Africa (**Figure 5.13**). The cercopithecines occupy a wide range of habitats and are quite variable in body size and dietary preferences. The social behavior, reproductive behavior, life history, and ecology of a number of cercopithecine species (particularly baboons, macaques, and vervets) have been studied extensively and will figure prominently in the discussions of mating strategies and social behavior in the next few chapters. Cercopithecines typically live in medium or large one-male or multimale groups. Females typically remain in their natal groups (the groups into which they are born) throughout their lives and establish close and enduring relationships with their maternal kin; males leave their natal groups and join new groups when they reach sexual maturity.

The superfamily Hominoidea includes two families of apes: Hylobatidae (gibbons) and Hominidae (orangutans, gorillas, chimpanzees, and humans).

The hominoids are different from the cercopithecoids in a number of ways. The most readily observed difference between apes and monkeys is that apes lack tails. But

(a)

(b)

(c)

FIGURE 5.13

Some representative cercopithecines: (a) Bonnet macaques are one of several species of macaques that are found throughout Asia and North Africa. Like other macaques, bonnet macaques form multimale, multifemale groups, and females spend their entire lives in their natal (birth) groups. (b) Vervet monkeys are found throughout Africa. Like macaques and baboons, females live among their mothers, daughters, and other maternal kin. Males transfer to nonnatal groups when they reach maturity. Vervets defend their ranges against incursions by members of other groups. (c) Blue monkeys live in one-male, multifemale groups. During the mating season, however, one or more unfamiliar males may join bisexual groups and mate with females.

(a)

(b)

FIGURE 5.14

(a) Gibbons and (b) siamangs live in pair-bonded groups and actively defend their territories against intruders. They have extremely long arms, which they use to propel themselves from one branch to another as they swing hand over hand through the canopy, a form of locomotion called brachiation. Siamangs and gibbons are confined to the tropical forests of Asia. Like other residents of tropical forests, their survival is threatened by the rapid destruction of tropical forests.

there are many other more subtle differences between apes and monkeys. For example, the apes share some derived traits, including broader noses, broader palates, and larger brains; and they retain some primitive traits, such as relatively unspecialized molars. In Old World monkeys the prominent anterior and posterior cusps are arranged to form two parallel ridges. In apes, the five cusps on the lower molars are arranged to form a side-turned Y-shaped pattern of ridges (Figure 5.6).

The family Hylobatidae, sometimes called lesser apes, includes gibbons and siamangs, and its living members are now found in Asia. The family Hominidae includes the larger-bodied great apes (orangutans, gorillas, bonobos, chimpanzees, and humans). Orangutans are found in Asia, while chimpanzees, bonobos, and gorillas are restricted to Africa.

The lesser apes are slightly built creatures with extremely long arms in relation to their body size (**Figure 5.14**). Gibbons and siamangs are strictly arboreal, and they use their long arms to perform spectacular acrobatic feats, moving through the canopy with grace, speed, and agility. Gibbons and siamangs are the only true brachiators among the primates, which means that they propel themselves by their arms alone and are in free flight between handholds. (To picture this, think about swinging on monkey bars in your elementary school playground.) Gibbons and siamangs typically live in pair-bonded family groups; vigorously defend their home ranges (the areas they occupy); and feed on fruit, leaves, flowers, and insects. Siamang males play an active role in caring for young, frequently carrying them during the day; male gibbons are less attentive fathers. In territorial displays, mated pairs of siamangs perform coordinated vocal duets that can be heard over long distances.

Orangutans, now found only on the Southeast Asian islands of Sumatra and Borneo, are among the largest and most solitary species of primates (**Figure 5.15**). Orangutans have been studied extensively by Birutė Galdikas in Tanjung Puting, Borneo,

FIGURE 5.15

(a) Orangutans are large, ponderous, and mostly solitary creatures. Male orangutans often descend to the ground to travel; lighter females often move through the tree canopy. (b) Today, orangutans are found only on the islands of Borneo and Sumatra, in tropical forests like this one.

(a)   (b)

for more than 30 years. Long-term studies of orangutans have also been conducted at Cabang Panti in Borneo, and at Ketambe and Suaq Balimbing in Sumatra. Orangutans feed primarily on fruit, but they also eat some leaves and bark. Adult females associate mainly with their own infants and immature offspring and do not often meet or interact with other orangutans. Adult males spend the majority of their time alone. A single adult male may defend a home range that encompasses the home ranges of several adult females; other males wander over larger areas and mate opportunistically with receptive females. When resident males encounter these nomads, fierce and noisy encounters may take place.

Gorillas, the largest of the apes, existed in splendid isolation from Western science until the middle of the nineteenth century (**Figure 5.16a and b**). Today, our knowledge of the behavior and ecology of gorillas is based mainly on detailed long-term studies of one subspecies, the mountain gorilla, at the Karisoke Research Center in Rwanda, which was founded by the late Dian Fossey. Mountain gorillas live in small groups that contain one or two adult males and a number of adult females and their young. Each day, mountain gorillas ingest great quantities of various herbs, vines, shrubs, and bamboo. They eat little fruit because fruiting plants are scarce in their mountainous habitat. Adult male mountain gorillas, called silverbacks because the hair on their backs and shoulders turns a striking silver-gray when they mature, play a central role

FIGURE 5.16

(a) Gorillas are the largest of the primates. Mountain gorillas usually live in one-male, multifemale groups, but some groups contain more than one adult male. (b) Most behavioral information about gorillas comes from observations of mountain gorillas who live in the Virunga Mountains of central Africa, pictured here. The harsh montane habitat may influence the nature of social organization and social behavior in these animals, and the behavior of gorillas living at lower elevations may differ.

(a)   (b)

in the structure and cohesion of their social groups. Males sometimes remain in their natal groups to breed, but most males leave their natal groups and acquire females by drawing them away from other males during intergroup encounters. The silverback largely determines the timing of group activity and the direction of travel. As data from newly established field studies of lowland gorilla populations become available, we are revising some elements of this view of gorilla social organization. For example, lowland gorillas seem to eat substantial amounts of fruit, spend more of their time in trees, and form larger and less cohesive social groups than mountain gorillas do.

As humankind's closest living relatives, chimpanzees (**Figure 5.17a**) have played a uniquely important role in the study of human evolution. Whether reasoning by homology or by analogy, researchers have found observations about chimpanzees to be important bases for hypotheses about the behavior of early hominins.

Detailed knowledge of chimpanzee behavior and ecology comes from a number of long-term studies conducted at sites across Africa. In the 1960s, Jane Goodall began her well-known study of chimpanzees at the Gombe Stream National Park on the shores of Lake Tanganyika in Tanzania (**Figure 5.17b**). About the same time, a second study was initiated by the late Toshisada Nishida at a site in the Mahale Mountains not far from Gombe. These studies are now moving into their sixth decade. Other important study sites have been established at Bossou, Guinea; in the Taï Forest of Ivory Coast; and at two sites in the Kibale Forest of Uganda: Kanyawara and Ngogo.

Bonobos (**Figure 5.17c**), another member of the genus *Pan,* live in inaccessible places and are much less well studied than common chimpanzees. Important field studies on bonobos have been conducted at two sites in the Democratic Republic of the Congo (formerly Zaire): Wamba and Lomako. Field studies of bonobos have been disrupted by civil conflicts that have ravaged central Africa over the last decades.

Chimpanzees and bonobos form large multimale, multifemale communities. These communities differ from the social groups formed by most other species of primates in two important ways. First, female chimpanzees usually disperse from their natal groups when they reach sexual maturity, while males remain in their natal groups throughout their lives. Second, the members of chimpanzee communities are rarely found together in a unified group. Instead, they split up into smaller parties that vary in size and composition from day to day. In chimpanzees, the strongest social bonds among adults are formed among males, while bonobo females form stronger bonds with one another and with their adult sons than males do. Chimpanzees modify natural objects for use as tools in the wild. At several sites, chimpanzees strip twigs and poke them into termite mounds and ant nests to extract insects, a much-prized delicacy. In the Taï Forest, chimpanzees crack hard-shelled nuts using one stone as a hammer and a heavy, flat stone or a protruding root as an anvil. At Gombe, chimpanzees wad leaves in their mouths and then dip these "sponges" into crevices to soak up water. New data also reveal tool use by wild orangutans, but chimpanzee tool use is more diverse and better studied.

FIGURE 5.17

(a) Chimpanzees live in multimale, multifemale social groups. In this species, males form the core of the social group and remain in their natal groups for life. Many researchers believe that chimpanzees and bonobos are our closest living relatives. (b) Like other apes, chimpanzees are found mainly in forests like this area on the shores of Lake Tanganyika in Tanzania. However, chimpanzees sometimes range into more open areas as well. (c) Bonobos are members of the same genus as chimpanzees and are similar in many ways. Bonobos are sometimes called "pygmy chimpanzees," but this is a misnomer because bonobos and chimpanzees are about the same size. This infant bonobo is sitting in a patch of terrestrial herbaceous vegetation, one of the staples of the bonobo's diet.

(a)

(b)

(c)

Primate Ecology

Much of the day-to-day life of primates is driven by two concerns: getting enough to eat and avoiding being eaten. Food is essential for growth, survival, and reproduction, and it should not be surprising that primates spend much of every day finding, processing, consuming, and digesting a wide variety of foods (**Figure 5.18**). At the same time, primates must always be on guard against predators like lions, pythons, and eagles that hunt them by day, and leopards that stalk them by night. As we will see in the chapters that follow, both the distribution of food and the threat of predation influence the extent of sociality among primates and shape the patterning of social interactions within and between primate groups.

In this section, we describe the basic features of primate ecology. Later we will draw on this information to explore the relationships among ecological factors, social organization, and primate behavior. It is important to understand the nature of these relationships because the same ecological factors are likely to have influenced the social organization and behavior of our earliest ancestors.

FIGURE 5.18

A female baboon feeds on corms in Amboseli, Kenya.

The Distribution of Food

Food provides energy that is essential for growth, survival, and reproduction.

Like all other animals, primates need energy to maintain normal metabolic processes; to regulate essential body functions; and to sustain growth, development, and reproduction. The total amount of energy that an animal requires depends on four components:

1. *Basal metabolism.* **Basal metabolic rate** is the rate at which an animal expends energy to maintain life when at rest. As **Figure 5.19** shows, large animals have higher basal metabolic rates than small animals have. However, large animals require relatively fewer calories *per unit* of body weight.

2. *Active metabolism.* When animals become active, their energy needs rise above baseline levels. The number of additional calories required depends on how much energy the animal expends. The amount of energy expended, in turn, depends on the size of the animal and how fast it moves. In general, to sustain a normal range of activities, an average-size primate like a baboon or macaque requires enough energy per day to maintain a rate about twice its basal metabolic rate.

3. *Growth rate.* Growth imposes further energetic demands on organisms. Infants and juveniles, which are gaining weight and growing in stature, require more energy than would be expected on the basis of their body weight and activity levels alone.

4. *Reproductive effort.* For female primates the energetic costs of reproduction are substantial. During the latter stages of their pregnancies, for example, primate females require about 25% more calories than usual; and during lactation, about 50% more calories than usual.

A primate's diet must satisfy the animal's energy requirements, provide specific types of nutrients, and minimize exposure to dangerous toxins.

The food that primates eat provides them with energy and essential nutrients, such as amino acids and minerals, that they cannot synthesize themselves. Proteins are essential for virtually every aspect of growth and reproduction and for the regulation of many body functions. As we saw in Chapter 2, proteins are composed of long chains of amino acids. Primates cannot synthesize amino acids from simpler molecules, so to build many essential proteins, they must ingest foods that contain sufficient amounts of a number of amino acids. Fats and oils are important sources of energy for animals and provide about twice as much energy as equivalent volumes of **carbohydrates**. Vitamins, minerals, and trace amounts of certain elements play an essential role in regulating many of the body's metabolic functions. Although specific vitamins, minerals, and trace elements are needed in only small amounts, deficiencies of these nutrients can cause significant impairment of normal body function. For example, trace amounts of the elements iron and copper are important in the synthesis of hemoglobin, vitamin C is essential for growth and healing of wounds, and sodium regulates the quantity and distribution of body fluids. Primates cannot synthesize any of these compounds and must acquire them from the foods they eat. Water is the major constituent of the bodies of all animals and most plants. For survival, most animals must balance their water intake with their water loss; moderate dehydration can be debilitating, and significant dehydration can be fatal.

At the same time that primates obtain nourishment from food, they must also take care to avoid **toxins**, substances in the environment that are harmful to them. Many plants produce toxins called **secondary compounds** to protect themselves from being eaten. Thousands of these secondary compounds have been identified: caffeine and morphine are among the secondary compounds most familiar to us. Some secondary compounds, such as **alkaloids**, are toxic to consumers because they pass through the stomach into various types of cells, where they disrupt normal metabolic functions. Common alkaloids include capsicum (the compound that brings tears to your eyes when you eat red peppers) and chocolate. Other secondary compounds, such as tannins (the bitter-tasting compound in tea), act in the consumer's gut to reduce the digestibility of plant material. Secondary compounds are particularly common among tropical plant species and are often concentrated in mature leaves and seeds. Young leaves, fruit, and flowers tend to have lower concentrations of secondary compounds, making them relatively more palatable to primates.

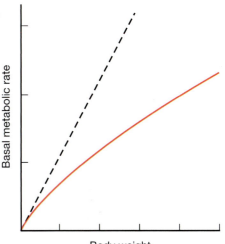

FIGURE 5.19

Average basal metabolism is affected by body size. The dashed line represents a direct linear relationship between body weight and basal metabolic rate. The solid line represents the actual relationship between body weight and basal metabolic rate. The fact that the curve bends means that larger animals use relatively less energy per unit of body weight.

Primates obtain nutrients from many different sources.

Primates obtain energy and essential nutrients from a variety of sources (**Table 5.4**). Carbohydrates are obtained mainly from the simple sugars in fruit, but animal prey, such as insects, also provide a good source of fats and oils. **Gum**, a substance that plants produce in response to physical injury, is an important source of carbohydrates for some primates, particularly galagos, marmosets, and tamarins. Primates get most of their protein from insect prey or from young leaves. Some species have special adaptations that facilitate the breakdown of cellulose, enabling them to digest more of the protein contained in the cells of mature leaves. Although seeds provide a good source of vitamins, fats, and oils, many plants package their seeds in husks or pods that shield their contents from seed predators. Many primates drink daily from streams, water holes, springs, or puddles of rainwater (**Figure 5.20**). Primates can also obtain water from fruit, flowers, young leaves, animal prey, and the underground storage parts (roots and tubers) of various plants. These sources of water are particularly important for arboreal animals that do not descend from the canopy and for terrestrial animals during times of the year when surface water is scarce. Vitamins, minerals, and trace elements are obtained in small quantities from many different sources.

Although primates display considerable diversity in their diet, some generalizations are possible:

1. All primates rely on at least one type of food that is high in protein and another that is high in carbohydrates. Strepsirrhines generally obtain protein from insects

TABLE 5.4

Source	Protein	Carbohydrates	Fats and oils	Vitamins	Minerals	Water
Animals	×	(×)	×	×	×	×
Fruit		×				×
Seeds	×		×	×		
Flowers		×				×
Young leaves	×			×	×	×
Mature leaves	(×)					
Woody stems	×					
Sap		×			×	×
Gum	×	(×)			×	
Underground parts	×	×				×

Sources of nutrients for primates. (x) indicates that the nutrient content is generally accessible only to animals that have specific digestive adaptations.

and carbohydrates from gum and fruit. Monkeys and apes usually obtain protein from insects or young leaves and carbohydrates from fruit.

2. Most primates rely more heavily on some types of foods than on others. Chimpanzees, for example, feed mainly on ripe fruit throughout their range from Tanzania to Ivory Coast. Scientists use the terms **frugivore**, **folivore**, **insectivore**, and **gummivore** to refer to primates who rely most heavily on fruit, leaves, insects, and plant gum, respectively. Closer Look 5.1 examines some of the morphological adaptations among primates with different diets.

3. In general, insectivores are smaller than frugivores, and frugivores are smaller than folivores (**Figure 5.21**). These differences in size are related to differences in energy requirements; small animals have relatively higher energy requirements than larger animals do, and they require relatively small amounts of high-quality

FIGURE 5.20

These savanna baboons are drinking from a pool of rainwater. Most primates must drink every day.

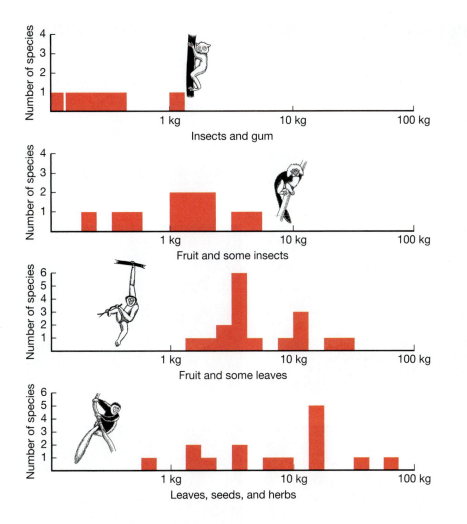

FIGURE 5.21

Body size and diet are related among primates. The smallest species eat mainly insects and gum; the largest species eat leaves, seeds, and herbs. Fruit-eating species fall in between.

foods that can be processed quickly. Larger animals are less constrained by the quality of their food than by the quantity because they can afford to process lower-quality foods more slowly.

The nature of dietary specializations and the challenge of foraging in tropical forests influence ranging patterns.

Nonhuman primates do not have the luxury of shopping in supermarkets, where abundant supplies of food are concentrated in a single location and are constantly replenished. Instead, the availability of their preferred foods varies widely in space and time, making their food sources patchy and often unpredictable. Most primate species live in tropical forests. Although such forests, with their dense greenery, seem to provide abundant supplies of food for primates, appearances can be deceiving. Tropical forests contain a very large number of tree species, and individual trees of any particular species are few in number.

Primates with different dietary specializations confront different foraging challenges (**Figure 5.22**). Plants generally produce more leaves than flowers or fruit, and they bear leaves for a longer period during the year than they bear flowers and fruit. As a result, foliage is normally more abundant than fruit or flowers at a given time during the year, and mature leaves are more abundant than young leaves. Insects and other suitable prey animals occur at even lower densities than plants. This means that folivores can generally find more food in a given area than frugivores or insectivores can. However, the high concentration of toxic secondary compounds in mature

FIGURE 5.22

(a) Some primates feed mainly on leaves, though many leaves contain toxic secondary plant compounds. The monkeys shown here are red colobus monkeys in the Kibale Forest of Uganda. (b) Some primates include a variety of insects and other animal prey in their diet. This capuchin monkey in Costa Rica is feeding on a wasp nest. (c) Mountain gorillas are mainly vegetarians. They consume vast quantities of plant material, like this fibrous stem. (d) This vervet monkey is feeding on grass stems. (e) Although many primates feed mainly on one type of food, such as leaves or fruit, no primate relies exclusively on one type of food. For example, the main bulk of the muriqui diet comes from fruit, but muriquis also eat leaves, as shown here. (f) Langurs are folivores. Here, gray langurs in Ramnagar, Nepal, forage for water plants.

(a)

(b)

(c)

(d)

(e)

(f)

leaves complicates the foraging strategies of folivores. Some leaves must be avoided altogether, and others can be eaten only in small quantities. Nonetheless, the food supplies of folivorous species are generally more uniform and predictable in space and time than the food supplies of frugivores or insectivores. Thus it is not surprising to find that folivores generally have smaller home ranges than frugivores or insectivores.

Activity Patterns

Primate activity patterns show regularity in seasonal and daily cycles.

Primates spend the majority of their time feeding, moving around their home ranges, and resting (**Figure 5.23**). Relatively small portions of each day are spent grooming, playing, fighting, or mating (**Figure 5.24**). The proportion of time devoted to various activities is influenced to some extent by ecological conditions. For primates living in seasonal habitats, for example, the dry season is often a time of scarce resources, and it is harder to find adequate amounts of appropriate types of food. In some cases, this

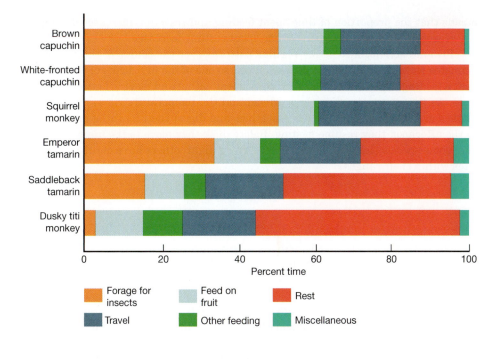

FIGURE 5.23

The amount of time that animals devote to various types of activities is called a "time budget." Time budgets of different species vary considerably. These six monkey species all live in a tropical rain forest in Manú National Park in Peru.

Legend:
- Forage for insects
- Feed on fruit
- Rest
- Travel
- Other feeding
- Miscellaneous

(a)

(b)

(c)

FIGURE 5.24

(a) All diurnal primates, like this capuchin monkey, spend some part of each day resting. (b) Immature monkeys spend much of their free time playing. These patas monkeys are play wrestling. (c) Gorillas often rest in close proximity to other group members and socialize during a midday rest period.

means that the proportion of time spent feeding and traveling increases during the dry season, while the proportion of time spent resting decreases.

Primate activity also shows regular patterns over the course of the day. When primates wake up, their stomachs are empty, so one of the first tasks of the day is to visit a feeding site. Much of the morning is spent eating and moving between feeding sites. As the sun moves directly overhead and the temperature rises, most species settle down in a shady spot to rest, socialize, and digest their morning meals. Later in the afternoon they resume feeding. Before dusk they move to the night's sleeping site; some species sleep in the same trees every night; others have multiple sleeping sites within their ranges.

Ranging Behavior

All primates have home ranges, but only some species are territorial—defending their home range against incursions by other members of their species.

In all primate species, groups range over a relatively fixed area, and members of a given group can be consistently found in a particular area over time. These areas are called home ranges, and they contain all of the resources that group members exploit in feeding, resting, and sleeping. However, the extent of overlap among adjacent home ranges and the nature of interactions with members of neighboring groups or strangers vary considerably among species. Some primate species, like gibbons, maintain exclusive access to fixed areas, called **territories**. Territory residents regularly advertise their presence by vocalizing, and they aggressively protect the boundaries of their territories from encroachment by outsiders (**Figure 5.25**). Although some territorial birds defend only their nest sites, primate territories contain all of the sites at which the residents feed, rest, and sleep and the areas in which they travel. Thus, among territorial primates, the boundaries for the territory are essentially the same as for their home range, and territories do not overlap.

Nonterritorial species, like squirrel monkeys and long-tailed macaques, establish home ranges that overlap considerably with those of neighboring groups (**Figure 5.26**). When members of neighboring nonterritorial groups meet, they may fight, avoid one another, or mingle peacefully together. This last option is unusual, but in some species, adult females sexually solicit males from other groups, males attempt to mate with females from other groups, and juveniles from neighboring groups play together when their groups are in proximity.

FIGURE 5.25

Siamangs and gibbons perform complex vocal duets as part of territorial defense.

The two main functions suggested for territoriality are resource defense and mate defense.

To understand why some primate species defend their home ranges from intruders and others do not, we need to think about the costs and benefits associated with defending resources from conspecifics. Costs and benefits are measured in terms of the impact on the individual's ability to survive and reproduce successfully. Territoriality is beneficial because it prevents outsiders from exploiting the limited resources within a territory. At the same time, however, territoriality is costly because the residents must be constantly vigilant against intruders, regularly advertise their presence, and be prepared to defend their ranges against encroachment. Territoriality is expected to occur only when the benefits of maintaining exclusive access to a particular piece of land outweigh the costs of protecting these benefits.

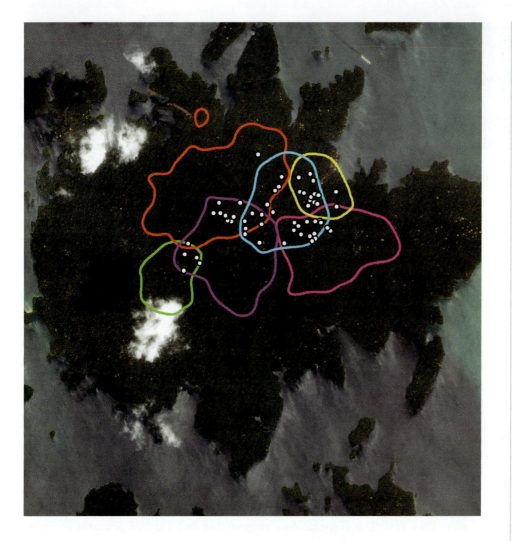

FIGURE 5.26

Overlapping home ranges of capuchin monkey groups on Barro Colorado Island, Panama. Sites of intergroup encounters are marked with a dot.

When will the benefits of territoriality exceed the costs? The answer to this question depends in part on the kinds of resources individuals need to survive and reproduce successfully, and in part on the way these resources are distributed spatially and seasonally. For reasons we will discuss more fully in Chapter 6, the reproductive strategies of mammalian males and females generally differ. In most cases, female reproductive success depends mainly on getting enough to eat for themselves and their dependent offspring, and males' reproductive success depends mainly on their ability to mate with females. As a consequence, females are more concerned about access to food, and males are more interested in access to females. Thus territoriality has two different functions. Sometimes females defend food resources, or males defend food resources on their behalf. Other times, males defend groups of females against incursions by other males. In primates, both resource defense and mate defense seem to have influenced the evolution of territoriality.

Predation

Predation is believed to be a significant source of mortality among primates, but direct evidence of predation is difficult to obtain.

Primates are hunted by a wide range of predators, including pythons, raptors, crocodiles, leopards, lions, tigers, and humans (**Figure 5.27**). In Madagascar, large lemurs

(a)

(b)

(c)

(d)

(e)

FIGURE 5.27

Primates are preyed upon by a variety of predators, including the (a) python, (b) lion, (c) leopard, (d) crowned hawk eagle, and (e) crocodile.

are preyed upon by fossas, pumalike carnivores. Primates are also preyed on by other primates. Chimpanzees, for example, hunt red colobus monkeys, and baboons sometimes prey on vervet monkeys.

The estimated rates of predation vary from less than 1% of the population per year to more than 15%. The available data suggest that small-bodied primates are more vulnerable to predation than larger ones and that immature primates are generally more susceptible to predation than adults. These data are not very solid, however, because systematic information about predation is quite hard to come by. Most predators avoid close contact with humans, and some predators, like leopards, generally hunt at night, when most researchers are asleep. Usually predation is inferred when a healthy animal that is unlikely to have left the group abruptly vanishes without a trace (**Figure 5.28**). Such inferences are, of course, subject to error.

Another approach is to study the predators, not their prey. Crowned hawk eagles are the only large raptors that live in the tropical rain forests of Africa. They are formidable predators; although they weigh only 3 to 4 kg (6.6 to 8.8 lb.), they have powerful legs and large talons and can take prey that weigh up to 20 kg (44 lb.). Crowned hawk eagles carry prey back to their nests and discard the bones. By sorting through the remains under crowned hawk eagle nests, researchers can figure out what they eat. Analyses of nest remains in the Kibale Forest of Uganda and the Taï Forest in Ivory Coast indicate that crowned hawk eagles prey on all of the primates in these forests except chimpanzees. Monkeys make up 60 to 80% of the crowned hawk eagles' diets at these sites, and the eagles kill a sizable fraction (2 to 16%) of the total populations of various primate species in these forests each year.

Susanne Shultz now at the University of Manchester and her colleagues compared the characteristics of mammalian prey taken by crowned hawk eagles, leopards, and chimpanzees in the Taï Forest (**Figure 5.29**). In general, terrestrial species are more vulnerable than arboreal species, and species that live in small groups are more vulnerable than animals that live in large groups. Thus arboreal monkeys that live in large groups face the lowest risks. Shultz and her colleagues suggest that these results

(a)   (b)   (c)

FIGURE 5.28

In some cases, researchers are able to confirm predation. Here, an adult female baboon in the Okavango Delta, Botswana, was killed by a leopard. You can see (a) the depression in the sand that was made when the leopard dragged the female's body out of the sleeping tree and across a small sandy clearing, (b) the leopard's footprints beside the drag marks, and (c) the remains of the female the following morning—her jaw, bits of her skull, and clumps of hair.

may explain some aspects of the distribution of terrestrial primates in Africa, Asia, and the neotropics. In Africa, with crowned hawk eagles and at least two large predatory felids, terrestrial primates are large bodied or live in large groups. In Asia, where there are no large forest raptors and few large felids, there are several semiterrestrial macaque species. And in the neotropics, where there are several species of large felids and forest raptors, there are no terrestrial monkeys at all.

Primates have evolved an array of defenses against predators.

Many primates give alarm calls when they sight potential predators, and some species have specific vocalizations for particular predators. Vervet monkeys, for example, give different calls when they are alerted to the presence of leopards, small carnivores, eagles, snakes, baboons, and unfamiliar humans. In many species, the most common response to predators is to flee or take cover. Small primates sometimes try to conceal themselves from predators; larger ones may confront potential predators. When slow-moving pottos encounter snakes, for example, they fall to the ground, move a short distance, and freeze. At some sites, adult red colobus monkeys aggressively attack chimpanzees that stalk their infants.

Another antipredator strategy that some primates adopt is to associate with members of other primate species. In the Taï Forest, a number of monkey species share the canopy and form regular associations with one another. For example, groups of red colobus monkeys spend approximately half their time with groups of Diana monkeys. Interspecific associations may enhance predator detection if each species occupies a

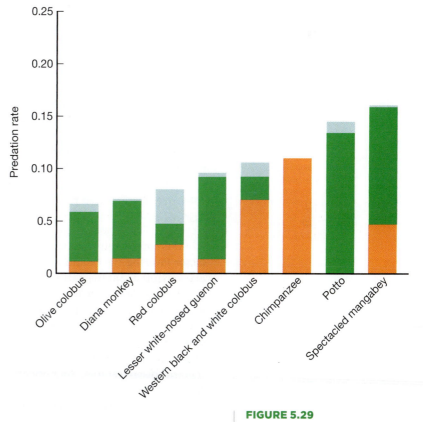

FIGURE 5.29

The rate of predation by leopards (orange), eagles (green), and chimpanzees (blue) in the Taï Forest on different primate species is shown here. Note that the preferred prey of chimpanzees are red colobus monkeys, and chimpanzees' only predators are leopards.

different portion of the canopy and is oriented toward different predators. In addition, by associating with members of different species, monkeys may increase group size without increasing levels of competition from conspecifics who have similar dietary preferences.

Primate Sociality

Sociality has evolved in primates in response to ecological pressures. Social life has both costs and benefits.

Nearly all primates live in social groups of one kind or another. Sociality has evolved in primates because there are important benefits associated with living in groups. Primates that live in groups may be better able to acquire and control resources. Animals that live in groups can chase away lone individuals from feeding trees and can protect their own access to food and other resources against smaller numbers of intruders. As we saw earlier, grouping also provides safety from predators because groups provide the three Ds: detection, deterrence, and dilution. Animals in groups are more likely to detect predators because there are more pairs of eyes on the look-out for predators. Animals in groups are also more effective in deterring predators by actively mobbing or chasing them away. Finally, the threat of predation to any single individual is diluted when predators strike at random. If there are two animals in a group, and a predator strikes, each animal has a 50% chance of being eaten. If there are 10 individuals, the individual risk is decreased to 10%.

Although there are important benefits associated with sociality, there are equally important costs. Animals that live in groups may encounter more competition over access to food and mates, become more vulnerable to disease, and face various hazards from conspecifics (such as cannibalism, cuckoldry, inbreeding, or infanticide).

The size and composition of the groups that we see in nature are expected to reflect a compromise between the costs and benefits of sociality for individuals. The magnitude of these costs and benefits is influenced by both social and ecological factors.

Primatologists are divided over whether feeding competition or predation is the primary factor favoring sociality among primates.

It is not entirely clear whether resource competition or predation was the primary factor favoring the evolution of sociality in primates. However, many primatologists are convinced that the nature of resource competition affects the behavioral strategies of primates, particularly females, and influences the composition of primate groups (Closer Look 5.2). Females come first in this scenario because their fitness depends mainly on their nutritional status: well-nourished females grow faster, mature earlier, and have higher fertility rates than do poorly nourished females. In contrast, males' fitness depends primarily on their ability to obtain access to fertile females, not on their nutritional status. Thus ecological pressures influence the distribution of females, and males distribute themselves to maximize their access to females. (We will discuss male and female reproductive strategies more fully in Chapter 6.)

Primate Conservation

Many species of primates are in real danger of extinction in the wild.

Sadly, no introduction to the primate order would be complete without noting that the prospects for the continued survival of many primate species are grim. According to

5.2 Forms of Social Groups among Primates

Most primates live in groups. A group is a social unit that is composed of animals that share a common home range or territory and interact more with one another than with other members of their species. Groups can vary in their size, age–sex composition, and degree of cohesiveness. We use the term **social organization** to describe variation along these dimensions. There are five basic types of social systems among primates (**Figure 5.30**):

Solitary: Females maintain separate home ranges or territories and associate mainly with their dependent offspring. Males establish their own territories or home ranges, which may encompass the ranges of one or more adult females.

All of the **solitary** primates are strepsirrhines, except for orangutans.

Pairs: Groups are composed of one adult male, one adult female, and immature offspring. Species that live in pairs usually defend the boundaries of their territories. Gibbons live in pairs, along with a few platyrrhine monkeys and a few strepsirrhines. In some pair-living species, males and females remain close together, but in others, they may travel independently within their territories much of the time.

Multiple males, one female: One adult female shares a territory or home range with more than one adult male and offspring. This form of social

organization is only found in marmosets and tamarins.

One male, multiple females: Groups are composed of a number of adult females, one resident adult male, and immature offspring. Males compete vigorously over residence in these kinds of groups, and males may band together to oust established residents. This form of social organization is characteristic of howler monkeys, some langurs, and gelada baboons.

Multiple males, multiple females: Groups are composed of a number of adult females, a number of adult males, and immatures. This form of social organization is characteristic of macaques, baboons, capuchin

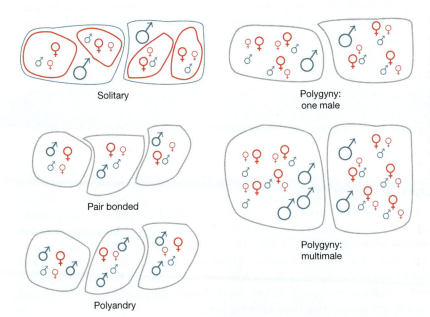

Solitary

Pair bonded

Polyandry

Polygyny: one male

Polygyny: multimale

FIGURE 5.30

The major types of social groups that primates form. When males and females share their home ranges, their home ranges are drawn here in brown. When the ranges of the two sexes differ, male home ranges are drawn in blue and female home ranges are drawn in red. The sizes of the male and female symbols reflect the degree of sexual dimorphism among males and females.

monkeys, squirrel monkeys, and some colobines. Some species, such as chimpanzees and spider monkeys, that live in these kinds of groups often divide up into smaller temporary parties (fission–fusion groups).

Primates also vary in their **mating systems**, the pattern of mating activity and reproductive outcomes. There is a close, but not perfect, relationship between social organization and mating systems. There are four main forms of mating systems in primates.

Monogamy/pair bonding: In a strictly monogamous mating system, each male and female mates with only one member of the opposite sex. Most primates that live in pairs mate mainly with each other, but there are reports of extra-pair matings in a number of pair-living primate species, and extra-pair paternity has been confirmed in at least one pair-living primate, the fork-marked lemur. Thus the term **pair bonding** may be a more accurate description of the mating system of most pair-living primates than monogamy.

Polyandry: Females mate with multiple males, but each of the males mates with only one female. **Polyandry** is an uncommon mating system among mammals but may characterize some of the marmosets and tamarins. In these species, one female usually monopolizes reproduction. The breeding female may mate with all of the unrelated males in the group, but the limited available genetic data suggest that not all males are equally successful in fathering offspring.

Polygyny: Males mate with multiple females, but each female mates with a single male. This mating system characterizes most of the species that live in one-male, multifemale groups. **Polygyny** generates considerable skew in male reproductive success, as resident males largely control access to receptive females. However, in some of these species, including blue monkeys, males from outside the group sometimes enter groups and mate with females.

Polygynandry (promiscuity): Both males and females mate with more than one partner. This mating system is generally associated with species that live in multimale, multifemale groups and might also characterize some solitary species. In most species that form multimale, multifemale groups males compete over access to mating females, and there is considerable skew in male reproductive success.

These classifications of social organization and mating systems represent idealized descriptions of residence and mating patterns. The reality is inevitably more complicated. Not all groups of a particular species may have the same social organization or mating system. For example, some groups of tarsiers are composed of a single mated pair, while others include additional females. Hamadryas and gelada baboons form one-male, multifemale units, but several of these units collectively belong to larger aggregations.

the International Union for the Conservation of Nature (IUCN), which assesses the conservation status of plant and animal species around the globe, nearly half of all primate species are now threatened in the wild (**Figure 5.31**). In Asia, 54% of all primate species are at risk of extinction. On the island of Madagascar, the conservation status of many species is not known, but of those that can be assessed, half are endangered or critically endangered and one has already become extinct. A smaller proportion of species in Africa and Central and South America are in threatened categories, but the prospects are not encouraging. All around the world, the populations of nearly all primate species are decreasing, some very rapidly.

All of the great apes are now endangered. In West Africa, chimpanzee populations have been decimated over the last two decades. In 1990, Ivory Coast was home to 8,000 to 12,000 chimpanzees. By 2007, that number had declined by 90%, according to a

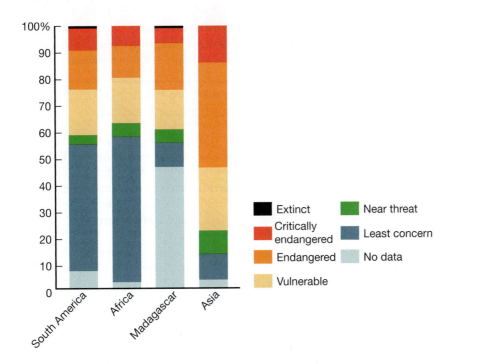

FIGURE 5.31

Conservation status of primate populations in the wild.

Legend:
- Extinct
- Critically endangered
- Endangered
- Vulnerable
- Near threat
- Least concern
- No data

census conducted by Christophe Boesch and his colleagues. The decline is attributed to a 50% increase in the size of the human population, which created more poaching and habitat destruction and was exacerbated by civil unrest within the country. There are only 6,600 orangutans left in Sumatra, where forests are being logged or converted to oil palm plantations.

It is particularly disturbing that some of the most endangered primate species are ones that we know the least about. For example, in 2005 researchers encountered a previously unknown type of monkey in the highlands of Tanzania (**Figure 5.32**). Genetic data indicate that these monkeys are sufficiently different from other species

FIGURE 5.32

The kapunji monkey was first discovered by scientists in 2005.

to be placed in their own genus, *Rungwecebus*, and are most closely related to baboons. This species is now restricted to two small areas of evergreen forest, 350 km (230 mi.) apart, and the total population is estimated to be only 1,100 individuals.

The main threats to primates in the wild are habitat destruction, hunting, disease, and live capture for trade and export.

As arboreal residents of the tropics, most primate populations are directly affected by the rapid and widespread destruction of the world's forests. Colin Chapman of the University of Florida and Carlos Peres of the University of East Anglia, reviewed the conservation status of the world's primate populations in the 1990s. Their analysis is quite sobering. Between 1980 and 1995, approximately 10% of the forests in Africa and Latin America were lost, and 6% of the forests of Asia disappeared (**Figure 5.33**).

The destruction of tropical forests is the product of economic and demographic pressures acting on governments and local residents. Many developing countries have huge foreign debts that must be repaid. The need to raise funds to pay off these debts generates intense pressure for timber harvesting and more intensive agricultural activity. Each year, 5 million to 6 million hectares of forest are logged, seriously disrupting the lives of the animals that live in them. (A hectare is a square measuring 100 m on a side, or about 2.5 acres.)

Forests are also cleared for agricultural activities. Rapid increases in the population of underdeveloped countries in the tropics have created intense demand for additional agricultural land. In West Africa, Asia, and South America, for example, vast expanses of forests have been cleared to accommodate the demands of subsistence farmers trying to feed their families as well as the needs of large-scale agricultural projects. In Central and South America, massive areas have been cleared for large cattle ranches.

FIGURE 5.33

Deforestation in Borneo. Tropical forests are disappearing all over the world, threatening the continuing survival of primates and other animals that live in them. In Borneo, deforestation has greatly reduced the availability of suitable habitats for orangutans and other primates.

In the last few decades, a new threat to the forests of the world has emerged: wildfire. Major fires destroyed massive tracts of forest in Southeast Asia and South America. Ecologists believe that natural fires in tropical forests are relatively rare and that these devastating fires are the product of human activity. In Indonesia, massive fires in the late 1990s left thousands of orangutans dead, reducing their numbers by nearly a third.

In many areas around the world, particularly South America and Africa, primates are also hunted for meat. Although systematic information about the impact of hunting on wild primate populations is scant, some case studies reveal troubling trends. In one forest in Kenya, for example, 1,200 blue monkeys and nearly 700 baboons were killed by subsistence hunters in one year. In the Brazilian Amazon, one family of rubber tappers killed 200 woolly monkeys, 100 spider monkeys, and 80 howler monkeys during an 18-month span. In addition to subsistence hunting, there is also an active market for "bushmeat" in many urban areas.

In equatorial Africa, primate populations have also been decimated by outbreaks of epidemic disease. About 26% of one habituated chimpanzee group in the Taï Forest of Ivory Coast died of the Ebola virus during a one-month period. Later, anthrax killed more members of the same community. Several hundred gorillas, belonging to more than 100 groups, regularly foraged in a swampy clearing in Odzala-Kokoua National Park in the Congo. Over the course of a two-year period, 95% of these gorillas died from Ebola.

The capture and trade of live primates has been greatly reduced since the Convention on International Trade in Endangered Species of Wild Fauna and Flora (CITES) was drafted in 1973. The parties to CITES, which now number 180 countries, ban commercial trade of all endangered species and monitor the trade of those that are at risk of becoming endangered. CITES has been an effective weapon in protecting primate populations around the world. The United States imported more than 100,000 primates each year before ratifying CITES but had reduced this number to approximately 13,000 a decade after signing the international agreement.

Although CITES has made a major impact, some problems persist. Live capture for trade remains a major threat to certain species, particularly the great apes, whose high commercial value creates strong incentives for illegal commerce. In many communities, young primates are kept as pets. For each animal taken into captivity, many other animals are put at risk because hunters cannot obtain young primates without capturing their mothers, who are usually killed in the process. In addition, many prospective pets die from injuries suffered during capture and transport or from poor housing conditions and inappropriate diets while in captivity.

Efforts to save endangered primate populations have met with some success.

Although much remains to be done, conservation efforts have significantly improved the survival prospects of a number of primate species. These efforts have helped preserve muriquis and golden lion tamarins in Brazil and golden bamboo lemurs in Madagascar. But there is no room for complacency. Promising efforts to save orangutans in Indonesia and mountain gorillas in Rwanda have been severely impeded by regional political struggles and armed conflict, putting the apes' habitats and their lives in serious jeopardy. A number of different strategies to conserve forest habitats and preserve animal populations are on the table. These include land-for-debt swaps in which foreign debts are forgiven in exchange for commitments to conserve natural habitats, to develop ecotourism projects, and to promote sustainable development of forest resources. But as conservationists study these solutions and try to implement them, the problems facing the world's primates become more pressing. More and more forests disappear each year, and many primates are lost, perhaps forever.

Key Terms

viviparity
nocturnal
diurnal
conspecifics
sexual dimorphism
binocular vision
stereoscopic vision
strepsirrhine
haplorrhine
opposable
prehensile
hind-limb dominated
olfactory
molars
incisors
canine
premolars
dental formula
maxilla
mandible

bilaterally symmetrical
infraorder
basal metabolic rate
carbohydrates
toxins
secondary compounds
alkaloids
gum
frugivore
folivore
insectivore
gummivore
territories
social organization
solitary
mating systems
pair bonding
polyandry
polygyny

Study Questions

1. What is the difference between homology and analogy? What evolutionary processes correspond to these terms?

2. Suppose that a group of extraterrestrial scientists lands on Earth and enlists your help in identifying animals. How do you help them recognize members of the primate order?

3. What kinds of habitats do most primates occupy? What are the features of this kind of environment?

4. Large primates often subsist on low-quality food such as leaves; small primates specialize in high-quality foods such as fruit and insects. Why is body size associated with dietary quality in this way?

5. For folivores, tropical forests seem to provide an abundant and constant supply of food. Why is this not an accurate assessment?

6. Territorial primates do not have to share access to food, sleeping sites, mates, and other resources with members of other groups. Given that territoriality reduces the extent of competition over resources, why are not all primates territorial?

7. Territoriality is often linked to group size, day range, and diet. What is the nature of the association, and why does the association occur?

8. Most primates specialize in one type of food, such as fruit, leaves, or insects. What benefits might such specializations have? What costs might be associated with specialization?

9. Nocturnal primates are smaller, more solitary, and more arboreal than diurnal primates. What might be the reason(s) for this pattern?

10. Sociality is a relatively uncommon feature in nature. What are the potential advantages and disadvantages of living in social groups? Why are (virtually all) primates social?

11. The future of primates, and other occupants of tropical forests, is precarious. What are the major hazards that primates face?

12. How can we balance the needs and rights of people living in the developing nations of the tropics with the needs of the animals who live in tropical forests?

Further Reading

Campell, C. J., A. Fuentes, K. C. MacKinnon, M. Panger, and S. K. Bearder, eds. 2007. *Primates in Perspective*. New York: Oxford University Press.

Cowlishaw, G. and R. I. M. Dunbar. 2000. *Primate Conservation Biology*. Chicago: University of Chicago Press.

IUCN 2010. *IUCN Red List of Threatened Species*. Version 2010.3. www.iucnredlist.org.

Kappeler, P. M. and M. Pereira, eds. 2003. *Primate Life Histories and Socioecology*. Chicago: University of Chicago Press.

Kramer, R., C. van Schaik, and J. Johnson, eds. 1997. *Last Stand: Protected Areas and the Defense of Tropical Biodiversity*. New York: Oxford University Press.

Mitani, J., J. Call, P. Kappeler, R. Palombit, and J. B. Silk, eds. 2012. *The Evolution of Primate Societies*. Chicago: University of Chicago Press.

Strier, K. B. 2010. *Primate Behavioral Ecology*. 4th ed. Boston: Allyn & Bacon.

6

CHAPTER OBJECTIVES

By the end of this chapter you should

- Explain why reproduction is the central act of all living things.

- Understand how mammalian reproductive biology influences the reproductive strategies of primate females.

- Discuss the factors that influence female reproductive success.

- Describe the process of sexual selection and explain why it favors traits that would not be favored by normal natural selection.

- Describe how competition among males over access to females influences male reproductive strategies.

- Explain why infanticide is an adaptive strategy for male primates in some circumstances.

PRIMATE MATING SYSTEMS

The Language of Adaptive Explanations

The Evolution of Reproductive Strategies

Reproductive Strategies of Females

Sexual Selection and Male Mating Strategies

Male Reproductive Tactics

Reproduction is the central act in the life of every living thing. Primates perform a dizzying variety of behaviors: gibbons fill the forest with their haunting duets, baboons threaten and posture in their struggle for dominance over other members of their group, and chimpanzees use carefully selected stone hammers to crack open tough nuts. But all of these behaviors evolved for a single ultimate purpose: to enhance reproduction. According to Darwin's theory, complex adaptations exist because they evolved step by step through natural selection. At each step, only those modifications that increased reproductive success were favored and retained in subsequent generations of offspring. Thus each morphological feature and every behavior exists only because it was part of an adaptation that contributed to reproduction in ancestral populations. As a consequence, mating systems (the way animals find mates and care for offspring) play a crucial role in our understanding of primate societies.

Understanding the diverse reproductive strategies of nonhuman primates illuminates human evolution because we share many elements of our reproductive physiology with other species of primates.

To understand the evolution of primate mating systems, we must take into account that the reproductive strategies of living primates are influenced by their phylogenetic heritage as mammals. Mammals reproduce sexually. After conception, mammalian females carry their young internally. After they give birth, mothers suckle their young for an extended period of time. The mammalian male's role in the reproductive process is more variable than that of the female. In some species, males' only contribution to their offspring is a single sperm at the moment of conception. In other species, males defend territories; provide for their mates; and feed, carry, and protect their offspring.

Although mammalian physiology constrains primate reproductive strategies, there is still considerable diversity in primate mating systems and reproductive behavior. Patterns of courtship, mate choice, and parental care vary greatly within the primate order. In some species, male reproductive success is determined mainly by success in competition with other males over access to mates; in others, it is strongly influenced by female preferences. In many pair-bonded species, both males and females care for their offspring; in most non-pair-bonded species, females provide almost all care for offspring and males focus mainly on gaining access to females.

What aspects of mating do humans share with other primates? Until very recent times, all pregnant women nursed their offspring for an extended period, as do other primates. In nearly all traditional human societies, fathers contribute extensively to their children's welfare, providing resources, security, and social support. An understanding of the phylogenetic and ecological factors that shape the reproductive strategies of other primates may help us understand how evolutionary forces shaped the reproductive strategies of our hominin ancestors and give us insight about the reproductive behavior of men and women in contemporary human societies.

The Language of Adaptive Explanations

In evolutionary biology, the term *strategy* is used to refer to behavioral mechanisms that lead to particular courses of behavior in particular functional contexts, such as foraging or reproduction.

Biologists often use the term **strategy** to describe the behavior of animals. For example, folivory is characterized as a foraging strategy, and monogamy is described as a mating strategy. When evolutionary biologists use the term, they mean something very different from what we normally mean when we use *strategy* to describe, say, a general's military maneuvers or a baseball manager's tactics. In common usage, *strategy* implies a conscious plan of action. Evolutionary biologists do not think other animals consciously decide to defend their territories, wean their offspring at a particular age, monitor their ingestion of secondary plant compounds, and so on. Instead, *strategy* refers to a set of behaviors occurring in a specific functional context, such as mating, parenting, or foraging. Strategies are the product of natural selection acting on individuals to shape the motivations, reactions, preferences, capacities, and choices that influence behavior. Strategies that led to greater reproductive success in ancestral populations have been favored by natural selection and represent adaptations.

Cost and benefit refer to the effect of particular behavioral strategies on reproductive success.

Different behaviors have different impacts on an animal's genetic fitness. Behaviors are said to be beneficial if they increase the genetic fitness of individuals, and costly if they reduce the genetic fitness of individuals. For example, we argued in Chapter 5 that ranging behavior involves a trade-off between the benefits of exclusive access to a particular area and the costs of territorial defense. Ultimately, benefits and costs should be measured as changes in reproductive success, but this is often very difficult to do, particularly in long-lived animals like primates. Instead, researchers rely on indirect measures, such as foraging efficiency (measured as the quantity of nutrients obtained per unit time) and assume that, all other things being equal, behavioral strategies that increase foraging efficiency also enhance genetic fitness and will be favored by natural selection. We will encounter many other examples of this type of reasoning in the chapters that follow.

The Evolution of Reproductive Strategies

Primate females always provide lots of care for their young, but males do so in only a few species.

The amount of parental care varies greatly within the animal kingdom. In most species, parents do little for their offspring. For example, most frogs lay their eggs and never see their offspring again. In such species, the nutrients that females leave in the egg are the only form of parental care. In contrast, primates—like almost all birds and mammals, and some invertebrates and fish—provide much more than just the resources included in gametes. At least one parent—and sometimes both—shelters its young from the elements, protects them from predators, and provides them with food.

The *relative* amount of parental care provided by mothers and fathers also varies within the animal kingdom. In species without parental care, females produce large, nutrient-rich gametes, and males produce small gametes and supply only genes. Among species with parental care, however, all possible arrangements occur. Primate mothers always nurse their offspring and often provide extensive care (**Figure 6.1**). The behavior of fathers is much more variable. In many species, fathers give nothing to their offspring other than the genes contained in their sperm. In a minority of species, however, males are devoted parents. In other taxa, patterns differ. For example, in most bird species, males and females form pairs and raise their young together (**Figure 6.2**).

The amount of time, energy, and resources that the males and females of a species invest in their offspring has profound consequences for the evolution of virtually every aspect of their social behavior and many aspects of their morphology. The selection pressures that affect males and females in species with equal parental investment are very different from the selection pressures that affect males and females in species in which females invest much more than males do. Thus it is important to understand why the amounts and patterns of parental investment differ among species.

Males do not care for their offspring (1) when they can easily use their resources to acquire many additional matings or (2) when caring for their offspring would not appreciably increase the offspring's fitness.

At first glance, it seems odd that most primate males fail to provide much care for their offspring. Surely, if the males helped their mates, they would increase the

FIGURE 6.1

In all primate species, females nurse their young. In baboons and many other species, females provide most of the direct care that infants receive.

FIGURE 6.2

In most species of birds, the male and female form a pair bond and jointly raise their young. Here a bald eagle carries food to its hungry brood.

FIGURE 6.3

In most non-pair-bonded species, males have relatively little contact with infants. Although males like this bonnet macaque are sometimes quite tolerant of infants, they rarely carry, groom, feed, or play with them.

chances that their offspring would survive to adulthood. Therefore, we might expect paternal care to be favored by natural selection (**Figure 6.3**).

If time, energy, and other resources were unlimited, this reasoning would be correct. In real life, though, time, energy, and material resources are always in short supply. The effort that an individual devotes to caring for offspring (parenting effort) diverts time and energy away from mate competition (mating effort). Natural selection will favor individuals that allocate effort among these competing demands so as to maximize the number of surviving offspring they produce.

To understand the evolution of unequal parental investment, we must identify the conditions under which one sex can profitably reduce its parental effort at the expense of its partner. Consider a species in which most males help their mates feed and care for their offspring. Even in such a species, a few males will have a heritable tendency to invest less in their offspring. We will refer to these two types as "investing" and "noninvesting" fathers. Because time, energy, and resources are always limited, males that invest more in parenting effort must invest less in mating effort. On average, the offspring of such males will receive less care than will the offspring of other males, making them less likely to survive and to reproduce successfully when they mature. On the other hand, because these males invest less in parenting effort, on average they will acquire more mates than will investing males. Mutations favoring the tendency to invest less in parenting effort will increase in frequency when the benefits to males (measured in terms of the increase in fitness gained from additional matings) outweigh the costs to males (measured as the decrease in offspring fitness due to a reduction in paternal care).

This reasoning suggests that unequal parental investment will be favored when one or both of the following are true:

1. Acquiring additional mates is relatively easy, so considerable gains are achieved by investing in mating effort.

2. The fitness of offspring raised by only one parent is high, so the payoff for investing in parenting effort is relatively low.

The key factors are the costs of finding additional mates and the benefits associated with incremental increases in the amount of care that offspring receive. When females are widely separated, for example, it may be difficult for males to locate them. In these cases, males may profit more from helping their current mates and investing in their offspring than from searching for additional mates. On the other hand, if females are capable of rearing their offspring alone and need little help from males, then investing males may be at a reproductive disadvantage compared with males that abandon females after mating and devote their efforts to finding eligible females.

The mammalian reproductive system commits primate females to investing in their offspring.

So far, there is nothing in our reasoning to say that if only one sex invests, it should always be the female. Why aren't there primate species in which males do all the work and females compete with each other for access to males? This is not simply a theoretical possibility: female sea horses deposit their eggs in their mate's brood pouch and then swim away and look for a new mate (**Figure 6.4**). There are whole families of fish in which male parental care is more common than female parental care; and in several species of birds—including rheas, spotted sandpipers, and jacanas—females abandon their clutches after the eggs are laid, leaving their mates to feed and protect the young.

In primates and other mammals, selection tends to favor high female investment because females lactate and males do not. Pregnancy and lactation commit mammalian females to invest in their young and limit the benefits of male investment in offspring. Because offspring depend on their mothers for nourishment during pregnancy and after birth, mothers cannot abandon their young without greatly reducing their offspring's chances of surviving. On the other hand, males are never capable of

FIGURE 6.4

Male sea horses carry fertilized eggs in a special pouch and provide care for their offspring as the young grow.

rearing their offspring without help from females. Therefore, when only one sex invests in offspring, it is invariably the female. Sometimes males can help females by defending territories or by carrying infants so that the mother can feed more efficiently, as siamangs and owl monkeys do. In most cases, however, these benefits are relatively insignificant, and selection favors males that allocate more time and energy to mating than to caring for their offspring.

You may be wondering why selection has not produced males that are able to lactate. This would seem like a highly desirable adaptation because it would enable males to make important contributions to offspring care and protect infants from the consequences of maternal mortality. But, as we noted in Chapter 3, most biologists believe the developmental changes that would enable males to lactate would also make them sterile. This is an example of a developmental constraint.

Reproductive Strategies of Females

Female primates invest heavily in each of their offspring.

Pregnancy and lactation are time-consuming and energetically expensive activities for female primates. The duration of pregnancy plus lactation ranges from 59 days in the tiny mouse lemur to 255 days in the hefty gorilla. In primates, as in most other animals, larger animals tend to have longer pregnancies than do smaller animals (**Figure 6.5**), but primates have considerably longer pregnancies than we would expect on the basis of their body sizes alone. The extended duration of pregnancy in primates is related to the fact that brain tissue develops very slowly. Primates have very large brains in relation to their body sizes, so extra time is needed for fetal brain growth and development during pregnancy. Primates also have an extended period of dependence after birth, further increasing the amount of care mothers must provide. Throughout this period, mothers must meet not only their own nutritional requirements but also those of their growing infants. In some species, offspring may weigh as much as 30% of their mother's body weight at the time of weaning.

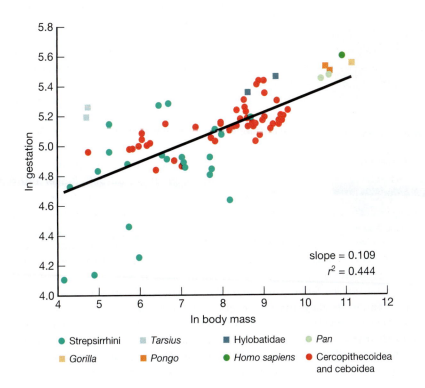

FIGURE 6.5

As in other mammalian taxa, maternal body size is correlated with gestation length. Great apes have the longest pregnancies, and small-bodied strepsirrhine primates have relatively short pregnancies.

FIGURE 6.6

This female bonnet macaque produced twins, but only one survived beyond infancy. Twins are common among marmosets and tamarins but are otherwise uncommon among monkeys and apes.

The energy costs of pregnancy and lactation impose important constraints on female reproductive behavior. Because it takes so much time and energy to produce an infant, each female can rear only a relatively small number of surviving infants during her lifetime (**Figure 6.6**). For example, a female toque macaque who gives birth for the first time when she is 5 years old and survives to the age of 20 would produce 15 infants if she gave birth annually and all of her infants survived. This number undoubtedly represents an upper limit; in the wild, a substantial fraction of all toque macaque infants die before they reach reproductive age, intervals between successive live births often last two years, and some females die before they reach old age. Thus most toque macaque females will produce a relatively small number of surviving infants over the course of a lifetime, and each infant represents a substantial proportion of a female's lifetime fitness. Therefore, we would expect mothers to be strongly committed to the welfare of each of their offspring.

A female's reproductive success depends on her ability to obtain enough resources to support herself and her offspring.

In most species of primates, including humans, females must achieve a minimum nutritional level in order to ovulate and to conceive. For animals living in the wild, without takeout pizza or 24-hour grocery stores, getting enough to eat each day is usually a serious challenge. There is considerable evidence that female reproductive success is limited by the availability of resources within the local habitat. When females have better access to high-quality resources, they grow faster, mature earlier, and give birth at shorter intervals. At a number of sites in Japan, for example, free-ranging monkeys' natural diets have been supplemented with wheat, sweet potatoes, rice, and other foods by humans for many years (**Figure 6.7**). This led to rapid increases in group size (**Figure 6.8**). Comparisons of wild and provisioned primates elsewhere tell a very similar story.

Sources of Variation in Female Reproductive Performance

Very young and very old females do not reproduce as successfully as middle-aged females.

FIGURE 6.7

At a number of locations in Japan, indigenous monkeys are fed regularly. The size of these artificially fed groups has risen rapidly, indicating that population growth is limited by the availability of resources.

Using data on births to females of known ages, researchers can compute age-specific fertility rates that provide estimates of the likelihood that a female of a given age will produce an infant. These analyses reveal that young females typically reproduce at lower rates than middle-aged females do. For example, **Figure 6.9** shows that young female baboons and gorillas have lower birth rates than older females do. First-time (**primiparous**) mountain gorilla mothers have 50% higher rates of infant mortality and 20% longer interbirth intervals after surviving births than older females do. Even among Japanese macaques, whose diets are enriched by provisioning, young mothers have longer interbirth intervals than older females do: 67% of first-time mothers skip a year before producing a second infant, while only 33% of experienced (**multiparous**) mothers skip years between births.

The relatively low fertility and high infant mortality of young females reflect the fact that when female monkeys and apes begin to reproduce, they are not yet fully grown. As a consequence, energetic investment in infants competes directly with energetic investment in their own skeletal growth and development. Younger females also may lack experience in handling newborn infants and may not provide appropriate care for them.

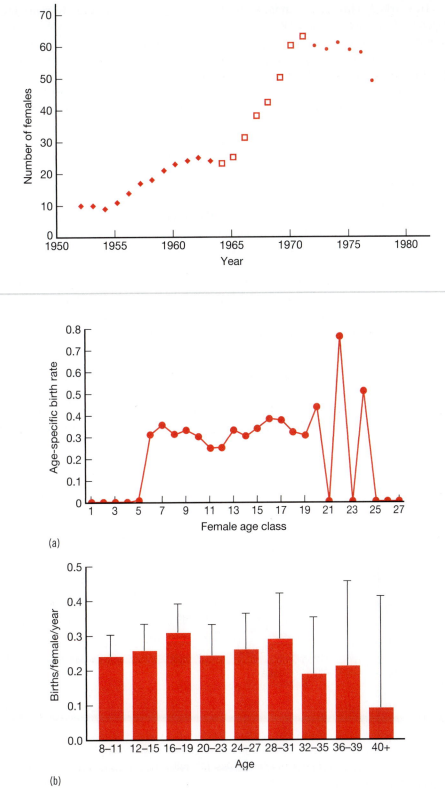

FIGURE 6.8

The size of the Koshima troop of Japanese macaques grew rapidly when they were provisioned intensively (*squares*) and then dropped when provisioning was restricted (*circles*).

(a)

(b)

FIGURE 6.9

The number of births per female are given for (a) baboons and (b) gorillas of different ages. In both species, birth rates remain fairly steady until females reach advanced ages and then decline. The variation in birth rates among old female baboons is partly because most females die before they reach such advanced ages, so samples are small.

In marked contrast to humans, most primate females continue to reproduce throughout their lives. Susan Alberts of Duke University led a team of researchers who examined the survivorship and reproductive activity of females in several well-studied populations of primates, ranging from sifakas to gorillas. Their analyses demonstrate that the age of last reproduction is close to the age at death for most females (**Figure 6.10**). The postreproductive period represents only 1% to 6% of the lifespan in these species, but 43% of the lifespan in a representative population of human foragers, the !Kung.

Longevity is a major source of variation in female fitness.

To borrow from Woody Allen, 80% of success is showing up. This seems to be true for primate females as well. The longer females live, the more newborns they produce and the more surviving offspring they raise. Variation in longevity is a major contributor to variation in lifetime fitness among females. For example, longevity accounts for as much as 50% to 70% of the variance in lifetime reproductive success among female baboons who reach reproductive age, swamping variance from other sources. Although we have some idea of the sources of mortality among adult females, such as predation and disease, we know very little about why some females live longer than others.

High-ranking females tend to reproduce more successfully than do low-ranking females.

As we explained in Chapter 5, females often compete for access to food resources that they need in order to reproduce successfully. In some situations, females form dominance hierarchies (Closer Look 6.1), which regulate access to resources. High-ranking females tend to have priority of access to the best feeding sites and can keep others

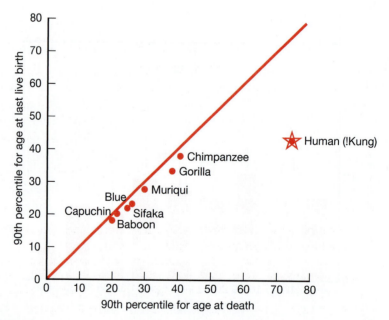

FIGURE 6.10

Female longevity is plotted against the age at last birth for a range of primates. The 90th percentile for age at death represents the age by which 90% of the females in the sample have died (in other words, 10% of the females live past this age). The 90th percentile for age at last birth represents the age at which 90% of the females in the sample produced their last infant. The close association between age at death and age at last infant means that most primate females continue to reproduce throughout their lives.

6.1 Dominance Hierarchies

In many animal species, ranging from crickets to chickens to chimpanzees, competitive encounters within pairs of individuals are common. The outcome of these contests may be related to the participants' relative size, strength, experience, or willingness to fight. In many species, for example, larger and heavier individuals regularly defeat smaller individuals. If there are real differences in power (based on size, weight, experience, or aggressiveness) between individuals, then we would expect the outcomes of dominance contests to be more or less the same from day to day. This is often

the case. When dominance interactions between two individuals have predictable outcomes, we say that a **dominance** relationship has been established.

When dominance interactions have predictable outcomes, we can assign dominance rankings to individuals. Consider the four hypothetical females in **Figure 6.11a**, which we shall call Blue, Turquoise, Green, and Purple. Blue always beats Turquoise, Green, and Purple. Turquoise never beats Blue but always beats Green and Purple. Green never beats Blue or Turquoise but always beats Purple.

Poor Purple never beats anybody. We can summarize the outcome of these confrontations between pairs of females in a **dominance matrix** such as the one in **Figure 6.11b**, and we can use the data to assign numerical ranks to the females. In this case, Blue ranks first, Turquoise second, Green third, and Purple fourth. When females can defeat all the females ranked below them and none of the females ranked above them, dominance relationships are said to be **transitive**. When the relationships within all sets of three individuals (trios) are transitive, the hierarchy is linear.

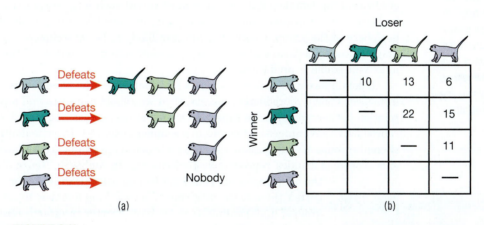

(a)   (b)

FIGURE 6.11

(a) Suppose that four hypothetical females—named Blue, Turquoise, Green, and Lavender—have the following transitive dominance relationships: Blue defeats the other three in dominance contests. Turquoise cannot defeat Blue but can defeat Green and Lavender. Green loses to Blue and Turquoise but is able to defeat Lavender. Lavender can't defeat anyone. (b) The results of data like those in part a are often tabulated in a dominance matrix, with the winners listed down the left side and the losers across the top. The value in each cell of the matrix represents the number of times one female defeated the other. Here, Blue defeated Turquoise 10 times and Green defeated Lavender 11 times. There are no entries below the diagonal because females were never defeated by lower-ranking females.

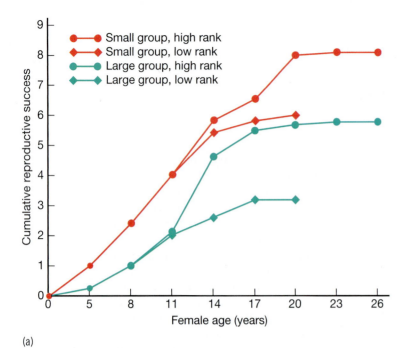

(a)

(b)

FIGURE 6.12

(a) In free-ranging groups of long-tailed macaques, both group size and dominance rank influence females' lifetime reproductive success. In general, females living in small groups reproduce more successfully than do females living in larger groups. But in both large and small groups, high-ranking females reproduce more successfully than do low-ranking females. (b) A long-tailed macaque and her nursing infant.

from food. This may enable high-ranking females to obtain larger quantities of food or higher-quality food, or forage more efficiently than lower-ranking females. For example, in a study of baboons, Robert Barton and Andrew Whiten found that the daily food intake of high-ranking females was 30% higher than the daily food intake of low-ranking females. But not all studies reveal such large disparities. This may be because low-ranking females compensate for their low status by feeding on the periphery of the group, where they are less likely to be interrupted. Although this may reduce competition for food, it may make low-ranking females and their offspring more vulnerable to predators.

If dominance rank influences access to valuable resources and access to resources influences female reproductive success, then we should expect to find a positive correlation between dominance rank and reproductive success. High rank does confer reproductive advantages on females in a number of species. In some multimale, multifemale groups of Old World monkeys, female dominance rank is correlated with various aspects of females' reproductive performance. In Amboseli, Kenya, for example, the offspring of high-ranking female baboons grow faster and mature earlier than do the offspring of low-ranking females. In captive vervet groups, high-ranking females have shorter interbirth intervals than lower-ranking females have. In some macaque populations, the offspring of high-ranking females are more likely to survive to reproductive age than the offspring of lower-ranking females. Associations between dominance rank and reproductive success may produce variation in lifetime fitness among females, particularly if females maintain the same rank over the course of their lives, as female macaques and baboons typically do. Thus Maria van Noordwijk and Carel van Schaik have found substantial differences in the lifetime reproductive success of high-, middle-, and low-ranking long-tailed macaques (**Figure 6.12**).

In gray langurs, female rank also influences female reproductive performance. In this species, female rank is inversely related to age, so young females typically outrank older ones (**Figure 6.13**). Long-term studies of hanuman langurs near Jodhpur, India, conducted by a group of German primatologists, including Carola Borries (now at Stony Brook University in New York) and Volker Sommer (now at University College London), have shown

FIGURE 6.13

A female gray langur at Jodhpur threatens another group member.

that young, high-ranking females reproduce more successfully than do older, lower-ranking females (**Figure 6.14**). Studies of gray langurs at Ramnagar in southern Nepal conducted by another group of German primatologists, including Andreas Koenig, Carola Borries, and Paul Winkler, have found that high-ranking females manage to commandeer higher-quality food patches and are consequently able to maintain higher levels of body fat. Females in good condition have higher fertility rates than do females in poor condition.

Anne Pusey, now at Duke University, and her colleagues have found that the offspring of high-ranking female chimpanzees are more likely to survive to the age of weaning than are the offspring of low-ranking females. In addition, their daughters grow faster and mature earlier than do the daughters of low-ranking females. These differences create substantial differences in lifetime fitness for high- and low-ranking female chimpanzees at Gombe Stream National Park, Tanzania (**Figure 6.15**). Recent analyses of long-term data on female mountain gorillas by Martha Robbins of the Max Planck

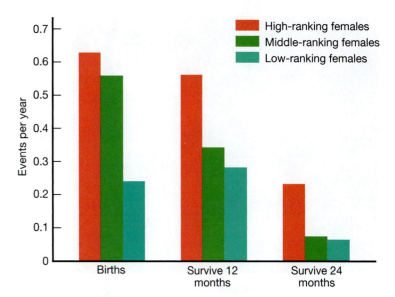

FIGURE 6.14

Female gray langurs reproduce more successfully when they are young and hold higher rank than when they are older and have lower rank. The three bars on the left represent the proportion of females of each rank category who give birth each year. The other sets of bars represent the proportion of females in each rank category who give birth each year to infants who survive to 12 months and 24 months. Dominance rank influences both the likelihood of giving birth and the likelihood that infants will survive.

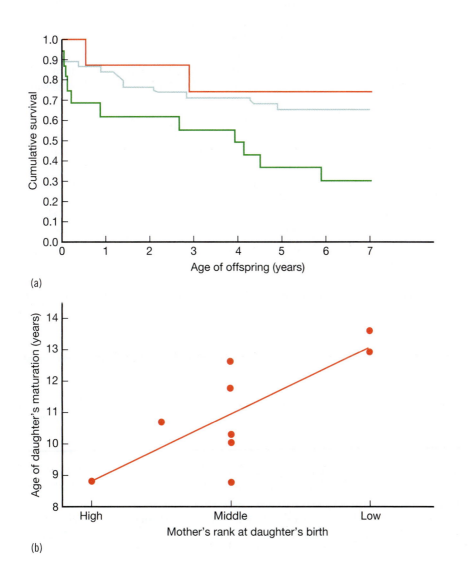

(a)

(b)

FIGURE 6.15

Among chimpanzees at Gombe Stream National Park, Tanzania, female rank influences reproductive performance. (a) The offspring of high- (*red line*) and middle-ranking (*blue line*) females are more likely to survive to weaning age than are the offspring of low-ranking females (*green line*). (b) Daughters of high-ranking females mature at earlier ages than do the daughters of lower-ranking females.

FIGURE 6.16

In many primate species, females spend considerable amounts of time in the company of other group members. Here adult female langurs rest and groom.

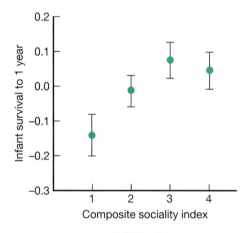

FIGURE 6.17

The sociality index captures information about how much time females spent in close association with other group members. High values represent more sociable females. More sociable females have higher survivorship among their offspring, and these effects are not due to differences in female rank or the size of their families.

Institute for Evolutionary Anthropology and her colleagues show that high-ranking females have substantially shorter interbirth intervals than low-ranking females.

Marmoset and tamarin groups in the wild often contain more than one adult female, but the dominant female is usually the only one who breeds successfully. Reproductive activity of subordinate females is suppressed in the presence of dominant females because subordinate females do not cycle normally. When subordinate females do breed, their infants may be killed by dominant females who have infants of their own.

The quality of social bonds may also influence female reproductive success.

In some species of primates, females spend a considerable amount of time sitting near, grooming, and interacting peacefully with other group members. Females save time for socializing, even when times are tough (**Figure 6.16**). For example, female baboons are forced to spend more time foraging and moving between feeding sites in the dry season than in the wet season. In response, they cut down on the amount of time that they spend resting, but they preserve time for socializing. Social bonds seem to matter to females. Anne Engh, now at Kalamazoo College, and colleagues from the University of Pennsylvania found that female baboons who lose close companions to predators experience substantial increases in cortisol levels, a hormonal indicator of stress. Now, you might think that females are simply stressed about living through a predator attack; but females who were present in the group but who didn't lose close associates were not affected.

Archival analyses of data derived from long-term studies of two different baboon populations suggest that females who have stronger social bonds reproduce more successfully than other females. Females who spent more time grooming and in proximity to other group members had more surviving infants than other females, and these effects were independent of the females' dominance rank (**Figure 6.17**). In fact, sociality seems to insulate females from some of the costs of low rank. The most sociable low-ranking females reproduce as successfully as the most sociable high-ranking females. We do not yet know why females who spend more time interacting with others enjoy these reproductive advantages. It's possible that they derive material benefits from their associations with others, such as better protection from predators. It's also possible that social contact reduces females' levels of stress, and this has beneficial effects on their health and the welfare of their offspring.

Reproductive Trade-offs

Females must make a trade-off between the number of offspring they produce and the quality of care they provide.

Just as both males and females must allocate limited effort to parental investment and mating, females must apportion resources among their offspring. All other things being equal, natural selection will favor individuals that are able to convert effort into offspring most efficiently. Because mothers have a finite amount of effort to devote to offspring, they cannot maximize both the quality and the quantity of the offspring they produce. If a mother invests great effort in one infant, she must reduce her investment in others. If a mother produces many offspring, she will be unable to invest very much in any of them.

In nature, maternal behavior reflects this trade-off when a mother modifies her investment in relation to an offspring's needs. Initially, infants spend virtually all of their time in contact with their mothers. The very young infant depends entirely on its mother for food and transportation and is unable to anticipate or to cope with environmental hazards. At this stage, mothers actively maintain close contact with their infants (**Figure 6.18**), retrieving them when they stray too far and scooping them up when danger arises.

As infants grow older, however, they become progressively more independent and more competent. They venture away from their mothers to play with other infants and to explore their surroundings. They begin to sample food plants, sometimes mooching scraps of their mother's food. They become aware of the dangers around them, attending to alarm calls given by other group members and reacting to disturbances within the group. Mothers use a variety of tactics to actively encourage their infants to become more independent. They may subtly resist their infants' attempts to suckle. They may also encourage their infants to travel independently. Nursing is gradually limited to brief and widely spaced bouts that may provide the infant with more psychological comfort than physical nourishment. At this stage, infants are carried only when they are ill, injured, or in great danger.

The changes in maternal behavior reflect the shifting balance between the requirements of the growing infant and the energy costs to the mother of catering to her infant's needs. As infants grow older, they become heavier to carry and require more food, imposing substantial burdens on mothers. However, as infants grow older they also become more capable of feeding themselves and of traveling independently, and this means that mothers can gradually limit investment in their older infants without jeopardizing their welfare (**Figure 6.19**). Mothers are thus able to conserve resources that can be allocated to subsequent infants. Moreover, because lactation inhibits ovulation in many primate species, a mother must wean her present infant before she can conceive another.

FIGURE 6.18

A female chimpanzee sits beside her youngest infant in Gombe Stream National Park in Tanzania.

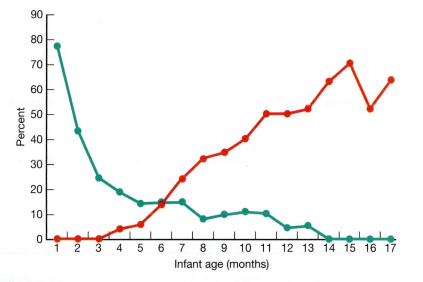

FIGURE 6.19

In free-ranging baboons, rates of suckling (*blue circles*) decline as infants mature. As suckling time declines, infants spend more and more time feeding on their own (*red circles*). These changes reflect changes in the costs and benefits of infant care for mothers.

Sexual Selection and Male Mating Strategies

Sexual selection leads to adaptations that allow males to compete more effectively with other males for access to females.

So far, we have seen that primate females invest heavily in each of their young and produce relatively few offspring over the course of their lives. Moreover, most primate females can raise their offspring without help from males. Female reproductive success is limited by access to food, not access to mates. Males can potentially produce progeny from many females, and as a result, males compete for access to females. Characteristics that increase male success in competition for mates will spread as a result of what Darwin called **sexual selection**.

It is important to understand the distinction between natural selection and sexual selection. Most kinds of natural selection favor phenotypes in both males and females that enhance their ability to survive and reproduce. Many of these traits are related to resource acquisition, predator avoidance, and offspring care. Sexual selection is a special category of natural selection that favors traits that increase success in competition for mates, and it will be expressed most strongly in the sex whose access to members of the opposite sex is most limited. Sexual selection may favor traits that increase the animal's attractiveness to potential mates, such as the peacock's tail, the red deer's antlers, and the hamadryas baboon's mane, even if those traits reduce the ability of the animal to survive or acquire resources—outcomes not usually favored by natural selection (**Figure 6.20**).

Sexual selection is often much stronger than ordinary natural selection.

In mammalian males, sexual selection can have a greater effect on behavior and morphology than other forms of natural selection because male reproductive success usually varies much more than female reproductive success. Data from long-term studies of lions conducted by Craig Packer of the University of Minnesota and Anne Pusey demonstrate that the lifetime reproductive success of the most successful males is often much greater than that of even the most successful females (**Figure 6.21**). The same pattern is likely to hold for non-pair-bonded primates. A primate male who succeeds in competition with other males may sire many offspring; a successful female might give birth to 5 or 10 offspring. Unsuccessful males and females will fail to reproduce at all. Because the strength of selection depends on how much variation in fitness there is among individuals, sexual selection acting on male primates can be much stronger than selective forces acting on female primates. (Incidentally, in species like sea horses, in which males invest in offspring and females do not, the entire pattern is reversed: sexual selection acts much more strongly on females than on males.)

There are two types of sexual selection: (1) intrasexual selection results from competition among males, and (2) intersexual selection results from female choice.

Many students of animal behavior subdivide sexual selection into two categories: intrasexual selection and intersexual selection. In species in which females cannot choose their mates, access to females will be determined by competition among males. In such species, **intrasexual selection** favors traits that enhance success in male–male competition. In species in which females can choose the partner(s) with which they mate, selection favors traits that make males more attractive to females. This is called **intersexual selection**. There is not much evidence that intersexual selection plays an important role in primates, so we will focus our attention on intrasexual selection.

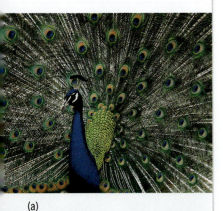

(a)

(b)

FIGURE 6.20

Sexual selection can favor traits not favored by natural selection. (a) The peacock's tail hinders his ability to escape from predators, but it enhances his attractiveness to females. Female peahens are attracted to males that have the most eyespots in their trains. (b) Male red deer use their antlers when they fight with other males. Red deer antlers are a good example of a trait that has been favored by sexual selection.

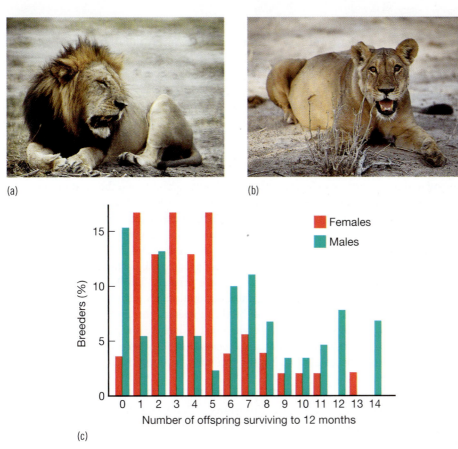

(a)

(b)

(c)

FIGURE 6.21

The reproductive success of (a) male lions is considerably more variable than the reproductive success of (b) female lions. (c) In Serengeti National Park and the Ngorongoro Crater of Tanzania, few female lions fail to produce any surviving cubs, but most females produce fewer than six surviving cubs over the course of their lives. Many males fail to produce any cubs, and a few males produce many cubs.

Intrasexual Selection

Competition among males for access to females favors large body size, large canine teeth, and other weapons that enhance male competitive ability.

For primates and most other mammals, intrasexual competition is most intense among males. In the most basic form of male–male competition, males simply drive other males away from females. Males who regularly win such fights have higher reproductive success than those who lose. Thus intrasexual selection favors features such as large body size, horns, tusks, antlers, and large canine teeth that enable males to be effective fighters. For example, male gorillas compete fiercely over access to groups of females, and males weigh twice as much as females and have longer canine teeth.

As explained in Chapter 5, when the two sexes consistently differ in size or appearance, they are said to be sexually dimorphic (**Figure 6.22**). The body sizes of males and females represent compromises among many competing selective pressures. Larger animals are better fighters and are less vulnerable to predation, but they also need more food and take longer to mature. Intrasexual competition favors larger body size, larger teeth, and other traits that enhance fighting ability. Males compete over females; females compete over resources but generally do not compete over mates. The effect of intrasexual competition among males, however, is quantitatively greater than the effect of competition among females because the fitness payoff to a very successful

FIGURE 6.22

Adult male baboons are nearly twice the size of adult females. The degree of sexual dimorphism in body size is most pronounced in species with the greatest competition among males over access to females.

male is greater than it is to a very successful female. Therefore, sexual selection is much more intense than ordinary natural selection. As a result, intrasexual selection leads to the evolution of sexual dimorphism.

The fact that sexual dimorphism is greater in primate species forming one-male, multifemale groups than in pair-bonded species indicates that intrasexual selection is the likely cause of sexual dimorphism in primates.

If sexual dimorphism among primates is the product of intrasexual competition among males over access to females, then we should expect to see the most pronounced sexual dimorphism in the species in which males compete most actively over access to females. One indirect way to assess the potential extent of competition among males is to consider the ratio of males to females in social groups. In general, male competition is expected to be most intense in social groups in which males are most outnumbered by females. At first, this prediction might seem paradoxical, because we might expect to have more competition when more males are present. The key to resolving this paradox is to remember that in most natural populations, there are approximately equal numbers of males and females at birth. In species that form one-male groups, there are many **bachelor males** (males who don't belong to social groups) who exert constant pressure on resident males. In species that form pair bonds, each male is paired with a single female, reducing the intensity of competition among males over access to females.

Comparative analyses originally conducted by Paul Harvey of the University of Oxford and Tim Clutton-Brock of the University of Cambridge have demonstrated that the extent of sexual dimorphism in primates corresponds roughly to the composition of the groups in which the males live (**Figure 6.23**). There is little difference in body weight or canine size between males and females in species that typically form pair bonds, such as gibbons, titi monkeys, and marmosets. At the other extreme, the most pronounced dimorphism is found in species, such as gorillas and black-and-white colobus monkeys, that live in one-male, multifemale groups. And in species that form multimale, multifemale groups, the extent of sexual dimorphism is generally intermediate between these extremes. Thus sexual dimorphism is most pronounced in the species in which the ratio of males to females living in bisexual groups is lowest (that is, the relative number of females is the highest).

FIGURE 6.23

The degree of sexual dimorphism is a function of the ratio of males to females in social groups. (a) Relative canine size (male canine length divided by female canine length) and (b) body size dimorphism (male body weight divided by female body weight) are greater in species that form one-male, multifemale groups than in species that form multimale, multifemale groups or pair-bonded groups.

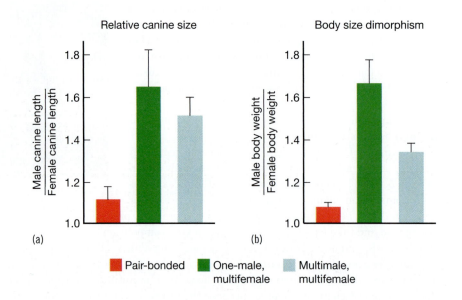

In multimale, multifemale groups, in which females mate with several males during a given estrous period, sexual selection favors increased sperm production.

In most primate species, as with mammals in general, the female is receptive to mating mainly during the portion of her reproductive cycle when fertilization is possible. That period of time is called **estrus**. In primate species that live in multimale, multifemale groups, females can often mate with several different males during a single estrous period. In such species, sexual selection favors increased sperm production because males who deposit the largest volume of sperm in the female reproductive tract have the greatest chance of impregnating them. Competition in the quantity of sperm is likely to be relatively unimportant in pair-bonded species because females mate mainly with their own partners. Because sperm production involves some cost to males, pair-bonded males may do better by guarding their partners when they are sexually receptive than by producing large quantities of sperm. Similarly, competition in sperm quantity probably does not play an important role in species that form one-male, multifemale groups. In these species, competition among males is over access to groups of females, which favors traits related to fighting ability. If resident males are able to exclude other males from associating with females in their groups, there may be little need to produce large quantities of sperm.

Social organization is associated with testis size, much as we would expect. Males with larger testes typically produce more sperm than do males with smaller testes, and males who live in multimale groups have much larger testes in relation to their body size than do males who live in either pair-bonded or one-male, multifemale groups (**Figure 6.24**).

Male Reproductive Tactics

Morphological evidence suggests that male–male competition is less intense in pair-bonded species than in species without pair bonds. As we will see in the remainder of this chapter, sexual selection has shaped male mating strategies as well as male morphology.

Investing Males

Pair bonding is generally associated with relatively high levels of paternal investment.

In species that form pair bonds, males do not compete directly over access to females. In these species, males' reproductive success depends mainly on their ability to establish territories, find mates, and rear surviving offspring. In such pair-bonded species, mate guarding and offspring care are important components of males' reproductive tactics.

Mate guarding may be an important component of pair-bonded males' reproductive effort. Numerous genetic studies of pair-bonded birds have demonstrated that a significant fraction of the young are not sired by the female's mate. (This is why biologists now avoid using the term *monogamy* to describe pair-bonded species.) Primatologists have known for some time that pair-bonded primates sometimes mate with individuals other than their social partners, but it has not been clear whether "extrapair" matings lead to offspring. Recent analyses of paternity in a population of white-handed gibbons that have been studied for many years by Ulrich Reichard of Southern Illinois University, indicate that about 10% of offspring are the product of extrapair matings. If females occasionally participate in extrapair copulations, their

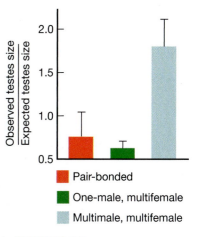

FIGURE 6.24

The average size of testes in species that typically form pair-bonded and one-male, multifemale groups is relatively smaller than the average size of testes in multimale, multifemale groups. Here, observed testes weight is divided by the expected testes weight to produce relative testes size. The expected testes weight is derived from analyses that correct for the effects of body size.

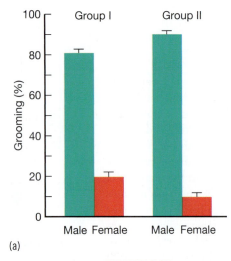

(a)

(b)

FIGURE 6.25

(a) In two white-handed gibbon groups, males groom their mates far more than they are groomed in return. The blue bar is the proportion of grooming from the male to the female, and the red bar is the proportion of grooming from the female to the male. Males' solicitous attention to females may be a form of mate guarding. (b) A pair of white-handed gibbons (*Hylobates lar*) grooms.

partners may benefit from keeping close watch on them. Ryne Palombit of Rutgers University, who has studied the dynamics of pair bonding in gibbons, suspects that males do just that. Male gibbons are principally responsible for maintaining proximity to their female partners, and most males groom their mates more than they are groomed in return (**Figure 6.25**).

Pair-bonded males tend to invest heavily in their mates' offspring. In titi monkeys and owl monkeys, adult males play an active role in caring for infants. They carry them much of the time, share food with them, groom them, and protect them from predators. Male siamangs are also helpful fathers, carrying their infants for long periods every day.

FIGURE 6.26

Some marmoset and tamarin groups contain more than one adult male and a single breeding female. In at least some of these groups, mating activity is limited to the group's dominant male, even though all the males participate in the care of offspring.

In cooperatively breeding species, males invest heavily in offspring, but the reproductive benefits to males are not clear.

Groups of cooperatively breeding primates, which include marmosets and tamarins, typically consist of one dominant pair and helpers of both sexes (**Figure 6.26**). Behavioral and genetic data suggest that reproductive benefits are not divided equally among males in these species. In most species of marmosets and tamarins, the dominant male monopolizes matings with receptive females.

The presence of multiple male helpers seems to enhance female fertility. Marmosets and tamarins are unusual among primates because they usually produce twins, and females produce litters at relatively short intervals, sometimes twice a year. Males play an active role in child care, frequently carrying infants, grooming them, and sharing food with them. Even in the cushy conditions of captivity, infant care is costly for males. Males typically lose weight while they are caring for infants.

Data compiled by Paul Garber of the University of Illinois at Urbana-Champaign show that groups with multiple adult males reared more surviving infants than did groups with only one male (**Figure 6.27**). In contrast, groups with multiple females produced slightly fewer infants than did groups with only one female resident.

Male–Male Competition in Groups without Pair Bonds

In non-pair-bonded groups, the reproductive success of males depends on their ability to gain access to groups of unrelated females and to obtain matings with receptive females.

As we explained in Chapter 5, males often leave their natal groups at puberty and attempt to join new groups. When females are philopatric, male dispersal is obligatory. Dispersal is often a dangerous and stressful time for males. In some species, males disperse alone and spend some time on their own before they join new groups. During this period, males are likely to become more vulnerable to predators and may have trouble gaining access to desirable feeding sites. One way to reduce the costs of dispersal and increase the chances of establishing residence in new groups may be to transfer in the company of other males. Peer migration is observed in a number of species, including squirrel monkeys, ring-tailed lemurs, and several species of macaques. Alternatively, males might transfer to groups that contain males from their natal groups. In Amboseli, Kenya, vervet males often join neighboring groups that kin or former group members have already joined.

In species that normally form one-male groups, males compete actively to establish residence in groups of females.

In primate species that form one-male groups, resident males face persistent pressure from nonresidents. In the highlands of Ethiopia, gelada baboons challenge resident males and attempt to take over their social groups, leading to fierce confrontations that may last for several days (**Figure 6.28**). Among gray langurs, males form all-male bands that collectively attempt to oust resident males from bisexual (coed) groups. Once they succeed in driving out the resident male, the members of the all-male band compete among themselves for sole access to the group of females. One consequence of this competition is that male tenure in one-male groups is often short.

Residence in one-male groups does not always ensure exclusive access to females.

Surprisingly, the male residents of one-male, multifemale groups sometimes face competition over access to females within their groups. In patas and blue monkeys, for example, researchers have discovered that the resident male is sometimes unable to prevent other males from associating with the group and mating with sexually receptive females. Such incursions are concentrated during the mating season and may last for hours, days, or weeks and involve one or several males.

Some primate species form both one-male and multimale groups, depending on the circumstances. For example, Teresa Pope and Carolyn Crockett have found that in Venezuelan forests that are relatively sparsely populated by red howlers and where it is relatively easy to establish territories, one-male groups predominate. But when the forests become more densely populated and dispersal opportunities are more limited, males adopt a different strategy: they pair up with other males and jointly defend access to groups of females. These partnerships enable males to defend larger groups of females and to maintain residence in groups longer.

In gelada baboons, approximately one-third of all social units include a leader and one or more "follower" males. Follower males are sometimes former leaders who remain in the group after being deposed in a takeover. In other cases, bachelor males team up to take over social units; afterward, one male becomes the leader and one or more other males may remain in the group as followers. Noah Snyder-Mackler now at Duke University and his colleagues Jacinta Beehner and Thore Bergman at the University of Michigan have found that followers tend to be found in units containing

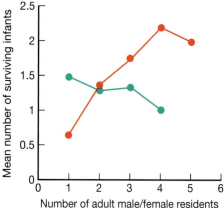

FIGURE 6.27

In tamarin groups, males clearly contribute to the reproductive success of breeding females. Tamarin groups that contain more adult males (*red circles*) produce higher numbers of surviving infants, but the effects flatten out when there are more than four males in the group. In contrast, the presence of additional females (*blue circles*) does not enhance infant survivorship.

FIGURE 6.28

Most gelada groups contain only one male. Males sometimes attempt to take over groups and oust the resident male; in other cases, males join groups as followers and establish coresidence. Takeovers are risky because they do not always succeed and males are sometimes badly injured.

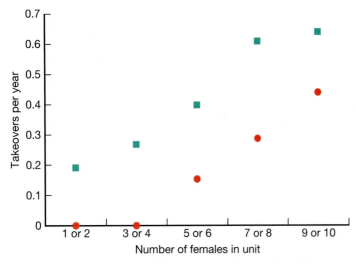

FIGURE 6.29

The rate of takeover attempts rises as the number of females in social units increases. However, units with more than one male (*circles*) experience fewer takeover attempts than units with only one male (*squares*).

larger numbers of females and the presence of additional males increases leader males' tenure and reduces the rate of takeover attempts (**Figure 6.29**). Followers actively defend the group against challenges by groups of bachelor males. Leader males sire about 83% of the infants born within their groups, and followers sire the remainder. These data suggest that leaders may tolerate the presence of followers because they help them maintain their position, while followers may accept their subordinate positions within social units because they gain some, albeit limited, reproductive success.

For males in multimale groups, conflict arises over group membership and access to receptive females.

In multimale groups, there is more competition over gaining access to mating partners than over establishing group membership. Nonetheless, it is not necessarily easy to join a new group; no one puts out the welcome mat. In some macaque species, males hover near the periphery of social groups, avoid aggressive challenges by resident males, and attempt to ingratiate themselves with females. In chacma baboons, immigrant males sometimes move directly into the body of the group and engage high-ranking resident males in prolonged vocal duels and chases. Although there may be conflict when males attempt to join nonnatal groups, males spend most of their adult lives in groups that contain both males and females.

In multimale groups, males often compete directly over access to receptive females. Sometimes males attempt to drive other males away from females, to interrupt copulations or to prevent other males from approaching or interacting with females. More often, however, male–male competition is mediated through dominance relationships that reflect male competitive abilities. These relationships are generally established in contests that can involve threats and stereotyped gestures but that can also lead to escalated conflicts in which males chase, wrestle, and bite one another (**Figure 6.30**). Male fighting ability and dominance rank are generally closely linked to physical condition: prime-age males in good physical condition are usually able to dominate others (**Figure 6.31**).

It seems logical that male dominance rank would correlate with male reproductive success in multimale groups, but this conclusion has been energetically debated. The issue has been difficult to resolve because it is difficult to infer paternity from behavioral observations of mating. However, genetic techniques now make it possible to assess paternity with a much higher degree of precision.

As more and more genetic information about paternity has become available, the links between male dominance rank and reproductive success have become stronger. For example, Susan Alberts and her colleagues have compiled information about the reproductive performance of more than 100 adult males who lived in seven baboon social groups over a 13-year period. High-ranking males sired substantially more offspring than other males (**Figure 6.32**). In addition, the highest-ranking males were more likely to mate-guard females during estrous cycles in which they actually conceived than during cycles in which they did not conceive. Among chimpanzees in the Taï Forest, Christophe Boesch and his colleagues at the Max Planck Institute for Evolutionary Anthropology have found that the highest-ranking male sires nearly half of all the infants born in the group (**Figure 6.33**). Another team led by Susan Perry of the University of California, Los Angeles, showed that the top-ranking male sired 38% to 70% of all infants born in three multimale groups of white-faced capuchins. Genetic analyses of paternity in multimale groups of hanuman langurs, long-tailed macaques,

FIGURE 6.30

Male baboons compete over access to an estrous female.

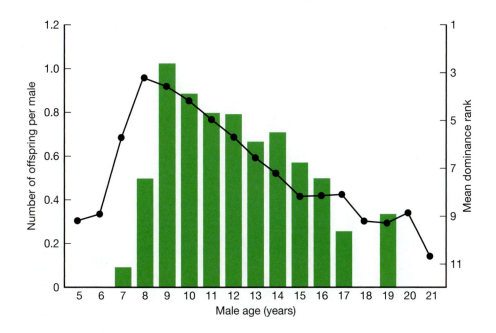

FIGURE 6.31

In baboons, male rank (*black dots*) is closely linked to male age and physical condition. Males reach their highest ranks, on average, when they are about 8 years old and then gradually fall in rank as they age. Male reproductive success (*green bars*) closely corresponds to male age and male rank.

howler monkeys, patas monkeys, and chimpanzees also show that high-ranking males reproduce more successfully than do other males.

These genetic analyses also reveal that dominance rank is not the only factor that influences males' reproductive performance. Among both baboons and chimpanzees, the highest-ranking male is able to monopolize access to receptive females most effectively when there are relatively few other males present in the group and when there are relatively few estrus females present at the same time. In most species, males disperse from groups before their own daughters become sexually mature, thus reducing the likelihood of father–daughter matings. However, in white-faced capuchins, Perry's group found that some high-ranking males remain in groups long enough to potentially mate with their own daughters. Nonetheless, father–daughter matings are largely avoided. The alpha males sired 79% of the offspring produced by unrelated females, but only 6% of their own daughters' offspring.

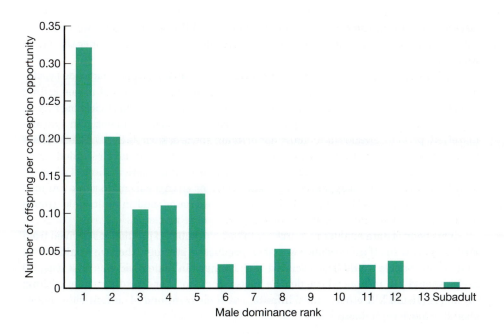

FIGURE 6.32

In baboons, male reproductive success is closely related to dominance rank. The highest-ranking male obtains the highest proportion of conceptions but does not monopolize conceptions entirely.

FIGURE 6.33

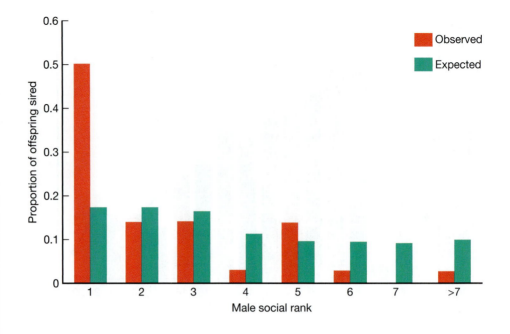

Infanticide

Infanticide is a sexually selected male reproductive strategy.

We have seen that high-ranking males are able to monopolize access to receptive females, and this generates fierce competition over residence in one-male groups and competition for high-ranking positions within multimale groups. Sarah Blaffer Hrdy, now retired from the University of California, Davis, was the first to see that these circumstances might favor the evolution of infanticide as a male reproductive tactic. Her reasoning was based on the following logic: when a female monkey gives birth to an infant, she nurses it for a number of months and does not become pregnant again for a considerable period of time. After the death of an infant, however, lactation ends abruptly and females resume cycling. Thus the death of nursing infants hastens the resumption of maternal receptivity. A male who takes over a group or rises to the top-ranking position may benefit from killing nursing infants because their deaths cause their mothers to become sexually receptive much sooner than they would otherwise.

This hypothesis, which has become known as the **sexual selection infanticide hypothesis**, was initially controversial. There were no direct observations of males killing infants, and some researchers found it hard to believe that this form of violence was an evolved strategy. However, infanticide by males has now been documented in approximately 40 primate species (and many nonprimate species, such as lions). Researchers have witnessed at least 60 infanticidal attacks in the wild and have recorded many nonlethal attacks on infants by adult males. There are many more instances in which healthy infants have disappeared after takeovers or changes in male rank. Infanticide occurs in species that typically form one-male groups, and in multimale groups of savanna baboons, langurs, capuchins, and Japanese macaques.

This body of data enables researchers to test a number of predictions derived from Hrdy's hypothesis. If infanticide is a male reproductive strategy, then we would expect that (1) infanticide would be associated with changes in male residence or status; (2) males should kill infants whose deaths hasten their mothers' resumption of cycling; (3) males should kill other males' infants, not their own; and (4) infanticidal males should achieve reproductive benefits.

FIGURE 6.34

A male baboon in the Moremi Game Reserve of the Okavango Delta in Botswana holds the body of an infant that he has just killed. The male had recently acquired the top-ranking position in the group.

All of these predictions have been supported. Carel van Schaik compiled information about 55 infanticides in free-ranging groups that were actually witnessed by observers. He found that nearly all infanticides (85%) followed changes in male residence or dominance rank. He also found that most infanticides involve unweaned infants, whose deaths will have the greatest impact on female sexual receptivity. Males largely avoid killing related infants. Only 7% of infanticides were committed by males who were sexually active in the group at the time the infants were conceived. Finally, in at least 45%—and possibly as much as 70%—of these cases, the infanticidal male later mated with the mother of the infant that he killed.

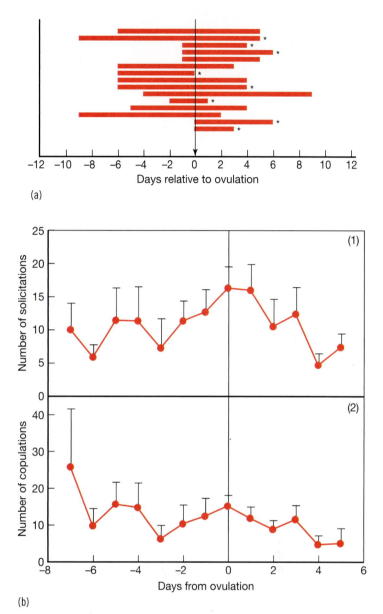

(a)

(b)

Infanticide is sometimes a substantial source of mortality for infants.

Among mountain gorillas in the Virunga Mountains of Rwanda, savanna baboons in the Moremi Game Reserve in Botswana (**Figure 6.34**), gray langurs in Ramnagar in Nepal, and red howlers in Venezuela approximately one-third of all infant deaths are due to infanticide. Among the gelada baboons of the Simien Mountains in Ethiopia, approximately 40% of infants are killed after takeovers.

Females have evolved a battery of responses to infanticidal threats.

Although infanticide may enhance male reproductive success, it can have a disastrous effect on females who lose their infants. Thus we should expect females to evolve counterstrategies to infanticidal threats. The most obvious counterstrategy would be for females to try to prevent males from harming their infants. However, females' efforts to defend their infants are unlikely to be effective. Remember that males are generally larger than females in species without pair bonds, and the extent of sexual dimorphism is most pronounced in species that form one-male groups.

Females may try to confuse males about paternity. As we have seen already, males seem to kill infants when there is no ambiguity about their paternity; if females can increase uncertainty about paternity, they may reduce the risk of infanticide. Females might confuse males about paternity by obscuring information about their reproductive state, by mating with multiple males when they are sexually receptive, and by mating with males at times when they are not likely to conceive. All of these strategies have been documented among primates. A group of researchers led by Michael Heistermann of the German Primate Center has examined the patterns of sexual behavior and ovulatory status among female gray langurs in multimale groups. The found that females are sexually receptive for about nine days, on average, and they can ovulate anytime within that period (**Figure 6.35a**). Females sexually solicit males throughout this period, and male mating behavior

FIGURE 6.35

In some species, females have evolved counterstrategies to infanticide. Grey langurs seem to obscure information about the timing of ovulation. (a) Females are sexually receptive for about nine days, and ovulation can occur anytime within that period. Asterisks indicate receptive periods in which conceptions occurred. (b) Sexual activity is not concentrated around the time of ovulation. Females solicit males, and males copulate with females at fairly consistent rates throughout the receptive period.

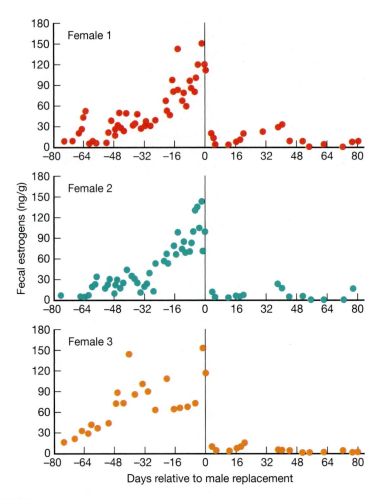

FIGURE 6.36

Gelada females terminate pregnancies immediately after takeovers. Levels of estrogen fall precipitously after takeovers, indicating that pregnancies have ended. Before takeovers, the hormone levels of females that terminated their pregnancies cannot be distinguished from the hormone levels of females that carry pregnancies to term.

FIGURE 6.37

After they give birth, many females begin to associate closely with one or two adult males. Here, a high-ranking female and her infant sit with the mother's male associate.

is not concentrated around the day of ovulation (**Figure 6.35b**), suggesting that males can't tell when females are likely to conceive. Female langurs also mate with multiple males and sometimes solicit males after takeovers when they are already pregnant.

Gelada females have adopted a different strategy to reduce the impact of infanticide. Eila Roberts, now at Arizona State University, and her colleagues used hormonal data to monitor the reproductive status of females before and after takeovers. They discovered that females terminate pregnancies in the days that follow takeovers (**Figure 6.36**). Although this may seem like a very costly strategy for females, it may actually provide a net benefit. Females who aborted pregnancies after takeovers had shorter interbirth intervals than females that carried their pregnancies to term and then lost their infants before they were weaned. It may be advantageous for females to terminate their investment in an infant that is very likely to be killed by the new leader male and to reallocate maternal effort to another reproductive attempt.

The threat of infanticide seems to influence the nature of male–female relationships in baboons.

It has been known for some time that mothers of newborn infant baboons sometimes form close relationships ("friendships") with one or sometimes two adult males (**Figure 6.37**). Females are primarily responsible for maintaining proximity to their male associates and grooming them. Males defend their female associates when the females are threatened. Males also hold, carry, and groom their female associates' infants, and they sometimes intervene on behalf of immatures who become involved in aggressive encounters.

A growing body of evidence suggests that these relationships protect infants from infanticidal attacks. In Moremi, Botswana, where male–female relationships are prominent and infanticide is common, female baboons are extremely agitated in the presence of new males. Jacinta Beehner and her colleagues have found that females' cortisol levels, which provide a physiological index of stress, rise sharply when immigrant males enter the group (**Figure 6.38**). The presence of a male "friend," however, reduces new mothers' agitation. Ryne Palombit has found that males are acutely sensitive to the distress of their female associates, but their responsiveness is directly tied to the infant's presence. If the infant dies, males stop responding.

If the data on infanticide are so consistent, why is the idea so controversial?

When Hrdy first proposed the idea that infanticide is an evolved male reproductive strategy, there was plenty of room for skepticism and dispute. Now, however, we have good evidence that the patterning of infanticidal attacks fits predictions derived from the sexual selection infanticide hypothesis. But controversy still lingers. Volker Sommer, whose own work on infanticide in gray langurs has been attacked by critics of Hrdy's hypothesis, believes that the criticism comes from a tendency to commit what is called the "naturalistic fallacy," the tendency to assume that what we see in nature is somehow right, just, and inevitable. Critics are concerned that if we accept the idea that infanticide is an adaptive strategy for langurs or baboons, it will justify similar behavior in humans. As we will discuss more fully in Part Four, it is misguided to try to extract moral meaning from the behavior of other animals. That is what makes the naturalistic fallacy an erroneous form of reasoning.

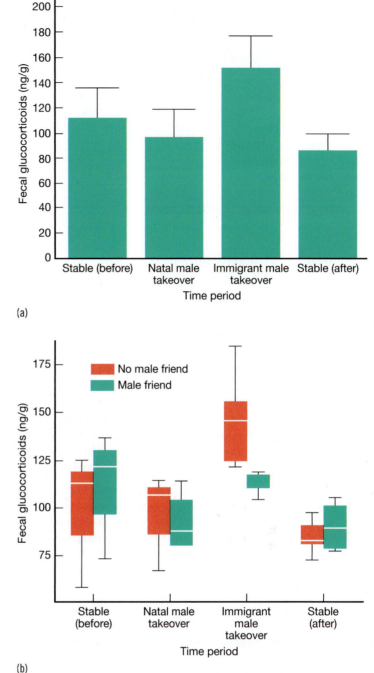

(a)

(b)

FIGURE 6.38

(a) The cortisol levels of female baboons increased when a new male immigrated into the group and took over the alpha position. (b) This effect was most pronounced for females who did not have a close male associate.

Key Terms

strategy
primiparous
dominance
dominance matrix
transitive
sexual selection
intrasexual selection
intersexual selection
bachelor males
estrus
sexual selection infanticide hypothesis

Study Questions

1. Explain why reproductive success is a critical element of evolution by natural selection. When biologists use the terms *cost* and *benefit*, what currency are they trying to measure?

2. What is the difference between polygyny and polyandry? It seems likely that females might prefer polyandry over polygyny, and at the same time males would favor polygyny. Explain why males and females might prefer different types of mating systems. If this conflict of interest occurs, why is polygyny more common than polyandry?

3. In many primate species, reproduction is highly seasonal. Some researchers have suggested that reproductive seasonality has evolved as a means for females to manipulate their reproductive options. How would reproductive seasonality alter females' options? Why do you think this strategy might be advantageous for females?

4. Imagine that you came upon a species in which males and females were the same size, but males had very large testes in relation to their body size. What would you infer about their social organization? Now suppose you found another species in which males were much larger than females but had relatively small testes. What would you deduce about their social system? Why do these relationships hold?

5. Among mammalian species, male fitness is typically more variable than female fitness. Explain why this is often the case. What implications does this have for evolution acting on males and females?

6. What factors influence the reproductive success of females? How do these factors contribute to variance in female reproductive success?

7. Biologists use the term *investment* to describe parental care. What elements of the selective forces acting on parental strategies does this term capture?

8. Explain the logic underlying the sexual selection infanticide hypothesis. What predictions follow from this hypothesis? List the predictions, and explain why they follow from the hypothesis.

9. In general, infanticide seems to be more common in species that form one-male groups than in species that form multimale, multifemale groups or pair-bonded groups. Explain why this might be the case.

10. Why is the naturalistic fallacy considered a fallacy in thinking?

Further Reading

Altmann, J. 2001. *Baboon Mothers and Infants.* Chicago: University of Chicago Press.

Kappeler, P. M. and C. P. van Schaik, eds. 2004. *Sexual Selection in Primates: New and Comparative Perspectives.* New York: Cambridge University Press.

Mitani, J., J. Call, P. Kappeler, R. Palombit, and J. B. Silk, eds. 2012. *The Evolution of Primate Societies.* Chicago: University of Chicago Press.

Van Schaik, C. P. and C. H. Janson, eds. 2000. *Infanticide by Males and Its Implications.* New York: Cambridge University Press.

Westneat, D. F. and C. W. Fox, eds. 2010. *Evolutionary Behavioral Ecology.* Section V. Oxford: Oxford University Press.

7

CHAPTER OBJECTIVES

By the end of this chapter you should

- Understand why altruism is unlikely to evolve in most circumstances.

- Understand how evolution can favor altruism through the processes of kin selection and reciprocal altruism.

- Discuss the mechanisms that allow primates to recognize their relatives.

- Explain how kinship influences the distribution of altruism in primate groups.

- Evaluate arguments about the importance of reciprocal altruism in primate groups.

THE EVOLUTION OF COOPERATION

Altruism: A Puzzle

So far, we have explained the evolution of morphology and behavior in terms of individual reproductive success. Natural selection favored deeper beaks in Darwin's finches during the drought because deeper beaks allowed individuals to crack tougher seeds. It favors infanticide by male langurs and lions because it allows them to sire offspring with the dead infants' mothers. However, primates (and many other creatures) perform **altruistic behaviors** that benefit others but at a personal cost. For example, virtually all social primates groom other group members, removing parasites, cleaning scabs, and picking debris from their hair (**Figure 7.1**). Grooming other individuals consumes time that could be spent looking for food, courting prospective mates, caring for offspring, or scanning for predators. The recipient gets a thorough cleaning of parts of her body that she might find difficult to reach and may enjoy a period of pleasant relaxation. And grooming isn't the only altruistic behavior; primates warn others about the presence of predators, even though doing so makes them more conspicuous. They risk injury to help others in dominance contests, and

FIGURE 7.1

Gray langurs groom one another. Grooming is usually considered altruistic because the groomer expends time and energy when it grooms another animal, and the recipient benefits from having ticks removed from its skin, wounds cleaned, and debris removed from its hair.

FIGURE 7.2

The pyramid will collapse if anyone slacks off.

in some species, individuals share food. If natural selection favors individually advantageous traits, how can we explain the evolution of such altruistic behaviors?

The answer to this question is one of the triumphs of evolutionary biology. Beginning in the 1960s and 1970s with the work of William D. Hamilton and Robert Trivers, biologists have developed a rich theory that explains why selection sometimes favors altruistic behavior and why it often does not. This theory has transformed our understanding of the evolution of social behavior. In this chapter, we show how natural selection can favor the evolution of altruistic behavior and describe how it explains the form and pattern of cooperation in primate groups.

Mutualism

Sometimes helping others benefits the actor as well as the recipient. Such behaviors are mutualistic.

Mutualistic interactions provide benefits to both participants. This seems like a win–win proposition, and you might think these kinds of interactions would be very common in nature. But there is a catch. To see what it is, think back to those group projects you worked on in elementary school. The problem with group projects is that if someone doesn't do his share, the rest of the group has to take up the slack. You could punish the slacker, but that just compounds the problem because doing so is a lot of trouble. So you grumble and finish the project yourself. The general lesson here is that mutualistic cooperation is fragile when slacking is profitable for individuals. Mutualism is most likely to work in situations in which slacking off isn't profitable for any of the participants. Imagine that you are entering a human-pyramid contest (**Figure 7.2**). The group that can construct the largest pyramid wins a big prize. If someone doesn't hold up his or her end, the pyramid collapses, and everyone loses. So no one is motivated to slack off.

Coalitions among male baboons may be an example of mutualism. In East Africa, male baboons guard receptive females. The highest-ranking male usually attempts to monopolize access to females on the days when females are most likely to conceive. Two males may jointly challenge a mate-guarding male and try to gain control of the female (**Figure 7.3**). These interactions can escalate to energetically costly chases and physical confrontations. The challengers often succeed in driving the male away, and one of them begins to mate-guard the female. Males that hold middle-ranking positions are most likely to form coalitions. These males have very little chance of gaining access to receptive females on their own, but two middle-ranking males are a formidable force when they work together. As long as each male has some probability of ending up with the female, it may be profitable for both to participate in the coalition. There is no incentive to slack off, because slacking off guarantees failure.

Like male baboons, chimpanzees also mate-guard receptive females. In the Kibale Forest, some pairs of high-ranking males jointly defend access to females. Cooperation allows males to fend off other males' approaches and keep close tabs on females at the same time. Coalition partners share matings with

FIGURE 7.3

Two male baboons (on the right) jointly challenge a third male over access to a receptive female.

the female they are guarding. Males switch from mate guarding alone to joint mate guarding when they are in large parties with many potential competitors. Again, this strategy may pay off for males if they are able to obtain more matings when they cooperate with other males than when they attempt to monopolize females on their own.

The Problem with Group-Level Explanations

Altruistic behaviors cannot be favored by selection just because they are beneficial to the group as a whole.

You might think that if the average effect of an act on all members of the group is positive, then it would be beneficial for all individuals to perform it. For example, suppose that when one monkey gives an alarm call, the other members of the group benefit, and the total benefits to all group members exceed the cost of giving the call. Then, if every individual gave the call when a predator was sighted, all members of the group would be better off than if no warning calls were ever given. You might think that alarm calling would be favored because every individual in the group benefits.

This inference is wrong because it confuses the effect on the group with the effect on the actor. In most circumstances, the fact that alarm calls are beneficial to those hearing them doesn't affect whether the trait of alarm calling evolves; all that matters is the effect that giving the alarm call has on the caller. To see why this is true, imagine a hypothetical monkey species in which some individuals give alarm calls when they are the first to spot a predator. Monkeys who hear the call have a chance to flee. Suppose that one-fourth of the population ("callers") give the call when they spot predators, and three-fourths of the individuals ("noncallers") do not give an alarm call in the same circumstance. (These proportions are arbitrary; we chose them because it's easier to follow the reasoning in examples with concrete numbers.) Let's suppose that in this species the tendency to give alarm calls is genetically inherited.

Now we compare the fitness of callers and noncallers. Because everyone in the group can hear the alarm calls and take appropriate action, alarm calls benefit

(a) Altruist gives alarm call to group.

(b) Nonaltruist doesn't give alarm call to group.

FIGURE 7.4

Two groups of monkeys are approached by a predator. (a) In one group, one individual (*pink*) has a gene that makes her call in this context. Giving the call lowers the caller's fitness but increases the fitness of every other individual in the group. Like the rest of the population, one out of four of these beneficiaries also carries the genes for calling. (b) In the second group, the female who detects the predator does not carry the gene for calling and remains silent. This lowers the fitness of all members of the group a certain amount because they are more likely to be caught unaware by the predator. Once again, one out of four is a caller. Although members of the caller's group are better off on average than members of the noncaller's group, the gene for calling is not favored, because callers and noncallers in the caller's group both benefit from the caller's behavior but callers incur some costs. Callers are at a disadvantage relative to noncallers. Thus calling is not favored, even though the group as a whole benefits.

everyone in the group to the same extent (**Figure 7.4**). Calling has no effect on the *relative* fitness of callers and noncallers because, on average, one-fourth of the beneficiaries will be callers and three-fourths of the beneficiaries will be noncallers—the same proportions we find in the population as a whole. Calling reduces the risk of mortality for everyone who hears the call, but it does not change the frequency of callers and noncallers in the population because everyone gains the same benefits. However, callers are conspicuous when they call, so they are more vulnerable to predators. Although all individuals benefit from hearing alarm calls, callers are the only ones who suffer the costs from calling. This means that, on average, noncallers will have a higher fitness than callers. Thus genes that cause alarm calling will not be favored by selection, even if the cost of giving alarm calls is small and the benefit to the rest of the group is large. Instead, selection will favor genes that suppress alarm calling because noncallers have a higher fitness than callers. (See Closer Look 7.1 for more about the role of group selection in nature.)

Kin Selection

Natural selection can favor altruistic behavior if altruistic individuals are more likely to interact with each other than chance alone would dictate.

If altruistic behaviors can't evolve by ordinary natural selection or by group selection, then how do they evolve? A clear answer to this question did not come until 1964, when a young biologist named William D. Hamilton published a landmark paper. This paper was the first of a series of fundamental contributions that Hamilton made to our understanding of the evolution of behavior.

The argument made in the previous section contains a hidden assumption: altruists and nonaltruists are equally likely to interact with one another. We supposed that

7.1 Group Selection

Group selection was once thought to be the mechanism for the evolution of altruistic interactions. In the early 1960s, the British ornithologist V. C. Wynne-Edwards contended that altruistic behaviors like those we have been considering here evolved because they enhanced the survival of whole groups of organisms. Thus individuals gave alarm calls, despite the costs of becoming more conspicuous to predators, because calling protected the group as a whole from attacks. Wynne-Edwards reasoned that groups containing a higher number of altruistic individuals would be more likely to survive and prosper than groups containing fewer altruists, and the frequency of the genes leading to altruism would increase.

Wynne-Edwards's argument is logical because Darwin's postulates logically apply to groups as well as individuals. However, group selection is not an important force in nature because there is generally not enough genetic variation among groups for selection to act on. Group selection can occur if groups vary in their ability to survive and to reproduce and if that variation is heritable. Then group selection may increase the frequency of genes that increase group survival and reproductive success. The strength of selection among groups depends on the amount of genetic variation among groups, just as the strength of selection among individuals depends on the amount of genetic variation among individuals. However, when individual selection and group selection are opposed and group selection favors altruistic behavior while individual selection favors selfish alternatives, individual selection has a tremendous advantage. This is because the amount of variation among groups is much smaller than the amount of variation among individuals, unless groups are very small or there is very little migration among them. Thus individual selection favoring selfish behavior will generally prevail over group selection, making group selection an unlikely source of altruism in nature.

callers give alarm calls when they hear a predator, no matter who is nearby. Hamilton's insight was to see that any process that causes altruists to be more likely to interact with other altruists than they would by chance could facilitate the evolution of altruism.

To see why this is such an important insight, let's modify the previous example by assuming that our hypothetical species lives in groups composed of full siblings, offspring of the same mother and father. The frequencies of the calling and noncalling genes don't change, but their distribution will be affected by the fact that siblings live together (**Figure 7.5**). If an individual is a caller, then, by the rules of Mendelian genetics, there is a 50% chance that the individual's siblings will share the genes that cause calling behavior. This means that the frequency of the genes for calling will be higher in groups that contain callers than in the population as a whole and, therefore, more than one-fourth of the beneficiaries will be callers themselves. When a caller gives an alarm call, the audience will contain a higher fraction of callers than the population at large does. Thus the caller raises the average fitness of callers relative to noncallers. Similarly, because the siblings of noncallers are more likely to be noncallers than chance alone would dictate, callers are less likely to be present in such groups than in the population at large. Therefore, the absence of a warning call lowers the relative fitness of noncallers relative to callers.

When individuals interact selectively with relatives, callers are more likely to benefit than noncallers and, all other things being equal, the benefits of calling will favor

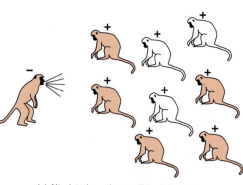

(a) Altruist gives alarm call to siblings.

(b) Nonaltruist doesn't give alarm call to siblings.

FIGURE 7.5

Two groups of monkeys are approached by a predator. Each group is composed of nine sisters. (a) In one group there is a caller (*pink*), an individual with a gene that makes her call in this context. Her call lowers her own fitness but increases the fitness of her sisters. (b) In the second group, the female who detects the predator is not a caller and does not call when she spots the predator. As in Figure 7.4, calling benefits the other group members but imposes costs on the caller. However, there is an important difference between the situations portrayed here and in Figure 7.4. Here the groups are made up of sisters, so five of the eight recipients of the call also carry the calling gene. In any pair of siblings, half of the genes are identical because the siblings inherited the same gene from one of their parents. Thus, on average, half of the caller's siblings also carry the calling allele, because they inherited it from their mom or dad. The remaining four siblings carry genes inherited from the other parent; and, like the population as a whole, one out of four of them is a caller. The same reasoning shows that in the group with the noncaller, there is only one caller among the beneficiaries of the call. Half are identical to their sister because they inherited the same noncalling gene from one of their parents; one of the remaining four is a caller. In this situation, callers are more likely to benefit from calling than noncallers, and so calling alters the relative fitness of callers and noncallers. Whether the calling behavior actually evolves depends on whether these benefits are big enough to compensate for the reduction in the caller's fitness.

the genes for calling. However, we must remember that calling is costly, and this will tend to reduce the fitness of callers. Calling will be favored by natural selection only if its benefits are sufficiently greater than its costs. The exact nature of this trade-off is specified by what we call Hamilton's rule.

Hamilton's Rule

Hamilton's rule predicts that altruistic behaviors will be favored by selection if the costs of performing the behavior are less than the benefits discounted by the coefficient of relatedness between actor and recipient.

Hamilton's theory of **kin selection** is based on the idea that selection could favor altruistic alleles if animals interacted selectively with their genetic relatives. Hamilton's theory also specifies the quantity and distribution of help among individuals. According to **Hamilton's rule**, an act will be favored by selection if

$$rb > c$$

where

r = the average coefficient of relatedness between the actor and the recipients
b = the sum of the fitness benefits to all individuals affected by the behavior
c = the fitness cost to the individual performing the behavior

The **coefficient of relatedness**, r, measures the genetic relationship between interacting individuals. More precisely, r is the probability that two individuals will acquire the same allele through descent from a common ancestor. **Figure 7.6** shows how these probabilities are derived in a simple genealogy. Female A obtains one allele at a given locus from her mother and one from her father. Her half sister, female B, also obtains one allele at the same locus from each of her parents. We obtain the probability that both females receive the same allele from their mother by multiplying the probability that female A obtains the allele (0.5) by the probability that female B obtains the same allele (0.5); the result is 0.25. Thus half sisters have, on average, a 25% chance of obtaining the same allele from their mothers. Now consider the relatedness between female B and her brother, male C. In this case, note that female B and male C are full siblings: they have the same mother and the same father. The probability that both siblings will acquire the same allele from their mother is still 0.25, but female B and male C might also share an allele from their father. The probability of this event is also 0.25. Thus the probability that female B and male C share an allele is equal to the sum of 0.25 and 0.25, or 0.5. This basic reasoning can be extended to calculate the degrees of relatedness among various categories of kin (**Table 7.1**).

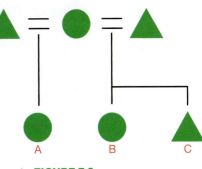

FIGURE 7.6

This genealogy shows how the value of r is computed. Triangles represent males, circles represent females, and the equals sign represents mating. The relationships between individuals labeled in the genealogy are described in the text.

Hamilton's rule leads to two important insights: (1) altruism is limited to kin and (2) closer kinship facilitates more costly altruism.

If you reflect on Hamilton's rule for a while, you will see that it produces two predictions about the conditions that favor the evolution of altruistic behaviors. First, altruism is not expected to be directed toward nonkin, because the coefficient of relatedness, r, between nonkin is 0. The condition for the evolution of altruistic traits will be satisfied only for interactions between kin, when $r > 0$. Thus altruists are expected to be nepotistic, showing favoritism toward kin.

Second, close kinship is expected to facilitate altruism. If an act is particularly costly, it is most likely to be restricted to close kin. **Figure 7.7** shows how the benefit:cost ratio scales with the degree of relatedness among individuals. Compare what happens when $r = \frac{1}{16}$ (or 0.0625) and when $r = \frac{1}{2}$ (or 0.5). When $r = \frac{1}{16}$, the benefits must be more than 16 times as great as the costs for Hamilton's inequality $rb > c$ to be satisfied. When $r = \frac{1}{2}$, the benefit needs to be just over twice as large as the costs. All other things being equal, Hamilton's rule will be easier to satisfy for close kin than for distant kin, and altruism will be more common among close relatives than among distant ones.

TABLE 7.1

Relationship	r
Parent and offspring	0.5
Full siblings	0.5
Half siblings	0.25
Grandparent and grandchild	0.25
First cousins	0.125 or 0.0625
Unrelated individuals	0

The value of r for selected categories of relatives. (When cousins are offspring of full siblings, they are related by 0.125, but when they are the offspring of half siblings they are related by 0.0625.)

FIGURE 7.7

As the degree of relatedness (*r*) between two individuals declines, the value of the ratio of benefits to costs (*b:c*) required to satisfy Hamilton's rule for the evolution of altruism rises rapidly.

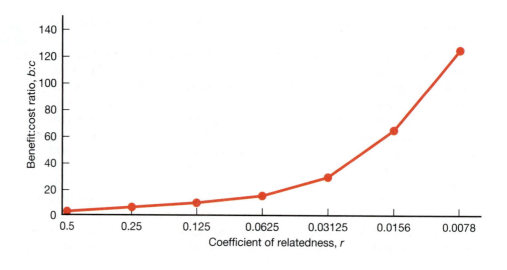

Kin Recognition

Primates may use contextual cues to recognize maternal relatives.

In order for kin selection to provide an effective mechanism for the evolution of cooperative behavior, animals must be able to distinguish relatives from nonrelatives and close relatives from distant ones. Some organisms are able to recognize their kin by their smell or likeness to themselves. This is called **phenotypic matching**. Others learn to recognize relatives using contextual cues—such as familiarity and proximity—that predict kinship (**Figure 7.8**). In the past, primatologists assumed that primates rely solely on contextual cues to identify their relatives, but new data suggest that phenotypic matching may also play a role in primate kin recognition.

Mothers seem to make use of contextual cues to recognize their own infants. After they give birth, females repeatedly sniff and inspect their newborns. By the time their infants are a few weeks old, mothers are clearly able to recognize them. After this, females of most species nurse only their own infants and respond selectively to their own infants' distress calls. Primate mothers don't really need innate means of recognizing their young, because young infants spend virtually all of their time in

FIGURE 7.8

(a) Even mothers must learn to recognize their own infants. Here, a female bonnet macaque peers into her infant's face. (b) Primates apparently learn who their relatives are by observing patterns of association among group members. Here, a female inspects another female's infant.

(a)

(b)

physical contact with their mothers. Thus mothers are unlikely to confuse their own newborn with another.

Monkeys and apes may learn to recognize other maternal kin through contact with their mothers. Offspring continue to spend considerable amounts of time with their mothers even after their younger siblings are born. Thus they have many opportunities to watch their mothers interact with their new brothers and sisters. Similarly, the newborn infant's most common companions are its mother and siblings (**Figure 7.9**). Because adult females continue to associate with their mothers, infants also become familiar with their grandmothers, aunts, and cousins.

(a)

(b)

Contextual cues may play some role in paternal kin recognition as well.

Primatologists were once quite confident that most primates were unable to recognize their paternal kin. This conclusion was based on the following reasoning: First, pair bonds are uncommon in most primate species, so patterns of association between males and females do not provide accurate cues of paternal kinship. Second, females may mate with several different males near the time of conception, creating confusion about paternity. Even in pair-bonded species, like gibbons and titi monkeys, females sometimes mate with males from outside their groups.

New evidence from field studies on macaques and baboons suggests that monkeys use contextual cues to assess paternal kinship. Jeanne Altmann of Princeton University pointed out that age may provide a good proxy measure of paternal kinship in species in which a single male typically dominates mating activity within the group. When this happens, all infants born at about the same time are likely to have the same father. Recent studies suggest that Altmann's logic is correct—monkeys do use age to identify paternal kin. Female baboons in the population that Altmann studied distinguish between paternal half sisters and unrelated females, and they seem to rely on age proximity to make these discriminations. Anja Widdig of the Max Planck Institute for Evolutionary Anthropology in Leipzig, Germany, and her colleagues have also found that females show strong affinities for paternal half sisters (**Figure 7.10**). Their affinities for paternal kin seem to be based partly on strong preferences for interacting with age-mates. However, females also distinguished *among* their age-mates, preferring paternal half sisters over unrelated females of the same age.

It is not entirely clear what cues females use to distinguish their paternal half sisters from other age mates. However, new research suggests that facial resemblances among relatives might play some role. In one study, researchers measured multiple features of rhesus macaque faces and compared the similarity of the faces of kin and nonkin. Not surprisingly, kin tend to resemble one another. In a second study, humans were asked to rate the similarity between an adult face and the faces of two immature macaques of the same age and sex. One of the immatures was the adult's

FIGURE 7.9

Monkey and ape infants grow up surrounded by various relatives. (a) These adult baboon females are mother and daughter. Both have young infants. (b) An adolescent female bonnet macaque carries her younger brother while her mother recovers from a serious illness.

FIGURE 7.10

Female macaques are able to identify paternal siblings. Females interact far more often with maternal half siblings (*blue bar*) than with paternal siblings, but they interact more often with paternal siblings than with nonkin. Age similarity seems to provide a cue for paternal kinship: Females interact more often with paternal half-sibling peers (*red hatched bar*) than with paternal half siblings that are not close in age (*solid red bar*). But note that females also distinguish among peers, preferring half-sibling peers over unrelated peers (*purple hatched bar*).

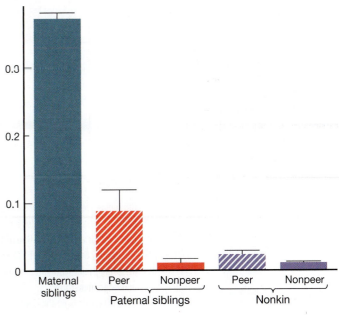

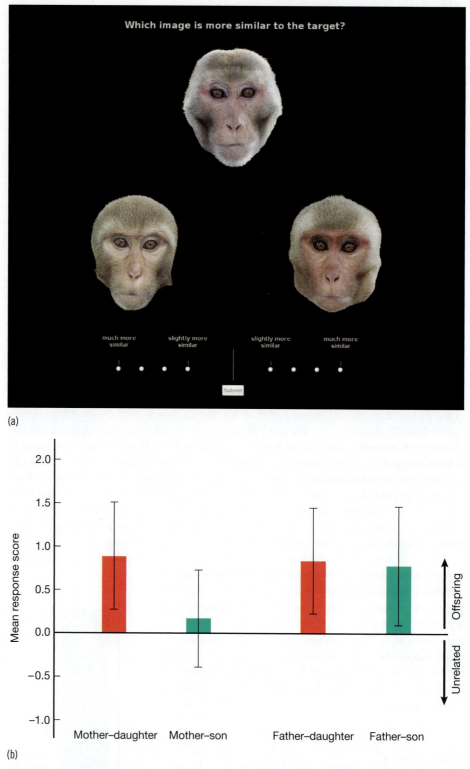

(a)

(b)

FIGURE 7.11

Kin recognition may be based in part on facial resemblances among relatives. (a) In a recent study, human subjects were asked to rate the facial resemblances between an adult rhesus macaques and two immatures matched for age and sex. One of the immatures was the adult's offspring and the other was unrelated. You can try this yourself. (b) The human subjects perceived adults to be significantly more similar to their offspring than to unrelated immatures. A value of zero indicates no difference in similarity to offspring and unrelated immatures.

*The offspring is on the right side.

(a)

(b)

(c)

(d)

FIGURE 7.12

Some of the many species of primates that groom are (a) capuchin monkeys, (b) blue monkeys, (c) baboons, and (d) gorillas.

offspring and the other was unrelated (**Figure 7.11a**). Human raters, even those with no previous experience working with macaques, were significantly more accurate than expected by chance (**Figure 7.11b**). Taken together, these studies suggest that facial resemblances among kin may provide cues about kinship.

Kin Biases in Behavior

A considerable body of evidence suggests that the patterns of many forms of altruistic interactions among primates are largely consistent with predictions derived from Hamilton's rule. Here we consider several examples.

Grooming is more common among kin than nonkin.

Social **grooming** plays an important role in the lives of most gregarious primates (**Figure 7.12**). Grooming is likely to be beneficial to the participants in at least two ways: First, grooming serves hygienic functions because bits of dead skin, debris, and parasites are removed and wounds are kept clean and open. Second, grooming may provide a means for individuals to establish relaxed, **affiliative** (friendly) contact and to reinforce social relationships with other group members (Closer Look 7.2). Grooming is costly because the actor expends both time and energy in performing these services. Moreover, Marina Cords of Columbia University has shown that blue monkeys are less vigilant when they are grooming, perhaps exposing themselves to some risk of being captured by predators.

Grooming is more common among kin, particularly mothers and their offspring, than among nonkin. For example, Ellen Kapsalis and Carol Berman of the University at Buffalo have documented the effect of maternal relatedness among rhesus macaques on Cayo Santiago. In this population, females groom close kin at higher rates than nonkin, and close kin are groomed more often than distant kin (**Figure 7.13**).

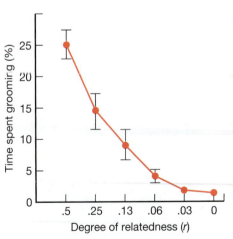

FIGURE 7.13

Rhesus monkeys on Cayo Santiago groom close relatives more often than they groom distant relatives or nonkin.

7.2 How Relationships Are Maintained

Conflict and competition are fundamental features of social life for many primates: females launch unprovoked attacks on unsuspecting victims, males battle over access to receptive females, subordinates are supplanted from choice feeding sites, and dominance relationships are clearly defined and frequently reinforced. Although violence and aggression are not prevalent in all primates (muriquis, for example, are so peaceful that dominance hierarchies cannot be detected), many primates can be charitably characterized as contentious. This raises an intriguing question: How is social life sustained in the face of such relentless conflict? After all, it seems inevitable that aggression and conflict will drive animals apart, disrupt social bonds, and reduce the cohesiveness of social groups.

Social relationships matter to primates. They spend a considerable portion of every day grooming other group members. Grooming is typically focused on a relatively small number of partners and is often reciprocated. Robin Dunbar of the University of Oxford contends that in Old World monkeys, grooming has transcended its original hygienic function and now serves as a means to cultivate and maintain social bonds. Social bonds may have real adaptive value to individuals. For example, grooming is sometimes exchanged for support in coalitions, and grooming partners may be allowed to share access to scarce resources.

When tensions do erupt into violence, certain behavioral mechanisms may reduce the disruptive effects of conflict on social relationships. After conflicts end, victims often flee from their attackers—an understandable response. In some cases, however, former opponents make peaceful contact in the minutes that follow conflicts. For example, chimpanzees sometimes kiss their former opponents, female baboons grunt quietly to their former victims, and golden monkeys may embrace or groom their former adversaries. The swift transformation from aggression to affiliation prompted Frans de Waal of Emory University to suggest that these peaceful postconflict interactions are a form of reconciliation, a way to mend relationships that were damaged by conflict. Inspired by de Waal's work, a number of researchers have documented reconciliatory behavior in a wide range of primate species.

Peaceful postconflict interactions seem to have a calming effect on former opponents. When monkeys are nervous and anxious, rates of certain self-directed behaviors, such as scratching, increase. Thus self-directed behaviors are a good behavioral index of stress. Filippo Aureli of Liverpool John Moores University and his colleagues at Utrecht University and Emory University have studied the effects of fighting and reconciliation on the rate of self-directed behaviors. They found

FIGURE 7.14

Two baboons form an alliance against an adult female.

It is interesting to note that as relatedness declined, the differences in the proportions of time spent grooming kin and nonkin were essentially eliminated. This may mean that monkeys cannot recognize more distant kin or that the conditions of Hamilton's rule ($rb > c$) are rarely satisfied for distant kin.

Primates most often form coalitions with close kin.

Most disputes in primate groups involve two individuals. Sometimes, however, several individuals jointly attack another individual or one individual comes to the support of another individual involved in an ongoing dispute (**Figure 7.14**). We call these kinds of interactions **coalitions** or **alliances**. Support is likely to be beneficial to the individual who receives aid because support alters the balance of power among the original contestants. The beneficiary may be more likely to win the contest or less likely to be injured in the confrontation. At the same time, however, intervention may

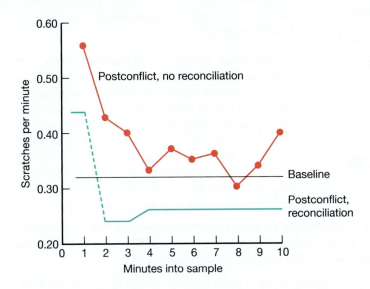

FIGURE 7.15

Rates of scratching, an observable index of stress, by victims of aggression are elevated over normal levels in the minutes that follow aggressive encounters. If some form of affiliative contact (reconciliation) between former opponents occurs during the postconflict period, however, rates of scratching drop rapidly below baseline levels. If there is no reconciliatory contact during the first few minutes of the postconflict period, rates of scratching remain elevated above baseline levels for several minutes. These data suggest that affiliative contact between former opponents has a calming effect. Similar effects on aggressors have also been detected.

that levels of self-directed behavior, and presumably stress, rise sharply above baseline levels after conflicts. Both victims and aggressors seem to feel the stressful effects of conflicts. If former opponents interact peacefully in the minutes that follow conflicts, rates of self-directed behavior fall rapidly to baseline levels (**Figure 7.15**). If they do not reconcile, rates of self-directed behavior remain elevated above baseline levels for several minutes longer. If reconciliation provides a means to preserve social bonds, then we would expect primates to reconcile selectively with their closest associates. In a number of groups, former opponents who have strong social bonds are most likely to reconcile. Kin also reconcile at high rates in some groups, even though some researchers have argued that kin have little need to reconcile, because their relationships are unlikely to be frayed by conflict.

Reconciliation may also play a role in resolving conflicts among individuals that do not have strong social bonds. Like many other primates, female baboons are strongly attracted to newborn infants and make persistent efforts to handle them. Mothers reluctantly tolerate infant handling, but they do not welcome the attention. Female baboons reconcile at particularly high rates with the mothers of young infants, even when they do not have close relationships with them. Reconciliation greatly enhances the likelihood that aggressors will be able to handle their former victims' infants in the minutes that follow conflicts. Thus, in this case, reconciliation seems to be a means to an immediate end but not a means to preserve long-term relationships.

be costly to the supporter, who expends time and energy and risks defeat or injury when it becomes involved. Hamilton's rule predicts that support will be preferentially directed toward kin and that the greatest costs will be expended on behalf of close relatives.

Many studies have shown that support is selectively directed toward close kin. Female macaques and baboons defend their offspring and close kin more often than they defend distant relatives or unrelated individuals (**Figure 7.16**). Females run some risk when they participate in coalitions, particularly when they are allied against higher-ranking individuals. Coalitions against high-ranking individuals are more likely to result in retaliatory attacks against the supporter than are coalitions against lower-ranking individuals. Female macaques are much more likely to intervene against higher-ranking females on behalf of their own offspring than on behalf of unrelated females or juveniles. Thus macaque females take the greatest risks on behalf of their closest kin.

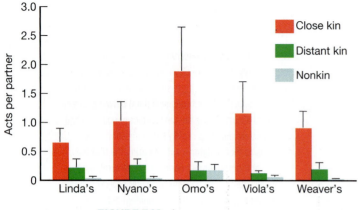

FIGURE 7.16

In five groups of wild baboons, rates of coalitionary support provided by close kin (mothers, daughters, and sisters), more distant maternal kin, and all others are shown. In all five groups, support is biased toward close kin.

Kin-based support in conflicts affects the social structure of macaque, vervet, and baboon groups.

Maternal support in macaques, vervets, and baboons influences the outcome of aggressive interactions and dominance contests. Initially, an immature monkey is able to defeat older and larger juveniles only when its mother is nearby. Eventually, regardless of their age or size, juveniles are able to defeat everyone their mothers can defeat, even when the mother is some distance away. Maternal support contributes directly to several remarkable properties of dominance hierarchies within these species:

- Maternal rank is transferred with great fidelity to offspring, particularly daughters. In a group of baboons at Gilgil, Kenya, for example, maternal rank is an almost perfect predictor of the daughter's rank (**Figure 7.17**).

- Maternal kin occupy adjacent ranks in the dominance hierarchy, and all the members of one **matrilineage** (maternal kin group) rank above or below all members of other matrilineages.

- Ranking within matrilineages is often quite predictable. In most cases, mothers outrank their daughters, and younger sisters outrank their older sisters.

- Female dominance relationships are amazingly stable over time. In many groups, they remain the same over months and sometimes over years. The stability of dominance relationships among females may be a result of the tendency to form alliances in support of kin.

Kin-biased support plays an important role in the reproductive strategies of red howler males.

Behavioral and genetic studies of red howlers in Venezuela conducted by Teresa Pope have shown that kinship influences howler males' behavior in important ways. Red howlers live in groups that contain two to four females and one or two males. Males sometimes join up with migrant females and help them establish new territories. Once such groups have been established, resident males must defend their position and their progeny from infanticidal attacks by alien males. When habitats are crowded, males can gain access to breeding females only by taking over established groups and evicting male residents. This is a risky endeavor because males are often injured in takeover attempts. Moreover, as habitats become more saturated and dispersal opportunities become more limited, males tend to remain in their groups longer. Maturing males help their fathers defend their groups against takeover attempts. Collective defense is crucial to males' success because single males are unable to defend their group against incursions by rival males.

This situation leads to a kind of arms race because migrating males also form coalitions and cooperate in efforts to evict residents. After they have established residence, males collectively defend the group against incursions by extragroup males. Cooperation among males is beneficial because it helps deter rivals. But it also involves clear fitness costs because, as behavioral and genetic data have demonstrated, only one male succeeds in siring offspring within the group. Not surprisingly, kinship influences the duration and stability of male coalitions. Coalitions that are made up of related males last nearly four times as long as coalitions composed of unrelated males. Coalitions composed of related males are also less likely to experience rank reversals. In this case, the costs of cooperation may be balanced by gains in inclusive fitness.

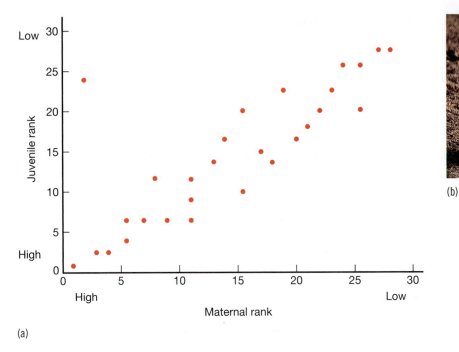

(a)

(b)

FIGURE 7.17

Juvenile female baboons acquire ranks very similar to their mother's ranks. (a) The anomalous point at maternal rank 2 belongs to a female whose mother died when she was an infant. (b) Here, the dominant female of a baboon group is flanked by her two daughters, ranked 2 and 3.

Kin selection plays an important role in cooperatively breeding primate groups.

In marmosets and tamarins, reproduction is usually monopolized by a single breeding pair, and all group members help care for offspring. This raises an obvious question: Why do helpers help? The answer seems to be linked to kin selection. When infants mature, they often remain in their natal groups for several years and help rear their younger siblings. At some point, older offspring disperse with same-sex siblings and form new groups when they meet appropriate members of the opposite sex. Then, one of the siblings becomes the dominant breeder, and the others become helpers. Again, helpers are closely related to the infants that they care for.

Kinship seems to reduce the extent of competition among females to some degree. Recall from Chapter 6 that there is competition among females over reproductive opportunities. When subordinate females produce infants, the dominant female often kills them. However, in golden lion tamarins (**Figure 7.18**), there are some groups in which females share reproduction with subordinate females for one or two years. Females are most likely to share breeding with their own daughters, less commonly with sisters, and rarely with unrelated females.

Sometimes biology is even stranger than fiction. Genetic **chimeras** are organisms that carry more than one genetically distinct population of cells derived from more than one zygote. Chimerism is generally rare in mammals but occurs in marmosets, which commonly produce fraternal twins. The twins share a common placenta and **chorion**, the membrane that surrounds the embryo in the uterus, and stem cells are passed between them. The twins are genetic chimeras with tissues derived from both their own and their siblings' cell lines. Although this phenomenon has been known for some time, it was thought that chimeric tissues were limited to tissues that produce blood cells. However, Corinna Ross and her colleagues from the University of Nebraska have discovered that chimerism extends to all bodily tissues, including the gametes. This means that individuals sometimes pass along their siblings' genes, not their own genes, to their offspring. This would raise the relatedness between nonbreeding helpers and infants and might be one of the factors that favors such high levels of cooperation in these species.

FIGURE 7.18

Golden lion tamarins are cooperative breeders, but there is sometimes conflict over breeding opportunities.

Parent–Offspring Conflict

Kin selection helps to explain why there is conflict between parents and offspring and among siblings.

As we explained in the last chapter, mothers must wean their infants so that they can conserve energy for subsequent infants. As mothers begin to curtail investment, their infants often resist, sometimes vigorously. Chimpanzee infants throw full-fledged tantrums when their mothers rebuff their efforts to nurse, and baboons whimper piteously when their mothers refuse to carry them. These weaning conflicts arise from a fundamental asymmetry in the genetic interests of mothers and their offspring. Mothers are equally related to all of their offspring ($r = 0.5$), but offspring are more closely related to themselves ($r = 1.0$) than to their siblings ($r = 0.5$ or 0.25). This phenomenon was labeled **parent–offspring conflict** by Rutgers biologist Robert Trivers, who was the first to recognize the evolutionary rationale underlying the conflict between parents and their offspring.

To understand why there is parent–offspring conflict, imagine a mutation that increases the amount of maternal investment in the current infant by a small amount, thereby reducing investment in future infants by the same amount. According to Hamilton's rule, selection will favor the expression of this gene in mothers if

$$0.5 \times \text{(increase in fitness of current infant)} >$$
$$0.5 \times \text{(decrease in fitness of future offspring)}$$

Because the mother shares half of her genes with each of her offspring, 0.5 appears on both sides of the inequality. The inequality tells us that selection will increase investment in the current offspring until the benefits to the current offspring are equal to the costs to future offspring. The result is quite different if the genes expressed in the current infant control the amount of maternal investment. This time, consider a gene expressed in the current infant that increases the investment the infant receives by a small amount. Once again, we use Hamilton's rule, this time from the perspective of the current infant:

$$1.0 \times \text{(increase in fitness of current fetus)} >$$
$$0.5 \times \text{(decrease in fitness of future offspring)}$$

In this case, the infant is related to itself by 1.0 and to its full sibling by 0.5. Now selection will increase the amount of maternal investment until the incremental benefit of another unit of investment in the current infant is twice the cost to future brothers and sisters of the fetus (and four times for half siblings). Thus genetic asymmetries lead to a conflict of interest between mothers and their offspring. Selection will favor mothers that provide less investment than their infants desire, and selection will favor offspring that demand more investment than their mothers are willing to give. This conflict of interest plays out in weaning tantrums and sibling rivalries.

Reciprocal Altruism

Altruism can also evolve if altruistic acts are reciprocated.

The theory of **reciprocal altruism** relies on the basic idea that altruism among individuals can evolve if altruistic behavior is balanced between partners (pairs of interacting individuals) over time. In reciprocal relationships, individuals take turns being actor and recipient—giving and receiving the benefits of altruism (**Figure 7.19**). Reciprocal altruism is favored because over time the participants in reciprocal acts obtain benefits that outweigh the costs of their actions. This theory was first formulated by Robert Trivers and later amplified and formalized by others.

Three conditions occurring together favor the development of reciprocal altruism:

individuals must (1) have an opportunity to interact often, (2) be able to keep track of support given and received, and (3) provide support only to those who help them. The first condition is necessary so that individuals will have the opportunity for their own altruism to be reciprocated. The second condition allows individuals to balance altruism given to and received from particular partners. The third condition produces the nonrandom interaction necessary for the evolution of altruism. If individuals are unrelated, initial interactions will be randomly distributed to altruists and nonaltruists. However, reciprocators will quickly stop helping those who do not help in return, while continuing to help those who do. Thus as in the case of kin selection, reciprocal altruism can be favored by natural selection because altruists receive a disproportionate share of the benefits of altruistic acts. Note that altruistic acts need not be exchanged in kind; it is possible for one form of altruism (such as grooming) to be exchanged for another form of altruism (such as coalitionary support).

FIGURE 7.19

Two old male chimpanzees groom each other. Reciprocity can involve taking turns or interacting simultaneously. Male chimpanzees remain in their natal communities throughout their lives and develop close bonds with one another.

In primates, the conditions for the evolution of reciprocal altruism probably are satisfied often, and there is some evidence that it occurs.

Most primates live in social groups that are fairly stable, and they can recognize all of the members of their groups. We do not know whether primates have the cognitive capacity to keep track of support given and received from various partners, but we do know that they are very intelligent and can solve complex problems. Thus primates provide a good place to look for examples of contingent forms of reciprocity.

In several species of macaques, baboons, vervet monkeys, and chimpanzees, individuals tend to spend the most time grooming those that spend the most time grooming them, and they most often support those from whom they most often receive support. In some cases, monkeys seem to exchange grooming for support. Sometimes monkeys switch roles during grooming bouts so that the amount of grooming given and received during each grooming bout is balanced; sometimes grooming is balanced across bouts.

Among male chimpanzees, social bonds seem to be based on reciprocal exchanges in many different currencies (Figure 7.19). For example, John Mitani of the University of Michigan and David Watts of Yale University have found that male chimpanzees at Ngogo, a site in the Kibale Forest of Uganda, share meat selectively with males who share meat with them and with males who regularly support them in agonistic interactions. Males who hunt together also tend to groom one another selectively, support one another, and participate in border patrols together. Interestingly, close associates are often not maternal or paternal kin, suggesting that males' relationships are based on reciprocity, not kinship.

These correlational findings are consistent with predictions derived from the theory of reciprocal altruism, but they do not demonstrate that altruism is contingent on reciprocation.

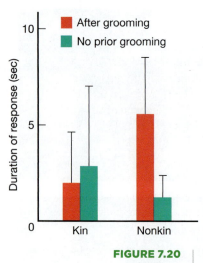

FIGURE 7.20

Vervet monkeys responded more strongly to recruitment calls played from a hidden speaker if the caller had previously groomed them than if the caller had not.

Robert Seyfarth and Dorothy Cheney conducted the first study to examine the contingent nature of altruistic exchanges. Like most other monkeys, vervets spend much of their free time grooming. Vervets also form coalitions and use specific vocalizations to recruit support. In this experiment, Seyfarth and Cheney played tape-recorded recruitment calls to individuals in two different situations. Vervet A's recruitment call was played to vervet B from a hidden speaker (1) after A had groomed B and (2) after a fixed period of time in which A and B had not groomed. It was hypothesized that if grooming were associated with support in the future, then B should respond most strongly to A's recruitment call after being groomed. And that's just what the vervets did (**Figure 7.20**). Seyfarth and Cheney have replicated these results with baboons, adding several controls that help rule out alternative explanations for the subjects' responses to the playbacks.

Although several naturalistic experiments suggest that primates respond to previous help in a contingent way, more controlled experiments conducted in the laboratory have been largely unsuccessful. For example, Alicia Melis, now at the University of Warwick, and her colleagues conducted an experiment in which one chimpanzee needed help from a second chimpanzee to get into a locked room. Each subject was paired with two different helpers, one who provided help and another who did not provide help. Then the roles were reversed, and the individual who had needed help was able to provide help to the previously helpful and unhelpful partners. The chimpanzees were as likely to help the unhelpful partner as they were to help the helpful partner.

At this point it is not entirely clear how to interpret the data. Some researchers think that primates selectively help those from whom they have previously received help and focus on the correlational evidence and the naturalistic experiments. Others emphasize the shortcomings of correlational studies, such as the lack of evidence from carefully controlled studies in the laboratory, and speculate that primates may not have the cognitive ability to keep track of help given and received from multiple partners over extended time periods. However, most researchers would agree on one point: Kin selection plays a more important role in regulating the distribution of altruism in primate groups than does reciprocity.

Key Terms

altruistic behaviors
kin selection
Hamilton's rule
coefficient of relatedness (*r*)
phenotypic matching
grooming
affiliative
coalitions
alliances
matrilineage
chimeras
chorion
parent–offspring conflict
reciprocal altruism

Study Questions

1. Consider the kinship diagram shown below. What is the kinship relationship (for example, mother, aunt, or cousin) and degree of relatedness (such as 0.5 or 0.25) for each pair of individuals?

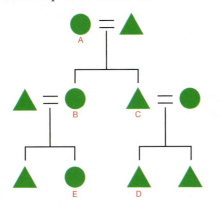

2. In biological terms, what is the difference between the following situations: (a) A male monkey sitting high in a tree gives alarm calls when he sees a lion at a distance; (b) A female monkey abandons a desirable food patch when she is approached by another female.

3. In documentaries about animal behavior, animals are often said to do things "for the good of the species." For example, when low-ranking animals do not reproduce, they are said to give up reproducing to prevent the population from becoming too numerous and exhausting its resource base. What is wrong with this line of reasoning?

4. Why is some sort of nonrandom interaction among altruists necessary for altruism to be maintained?

5. Suppose that primates are not able to recognize paternal kin, as many primatologists have assumed. What would that tell you about how natural selection produces adaptations?

6. Data from a number of studies indicate that primates are more likely to behave altruistically toward kin than toward nonkin. However, many of the same studies show that rates of aggression toward kin and nonkin are basically the same. How does this fit with what you have learned about kin selection? Why are monkeys as likely to fight with kin as with nonkin?

7. There are relatively few good examples of reciprocal altruism in nature. Why is reciprocal altruism uncommon? Why might we expect reciprocal altruism to be more common among primates than among other kinds of animals?

8. Seyfarth and Cheney found that vervet monkeys tended to respond more strongly to the calls of the animals who had groomed them earlier in the day than to the calls of animals who had not groomed them. However, this effect held only for unrelated animals, not for kin. The vervets responded as strongly to the calls of grooming relatives as to those of nongrooming relatives. How might we explain kinship's influence on these results?

9. In addition to kin selection and reciprocal altruism, a third mechanism leading to nonrandom interaction of altruists has been suggested. Suppose altruists had an easily detected phenotypic trait, perhaps a green beard. Then they could use the following rule: "Do altruistic acts only for individuals who have green beards." Once the allele became common, most individuals carrying green beards would not be related to one another, so this would not be a form of kin selection. However, there is a subtle flaw in this reasoning. Assuming that the genes controlling beard color are at different genetic loci than the genes controlling altruistic behavior, explain why green beards would not evolve.

10. Explain why punishment does not provide a ready solution to the problem of cheating in mutualistic interactions.

Further Reading

Chapais, B. and C. M. Berman, eds. 2004. *Kinship and Behavior in Primates.* New York: Oxford University Press.

Dugatkin, L. A. 1997. *Cooperation among Animals: An Evolutionary Perspective.* New York: Oxford University Press.

Kappeler, P. M. and C. P. van Schaik, eds. 2006. *Cooperation in Primates and Humans: Mechanisms and Evolution.* New York: Springer.

Mitani, J., J. Call, P. Kappeler, R. Palombit, and J. B. Silk, eds. 2012. *The Evolution of Primate Societies.* Chicago: University of Chicago Press.

Westneat, D. F. and C. W. Fox, eds. 2010. *Evolutionary Behavioral Ecology.* Oxford: Oxford University Press.

8

CHAPTER OBJECTIVES

By the end of this chapter you should

- Explain how life history theory helps us understand why certain features, such as fertility and longevity, are correlated.

- Understand how the evolution of big brains has shaped primate life history strategies.

- Explain why primatologists think natural selection has favored large brains in monkeys and apes.

- Describe what primates know about their physical environment.

- Describe what primates know about their social world.

PRIMATE LIFE HISTORIES AND THE EVOLUTION OF INTELLIGENCE

Big Brains and Long Lives

Large brains and long life spans are two of the features that define the primate order (**Figure 8.1**). Compared to most other animals, primates rely more heavily on learning to acquire the knowledge and skills that they need to survive and reproduce successfully. The complex behavioral strategies that we have explored in the last few chapters depend on primates' ability to respond flexibly in novel situations. Primates also have long periods of development and long life spans. Cognitive complexity and longevity have become even more exaggerated among modern humans, who live longer than any other primates and have relatively larger brains than any other creatures on the planet. It is not a coincidence that primates have both big brains and long lives; these traits are correlated across mammalian species. As we complete our discussion of the behavior and ecology of contemporary primates and turn our attention to the history of the human lineage, it is important to consider the forces that have shaped the evolution of large brains and long life spans in the primate order.

Selection for larger brains generates selection for long lives.

Correlations tell us that two traits are related but not why this relationship exists. In this case, we have some reason to think that the causal arrow goes from brain size to life span, not vice versa. We come to this conclusion because brains are expensive organs to maintain. Our brains account for just 2% of our total body weight, but they consume about 20% of our metabolic energy.

Natural selection does not maintain costly features like the brain unless they confer important adaptive advantages. Moreover, the extent of investment that organisms make in a particular feature will be linked to the benefit that is derived from the investment. This is the same reason that you are usually willing to spend more for something that you will use for a long time than for something you will use only once. Animals that live for a long time will derive a greater benefit from the energy they expend on building and maintaining their brains than will animals that live for only a short time.

FIGURE 8.1

Primates are intelligent and long-lived. The first ape in space was a 4-year-old chimpanzee named Ham, who was trained to perform a variety of tasks as he hurtled into space. In May 1961, three months after Ham's flight, Alan Shepard followed the chimp into space. Ham was one of several dozen chimpanzees that NASA used to test the safety of space travel for humans. Although Ham died at the age of 27, a number of his fellow "astrochimps" are still alive in their 40s. The survivors and some of their descendants are now living in sanctuaries in New Mexico and southern Florida.

Life History Theory

Life history theory focuses on the evolutionary forces that shape trade-offs between the quantity and quality of offspring and between current and future reproduction.

Birth and death mark the beginning and end of every individual's life cycle. Between these two end points, individuals grow, reach sexual maturity, and begin to reproduce. Natural selection has generated considerable variation around this basic scheme. For example, Pacific salmon are hatched in freshwater but spend their adult lives in the open ocean. After years in the sea, they return to the streams where they were hatched to lay or fertilize their eggs; they die soon after they complete this journey. Opossums, the only North American marsupial, produce their first litter at the age of 1 year. Females have one to two litters per year and live less than 3 years (**Figure 8.2**). Lion females produce litters of up to six cubs at 2-year intervals. Elephants conceive for the first time at 10 years of age, have 22-month pregnancies, and give birth to single infants at 4- to 9-year intervals.

If natural selection favors increased reproductive success, why doesn't it extend the opossum's life span, reduce the lion's interbirth interval, or increase the elephant's litter size? The answer is that all organisms face trade-offs that constrain their reproductive options. As we explained in Chapter 6, investment in one infant limits investment in other offspring, so parents must make trade-offs between the quality and quantity of offspring they produce. Organisms also face trade-offs between current and future reproduction. All other things being equal, fast maturation and early reproduction are advantageous because they increase the length of the reproductive life span and reduce generation time. However, energy devoted to current reproduction diverts energy from growth and maintenance. If growth enhances reproductive success, then it may be advantageous to grow large before beginning to reproduce. Thus many kinds of organisms have a juvenile phase in which they do not reproduce at all. They do not become sexually mature until they reach a size at which the payoffs of allocating energy to current reproduction exceed the payoffs of continued growth. The same kind of argument applies to maintenance. Energy that is diverted from current reproduction to maintenance enables individuals to survive and reproduce successfully in the future.

Aging and death result from trade-offs between reproduction at different ages and survivorship.

Like humans, other primates age; as they get older, their physical abilities deteriorate. They don't run as fast, jump as high, or react as quickly (**Figure 8.3**). Their teeth wear down, making it harder for them to chew their food, and their joints deteriorate. Although humans are the only primates to experience menopause, the fertility of female primates of all species declines when they reach old age. Males seem to reach peak physical condition in early adulthood and then decline.

At first glance, aging and death seem to be the inevitable effects of wear and tear on bodies. Organisms are complicated machines, like cars or computers. A machine has many components that must function together for it to work. It seems logical that the components in animals' bodies simply wear out and break down, like a worn clutch or faulty hard disk. But this explanation of aging is flawed because the analogy between organisms and machines is not really apt. Every cell in an organism contains all of the genetic information necessary to build a complete, new body, and this genetic information can be used to repair damage. Wounds heal and bones mend, and some organisms, such as frogs, can regenerate entire limbs. Some organisms that reproduce asexually by budding or fission do not experience senescence at all.

If senescence is not inevitable, why doesn't natural selection do away with it? The answer has to do with the relative magnitude of the benefits that animals can derive from current reproduction or from living longer. Organisms could last longer if they were built better. A Subaru costs much less to build than a Lexus, but it is also of lower quality. As a consequence, a Lexus is not expected to break down as often as a Subaru is. The same trade-off applies to organisms. Our teeth would last longer if they were protected by a thicker covering of enamel, but building stronger teeth would require more nutrients, particularly calcium. Building higher-quality organisms consumes time and resources, thus reducing the organism's growth rate and early fertility.

The trade-off between survival and reproduction is strongly biased against characteristics that prolong life at the expense of early survival or reproduction.

Senescence is at least partly the consequence of genes that increase fitness at early ages and decrease it at later ages. Aging is favored by selection because traits that increase fertility at young ages are favored at the expense of traits that increase longevity.

The key to understanding this idea is to realize that selective pressures are much weaker on traits that affect only the old. To see why, think about the fate of two mutant alleles. One allele kills individuals before they reach adulthood, and the other kills individuals late in their lives. Carriers of the allele that kills infants and juveniles have a fitness of zero because none survives long enough to transmit the gene to their descendants. Therefore, there will be strong selection against alleles with deleterious effects on the young. In contrast, selection will have much less impact on a mutant allele that kills animals late in their lives. Carriers of a gene that kills them late in life will have already produced offspring before the effects of the gene are felt. Thus a mutation that affects the old will have limited effects on reproductive performance, and there will be little or no selection against it. This means that genes with pleiotropic effects that enhance early fertility but reduce fitness at later ages may be favored by natural selection because they increase individual fitness.

FIGURE 8.2

The Virginia opossum, *Didelphis virginiana*, is the only marsupial mammal in North America. Females produce many tiny fetuses, which make their way into the mother's pouch, attach themselves to a nipple, and nurse for two to three months. Then they emerge from the pouch and cling to their mother's back.

FIGURE 8.3

Virtually all organisms experience senescence (aging). When this photograph was taken, this old male chimpanzee, named Hugo, was missing a lot of hair on his shoulders and back, he had lost a considerable amount of weight, and his teeth had been worn down to the gums. Hugo died a few weeks later.

FIGURE 8.4

Elephants are an example of a species at the slow/long end of the life history continuum. They are very large (approximately 6,000 kg, or 13,200 lb.) and can live up to 60 years in the wild. Females mature at about 10 years of age, have a 22-month gestation period, and give birth to single offspring at 4- to 9-year intervals.

The trade-offs between current and future reproduction and between the quantity and quality of offspring generate constellations of interrelated traits.

Animals that begin to reproduce early also tend to have small body sizes, small brains, short gestation times, large litters, high rates of mortality, and short life spans. Animals that begin to reproduce at later ages tend to have larger body sizes, larger brains, longer gestation times, smaller litters, lower rates of mortality, and longer life spans (**Figure 8.4**). Life history traits are clustered together in this way because of the inherent trade-offs between current and future reproduction and between the quantity and quality of offspring. Animals that begin to reproduce early divert energy from growth and remain small. Animals that have small litters are able to invest more in maintenance and extend their life spans. These clusters of correlated traits create a continuum of life history strategies that runs from fast to slow, or from short to long. Opossums fall somewhere along the fast/short end of the continuum; elephants lie at the slow/long end.

The trade-off between current and future reproduction depends on ecological factors that influence survival rates.

It makes little sense to divert energy to future reproduction if the prospects for surviving into the future are slim. For example, selection is likely to favor fast/short life histories in species that experience intense predation pressure. If predators are abundant and the prospects of surviving from one day to another are low, it makes little sense to postpone reproducing. In this situation, individuals that mature quickly and begin reproducing at early ages are likely to produce more surviving offspring than those that mature more slowly, so selection will favor faster/shorter life history strategies. Other kinds of ecological factors may favor slower/longer life histories. Suppose that there is severe competition for access to the resources that animals need to reproduce successfully and that larger animals are more successful in competitive encounters than small animals are. In this situation, small animals will be at a competitive disadvantage, and it may be profitable to invest more energy in growth, even if such an investment delays maturation. The life history strategies that characterize organisms reflect the net effects of these kinds of ecological pressures.

Natural selection shifts life history traits in response to changes in environmental conditions.

Natural selection adjusts life history traits in response to changes in prevailing conditions. Because life history traits are tightly clustered together, selection pressures acting on one trait often influence the value of other traits as well. For example, Steven Austad, a biologist at the University of Texas, compared the effect of predation on the life histories of two populations of opossums. One population lived on the mainland and was vulnerable to a variety of predators. Another population lived on an island that had very few predators for several thousand years. Opossums on the island aged more slowly, lived longer, and had smaller litters than opossums on the mainland. In this case, reduction of predation pressure favored a decelerated life history.

In some cases, organisms adjust their life histories in relation to current ecological conditions. Recall from Chapter 6 that female monkeys mature more quickly and reproduce at shorter intervals when food is abundant. This is not simply an inevitable response to the availability of food, it is an evolved capacity to adjust development in response to local conditions.

FIGURE 8.5

Variation in the availability of fruit may influence the life history strategies of orangutans in Borneo and Sumatra.

Primates fall toward the slow/long end of the life history continuum.

As a group, primates tend to delay reproduction and grow to relatively large sizes, and they also have relatively long gestation times, small litters, low rates of mortality, long life spans, and large brains in relation to their body size. However, there is also variation within the primate order: Monkeys have relatively larger brains and slower life histories than strepsirrhines, and great apes have larger brains and slower life histories than monkeys.

As in other taxa, there is some evidence that ecological conditions influence life history variables in primates. Orangutans live in tropical rain forests on the islands of Borneo and Sumatra. Soil quality is higher in Sumatra than Borneo, and Sumatran forests have more fruit than Bornean forests. In addition, there is less temporal variation in fruit availability in Sumatra than Borneo. Sumatran orangutans feed mainly on fruit throughout the year, while orangutans living in the relatively unproductive forests of eastern and northeastern Borneo experience long periods in which fruit is scarce and they must rely on lower-quality foods, such as bark (**Figure 8.5**). Andrea Taylor of Duke University and Carel van Schaik of the University of Zürich suggest that these conditions have favored the evolution of relatively smaller brains and substantially shorter interbirth intervals in Bornean orangutans than Sumatran orangutans.

Selective Pressures Favoring Large Brains in Monkeys and Apes

Social or ecological pressures may have favored cognitive evolution in monkeys and apes.

Most primatologists now believe that the enlargement and reorganization of the brain in monkeys and apes was linked to the competitive pressures produced by sociality. In

FIGURE 8.6

Many primates live in complex social groups. Geladas form one-male units, which aggregate together to form large bands composed of hundreds of individuals.

social groups, animals compete for food, mates, grooming partners, and other valuable resources. They also form social bonds that influence their participation in coalitions, exchange networks, access to resources, and so on (**Figure 8.6**). The larger a group becomes, the more difficult it gets to sustain social bonds and keep track of relationships within the group. The ability to operate effectively in this complicated social world may reward greater flexibility in behavior and favor expansion of the parts of the brain that are linked to learning and planning. This idea is called the **social intelligence hypothesis**.

An alternative set of hypotheses links increased brain size to ecological challenges, behavioral flexibility, innovation, and social learning capacities. Simon Reader of Utrecht University and Kevin Laland of the University of St. Andrews propose that natural selection has favored changes in the primate brain that enhance behavioral flexibility and enable animals to invent appropriate solutions to novel problems and to learn new behaviors from conspecifics (**Figure 8.7**). The benefits derived from innovation and social learning generated selective pressures that favored expansion and development of the parts of the brain linked to learning, planning, and behavioral flexibility. The ability to innovate and learn from others might enhance animals' ability to cope with ecological challenges. Monkeys feed mainly on plants and include many different plant species in their diets. They must evaluate the ripeness, nutritional content, and toxicity of their food items. Moreover, some primates rely heavily on **extracted foods** that require complex processing techniques. For example, chimpanzees and capuchin monkeys eat hard-shelled nuts that must be cracked open with stones or smashed against a tree trunk; baboons dig up roots and tubers; aye-ayes extract insect larvae from underneath tree bark (**Figure 8.8**). Extracted foods are valuable elements in primate diets because they tend to be rich sources of protein and energy. However, they require complicated, carefully coordinated techniques to process.

Comparative analyses provide some support for both types of hypotheses about cognitive evolution in primates.

These models of the evolution of cognitive complexity generate specific predictions about the pattern of variation in the brains and cognitive abilities of living primates. For example, the social intelligence hypothesis predicts a link between social complexity and cognitive complexity, and the behavioral flexibility hypothesis predicts that innovations and social learning will be linked to brain size.

To test these hypotheses, we need a reliable measure of cognitive ability. Unfortunately, it is very difficult to assess cognitive ability in other species. Instead, most work in this area has relied on measurements of the size or organization of particular parts of the brain. Researchers focus on the development of the forebrain, particularly the **neocortex**, because this is the site of the most substantial evolutionary changes in size and complexity (**Figure 8.9**). Moreover, the neocortex seems to be the part of the brain most closely associated with problem solving and behavioral flexibility. Neocortex size alone is not a very useful measure because larger animals generally have larger brains (and larger neocortexes) than smaller animals. Thus researchers make

FIGURE 8.7

Wolfgang Köhler was one of the first scientists to systematically study cognitive abilities in captive chimpanzees. He hung a bunch of bananas out of the chimpanzees' reach and put several wooden crates in the room. Eventually, one individual, named Sultan, managed to stack the crates, clamber onto the precarious tower, and grab the bananas.

(a)

(b)

FIGURE 8.8

Primates sometimes exploit foods that are difficult to extract. Here (a) a male chimpanzee pokes a long twig into a hole in a termite mound and extracts termites, and (b) a capuchin monkey punctures an eggshell and extracts the contents.

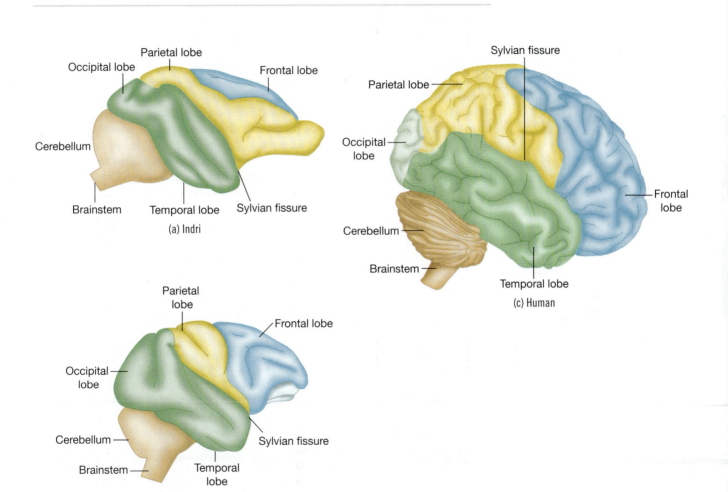

FIGURE 8.9

The brains of (a) an indri, a large strepsirrhine; (b) a macaque; and (c) a human. There are three main components of the brain: the hindbrain, which contains the cerebellum and medulla (part of the brainstem); the midbrain, which contains the optic lobe (not visible here); and the forebrain, which contains the cerebrum. The cerebrum is divided into four main lobes: occipital, parietal, frontal, and temporal. The forebrain is greatly expanded in primates and other mammals, and much of the gray matter (which is made up of cell bodies and synapses) is located on the outside of the cerebrum in a layer called the cerebral cortex. The neocortex is a component of the cerebral cortex, and in mammals the neocortex covers the surface of virtually the entire forebrain.

(a)

(b)

FIGURE 8.10

Chimpanzees use tools to help them obtain certain kinds of foods. (a) This chimpanzee at Gombe Stream National Park in Tanzania is using a long stick to dip for ants. (b) Here a chimpanzee uses a large stone to hammer open hard-shelled nuts.

use of measures that control for these effects. Robin Dunbar, for example, measures the **neocortex ratio**, the ratio between the volume of the neocortex and the volume of the rest of the brain. Dunbar's analyses indicated that animals living in larger groups have larger neocortex ratios than animals living in smaller groups.

There is also evidence that behavioral flexibility and social learning are linked to brain evolution. Reader and Laland surveyed the primate literature for information about three measures of behavioral flexibility: (1) reports of behavioral innovation, which they defined as novel solutions to ecological or social problems; (2) examples of social learning, the acquisition of skills and information from others; and (3) observations of tool use. They demonstrated that these measures of behavioral flexibility are closely linked to the executive brain ratio (the size of the executive brain in relation to the brainstem). Primates with relatively large executive brains are more likely to innovate, learn from others, and use tools than primates with relatively small executive brains. In addition, primates seem to be more flexible in their foraging behavior than in their social behavior. In the long list of examples of innovations and socially learned behaviors that Reader and Laland compiled, foraging innovations predominate. In these comparative analyses, there is no consistent relationship between social learning and group size.

It is important to point out that these two hypotheses are not mutually exclusive. Primates may have derived benefits from being able to cope more effectively with social challenges and from being able to master ecological challenges. Alternatively, cognitive abilities that evolved for one purpose may be applied in other contexts.

Great apes do not fit the social intelligence hypothesis very well.

Great apes have larger brains in relation to their body size than monkeys do, but they live in smaller groups than many monkeys. Although chimpanzees and bonobos may live in communities that include as many as 50 individuals, gorillas live in much smaller groups, and orangutans are largely solitary. This obviously poses a problem for the social intelligence hypothesis.

Richard Byrne points out that great apes make use of more complicated foraging techniques than other primates, enabling them to feed on some foods that other primates cannot process. For example, virtually all plant foods that mountain gorillas rely on are well defended by spines, hard shells, hooks, and stingers. Each of their food items requires a particular routine—a complicated sequence of steps structured in a particular way. Many of the foods that orangutans feed on are also difficult to process.

Great apes sometimes use tools to obtain access to certain foods that are not otherwise available to them. Chimpanzees poke twigs into holes of termite mounds and anthills, use leaves as sponges to mop up water from deep holes, and employ stones as hammers to break open hard-shelled nuts (**Figure 8.10**). Sumatran orangutans use sticks to probe for insects and to pry seeds out of the husks of fruit.

What Do Monkeys Know about One Another?

Although the selective forces that favored the evolution of large brains and slow life histories among primates are not fully understood, it is clear that primates know a lot about the other members of their groups. One of the most striking things about primates is the interest they take in one another. Newborns are greeted and inspected with interest (**Figure 8.11**). Adult females are sniffed and visually inspected regularly during their estrous cycles. When a fight breaks out, other members of the group watch attentively. As we have seen in previous chapters, monkeys know a considerable amount about their own relationships to other group members. A growing body of evidence suggests that monkeys also have some knowledge of the nature of relationships among other individuals, or **third-party relationships**. Monkeys' knowledge of social relationships may enable them to form effective coalitions, compete effectively, and manipulate other group members to their own advantage.

Monkeys and apes know something about kinship relationships among other members of their groups.

One of the first indications that monkeys understand the nature of other individuals' kinship relationships came from a playback experiment on vervet monkeys conducted by Dorothy Cheney and Robert Seyfarth in Kenya's Amboseli National Park. Several female vervets heard a tape-recorded scream of a juvenile vervet piped from a hidden speaker. When the call was played, the mother of the juvenile stared in the direction of the speaker longer than other females did. This response suggests that mothers recognized the call of their own offspring. Even before the mother reacted, however, other females in the vicinity looked directly at the juvenile's mother. This response suggests that other females understood which monkey the juvenile belonged to, and that they were aware that a special relationship existed between the mother and her offspring.

FIGURE 8.11

In many primate species, all group members take an active interest in infants. Here, a female baboon greets a newborn infant. Evidence from playback experiments, laboratory experiments, and naturalistic observations suggests that monkeys know something about the relationships among group members.

FIGURE 8.12

Monkeys may also have broader knowledge of kinship relationships (**Figure 8.12**). The evidence for this claim also comes from Cheney and Seyfarth's work on vervet monkeys. When monkeys are threatened or attacked, they often respond by threatening or attacking a lower-ranking individual who was not involved in the original incident—a phenomenon we call **redirected aggression**. Vervets selectively redirect aggression toward the maternal kin of the original aggressor. So, if female A threatens female B, then B threatens AA, a close relative of A. If monkeys were simply blowing off steam or venting their aggression, they would choose a target at random. Thus the monkeys seem to know that certain individuals are somehow related.

Monkeys probably understand rank relationships among other individuals.

Because kinship and dominance rank are major organizing principles in most primate groups, it makes sense to ask whether monkeys also understand third-party rank relationships. The most direct evidence that monkeys understand third-party rank relationships comes from two playback experiments conducted on a group of baboons in the Okavango Delta of Botswana who have been studied for the last 15 years by Seyfarth, Cheney, and their colleagues. In this group, dominance relationships were stable, and females never responded submissively toward lower-ranking females.

In one experiment that Seyfarth and Cheney designed, females listened to a recording of a female's grunt followed by another female's submissive fear barks. Female baboons responded more strongly when they heard a higher-ranking female responding submissively to a lower-ranking female's grunt than when they heard a lower-ranking female responding submissively to a higher-ranking female's grunt. Thus females were more attentive when they heard a sequence of calls that did not correspond to their knowledge of dominance rank relationships among other females. Control experiments excluded the possibility that females were reacting simply to the fact that they had not heard a particular sequence of calls before. The pattern of responses suggests that females knew the relative ranks of other females in their group and were particularly interested in the anomalous sequence of calls.

In a second experiment, Thore Bergman and Jacinta Beehner collaborated with Seyfath and Cheney to probe the baboons' knowledge of the hierarchical nature of rank relationships in groups with matrilineal dominance ranks. Using the same basic experimental paradigm, researchers played sequences of vocalizations that simulated rank reversals within lineages and rank reversals between lineages. As young female baboons mature, they often rise in rank above their older sisters and other female kin. Thus changes in the relative rank of females in the same lineage are part of the normal course of rank acquisition. However, changes in the relative ranks of unrelated females are much less common. The baboons reacted much more strongly to simulated rank reversals between lineages than to simulated rank reversals within lineages. Again, the researchers were careful to control for confounding variables, such as rank distance and novelty. This result suggests that the females understood the relative ranks of other females and that they understood that changes in rank relationships within lineages are not the same as changes in rank relationships between lineages.

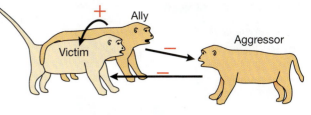

FIGURE 8.13

Complex fitness calculations may be involved in decisions about whether to join a coalition. By helping the victim against the aggressor, the ally increases the fitness of the victim and decreases the fitness of the aggressor.

Participation in coalitions probably draws on sophisticated cognitive abilities.

Even the simplest coalition is a complex interaction. When coalitions are formed, at least three individuals are involved, and several different kinds of interactions are going on simultaneously (**Figure 8.13**). Consider the case in which one monkey (the aggressor) attacks another monkey (the victim). The victim then solicits support from a third party (the ally), and the ally intervenes on behalf of the victim against the aggressor. The ally behaves altruistically toward the victim, giving support to the victim at some potential cost to itself. At the same time, however, the ally behaves aggressively toward the aggressor, imposing harm or energy costs on the aggressor. Thus the ally simultaneously has a positive effect on the victim and a negative effect on the aggressor. Under these circumstances, decisions about whether or not to intervene in a particular dispute may be quite complicated. Consider a female who witnesses a dispute between two of her offspring. Should she intervene? If so, which of her offspring should she support? When a male bonnet macaque is solicited by a higher-ranking male against a male who frequently supports him, how should he respond? In each case, the ally must balance the benefits to the victim, the costs to the opponent, and the costs to itself (**Figure 8.14**).

Given the complexity of even simple coalitions, knowledge of third-party relationships may be valuable because it enables individuals to predict how others will behave. Thus animals who understand the nature of third-party relationships may have a good idea about who will support them and who will intervene against them in confrontations with particular opponents, and they may also be able to tell which of their potential allies are likely to be most effective in coalitions against their opponents.

Susan Perry and her colleagues at the University of California, Los Angeles, have studied capuchin monkeys' use of third-party information in coalitions. Their analysis reveals that capuchins follow three basic rules when they form coalitions: (1) support females against males, (2) support dominants against subordinates, and (3) support close associates against others. If capuchins understand these rules, particularly the last one, they are not expected to recruit support against dominant opponents or from males who have closer relationships with their opponents than with themselves. This is exactly what they do. Their ability to adhere to these rules suggests that they understand the nature of relationships among other group members.

(a)

(b)

FIGURE 8.14

Primates form coalitions that are more complicated than the coalitions of most other animals. (a) In a captive bonnet macaque group, members of opposing factions confront one another. (b) Two capuchins jointly threaten a third individual who is not visible in the picture.

FIGURE 8.15

In Menzel's experiments, a researcher showed a young chimpanzee where food was hidden in the chimp's enclosure, as pictured here. Then the chimpanzee was reunited with the other members of the group, and the group was released inside the enclosure. The young chimpanzee often led the group back to the hidden food, but it also learned to divert the group so that it could get bits of food before others found the cache.

We are beginning to gain insight into what monkeys and apes know about others' minds.

Monkeys and apes seem to be very good at predicting what other animals will do in particular situations. For example, we have seen that vervets groom monkeys who support them in coalitions, female langurs with newborn infants are fearful of new resident males, baboons express surprise when low-ranking animals elicit signs of submission from higher-ranking animals, and capuchins don't try to recruit support from monkeys who have closer bonds to their opponents than to themselves. These examples indicate that monkeys can predict what others will do and adjust their behavior accordingly.

Monkeys' ability to predict what other individuals will do may not seem very remarkable. After all, we know that many animals are very good at learning to make associations between one event and another. In the laboratory, rats, pigeons, monkeys, and many other animals can learn to pull a lever, push a button, or peck a key to obtain food. These are examples of associative learning, the ability to track contingencies between one event and another. Monkeys' ability to predict what others will do in particular situations might be based on sophisticated associative learning capacities, prodigious memory of past events, and perhaps some understanding of conceptual categories like kinship and dominance. On the other hand, it is also possible that monkeys' ability to predict what others will do is based on their knowledge of the mental states of others—what psychologists call a **theory of mind**.

It may seem relatively unimportant whether monkeys and apes rely on associative learning to predict what others will do or whether they have a well-developed theory of mind. However, there may be some things that animals cannot do unless they understand what is going on in other animals' minds. For example, some researchers think that effective deception requires the ability to manipulate or take advantage of others' beliefs about the world. In the 1960s, the late Emil Menzel conducted a landmark set of experiments about chimpanzees' ability to find and communicate about the location of hidden objects (**Figure 8.15**). In a set of experiments, Menzel showed one chimpanzee where a food item was hidden, then released the knowledgeable chimpanzee and his companions into their enclosure. The group quickly learned to follow their knowledgeable companion; but he just as quickly learned that when he led others to the hidden food, he would not get a very big share of it. Menzel noticed that the knowledgeable chimpanzee sometimes led his companions in the wrong direction and then dashed off and grabbed the hidden treasure. How did the knowledgeable chimpanzee work out this tactic? He might have understood that his knowledge differed from the knowledge of other group members and then have come up with a way to take advantage of this discrepancy effectively. If this is what he did, then we would conclude that he had a well-developed theory of mind.

Although some researchers suggest that deception does not rely on a theory of mind, it seems clear that a theory of mind would allow for more complicated and successful deceptions. Similarly, the ability to pretend, empathize, take another's perspective, read minds, console, imitate, and teach relies on knowing what others know or how they feel. Humans do all of these things, but it is not clear whether other primates do.

It is difficult to be sure what nonhuman primates know about the minds of other individuals. However, primatologists have begun to make some progress in this area.

Bryan Hare, now at Duke University, Josep Call, and Michael Tomasello of the Max Planck Institute for Evolutionary Anthropology in Leipzig, Germany, developed a

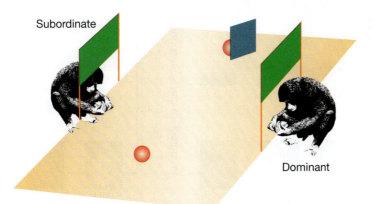

Subordinate

Dominant

FIGURE 8.16

In this experiment, one food item was hidden behind a barrier so that it could be seen by only the subordinate animal, and one food item was in plain sight of the dominant. Subordinates are unlikely to obtain food rewards when dominant animals are present. So if the subordinate knew what the dominant could see, it was expected to head for the item that was hidden from the dominant. This is what the chimpanzees did most of the time.

protocol that evaluates individuals' ability to take advantage of discrepancies between their own knowledge and other individuals' knowledge in a competitive situation. In their experiments, they paired subordinate and dominant chimpanzees in the configuration illustrated in **Figure 8.16**. The experiments take advantage of the fact that subordinates cannot obtain food when dominants are present. Here, two pieces of food are visible to the subordinate, but the dominant can see only one; the other is hidden behind a barrier. Hare and his colleagues predicted that if the subordinate *knew* what the dominant could see, the subordinate would head for the piece of food that the dominant could not see, hoping to consume the hidden food item while the dominant was occupied with the other piece. This is exactly what the subordinate chimpanzees did. So the chimpanzees seemed to understand what other chimpanzees know.

Laurie Santos of Yale University and her colleagues applied the same reasoning in designing experiments with free-ranging rhesus macaques on Cayo Santiago. In these experiments, monkeys were given the chance to "steal" food from two human experimenters. In one experiment, one experimenter was facing toward the monkey, and the other was facing away. The monkeys were more likely to approach the experimenter who was facing away than the experimenter who was facing forward. In other experiments, the monkeys selectively approached experimenters whose faces were pointed away and experimenters whose eyes were averted (**Figure 8.17**). In another

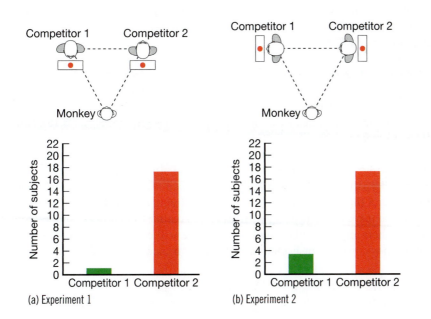

(a) Experiment 1

(b) Experiment 2

FIGURE 8.17

In this set of experiments, monkeys were presented with two human competitors who had food that they could potentially steal. The graphs show that monkeys were much more likely to approach the person who was looking away from them than the person who was facing them, and they were more likely to approach the person who was looking away from the food than the person who was looking toward the food. This suggests that monkeys know what others can and cannot see.

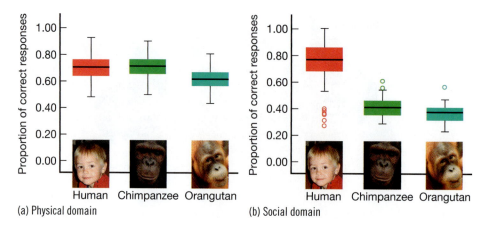

FIGURE 8.18

Children and apes were presented with an identical set of tasks that examined their physical and social cognition. Children and apes showed no differences in tasks based on physical cognition. But children were considerably more successful than apes on tasks that were based on social cognition.

set of experiments, Santos placed food rewards in two transparent boxes covered with bells. In one box, the ringers on the bells were removed, creating one noisy box and one quiet box. The experimenter baited the boxes, shook the boxes to display their auditory qualities, and then walked away and hid his face. The monkeys showed strong preferences for the quiet container, suggesting that they knew what the experimenter could hear. Santos and her colleagues argue that rhesus monkeys have accurate perceptions about what others see and hear in these competitive situations.

Human social cognition is more sophisticated than that of apes.

Although apes and monkeys are able to solve many complex cognitive tasks, there are still substantial differences between the cognitive skills of humans and other primates. These differences are most pronounced in tasks that involve social learning, communication, and knowledge of others' minds. In a comprehensive comparative study of ape cognition, Esther Herrmann and her colleagues from the Max Planck Institute of Evolutionary Anthropology evaluated the performance of 105 two-year-old humans on a battery of cognitive tasks and compared this with the performance of 106 chimpanzees and 32 orangutans of all ages on the same tasks. Some tasks focused on cognition about the physical world, such as tracking a reward after it has been moved or using a tool to retrieve a reward that is out of reach. Other tasks focused on social cognition, such as solving a novel problem after observing the demonstration of a solution or following a gaze to a target. There was little difference in the performance of children and apes on tasks that involved physical cognition (**Figure 8.18**). However, there were greater differences in the social domain. The human children were significantly more successful than the chimpanzees and orangutans on tasks that required social learning, communication, and knowledge of others' minds. Herrmann and her colleagues hypothesize that humans have "evolved some specialized socio-cognitive skills (beyond those of primates in general) for living and exchanging knowledge in cultural groups: communicating with others, learning from others, and 'reading the mind' of others in especially complex ways." We will come back to this idea in Part Four, when we discuss the evolution of the human capacity for culture.

The Value of Studying Primate Behavior

As we come to the end of Part Two, it may be useful to remind you why information about primate behavior and ecology plays an integral role in the story of human evolution. First, humans are primates, and the first members of the human species were probably more similar to living nonhuman primates than to any other animals on Earth. Thus by studying living primates we can learn something about the lives of our ancestors. Second, humans are closely related to primates and similar to them in many ways. If we understand how evolution has shaped the behavior of animals who are so much like ourselves, we may have greater insights about the way evolution has shaped our own behavior and the behavior of our ancestors. Both of these kinds of reasoning will be apparent in Part Three, which covers the history of our own lineage.

Key Terms

social intelligence hypothesis
extracted foods
neocortex
neocortex ratio
third-party relationships
redirected aggression
theory of mind

Study Questions

1. There is a positive correlation between brain size and longevity in animal species. One interpretation of this correlation is that selection for longer life spans was the primary force driving the evolution of large brains. An alternative interpretation is that selection for larger brains was the primary force driving the evolution of longer life spans. Explain which of these interpretations is more likely to be correct and why this is the case.

2. We have argued that natural selection is a powerful engine for generating adaptations. If that is the case, then why do organisms grow old and die? Why can't natural selection design an organism that lives forever?

3. Life history traits tend to be bundled together in particular ways. Explain how these traits are combined and why we see these kinds of combinations in nature.

4. Primates evolved from small-bodied insectivores that were arrayed somewhere along the fast/short end of the life history continuum. What ecological factors are thought to have favored the shifts toward slower/longer life histories in early primates, monkeys, and apes?

5. Primates take a relatively long time to grow up, compared to other animals. Consider the costs and benefits of this life history pattern from the point of view of the growing primate and its mother.

6. What do comparative studies of the size and organization of primate brains tell us about the selective factors that shaped the evolution of primate brains? What are the shortcomings of these kinds of analyses?

7. Monkeys are quite skilled in navigating complicated social situations that they encounter in their everyday lives. They seem to know what others will do in particular situations and are able to respond appropriately. However, monkeys consistently fail theory-of-mind tests in the laboratory. How can we reconcile these two observations?

8. Monkeys seem to have some concept of kinship. What evidence supports this idea? What kind of

variation might you expect to find in monkeys' concepts of kinship within and between species?

9. Suppose that you were studying a group of monkeys and you discovered convincing evidence of empathy or deception. How and why would these data surprise your colleagues?

10. Detailed studies of coalitionary behavior have provided an important source of information about primate cognitive abilities. Explain why coalitions are useful sources of information about social knowledge. What does the pattern of coalitionary support tell us about what monkeys know about other group members?

Further Reading

Byrne, R. W. and A. Whiten, eds. 1988. *Machiavellian Intelligence: Social Expertise and the Evolution of Intellect in Monkeys, Apes, and Humans.* New York: Oxford University Press.

Cheney, D. L. and R. M. Seyfarth. 2007. *Baboon Metaphysics: The Evolution of a Social Mind.* Chicago: University of Chicago Press.

Mitani, J., J. Call, P. Kappeler, R. Palombit, and J. B. Silk, eds. 2012. T*he Evolution of Primate Societies.* Chicago: University of Chicago Press.

Reader, S. M. and K. N. Laland. 2002. "Social Intelligence, Innovation, and Enhanced Brain Size in Primates." *Proceedings of the National Academy of Sciences U.S.A.* 99: 4436–4441.

Whiten, A. W. and R. W. Byrne, eds. 1997. *Machiavellian Intelligence II: Extensions and Evaluations.* New York: Cambridge University Press.

3

PART THREE

THE HISTORY OF THE HUMAN LINEAGE

9

CHAPTER OBJECTIVES

By the end of this chapter you should be able to

- Explain how the major changes in the position of the continents and world climates have influenced the course of primate evolution.

- Understand how paleontologists establish the age of fossils.

- Describe what we know about the earliest members of the primate lineage.

- Identify when and where apelike primates first appear in the fossil record.

- Understand that apes once flourished in the tropical forests of Africa and Asia, but most species became extinct as climates changed.

FROM TREE SHREW TO APE

Continental Drift and Climate Change

The Methods of Paleontology

The Evolution of the Early Primates

The First Haplorrhines

The Emergence of the Hominoids

During the Permian and early Triassic periods (**Table 9.1**), much of the world's fauna was dominated by therapsids, a diverse group of reptiles that possessed traits, such as being warm-blooded and covered with hair (**Figure 9.1**), that linked them to the mammals that evolved later. At the end of the Triassic, most therapsid groups disappeared, and dinosaurs radiated to fill all of the niches for large, terrestrial animals. One therapsid lineage, however, evolved and diversified to become the first true mammals. These early mammals were probably mouse-size, nocturnal creatures that fed mainly on seeds and insects. They had internal fertilization but still laid eggs. By the end of the Mesozoic era, 65 million years ago (mya), placental and marsupial mammals that bore live young had evolved. With the extinction of the dinosaurs at the beginning of the next era (the Cenozoic) came the spectacular radiation of the mammals. All of the modern descendants of this radiation—including horses, bats, whales, elephants, lions, and primates—evolved from creatures that were something like a contemporary shrew (**Figure 9.2**).

TABLE 9.1 The Geological Timescale

Era	Period	Epoch	Period begins (mya)	Notable events
Cenozoic	Quaternary	Recent	0.012	Origins of agriculture and complex societies
		Pleistocene	1.8	Appearance of *Homo sapiens*
	Tertiary	Pliocene	5	Dominance of land by angiosperms, mammals, birds, and insects
		Miocene	23	
		Oligocene	34	
		Eocene	54	
		Paleocene	65	
Mesozoic	Cretaceous		136	Rise of angiosperms, disappearance of dinosaurs, second great radiation of insects
	Jurassic		190	Abundance of dinosaurs, appearance of first birds
	Triassic		225	Appearance of first mammals and dinosaurs
Paleozoic	Permian		280	Great expansion of reptiles, decline of amphibians, last of trilobites
	Carboniferous		345	Age of Amphibians; first reptiles, first great insect radiation
	Devonian		395	Age of Fishes; first amphibians and insects
	Silurian		430	Land invaded by a few arthropods
	Ordovician		500	First vertebrates
	Cambrian		570	Abundance of marine invertebrates
Precambrian				Primitive marine life

To have a complete understanding of human evolution, we need to know how the transition from a shrew-like creature to modern humans took place. Remember that, according to Darwin's theory, complex adaptations are assembled gradually, in many small steps—each step favored by natural selection. Modern humans have many complex adaptations, like grasping hands, **bipedal** locomotion (walking upright on two legs), toolmaking abilities, language, and large-scale cooperation. To understand human evolution fully, we have to consider each of the steps in the lengthy process that transformed a small, solitary, shrewlike insectivore scurrying through the leaf litter of a dark Cretaceous forest into someone more or less like you. Moreover, it is not enough to chronicle the steps in this transition. We also need to understand why each step was favored by natural selection. We want to know, for example, why claws were traded for flat nails, why quadrupedal locomotion gave way to upright bipedal locomotion, and why brains were so greatly enlarged.

In this part of the text, we trace the history of the human lineage. We begin in this chapter by describing the emergence of creatures that resemble modern lemurs and tarsiers, then we document the appearance of animals that look more like modern monkeys, and finally we investigate the origins of animals something like contemporary

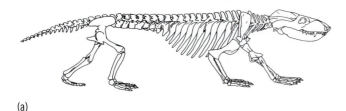
(a)

(b)

FIGURE 9.1

Therapsids dominated the Earth about 250 mya, before dinosaurs became common. The therapsids were reptiles, but they may have been warm-blooded and they had hair instead of scales. The therapsid *Thrinaxodon*, whose (a) skeleton and (b) reconstruction are shown here, was about 30 cm (12 in.) long and had teeth suited for a broad carnivorous diet.

apes. In later chapters, we recount the transformation from hominoid to hominin. We will introduce the first members of the human tribe, Hominini; and then the first members of our own genus, *Homo*; and finally the first known representatives of our own species, *Homo sapiens*. We know something about each step in this process, although far more is known about recent periods than about periods in the most distant past. We will see, however, that there is still a great deal left to be discovered and understood.

Continental Drift and Climate Change

To understand the evolution of our species, it is important to understand the geological, climatic, and biological conditions under which these evolutionary changes occurred.

When we think about the evolution of modern humans, we usually picture early humans wandering over open grasslands dotted with acacia trees—the same breathtaking scenery that we see in African wildlife documentaries. As we shift the time frame forward through millions of years, the creatures are altered but the backdrop is unchanged. This image is misleading, however, because the scenery has changed along with the cast of characters (**Figure 9.3**).

It is important to keep this fact in mind because it changes our interpretation of the fossil record. Remember that evolution produces adaptation, but what is adaptive in one environment may not be adaptive in another. If the environment remained the same over the course of human evolution, then the kinds of evolutionary changes observed in the hominin fossil record (such as increases in brain size, bipedalism, and prolonged juvenile dependence) would have to be seen as steady improvements in the perfection of human adaptations: evolution would progress toward a fixed goal. But if the environment varied through time, then evolution would have to track a moving target. In this scenario, new characteristics seen in fossils would not have to represent progress in a single direction. Instead,

FIGURE 9.2

The first mammals probably resembled the modern-day Belanger's tree shrew.

FIGURE 9.3

Today, East African savannas look much like this. In the past, the scenery is likely to have been quite different.

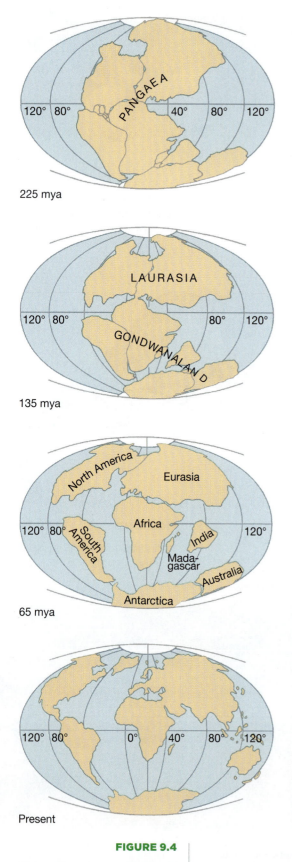

225 mya

135 mya

65 mya

Present

FIGURE 9.4

The arrangement of the continents has changed considerably over the last 180 million years.

these changes might have been adaptations to changing environmental conditions. As we will see, the world has become much colder and drier in the last 20 million years and has been extremely variable in the last 800,000 years, and these changes likely altered the course of human evolution. If the world had become warmer rather than colder during this period, then our human ancestors would probably have remained in the safety of the trees and would not have become terrestrial or bipedal. We would probably be stellar rock climbers but poor marathon runners.

The positions of the continents have changed relative to each other and to the poles.

The world has changed a lot in the last 200 million years. One of the factors that has contributed to this change is the movement of the continents, or **continental drift**. The continents are not fixed in place; instead, the enormous, relatively light plates of rock that make up the continents slowly wander around the globe, floating on the denser rock that forms the floor of the deep ocean. About 200 mya, all of the land making up the present-day continents was joined together in a single, huge landmass called **Pangaea**. About 150 mya, Pangaea began to break apart into separate pieces (**Figure 9.4**). The northern half, called **Laurasia**, included what is now North America and Eurasia minus India; the southern half, **Gondwanaland**, was composed of the rest. By the time the dinosaurs became extinct 65 mya, Gondwanaland had broken up into several smaller pieces. Africa and India separated, and India headed north, eventually crashing into Eurasia, while the remainder of Gondwanaland stayed in the south. Eventually, Gondwanaland separated into South America, Antarctica, and Australia, and these continents remained isolated from each other for many millions of years. South America did not drift north to join North America until about 5 mya.

Continental drift is important to the history of the human lineage for two reasons. First, oceans serve as barriers that isolate certain species from others, so the position of the continents plays an important role in the evolution of species. As we will see, the long isolation of South America creates one of the biggest puzzles in our knowledge of primate evolution. Second, continental drift is one of the engines of climate change, and climate change has fundamentally influenced human evolution.

The climate has changed substantially during the last 65 million years—first becoming warmer and less variable, then cooling, and finally fluctuating widely in temperature.

The size and orientation of the continents have important effects on climate. Very large continents tend to have severe weather. This is why Chicago has much colder winters than London, even though London is much farther north. Pangaea was much larger than Asia and is likely to have had very cold weather in winter. When continents restrict the circulation of water from the tropics to the poles, world climates seem to become cooler. These changes, along with other poorly understood factors, have led to substantial climate change. **Figure 9.5** summarizes changes in global temperature during the Cenozoic era. Closer Look 9.1 explains how climatologists reconstruct ancient climates.

To give you some idea what these changes in temperature mean, consider that during the period of peak warmth in the early Miocene, palm trees grew as far north as what is now Alaska, rich temperate

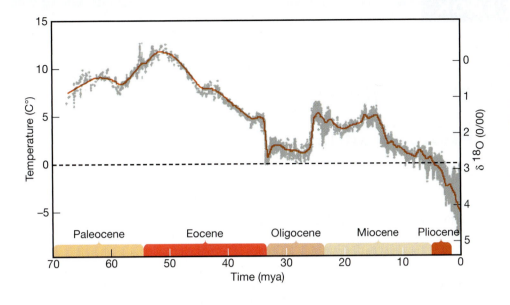

FIGURE 9.5

The gray points are estimates of average world temperature based on the ratio of ^{16}O to ^{18}O taken from deep-sea cores. The red line plots a statistically smoothed average value. The variability around the line represents both measurement error and rapid temperature fluctuations that last less than a million years. As we will see (Figure 12.4), the increase in variability in the last several million years has been the result of fluctuations in world temperature, some lasting only a few centuries.

forests (like those in the eastern United States today) extended as far north as Oslo, Norway, and only the tallest peaks in Antarctica were glaciated.

The Methods of Paleontology

Much of our knowledge of the history of life comes from the study of fossils, the mineralized bones of dead organisms.

In certain kinds of geological settings, the bones of dead organisms may be preserved long enough for the organic material in the bones to be replaced by minerals (**mineralized**) from the surrounding rock. Such natural copies of bones are called **fossils**. Scientists who recover, describe, and interpret fossil remains are called **paleontologists**.

A great deal of what we know about the history of the human lineage comes from the study of fossils. Careful study of the shapes of different bones tells us what early hominins were like—how big they were, what they ate, where they lived, how they moved, and even something about how they lived. When the methods of systematics described in Chapter 4 are applied to these materials, they also can tell us something about the phylogenetic history of long-extinct creatures. The kinds of plant and animal fossils found in association with the fossils of our ancestors tell us what the environment was like—whether it was forested or open, how much it rained, and whether rainfall was seasonal.

There are several radiometric methods for estimating the age of fossils.

To assign a fossil to a particular position in a phylogeny, we must know how old it is. As we will see in later chapters, the date that we assign to particular specimens can profoundly influence our understanding of the evolutionary history of certain lineages or traits.

Radiometric methods provide one of the most important ways to date fossils. To understand how radiometric techniques work, we need to review a little chemistry. All of the atoms of a particular element have the same number of protons in their nucleus. For example, all carbon atoms have six protons. However, different **isotopes** of a particular element have different numbers of neutrons in their nucleus. Carbon-12, the most common isotope of carbon, has six neutrons, and carbon-14 has eight. Radiometric

9.1 Using Deep-Sea Cores to Reconstruct Ancient Climates

Beginning about 50 years ago, oceanographers launched a program of extracting long cores from the sediments that lie on the floor of the deep sea (about 6,000 m, or 20,000 ft., below the surface). Data from these cores have allowed scientists to make much more detailed and accurate reconstructions of ancient climates. Figure 9.5 shows the ratio of two isotopes of oxygen, ^{16}O and ^{18}O, derived from different layers of a deep-sea core. Because different layers of the cores were deposited at different times over the last 65 million years and have remained nearly undisturbed ever since, they give us a snapshot of the relative amounts of ^{16}O and ^{18}O in the sea when the layer was deposited on the ocean floor.

The ratio of ^{16}O to ^{18}O allows us to estimate ocean temperatures in the past. Water molecules containing the lighter isotope of oxygen, ^{16}O, evaporate more readily than molecules containing the heavier isotope, ^{18}O. Snow and rain have a higher concentration of ^{16}O than the sea does because the water in clouds evaporates from the sea. When the world is warm enough that few glaciers form at high latitudes, the precipitation that falls on the land returns to the sea, and the ratio of the two isotopes of oxygen remains unchanged (**Figure 9.6a**). When the world is colder, however, much of the snow falling at high latitudes is stored in immense continental glaciers like those now covering Antarctica (**Figure 9.6b**). Because the water locked in glaciers contains more ^{16}O than the ocean does, the proportion of ^{18}O in the ocean increases. Therefore, the concentration of ^{18}O in seawater increases when the world is cold and decreases when it is warm. This means that scientists can estimate the temperature of the oceans in the past by measuring the ratio of ^{16}O to ^{18}O in different layers of deep-sea cores.

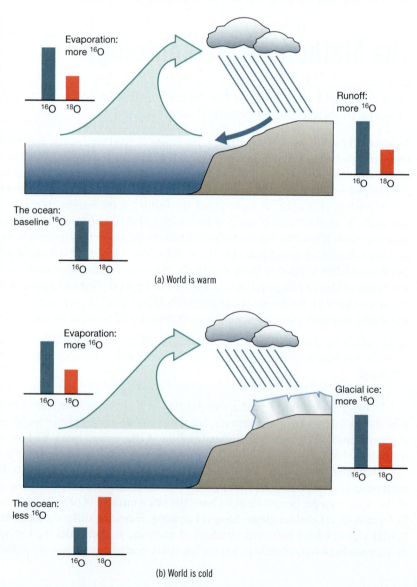

FIGURE 9.6

Because water evaporating from the sea is enriched in ^{16}O, so is precipitation. (a) When the world is warm, this water returns rapidly to the sea, and the concentration of ^{16}O in seawater is unchanged. (b) When the world is cold, much precipitation remains on land as glacial ice, and so the sea becomes depleted in ^{16}O.

Evaporation: more ^{16}O

Runoff: more ^{16}O

The ocean: baseline ^{16}O

(a) World is warm

Evaporation: more ^{16}O

Glacial ice: more ^{16}O

The ocean: less ^{16}O

(b) World is cold

methods are based on the fact that the isotopes of certain elements are unstable. This means they change spontaneously from one isotope to another of the same element or to an entirely different element. For example, carbon-14 changes to nitrogen-14, and potassium-40 changes spontaneously to argon-40. For any particular isotope, such changes (or **radioactive decay**) occur at a constant, clocklike rate that can be measured with precision in the laboratory. There are several different radiometric methods:

1. **Potassium–argon dating** is used to date the age of volcanic rocks found in association with fossil material. Molten rock emerges from a volcano at a very high temperature. As a result, all of the argon gas is boiled out of the rock. After this, any argon present in the rock must be due to the decay of potassium. Because this occurs at a known and constant rate, the ratio of potassium to argon can be used to date volcanic rock. Then, if a fossil is discovered in a geological **stratum** ("layer"; plural *strata*) lying under the stratum that contains the volcanic rock, paleontologists can be confident that the fossil is older than the rock. A new variant of this technique, which is called **argon–argon dating** because the potassium in the sample is converted to an isotope of argon before it is measured, allows more accurate dating of single rock crystals.

2. **Carbon-14 dating** (or **radiocarbon dating**) is based on an unstable isotope of carbon that living animals and plants incorporate into their cells. As long as the organism is alive, the ratio of the unstable isotope (carbon-14) to the stable isotope (carbon-12) is the same as the ratio of the two isotopes in the atmosphere. Once the animal dies, carbon-14 starts to decay into nitrogen-14 at a constant rate. By measuring the ratio of these elements, paleontologists can estimate the amount of time that has passed since the organism died.

3. **Thermoluminescence dating** is based on an effect of high-energy nuclear particles traveling through rock. These particles come from the decay of radioactive material in and around the rock and from cosmic rays that bombard the earth from outer space. When they pass through rock, these particles dislodge electrons from atoms, so the electrons become trapped elsewhere in the rock's crystal lattice. Heating a rock relaxes the bonds holding the atoms in the crystal lattice together. All of the trapped electrons are then recaptured by their respective atoms—a process that gives off light. Researchers often find flints at archaeological sites that were burned in ancient campfires. It is possible to estimate the number of trapped electrons in these flints by heating them in the laboratory and measuring the amount of light given off. If the density of high-energy particles currently flowing through the site is also known, scientists can estimate the length of time that has elapsed since the flint was burned.

4. **Electron-spin-resonance dating** is used to determine the age of **apatite crystals**, an inorganic component of tooth enamel, according to the presence of trapped electrons. Apatite crystals form as teeth grow, and initially they contain no trapped electrons. These crystals are preserved in fossil teeth and, like the burned flints, are bombarded by a flow of high-energy particles that generate trapped electrons in the crystal lattice. Scientists estimate the number of trapped electrons by subjecting the teeth to a variable magnetic field—a technique called "electron spin resonance." To estimate the number of years since the tooth was formed, paleontologists must once again measure the flow of radiation at the site where the tooth was found.

5. **Uranium-lead dating** has long been used by geologists to date zirconium crystals found in igneous rocks. It is based on the fact that uranium decay produces a series of unstable elements but eventually yields a stable isotope of lead. By measuring the ratio of uranium to lead, the date of the formation of the crystal can be estimated. It is possible to use this method to date speleothems—stalactites, stalagmites, and flow stone formed by precipitation in limestone caves. This technology is used to date hominin sites in South Africa that lack the volcanic rocks necessary for potassium-argon methods.

Different radiometric techniques are used for different time periods. Methods based on isotopes that decay very slowly, such as potassium-40, work well for fossils from the distant past. However, they are not useful for more recent fossils, because their "clock" doesn't run fast enough. When slow clocks are used to date recent events, large errors can result. For this reason, potassium–argon dating usually cannot be used to date samples less than about 500,000 years old. Conversely, isotopes that decay quickly, such as carbon-14, are useful only for recent periods because all of the unstable isotopes decay in a relatively short period of time. Thus carbon-14 can be used only to date sites that are less than about 40,000 years old. The development of thermoluminescence dating and electron-spin-resonance dating is important because these methods allow us to date sites that are too old for carbon-14 dating but too young for potassium–argon dating.

Absolute radiometric dating is supplemented by relative dating methods based on magnetic reversals and comparison with other fossil assemblages.

Radiometric dating methods are problematic for two reasons. First, a particular site may not always contain material that is appropriate for radiometric dating. Second, radiometric methods have relatively large margins for error. These drawbacks have led scientists to supplement such absolute methods with other, relative methods for dating fossil sites.

One such relative method is based on the remarkable fact that, every once in a while, the earth's magnetic field reverses itself. This means, for example, that compasses now pointing north would at various times in the past have pointed south (if compasses had been around then, that is). The pattern of magnetic reversals is not the same throughout time, so for any given time period the pattern is unique. But the pattern for a given time *is* the same throughout the world. We know what the pattern is because when certain rocks are formed, they record the direction of the earth's magnetic field at that time. Thus by matching up the pattern of magnetic reversals at a particular site with the well-dated sequence of reversals from the rest of the world, scientists are able to date sites.

Another approach is to make use of the fact that sometimes fossils of interest are found in association with fossils of other organisms that existed for only a limited period of time. For example, during the last 20 million years or so there has been a sequence of distinct pig species in East Africa. Each pig species lived for a known period of time (according to securely dated sites). This means that some East African materials can be accurately dated from their association with fossilized pig teeth.

The Evolution of the Early Primates

The evolution of flowering plants created a new set of ecological niches. Primates were among the animals that evolved to fill these niches.

During the first two-thirds of the Mesozoic, the forests of the world were dominated by the **gymnosperms**, trees like contemporary redwood, pine, and fir. With the breakup of Pangaea during the Cretaceous, a revolution in the plant world occurred. Flowering plants, called **angiosperms**, appeared and spread. The evolution of the angiosperms created a new set of ecological niches for animals. Many angiosperms depend on animals to pollinate them, and they produce showy flowers with sugary nectar to attract pollinators. Some angiosperms also entice animals to disperse their seeds by providing nutritious and easily digestible fruits. Arboreal animals that could find, manipulate, chew, and digest these fruits could exploit these new niches. Primates were one of the taxonomic groups that evolved to take advantage of these opportunities. Tropical birds, bats, insects, and some small rodentlike animals probably competed with early primates for the bounty of the angiosperms.

The ancestors of modern primates were small-bodied nocturnal quadrupeds much like contemporary shrews.

To understand the evolutionary forces that shaped the early radiation of the primates, we need to consider two related questions. First, what kind of animal did natural selection have to work with? Second, what were the selective pressures that favored this suite of traits in ancient primates? Answers to the first question come from the fossil record. Answers to the second question come from comparative studies of living primates.

The **plesiadapiforms**, a group of fossil animals found in what is now Montana, Colorado, New Mexico, and Wyoming, give us some clue about what the earliest primates were like. Plesiadapiforms are found at sites that date from the Paleocene epoch, 65 to 54 mya, a time so warm and wet that broadleaf evergreen forests extended to 60°N (near present-day Anchorage, Alaska). The plesiadapiforms varied from tiny, shrew-size creatures to animals as big as marmots (**Figure 9.7**). It seems likely that they were solitary quadrupeds with a well-developed sense of smell. The teeth of these

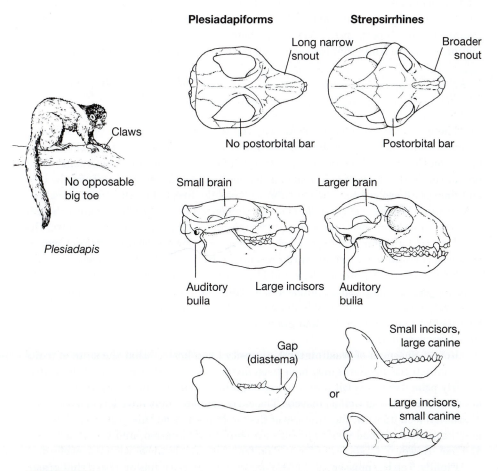

Plesiadapis

FIGURE 9.7

Plesiadapiforms were once thought to be primates, but closer analysis indicates they lack many of the defining characteristics of early modern primates. For example, they had claws instead of nails; their eye orbits were not fully encased in bone; their eyes were placed on the sides of the head, so the fields of vision of the two eyes did not converge; and in some species, the big toe was not opposable.

FIGURE 9.8

An artist's reconstruction of the plesiadapiform *Carpolestes simpsoni*. This creature, which lived about 56 mya, had grasping hands and feet.

animals are quite variable, suggesting that they had a wide range of dietary specializations. Some members of this group were probably terrestrial, some were arboreal quadrupeds, and others may have been adapted for gliding. Most of the plesiadapiforms had claws on their hands and feet, and they did not have binocular vision.

The discovery of a 56-million-year-old plesiadapiform by Jonathan Bloch of the Florida Museum of Natural History and Doug Boyer of Duke University provides important clues about primate origins. *Carpolestes simpsoni* (**Figure 9.8**) had an opposable big toe with a flat nail, but claws on its other digits. The claws on its feet and hands probably helped it climb large-diameter tree trunks, but it was also able to grasp small supports. *C. simpsoni* had low-crowned molars, which are suited for eating fruit. Its eyes were on the sides of the head, and the fields of vision did not overlap. These creatures probably used their hands and feet to grasp small branches as they climbed around in the terminal branches of fruiting trees and used their hands to handle fruit as they were feeding.

Experts disagree about whether plesiadapiforms ought to be included within the Primate order. They possess some but not all of the suite of traits that characterize modern primates, and the decision about how to classify these creatures depends on a relatively arbitrary assessment of how similar they are to other primates. The plesiadapiforms are important to know about, however, because they provide some information about the traits that characterized the common ancestor of modern primates.

The discovery of C. simpsoni helps explain why natural selection favored the basic features of primate morphology.

There are several theories about why the traits that are diagnostic of primates evolved in early members of the Primate order. Matt Cartmill, an anthropologist now at Boston University, has argued that forward-facing eyes (orbital convergence) that provide binocular stereoscopic vision, grasping hands and feet, and nails on the toes and fingers all evolved together to enhance visually directed predation on insects in the terminal branches of trees. This idea is supported by the fact that many arboreal predators, including owls and ocelots, have eyes in the front of the head. However, the discovery that grasping hands and feet evolved in a frugivorous plesiadapiform species before the eyes were shifted forward presents problems for this hypothesis.

Fred Szalay of Hunter College and Marian Dagosto of Northwestern University have suggested that grasping hands and feet and flat nails on the fingers and toes all coevolved to facilitate a form of leaping locomotion. *C. simpsoni* also poses a problem for this hypothesis because it had grasping hands and feet but evidently didn't leap from branch to branch.

Robert Sussman of Washington University hypothesized that the suite of traits that characterize primates may have been favored because they enhanced the ability of early primates to exploit a new array of plant resources—including fruit, nectar, flowers, and gum—as well as insects. The early primates may have foraged and handled small food items in the dimness of the forest night, and this nocturnal behavior may have favored good vision, precise eye–hand coordination, and grasping hands and feet. However, *C. simpsoni* foraged on fruit before orbital convergence evolved.

Finally, Tab Rasmussen, also of Washington University, has proposed that grasping hands and feet allowed early primates to forage on fruit, flowers, and nectar in the terminal branches of angiosperms. Later, the eyes were shifted forward to facilitate visually directed predation on insects. The idea that the evolution of grasping hands and feet preceded the movement of the eyes to the front of the face fits with the evidence from *C. simpsoni*.

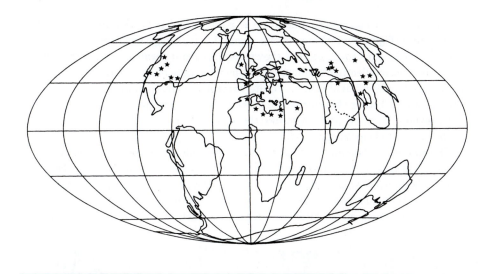

FIGURE 9.9

Sites where Eocene prosimian fossils have been found. The continents are arranged as they were during the early Eocene.

Primates with modern features appeared in the Eocene epoch.

The Eocene epoch (54 to 34 mya) was even wetter and warmer than the preceding Paleocene, with great tropical forests covering much of the globe. At the beginning of the Eocene, North America and Europe were connected, but then the two continents separated and grew farther apart. The animals within these continents evolved in isolation and became progressively more different. There was some contact between Europe and Asia and between India and Asia during this period, but South America was completely isolated. Primate fossils from this period have been found in North America, Europe, Asia, and Africa (**Figure 9.9**). More than 200 species of fossil strep-sirrhines have now been identified. The Eocene primates were a highly successful and diverse group, occupying a range of ecological niches.

It is in these Eocene primates that we see at least the beginnings of all the features that define modern primates (see Chapter 5). They had grasping hands and feet with nails instead of claws, hind limb–dominated posture, shorter snouts, eyes moved forward in the head and encased in a bony orbit, and relatively large brains.

The Eocene primates are classified into two families: Omomyidae and Adapidae (**Figure 9.10**). Although their phylogenetic affinities to modern primates are not known,

FIGURE 9.10

Adapids were larger than omomyids, and they had longer snouts and smaller orbits than the omomyids had. (a) The size of the orbits suggests that the adapids were active during the day, and the shape of their teeth suggests that they fed on fruit or leaves.
(b) Omomyids were small primates that fed mainly on insects, fruit, or gum. The large orbits suggest that they may have been nocturnal. They are similar in some ways to modern tarsiers.

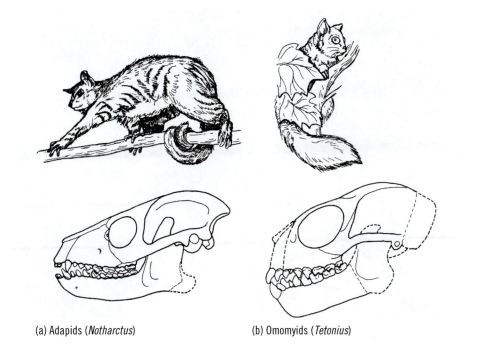

(a) Adapids (*Notharctus*)   (b) Omomyids (*Tetonius*)

most researchers compare the omomyids to galagos and tarsiers and the adapids to living lemurs (**Figure 9.11**). Some of the omomyids had huge eye orbits, like modern tarsiers. This feature suggests that they were nocturnal because nocturnal primates that do not have a reflecting **tapetum**, such as owl monkeys and tarsiers, have extremely large orbits. Omomyid dentition was quite variable: Some seem to have been adapted for frugivory, and others for more insectivorous diets. Some omomyids have elongated calcaneus bones in their feet, much like those of modern dwarf lemurs, and they may have been able to leap from branch to branch.

The adapids had smaller eye orbits and were likely diurnal. They resemble living lemurs in many aspects of their teeth, skull, nasal, and auditory regions. However, the adapids do not display some of the unique derived traits that are characteristic of modern lemurs, such as the toothcomb, a specialized formation of incisors used for grooming. They had a range of dietary adaptations, including insectivorous, folivorous,

FIGURE 9.11

The behavior of adapids and omomyids likely differed. (a) Adapids were probably diurnal. Here a group forages for leaves. (b) Omomyids were probably nocturnal. Several species are shown here.

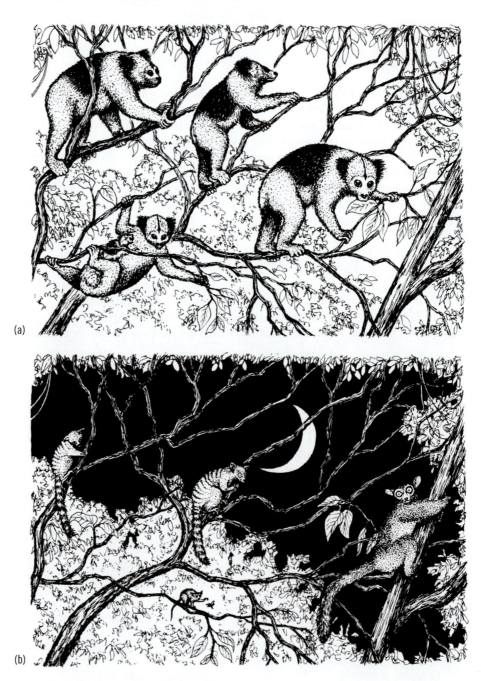

(a)

(b)

and frugivorous diets. They were generally larger than the omomyids, and their **postcranial** bones (the bones that make up the skeleton below the neck) indicate that some were active arboreal quadrupeds like modern lemurs, while others were slow quadrupeds similar to contemporary lorises. At least one species showed substantial sexual dimorphism, a feature that points to life in nonpair-bonded social groups.

One spectacular Eocene primate specimen, *Darwinius masillae*, was introduced to the world with great fanfare in 2009. The fossil, nicknamed Ida, was discovered at a well-known fossil site near Frankfurt, Germany, and dated to 47 mya. As you can see in **Figure 9.12**, Ida is so well preserved that you can see the outline of her furry body and the contents of her last meal in her stomach cavity. Ida was originally billed as a "missing link," the earliest ancestor of modern monkeys and apes because she lacked some of the derived features of modern lemurs, including the toothcomb. However, most scientists now consider Ida to be an adapid.

The First Haplorrhines

During the Oligocene epoch, many parts of the world became colder and drier.

By the end of the Eocene epoch, 34 mya, the continents were more or less positioned on the globe as they are today. However, South America and North America were not yet connected by Central America; Africa and Arabia were separated from Eurasia by the Tethys Sea, a body of water that connected the Mediterranean Sea and the Persian Gulf. South America and Australia had completed their separation from Antarctica, creating deep, cold currents around Antarctica (see Figure 9.4). Some climatologists believe that these cold currents reduced the transfer of heat from the equator to Antarctic regions and may have been responsible for the major drop in global temperatures that occurred during this period. During the Oligocene epoch, 34 to 23 mya, temperatures dropped, and the range in temperature variation over the course of the year increased. Throughout North America and Europe, tropical broad-leaf evergreen forests were replaced by broadleaf deciduous forests. Africa and South America remained mainly warm and tropical.

Primates similar to modern monkeys may have first evolved during the Eocene, but they radiated during the Oligocene.

The origins of the haplorrhines may extend back into the Eocene epoch. *Algeripithecus minutus,* known from fragmentary fossils in North Africa, possessed some cranial features that we find in modern haplorrhines, but it was otherwise quite primitive. These finds are dated to about 50 mya. *Eosimias,* a tiny primate with small incisors, large canines, and broad premolars, lived in southern China during the middle of the Eocene epoch.

The earliest unambiguous haplorrhine fossils are found at a site in the Fayum (also spelled "Faiyûm") Depression of Egypt. The Fayum deposits straddle the Eocene–Oligocene boundary, 36 to 33 mya. The Fayum is now one of the driest places on Earth, but it was very different at the beginning of the Oligocene. Sediments of soil recovered from the Fayum tell us that it was a warm, wet, and somewhat seasonal habitat then.

FIGURE 9.12

An Eocene primate specimen, *Darwinius masillae*, named Ida, was discovered in Germany in 2009 and dated to 47 mya.

FIGURE 9.13

Although the Fayum Depression is now a desert, it was a swampy forest during the Oligocene.

FIGURE 9.14

The Fayum was home to a diverse group of primates, including propliopithecids like *Aegyptopithecus zeuxis* (upper left) and *Propliopithecus chirobates* (upper right), and parapithecids like *Apidium phiomense* (bottom).

The plants were most like those now found in the tropical forests of Southeast Asia. The soil sediments contain the remnants of the roots of plants that grow in swampy areas, like mangroves, and the sediments suggest that there were periods of standing water at the site. There are also many fossils of waterbirds. All this suggests that the Fayum was a swamp during the Oligocene (**Figure 9.13**). Among the mammalian fauna at the Fayum are representatives of the suborder that includes porcupines and guinea pigs, opossums, insectivores, bats, primitive carnivores, and an archaic member of the hippopotamus family.

The Fayum contains one of the most diverse primate communities ever documented. This community included at least five groups of strepsirrhines, one group of omomyids, and three groups of haplorrhine primates: the oligopithecids, parapithecids, and propliopithecids (**Figure 9.14**). To introduce a theme that will become familiar in the chapters that follow, the more that paleontologists learn about early primates from the Fayum, the more complicated the primate family tree becomes. Instead of a neat tree with a few heavy branches that connect ancient fossils with living species, we have a messy bush with many fine branches and only the most tenuous connections between most living and extinct forms. Nevertheless, we can detect certain trends in the primate fossil record at the Fayum that provide insight about the selective pressures that shaped adaptation within the primate lineage.

The parapithecids were a very diverse group; currently they are divided into four genera and eight species. The largest parapithecids were the size of guenons (3 kg, or about 6.5 lb.) and the smallest were the size of marmosets (150 g, or about 5 oz.). These creatures have the primitive dental formula 2.1.3.3/2.1.3.3, which has been retained in New World monkeys but has been modified in Old World monkeys and apes, whose dental formula is 2.1.2.3/2.1.2.3. (Dental formulas were discussed in Chapter 5.) Many aspects of parapithecid teeth and postcranial anatomy are also primitive, suggesting that they may have been the unspecialized ancestors both of more derived Old World monkey lineages and of the New World monkeys (see Closer Look 9.2).

The propliopithecids are represented by two genera and five species. These primates had the same dental formula as modern Old World monkeys and apes, but they lack other derived features associated with Old World monkeys. The largest and most famous of the propliopithecids is named *Aegyptopithecus zeuxis,* who is known from several skulls and a number of postcranial bones (**Figure 9.16**, p. 226). *A. zeuxis* was a medium-size monkey, perhaps as big as a female howler monkey (6 kg, or 13.2 lb.). It was a diurnal, arboreal quadruped with a relatively small brain. The shape and size of the teeth suggest that it ate mainly fruit. Males were much larger than females, indicating that they probably did not live in pair-bonded groups. Other propliopithecids were smaller than *A. zeuxis,* but their teeth suggest that they also ate fruit, as well as seeds and perhaps gum. They too were probably arboreal quadrupeds with strong, grasping feet. Modern Old World monkeys and apes may have been derived from members of this family.

The third group of Fayum haplorrhines, the oligopithecids, were among the earliest Fayum monkeys. The oligopithecids,

9.2 Facts That Teeth Can Reveal

Much of what we know about the long-dead early primates comes from their teeth. Fortunately, teeth are more durable than other bones, and they are also the most common elements in the fossil record. If paleontologists had to choose only one part of the skeleton to study, most would choose teeth. There are several reasons for this choice. First, teeth are complex structures with many independent features, which makes them very useful for phylogenetic reconstruction. Second, tooth enamel is not remodeled during an animal's life, and it carries an indelible record of an individual's life history. Third, teeth show a precise developmental sequence that allows paleontologists to make inferences about the growth and development of long-dead organisms. Finally, as we saw in Chapter 5, each of the major dietary specializations (frugivory, folivory, insectivory) is associated with characteristic dental features.

Figure 9.15 shows one side of the upper jaw of three modern species of primates: an insectivore, a folivore, and a frugivore. The insectivorous tarsier (**Figure 9.15a**) has relatively large, sharp incisors and canines, which are used to bite through the tough external skeletons of insects. In contrast, the folivorous indri (**Figure 9.15b**) has relatively small incisors, and large premolars with sharp crests that allow it to shred tough leaves. Finally, the frugivorous mangabey (**Figure 9.15c**) has large incisors that are used to peel the rinds from fruit. Its molars are small because the soft, nutritious parts of fruit require less grinding than leaves do.

Knowing what an animal eats enables researchers to make sensible guesses about other characteristics as well. For example, there is a good correlation between diet and body size in living primates: insectivores are generally smaller than frugivores, and frugivores are generally smaller than folivores.

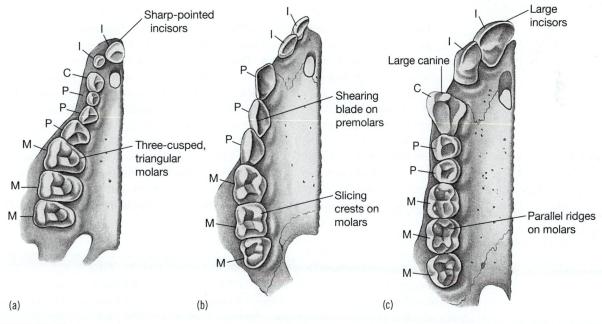

FIGURE 9.15

The right half of the upper jaws of (a) a tarsier, an insectivore; (b) an indri, a folivore; and (c) a mangabey, a frugivore. I = incisor, C = canine, P = premolar, M = molar.

FIGURE 9.16

In this reconstruction of the skeleton of *Aegyptopithecus*, the postcranial bones that have been found are shown in red.

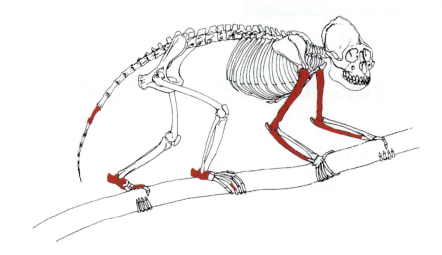

who may have ranged beyond the Fayum through North Africa and the Arabian Peninsula, share many primitive features with the Eocene strepsirrhines. However, they also share some derived features with contemporary haplorrhines. For example, the orbits are fully enclosed in bone. The dental formula of some oligopithecids was the same as that of modern Old World monkeys and apes. It is not clear whether the reductions in the number of premolars in oligopithecids and propliopithecids represent independent evolutionary events or common ancestry.

Primates appear in South America for the first time during the Oligocene, but it is unclear where they came from or how they got there.

The earliest New World monkey fossils come from a late Oligocene site in Bolivia. The monkeys at this site have three premolars like modern New World monkeys and were about the size of owl monkeys. The shape of their molars suggests they were frugivores. Sites in Argentina and Chile contain a number of monkey genera dating to the early and middle Miocene. They were part of a diverse animal population that included rodents, ungulates, sloths, and marsupial mammals. Most of these Patagonian primates were about the size of squirrel monkeys (800 g, or 1.8 lb.), though some may have been as large as sakis (3 kg, or 6.6 lb.). In Colombia, Miocene sites dated to 12 to 10 mya contain nearly a dozen species of fossil primates. Many of these species closely resemble modern New World monkeys (**Figure 9.17**). Pleistocene sites in Brazil and the Caribbean islands have yielded a mixture of extinct and extant species. Evidently, several species were considerably larger than any living New World primates. Although there are no indigenous primates in the Caribbean now, these islands once housed a diverse community of primates.

The origin of New World primates is a mystery. It is not clear how monkeys got to South America or how they found their way to the islands of the Caribbean. The absence of Oligocene primate fossils in North America and the many similarities between New World monkeys and the Fayum primates suggest to many scientists that the ancestor of the New World monkeys came from Africa. The problem with this idea is that we don't know how they could have gotten from Africa to South America. By the late Oligocene, the two continents were separated by at least 3,000 km (about 2,000 miles) of open ocean. Some authors have suggested that primates could have rafted across the sea on islands of floating vegetation. Although there are no well-documented examples of primates rafting such distances, fossil rodents appear in South America about the same time and are so similar to those found in Africa that it seems very likely that rodents managed to raft across the Atlantic.

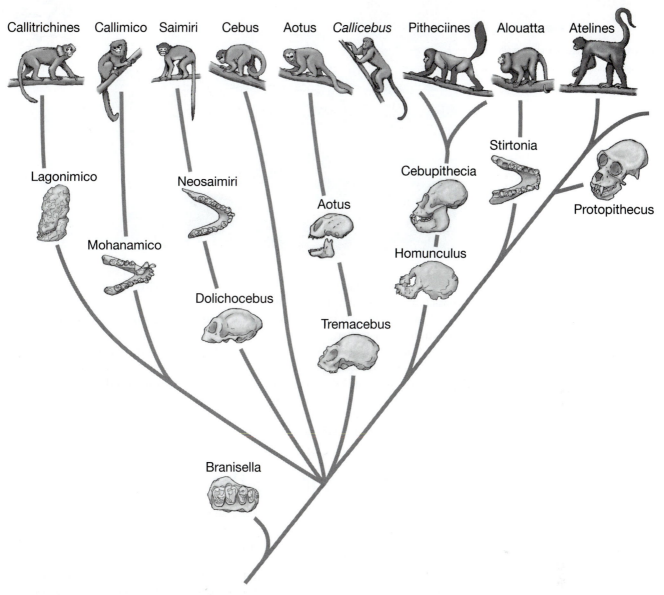

FIGURE 9.17

A considerable amount of new New World fossil evidence has been discovered. A number of species bear close resemblances to modern primate species. There were once many more species of primates than we find in the same areas today.

Other researchers suggest that New World monkeys are descended from a North American primate. But there are two problems with this hypothesis. One is that although there is evidence of Eurasian *strepsirrhines* reaching North America earlier (during the Eocene), there are no known *haplorrhine* fossils from North America—for any time period. If we assume that an early haplorrhine reached North America at about the same time, then the extensive similarities between Old World and New World monkeys could be readily explained. Otherwise we would have to reach the improbable conclusion that New World monkeys are descended from a strepsirrhine ancestor and that the many similarities between New World and Old World monkeys are due to convergence.

The second difficulty with this hypothesis is geographic. Because North America did not join South America until 5 mya, this scenario also requires the haplorrhine ancestor to have made an ocean voyage, though it may have been possible to break

FIGURE 9.18

Perhaps this is how early monkeys *really* got from Africa to South America.

up the voyage by hopping across the islands that dotted the Caribbean. Still other possibilities may exist (**Figure 9.18**).

The most intriguing hypothesis is that haplorrhine primates actually appeared in Africa much earlier, when a transatlantic journey would have been easier to complete. Atlantic sea levels were lowest during the middle of the Oligocene. The Fayum primates with the closest affinities to New World monkeys are considerably younger than this. However, this may not be a fatal liability for the hypothesis. There is good reason to believe that the date of the earliest fossil we have discovered usually underestimates the age of a lineage. The method outlined in Closer Look 9.3 suggests that haplorrhines actually originated at least 52 mya.

The Emergence of the Hominoids

The early Miocene was warm and moist, but by the end of the epoch, the world had become much cooler and more arid.

The Miocene epoch began approximately 23 mya and ended 5 mya. In the early Miocene, the world became warmer, and once again Eurasian forests were dominated by broadleaf evergreens like those in the tropics today. At the end of the Miocene, the world became considerably colder and more arid. The tropical forests of Eurasia retreated southward, and there was more open, woodland habitat. India continued its slow slide into Asia, leading to the uplifting of the Himalayas. Some climatologists believe that the resulting change in atmospheric circulation was responsible for the late Miocene cooling. About 18 mya, Africa joined Eurasia, splitting the Tethys Sea and creating the Mediterranean Sea. Because the Strait of Gibraltar had not yet opened, the Mediterranean Sea was isolated from the rest of the oceans. At one point, the Mediterranean Sea dried out completely, leaving a desiccated, searing hot valley thousands of feet below sea level. About the same time, the great north–south mountain ranges of the East African Rift began to appear. Because clouds decrease their moisture as they rise in elevation, there is an area of reduced rainfall, called a **rain shadow**, on the lee (downwind) side of mountain ranges. The newly elevated rift mountains caused the tropical forests of East Africa to be replaced by drier woodlands and savannas.

Contemporary apes differ from monkeys in posture and forms of locomotion, and this is reflected in their skeletal anatomy.

Some of the anatomical features that distinguish living apes from monkeys are related to their posture and locomotor behavior. Monkeys move along the tops of

9.3 Missing Links

Anthropologist Robert Martin of Chicago's Field Museum has pointed out that most lineages are probably older than the oldest fossils we have discovered. The extent of the discrepancy between the dates of the fossils and the actual origin of the lineage depends on the fraction of fossils that have been discovered. If the primate fossil record were nearly complete, then the fact that no haplorrhines living more than 35 mya have been found would mean that they didn't exist that long ago.

However, we have reason to believe that the primate fossil record is quite incomplete (**Figure 9.19**).

Just as not all fossils of a given species are ever found, not all species are known to us either. How many species are missing from our data? Martin's method for answering this question is based on the assumption that the number of species has increased steadily from 65 mya, when the first primates appeared, to the present. This means that there were half as many species 32.5 mya as there are now, three-fourths as many species 16.25 mya as there are now, and so on.

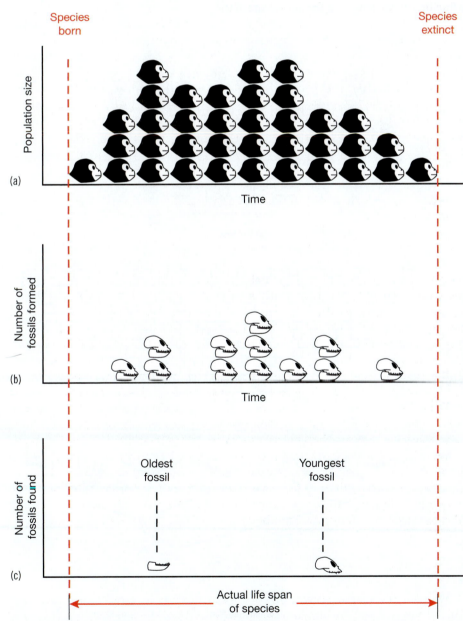

FIGURE 9.19

The sparseness of the fossil record virtually guarantees that the oldest fossil found of a particular species underestimates the age of the species. (a) The population size of a hypothetical primate species is plotted here against time. In this case, we imagine that the species becomes somewhat less populous as it approaches extinction. (b) The number of fossils left by this species is less than the population size. It is unlikely that the earliest and latest fossils date to the earliest and latest living individuals. (c) The number of fossils found by paleontologists is less than the total number of fossils.

Assuming that each species has lived about 1 million years, the average life span of a mammalian species, Martin summed these figures to obtain the number of primate species that have ever lived. Then he took the number of fossil species discovered so far and divided that number by his estimate of the total number of species that have ever lived. According to these calculations, only 3% of all fossil primate species have been found so far.

Next, Martin constructed a phylogenetic tree with the same number of living species that we now find in the Primate order. One such tree is shown in **Figure 9.20a.** He then randomly "found" 3% of the fossil species. In **Figure 9.20b** the gray lines give the actual pattern of descent, and the red lines show the data that would be available if we knew the characteristics of all the living species but had recovered only 3% of the fossil species. The best phylogeny possible, given these data, is shown in **Figure 9.20c.**

Then Martin computed the difference between the age of the lineage based on this estimated phylogeny, and the actual age of the lineage based on the original phylogeny. The discrepancy between these values represents the error in the age of the lineage that is due to the incompleteness of the fossil record. By repeating this procedure over and over on the computer, Martin was able to produce an estimate of the average magnitude of error, which turned out to be about 40%. Thus if Martin is correct, living lineages are, on average, about 40% older than the age of the oldest fossil discovered.

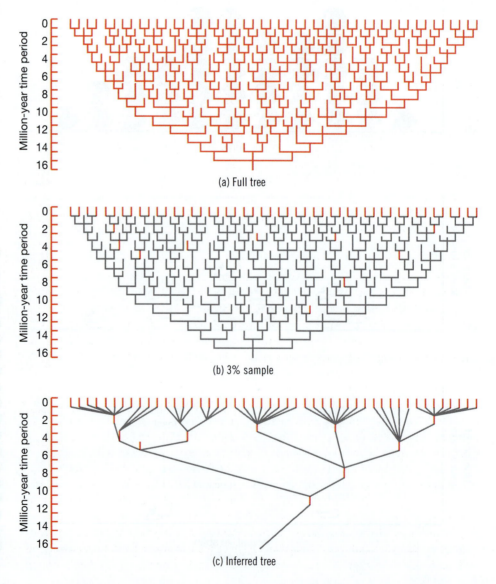

FIGURE 9.20

(a) This tree shows the complete phylogeny of a hypothetical lineage. (b) This tree shows the same phylogeny when only a small percentage of the fossil species have been discovered. The red lines show the species that have been discovered, and the gray lines show the missing species. Note that all *living* species are known, but only 3% of the fossil species have been discovered. (c) The tree we would have to infer from the incomplete data at hand differs from the actual tree in two respects: (1) It links each species to its closest known ancestor, which often means assigning inappropriate ancestors to fossil and modern species, and (2) it frequently underestimates the age of the oldest member of a clade.

(a) Full tree

(b) 3% sample

(c) Inferred tree

branches, using their hands and feet to grip branches, and their tails for balance. They leap between gaps in the canopy. They sit on branches while they feed and have fleshy sitting pads to cushion their bottoms. In contrast, apes often hang below branches to feed (**Figure 9.21**), move underneath branches when they travel, and have no tails or fleshy pads on their bottoms. They use their long arms to "bridge" gaps in the canopy, rather than leaping. By hanging below branches and using multiple branches to support their body weight, large-bodied apes are able to navigate the slender terminal branches of trees. Apes have little need of tails for balance, and the tail muscles have been restructured to strengthen the pelvic floor and provide support for the internal organs. This in turn allows apes to sustain upright postures. Suspensory feeding and locomotion have also favored relatively long arms and short legs, long fingers, more mobile limbs, and a short and stiff lumbar spine.

The first evidence of adaptations for suspensory locomotion comes from Miocene fossils collected nearly 50 years ago but overlooked until recently.

Fossils that are now assigned to the species *Morotopithecus bishopi* were first collected at the site of Moroto, in Uganda, in the late 1950s and early 1960s. These finds were dated to about 20 mya and classified as hominoids, but they were not officially named until the mid-1990s, when Daniel Gebo of Northern Illinois University, Laura MacLatchy of the University of Michigan, and their colleagues resumed work in Moroto and collected additional material (**Figure 9.22**). According to MacLatchy and her colleagues, *M. bishopi* possessed a number of skeletal features that allowed it to move like an ape, not like a monkey. For example, several aspects of the femur suggest that *M. bishopi* might have climbed slowly and cautiously, it had a stiff lower back like apes, and the shape of the scapula indicates that it could have hung by its arms and brachiated slowly through the trees. These features are shared with modern apes but not with the contemporary Miocene apes that we will meet next.

Other early Miocene apes were similar to *Morotopithecus* in their dentition but more like monkeys in their postcranial anatomy.

Before *Morotopithecus* made its debut in the pages of anthropological journals, most paleontologists believed that the oldest hominoids were members of the family Proconsulidae (**Figure 9.23**). This family includes 10 genera and 15 species. The smallest **proconsulids** were about the size of capuchin monkeys (3.5 kg, or about 7.5 lb.), and the largest were the size of female gorillas (50 kg, or a little over 100 lb.). The proconsulids seem to have occupied a range of habitats, including the tropical rain forests in which we find apes today and the open woodlands where we now find only monkeys.

The earliest members of *Proconsul*, the best-known genus of these early hominoids, were found at a site called Losidok in northern Kenya and date to about 27 mya. The most recent fossils have been found at sites in Africa dated to 17 mya. *Proconsul* species share several derived features with living apes and humans that we don't see in haplorrhine primates. For example, *Proconsul* didn't have a tail and did not have the fleshy sitting pads that Old World monkeys and gibbons have. *Proconsul* species also had somewhat larger brains in relationship to body size than similarly sized monkeys. Otherwise, members of the genus *Proconsul* were similar to *Aegyptopithecus* and the other Oligocene primates. Their teeth had thin enamel, which is consistent with a frugivorous diet. Their postcranial anatomy, including the relative length of their arm and leg bones and narrow and deep shape of their thorax, were much like that of quadrupedal monkeys, but

FIGURE 9.21

Apes sometimes hang below branches while they feed.

FIGURE 9.22

These fossil bones of *Morotopithecus* include parts of the right and left femurs, vertebrae, shoulder socket, and upper jaw. These remains suggest that these creatures moved like apes, not like monkeys.

FIGURE 9.23

Members of the genus *Proconsul* were relatively large (15 to 50 kg, or 33 to 110 lb.), sexually dimorphic, and frugivorous. The skeleton of *Proconsul africanus,* reconstructed here, shows that it had limb proportions much like those of modern-day quadrupedal monkeys.

certain features of their feet and lower legs were more apelike. *Proconsul* had a large grasping thumb, a feature that we see in humans but not in living apes or monkeys. Based on its postcranial anatomy, functional morphologists believe that *Proconsul* clambered through the trees, using its flexible, grasping limbs to reach branches on all sides and distribute its weight on multiple supports. All of the *Proconsul* species show considerable sexual dimorphism, suggesting that they were not pair-bonded.

Besides *Morotopithecus* and *Proconsul,* there were a number of other early Miocene apes in Africa. These creatures have derived features of apes in their faces and teeth but not in their postcranial anatomy (**Figure 9.24**).

The middle Miocene epoch saw a new radiation of hominoids and the expansion of hominoids throughout much of Eurasia.

Exploration of middle Miocene (15 to 10 mya) deposits has yielded a great abundance of hominoid species in Africa, Europe, and Asia. Examples include *Kenyapithecus* and *Nacholapithecus* from what is now East Africa; *Lufengpithecus* and *Sivapithecus* from Asia; and *Oreopithecus* (**Figure 9.25**), *Dryopithecus, Pierolapithecus,* and *Anoiapithecus* (aptly named, you might think) from Europe. The skulls and teeth of these hominoids typically differ from those of the proconsulids in a number of ways that indicate they ate harder or more fibrous foods than their predecessors. Their molars had thick enamel for longer wear and rounded cusps, which are better suited to grinding. Their **zygomatic arches** (cheekbones) flared farther outward to make room for larger jaw muscles, and the lower jaw was more robust to carry the forces produced by those muscles. It seems likely that these features were a response to the climatic shift from a moist, tropical environment to a drier, more seasonal environment with tougher vegetation and harder seeds.

There was considerable diversity in the range of locomotor and postural adaptations of the middle Miocene apes. The traits that distinguish contemporary apes from monkeys were combined in different ways in different Miocene ape lineages. For example, *Nacholapithecus* was adapted for more extensive forelimb-dominated climbing and locomotion than were earlier hominoids but did not possess the full range of adaptations for below-branch feeding and travel that are seen in modern apes. It had relatively long arms relative to its legs as modern apes do, but the torso had not been restructured, and the shoulder was more monkeylike than apelike.

Sivapithecus, known from sites in Asia, is thought to be closely related to modern orangutans based on the morphology of the skull and facial structure. *Sivapithecus* had some traits that we find in modern apes that practice suspensory locomotion, including long fingers and toes, a strong big toe, and a flexible elbow. However, the

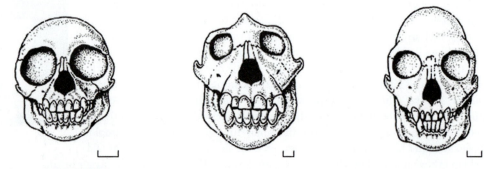

FIGURE 9.24

Miocene hominoids exhibit a diverse range of cranial morphology, but they share a number of derived characteristics with modern apes. From left to right: *Turkanapithecus, Micropithecus, Afropithecus,* and *Proconsul.*

orientation of the humerus, the upper arm bone, suggests that the shape of the thorax was more monkeylike. If this interpretation is correct, then some of the features that the modern great apes share may be the product of convergence rather than common descent. It is important to note that *Sivapithecus* had a large brain and a pattern of tooth development reflecting a long juvenile period, suggesting a prolonged life history strategy like that of modern great apes.

Oreopithecus, from Italy, provides another variation on suspensory adaptations. Its arms were considerably longer than its legs; it had a somewhat shortened lumbar spine and flexible hips. Although it seems to have been adapted for below-branch movement, it does not have long, curved fingers as modern apes do.

The mosaic nature of ape adaptations is also illustrated by the middle Miocene ape *Pierolapithecus catalaunicus* (**Figure 9.26**). This specimen is important because it includes well-preserved cranial, dental, and postcranial material from a single individual that lived about 13 mya. *Pierolapithecus* had a small, apelike face as well as a number of morphological features associated with upright posture and locomotion. The wrist is flexible, the rib cage is wide and shallow, and the lumbar region of the spine is somewhat short and stiff, but these features are not as developed as they are in modern great apes. However, the finger bones are not as long and curved as the fingers of orangutans. Again, this suggests that some features of modern ape morphology may have evolved independently after apes diverged from a common ancestor.

Climatic changes in the late middle Miocene reduced hominoid diversity in Asia and Europe.

During the middle Miocene, there was a gradual cooling and the climate became more seasonal in western and central Europe. Subtropical evergreen forests gave way to deciduous broadleaf woodlands. These climatic changes had dramatic effects on the mammalian fauna; many of the ape lineages that flourished in Africa, Asia, and Europe became extinct. A few species, including the ancestors of orangutans, survived in the remaining areas of evergreen forests. Others evolved adaptations that enabled them to survive in drier, more open, and more seasonal habitats.

Apes of the late Miocene are not well known, particularly in Africa. Recent finds fill in some of the gaps.

Crucial events in the history of the human lineage occurred during the late Miocene, 10 to 5 mya. Genetic data tell us that the last common ancestor of humans, gorillas, and chimpanzees lived between 9 and 8 mya and the last common ancestor of humans and chimpanzees lived about 7 to 5 mya. As we will see in Chapter 10, the oldest hominin fossils come from Africa, so it seems likely that the last common ancestor of humans and chimpanzees probably lived in Africa as well. Until recently, however, this logic did not fit the evidence because late Miocene apes were known only from sites in Europe. The presence of several species of late Miocene apes in Europe and Asia has led some researchers to suggest that the last common ancestor of the African apes diverged there and then migrated back to Africa. However, several discoveries of late Miocene apes in Africa have shifted the geographic focus of human origins back to Africa.

Chororapithecus abyssinicus was discovered at a site in Ethiopia dated 10.5 to 10 mya by a research team led by Gen Suwa of the University of Tokyo. The finds consist of teeth from at least three individuals. The molars have shearing crests for shredding foliage and thick enamel for feeding on hard and abrasive foods. Suwa and his colleagues have emphasized the similarity between the teeth of *Chororapithecus* and gorillas and suggest that *Chororapithecus* may be ancestral to modern gorillas. However, others have pointed out that this is not consistent with divergence dates derived from genetic data and suggest that the dental similarities might not be evidence of shared ancestry.

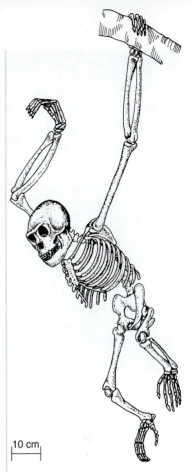

|10 cm|

FIGURE 9.25

Oreopithecus had a number of traits that are associated with suspensory locomotion, including a relatively short trunk, long arms, short legs, long and slender fingers, and great mobility in all joints. The phylogenetic affinities of this late-Miocene ape from Italy are not well established.

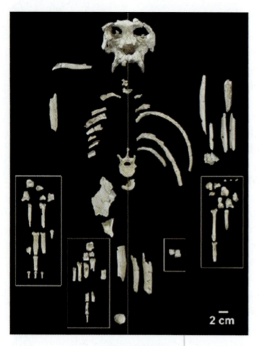

FIGURE 9.26

This remarkably complete skeleton of the Miocene ape *Pierolapithecus catalaunicus* does not show morphological features associated with suspensory locomotion. This finding suggests that suspensory locomotion evolved independently in gibbons and the great apes after they diverged from a common ancestor.

Another large-toothed ape, *Nakalipithecus nakayamai*, dated 9.9 to 9.8 mya, comes from a site along the eastern edge of the Rift Valley in Kenya. Based on the size of its teeth and mandible, *Nakalipithecus* is thought to have been the size of a female gorilla. It had thick enamel on its molars, which suggests that its diet included some hard foods. *Nakalipithecus* bears a number of similarities to *Ouranopithecus*, a slightly more recent late Miocene ape known from sites in Greece and Turkey but is more primitive. The third late Miocene ape from East Africa, *Samburupithecus kiptalami*, is known from a partial maxilla, premolars, and molars. This ape was found at a site dated 9.6 mya and is thus slightly younger than *Nakalipithecus*. Its teeth retain more primitive traits than the teeth of any of the modern great apes.

There are no clear candidates for the ancestors of humans or any modern apes except perhaps orangutans.

The evolutionary history of the apes of the Miocene is still poorly understood. There were many different species, and the phylogenetic relationships among them remain unclear. We have no strong candidates for the ancestors of any modern apes except for the orangutan, which shares a number of derived skull features with *Sivapithecus* of the middle Miocene. The teeth of *Chororapithecus* and *Nakalipithecus* bear similarities to those of modern gorillas, but it is not clear whether these similarities reflect common ancestry or convergence.

Carol Ward of the University of Missouri emphasizes that the suite of suspensory adaptations that generally characterize the hominoids developed piecemeal within lineages over time. There may have been multiple instances of convergence as various large-bodied apes evolved similar, but not identical, solutions to the challenges of terminal branch feeding and movement through the canopy. The last common ancestor of the great apes and humans may have been a fairly generalized ape, which lacked many of the highly specialized locomotor and postural adaptations that have evolved in extant apes, including knuckle walking. As we will see in Chapter 10, this view fits with new discoveries about what may be the oldest members of the human lineage.

During the early and middle Miocene, ape species were plentiful and monkey species were not. In the late Miocene and early Pliocene, many ape species became extinct and were replaced by monkeys.

Apes flourished during the Miocene, but all but a few genera and species eventually became extinct. Today there are only gibbons, orangutans, gorillas, and chimpanzees. We don't know why so many ape species disappeared, but it seems likely that many of them were poorly suited to the drier conditions of the late Miocene and early Pliocene. The fossil record of Old World monkeys is quite different from that of the apes. Monkeys were relatively rare and not particularly variable in the early and middle Miocene, but the number and variety of fossil monkeys increased in the late Miocene and early Pliocene.

Once again, the fossil record reminds us that evolution does not proceed on a steady and relentless path toward a particular goal. *Evolution* and *progress* are not synonymous. During the Miocene, there were dozens of ape species but relatively few species of Old World monkeys. Today there are many monkey species and only a handful of ape species. Despite our tendency to think of ourselves as the pinnacle of evolution, the evidence suggests that, taken as a whole, our lineage was poorly suited to the changing conditions of the Pliocene and Pleistocene.

Key Terms

bipedal	radiometric methods	thermoluminescence dating	tapetum
continental drift	isotopes	electron-spin-resonance	postcranial
Pangaea	radioactive decay	dating	rain shadow
Laurasia	potassium–argon dating	apatite crystals	proconsulids
Gondwanaland	stratum	uranium–lead dating	zygomatic arches
mineralized	argon–argon dating	gymnosperms	
fossils	carbon-14 dating/	angiosperms	
paleontologists	radiocarbon dating	plesiadapiforms	

Study Questions

1. Briefly describe the motions of the continents over the last 180 million years. Why are these movements important to the study of human evolution?

2. What has happened to the world's climate since the end of the Age of Dinosaurs? Explain the relationship between climate change and the notion that evolution leads to steady progress.

3. What are angiosperms? What do they have to do with the evolution of the primates?

4. Why are teeth so important for reconstructing the evolution of past animals? Explain how to use teeth to distinguish among insectivores, folivores, and frugivores.

5. Which primate groups first appear during the Eocene? Give two explanations for the selective forces that shaped the morphologies of these groups.

6. Why is there a problem in explaining how primates arrived in the New World?

7. Why does the oldest fossil in a particular lineage underestimate the true age of the lineage? Explain how this problem is affected by the quality and completeness of the fossil record.

8. Explain how potassium–argon dating works. Why can it be used to date only volcanic rocks older than about 500,000 years?

9. Some evidence suggests that the last common ancestor of humans and great apes evolved in Europe, while other evidence suggests the last common ancestor was an African species. Describe the logic and evidence underlying these two positions. What kind of evidence would help resolve this issue?

Further Reading

Begun, D. R. 2007. "The Fossil Record of Miocene Apes." In W. Henke and I. Tattersall, eds., *Handbook of Paleontology*, Vol. 2, pp. 922–976. Berlin: Springer-Verlag.

Fleagle, J. G. 1999. *Primate Adaptation and Evolution*. 2nd ed. San Diego, CA: Academic Press.

Klein, R. G. 2009. *The Human Career: Human Biological and Cultural Origins*. 3rd ed. Chicago: University of Chicago Press.

MacLatchy, L. 2004. "The Oldest Ape." *Evolutionary Anthropology* 13: 90–103.

Ward, C. V. 2007. "The Locomotor and Postcranial Adaptations of Hominoids." In W. Henke and I. Tattersall, eds., *Handbook of Paleontology*, Vol. 2, pp. 1011–1030. Berlin: Springer-Verlag.

FROM HOMINOID TO HOMININ

At the Beginning

The Adaptive Advantages of Bipedalism

The Hominin Community Diversifies

Hominin Phylogenies

CHAPTER OBJECTIVES

By the end of this chapter you should be able to

- Describe why the earliest members of the human lineage were basically bipedal apes.

- Understand that the evolution of bipedal locomotion altered the postcranial skeleton in many important ways.

- Discuss why natural selection may have favored bipedal locomotion in early hominins.

- Summarize the key attributes of the hominin species that lived in Africa 5 to 2 mya.

- Understand why efforts to construct phylogenies of early hominins are unproductive.

During the Miocene, the earth's temperature began to fall. This global cooling caused two important changes in the climate of the African tropics. First, the total amount of rain that fell each year declined. Second, rainfall became more seasonal, so there were several months each year when no rain fell. As the tropical regions of Africa became drier, moist tropical forests shrank and woodlands and grasslands expanded. Like other animals, primates were affected by these ecological changes. Some species, including many of the Miocene ape lineages, apparently failed to adapt and became extinct. The ancestors of chimpanzees and gorillas remained in the shrinking forests and carried on their lives much as before. Changes brought about through generations of natural selection allowed a few species to move down from the trees, out of the rain forests, and into the woodlands and savannas. Our ancestors, the earliest **hominins**, were among these pioneering species.

The first hominins appear in the fossil record about 6 mya. Between 4 and 2 mya, a diverse community of hominin species ranged through eastern and southern Africa.

These creatures were different from any of the Miocene apes in two ways. First, and most important, they walked upright. This shift to bipedal locomotion led to major morphological changes in their bodies. Second, some of the hominin species began to exploit new savanna and woodland habitats, and new kinds of food became available. As a result, the hominin chewing apparatus—including many features of the teeth, jaws, and skull—changed. Otherwise, the behavior and life history of the earliest hominins were probably not much different from those of modern apes.

A number of shared derived characters distinguish modern humans from other living hominoids: bipedal locomotion, a larger brain, slower development, several features of dental morphology, and cultural adaptation.

To appreciate the evolutionary transitions that occurred in the human lineage, it is useful to think about how modern humans differ from other apes. Five categories of derived traits distinguish modern humans from contemporary apes:

1. We habitually walk bipedally.

2. Our dentition and jaw musculature are different from those of apes in a number of ways. For example, we have a wide parabolic dental arcade, thick molar enamel, reduced canine teeth, and larger molars in relation to the other teeth.

3. We have much larger brains in relation to our body size.

4. We develop slowly, with a long juvenile period.

5. We depend on an elaborate, highly variable material and symbolic culture, transmitted in part through spoken language.

In this chapter, we describe the species that constituted this early hominin community, and we discuss the selective forces that transformed an ancestral, arboreal ape into a diverse community of bipedal apes living in the forests, woodlands, and savannas of Pliocene Africa. In subsequent chapters, we consider how one of these savanna apes became human.

Many of the morphological features that we focus on in this chapter may seem obscure, and you may wonder why we spend so much time describing them. These features help us identify hominin species and allow us to trace the origins of traits that we see in later species. We can also use some of these characteristics to reconstruct aspects of diet, social organization, and behavior.

At the Beginning

Genetic data indicate that the last common ancestor of humans and chimpanzees lived between 7 and 5 mya. In the last decade, fossil discoveries of several kinds of creatures have begun to shed light on this important period in the history of the human lineage. During this period, we see the first hints of some of the distinctive features that differentiate hominins from apes—some evidence of bipedal locomotion (see Closer Look 10.1), large posterior teeth, and canine reduction.

10.1 What It Takes To Be a Biped

Bipedal locomotion distinguishes hominins from hominoids. The transition from a forest ape to a terrestrial biped involves many new adaptations. A number of these changes are reflected in the morphology of the skeleton. Thus by studying the shape of fossils we can make inferences about the animal's mode of locomotion. Changes in the pelvis provide a good example. In terms of shape and orientation, the human pelvis is very different from that of forest-dwelling apes like the chimpanzee (**Figure 10.1**).

Other changes are more subtle but also diagnostic. When modern humans walk, a relatively large proportion of the time is spent balanced on one foot. Each time you take a step, your body swings over the foot that is on the ground, and all of your weight is balanced over that foot. At that moment, the weight of your body pulls down on the center of the pelvis, well inward from the hip joint (**Figure 10.2**). This weight creates a twisting force, or **torque**, that acts to rotate your torso down and away from the weighted leg. But your torso does not tip because the torque is opposed by **abductors**, muscles that run from the outer side of the pelvis to the femur. At the appropriate moment during each stride, these muscles tighten and keep you upright. (You can demonstrate this by walking around with your open hand on the side of your hip. You'll feel your abductors tighten as you walk and your torso tip if you relax these muscles. You might want to do this in private.) The abductors are attached to the **ilium** (plural *ilia*), a flaring blade of bone on the upper end of the pelvis). The widening and thickening of the ilium and the lengthening of the neck of the **femur** (the thighbone) add to the leverage that the abductors can exert and make bipedal walking more efficient. In addition, the distribution of cortical bone in the femur is diagnostic of locomotor patterns. In humans the cortical bone is thickest along the lower edge of the femoral neck, while in chimpanzees cortical bone is evenly distributed on the upper and lower edge.

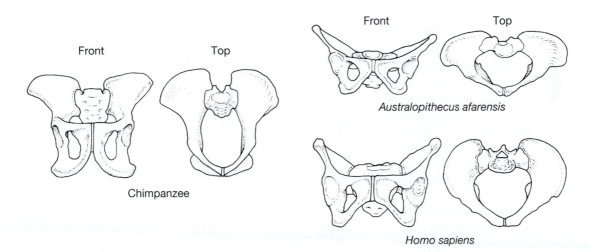

FIGURE 10.1

The pelvis of *Australopithecus afarensis,* an early hominin species (see page 251), resembles the modern human pelvis more than it resembles the chimpanzee pelvis. Notice that the australopithecine pelvis is flattened and flared like that of the modern human. These features increase the efficiency of bipedal walking. The australopithecine pelvis is, however, much wider side to side and narrower front to back than that of modern humans. Some anthropologists believe these differences indicate that australopithecines did not walk the same way that modern humans do.

FIGURE 10.2

The lower body at the point of the stride when all the weight is on one leg. Note that the body weight pulls down through the centerline of the pelvis, creating a torque, or twisting force, around the hip joint of the weighted leg. (a) If this torque were unopposed, the torso would twist down and to the left. (b) During each stride the abductor muscles tighten to create a second torque that keeps the body erect.

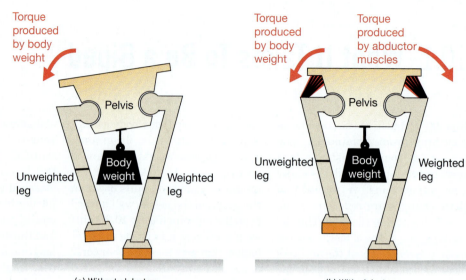

Torque produced by body weight

Pelvis

Unweighted leg

Body weight

Weighted leg

(a) Without abductors

Torque produced by body weight

Torque produced by abductor muscles

Pelvis

Unweighted leg

Body weight

Weighted leg

(b) With abductors

The modern human knee joint is quite different from the chimpanzee knee joint (**Figure 10.3**). Efficient bipedal locomotion requires the knees to lie close to the centerline of the body. As a result, the human femur slants down and inward, and its lower end is angled at the knee joint to make proper contact with the bones of the lower leg. In contrast, the chimpanzee femur descends vertically from the pelvis, and the end of the femur at the knee joint is not slanted. The feet also show a number of derived features associated with bipedal locomotion, including a longitudinal arch and a humanlike ankle.

The presence or absence of these features in fossil skeletal material allows paleontologists to make strong inferences about the mode of locomotion that the animals used.

FIGURE 10.3

The knees of *Australopithecus afarensis* are more like the knees of modern humans than like the knees of chimpanzees. Consider the lower end of the femur, where it forms one side of the knee joint. In chimpanzees, this joint forms a right angle with the long axis of the femur. In humans and australopiths, the knee joint forms an oblique angle, causing the femur to slant inward toward the centerline of the body. This slant causes the knee to be carried closer to the body's centerline, which increases the efficiency of bipedal walking.

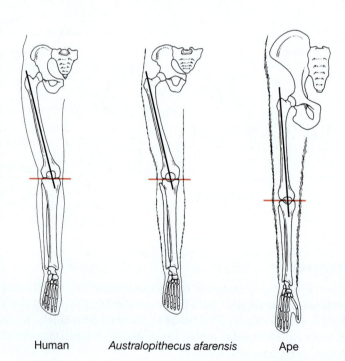

Human   *Australopithecus afarensis*   Ape

Sahelanthropus tchadensis

Sahelanthropus tchadensis, the earliest known hominin, has a surprising mix of derived and primitive features.

In 2002, a team of researchers led by Michel Brunet of the University of Poitiers in France announced a remarkable find from a site in Chad. The fossil material consists of a nearly complete cranium (the skull minus the lower jawbone), four partial mandibles, and four teeth (**Figure 10.4**). Brunet and his colleagues named the fossil *Sahelanthropus tchadensis*. (The word *Sahelanthropus* comes from "Sahel," the vast dry region south of the Sahara, and *tchadensis* comes from "Chad," the country in which the fossil was found.) Although the site at which *Sahelanthropus tchadensis* was found is now a barren desert, it was much different millions of years ago. Lakes and rivers sustained forests and wooded grasslands there.

This fossil shook up the paleontological community because of its age and location. The geology of the site does not allow radiometric or paleomagnetic dating. However, there is a close match between the other fossil animals found at the site and the fauna found at two sites in East Africa securely dated to between 7 and 6 mya. This means that *Sahelanthropus* represents the oldest known hominin. In addition, all other early hominin sites are located in East Africa, a long way from Chad. This find indicates that hominins had a much larger range than was previously believed.

Sahelanthropus possesses a surprising mix of anatomical features. The **foramen magnum**, the hole in the skull through which the spinal cord passes, is located under the skull, rather than at the back—a feature that is associated with bipedal locomotion. Because of this, Brunet and his colleagues think that these creatures walked upright. However, their brains were no bigger than the brains of chimpanzees. *Sahelanthropus tchadensis*'s brains were 320 to 350 cc (cubic centimeters); for comparison, chimpanzee brains are about 350 to 380 cc. The teeth are different from the teeth of chimpanzees in several ways: The canines are smaller, the upper canine is not sharpened against the lower premolar as it is in chimpanzees, and the enamel is thicker. The face is relatively flat, and there is a massive browridge over the eyes. These features are associated with hominins that date to later than 2 mya but not with chimpanzees or with the australopiths, the hominins that dominate the fossil record between 4 and 2 mya.

Orrorin tugenensis

Orrorin tugenensis is a second early fossil with similarities to humans.

A team led by Brigitte Senut of the National Museum of Natural History in Paris and Martin Pickford of the Collège de France discovered 12 hominin fossil specimens in the highlands of Kenya. These fossils, which include parts of thigh and arm bones, a finger bone, two partial mandibles (lower jaws), and several teeth, are securely dated to 6 mya (**Figure 10.5**). Senut and Pickford assigned their finds to a new species, *Orrorin tugenensis*. The genus name means "original man" in the language of the local people, and it reminded Senut and Pickford of the French word for "dawn," *aurore*. Fossils of forest creatures, such as colobus monkeys, and open-country dwellers, such as impala, were found in the same strata as *O. tugenensis*, indicating that the habitat was a mix of woodland and savanna.

Like the fossils of *Sahelanthropus*, these specimens are similar to chimpanzees in some ways and to humans in others. The incisors, canines, and one of the premolars

FIGURE 10.4

The cranium of *Sahelanthropus tchadensis* found in Chad dates to between 7 and 6 mya. It has a flat face and large browridge. Australopiths dated to between 4 and 2 mya have more apelike prognathic faces and lack browridges.

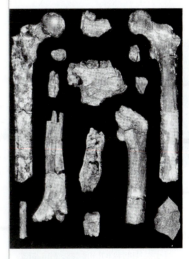

FIGURE 10.5

The fossils of *Orrorin tugenensis* include parts of the femur, lower jaw, a finger bone, and teeth.

are more like the teeth of chimpanzees than of later hominins. The molars are smaller than those of *Ar. ramidus*, whom you will meet next, and later apelike hominins, and they have thick enamel like human molars. As in chimpanzees and some later hominins, the arm and finger bones have features that are believed to be adaptations for climbing. Senut and her colleagues argue that several features of the femur (thighbone), such as the long femoral neck that connects the shaft to the head of the femur, are more similar to those of later bipedal hominins than to those of quadrupedal apes. The research team has also used computerized tomography (CT) to assess the distribution of cortical bone in the *Orrorin tugenensis* femur. In modern humans, the cortical bone is thicker along the lower edge of the femoral neck than it is along the upper edge, while in chimpanzees the cortical thickness is the same in both. Senut's team argues that the distribution of cortical bone in *Orrorin tugenensis* is more humanlike than apelike, which suggests that these creatures were bipedal. Not all experts are convinced by these analyses, and the issue will not be settled until additional skeletal material is recovered.

Ardipithecus

The genus *Ardipithecus* includes two species, *Ar. kadabba* and *Ar. ramidus*, from the middle Awash region of Ethiopia.

Some of the most important evidence of human origins comes from the northern end of the Rift Valley, in the middle Awash region of Ethiopia. Although this area is now dry and desolate, it was once the site of woods and grasslands. As we will see, this is where many crucial events in the history of the human lineage unfolded and a number of spectacular discoveries of hominin ancestors have been made.

Ar. kadabba

About 5.8 to 5.2 mya, the middle Awash region was occupied by an apelike hominin named *Ardipithecus kadabba*. This species was discovered by Yohannes Haile-Selassie, who is now with the Cleveland Museum of Natural History. The finds, which consist mainly of teeth and a single foot bone, were made at a site called Aramis, in the Middle Awash basin. Like *Sahelanthropus*, *Ardipithecus kadabba* possesses a mixture of primitive and derived dental traits. For example, the canine sharpens itself against the first premolar, a trait that is found in chimpanzees but not in modern humans. On the other hand, *Ar. kadabba* has thicker enamel on its molars than chimpanzees do, and the shape of its canines is like that of hominins that succeeded it in the area (**Figure 10.6**). A single toe bone dated to 5.2 mya is similar to the toe bones of other bipedal hominins and may be diagnostic of bipedal locomotion. Again, more postcranial material is needed to confirm this interpretation.

Ar. ramidus

Another member of the same genus, *Ar. ramidus,* appears in the fossil record about a million years after *Ardipithecus kadabba.*

Fossils later assigned to *Ardipithecus ramidus* were discovered in 1992 by the members of an expedition led by Tim White of the University of California, Berkeley. During their first field season the team found parts of the teeth and jaws, the lower part of the skull, and parts of the upper arms. The fossils were dated to 4.4 mya. White, and his colleagues Gen Suwa of the University of Tokyo and Berhane Asfaw of the Rift Valley Research Service in Addis Ababa, named the species *Ar. ramidus*, from the words *ardi* (meaning "ground" or "floor") and *ramis* (meaning "root") in the local Afar language. In hopes of finding additional material, the team returned to Aramis and combed the site for more fossils. Their efforts produced a wealth of skeletal material.

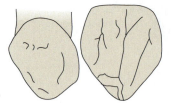

Australopithecus afarensis

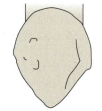

Ardipithecus ramidus

Ardipithecus kadabba

FIGURE 10.6

In *Ardipithecus kadabba* and chimpanzees, the canines are sharpened against the first premolar. This is not the case with later australopithecines (top). However, the shape of the canine of *Ar. kadabba* is similar to *Ar. ramidus* and *Ar. afarensis*, which follow *Ardipithecus kadabba*.

Altogether, White's team collected more than 150,000 fossils of animals and plants, including 110 fossils from *Ardipithecus*.

The announcement of these finds created great anticipation in the paleontological community. No other hominins from this time period were known, and there were tantalizing hints that *Ar. ramidus* might substantially change our picture of human origins. However, the fossils were in very poor condition—the bones crumbled when they were touched, and many of them had been trampled, crushed, and broken into many small pieces. It took painstaking care to excavate each specimen and reconstruct the bones. The process was finally completed and a comprehensive description of *Ar. ramidus* was published in 2009.

Additional specimens of *Ar. ramidus* come from a second site near Aramis called Gona. At Gona, a team led by Sileshi Semaw of Consorcio CENIEH in Burgos, Spain, found fossils representing at least nine individuals.

ARA-VP-6/500, more commonly known as Ardi, represents most of the skeleton of a single individual.

White and his colleagues were able to piece together a nearly complete skeleton of one individual, which was assigned the official identifier ARA-VP-6/500 (**Figure 10.7**). Paleontologists assign numbers to specimens to help them keep track of the material in their collections. But because it's easier to remember names than accession numbers, particularly important fossils sometimes get nicknames as well. In this case, ARA-VP-6/500 is informally known as "Ardi."

Ardi weighed about 51 kg (112 lb.), stood 1.2 m tall (3.9 ft.), and was probably female. This makes her somewhat larger than a wild chimpanzee male and smaller than a female gorilla. Her limb proportions were similar to those of quadrupedal Old World monkeys and the Miocene ape *Proconsul*, and she did not have the elongated arms and relatively short legs that we see in modern apes that are specialized for suspensory locomotion and below-branch feeding.

The thousands of fossils of plants and animals from Aramis provide a detailed picture of Ardi's habitat. Aramis was much wetter 4.4 mya than it is today. Ardi lived in a woodland habitat dotted with patches of denser forest. Monkeys, including colobus monkeys and a small baboonlike monkey, were abundant. Kudu, large ungulates that now favor wooded areas, were also common.

Ar. ramidus resembles *Sahelanthropus* and *Orrorin* in many features of its skull, face, and dentition.

Ardi had an ape-size brain, with a cranial capacity of 300 to 350 cc. The upper part of her face was flatter than chimpanzee faces, while the prognathism of the middle part of the face was similar to that of chimpanzees. The skull was perched on top of the spine, indicating an upright posture. In all of these features, *Ar. ramidus* resembles *Sahelanthropus* and what is known of *Orrorin*.

Ar. ramidus provides a preview of a distinctive suite of dental traits that characterize later hominins: thicker molar enamel, general reduction in the size and extent of sexual dimorphism in the canines, and no honing by the premolars.

The dental material includes 145 teeth, a wealth of material by paleontological standards. These teeth, which were analyzed by a team led by Suwa, provide important clues about the diet and social organization of *Ar. ramidus*. The dentition also reveals the first evidence of a number of distinctive features that are shared by hominin species that we will meet later in this chapter.

Overall, the teeth were similar in size to the teeth of chimpanzees, and the dental arcade is U-shaped, as it is in chimpanzees. *Ar. ramidus* had smaller incisors than

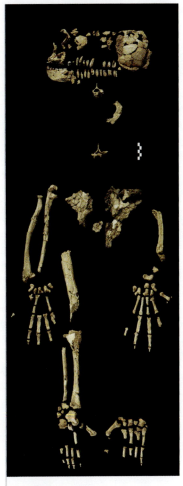

FIGURE 10.7

Ar. ramidus (ARA-VP-6/500) skeleton, known as Ardi.

FIGURE 10.8

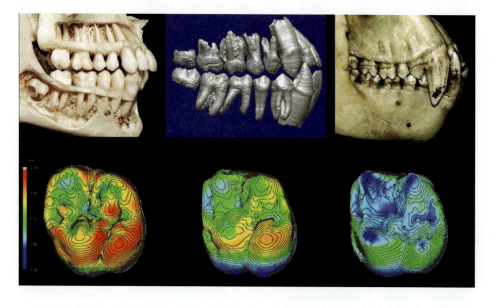

The teeth and jaws of (left) a modern human, (middle) *Ar. ramidus*, and (right) a modern chimpanzee. The top panel shows that *Ar. ramidus* had larger molars than modern humans or chimpanzees. The lower panel shows the molars of the three species, and the color indicates enamel thickness ranging from thin enamel (*blue*) to thick enamel (*red*).

chimpanzees. Chimpanzees use their incisors to process fruit before they chew it, so this suggests that *Ar. ramidus* was less frugivorous than modern chimpanzees.

The *Ar. ramidus* material includes 23 upper and lower canines from 21 individuals. The canines are about the size of the canines of female chimpanzees, but are not honed by the lower premolar as they are in other primates with large canines. As we discussed in Chapter 6, canines of a primate species provide important information about its social organization. In pair-bonded species, there is little sexual dimorphism in canine size, but in species that are not pair-bonded, male canines are generally much larger than female canines. Male chimpanzee canines are 19% to 47% larger than female canines, while in modern humans, males' canines are 4% to 9% larger than those of females (**Figure 10.8**).

Suwa and his colleagues cannot tell which teeth come from males and which teeth come from females, so they cannot assess the extent of sexual dimorphism directly. But they can assess the extent of variation within the full sample of canines to see whether there seemed to be some individuals with large canines, which could be males, and some individuals with small canines, which could be females. When they did this, they found surprisingly little variation in canine dimensions (**Figure 10.9**). They estimate that the canines of *Ar. ramidus* males might have been 10% to 15% larger than the

FIGURE 10.9

Sex differences in canine dimensions in great apes and hominins. The rectangles give the central 50% of each sample. *6 Ma hominins* refers to teeth from *Ar. Kadabba* and *O. tugenensis*. The *labial crown height* is the height of the canine on the inside next to the tongue.

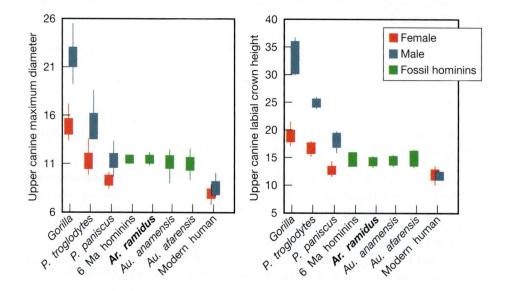

canines of females. However, it is not yet clear whether a reduction in sexual dimorphism in canine size is linked to a reduction in sexual dimorphism in body size as well.

Ar. ramidus molar morphology also differs from the morphology of other great apes. Gorilla molars have thin enamel and tall shearing crests for shredding foliage; chimpanzee molars also have thin enamel, a broad basin in the middle of the tooth for crushing soft fruits, and moderate cusps for processing herbaceous plant material. *Ar. ramidus* had thicker enamel and more generalized low cusps on its molars (Figure 10.8).

Taken together, these features suggest that *Ar. ramidus* was a generalized omnivore and frugivore. They may have relied less on ripe fruit than modern chimpanzees do, less on tough fibrous material than gorillas do, and less on hard, tough foods than orangutans do.

The postcranial anatomy of *Ar. ramidus* provides important clues about its locomotor patterns. Characteristics of the feet and pelvis indicate that *Ar. ramidus* walked upright.

Both *Sahelanthropus* and *Orrorin* have traits that are associated with bipedality, but the limited postcranial material makes it hard to determine their locomotor patterns. For *Ardipithecus*, it is possible to reconstruct the postcranial skeleton and to assess its locomotor behavior in much greater detail. Characteristics of the feet, pelvis, and hands provide important insights about how *Ardipithecus* moved around.

The *Ardipithecus ramidus* foot combines characteristics that we see in modern apes and humans. Apes have flexible feet and an opposable (grasping) big toe, allowing them to climb trees and support their weight by grasping multiple small supports. By comparison, the human foot is fairly rigid, creating a better platform for transferring energy during walking and running. The big toe is not opposable, and we cannot grasp things with our feet. *Ar. ramidus* retained the opposable toe, but the other four toes were modified for bipedal walking.

The *Ardipithecus* pelvis has also been reconfigured for upright posture and bipedal locomotion. To understand the transformation of the pelvis, you need to know something about its structure. The pelvis, which is composed of three bones, forms a circle of bone that supports the lower part of the vertebral column and protects the internal organs. The top part of the pelvis is called the ilium (or iliac crest), the central part is called the pubis, and the lower part is called the ischium. The pelvis rests on the leg bones and forms the hip joint. The neck of the femur is bent inward so the round head of the femur fits into a circular depression in the lower part of the pelvis. (Oddly, the bony protuberance below your waist is not your hip, it is your pelvis.)

There are striking differences in the pelvis of modern humans and chimpanzees (**Figure 10.10**). In modern humans, the ilium is shorter and broader than in

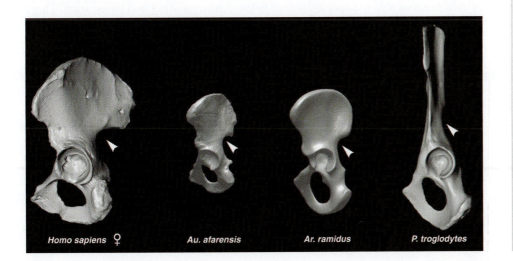

Homo sapiens ♀   Au. afarensis   Ar. ramidus   P. troglodytes

FIGURE 10.10

Pelvises of modern humans, *Au. afarensis, Ar. ramidus,* and modern chimpanzees. The arrows point to the sciatic notch.

chimpanzees. This provides more room for the attachment of powerful muscles that keep the body upright during bipedal walking. The broadening of the top part of the ilium creates a distinctive curve (sciatic notch) in the lower part of the ilium, which is not seen in chimpanzees. The *Ar. ramidus* ilium is shorter and broader than the chimpanzee ilium and contains a sciatic notch. However, the lower part of the *Ar. ramidus* pelvis is more apelike and lacks some distinctive features that we see in modern humans. As in the foot, this combination of traits suggests that *Ar. ramidus* walked upright, but its gait may have been somewhat different from ours.

Characteristics of the hands and forelimbs suggest that *Ardipithecus* lacked some of the locomotor specializations we see in modern apes.

Gorillas, chimpanzees, and bonobos all bear their weight on their knuckles when they walk, so most researchers assumed that this trait characterized the last common ancestor of the great apes and humans and was subsequently lost in the human lineage. However, as we explained in Chapter 9, there is growing evidence of diversity in the locomotor adaptations of the Miocene apes and multiple instances of convergence. Detailed analyses of the hands of chimpanzees and gorillas by Tracy Kivell of the University of Kent and Daniel Schmitt of Duke University indicate that there are important differences in the biomechanics of knuckle walking in these species. This is not surprising if knuckle walking evolved independently in these lineages.

From this perspective, it is not entirely surprising that *Ar. ramidus*'s hands are quite different from the hands of other African apes. Gorillas and chimpanzees have long metacarpals (the bones in the palm of the hand), long phalanges (finger bones), and relatively short thumbs. These are derived traits linked to suspensory postures and below-branch locomotion. In *Ar. ramidus,* the palms and fingers are shorter, and their thumbs are longer and more robust. White and his colleagues hypothesize that *Ar. ramidus* walked along the tops of branches, bearing weight on its palms, and carefully bridged gaps in the canopy.

The analyses of *Ar. ramidus's* morphology have surprised paleontologists in a number of ways.

Paleontologists had been anticipating the comprehensive descriptions of the *Ar. ramidus* material for many years. Now that it has been published, it will take some time for the scientific community to evaluate the analyses and come to a consensus about Ardi's place in the hominin family tree. There is likely to be lively debate about some of the conclusions that White, Lovejoy, Suwa, and their colleagues have reached. Most surprising, perhaps, is the evidence that Ardi's limb proportions were like that of monkeys, not modern great apes, and the conjecture that the last common ancestor of chimpanzees was not specialized for below-branch feeding and suspension. There is already debate about how these analyses influence our use of comparative data to reconstruct the behavior and social organization of early hominins.

The Adaptive Advantages of Bipedalism

The shift from quadrupedal to bipedal locomotion is a defining feature of the hominins. However, it is not entirely clear why bipedality was favored by natural selection.

We take walking on two legs for granted, but it's actually a very unusual adaptation. Among mammals, the only habitual bipeds are macropods (kangaroos and wallabies), kangaroo rats, and springhares. Biomechanical analyses suggest that bipedalism and quadrupedalism are roughly equivalent in efficiency. If that's the case, then why did hominins adopt this odd form of locomotion? There are several possible explanations for the evolution of bipedalism in the hominins.

Bipedalism first evolved among arboreal Miocene apes as a feeding adaptation and was retained in hominins. A number of the Miocene apes seem to have had upright postures and may have been facultative arboreal bipeds. According to Robin Crompton of the University of Liverpool and his colleagues, these apes might have used their feet to grasp multiple small branches to support their body weight and used their hands for balance, grasping branches to steady themselves, and collecting food items. This may have allowed them to move in the slender terminal branches of trees where fruits are found and to make crossings from one tree to another. Today, orangutans and chimpanzees sometimes adopt bipedal postures when they are feeding in trees.

One problem with this explanation is that it does not fit neatly with the evidence that *Ar. ramidus* had monkeylike limb proportions and lacked the derived locomotor adaptations of living great apes.

Bipedal posture allows efficient harvesting of fruit from small trees. Kevin Hunt, an anthropologist at Indiana University, thinks that bipedal posture was favored because it allows efficient harvesting of fruit from the small trees that predominate in African woodlands. Hunt found that chimpanzees rarely walk bipedally, but they spend a lot of time standing bipedally as they harvest fruit from small trees (**Figure 10.11**). Using their hands for balance, they pick the fruit and slowly shuffle from depleted patches to fresh ones. Standing upright allows the chimpanzees to use both hands to gather fruit, and the slow bipedal shuffling allows them to move from one fruit patch to another without lowering and raising their body weight.

Erect posture allowed hominins to keep cool. Heat stress is a more serious problem in open habitats than in the shade of the forest. If an animal is active in the open during the middle of the day, it must have a way to prevent its body temperature, particularly the temperature of its brain, from rising too high. Peter Wheeler of Liverpool John Moores University has pointed out that standing upright reduces heat stress in several different ways (**Figure 10.12**).

This explanation does not seem to fit evidence that bipedality evolved while hominins were living in wooded habitats, where heat stress would not be a major problem. However, there is some evidence that hominins occupied mosaic habitats, and it is possible that hominins sometimes ventured beyond the boundaries of the forest to forage.

Bipedal locomotion leaves the hands free to carry things. The ability to carry things is, in a word, handy. Quadrupeds can't carry things in their hands without interfering with their ability to walk and to climb. As a consequence, they must carry things in their mouths. Some Old World monkeys pack great quantities of food into their cheeks to be chewed and swallowed later. Other primates must eat their

FIGURE 10.11

Chimpanzees sometimes stand bipedally as they harvest fruit from small trees. They use one hand for balance and feed with the other, shuffling slowly from one food patch to another.

FIGURE 10.12

Bipedal locomotion helps an animal living in warm climates to keep cool by reducing the amount of sunlight that falls on the body, by increasing the animal's exposure to air movements, and by immersing the animal in lower-temperature air.

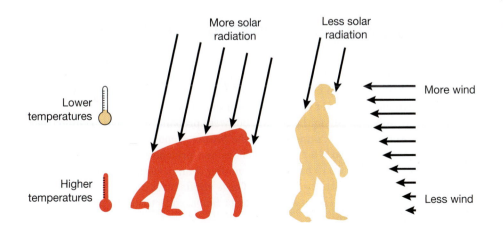

food where they find it—a necessity that can cause problems when food is located in a dangerous place or when there is a lot of competition over food. Bipedal hominins can carry larger quantities of food in their hands and arms, and they can also transport tools from one place to another.

Any or all of these hypotheses may be correct. Bipedalism might have been favored by selection because it was more efficient, because it allowed early hominins to keep cool, because it enabled them to carry food or tools from place to place, or because it enabled them to feed more efficiently. And once bipedalism had evolved, it might have facilitated other forms of behavior, such as the use of tools.

The Hominin Community Diversifies

A number of hominin species lived in Africa between 4 and 2 mya. They are divided into four genera: Australopithecus, Paranthropus, Kenyanthropus, and Homo.

Beginning about 4 mya the hominin lineage proliferated, and over the next 2 million years there were between four and seven species of relatively small-brained bipedal hominins living in Africa at any given time. A number of different taxonomic schemes have been used to classify these creatures, although there is no consensus about their phylogenetic relationships. We adopt the following taxonomic scheme:

1. *Australopithecus* includes five species: *Au. anamensis, Au. afarensis, Au. africanus, Au. garhi,* and *Au. sediba.* The genus name means "southern ape" and was first applied to an *Au. africanus* skull found in South Africa in the 1920s. These creatures were small bipeds with teeth, skull, and jaws adapted to a generalized diet.

2. *Paranthropus* includes three species: *P. aethiopicus, P. robustus,* and *P. boisei.* The genus name means "parallel to man" and was coined by Robert Broom, who discovered the first specimens of *P. robustus.* These species were similar to the members of the genus *Australopithecus* from the neck down, but they had massive teeth and jaws adapted to heavy chewing of tough plant materials and a skull modified to carry the enormous muscles necessary to power this chewing apparatus.

3. *Kenyanthropus* includes only one species: *K. platyops.* The genus name means "Kenyan man" and was given to a specimen found in northern Kenya. We do not yet know much about these creatures, but they are distinguished by a flattened face and small teeth.

4. The first members of the genus *Homo* probably coexisted with several other hominin species in East Africa. They had somewhat larger brains and smaller teeth than contemporary hominin species. We will discuss these creatures in Chapter 12.

The sites at which early hominin fossils have been found in Africa are identified on the map in **Figure 10.13**. In this section, we briefly describe the history and characteristics of each of these fossil species and then turn to a discussion of their common features.

You are excused if you feel as though you had mistakenly picked up a Russian novel with a long cast of characters filled with tongue-twisting, hard-to-remember names. Keep in mind, however, that all of these species share some important characteristics. They were bipedal on the ground but were probably also able to climb trees; their brains were about the same size as the brains of modern apes; and they had smaller canines and incisors but bigger molars and premolars with thicker enamel than chimpanzees. They were considerably smaller than modern humans, and sexual dimorphism in body size was pronounced. These similarities have led many anthropologists to refer to all of these creatures, except *Homo,* collectively as "australopiths," a usage we will adopt here.

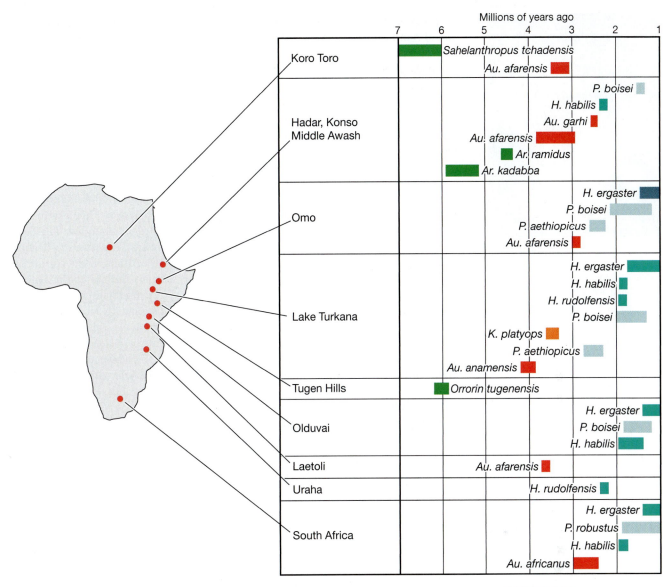

FIGURE 10.13

Hominin fossils have been discovered at a number of sites in eastern and southern Africa. Fossils belonging to each genus have been assigned a different color. Fossils discovered at Bahr el Ghazal in Chad have been provisionally assigned to the species *Au. afarensis*, pending more detailed analysis.

Australopithecus

Au. anamensis

Australopithecus anamensis was bipedal but had a more apelike skull than later australopithecines.

In 1994, members of an expedition led by Meave Leakey of the National Museums of Kenya found fossils of a new hominin species at Kanapoi and Allia Bay, two sites near Lake Turkana in Kenya (**Figure 10.14**). Among these specimens are parts of the upper and lower jaw, part of a **tibia** (the larger of the two bones in the lower leg), and numerous teeth. In addition, parts of a **humerus** (the upper arm bone) found at Kanapoi in the early 1970s can now be associated with the new finds. Leakey assigned them to the species *Australopithecus anamensis*. The species name is derived from *anam*, the word for "lake" in the language of the people living around Lake Turkana. Subsequent discoveries have expanded the sample to more than 50 specimens from the Turkana region, and 30 additional specimens attributed to this

FIGURE 10.14

Australopithecus anamensis lived about 4 mya, half a million years before *Au. afarensis*. Fragments of limb bones, the upper and lower jaws, and many teeth have been recovered.

species have been found by Tim White and his colleagues at Aramis and the nearby site of Asa Issie in the Middle Awash region of Ethiopia. These fossils are dated to between 4.2 and 3.9 mya.

Au. anamensis was bipedal. We know this from the shape of the tibia (the lower leg bone) and its articulation with the ankle. In humans, the shaft of the tibia is perpendicular to the ankle plane, while in chimpanzees and gorillas the angle is oblique. The oblique angle provides more flexibility in the ankle joint, allowing apes to bend their feet forward when they climb vertical tree trunks. *Au. anamensis* was more like modern humans in these features than like other apes. *Au. anamensis* also had relatively long foreams and curved fingers, suggesting that it might have been a good tree climber.

However, *Au. anamensis* lacks several derived traits seen in later australopiths. For example, the ear holes are small and shaped like ellipses, as they are in living apes; the ear holes of later australopiths are larger and more rounded. The dental arcade is U-shaped, as it is in *Ar. ramidus* and chimpanzees. The chin recedes more sharply than it does in other australopiths (**Figure 10.15**). Although the canines are relatively small compared to those of apes, they are larger than the canines of later australopiths. There may be more variability in canine size (and perhaps more sexual dimorphism) in *Au. anamensis* than in *Ar. ramidus* or later australopiths.

The fossils of other animals found along with *Au. anamensis* specimens provide information about the habitat these creatures lived in. At Asa Issie, there are numerous remains of colobine monkeys and bovids (the family including antelope and buffalo), which prefer closed or grassy woodlands. The habitat was quite similar to the habitat occupied by *Ar. ramidus* in the same area 200,000 years earlier. The faunal remains at Kanapoi and Allia Bay suggest that *Au. anamensis* at these sites occupied a more diverse set of habitats, including dry woodlands, riverine gallery forests, and more open grasslands.

Au. anamensis is likely to be the ancestor of the next-oldest known hominin, *Au. afarensis*. New discoveries in Ethiopia may link these two species.

As we noted earlier, *Au. anamensis* fossils are dated to 4.2 to 3.9 mya. The next known hominin species, *Au. afarensis*, appears in the fossil record about 3.6 mya. The pattern of similarities and differences between *Au. anamensis* and *Au. afarensis* has led many researchers to believe that *Au. afarensis* evolved from *Au. anamensis*. However, the gap in the fossil record between 3.9 and 3.6 mya creates uncertainties about how and when this transformation occurred.

In 2010, a team led by Haile-Selassie announced the discovery of hominin fossil specimens at the site of Woranso-Mille in the Afar region of Ethiopia; these specimens are dated from 3.8 to 3.6 mya. The finds consist mainly of isolated teeth, although there are also some fragments of the mandible and postcranial material. Careful analyses of this material indicate that these creatures shared some characteristics with *Au. anamensis* and other characteristics with *Au. afarensis*.

The fact that the Woranso-Mille hominins are intermediate in time and in their morphology suggests that *Au. anamensis* and *Au. afarensis* may be part of a single lineage that evolved over time. If so, we might eventually reconsider the taxonomic status of these two species and reclassify all of the *Au. anamensis* and *Au. afarensis* material into a single taxon.

FIGURE 10.15

Australopithecus anamensis had a more receding chin than later australopiths had, as is evident when side views of the lower jaws of *Au. anamensis* (*beige*) and *Au. afarensis* (*blue*) are superimposed.

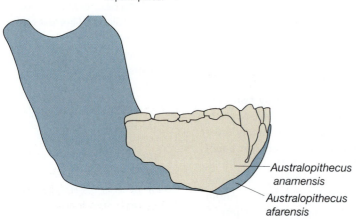

Australopithecus anamensis

Australopithecus afarensis

Au. afarensis

Hominin fossils assigned to the species *Australopithecus afarensis* are found at sites in East Africa that date from 3.6 to 3.0 mya.

Australopithecus afarensis is well known from specimens found at several sites in Africa (see Figure 10.13), but the most extensive fossil collections come from several sites in Ethiopia. In the early 1970s, a French and American team headed by Maurice Taieb and Donald Johanson began searching for hominid fossils at Hadar, in the Afar Depression of northeastern Ethiopia (**Figure 10.16**). In 1973, this team made a startling discovery: They found the bones of a 3-million-year-old knee that showed striking similarities to a modern human knee. The next year the team returned and found a sizable fraction of the skeleton of a single individual. They dubbed the skeleton "Lucy," after the Beatles song "Lucy in the Sky with Diamonds" (**Figures 10.17** and **10.18**). Lucy, who is 3.2 million years old, was not the only remarkable find at Hadar. During the next field season, the team found the remains of 13 more individuals.

Just after these fossils were discovered, the excavations were interrupted by civil war in Ethiopia, and paleontologists were unable to resume work at Hadar for more than a decade. Then, a team led by Johanson returned to Hadar, while a separate team led by White searched for fossils in the nearby Middle Awash basin. Both groups were successful in discovering fossils from many *Au. afarensis* individuals, including a nearly complete skull (labeled AL 444-2). In 2001, the Ethiopian researcher Zeresenay Alemseged announced the discovery of a very well-preserved partial skeleton of a child at a site called Dikika in the Afar region of Ethiopia (**Figure 10.19**). The skeleton was embedded in sandstone, and it required painstaking efforts to extract the delicate fossils. The result was clearly worth the effort; the Dikika child's skeleton is even more complete than Lucy's and reveals elements of anatomy that are not known from any other early hominins. For example, the delicate hyoid bone, which anchors the tongue, has been preserved intact. A partial skeleton, dated 3.6 mya, has also been found at the Woranso-Mille site. This find includes some delicate rib bones and one of the most complete *Au. afarensis* scapulas (shoulder blade) yet found.

Australopithecus afarensis fossils have also been found at several sites elsewhere in Africa. During the 1970s, members of a team led by Mary Leakey discovered fossils of *Au. afarensis* at Laetoli in Tanzania. The Laetoli specimens are 3.5 million years old, several hundred thousand years older than Lucy. In 1995, researchers announced interesting finds from Chad and South Africa. A French team published a description of a lower jaw from Bahr el Ghazal in Chad. This fossil, provisionally identified as *Au. afarensis*, is between 3.1 and 3.4 million years old, judging by the age of associated fossils. In South Africa, Ronald Clarke of the University of Witswatersrand, Johannesburg, and the late Phillip Tobias found several foot bones that may also belong to *Au. afarensis*.

Reconstructions of the environments at these sites indicate that *Au. afarensis* lived in habitats ranging from woodland to dry savanna. Between 4 and 3 mya, the environment at Hadar was a mix of woodland, scrub, and grassland; at Laetoli, it was a dry grassland sparsely dotted with trees.

Australopithecus afarensis was quite apelike in its skull and dentition.

The cranium of *Au. afarensis* is quite apelike, with a small brain and powerful chewing capacities. Its **endocranial volume** (the capacity of its brain cavity) is about 450 cc—less than a pint. This is about the same size as the brain of a modern chimpanzee. The cranium of *Au. afarensis* also shows many other apelike cranial

FIGURE 10.16

The Awash River basin in Ethiopia is the site of several important paleontological discoveries, including many specimens of *Australopithecus afarensis*.

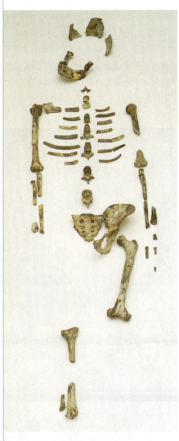

FIGURE 10.17

A sizable fraction of the skeleton of a single individual was recovered at Hadar. Because the skeleton is bilaterally symmetrical, most of the skeleton of this *Australopithecus afarensis* female, popularly known as Lucy, can be reconstructed.

characteristics. For example, the base of the cranium is flared at the bottom, and the bone is pneumatized; the front of the face below the nose is pushed out—a condition known as **subnasal prognathism**; and the jaw joint is shallow (**Figure 10.20**). There are also many apelike features of the dentition, including substantial sexual dimorphism in canine size, relatively large and procumbent (forward-slanting) incisors, and the presence of a **diastema** (space between the upper canine and incisor that accommodates the lower canine) in many specimens (**Figure 10.21**).

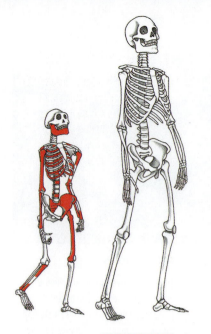

The Dikika child's skeleton included one tiny bone that is rarely found intact in fossil specimens, the hyoid.

The hyoid connects the muscles of the tongue to the muscles of the larynx. The anatomy of the throat affects the range of sounds that can be made. The shape of the Dikika child's hyoid is very similar to the hyoid of extant apes, rather than to the hyoid of modern humans, which suggests that *Au. afarensis* shared the limited vocal capacities of extant great apes.

Au. afarensis may have developed more slowly than chimpanzees do. This conclusion is based on the pattern of tooth eruption and brain development in the Dikika child.

Based on a CT scan of the Dikika child's skull, researchers have been able to reconstruct the sequence of dental development. At the time of its death, the child's deciduous teeth had erupted, and the crown of the first permanent molar was fully formed (**Figure 10.22**). Based on the dental development pattern of chimpanzees, the researchers estimate that the child was about three years old when it died. The Dikika child's cranial capacity is about 300 cc, about the same size as the brain of a chimpanzee. But in chimpanzees, 90% of brain growth is completed by the age of three. In contrast, the Dikika child's cranial capacity seems to have been only about 75% as big as an adult cranium. If the age estimates of the Dikika child are correct, then this would indicate that *Au. afarensis* matured more slowly than do modern chimpanzees.

Anatomical evidence clearly indicates that *Australopithecus afarensis* was fully bipedal.

From the neck down, *Au. afarensis* looks much more like you than it does like a chimpanzee (see Closer Look 10.1). The pelvis is short and wide, and the femoral neck is long. The femur of *Au. afarensis* slants inward, and the foot is arched and has a nonopposable big toe. These are all traits associated with bipedalism.

Although there is no doubt that *Au. afarensis* was bipedal, many features of the pelvis and legs of *Au. afarensis* are different from the pelvis and legs of modern humans. These differences have convinced some researchers that Lucy and her colleagues walked with an inefficient, bent-legged gait. For example, the ilium is oriented more toward the back than in modern humans, and biomechanical calculations suggest that the abductors would be less efficient in this orientation. The legs of *Au. afarensis* were also much shorter in relation to body size than are the legs of modern humans, and this would reduce the efficiency and speed of their walking. However, other researchers have argued that *Au. afarensis* was an efficient biped even though it did not walk in exactly the same way modern humans do. These researchers note, for example, that the pelvis of *Au. afarensis* is much wider in relation to its body size, compared with the modern human pelvis. This extra width may have minimized vertical motion of the body during walking. The longer legs of modern humans produce the same effect.

FIGURE 10.18

Here, Lucy's skeleton (left) stands beside the skeleton of a modern human female. The parts of the skeleton that have been discovered are shaded. Lucy was shorter than modern females and had relatively long arms and a relatively small brain.

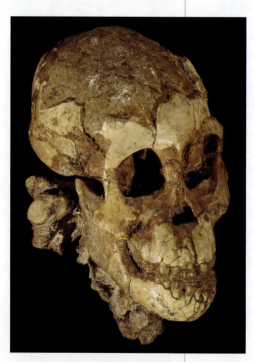

FIGURE 10.19

Young, but old. The Dikika child's flat nose and projecting face look chimplike, but the Ethiopian fossil comes from a 3.3-million-year-old human ancestor that belongs to the same species as the famous Lucy skeleton.

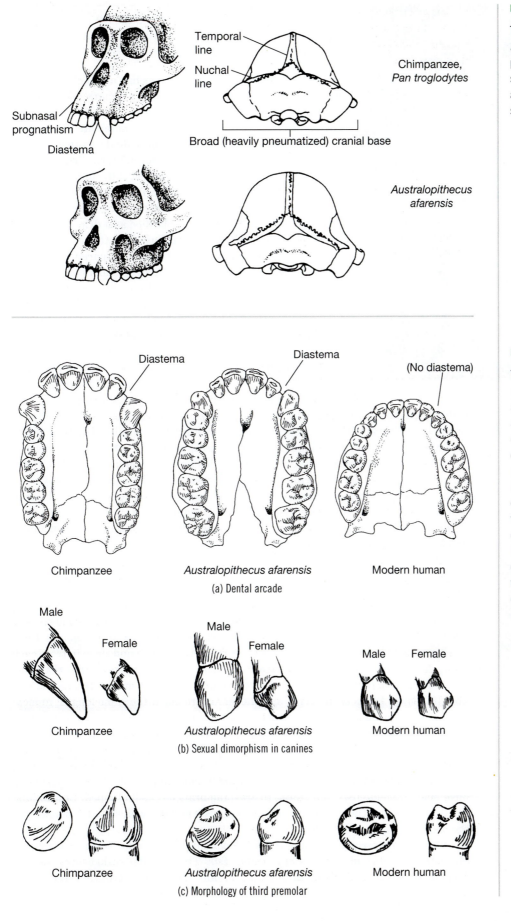

Temporal line

Nuchal line

Chimpanzee, *Pan troglodytes*

Subnasal prognathism

Diastema

Broad (heavily pneumatized) cranial base

Australopithecus afarensis

FIGURE 10.20

The cranium of *Australopithecus afarensis* possesses a number of primitive features, including a small brain, a shallow jaw joint, a pneumatized cranial base, and subnasal prognathism in the face.

Diastema

Diastema

(No diastema)

Chimpanzee

Australopithecus afarensis

Modern human

(a) Dental arcade

Male

Female

Male

Female

Male   Female

Chimpanzee

Australopithecus afarensis

Modern human

(b) Sexual dimorphism in canines

FIGURE 10.21

The teeth and jaws of *Australopithecus afarensis* have several features that are intermediate between those of apes and modern humans. (a) The dental arcade is less U-shaped than in chimpanzees but less parabolic than in modern humans. (b) Chimpanzees have larger and more sexually dimorphic canines than did *Au. afarensis,* who in turn had larger and more dimorphic canines than modern humans have. (c) The lower third premolars of chimpanzees have only one cusp, but those of modern humans have two cusps. In *Au. afarensis*, the second cusp is small but clearly present.

Chimpanzee

Australopithecus afarensis

Modern human

(c) Morphology of third premolar

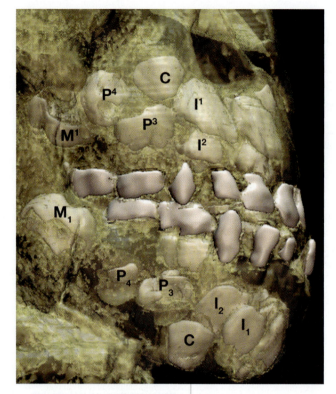

FIGURE 10.22

A three-dimensional reconstruction of the Dikika child's teeth and skull. Only permanent teeth of the right side are labeled.

FIGURE 10.23

Several bipedal creatures walked across a thick bed of wet volcanic ash about 3.5 mya. Their footprints were preserved when the ash solidified as it dried.

A trail of fossil footprints proves that a striding biped lived in East Africa at the same time as *Australopithecus afarensis.*

The conclusion that *Au. afarensis* had an efficient striding gait was dramatically strengthened by a remarkable discovery by Mary Leakey and her co-workers at Laetoli in Tanzania. They uncovered a trail of footprints 30 m (about 100 ft.) long that was made by three bipedal individuals as they crossed a thick bed of wet volcanic ash about 3.5 mya (**Figure 10.23**). Paleontologists estimate that the tallest of the individuals who made these prints was 1.45 m (4.75 ft.) and the shortest was 1.24 m (4 ft. 1 in.) tall. The path of these three individuals was preserved because the wet ash solidified as it dried, leaving us a tantalizing glimpse of the past. Russell Tuttle, an anthropologist at the University of Chicago, has compared the Laetoli footprints with the footprints made by members of a group of people called the Machigenga, who live in the tropical forests of Peru. Tuttle chose the Machigenga because their average height is close to that of the makers of the Laetoli footprints, and they do not wear shoes. Tuttle found that the Laetoli footprints are functionally indistinguishable from those made by the Machigenga, and he concluded that the creatures who made the footprints walked with a fully modern striding gait.

Who made these footprints? The prime suspects are *Australopithecus afarensis* and *Kenyanthropus platyops* (a hominin you will meet later in this chapter) because they are the only hominins known to have lived in East Africa at the time the tracks were made. *Australopithecus afarensis* is the most likely culprit because it is the only hominin whose remains have been found at Laetoli. If *Au. afarensis* did make the footprints, then the researchers who doubt that they were striding bipeds are wrong. However, some anthropologists are convinced by the anatomical evidence that *Au. afarensis* was not a modern biped. If they are correct, then *K. platyops* made the footprints, or there was another, as yet undiscovered, hominin species living in East Africa 3.5 mya.

Australopithecus afarensis probably spent a good deal of time in trees.

All nonhuman primates, except some gorillas, spend the night perched in trees or huddled on cliffs to protect themselves from nocturnal predators like leopards. Even chimpanzees, who are about the size of Lucy, make leafy nests and sleep in trees each night. A number of features of the skeleton of *Au. afarensis* suggests that they may have slept and foraged in trees, too. In chimpanzees, the humerus, the radius and ulna (the lower bones of the arm), and the femur are about the same length; in modern humans, the bones of the forearm have become shorter and the femur has become longer than the humerus. *Australopithecus afarensis* resembles chimpanzees in the proportions of these bones. In addition, the bones of their fingers and toes curved like those of modern apes. Their thumbs were short and the tips of their fingers tapered, while modern humans have longer thumbs and broader fingertips. These traits would have made *Au. afarensis* well suited to grasping branches as it climbed. Certain distinctive features of their scapulae (shoulder blades) are also well suited to supporting the body in a hanging position.

The well-preserved scapulae of the Dikika child have added to the controversy about the arboreal adaptations of *Au. afarensis*. The shoulder socket faces upward as in apes, not to the side as in modern humans. This may facilitate the kinds of movements that apes use when they are climbing. Alemseged and his colleagues think that the Dikika child's scapula is more similar to the scapula of modern gorillas, which spend most of their time on the ground, than to the scapula of chimpanzees, which are partly arboreal (**Figure 10.24**).

Australopithecus afarensis was sexually dimorphic in body size.

Anatomical evidence suggests that there was considerable variation in the body size of *Au. afarensis* adults in the Hadar population. The bigger individuals were 1.51 m (5 ft.) tall and weighed about 45 kg (100 lb.). The smaller ones were about 1.05 m (3.5 ft.) tall and weighed about 30 kg (65 lb.). Thus the big ones were about 1.5 times larger than the small ones. There are two possible explanations for variation in the Hadar population. The variation could represent sexual dimorphism, with the larger adults being male and the smaller ones female. The difference between the Hadar males and females approaches the magnitude of sexual dimorphism in modern orangutans and gorillas and is considerably greater than that in modern humans, bonobos, and chimpanzees.

On the other hand, it is possible that large and small individuals represent two different species. This interpretation was initially supported by the fact that larger individuals were much more common at Laetoli, which was then a savanna, while the smaller ones were found mainly in what were then forested environments. Some researchers also believe that the smaller individuals were less suited to bipedal locomotion than the bigger ones were. This suggests that one species was big, fully bipedal and adapted for savanna life. The morphology of the smaller species represented a compromise between tree climbing and walking—an adaptation for life in the forest.

The fossils discovered in Ethiopia by White and Johanson suggest that the two-species theory is wrong. The new fossils encompass the full range of variation in size at a single site and over a fairly narrow range of dates. Moreover, a large femur shows many of the same features seen in Lucy's more petite femur. These data also suggest that both large and small forms were found in the full range of environments from forest to savanna. All of these facts suggest that this assemblage of fossils represents a single, sexually dimorphic species. Most paleoanthropologists now accept this conclusion, although there is some dispute about whether the degree of dimorphism was large like modern gorillas or orangutans, or smaller, more like chimpanzees and humans.

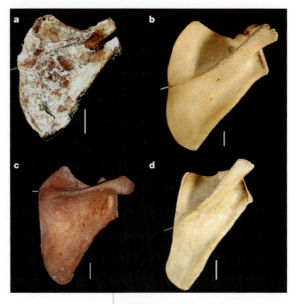

FIGURE 10.24

The shape and orientation of the scapula (shoulder) of the (a) Dikika child is compared to the scapula of a (b) gorilla, (c) modern human, (d) and chimpanzee of approximately the same age. The green line indicates where the spine meets the scapula. It is somewhat surprising to find that the scapula of the Dikika child looks more like the scapula of gorillas than chimpanzees because gorillas use suspensory postures less than chimpanzees do.

Au. garhi

Australopithecus garhi lived about 2.5 mya in East Africa.

In 1999, a research team led by Asfaw and White announced the discovery of a new species, *Australopithecus garhi*, from the Awash valley of Ethiopia. *Garhi* means "surprise" in the Afar language. In 1996, Asfaw, White, and their colleagues had recovered hominin remains from a site called Bouri, the ancient site of a shallow freshwater lake, not far from where *Au. afarensis* was found. The findings included a number of postcranial bones and the partial skeleton of one individual. These specimens are well preserved and securely dated to 2.5 mya, but they don't contain diagnostic features that can be used to assign them to a specific species. In 1997, however, the research team discovered a number of cranial remains about 300 m (1,000 ft.) away from the original site. These pieces of the skull, maxilla (upper jaw), and teeth come from the same stratigraphic level as the postcranial remains, and they reveal more about the taxonomic identity of the Bouri hominins.

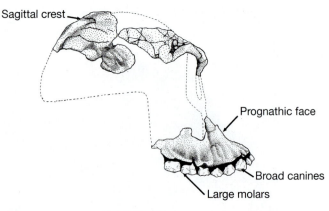

Sagittal crest

Prognathic face

Broad canines

Large molars

FIGURE 10.25

In 1999, the first descriptions of a 2.5-million-year-old hominin species from Ethiopia were published. This species, named *Australopithecus garhi,* had a small brain and a prognathic face. It also had a sagittal crest, a fin of bone that runs along the top of the skull. Compared to *Au. afarensis* and *Au. africanus, Au. garhi* had broader canines and larger molars.

These creatures had small brains (approximately 450 cc), like *Au. afarensis,* perched above a very prognathic face (**Figure 10.25**). The canines, premolars, and molars of *Au. garhi* were generally larger than those of *Au. afarensis.* Certain detailed features of the dentition differed from *Au. afarensis* as well. This creature also had a **sagittal crest,** a fin of bone that runs along the centerline of the skull, making it look a bit like a punk rocker's Mohawk haircut. The Bouri specimens were assigned to a new species of the genus *Australopithecus* because they differ from any members of the genus but lack the derived characteristics associated with other hominins.

So far, the postcranial remains found near the type specimen of *Au. garhi* cannot be assigned to a particular species, but they do reveal some interesting developments in the hominin lineage. Reconstructions of the humerus, radius, ulna, and femur of the hominins at Bouri suggest that these creatures' femurs had become longer in relation to the humerus than in *Au. afarensis,* while the relationship between the bones of the upper and lower arm remained the same as in *Au. afarensis.* The postcranial remains suggest that there was considerable variation in the size and robustness of the Bouri hominins. This variation may reflect the fact that males were larger than females, but there is not yet enough evidence to be certain that this was the case.

Au. africanus

Australopithecus africanus is known from several sites in South Africa that date from 3 to 2.2 mya.

At about the same time that *Au. afarensis* and then *Au. garhi* were living in East Africa, another australopith was living in South Africa. *Australopithecus africanus* was first identified in 1924 by Raymond Dart, an Australian anatomist living in South Africa. Miners brought him a piece of rock from which he painstakingly extracted the skull of an immature, small-brained creature (**Figure 10.26**). Dart formally named this fossil *Australopithecus africanus,* which means "the southern ape of Africa," and there is now evidence that members of the same species may have been distributed throughout southern Africa. Dart's fossil is popularly known as "the Taung child." Dart believed that the Taung child was bipedal because the position of the foramen magnum was more like that of modern humans than that of apes. At the same time, he observed many similarities between the Taung child and modern apes, including a relatively small brain. Thus he argued that this newly discovered species was intermediate between apes and humans. His conclusions were roundly rejected by members of the scientific community because in those days most physical anthropologists believed that large brains had evolved in the human lineage before bipedal locomotion. Controversy about the taxonomic status of *Au. africanus* continued for the next 30 years.

The creature who caused all the controversy was a small biped with relatively modern dentition and postcranial skeleton. As with *Au. afarensis,* there is pronounced sexual dimorphism, in both canine and body size. Males stood 1.38 m (4.5 ft.) tall and weighed 41 kg (90 lb.), and females were 1.15 m (3.75 ft.) tall and tipped the scales at about 30 kg (66 lb.). The teeth are more modern than those of *Au. afarensis* in several ways. The brain averaged about 460 cc, somewhat larger than the average for *Au. afarensis.* However, the difference in cranial capacity between *Au. afarensis* and *Au. africanus* is small compared with that among individuals and is likely due to sampling variation. Members of this species lived from 3 to 2.2 mya. The postcranial skeleton is virtually identical to that of *Au. afarensis.* Dart's notion that the Taung child was bipedal was controversial because it relied primarily on the location of the foramen magnum, and he had no postcranial bones to corroborate his conclusions. Subsequently, many adult skulls and postcranial bones were found at two other sites in South Africa: Makapansgat and Sterkfontein. The hip bone, pelvis, ribs, and vertebrae of *Au. africanus* are much like those of *Au. afarensis*. Dart's claim that the Taung child was bipedal has been strongly supported.

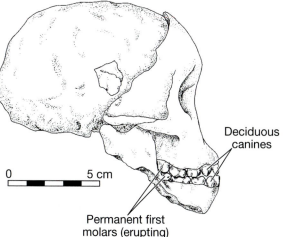

Deciduous canines

Permanent first molars (erupting)

FIGURE 10.26

The first australopithecine specimen was identified in South Africa by Raymond Dart in 1924. Dart named it *Australopithecus africanus*, which means "the southern ape of Africa," but the specimen is often called the Taung child. Dart concluded that the Taung child was bipedal. Even though it had a very small brain, he believed it to be intermediate between humans and apes. His conclusions were not generally accepted for nearly 30 years.

The skull of *Australopithecus africanus* has a number of derived features. Only some of these are shared with modern humans.

Au. africanus differs from *Au. afarensis* in a number of important details above the neck. For example, the base of the skull has fewer air pockets, the face is shorter and less protruding below the nose, the front teeth are smaller, the canines are shorter and considerably less dimorphic, and the base of the cranium is bent further upward, or flexed. In all these traits *Au. africanus* is more like modern humans and less like earlier primates.

However, *Au. africanus* exhibits a number of derived characters that it does not share with modern humans. Most of these characters seem to have to do with food processing. The premolars and molars are quite big, the enamel is thick, the lower jaw is large and sturdy, and the face is heavily buttressed to withstand the stress of forces exerted during chewing. Finite element analysis, an engineering technique that is designed to assess how complex structures respond to external loads, suggests that facial buttressing in *Au. africanus* may have enabled it to process large, hard-shelled food items with its premolars. Such foods, including nuts and fruits, might have been an important fallback food when other resources were unavailable.

New methods for analyzing dental enamel and the load-bearing properties of the facial skeleton provide additional clues about what kinds of foods *Australopithecus africanus* ate.

While the old saw "You are what you eat" might not be right in general, it is true of your tooth enamel. To understand this, we need to do a little bit of botany and chemistry. Plants use one of two chemically distinct kinds of photosynthesis. Woody plants like trees, bushes, and shrubs use one type, which is called C_3 photosynthesis, while grasses and sedges use a second type, called C_4 photosynthesis. C_4 plants have higher concentrations of the heavy isotope of carbon, ^{13}C, than do C_3 plants. Animals that eat plants (or eat things that eat plants) incorporate the carbon isotopes into the enamel of their teeth, and the ratio of the two carbon isotopes, ^{13}C versus ^{12}C, in tooth enamel tells us something about the kinds of foods the animals ate. Matt Sponheimer, now at the University of Colorado at Boulder, and Julia Lee-Thorpe, now at the University of Oxford, have used stable isotope mass spectrometry to analyze the composition of tooth enamel in *Au. africanus* and a number of other mammalian taxa from several sites in South Africa. The carbon isotope values for *Au. africanus* indicate that its diet was more variable than the diets of all but one of the other mammalian species sampled and included substantial amounts of C_4 foods. This suggests that *Au. africanus* ate things like seeds, roots, and tubers of grasses and sedges and may have eaten animals that feed on C_4 foods. This does not necessarily mean that *Au. africanus* hunted vertebrate prey. They could have scavenged for meat or fed on termites, birds' eggs, grubs, or honey. In contrast, the diet of chimpanzees, even those living in relatively open and arid habitats, is derived almost exclusively from C_3 foods, and their preferred prey feed on C_3 foods as well.

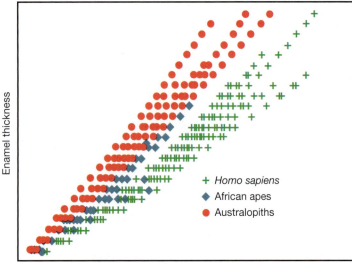

FIGURE 10.27

The rate of growth of enamel in the teeth of six australopiths was comparable to that of African apes. The enamel growth rate of modern humans is slower.

(Chart axes: Enamel thickness (vertical), Enamel formation time (horizontal). Legend: + Homo sapiens, ◆ African apes, ● Australopiths)

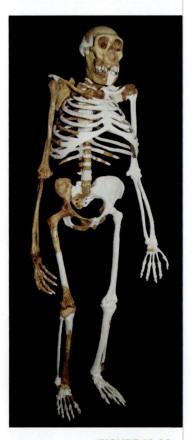

FIGURE 10.28

A reconstruction of the *Au. sediba* skeleton.

Australopithecus africanus matured rapidly like chimpanzees, not slowly like humans.

Among living primates, the age at which teeth, particularly molars, erupt is a very good predictor of the age of sexual maturity, age at first reproduction, and overall life span. Thus if we know the rate at which teeth developed in extinct hominins, we can estimate how rapidly they developed overall. Christopher Dean and his colleagues at University College, London, have found a way to tell how fast hominin teeth developed. Their method relies on the fact that enamel is secreted as teeth grow. Over the course of the day the rate of secretion varies, and this variation creates minute parallel lines that correspond to a day's growth. Dean and his colleagues used electron and polarizing-light microscopes to make highly magnified images of the teeth of six australopiths, and they carefully counted the daily layers of enamel. Then they calculated how long it took to grow to a particular stage of development. Their results indicate that these creatures developed rapidly, not slowly like modern humans (**Figure 10.27**). However, these results are inconsistent with interpretations of tooth development of the Dikika child discussed earlier.

As we will discuss more fully later, if correct, these results are important because they tell us that australopith infants did not have as long a period of dependency as human children do. Many anthropologists believe that a number of the fundamental features of human foraging societies, such as the establishment of home bases, sexual division of labor, and extensive food sharing, were necessitated by a long period of infant dependency. If australopith infants matured quickly, then it seems likely that these features were not yet part of the hominin adaptation.

Au. sediba

A new hominin species was discovered in South Africa.

In 2008, a team led by Lee Berger of the University of Witwatersrand in South Africa and Paul Dirks of John Cook University in Australia was searching for new hominin fossil sites in an area near Johannesburg that contains many caves. Near one cave, called Malapa, Berger's nine-year-old son spotted a hominin fossil embedded in a rock. Excavations in the Malapa cave eventually produced partial skeletons from two individuals, one an adult female and the other a juvenile, and the shinbone of a third individual. These finds are dated to 1.98 mya (**Figure 10.28**). Berger and his colleagues assigned these fossils to a new species and chose the name *Australopithecus sediba*, which means "well-spring" in the local Sesotho language and reflects their view that *Au. sediba* is the most likely candidate for ancestry of our own genus, *Homo*. Although this has proven to be a controversial claim, there is no doubt that these are interesting and important specimens that provide further evidence of the diversity among early hominin lineages. Berger and his colleagues were able to estimate the cranial capacity of the juvenile, which had probably achieved about 95% of its adult size at the time that it died. Its brain was about 420 cc, around the same size as the brains of the other small-bodied australopiths but smaller than the brains of the oldest specimens included in the genus *Homo*, which we will describe in Chapter 12.

Analyses of the dentition suggest that *Au. sediba* most closely resembles *Au. africanus* which preceded it in South Africa. However, their teeth, particularly their canines and premolars, were smaller than the teeth of *Au. africanus* and differ to some degree in their shape. *Au sediba* also has less-pronounced cheekbones and less postorbital constriction than *Au. africanus.*

The two partial skeletons provide a relatively complete picture of the morphology of the chest and upper limbs of *Au. sediba.* They had relatively long arms, like other australopiths, and probably continued to use their arms for climbing and suspensory locomotion and feeding. We don't know much about the shape of the thorax in other australopiths because delicate rib bones are not often preserved. But it is possible to reconstruct the thorax of the Malapa hominins (**Figure 10.29**). In modern humans, the thorax is like a cylinder, but in apes the thorax is more like a cone, with the narrower part at the top. The upper thorax of *Au. sediba* is much like that of other apes, while the lower part of the thorax is more like that of humans.

The most surprising features of *Au. sediba* are found below the waist. Like other australopiths, *Au. sediba* was bipedal. However, a group led by Jeremy DeSilva of Boston University has suggested that at least one of these creatures walked with a distinctive pronating gait. When most of us walk, we strike the ground with the outside edge of our heel, and our foot rotates about 15° inward as the forefoot comes into contact with the ground. This helps distribute the force of the impact with the ground and absorb shock. Then, as the stride continues, weight is transferred to the forefoot, and we push off evenly with our toes. However, pronators strike the ground with the heel and the foot rotates farther inward so that the inside edge of the forefoot comes into contact with the ground. This reduces the foot's ability to absorb shock and makes it harder for the foot and ankle to stabilize the body. Pronators then push off with their first and second toes. Based on the shape of the foot bones of the female from Malapa, DeSilva and his colleagues think that she struck the ground with her heel and the outside edge of her foot and then rotated the foot inward. The heel bone of the Malapa female was smaller and more pointed than the heel bones of modern humans (**Figure 10.30**) and would have provided less surface area to distribute her weight as her foot struck the ground. The researchers think her foot was arched so the heel and the outside edge of the foot hit the ground at the same time and then rolled inward. Modern humans who overpronate like this often need fancy running shoes or orthotics to correct their gait and avoid orthopedic problems, and researchers have detected some evidence of strain in the Malapa female's ankle, knee, and hip. However, there is also evidence of several adaptations in the foot that may have helped her compensate for these problems.

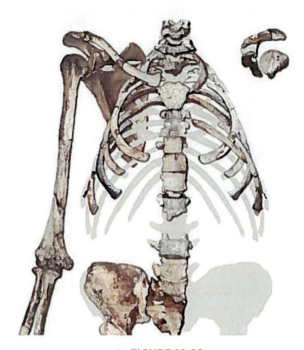

FIGURE 10.29

A reconstruction of *Au. sediba*'s thorax and rib cage.

The diet of *Au. sediba* was composed mainly of C₃ foods, much like that of chimpanzees that live in savanna environments today.

A group of researchers led by Amanda Henry of the Max Planck Institute for Evolutionary Anthropology used a number of different techniques to evaluate what *Au. sediba* ate. In addition to mass spectrometry, they also examined patterns of dental microwear and extracted phytoliths from tartar on the surface of the teeth.

Phytoliths are silica bodies that are produced by plants. Different types of plants produce different types of phytoliths, allowing researchers to figure out what the animals had been eating. Although C₄ foods were abundant in the area around Malapa, *Au. sediba* seemed to have a preference for C₃ foods, such as the leaves, fruit, wood, and bark of trees and grasses and sedges. In this way, their diet was more like that of *Ar. ramidus* than *Au. africanus.* Dental microwear analyses suggest that *Au. sediba* also relied more on hard foods than did the other australopiths that we have discussed this far.

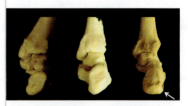

FIGURE 10.30

The heel bones of a modern chimpanzee (left), *Au. sediba* female (middle), and modern human (right). The *Au. sediba* heel bone is more like that of a chimpanzee than a modern human.

Paranthropus

Paranthropus aethiopicus is a hominin who has teeth and skull structures specialized for heavy chewing.

Alan Walker of Pennsylvania State University discovered the skull of a very robust australopith at a site on the west side of Lake Turkana in northern Kenya. Walker called it the "Black Skull" because of its distinctive black color, but its official name is KNM-WT 17000 (**Figure 10.31**). (*WT* stands for "West Turkana," the site at which the fossil was found.) This creature lived about 2.5 mya, and in some ways it is similar to *Au. afarensis*. For example, the hinge of the jaw in KNM-WT 17000 has the same primitive structure as the jaw in *Au. afarensis*, which is very similar to the jaw joints of chimpanzees and gorillas. Later hominins have a modified jaw hinge. In addition, both KNM-WT 17000 and *Au. afarensis* were probably quite sexually dimorphic; they had a similar postcranial anatomy, and they were equipped with relatively small brains in relation to body size.

However, as shown in **Figure 10.32**, KNM-WT 17000 is very different from the skulls of australopiths we have met so far. The molars are enormous, the lower jaw is very large, and the entire skull has been reorganized to support the massive chewing apparatus. For example, it has a pronounced sagittal crest, which enlarges the surface area of bone available for attaching the **temporalis muscle**, one of the muscles that works the jaw. You can easily demonstrate for yourself the function of the sagittal crest. Put your fingertips on your temple and clench your teeth; you will feel the temporalis muscle bunch up. As you continue clenching your teeth, slowly move your fingertips upward until you can't feel the muscle any more. This is the top point of attachment for your temporalis muscle, about 1 in. above your temple. All of the australopiths had bigger teeth than we do, and so they also needed larger temporalis muscles, and these muscles required more space for attachment to the skull. In *Au. africanus*, the muscles expanded so that they almost met at the top of the skull. The even larger teeth of *P. aethiopicus* required even more space for muscle attachment, and the sagittal crest served this function (**Figure 10.33**). Other distinctive features of *P. aethiopicus* are also accommodations to the enlarged teeth and jaw musculature. For example, the

Paranthropus aethiopicus
Sagittal crest (males)

Australopithecus africanus
No crest

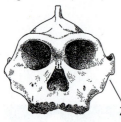

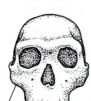

Zygomatic arches

(a)

(b)

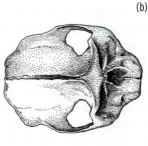

(c)

5 cm

cheekbones (zygomatic arches) are flared outward to make room for the enlarged temporalis muscle, which then cause the face to be flat, or even pushed in.

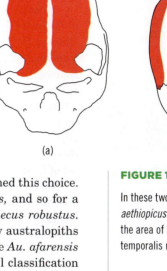

(a)   (b)

FIGURE 10.33

In these two skulls—(a) *Paranthropus aethiopicus* and (b) modern human— the area of attachment of the temporalis muscle is shown in color.

Paranthropus robustus is a more recent species found in southern Africa.

In the late 1930s, a retired Scottish physician and avid paleontologist named Robert Broom discovered fossils at Kromdraai that seemed very different from *Au. africanus* specimens previously found at the nearby site of Sterkfontein (**Figure 10.34**). The creatures at Kromdraai were much more robust (with more massive skulls and larger teeth) than their neighbors, so Broom called his find *Paranthropus robustus*. Many of his colleagues questioned this choice. They thought he had discovered another species of *Australopithecus,* and so for a time most paleontologists classified Broom's fossils as *Australopithecus robustus*. More recently, however, the consensus has been that the robust early australopiths are so different from the gracile (more lightly built) australopiths like *Au. afarensis* that they should be placed in a separate genus, and Broom's original classification has been restored.

There is now a large sample of *P. robustus* fossils from Kromdraai and the nearby sites of Swartkrans and Drimolen. These creatures appeared about 1.8 mya and disappeared about 1 mya. Their brains averaged about 530 cc. Their postcranial anatomy shows that they were undoubtedly bipedal. They share many of the same derived features with humans that *Au. africanus* does. In addition, they share with *Au. africanus* several specialized features for heavy chewing, but these features are much more pronounced in *P. robustus*.

There was substantial sexual dimorphism in body size in *Paranthropus robustus*. The males stood about 1.3 m (4.5 ft.) tall and weighed about 40 kg (88 lb.); females were about 1.1 m (3.5 ft.) tall and weighed 32 kg (70 lb.). It looks as if males in this species continued to grow for a longer time than did the females, as is the case in other sexually dimorphic primate species. The late Charles Lockwood and his colleagues analyzed the size and age of 35 fossil specimens. They limited their sample to mature individuals, whose third molars had erupted, and then assessed the extent of tooth wear to rank them according to age. Older individuals were substantially larger than younger individuals, suggesting that male growth continued into adulthood. In contrast, among the smallest specimens in the sample, which are considered to be females, there is no relationship between age and size. This suggests that males continued to grow longer than females did.

It is unclear what the robust australopiths were doing with this massive chewing apparatus. Many anthropologists believe that *P. robustus* relied more on plant materials that required heavy chewing than *Au. africanus* did. In other animals, large grinding teeth are often associated with a diet of tough plant materials, and omnivorous animals typically have relatively large canines and incisors. Moreover, the wear patterns on *P. robustus* teeth suggest that they ate very hard foods like seeds or nuts. However, the carbon isotope levels in the tooth enamel of *P. robustus* at Swartkrans are very similar to the values for *Au. africanus,* suggesting that the robust and gracile australopiths might have had considerable overlap in their diets. *Paranthropus robustus* obtained nearly a third of its diet from C4 foods, such as grasses, roots, and tubers or consumed animals that fed on these kinds of foods.

FIGURE 10.34

A nearly complete skull of *Paranthropus robustus* was found at Sterkfontein in South Africa in 1999. This species has very large jaws and molars and relatively small incisors and canines.

FIGURE 10.35

Olduvai Gorge in Tanzania has been the site of many important paleontological and archaeological finds. Louis and Mary Leakey worked in Olduvai for more than 30 years.

Paranthropus boisei was a robust robustus.

Another robust australopith with large molars was discovered by Mary Leakey at Olduvai Gorge, Tanzania, in 1959 (**Figure 10.35**). This specimen, officially labeled Olduvai Hominin 5 (OH 5), was first classified as *Zinjanthropus boisei*. *Zinj* derives from an Arabic word for "East Africa," and *boisei* comes from Charles Boise, who was funding Leakey's research at the time. Leakey's find was later reclassified *Paranthropus boisei* because of its affinities to the South African forms of *P. robustus*. (Those who advocate classifying *P. robustus* as *Australopithecus robustus* would assign Leakey's find to the same genus and call it *Au. boisei*.) The discovery of OH 5 was important partly because it ended nearly 30 frustrating years of work in Olduvai Gorge in which there had been no dramatic hominin finds. It was only the first of a very remarkable set of fossil discoveries at Olduvai.

Essentially, *P. boisei* is an even more robust *P. robustus*—that is, a hyperrobust australopith. Its body is somewhat larger than the body of *P. robustus,* and its molars are larger than those of *P. robustus,* even when the difference in body size is taken into account. The enamel is extremely thick, and the skull is even more specialized for heavy chewing.

In other primates, the proportion of leaves in the diet is inversely related to the ratio of the size of first and third molars. In *P. boisei,* this ratio is quite low, suggesting that their diet consisted of leaves or seeds. However, other elements of their teeth, including rounded molar cusps, suggest that they would not have processed leaves very efficiently. Instead, their diet might have consisted of things like seeds, tubers, bulbs, roots, and rhizomes.

Paranthropus boisei appears in the fossil record at about 2.2 mya in eastern Africa. It became extinct about 1.3 mya, although the exact date of its disappearance is not well established.

Kenyanthropus

Kenyanthropus platyops lived in East Africa between 3.5 and 3.2 mya.

In 1999, Justus Erus, a member of a research team led by Meave Leakey, found a nearly complete hominin cranium, labeled KNM-WT 40000, on the western side of Lake Turkana in Kenya (**Figure 10.36**). Argon dating methods indicate that KNM-WT 40000 is 3.5 million years old. This creature displays a distinctive mix of traits. As in chimpanzees, *Au. anamensis*, and *Au. ramidus*, the cranium has a small ear hole. Like most of the early hominins, the specimen has a chimpanzee-size braincase and thick enamel on its molars. However, its molars are substantially smaller than those of any other early hominin except *Au. ramidus*. As it has been reconstructed, the face is broad and very flat, like the faces of *P. boisei* and early members of the genus *Homo*, whom you will meet in Chapter 12. The fossils found in association with the cranium suggest that these creatures lived in a mix of woodland and savanna environments.

This specimen combines features not found in other hominins, so Leakey and her co-authors placed it and a fragmentary upper jaw found nearby some years earlier in a new genus. They called the new genus *Kenyanthropus,* meaning "Kenyan man." The species name, *platyops,* is from the Greek for "flat face" and refers to the most notable anatomical feature of this specimen. Some researchers are skeptical about this attribution because of the distortion in the cranium that occurred when it was in the ground; this controversy will persist until more fossil material is found.

FIGURE 10.36

The fossil cranium of *Kenyanthropus platyops* was found near Lake Turkana in northern Kenya. It dates to about 3.5 mya and has a unique combination of anatomical features.

Hominin Phylogenies

It is difficult to infer the phylogenetic relationships among the Plio-Pleistocene hominins.

One of the primary goals of our enterprise is to reconstruct the evolutionary history of the human lineage. To do so, we would like to understand the phylogenetic relationships among all of the early hominin species that we have described in this chapter and to identify the species that gave rise to the genus *Homo*, the genus to which modern humans belong. Unfortunately, as the hominin fossil record has become richer, this task has become harder.

The problem arises from the extensive convergence and parallelism in hominin evolution. Richard Klein of Stanford University points out that parallelisms are particularly likely to occur in a group of closely related species, like the australopiths, because they share genes that increase the probability that they will respond in the same way to similar types of selection pressures. This means that many alternative phylogenies are equally plausible, depending on what is assumed to be homologous and what is assumed to be convergent. This can lead to very different interpretations of the data.

To illustrate how these kinds of differences can arise, Randall Skelton of the University of Montana and Henry McHenry of the University of California at Davis, performed a phylogenetic analysis of 77 traits of the skulls of a number of the early hominin species you met in this chapter. They sorted the traits into groups according to their function and their location in the body. For example, one functional group of traits included features thought to be adaptations for heavy chewing, such as large teeth and a sagittal crest, and another group included all of the features of the bottom of the cranium. Then Skelton and McHenry constructed phylogenetic trees based on different combinations of traits. They found that the branching pattern of the best tree depends on which groups of traits are included. For example, the best fit based on traits in the heavy-chewing complex groups together all the robust australopiths and identifies *Au. afarensis* as the ancestor of the genus *Homo* (**Figure 10.37a**). In contrast, when the traits in the heavy-chewing complex are eliminated, the results are consistent with the radically different tree shown in **Figure 10.37b**. In this case, *P. aethiopicus* is unrelated to *P. robustus* and *P. boisei,* and *Au. africanus* is ancestral to *Homo*.

Richard Klein proposes a "working phylogeny" of the hominins (**Figure 10.38**) based on the geographic locations in which fossils have been found, the times that various fossil species are believed to have lived, and the morphological characteristics of the fossil species. Klein places *Ardipithecus* at the base of the lineage and groups all of the robust

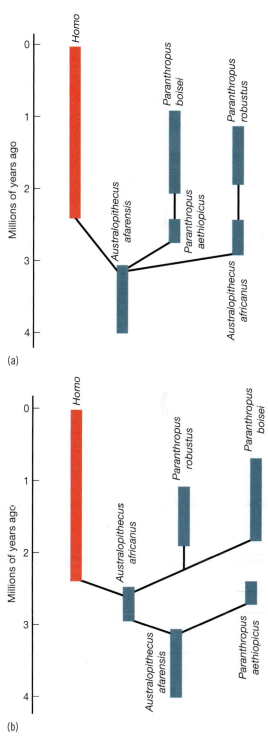

(a)

(b)

FIGURE 10.37

(a) Before the discovery of *Paranthropus aethiopicus* (KNM-WT 17000), there was a general consensus about the hominin phylogeny: that *Homo* species derive from *Australopithecus afarensis,* and that *Au. africanus* began a lineage of increasing robustness, culminating in *Paranthropus boisei.* (b) If we assume that the similarities in traits other than those involved in heavy chewing are homologous, then we might obtain the phylogeny shown here, in which *Au. afarensis* gives rise to *Au. africanus,* which in turn gives rise to *Homo* species and the later paranthropines. According to this phylogeny, the similarities between *P. aethiopicus* and the other paranthropines are due to parallel evolution.

FIGURE 10.38

A possible phylogeny of the Plio-Pleistocene hominins. Note that there are many uncertainties in the tree.

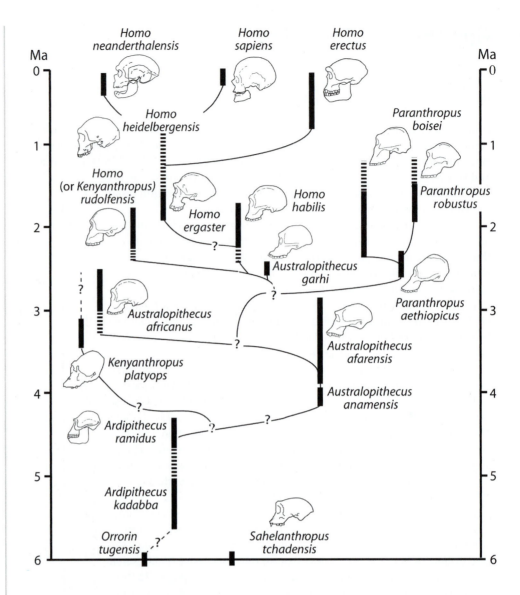

australopiths together. As you can see, there are uncertainties about the relationships among *Au. afarensis*, *Au. africanus*, and *Au. garhi*. Klein suggests that *Au. garhi* may be most closely related to early members of the genus *Homo*, but he emphasizes that this is a very tentative hypothesis.

The absence of a secure phylogeny for the early hominins does not prevent us from understanding human evolution.

It is easy to be discouraged by the uncertainties in the hominin fossil record and to doubt that we know anything concrete about our earliest ancestors. Although there are many gaps in the fossil record and much controversy about the relationship among the early hominin species, we do know several important things about them. In every plausible phylogeny, the human lineage is derived from a small biped who was adept in trees. Its teeth and jaws were suited for a generalized diet. The males were considerably taller and heavier than the females, their brains were the same size as those of modern apes, and their offspring developed faster than modern humans do. This is the kind of creature that linked the apes of the Miocene to the earliest members of our own genus, *Homo*.

Key Terms

hominins
torque
abductors
ilium
femur
foramen magnum
tibia
humerus
endocranial volume
subnasal prognathism
diastema
sagittal crest
temporalis muscle

Study Questions

1. What features distinguish modern humans from great apes?

2. Many researchers refer to the early hominins as bipedal apes. Is this description accurate? In what ways do you think early hominins may have differed from other apes?

3. What makes the discovery of fossil hominin material from Chad so startling?

4. What circumstances might have favored the divergence and subsequent diversification of hominin species in Africa 4 to 2 mya?

5. What do we mean when we label a trait "primitive"?

6. Outline three reasons natural selection may have favored bipedal locomotion in the hominin lineage.

In each case, explain why hominins became bipedal but other terrestrial primates, such as baboons, did not.

7. What evidence suggests that australopiths spent more time in trees than modern humans do?

8. What features do the *Australopithecus* species share? In what ways do they differ from *Paranthropus* and *Kenyanthropus*?

9. What features do the three earliest hominin species share? How are they different?

10. From the comparative and morphological evidence on hand, what can we say about the behavior and social organization of the early hominins?

Further Reading

Cartmill, M., F. H. Smith, and K. Brown, 2007. *The Human Lineage.* New York: Wiley-Blackwell.

Gibbons, A. 2007. *The First Human: The Race to Discover Our Earliest Ancestors.* New York: Doubleday.

Kimbel, W. 2007. "The Species and Diversity of Australopiths." In W. Henke and I. Tattersall, eds. *Handbook of Paleontology.* Vol. 3. pp. 1539–1574. Berlin: Springer-Verlag.

Klein, R. G. 2009. *The Human Career: Human Biological and Cultural Origins.* 3rd ed. Chicago: University of Chicago Press.

White, T. D., B. Asfaw, Y. Beyene, Y. Haile-Selassie, C. O. Lovejoy, G. Suwa, and G. WoldGabriel, 2009. "*Ardipithecus ramidus* and the Paleobiology of Early Hominids." *Science* 326: 75–86.

266

CHAPTER OBJECTIVES

By the end of this chapter you should be able to

- Describe the first stone tools made by hominins.

- Contrast the foraging techniques of modern foragers with the foraging techniques of other primates.

- Understand how reliance on complex foraging techniques has influenced human life history.

- Describe what we know about the foraging strategies of the creatures that make Oldowan tools.

- Explain why some experts think that Oldowan toolmakers hunted game and others think they mostly scavenged meat.

OLDOWAN TOOLMAKERS AND THE ORIGIN OF HUMAN LIFE HISTORY

The Oldowan Toolmakers

Complex Foraging Shapes Human Life History

Evidence for Complex Foraging by Oldowan Toolmakers

Back to the Future: The Transition to Modern Human Life Histories

The Oldowan Toolmakers

Early hominins are likely to have been tool users because tool use is common in apes. Tool use almost certainly precedes the divergence from the lineage that led to modern great apes. Chimpanzees use long, thin branches, vines, stems, sticks, and twigs to poke into ant nests, termite mounds, and bees' nests to extract insects and honey. They sometimes scrape marrow and other tissue from the bones and braincases of mammalian prey with wooden twigs. They wad up leaves, dip them into pools of rainwater that have collected in hollow tree trunks, and then suck water from their leafy "sponges." In West Africa, chimpanzees pound stone hammers against heavy flat stones, exposed rocks, and roots to crack open hard-shelled nuts (**Figure 11.1**). There are some examples of

FIGURE 11.1

In West Africa, chimpanzees use stones to crack open hard-shelled nuts.

tool use in other apes as well. For example, orangutans use sticks to pry open fruits, and lowland gorillas sometimes use sticks to probe the depth of water as they cross swamps.

Chimpanzees sometimes modify natural objects for specific purposes. Caroline Tutin of the Centre International de Recherches Médicales de Franceville (CIRMF), Gabon, and William McGrew of Cambridge University observed that chimpanzees at Mount Assirik in Senegal use twigs to extract termites from their mounds. The twigs are first detached from the bush or shrub; then leaves growing from the stem are stripped off, the bark is peeled back from the stem, and the twig is clipped to an appropriate length.

Chimpanzees do not modify all of the materials that they use as tools. The stone hammers and anvils they use to crack open hard-shelled nuts in West Africa are carefully selected, used repeatedly, and sometimes moved from one site in the forest to another, but they are not deliberately altered.

It seems reasonable to assume that hominins used tools much as chimpanzees do today, but the only tools that have left traces in the archaeological record were those made from durable substances, like stone.

Early hominins may have first used naturally occurring stones as tools and then begun to modify them.

At Dikika, researchers have found animal bones from 3.4 mya that may have been marked by stone tools. It is possible that hominins used sharp-edged stones to scrape the flesh off bones of animal prey. Because no stone tools have been found in association with these bones, it is hard to exclude the possibility that the marks on the bones were made by other predators or by other natural processes. But by 2.3 mya, hominins were using and producing stone tools and were already quite proficient at these tasks. At a site in West Turkana, researchers have found an extensive array of stone artifacts, including **flakes** (small, sharp chips), **cores**, hammer stones, and debris from manufacturing. Preservation conditions at the site were so good that workers were able to fit a number of flakes back onto the cores from which they had been struck. This reconstruction revealed that early hominins removed as many as 30 flakes from a single core, maintaining precise flaking angles during the entire toolmaking sequence.

These artifacts, collectively referred to as the **Oldowan tool industry**, are very simple. The tool kit consists of rounded stones, like the cobbles once used to pave city streets, that have been flaked (chipped) a few times to produce an edge (**Figure 11.2**). Toolmaking (**knapping**) leaves telltale traces on the cobble cores, so it's possible to distinguish natural breakage from deliberate modification. The Oldowan artifacts are quite variable in their shape and size, but this variation does not seem to be related to differences in how the tools were used, how they were made, or how toolmakers thought their tools should look. Instead, the tools vary because they were made out of different raw materials. There is evidence that the flakes struck from these cobbles were at least as useful as the cores themselves (Closer Look 11.1).

The Oldowan tool industry is an example of Mode 1 technology.

Tool industries like the Oldowan refer to collections of tools that are found in a particular region and time. It is also useful to have a name for a particular method of manufacturing tools so that we can compare industries from different times and places. The late J. Desmond Clark devised a scheme for classifying modes of production that we will use here. According to this scheme, crude flaked pebble tools like those associated with the Oldowan tool industry are classified as **Mode 1** technology. The distinction between industry and mode is not very meaningful for our discussion of early hominins, who used simple techniques to create a very limited set of tools, but it will become useful later when there are major regional and temporal variations in the composition of tool kits and modes of production.

We do not know which hominin species were responsible for making the tools.

As you learned in Chapter 10, a sizable number of hominin species were running around in East Africa between 3.5 and 2 mya, and it is not clear which of these species made the Oldowan tools. If the tools found at Dikika were modified before use, then the title of "first engineer" would probably go to *Australopithecus afarensis*. But if hominins used stones as tools before they began modifying them, then *Au. garhi* may deserve this title. At Bouri, animal bones bearing the distinctive marks made by stone tools are found in the same strata as the fossils of *Au. garhi*. Although no tools were found with the fossils at Bouri, many tools have been found at the nearby site of Gona, which is dated to 2.5 mya. Thus *Au. garhi* may have been the first stone toolmaker. But remember that several species were present in East Africa at the same time; they could have made the tools found at Gona but impolitely failed to leave their own fossils behind.

It is also possible that the earliest stone tools were made by species that do not appear until later in the fossil record. Stone tools are more durable than bones, so the archaeological record is usually more complete than the fossil record. This means that the earliest tools typically appear in the fossil record before the first fossil of the creature that made them (see Closer Look 9.3 for more discussion of this topic). Thus the first stone toolmaker may have been an australopith or an early member of the genus *Homo*, which will be discussed in more detail in Chapter 12. Because of this ambiguity, in the rest of this chapter we will refer to the hominins who made the tools of this period as Oldowan hominins or Oldowan toolmakers.

Because it is likely that Oldowan toolmakers were human ancestors, we can learn a lot about the processes that shaped human evolution by studying Oldowan archaeological sites.

By about 2 mya, one of the early hominin lineages had given rise to a new kind of hominid. These hominids were fully terrestrial with large bodies—about as big as modern humans. They developed more slowly than early hominins, and males and females were about as different in size as men and women are today. These creatures almost certainly made and used tools, although they may not have been the first ones to do so. By combining knowledge of contemporary foraging peoples with careful study of Oldowan tools, the sites where these tools were found, and the marks that they make on animal bones, we can learn a lot about the transition from hominin to hominid.

In the discussion that follows, we will first see how a reliance on highly productive but very hard to learn foraging skills distinguishes humans from other primates and how this novel foraging niche may have led to the evolution of other novel features of the human life cycle, such as slow maturation, reduced sexual dimorphism, and sexual division of labor. We will then consider the archaeological evidence from Oldowan sites indicating that these hominins had begun to shift to a subsistence economy based on more challenging foraging techniques.

Bifacial chopper

Hammer stone

Discoid

Flake scraper

Polyhedron

0   5 cm

Flake

Heavy-duty (core) scraper

FIGURE 11.2

Stone tools like these first appear in the archaeological record about 2.5 mya. Researchers are not sure how these tools were used. Some think that the large cores shown here were used for a variety of tasks; others think that the small flakes removed from these cores were the real tools.

11.1 Ancient Toolmaking and Tool Use

Kathy Schick and Nicholas Toth of Indiana University have done many experiments with simple stone tools. They have mastered the skills needed to manufacture the kinds of artifacts found at Oldowan sites and learned how to use them effectively. Their experiments have produced several interesting results. Schick and Toth believe the Oldowan artifacts that archaeologists have painstakingly collected and described are not really tools at all. They are cores left over after striking off small, sharp flakes, and the flakes are the real tools. Schick and Toth find that the flakes can be used for an impressive variety of tasks, even for butchering large animals like elephants. In contrast, although the cores can be used for some tasks, such as chopping down a tree to make a digging stick or a spear or cracking bones to extract marrow, they are generally much less useful. Schick and Toth's conclusion is supported by microscopic analysis of the edges of a small number of Oldowan flakes, which indicates that they were used for both woodworking and butchery.

Schick and Toth have also been able to explain the function of enigmatic objects that archaeologists call spheroids. These are smooth, approximately spherical pieces of quartz about the size of a baseball. Several suggestions for their function have been put forth, including processing plants and bashing bones to extract marrow. Some researchers thought the spheroids were part of a bola, a hunting tool used on the grasslands of Argentina. In a bola, three stones are connected by leather thongs and thrown so that they tangle the prey's legs. Schick and Toth have shown there is a much more plausible explanation for these stones. If a piece of quartz is used as a hammer to produce flakes, bits of the hammer stone are inadvertently knocked off. The hammer surface is no longer flat, so the hammer stone is shifted in the toolmaker's hand. Thus the hammer gradually becomes more and more spherical. After a while, a quartz hammer becomes a spheroid.

Perhaps the most remarkable conclusion that Schick and Toth drew from their experiments is that early hominin toolmakers were right-handed. Schick and Toth found that right-handers usually hold the hammer stone in their right hand and hold the stone to be flaked in the left hand. After driving off the first flake, they rotate the stone clockwise and drive off the second flake. This sequence produces flakes in which the **cortex** (the rough, unknapped surface of the stone) is typically on the right side of the flakes (**Figure 11.3**). On flakes made by left-handers, the cortex is typically on the left side. With these data in mind, Schick and Toth studied flakes from sites at Koobi Fora, Kenya, dated to 1.9 to 1.5 mya. Their results suggest that most of the individuals who made the flakes were right-handed.

Complex Foraging Shapes Human Life History

Anthropologists divide the foods acquired by foragers into three types according to the amount of knowledge and skill required to obtain them. These are, in order of increasing difficulty of acquisition, collected foods, extracted foods, and hunted foods.

Hillard Kaplan and Jane Lancaster of the University of New Mexico, along with Kim Hill and A. Magdalena Hurtado of Arizona State University, have argued that the evolution of modern human life history was driven by a shift to valuable but

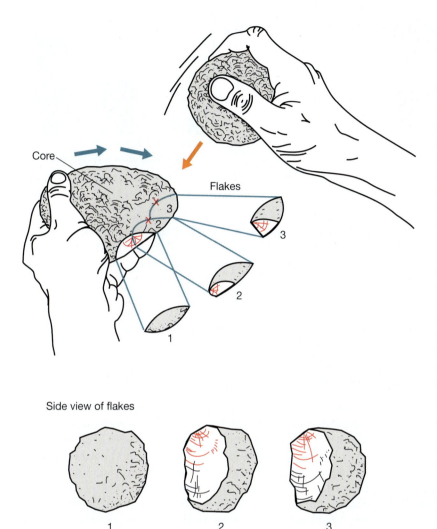

Core

Flakes

3
2
1

Side view of flakes

1   2   3

FIGURE 11.3

Demonstration of why right-handed flint knappers make distinctive flakes. When a right-handed person makes a stone tool, she typically holds the hammer stone in her right hand and the core to be flaked in the left hand. When the hammer stone strikes the core, a flake spalls off, leaving a characteristic pattern of rays and ripple marks centered around the point of impact (shown in *red*). The knapper then rotates the core and strikes it again. If she rotates the core clockwise, as shown, the second flake has the percussion marks from the first flake on the upper left and part of the original rough surface of the rock, or cortex (shown in *gray*), on the right. If she rotates the core counterclockwise, the cortex will be on the left and the percussion marks on the upper right. Modern right-handed flint knappers make about 56% right-handed flakes and 44% left-handed flakes, and left-handed flint knappers do just the opposite. A sample of flakes from Koobi Fora dated to between 1.9 and 1.5 mya contains 57% right-handed flakes and 43% left-handed flakes, suggesting that early hominin toolmakers were right-handed.

hard-to-acquire food resources. They rank food resources into three categories according to how difficult it is to acquire them:

1. **Collected foods** can be simply gathered from the environment and eaten. Examples include ripe fruit and leaves.

2. **Extracted foods** come from things that don't move but are protected in some way. These things must be processed before the food can be eaten. Examples include fruits in hard shells, tubers or termites that are buried deep underground, honey hidden in hives high in trees, and plants containing toxins that must be extracted before the plants can be eaten.

3. **Hunted foods** come from things that run away and must be caught or trapped. They may also need to be extracted and processed before consumption. Vertebrate prey are the prime example of hunted foods for both humans and chimpanzees.

FIGURE 11.4

(a) Chimpanzees spend most of their time feeding on collected foods like fruit and leaves, which can be eaten without processing. (b) Human foragers get most of their calories from extracted foods like tubers, which must be processed before they can be eaten, and hunted foods like animal game, which must be caught or trapped.

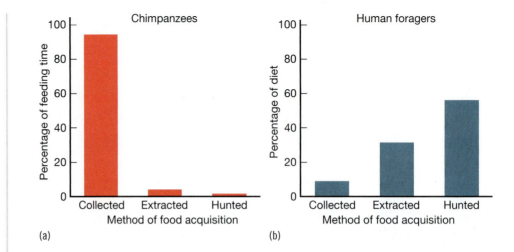

(a) (b)

Apes, especially chimpanzees, are the brainiacs of the primate world, at least when it comes to foraging. Gorillas and orangutans use elaborate routines to process some plant foods. Both orangutans and chimpanzees use tools to process some kinds of foods. Moreover, as we will see in Chapter 15, different ape populations use different techniques for the acquisition of extracted foods like hard-shelled nuts. Chimpanzees have a broader diet, including collected, hunted, and extracted foods, the latter two requiring considerable skill to acquire and process. However, even these clever apes do not come close to human expertise in foraging.

Humans depend on hard-to-learn skills to acquire food.

Kaplan and his colleagues emphasize the importance of the fact that contemporary foraging peoples depend on extracted and hunted foods to a much greater extent than chimpanzees do. **Figure 11.4** compares the average dependence of chimpanzees and humans on collected, extracted, and hunted foods. The general pattern is clear: chimpanzees are overwhelmingly dependent on collected resources, but human foragers get almost all of their calories from extracted or hunted resources.

Unlike other predators, humans must learn a very diverse set of hunting skills. Most large mammalian predators capture a relatively small range of prey species using one of two methods: They wait in ambush or they combine a stealthy approach with fast pursuit. Once the prey is captured, they process it with tooth and claw. In contrast, human hunters use a vast number of methods to capture and process a huge range of prey species. For example, the Aché, a group of foragers who live in Paraguay, hunt 78 different species of mammals, 21 species of reptiles, 14 species of fish, and over 150 species of birds using a vast array of techniques that depend on the prey type, the season, the weather, and many other factors (**Figure 11.5**). The Aché track some animals, a difficult skill that entails a great deal of ecological knowledge (see Chapter 14). Other animals they call by imitating the prey's mating or distress sounds. Still other animals they trap with snares or traps or smoke out of burrows. They capture and kill animals using their hands, arrows, clubs, or spears. And this is just the one group of foragers in one habitat; if we included the full range of human habitats, the list would be immeasurably longer.

It takes a long time to learn this range of skills. Among the Aché, men's hunting efficiency peaks at about age 35. Twenty-year-old men manage to capture only about a fourth of the maximum. Kaplan and Hill made strenuous efforts to become competent hunters when they were living with the Aché, but they could not come close to the production of the 20-year-olds.

Efficient extraction of resources also requires considerable skill. Nicholas Blurton Jones, an anthropologist at the University of California, Los Angeles, who has

FIGURE 11.5

Meat makes up about 70% of the diet of the Aché, a group of foragers from Paraguay. Here an Aché man takes aim at a monkey.

studied the Hadza and the !Kung, two foraging groups, describes digging up deeply buried tubers from rocky soil as a complex mining operation involving much clever engineering of braces and levers (**Figure 11.6**). Among the Hiwi, a group of foragers who live in the tropical savanna of Venezuela, women do not achieve maximum efficiency in gathering roots until they are between 35 and 45 years old. Ten-year-old girls get only 10% as much as older, highly skilled women. Among the Aché, rates of starch extraction from palms and honey extraction also peak when people are in their 20s.

FIGURE 11.6

A !Kung San woman carries her young child on her back and digs for roots and tubers in the Kalahari Desert of Botswana.

A reliance on hunting and extractive foraging favors food sharing and division of labor in contemporary foraging groups.

In all contemporary foraging groups, hunting and extractive foraging are associated with extensive food sharing and sexual division of labor. In nearly all foraging groups, men take primary responsibility for hunting large game, and women take primary responsibility for extractive foraging (**Figure 11.7**). This division of labor makes sense for two reasons. First, hard-to-learn techniques reward specialization. It takes a long time to learn how to be a good hunter, and it takes a long time to learn how to dig tubers. This means that everyone is better off if some individuals specialize in hunting and others specialize in extractive foraging. Second, because child care is more compatible with gathering than with hunting, and lactation commits women to child care for a substantial portion of their adult lives, it makes sense that men specialize in hunting and women specialize in extractive foraging. Of course, this all works only if members of the group regularly share food.

For people who rely on meat, food sharing may be a necessary form of social insurance. Hunting is an uncertain endeavor, and even the most skilled hunter sometimes comes home empty-handed. If his bad luck extends over several days or weeks, he will be very hungry and may starve. If several hunters share their catch, however, the chance of starvation is greatly reduced (Closer Look 11.2).

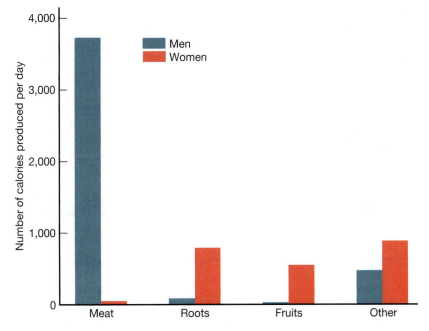

FIGURE 11.7

Data on foraging behavior for three well-studied modern foraging groups: the Aché, the Hadza, and the Hiwi. Men and women in these groups specialize in different foraging tasks. Men hunt, and women concentrate on extractive foraging.

11.2 Why Meat Eating Favors Food Sharing

Many anthropologists believe a heavy dependence on meat makes food sharing necessary. Let's examine how food sharing provides insurance against the risks inherent in hunting. Hunting, especially for hunters who concentrate on large game, is a boom-or-bust activity. When a hunter makes a kill, a lot of very high quality food becomes available. Hunters are often unlucky, however, and each time one sets out to hunt there is a fairly high probability of returning empty-handed and hungry. Food sharing greatly reduces the risks associated with hunting by averaging returns over a number of hunters.

To see why this argument has such force, consider the following simple hypothetical example. Suppose there are five hunters in a group that subsists entirely on meat. Hunters are able to hunt every day, and each hunter has a 1-in-5 (0.2) chance of making a kill and a 4-in-5 (0.8) chance of bringing back nothing. Further, suppose that people starve after 10 days without food. We can calculate the probability of starvation for each hunter over a 10-day period by multiplying the probability of failing on the first day (0.8) by the probability of failing on the second day (0.8), and so on, to get

$$0.8 \times 0.8 \times 0.8 \times 0.8 \times 0.8 \times 0.8 \times 0.8 \times 0.8 \times 0.8 \times 0.8 \approx 0.1$$

Thus there is about a 10% chance that a hunter will starve over any 10-day period. With these odds, it is impossible for people to sustain themselves by hunting alone.

A comparison with chimpanzee hunting provides good reason to think that these probabilities are realistic for early hominins. Craig Stanford of the University of Southern California and his colleagues have carefully analyzed records of hunting by chimpanzees at Gombe Stream National Park in Tanzania. In about half of the hunts, the chimpanzees succeeded in killing at least one monkey, and sometimes they made more than one kill. The average number of monkeys killed per hunt was 0.84. However, the hunting groups contained 7 males on average. Dividing 0.84 by 7 gives the average number of monkeys killed per male per hunt, which comes out to 0.12. Thus, on any given day, each male chimpanzee had only a 12% chance of making a kill, which is less than the 20% chance we posited for the five human hunters at the outset of our example.

Now let's consider how sharing food alters the probability of starvation for our human hunters. If each hunter has a 0.8 chance of coming back empty-handed, then the chance that all five hunters will come back on a given evening without food is

$$0.8 \times 0.8 \times 0.8 \times 0.8 \times 0.8 \approx 0.33$$

Thus on each day there is a 1-in-3 chance that no one will make a kill. If the kill is large enough to feed all members of the group, then no one will go hungry as long as someone succeeds. The chance that all five hunters will face starvation during any 10-day period is

$$0.33 \times 0.33 \times 0.33 \times 0.33 \times 0.33 \times 0.33 \times 0.33 \times 0.33 \times 0.33 \times 0.33 \approx 0.000015$$

Sharing reduces the chance of starvation from 1 chance in 10 to roughly 1 chance in 60,000. Clearly, the risks associated with hunting could be reduced even further if there were alternative sources of food that unsuccessful hunters might share. For example, suppose one member of the group hunted while the others foraged, and they all contributed food to a communal pot.

The fact that food sharing is mutually beneficial is not enough to make it happen. As we pointed out in Chapter 7, food sharing is an altruistic act. Each individual will be better off if he or she gets meat but does not share it. For sharing to occur among unrelated individuals, as it often does in contemporary foraging societies, those who do not share must be punished in some way, such as by being excluded from future sharing or by being forced to leave the group.

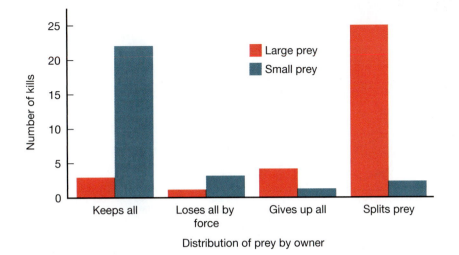

FIGURE 11.8

In the Taï Forest, chimpanzees sometimes share their kills. Infant and juvenile monkeys (small prey) are generally consumed by the captor, but adult monkey carcasses are generally divided by the captor and shared with other chimpanzees.

Food sharing occurs in chimpanzees but plays a much less important nutritional role than it does in humans. Once they are weaned, chimpanzees obtain virtually all of their own food themselves.

Unlike most other primates, chimpanzees sometimes share food. Mothers share plant foods with their infants, and adults sometimes share meat. The patterns of food sharing between mothers and their infants have been the most carefully analyzed at Gombe. There, mothers are most likely to share foods that are difficult for the infants to obtain or to process independently (see Chapter 7). For example, infants have a hard time opening hard-shelled fruits and extracting seeds from sticky pods. A mother will often allow an infant to take bits of these items from her own hand, or sometimes she will spontaneously offer them to her infant. When chimpanzees capture vertebrate prey, they dismember, divide, and sometimes redistribute the meat among members of the foraging party. In the Taï Forest, small prey are generally retained by the captor, and larger prey are typically divided among several individuals (**Figure 11.8**). The distribution of meat spans a continuum from outright coercion to apparently voluntary donations. High-ranking males sometimes take kills away from lower-ranking males, and adult males sometimes take kills away from females. At Gombe, about one-third of all kills are appropriated by higher-ranking individuals. More often, however, kills are retained by the captor and shared with others who cluster closely around. Males, generally the ones who control the kills, share food with other males, adult females, juveniles, and infants (**Figure 11.9**). However, in all of these communities, the amounts of food obtained through various forms of food sharing constitute a small fraction of all calories consumed.

FIGURE 11.9

Male chimpanzees sometimes share their kills with other males, sexually receptive females, and immature individuals.

In foraging societies, food sharing and division of labor lead to extensive flows of food between people of different ages and sexes.

It seems likely that such self-sufficiency after weaning is the ancestral state in the hominin lineage. The economy of human foragers is strikingly different: Some

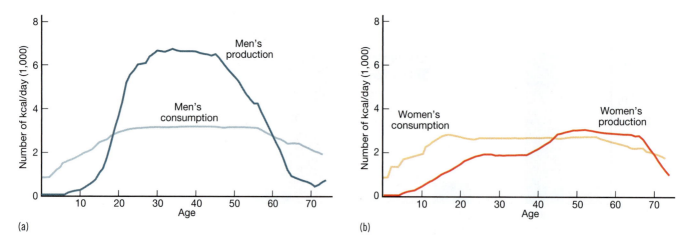

(a)

(b)

FIGURE 11.10

Data from three contemporary foraging groups show that both (a) men and (b) women do not become self-sufficient in terms of food production until they are adults. Adult men produce many more calories than they consume; adult women are approximately in balance.

people produce much more food than they consume, and others consume much more than they produce. Over the last 20 years, anthropologists have done careful quantitative studies of the subsistence economies of a number of different foraging groups. In these societies, anthropologists observed people's daily behavior, measuring how much food they produced and how much they consumed. For three of these groups—the Aché, the Hiwi, and the Hadza—researchers have meticulously computed average food production and consumption for men and women of different ages. Kaplan and his colleagues compiled these data to compare patterns of food production across societies. Their analysis reveals striking differences in the foraging economy of humans and chimpanzees and important changes in productivity over the life course.

Figure 11.10 shows that human young continue to depend on others for food long after they are weaned. Men become self-sufficient around the age of 17, and women do not produce enough to feed themselves until they are in their late 40s. Older men also depend on others for their daily needs. These deficits are made up by the production of young and middle-aged men and, to a lesser extent, postmenopausal women. In contrast, chimpanzees obtain very little of their food from others after they are weaned.

Less detailed data from other foraging groups are consistent with this pattern. **Figure 11.11** shows that men contribute more than half of the total calories consumed in seven of the nine foraging groups for which the necessary data are available. Notice that all of these groups live in tropical habitats. It seems likely from historical and ethnographic accounts that temperate and arctic foragers depend even more on meat than do tropical foragers, and thus in these societies men may make an even bigger caloric contribution.

Selection may have favored larger brains, a prolonged juvenile period, and a longer life span because these traits make it easier to learn complex foraging methods.

Complex, learned foraging techniques allow humans to acquire highly valuable or otherwise inaccessible food resources. Meat is a much better source of most nutrients that animals need than is the usual primate fare of leaves and ripe fruit. Meat is rich in energy, essential lipids, and protein. It is also dense enough to be economically transported from the kill site to home base. Some extracted resources like honey, insect

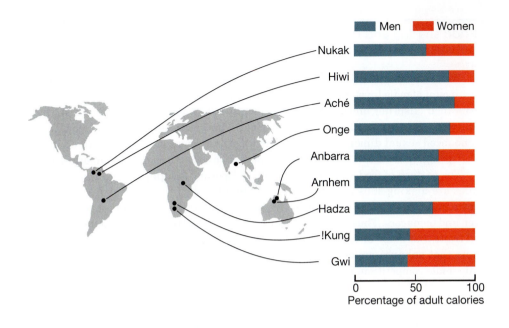

FIGURE 11.11

Males contribute significantly more calories than do women in nine contemporary foraging groups from different parts of the world.

larvae, and termites are also concentrated sources of important nutrients. Other kinds of extractive foraging unlock vast new food supplies. Tubers are a prime example. A number of tropical savanna plants store their reserve supplies of energy underground as various kinds of tubers, protected from the teeming herds of grazers and browsers by as much as a meter of rocky soil. By learning to recognize which plant species have tubers, how to use tools to dig them up, and when such work is likely to be profitable, humans were able to access a large supply of food for which there was relatively little competition from other organisms.

If learning is valuable, natural selection will favor adaptations that make a better learner. Thus a shift to hunting and extractive foraging would favor larger brains and greater intelligence. Reliance on complex learned foraging skills would also favor the evolution of a prolonged juvenile period. As we all know, learning takes time. You can't become a proficient skier, baker, or computer programmer in a day; practice and experience are needed. Similarly, learning the habits of animals and the lore of plants, acquiring the knowledge for tracking animals and the skills for shooting a bow or blowgun, and becoming adept at extracting starch from baobab pulp require years of practice. Thus it is plausible that selection favored a longer juvenile period to allow human children the time to acquire the skills they needed.

A prolonged juvenile period generates selection for a long life span. It is often said that time is money. In evolution, time is fitness. To see why, suppose that two genotypes, A and B, have the same number of children on average, but type A completes reproduction in 30 years and type B in 60 years. If you do a bit of math, you will see that type A will have twice the population growth rate as type B, and it will quickly replace type B in the population. This means that a prolonged juvenile period is costly and will not be favored by natural selection unless it causes people to have sufficiently more children over their life span. Human childhood is like a costly investment; it costs time, but the added time allows learning that produces more capable adults. Like any expensive investment, it will pay off more if it is amortized over a longer period. (The same logic explains why you are willing to spend more on something that you will use for a long time than on something you will use for a short time and then discard.) Selection favors a longer life because it allows people to get more benefit from the productive foraging techniques they learned during the necessary, but costly, extended juvenile period.

We saw in Chapter 6 that the intensity of competition between males depends on the amount of male investment in offspring. In most primate species, males do very little for their offspring, and selection consequently favors male traits that enhance their ability to compete with other males for matings. This increased competition leads to the pronounced sexual dimorphism seen in most primate species. When males do invest in offspring, there is less male–male competition and reduced sexual dimorphism.

The pattern of food sharing seen in contemporary foraging societies means that males are making substantial investments in offspring. This is clear from the data shown in Figure 11.10: males produce the bulk of the surplus calories that sustain children and teenagers. Thus we would expect selection to favor behavioral and morphological traits that make men good providers, and we would also expect selection-favoring traits that enhance male–male competitive ability to be reduced. The reduction in male–male competition, in turn, should lead to reduced sexual dimorphism.

Evidence for Complex Foraging by Oldowan Toolmakers

Let's stop and review for a second. So far, we have made two points. First, the Oldowan toolmakers (whoever they were) are plausible candidates for the species that links early apelike hominins to later hominins who have more humanlike life history patterns. Second, contemporary foragers rely on complex, hard-to-learn foraging techniques to a much greater extent than other primates do, and this shift can explain the evolution of the main features of human life history. To link these points, we need to consider the evidence that Oldowan hominins had begun to rely on hunting and extractive foraging to make a living.

As described in Closer Look 11.1, Schick and Toth have learned how to make the kinds of tools found at Oldowan sites. Then to get an idea what those tools were used for, they experimented, implementing them for different activities. They found that stone flakes can be used for a great number of tasks, whereas the cores are useful for a much narrower range of jobs

Extractive foraging, which is commonly done with wooden digging sticks by modern peoples, is likely to leave few traces in the archaeological record. However, one interesting piece of evidence suggests that hominins from this period were extractive foragers. During their excavations at Swartkrans, Robert Brain and his co-workers identified a sizable number of broken bones that had wear patterns suggesting that they had been used as tools. Lucinda Backwell of the University of the Witwatersrand and Francesco d'Errico of the Institut de Préhistoire et de Géologie du Quaternaire in France carefully analyzed these bones to find out how they were used. First the researchers used freshly broken bones to do a number of foraging tasks, including digging in hard soil for tubers and digging in a termite mound. Each activity creates a distinctive wear pattern that can be detected under microscopic analysis. Then they compared these wear patterns with those on the fossil bones found at Swartkrans.

Experimental tools used to dig

Swartkrans fossil   Tubers   Termites

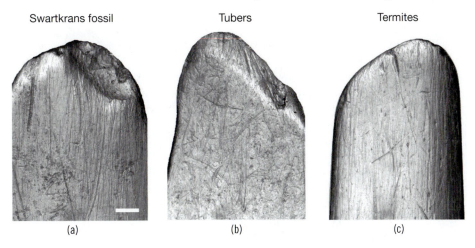

(a)   (b)   (c)

FIGURE 11.12

Experiments indicate that bone tools found at Swartkrans were used to excavate termite mounds. The tool shown in panel (a) is a cast of the original tool found at Swartkrans. The experimental tools in panels (b) and (c) were used for subsistence tasks, digging for tubers and digging for termites. The wear pattern on the Swartkrans fossils was most similar to that on the experimental tool used to dig for termites.

This analysis indicated that the fossil tools were used for digging in termite mounds. **Figure 11.12** shows the wear patterns on the fossil tool and two experimental tools, one used for digging in soil and the other used for excavating a termite mound. All of the tools have a smooth, rounded point. However, the tool experimentally used for digging in soil has deep marks of different depths going in all directions. In contrast, the tool used to dig in termite mounds has fine, parallel grooves. The fossil-bone tools closely resemble the experimental tool used for digging in termite mounds, so it seems likely that this is what these tools were used for. If this is correct, then Oldowan hominins were using tools to do extractive foraging.

Archaeological Evidence for Meat Eating

At several archaeological sites in East Africa, Oldowan tools have been found along with dense concentrations of animal bones.

Archaeological sites with early stone tools occur at the Olduvai Gorge of Tanzania, Koobi Fora in Kenya, and a number of sites in Ethiopia. Several sites in Bed I of the Olduvai Gorge excavated by Mary Leakey have been analyzed the most extensively. These sites, which are dated to 2 to 1.5 mya, measure only 10 to 20 m (33 to 66 ft.) in diameter, but they are littered with fossilized animal bones (**Figure 11.13**). The densities of animal bones in the archaeological sites are hundreds of times higher than those in the surrounding areas or in modern savannas. The bones belong to a wide range of animal species, including bovids (such as present-day antelope and wildebeests), pigs, equids (horses), elephants, hippopotamuses, rhinoceroses, and a variety of carnivores (**Figure 11.14**).

At some of these sites, Mary Leakey also found several kinds of stone artifacts: cores, flakes, battered rocks that may have been used as hammers or anvils and some stones that show no signs of human modification or use. The artifacts were manufactured from rocks that came from a number of different spots in the local area; some were made from rocks found several kilometers away (**Figure 11.15**).

The association of hominin tools and animal bones does not necessarily mean that early hominins were responsible for these bone accumulations.

It is easy to jump to the conclusion that the association of hominin tool and animal bones means that the Oldowan toolmakers hunted and processed the prey whose

FIGURE 11.13

In this site map for one level of Bed I at Olduvai Gorge, most of the bones are from an elephant. Tools are shown in black.

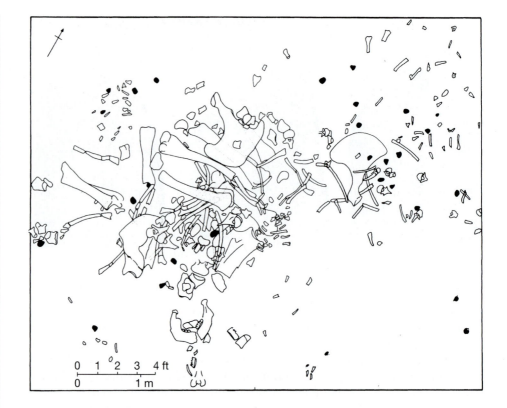

bones we find at these sites. If that is our assumption, these may have been sites where Oldowan hominins lived, like modern foragers' camps, or they may have been butchery sites where Oldowan hominins processed carcasses but did not live. However, there are also other possibilities. Bones may have accumulated at these sites without any help from early hominins. The bones may have been deposited there by moving water (which has now disappeared) or by other carnivores, such as hyenas. These sites also might be where many animals died of natural causes. Hominins might have visited the sites after the bones accumulated, perhaps hundreds of years later, and left their tools behind. Such sites are called **palimpsests**, a word that was originally used to describe the practice of scraping parchment manuscript pages and reusing them.

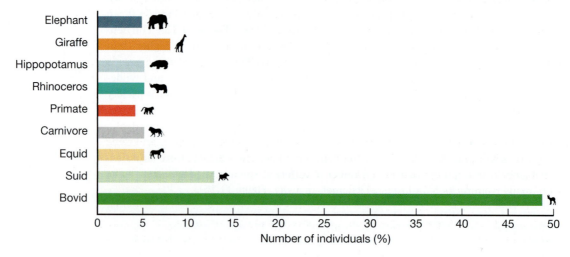

FIGURE 11.14

The bones of many different mammals were found at one archaeological site at Olduvai. Bovids (which include antelope, gazelles, sheep, goats, and cattle) clearly outnumber all other taxa.

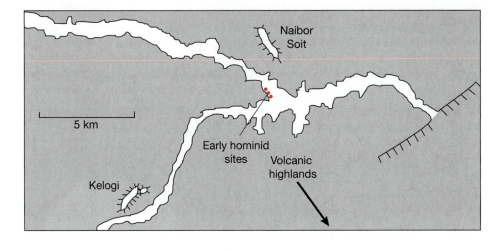

FIGURE 11.15

This map of Olduvai Gorge shows the major Bed I sites. Some of the tools were made of quartzite from Naibor Soit, others were made from gneiss from Kelogi, and some used lava cobbles that came from streams in the volcanic highlands to the south.

Archaeologists have resolved some of the uncertainty about these sites by studying how contemporary kill sites are formed.

Taphonomy provides one means of resolving questions about what happened at these sites. Taphonomy is the study of the processes that produce archaeological sites. Taphonomists examine the characteristics of contemporary kill sites—spots where animals have been killed, processed, and eaten by various predators, including contemporary human hunters. They monitor how each type of predator consumes its prey, noting whether limb bones are cracked open for marrow, which bones are carried away from the site, how human hunters use tools to process carcasses, and how bones are distributed by predators at the kill site.

They also examine the marks that are left on bones when they have been chewed on by predators, processed with stone tools, or left out in the open for long periods. When carnivores gnaw on meat, their teeth leave distinctive marks on the bones. Similarly, when humans use stone tools to butcher prey, their tools leave characteristic marks. Flaked-stone tools have microscopic serrations on the edges and make very fine parallel grooves when they are used to scrape meat away from bones (**Figure 11.16**).

These data enable archaeologists to develop a profile of the characteristics of kill sites created by different types of predators. Taphonomists can also assess many of the same characteristics in archaeological sites. By comparing the features of archaeological and contemporary sites, they are sometimes able to determine what happened at an archaeological site in the past.

Taphonomic analyses at Olduvai Gorge suggest that the bones at most of these sites were not accumulated by natural processes.

Taphonomic studies of the Olduvai sites where both animal bones and stone tools have been found tell us, first of all, that the bones were not deposited by moving water. Animals sometimes drown as they try to cross a swollen river or when they are swept away in flash floods (**Figure 11.17**). The bodies are carried downstream and accumulate in a sinkhole or on a sandbar. As the bodies decompose, the bones are exposed to the surrounding elements. The study of modern sites shows that sediments deposited by rapidly moving water have a number of distinctive characteristics. For example, such sediments tend to be graded by size because particles of different sizes and weights sink at different spots. Sediments surrounding Olduvai sites do not show any of the features characteristic of sediments deposited by rapidly moving water.

Taphonomic analyses also tell us that the dense concentrations of bones were not due to the deaths of a large number of animals at one spot. Sometimes many animals die in the same place. In severe droughts, for example, large numbers of animals may

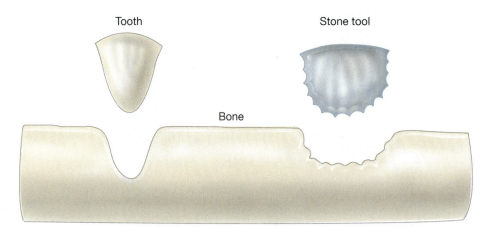

Tooth

Stone tool

Bone

(a)

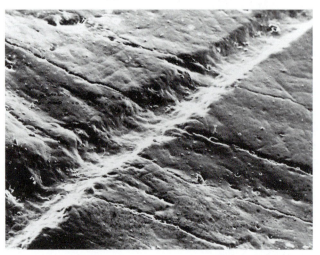

(b)

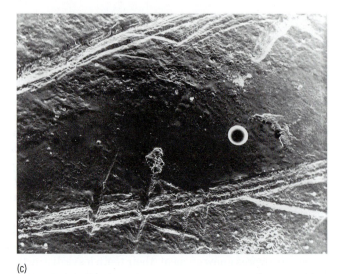

(c)

FIGURE 11.16

The marks made on bone by teeth differ from the marks made by stone tools. (a) The smooth surfaces of teeth leave broad, smooth grooves on bones; the edges of stone tools, on the other hand, have many tiny, sharp points that leave fine parallel grooves. Cut marks made by (b) carnivore teeth and (c) stone tools can be distinguished when they are examined with a scanning electron microscope. These are scanning electron micrographs of 1.8-million-year-old fossil bones from Olduvai Gorge.

die near water holes. Mass deaths usually involve members of a single species, and there is typically little mixing of bones from different carcasses. By contrast, the bones at the Olduvai sites come from a number of different species, and bones from different carcasses are jumbled together.

At some sites, however, bone accumulations seem to be the product of carnivore activity, without hominin involvement. There is one site where the pattern of bone accumulation is very similar to the pattern of bone accumulations near modern hyena dens. Hyenas often carry and drag carcasses from kill sites to their dens so that they can feed their young and avoid competition with other carnivores.

Taphonomic analyses suggest that hominins were active at two of the Olduvai sites and used tools at these sites to process carcasses.

At two sites, FLK Zinjanthropus and Bell's karongo, there is good evidence that hominins processed carcasses. There are large quantities of bones from multiple animal species and stone tools. Moreover, many of the bones bear cut marks and

FIGURE 11.17

Sometimes large numbers of wildebeest drown when trying to cross swollen rivers.

percussion marks (**Figure 11.18**), clear signs of hominin activity. Some of these bones also show tooth marks, suggesting that carnivores were also present at these sites.

Hunters or Scavengers?

There has been controversy about whether the Oldowan hominins were hunters or scavengers.

The archaeological evidence indicates that Oldowan hominins processed the carcasses of large animals, and we assume that they ate the meat they cut from the bones. But eating meat does not necessarily imply hunting. Some carnivores acquire meat by hunting, but many carnivores rely at least partly on scavenging. Scavengers steal kills from other predators or rely on opportunistic discoveries of carcasses.

There has been considerable dispute about how early hominins acquired the meat they ate. Some have argued that Oldowan hominins killed the prey found at the archaeological sites; others have argued that Oldowan hominins could not have captured large mammals because they were too small, too poorly armed, and too poorly encephalized. They contend that the Oldowan hominins were scavengers who occasionally appropriated kills from other predators or collected carcasses they found.

For most contemporary carnivores, scavenging is as difficult and dangerous as hunting.

To resolve the debate about whether early hominins were hunters or scavengers, we must first rethink popular conceptions of scavengers. Although scavengers have an unsavory reputation, scavenging is not an occupation for the cowardly or lazy. Scavengers must be brave enough to snatch kills from the jaws of hungry competitors, shrewd enough to hang back in the shadows until the kill is momentarily left unguarded, or patient enough to follow herds and take advantage of natural mortality. Studies of contemporary carnivores show that the great majority of scavenged meat is acquired by taking a kill away from

FIGURE 11.18

This bone shows linear cut marks (*A*) and round percussion marks (*B*).

(a)   (b)

FIGURE 11.19

Competition among predators at kill sites is frequently intense. Here (a) lions have scavenged prey from a pack of hyenas, and (b) the hyenas fight to get it back.

FIGURE 11.20

Male lions sometimes take kills from smaller carnivores and from female lions.

FIGURE 11.21

As dusk falls, three cheetah cubs wait for their mother to return from hunting.

another predator. Most predators respond aggressively to competition from scavengers. For example, lions jealously guard their prey from persistent scavengers that try to steal bits of meat or to drag away parts of the carcass. These contests can be quite dangerous (**Figure 11.19**).

Most large mammalian carnivores practice both hunting and scavenging.

We also tend to think that some carnivores, like lions and leopards, only hunt, and that others, like hyenas and jackals, only scavenge. But the simple dichotomy between scavengers and hunters collapses when we review the data on the behavior of the five largest African mammalian carnivores: lion, hyena, cheetah, leopard, and wild dog. The fractions of meat obtained by scavenging vary from none for the cheetah, to 33% for hyenas, with the others ranging somewhere in between. Contrary to the usual stereotypes, the noble lion is not above taking prey from smaller competitors, including female members of his own pride, and hyenas are accomplished hunters (**Figure 11.20**). For most large carnivores in eastern Africa, hunting and scavenging are complementary activities.

No mammalian carnivores subsist entirely by scavenging. It would be difficult for any large mammal to do so. For one thing, many prey species create movable feasts, migrating in large herds over long distances. Although natural mortality in these herds might make scavenging feasible, their migratory habits eliminate this option. Mammalian carnivores cannot follow these migrating herds very far, because they have dependent young that cannot travel long distances (**Figure 11.21**). Only avian scavengers that can soar over great distances, like the griffon vulture, rely entirely on scavenging (**Figure 11.22**). When migratory herds are absent, mammalian carnivores rely on other prey, such as waterbuck and impalas. Natural mortality among resident species is not high enough to satisfy the caloric demands of carnivores, so they must hunt and kill much of their own prey, though they still scavenge when the opportunity arises.

Scavenging might be more practical if carnivores switched from big game to other forms of food when migratory herds were not present. This is a plausible option for early hominins. Most groups of contemporary foraging people rely heavily on gathered foods—including tubers, seeds, fruit, eggs, and various invertebrates—in addition to meat. A few, such as the Hadza, obtain meat from scavenging as well as from hunting. It is possible that early hominins relied mainly on gathered foods and scavenged meat opportunistically.

FIGURE 11.22

Vultures, which soar on thermals and have enormous ranges, are the only carnivores that rely entirely on scavenging.

Taphonomic evidence suggests that early hominins acquired meat both by scavenging and by hunting.

As we saw earlier, predators often face stiff competition for their kills. An animal that tries to defend its kill risks losing it to scavengers. For this reason, leopards drag their kills into trees and eat the meat in safety. Other predators, like hyenas, sometimes rip off the meaty parts of the carcass, such as the hindquarters, and drag their booty away to eat in peace. This means that limb bones usually disappear from a kill site first, and less meaty bones, such as the vertebrae and skull, disappear later or remain at the kill site (**Figure 11.23**). If hominins obtained most of their meat from scavenging, we would expect to find cut marks made by tools mainly on bones typically left at kill sites by predators, such as vertebrae. If hominins obtained most of their meat from their own kills, we would expect to find tool marks mainly on large bones, like limb bones.

There is a vigorous debate about the taphonomic evidence for hunting versus scavenging. Robert Blumenschine of Rutgers University has argued that carnivores killed prey and partially consumed the flesh; then hominins acquired pieces of the carcass which they used to process marrow; finally other carnivores gnawed on the bones. He argues that opportunistic scavenging would not require novel technological skills or behavioral adaptations and is therefore an evolutionarily conservative hypothesis. However, scavenging would mark a departure from chimpanzees, which hunt often but very rarely take advantage of scavenging opportunities.

FIGURE 11.23

After other predators have left, vultures consume what remains at the kill site.

Manuel Domínguez-Rodrigo from the Universidad Complutense de Madrid takes a different view. He argues that hominins had first access to carcasses. He bases his conclusions on two sources of evidence. First, he believes that the carnivore–hominin–carnivore model is based on a misreading of the taphonomic evidence from one of the two sites at which hominins were active. He and his colleagues argue that some natural biochemical marks on bones may have been mistaken for carnivore tooth marks. Genuine tooth marks are mainly limited to the ends of long bones, which indicates that they were processed by carnivores after they were processed by hominins. Blumenschine rejects this interpretation, and the debate is not resolved.

Second, excavations of a second site at Olduvai, Bell's karongo, suggest that hominins initially processed carcasses that were later available to carnivores. Many of the bones bear cut marks and percussion marks (Figure 11.18), but tooth marks are relatively uncommon. Cut marks are common on fleshy limb bones that would already have been defleshed if carnivores had had first access to the carcasses.

Domestic Lives of Oldowan Toolmakers

We have reason to believe that Oldowan toolmakers used their tools for extractive foraging and to process prey carcasses. Oldowan hominins may have obtained these carcasses through a mix of hunting and scavenging. Thus they had probably come to

FIGURE 11.24

The Efe, a foraging people of central Africa, build temporary camps in the forest and shift camps frequently.

rely on complex foraging skills that were difficult to master. In modern foraging societies, reliance on complex foraging skills is also linked to food sharing, sexual division of labor, and the establishment of home bases. Nearly all contemporary foraging peoples establish a temporary camp (**home base**), where food is shared, processed, cooked, and eaten. The camp is also the place where people weave nets, manufacture arrows, sharpen digging sticks, string bows, make plans, resolve disputes, tell stories, and sing songs (**Figure 11.24**). Because foragers often move from one location to another, their camps are simple, generally consisting of modest huts or shelters built around several hearths. If Oldowan hominins established home bases, we might be able to detect traces of their occupation in the archaeological record.

> Some archaeologists have interpreted the dense accumulations of stones and bones as home bases, much like those of modern foragers, but this view is not consistent with some of the evidence.

Some archaeologists, particularly the late Glyn Isaac, have suggested that the dense accumulations of animal bones and stone tools found at some sites mark the location of hominin home bases. They have speculated that early hominins acquired meat by hunting or scavenging and then brought pieces of the carcass home, where it could be shared. The dense collections of bones and artifacts were thought to be the result of prolonged occupation of the home base (and sloppy housekeeping). At one Olduvai Bed I site, there is even a circle of stones (**Figure 11.25**), dated to 1.9 mya, that is similar to the circles of stones anchoring the walls of simple huts constructed by some foraging peoples in dry environments today. Many Oldowan tools and bone fragments from a variety of prey species are found at the same site.

However, a number of other observations are inconsistent with the idea that these sites were home bases:

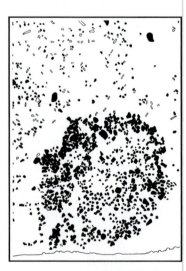

FIGURE 11.25

A circle of stones at one Olduvai Bed I site has been interpreted by some archaeologists as the remains of a simple shelter.

- Both hominins and nonhominin carnivores were active at many of the Olduvai sites. Many of the bones at the Olduvai sites were gnawed by nonhominin carnivores. Sometimes the same bones show both tooth marks and cut marks, but some show only the marks of nonhominin carnivores.

- Hominins and nonhominin carnivores apparently competed over kills. The bones of nonhominin carnivores occur more often than would be expected on the basis of their occurrence in other fossil assemblages or modern carnivore densities.

Perhaps the carnivores were killed (and eaten) when attempting to scavenge hominin kills or when hominins attempted to scavenge their kills. Hominins may not have always won such contests; some fossilized hominin bones show the tooth marks of other carnivores.

- Modern kill sites are often the scene of violent conflict among carnivores. This conflict occurs among members of different species as well as the same species. It is especially common when a small predator, like a cheetah, makes a kill. The kill attracts many other animals, most of which are able to displace the cheetah.

- The bones accumulated at the Olduvai sites are weathered. When bones lie on the surface of the ground, they crack and peel in various ways. The longer they remain exposed on the surface, the greater the extent of weathering. Taphonomists can calibrate the weathering process and use these data to determine how long fossil bones were on the ground before being buried. Some of the bones at the Olduvai sites were exposed to the elements for at least four to six years (**Figure 11.26**).

- The Olduvai sites do not show evidence of intensive bone processing. The bones at these sites show cut marks and tooth marks, and many bones were apparently smashed with stone hammers to remove marrow. However, the bones were not processed intensively, as they are by modern foragers.

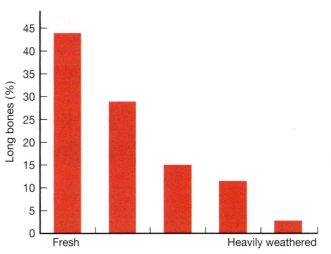

FIGURE 11.26

Many of the bones at Bed I sites at Olduvai are heavily weathered, suggesting that they were deposited and exposed to the elements over a fairly long period of time.

These observations are difficult to reconcile with the idea that the Olduvai sites were home bases—places where people eat, sleep, tell stories, and care for their children. First, foragers today do everything they can to prevent carnivores from entering their camps. They often pile up thorny branches to fence their camps and keep dogs that are meant to chase predators away. It is hard to imagine that early hominins could have occupied these sites if lions, hyenas, and saber-toothed cats were regular visitors. Second, bones at the Olduvai sites appear to have accumulated over a period of years. Contemporary foragers usually abandon their home bases permanently after a few months because the accumulating garbage attracts insects and other vermin. Even though they revisit the same areas regularly, they don't often reoccupy their old sites. Finally, the fossilized bones found at Olduvai were not processed as thoroughly as modern foragers process their kills.

Hominins may have brought carcasses to these sites and processed the carcasses with flakes made from previously cached stones.

Richard Potts, an anthropologist at the Smithsonian Institution, suggests that these sites were not home bases but butchery sites—places where hominins worked but did not live. He believes that hominins brought their kills to these sites and dismembered their carcasses there. Some of the carcasses were scavenged by hominins from other carnivores, and some of the hominins' kills were lost to scavengers. Hominins may have carried bones and meat away to other sites for more intensive processing. This would explain why bones accumulated over such a long time, why bones of non-hominin carnivores were present, and why bones were not completely processed.

At first glance, it might seem inconvenient for hominins to schlep their kills to butchery sites. Why not process the carcass at the kill site? We have seen that hominins used tools to process the meat. However, they couldn't be sure of finding appropriate rocks for toolmaking at the sites of their kills. And they couldn't leave their kills unguarded while they went off to fetch their tools, lest a hungry scavenger steal their supper. So they must have had to carry the meat to where their tools were kept or to keep their tools with them all the time. Remember that these tools were fairly heavy, and early hominins had no pockets or backpacks. Potts suggests that the best strategy would have been to cache tools at certain places and then to carry carcasses that they had acquired to the nearest cache.

Back to the Future: The Transition to Modern Human Life Histories

We have argued that complex foraging techniques favor food sharing, male parental investment, and sexual division of labor. These behavioral practices, in turn, create selective pressures for reduced sexual dimorphism and delayed maturation of off-spring. The Oldowan toolmakers were extractive foragers, hunters, and scavengers of meat. As we will see in the next chapter, reduced sexual dimorphism and somewhat delayed maturation characterize hominins who appear in the fossil record about 2 mya. It seems likely that these morphological and developmental features, which also characterize modern humans, represent adaptations to this new way of life.

Key Terms

flakes
cores
Oldowan tool industry
knapping
Mode 1
cortex
collected foods
extracted foods
hunted foods
palimpsests
taphonomy
home base

Study Questions

1. Who made the first stone tools? What kinds of evidence complicate this question?

2. What are the differences between collected, extracted, and hunted foods? How do comparative data help us understand the unique foraging adaptations of modern humans?

3. Why do complex foraging techniques favor slow development and long childhoods? What kinds of data enable us to draw inferences about developmental patterns in early hominins?

4. Suppose we discovered that Oldowan foraging technology was very easy to master and required

little skill. How would that change your ideas about the selective pressures acting on hominins? How would that change your ideas about who made Oldowan tools?

5. Why do we associate food sharing with meat eating rather than with vegetarianism?

6. What were Oldowan tools like, and what were they used for?

7. Researchers argue about whether Oldowan toolmakers were hunters or scavengers. What are the main arguments on each side of this debate?

8. How would it change our views of human evolution if we found convincing evidence that the Oldowan hominins scavenged but did not hunt?

9. Some researchers have argued that Olduvai Bed I sites are the remains of hominin home bases; others think that they are workplaces where hominins processed carcasses. If you were an archaeologist, how would you go about testing this idea? Think about the kinds of data you would need to collect to examine the merits of each hypothesis.

10. We have discussed the Oldowan toolmakers at length, even though we don't really know who they were. Why is this a profitable exercise?

Further Reading

Domínguez-Rodrigo, M. 2009. "Are Oldowan Sites Palimpsests? If So, What Can They Tell Us about Hominid Carnivory?" In E. Hovers and D. R. Braun, eds. *Interdisciplinary Approaches to the Oldowan*, pp. 129–147. Springer, Dordrecht: The Netherlands.

Kaplan, H., K. Hill, J. Lancaster, and A. M. Hurtado. 2000. "A Theory of Human Life History Evolution: Diet, Intelligence, and Longevity." *Evolutionary Anthropology* 9: 156–185.

McGrew, W. C. 1992. *Chimpanzee Material Culture: Implications for Human Evolution*. New York: Cambridge University Press.

Potts, R. 1984. "Home Bases and Early Hominins." *American Scientist* 72: 338–347.

Schick, K. D., and N. Toth, eds. 2009. *The Cutting Edge: New Approaches to the Archaeology of Human Origins*. Bloomington, IN: Stone Age Institute Press.

CHAPTER OBJECTIVES

By the end of this chapter you should be able to

- Describe the morphology of the earliest members of the human genus *Homo*.

- Describe the morphology, life history, and life ways of *Homo erectus/ergaster*.

- Explain how hominins left Africa.

- Describe the morphology, life history, and life ways of the larger-brained Middle Pleistocene hominins, including the Neanderthals.

- Discuss the difficulty in classifying Middle Pleistocene hominins.

FROM HOMININ TO *HOMO*

Early *Homo*

Homo ergaster

Hominins of the Early Middle Pleistocene (900 to 300 kya)

Hominins of the Later Pleistocene (300 to 50 kya)

The Sources of Change

The Muddle in the Middle

About 1.8 mya, a new kind of hominin appeared in Africa. These creatures, whom we will call *Homo ergaster*, were much more like modern humans than the apelike hominins who preceded them. Some of them had large, robust bodies with relatively long legs and short arms. They were fully committed to life on the ground and may have been good long-distance runners. *Homo ergaster* invented a new kind of tool technology and probably learned to master fire and to hunt large game. Although we can see much of ourselves in these creatures, important differences remain. They had smaller brains than we have, and their subsistence technology seems to have been much less flexible than ours.

We begin this chapter by describing what is known about the origins of the genus *Homo* in Africa. Then we describe the emergence of *Homo ergaster* in Africa and trace the evolution of hominins as they migrated out of Africa and spread throughout temperate Asia and into Europe. There is considerable controversy about what we should call the African, Asian, and European forms of early members of the genus *Homo*; uncertainty about their relationships to one another; and debate about how to explain the variation that is seen within and across regions of the world. However, these creatures all share many aspects of morphology and seem to have shared important elements of subsistence technology. We will see that hominins gradually evolved larger brains and more sophisticated subsistence technology and that these incremental changes eventually led to the emergence of our own species, *Homo sapiens,* about 200 kya (thousand years ago). We will track changes that took place over time and space as we reconstruct the transformation of *Homo ergaster* into *Homo sapiens.*

Early *Homo*

The earliest evidence of the genus *Homo* comes from East Africa about 2.3 mya. These creatures were distinguished by larger brains and more humanlike teeth.

In 1960, while working at Olduvai Gorge with his parents, the renowned paleoanthropologists Louis and Mary Leakey, Jonathan Leakey found pieces of a hominin jaw, cranium, and hand. The Leakeys assigned this specimen, labeled Olduvai Hominin 7 (OH 7), to the genus *Homo* because they believed the cranial bones indicated that it had a much larger brain than australopiths had. In addition, the teeth are smaller and have thinner enamel and the dental arcade is more parabolic than in the australopiths. The skulls are more rounded, there are fewer air pockets in the bottom of the skull, the face is smaller and protrudes less, and the jaw muscles are reduced in size compared with the australopiths.

More recent analyses of the early *Homo* material from Olduvai and other sites suggest that these creatures resembled australopiths in their development patterns and their limb proportions. Analyses of the layering of dental enamel suggest that early *Homo* juveniles had relatively rapid apelike development patterns. The first fragmentary postcranial material found at Olduvai Gorge suggested that OH 7 had longer arms and shorter legs than modern humans. Subsequent discoveries at Olduvai Gorge add credence to this picture. During an expedition led by Don Johanson, Tim White discovered a specimen that included an incomplete cranium and numerous postcranial bones. This specimen, labeled OH 62, was very short in stature and had surprisingly long arms, suggesting that the postcranial skeletons of the Olduvai early *Homo* specimens were similar to those of *Au. afarensis.*

Louis Leakey was convinced that OH 7 was evidence that a new, large-brained hominin was present in Africa by 2 mya, but others were skeptical.

Many paleoanthropologists doubted that the Leakeys had found the oldest member of our genus. After all, the Leakeys' estimate of OH 7's brain size was based on only part of the cranium, and even then the complete cranium was estimated to be at most 50% larger than the brains of the australopiths. There was plenty of room for skepticism.

Another member of the famous Leakey family helped prove that large brains were indeed present in a hominin living 1.9 mya. Mary and Louis Leakey's son Richard set up his own research team and began work at a site called Koobi Fora on the eastern shore of Lake Turkana. In 1972, a member of Richard Leakey's team, Bernard Ngeneo, found a nearly complete skull of a hominin. This find is usually referred to by its official collection number, KNM-ER 1470 (**Figure 12.1**).

FIGURE 12.1

The discovery of KNM-ER 1470 at a site on Lake Turkana confirmed that there was at least one large-brained hominin in East Africa about 2 mya.

(*KNM* stands for Kenya National Museum, and *ER* stands for East Rudolf—Lake Turkana was known as Lake Rudolf when Leakey began his work there.) The most striking thing about KNM-ER 1470 is that it had a much larger brain than any known australopith had. Its endocranial volume is 775 cc, 75% bigger than the brains of specimens of *Au. africanus*. Compared to OH 7, however, it had an australopith-like face and relatively large teeth.

Since the discovery of KNM-ER 1470, several other early *Homo* fossils have been found. These fossils have come from a number of sites in East Africa, including the Olduvai Gorge, the Omo River basin, and Ileret near Lake Turkana. Other fossils associated with early *Homo* come from Sterkfontein in South Africa and a site near Lake Malawi. The oldest of these fossils dates to 2.3 mya, and the youngest is dated to 1.4 mya. The skulls and teeth of these fossils are quite variable. Some of them, like KNM-ER 1813 (**Figure 12.2**), have more humanlike teeth and less robust skulls with smaller faces and teeth than KNM-ER 1470, but they also have smaller brains than KNM-ER 1470, often about 500 cc.

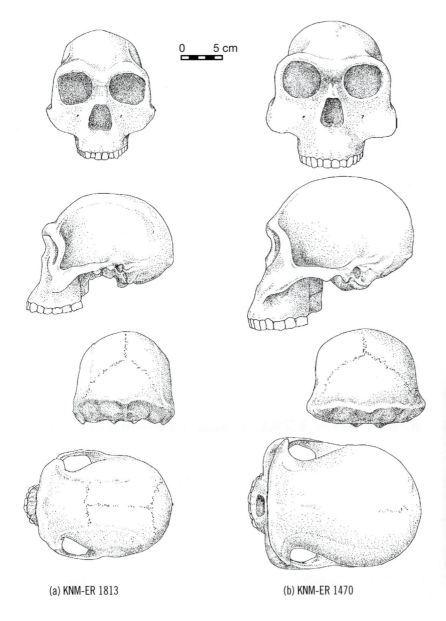

0 5 cm

(a) KNM-ER 1813   (b) KNM-ER 1470   (c)

FIGURE 12.2

(a, c) KNM-ER 1813 had more modern teeth but a smaller brain than (b) KNM-ER 1470. This variation led many investigators to argue that fossils assigned to the species *habilis* actually belonged to more than one species of hominin.

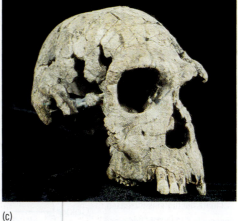

It is not clear whether the early *Homo* material from this period should be assigned to one, two, or perhaps even three species.

Some believe that the differences among these African specimens represent variation within a single sexually dimorphic species. Others have argued that there were two early *Homo* species present in East Africa 2 mya and that the smaller-brained, less robust individuals should be classified as *H. habilis,* while the more robust ones with larger brains are a second species that should be named *H. rudolfensis.* One specimen from Sterkfontein in South Africa, dated 1.9 to 1.8 mya, might represent a third species or might be subsumed under *H. habilis.*

Homo ergaster

The Pleistocene epoch began 1.8 mya and saw a cooling of the world's climate.

The Pleistocene is divided into three parts: the Lower, Middle, and Upper Pleistocene. The Lower Pleistocene began about 1.8 mya, a date that coincides with a sharp cooling of the world's climate. The beginning of the Middle Pleistocene is marked by sharply increased fluctuations in temperature and the first appearance of immense continental glaciers that covered northern Europe 900 kya, and its end is defined by the termination of the penultimate glacial period about 130 kya. The Upper Pleistocene ended about 12 kya when a warm, interglacial phase of the world climate began; this warm period has persisted into the present (**Figure 12.3**).

Homo ergaster appears in the African fossil record about 1.8 mya and disappears about 0.6 mya.

Fossils of *Homo ergaster* have been found at several sites in Kenya (Lake Turkana, Olorgesailie, and Ileret), as well as at Konso-Gardula (Ethiopia), Daka (Ethiopia), Olduvai Gorge (Tanzania), and Swartkrans (South Africa). **Figure 12.4** shows a very well preserved skull (labeled KNM-ER 3733) from Lake Turkana that was found in

FIGURE 12.3

The pattern of world temperature over the last 6 million years. These estimates are based on the ratio of ^{16}O to ^{18}O in cores extracted from deep-sea sediments. During the Pliocene, world temperatures declined, and in the Pleistocene climate fluctuations increased, especially during the Middle and Upper Pleistocene.

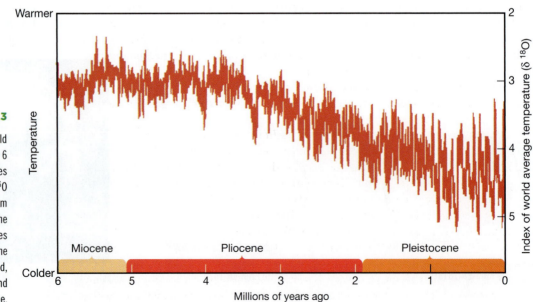

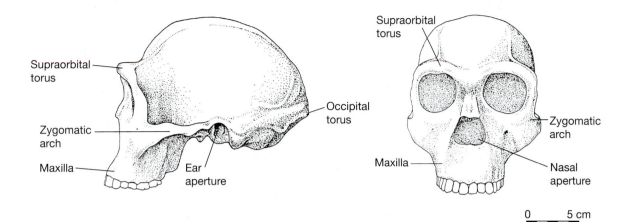

Supraorbital torus

Supraorbital torus

Occipital torus

Zygomatic arch

Zygomatic arch

Maxilla

Maxilla

Ear aperture

Nasal aperture

0 — 5 cm

FIGURE 12.4

Homo ergaster skulls, like the skull of KNM-ER 3733 illustrated here, show a mix of primitive and derived features.

1976 by a team led by Richard Leakey. When *H. ergaster* fossils first appear on the scene, they are associated with Oldowan tools. Finds in Ileret suggest that *H. habilis* and *H. ergaster* may have co-existed for almost half a million years in the Turkana basin of Kenya.

Until recently, most paleontologists had assigned these East African fossils to the species *Homo erectus* on the basis of their similarities to fossils that had been discovered in Indonesia at the end of the nineteenth century. However, a growing number of paleontologists have come to believe that the African specimens are distinctive enough to be assigned to a different species. Following the rules of zoological nomenclature, the Indonesian specimens retained the original name *H. erectus* because they were described first, and the African specimens were given a new name. Advocates of this view have given the African fossils the name *Homo ergaster,* or "work man." We will use *H. ergaster* to refer to African specimens of this group and *H. erectus* for the Asian fossils. Keep in mind that it is not entirely clear how many species these fossils represent.

Morphology

Skulls of *Homo ergaster* differ from those of both earlier hominins and modern humans.

Skulls of *Homo ergaster* retain many of the characteristics of earlier hominins (**Figure 12.5**), including a marked narrowing behind the eyes, a receding forehead, and no chin. *H. ergaster* also shows many derived features. Some of these are shared by modern humans, including a shorter and less prognathic face, a taller skull, smaller jaws and postcanine teeth, and reduction in the number of roots on the upper premolars. However, *H. ergaster* also has some derived features that we don't see in earlier hominins or modern humans. For example, *H. ergaster* has a horizontal ridge at the back of the skull (**occipital torus**), which gives it a pointed appearance when viewed from the side. It also has quite large browridges.

Many of the derived features of the skull of *Homo ergaster* may be related to diet. These hominins were probably better adapted for tearing and biting with their canines and incisors and less suited to heavy chewing with their molars. Thus all their teeth are smaller than the teeth of the australopiths and paranthropines, but their molars are reduced relatively more in comparison with their incisors. The large browridges and the point at the back of the skull may have been needed to buttress the skull against novel stresses created by an increased emphasis on tearing and biting.

Homo ergaster may also have been better adapted for life in a drier environment. In apes and earlier hominin species, the nose is relatively flat and the nostrils face forward. Like modern humans, *H. ergaster*'s nostrils face downward, and it probably had a projecting nose. This may have been an adaptation for preserving moisture during

FIGURE 12.5

Skulls of (a) *Australopithecus africanus*, (b) *Paranthropus robustus*, (c) *Homo ergaster*, and (d) modern *Homo sapiens*.

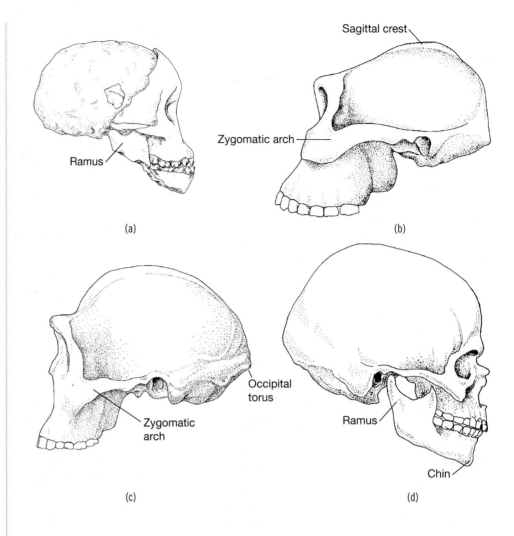

periods of physical exertion. The nose is generally cooler than the body, and moisture condenses inside the nose when we exhale. Richard Klein of Stanford University speculates that *H. ergaster* may also have been the first hominin species to have hairless skin, an adaptation that would enhance the effectiveness of sweating as a means of cooling the body and brain.

Homo ergaster had a substantially larger brain than earlier hominins, averaging about 800 cc. Some very small specimens of *H. ergaster* have brains that lie at the upper end of the distribution of brain sizes among earlier hominin species (500 to 700 cc), while other specimens have brains that are as large as 1,000 cc. It is not entirely clear how to interpret this variation in brain size. It might be associated with sexual dimorphism, but we cannot be certain of this because the skulls that provide brain-size estimates are not associated with skeletal material.

As we will see later in this chapter, some members of this species were considerably taller than earlier hominins while others were quite small. Brain size increases with body size in mammals, so it seems likely that *H. ergaster* did not have a substantially larger brain in relation to body size than earlier hominin species.

The postcranial skeleton of *Homo ergaster* is more similar to the skeleton of modern humans than to that of earlier hominins, but it still differs from ours in interesting ways.

Fossils attributed to *Homo ergaster* differ considerably in size. The smallest ones, like KNM-ER 42700 from Ileret, may have been the same size as *Homo habilis* and the australopiths, while others were considerably taller. The most complete information about the postcranial morphology of *H. ergaster* comes from a spectacular specimen discovered by Kimoya Kimeu (**Figure 12.6**), the leader of the Koobi Fora paleontological team. The find was made on the west side of Lake Turkana, the same region where fossils of *Australopithecus anamensis, Paranthropus aethiopicus,* and *Kenyanthropus platyops* were found. The skeleton, which is formally known as KNM-WT 15000, belonged to a boy who was about 12 years old when he died. The skeleton provides us with a remarkably complete picture of the *H. ergaster* body; even the delicate ribs and vertebrae are preserved (**Figure 12.7**). An extensive analysis of this skeleton, coordinated by Alan Walker, tells us a lot about this youngster's body and his way of life.

Remember that earlier hominins were bipeds but still had long arms, short legs, and other features suggesting that they spent a considerable amount of time in trees. In contrast, KNM-WT 15000 had the same body proportions as people who live in tropical savannas today: long legs, narrow hips, narrow shoulders, and barrel-shaped chest. KNM-WT 15000 also had short arms, compared with earlier hominins. Taken together, these features suggest that *H. ergaster* was fully committed to terrestrial life.

This skeleton and less complete bits of the skeletons of other *H. ergaster* individuals tell us several other interesting things about them:

- Some were quite tall. KNM-WT 15000 stood about 1.625 m (5.33 ft.) in height. If *Homo ergaster* growth patterns were comparable to those of modern humans, this boy would have been about 1.9 m (6 ft.) tall when he was fully grown. However, he was also robust and heavily muscled. Think of him as a young shooting guard or a small forward.

- Sexual dimorphism was reduced. *Homo ergaster* males were 20% to 30% larger than females, making *H. ergaster* much less dimorphic than the australopiths but still more dimorphic than modern humans.

- They may not have had spoken language. The vertebral canal in the thoracic (middle) region of the back is much larger in modern humans than it is in apes, and it contains a proportionally thicker spinal cord. Detailed studies of the neuroanatomy in the thoracic region suggest that all of the extra nerves that enlarge the spinal cord innervate the muscles of the rib cage and diaphragm. The thoracic vertebrae of KNM-WT 15000 are comparable to those of other primates. If this young male is typical, then *H. ergaster* would have had less precise control over the muscles of its rib cage and diaphragm than modern humans do. Ann MacLarnon, an anatomist at Roehampton University, argues that increased motor control of the diaphragm and thoracic muscles is an adaptation that allows people to regulate complex timing of breathing associated with speech.

- *Homo ergaster* was fully committed to life on the ground and was the first hominin that could run for long distances. Compared to most other mammals, modern humans are not good sprinters. However, we are able to outrun all but a few species over distances of several kilometers. Dennis Bramble, a biologist at the University of Utah, and Daniel Lieberman, an anthropologist at Harvard University, have argued that features of the *H. ergaster* boy, such as long legs, narrow hips, and a barrel-shaped chest, are evidence that the capacity for long-distance running first appeared in this species. They believe that this talent may have been useful in long-distance scavenging and hunting in open country.

Homo ergaster may have developed more slowly than early hominins but more rapidly than modern humans.

Remember from Chapter 10 that Christopher Dean and his colleagues used estimates of tooth enamel growth rate to show that australopiths developed relatively

FIGURE 12.6

Kimoya Kimeu is an accomplished field researcher. He has made many important finds, including KNM-WT 15000 (see Figure 12.7).

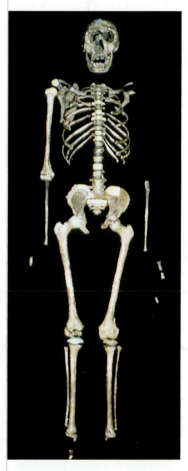

FIGURE 12.7

KNM-WT 15000, a *Homo ergaster* boy found on the west side of Lake Turkana, is amazingly complete.

quickly. Using the same methods, they estimate that *H. ergaster* developed more slowly than australopiths but still faster than modern humans. If this interpretation is correct, then *H. ergaster* did not have as long a childhood as modern humans have, suggesting that learning did not play as important a role in the lives of these creatures.

Tools and Subsistence

Homo ergaster made fancier tools than earlier hominins had made.

The earliest fossils of *Homo ergaster* both in Africa and in Eurasia are associated with Oldowan tools, the same tools that we described in Chapter 11. However, sometime between 1.6 and 1.4 mya in Africa, *H. ergaster* added a new and more sophisticated tool to its kit. This totally new kind of stone tool is called a **biface**. To make a biface, the toolmaker strikes a large piece of rock from a boulder to make a core and then flakes this core on all sides to create a flattened form with a sharp edge along its entire circumference. The most common type of biface, called a **hand ax**, is shaped like a teardrop and has a sharp point at the narrow end (**Figure 12.8**). A **cleaver** is a lozenge-shaped biface with a flat, sharp edge on one end; a **pick** is a thicker, more triangular biface. Bifaces are larger than Oldowan tools, averaging about 15 cm (6 in.) in length and sometimes reaching 30 cm (12 in.). Bifaces are categorized as **Mode 2** technology. Paleoanthropologists call the Mode 2 industries of Africa and western Eurasia (that is, Europe and the Middle East) the **Acheulean industry** after the French town of Saint-Acheul, where hand axes were first discovered. The oldest Acheulean tools found at West Turkana date to about 1.6 mya, just after *H. ergaster* first appeared in Africa. It is important to understand that Oldowan tools do not disappear when Acheulean tools make their debut. *Homo ergaster* continued making simple Mode 1 tools, perhaps when they needed a serviceable tool in a hurry—as foraging people do today.

The standardized form of hand axes and other Mode 2 tools in the Acheulean industry suggests that toolmakers had a specific design in mind when they made each tool. The Mode 1 tools of the Oldowan industry have a haphazard appearance; no two are alike. This lack of standardization suggests that makers of Oldowan tools simply picked up a core and struck off flakes; they didn't try to create a tool with a particular shape that they had in mind beforehand. They may have done this because the flakes were the actual tools.

It is easy to see how a biface might have evolved from an Oldowan chopper by extending the flaking around the periphery of the tool. However, Acheulean tools are not just Oldowan tools with longer edges; they are designed according to a uniform plan. Hand axes have regular proportions: The ratio of height to width to thickness is remarkably constant from one ax to another. *Homo ergaster* must have started with an irregularly shaped piece of rock and whittled it down by striking flakes from both sides until it had the desired shape. Clearly, all the hand axes would not have come out the same if their makers hadn't shared an idea for the design.

Hand axes were probably used to butcher large animals.

If hand axes were designed, what were they designed for? The answer to this question is not obvious, because hand axes are not much like the tools made by later peoples. A number of ideas about what hand axes were used for have been proposed:

1. *Butchering large animals.* *Homo ergaster* acquired the carcasses of animals like zebra or buffalo either by hunting or by scavenging and then used a hand ax as a modern butcher would use a cleaver—to dismember the carcass and cut it into useful pieces.

2. *Digging up tubers, burrowing animals, water.* Contemporary foragers in savanna environments spend a lot of their time digging up edible tubers. Although modern

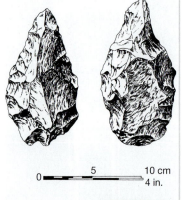

0   5   10 cm
        4 in.

FIGURE 12.8

Acheulean hand axes were teardrop-shaped tools created by removing flakes from a core. The smallest ones would fit in the palm of your hand, and the largest ones are more than 0.3 m (1 ft.) long.

peoples generally use sharpened sticks for digging, some archaeologists have suggested that *H. ergaster* may have used hand axes for this purpose. Digging tools would also have been useful for capturing burrowing animals, like warthogs and porcupines, and for making wells to acquire water.

3. *Stripping bark from trees to get at the nutritious cambium layer underneath.*

4. *Hurling at prey animals.*

5. *Dispensing flake tools.* Hand axes weren't tools at all. Instead they were "flake dispensers" from which *H. ergaster* struck flakes to be used for many everyday purposes.

Although we are not certain how hand axes were used, two kinds of evidence support the hypothesis that they were heavy-duty butchery tools. Kathy Schick and Nicholas Toth, whose investigations into the function of Oldowan tools we discussed in Chapter 11, have also done experiments using Acheulean hand axes for each of the tasks just listed. From these experiments, Schick and Toth conclude that hand axes are best suited to butchery. The sharp end of the hand ax easily cuts through meat and separates joints; the rounded end provides a secure handle. The large size is useful because it provides a long cutting edge, as well as the cutting weight necessary to be effective for a tool without a long handle. Schick and Toth's results are supported by the work of Lawrence Keeley, a paleoanthropologist at the University of Illinois at Chicago, who performed microscopic analysis of wear patterns on a small number of hand axes. He concluded that the pattern of wear is consistent with animal butchery.

Evidence from Olorgesailie, a site in Kenya at which enormous numbers of hand axes have been found, indicates that these axes may also have served as flake dispensers. A team led by Richard Potts of the Smithsonian Institution discovered most of the fossilized skeleton of an elephant, along with numerous small stone flakes dated to about 1 mya. Chips on the edges of the flakes suggest that they were used to butcher the elephant, and the elephant bones show cut marks made by stone tools. Careful examination of the flakes reveals that they were struck from an already flaked core, such as a hand ax, not from an unflaked cobble. Moreover, when the flakes were removed from the hand axes, they did not leave a sharper hand-ax edge. Taken together, these data suggest that *H. ergaster* struck flakes from hand axes and used both hand axes and flakes as butchery tools.

The Acheulean industry remained remarkably unchanged for almost 1 million years.

There is relatively little change over space and time in the Acheulean tool kit from its first appearance about 1.6 mya until it was replaced around 300 kya. Amazingly enough, Acheulean tools that were made half a million years apart are just as similar as tools made at about the same time at sites located thousands of miles apart. Essentially the same tools were made for more than 1 million years. In fact, as we will see shortly, the Acheulean industry was longer lived than *H. ergaster* itself, which disappeared from the fossil record in Africa about 1 mya. Most anthropologists assume that the knowledge necessary to make a proper hand ax was passed from one generation to the next by teaching and imitation. It is a remarkable notion that this form of knowledge might have been faithfully transmitted and preserved for so long in a small population of hominins spread from Africa to eastern Eurasia.

A number of lines of evidence suggest that *H. ergaster* ate meat regularly.

One line of evidence that these hominins ate meat comes from the skeleton of a *Homo ergaster* woman (KNM-ER 1808) that was discovered at Koobi Fora by Alan

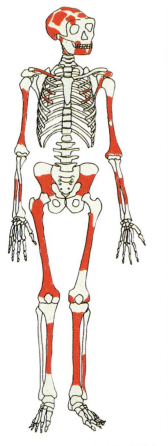

FIGURE 12.9

Much of the skeleton of a *Homo ergaster* female (KNM-ER 1808) was discovered at Koobi Fora. The bones marked in red are those that were recovered.

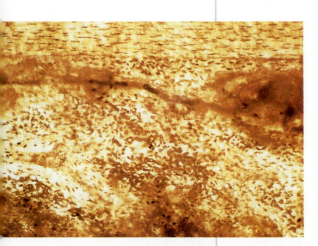

FIGURE 12.10

A microscopic view of the bone structure of KNM-ER 1808. Note that the small band of normal bone at the top looks very different from the puffy, irregular, diseased bone in the rest of the picture.

Walker and his colleagues (**Figure 12.9**). The long bones of this woman, who died about 1.6 mya, are covered with a thick layer of abnormal bone tissue. This kind of bone growth is symptomatic of vitamin A poisoning (**Figure 12.10**). How could a hunter-gatherer get enough vitamin A to poison herself? The most likely way would be to eat the liver of a large predator, like a lion or a leopard. The same symptoms have been reported for Arctic explorers who ate the livers of polar bears and seals. If this woman's bones were deformed because she ate a large predator's liver, then we can assume that *H. ergaster* ate meat. Of course, we don't know how this woman obtained the liver that poisoned her. She might have scavenged the liver from a predator's carcass or she might have killed the predator in a contest over a kill.

Several lines of circumstantial evidence also suggest that *H. ergaster* relied on meat, at least during part of the year. First, hand axes seem to be a suitable tool for the butchery of large animals. Second, the elephant bones associated with the hand axes at Olorgesailie show signs of cut marks from stone tools, suggesting that hominins used tools to cut meat from the carcass. Third, the teeth of *H. ergaster* are well suited for biting and tearing and less suited for chewing tough plant foods. As we pointed out in Chapter 11, meat, seeds, and fibrous plant materials are the main alternative food sources for primates during the dry season. If *H. ergaster* was not eating tough plant foods during the dry season, then it might have relied on meat. Fourth, as we will see shortly, *H. ergaster* moved from the tropics to more temperate habitats outside of Africa. Recall from Chapter 5 that other primates rely heavily on fruit and tender parts of plants for survival. To survive a temperate winter when such things are not available, *H. ergaster* might have relied on meat. Very few primates except humans live in places with severe winters, and these are only small, peripheral populations of species that are usually more tropical.

Additional evidence for meat eating comes from an unexpected source—our intestinal parasites. Humans are the terminal hosts of three species of tapeworm in the genus *Taenia*. African carnivores are the terminal hosts of closely related members of this genus. Tapeworms have a complex life cycle, diagrammed in **Figure 12.11**. Herbivores ingest tapeworm eggs while they are feeding, and the eggs develop into larvae, which are encased in cysts in the flesh of the host. When a carnivore consumes the cysts in meat, the larvae develop into adults and produce eggs, which are shed in the host's feces. Domestic cattle and pigs are now the intermediate hosts of human tapeworms, and it has been assumed that we acquired our tapeworms from domesticated livestock. However, studies of the molecular phylogeny of a number of *Taenia* species conducted by Eric Hoberg of the U.S. Department of Agriculture and his colleagues suggest otherwise. Two of the human tapeworm species, *T. saginata* and *T. asiatica,* diverged from a common ancestor 1.7 to 0.8 mya. This suggests that humans had become the terminal host for the ancestral species (and consumed meat regularly) before this point. This is well before humans domesticated animals and coincides with the emergence of *H. ergaster* in Africa.

Many questions about *Homo ergaster* lifestyles remain unresolved.

Homo ergaster apparently ate meat, but we do not know how they acquired it or how the meat was processed. There is considerable controversy about whether *H. ergaster* obtained meat from scavenging or from hunting. The issues and evidence about hunting are similar to the controversy surrounding hunting by Oldowan hominins. As we noted earlier, the bones of the elephant found at Olorgesailie show signs of cut marks from stone tools. It is not clear how hominins obtained the elephant carcass. The archaeological evidence indicates that the site was not repeatedly used by hominins or other animals. Perhaps the hominins killed the elephant and butchered it at the kill site. Perhaps they came upon the body of the elephant after it had died and butchered it there. It

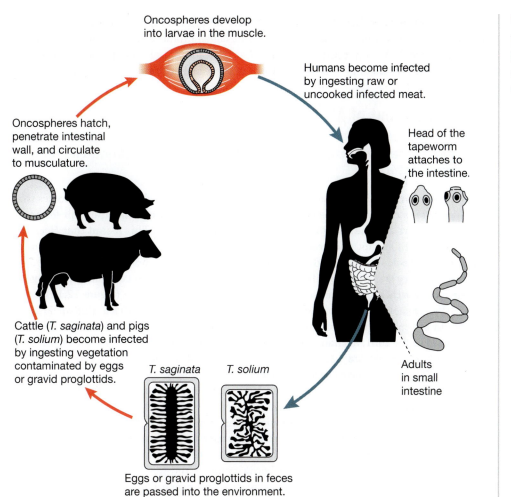

Oncospheres develop
into larvae in the muscle.

Humans become infected
by ingesting raw or
uncooked infected meat.

Oncospheres hatch,
penetrate intestinal
wall, and circulate
to musculature.

Head of the
tapeworm
attaches to
the intestine.

Cattle (*T. saginata*) and pigs
(*T. solium*) become infected
by ingesting vegetation
contaminated by eggs
or gravid proglottids.

T. saginata   *T. solium*

Adults
in small
intestine

Eggs or gravid proglottids in feces
are passed into the environment.

FIGURE 12.11

The life cycle of two tapeworm species.
Humans are the terminal hosts of sister
species *Taenia saginata* and *T. asiatica*,
and a third species, *T. solium*.

does not seem likely that they stole the kill from another predator, because there are
no tooth marks on the bones.

There is also some dispute about when early hominids gained control over fire.
Archaeologists have found areas of baked earth at two Kenyan sites dated to about 1.5
mya, but it is not certain if this represents the remains of a campfire or a slow-burning
natural fire. Excavations at Swartkrans Cave in South Africa have yielded thousands
of fragmented fossil bones of antelope, zebras, warthogs, baboons, and *Paranthropus robustus*. Burned bones have been found at 20 different levels dated from 1.5 to
1 mya. Oldowan tools and *H. ergaster* fossils were also found on some of these levels.
To determine whether these bones had been burned in campfires, C. K. Brain of the
Transvaal Museum in Pretoria and Andrew Sillen of the Synergos Institute compared
the fossils to modern antelope bones burned at a range of temperatures. They found
that the very high temperatures characteristic of long-burning campfires produce
clear changes in the microscopic structure of bone—changes that can also be seen in
the burned fossils at Swartkrans.

Stronger evidence for the use of fire comes from the site of Gesher Benot Ya'aqov in
northern Israel, which is dated to 790 kya. Carefully sifting through thousands of artifacts, researchers identified a number of burned seeds, wood, and flint artifacts. The
flint artifacts were concentrated in particular areas, which may have been hearths.
The burned items represent a small fraction of the material at the site, which makes
it unlikely that it was the product of a natural wildfire that swept through the site.

It is even harder to determine whether hominins used fire to cook their food.
Richard Wrangham of Harvard University has pointed out that cooking makes meat

easier to chew and digest. Moreover, tubers must be cooked before they are eaten. The use of fire to cook meat or tubers might have enhanced the foraging efficiency of *H. ergaster*. This might have been an important adaptation for these creatures, who had to support the higher energetic costs of their larger brains.

Dispersal out of Africa

Homo ergaster occupied almost all of Africa and extended its range into Eurasia.

Archaeological and paleontological evidence compiled by Richard Klein indicates that *H. ergaster*'s range encompassed almost all of the African continent, except for areas of arid desert and the rain forests of the Congo River basin. This meant that *H. ergaster* was able to adapt to a broad range of environmental conditions. Around 1.5 mya, *H. ergaster* colonized the high altitude plateaus of Ethiopia and made more intensive use of the dry edges of the Rift Valley. By 1 mya, *H. ergaster* had extended its range to the most northernmost and southernmost parts of the continent (**Figure 12.12**).

We are not exactly sure how and when hominins first left Africa. But we do know that by around 1.8 mya, hominins had reached the Caucasus Mountains of the Republic of Georgia. In 1991, archaeologists excavating beneath the ruins of a medieval town called Dmanisi (**Figure 12.13**) discovered the first of a remarkable series of hominin fossils. Their first discoveries were of a hominin lower jaw and Oldowan tools. In 1999, an international team of researchers, led by the late Leo Gabunia of the Republic of Georgia National Academy of Sciences, uncovered two nearly complete crania at Dmanisi that are very similar to African specimens of *H. ergaster* (**Figure 12.14**). Later, the team discovered a very well-preserved cranium and associated mandible of a subadult with a very small brain (700 cc), which shows striking similarities to the specimen from Ileret, Kenya. In 2007, David Lordkipanidze and his colleagues published the first detailed descriptions of postcranial material from one adolescent and three adults. The Dmanisi fossils are associated with more than 1,000 Oldowan (Mode 1) choppers,

FIGURE 12.12

The locations of fossil and archaeological sites mentioned in the text. *Homo ergaster* is found in Africa and Europe from 1.8 mya until about 1 mya. *Homo heidelbergensis* is found at sites in Africa and Europe that date to between 800 and 300 kya. Only *Homo erectus* is found in east Asia during this period. The Bose basin has yielded Mode 2 tools but no hominin fossils, so the identity of the toolmakers is unknown.

Early Middle Pleistocene, 1.8 mya–250 kya

- *Homo ergaster*
- *Homo erectus*
- *Homo heidelbergensis*

FIGURE 12.13

The excavation site at Dmanisi, at the foot of the Caucasus Mountains in the Republic of Georgia. Although archaeologists have worked there since 1936, it was only in 1983 that they began to uncover remains from the Lower Pleistocene.

scrapers, chopping tools, and flakes. The residents of Dmanisi manufactured their tools from local materials but clearly preferred fine-grained stones, such as quartzite and basalt, for making tools. Radiometric dating of shards of volcanic glass found at the same levels as the hominin fossils indicates that they are about 1.8 million years old. The fauna associated with the hominin fossils are consistent with this date.

In 2013, Lordkipanidze and his colleagues published the first description of a remarkably well-preserved and intact cranium (**Figure 12.15**). The cranium matches a mandible found several years earlier in the same spot, and together they represent the most complete skull of early *Homo* from any site. The skull presented paleontologists with a number of surprises. First, it had a very small brain. The cranial capacity was only 546 cc, making the brain smaller than any of the other specimens of early *Homo* from Dmanisi and at the very low end of the distribution for early *Homo* specimens from Africa. It also had a large and quite prognathic lower face with procumbent incisors. The large and robust jaws and teeth are similar to *H. erectus* in Java, which we will describe in the next section. The skull was robust, with robust supraorbital tori, postorbital constriction, and bulging glabellar region (the space between the eyebrows and above the nose). However, the skull also bears traits that link it to *Homo*, including the relatively vertical upper face and shape of the cranium. Based on postcranial elements that the researchers think belong to the same individual, they estimate that this individual was at the low end of the distribution of height for modern humans (1.5 to 1.7 m; 4 ft. 9 in. to 5 ft. 5 in.).

Lordkipanidze and his colleagues emphasize that the Dmanisi hominins display a diverse mix of primitive and derived features. They have relatively small brains (546 to 775 cc). Calculations based on the relationship between brain size and body size indicate that the Dmanisi hominins fall at the lower end of the distribution for African *H. ergaster* and appear more like *H. habilis* and the australopiths in their degree of encephalization. They also retain primitive features in certain elements of their shoulder morphology. In modern humans, the elbow joint is rotated so that our palms face inward when our arms hang by our sides. In the Dmanisi hominins, the palms would be oriented more toward the front of the body. The lower-limb morphology shows a number of derived features. The Dmanisi hominins have the same limb proportions as modern humans, and their lower limbs and feet were well suited

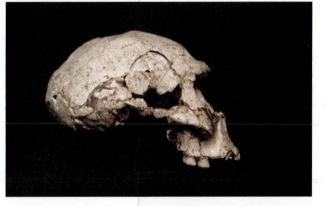

FIGURE 12.14

One of the crania found at Dmanisi. The Dmanisi fossils date to 1.2 to 1.8 mya and are very similar to *Homo ergaster* fossils of the same age from Africa. The Dmanisi site is at latitude 41° north, well out of the tropics, indicating that *Homo ergaster* was able to adapt to a wider range of habitats than previous hominins were.

FIGURE 12.15

A complete skull found at Dmanisi surprised paleontologists because it had a very small brain and large, robust jaws and teeth.

(a)　　　　　　　　　　　　　(b)

for long-distance walking and running. For example, they have relatively high femoral to tibia and humeral to femoral ratios, well-developed arches in their feet, and an adducted big toe (that is, it is in line with the rest of the toes).

The variation in the Dmanisi material raises new questions about the classification of the earliest members of the genus *Homo*.

The existence of such extensive variation at a single site, which represents a narrow time range and has affinities to fossil specimens from both Africa and Asia, has renewed the debate about how many species of early *Homo* there might have been. Researchers from Dmanisi believe the evidence supports the idea that all of the early *Homo* fossils in Africa, Europe, and Asia represent a single, variable lineage that should be called *H. erectus*, the species name with historical primacy. Others are not convinced and suggest there may be more than one species represented in Dmanisi and that lineages in Africa, Europe, and Asia represent distinct species. A consensus may eventually develop as more researchers have an opportunity to evaluate the new Dmanisi skull and compare this striking new find to materials from other sites.

Eastern Asia: *Homo erectus*

Homo erectus, a hominin similar to *Homo ergaster*, probably arrived in eastern Asia during the Lower Pleistocene.

Fossils quite similar to what we now call *Homo ergaster* were unearthed by Eugène Dubois near the Solo River in Java during the nineteenth century (Figure 12.12 and **Figure 12.16**). Dubois named the species *Homo erectus*, or "erect man." Dubois's fossils were very poorly dated, and for many years they were believed to be about 500,000 years old. In the 1990s, however, Carl Swisher now at Rutgers University and the late Garniss Curtis used argon–argon dating techniques to determine the age of small crystals of rock from the sites at which Dubois's fossils had originally been found. Their analyses indicate that the two *H. erectus* sites in Java were actually 1.6 to 1.8 million years old. However, because Dubois's excavations were made 100 years before

FIGURE 12.16

Eugène Dubois was a Dutch anatomist who discovered the first *Homo erectus* fossil at a site called Trinil, in what is now Indonesia.

geologists returned to assess the stratigraphic provenance of the finds, we need to treat these dates with some caution.

The main morphological differences between *Homo erectus* and *Homo ergaster* lie in the skull. In *H. erectus,* the face is more massive, the walls of the cranium are thicker, the cranium is lower and less domed, the brow-ridges are more pronounced, the sides of the skull slope more steeply, the occipital torus is more pronounced, and there is a **sagittal keel** (a longitudinal V-shaped ridge along the top of the skull) (**Figure 12.17**). As you may recall from Chapter 10, the sagittal crest expands the area of attachment of the temporalis muscles in paranthropines. The sagittal keel does not serve this function in *H. erectus.* In fact, we don't know what its function was.

Homo erectus was shorter and stockier than *H. ergaster.* Femurs from northern China indicate that adult males were only about 1.6 m (5.25 ft.) tall, about a head shorter than KNM-WT 15000 would have been.

Homo erectus is known from sites in Java and China, and persisted until about 30 kya. Over this period, *H. erectus* changed very little. This species does not show the same increase in cranial capacity, technological sophistication, and behavioral flexibility that characterizes contemporary hominin populations in Africa and western Eurasia. Even the most recent *H. erectus* fossils from eastern Asia are less like modern humans than are the African specimens of *H. ergaster,* which are 1 million years older.

Nonetheless, the presence of *Homo erectus* fossils in eastern Asia suggests that this species mastered difficult environmental challenges. Between 780 and 680 kya, *H. erectus* occupied a cave at Zoukoudian (also Zhoukoudian or Choukoutien) near Beijing. Fossil-pollen samples indicate that *H. erectus* occupied the cave during only the warmer interglacial periods. However, *warm* is a relative term; the climate of Zoukoudian during the interglacial periods was probably something like that of Chicago today. Imagine living through a winter in Chicago without a roof over your head or clothes to keep you warm. To survive the rigors of cold temperate winters, *H. erectus* may have relied on fire and taken shelter in caves like the one at Zoukoudian. Even this, however, might have been a challenge. The cave at Zoukoudian is littered with the bones of large game, particularly two species of deer. It is clear that they were brought to the cave by a predator, perhaps *H. erectus.* However, there are also fossilized hyena bones and coprolites (fossilized feces) in these caves. Many of the animal bones show evidence of hyena tooth marks, and most of the faces of the hominins are absent. Thus it is possible that *H. erectus* was sometimes the prey at Zoukoudian rather than the predator.

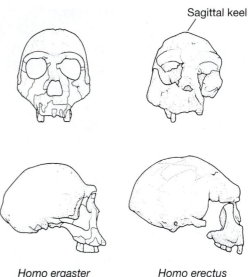

Sagittal keel

Homo ergaster
(KNM-ER 3733)

Homo erectus
(Sangiran 17)

FIGURE 12.17

Homo ergaster and *H. erectus* differed in a number of ways. Most notably, *H. erectus* had a sagittal keel and a more pronounced occipital torus, and the sides of the skull sloped more than in *H. ergaster.*

Homo erectus is associated with Mode 1 tools.

Acheulean tools appear by 1.6 mya in Africa, but they are rarely found in eastern Asia. Instead, *Homo erectus* is usually associated with the simpler Mode 1 tools, similar to those of the Oldowan industry. Some paleoanthropologists think that the differences in tool technology between eastern Asia and Africa provide evidence of cognitive differences between the two species; others think that environmental differences may be responsible for the tool differences. Remember that *H. ergaster* may have been present in eastern Asia by 1.7 mya. If so, then *H. ergaster* would have left Africa before Mode 2 tools first appeared there. It is possible that a cognitive change arose in the African *H. ergaster* population after the first members of the genus had migrated north into eastern Asia and that this cognitive adaptation enabled later members of *H. ergaster* to manufacture bifaces. The absence of more symmetrical Mode 2 tools in eastern Asia may mean that they lacked this cognitive ability.

Other researchers argue that differences in tool technology between *Homo erectus* and *Homo ergaster* tell us more about their habitats than about their cognitive abilities. During the Middle Pleistocene, *H. erectus* lived in regions that were covered with dense

bamboo forests. Bamboo is unique among woods because it can be used to make sharp, hard tools suitable for butchering game. *H. erectus* may not have made hand axes because they didn't need them. The discovery of a large number of hand axes in the Bose basin in southern China support this view (**Figure 12.18**). About 800 kya, a large meteor struck this area and set off fires that destroyed a wide area of the forest. Grasslands replaced the forest. While grasslands predominated, the residents of this area made Mode 2 tools like those seen in Africa around the same time. Before the forest was destroyed and after it regenerated, the inhabitants of this area made Oldowanlike Mode 1 tools. This evidence suggests that hand axes were an adaptation to open-country life. However, there are no hominin fossils associated with these tools, so we don't know whether *H. erectus* actually made them. It is possible that the Bose hand axes were made by members of more technologically advanced immigrant populations from farther west.

FIGURE 12.18

Hand axes found in the Bose Basin in southern China are the only Mode 2 tools discovered in east Asia. These tools date to about 800 kya. Mode 1 tools are found in the same area both before and after this date.

Hominins of the Early Middle Pleistocene (900 to 300 kya)

The world's climate became colder and much more variable during the Middle Pleistocene (900 to 130 kya).

During the Middle and Upper Pleistocene there were many long, cold glacial periods punctuated by short, warmer interglacial periods. **Figure 12.19** shows estimates of global temperatures for this time period. Notice that the world climate has fluctuated wildly in the last 700,000 years. From geological evidence, we know that during the cold periods, glaciers covered North America and Europe and arctic conditions prevailed. These cold periods were intermittently interrupted by shorter warm periods during which the glaciers receded and the forests returned.

During glacial periods, the world was dry, and Africa and Eurasia were isolated from each other by a massive desert. During interglacial periods, the world was much wetter, and animals moved from Africa to Eurasia.

These temperature fluctuations had massive effects on the world's biological habitats. **Figure 12.20a** shows the distribution of habitats about 7 kya during the warmest and wettest period of the current interglacial period. At this time, much of Eurasia and Africa was covered by forests, East and North Africa and Arabia were grasslands, and deserts were limited to small bits of southwest Africa and central Asia. **Figure 12.20b** shows what the world was like at the depth of the last glacial period, about 20 kya. The middle latitudes were dominated by vast expanses of extreme desert, as dry as the Sahara Desert today. North and south of this desert, grassland, scrub, and open woodland predominated, and forests were restricted to small regions of central Africa and Southeast Asia. Since the beginning of the Middle Pleistocene, the planet has oscillated between these two extremes, sometimes shifting from one extreme to the other in just a few hundred years.

These fluctuations had important effects on the dispersal of animal species, including hominins, in the Middle and Upper Pleistocene. During glacial periods, deserts spread across the northern part of Africa, making this region uninhabitable for most animal species. This corresponds to what we know from the fossil record: There was

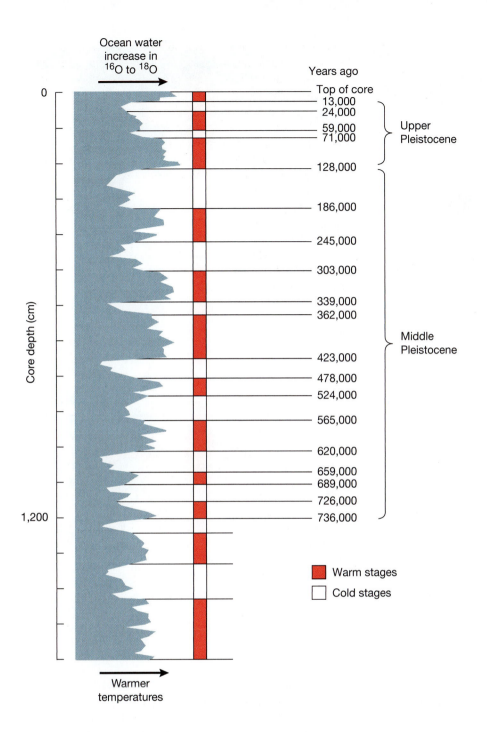

FIGURE 12.19

The ratio of ^{16}O to ^{18}O in seawater over the last 700,000 years indicates that there have been wide swings in world temperature. But on average, the world has been colder than it is now. Larger ocean values of ^{16}O to ^{18}O signify higher global temperatures.

little movement of animal species between Africa and Asia during glacial periods. Instead, animal species moved mainly east and west across Eurasia. When the world was warmer, grasslands and savannas replaced most deserts, and animals were able to move between Africa and Eurasia much more easily. The fossil record indicates that animal species generally moved from Africa to Eurasia, not vice versa. As we will see later, this fact has important implications for understanding human evolutionary history.

The evolutionary transition from *Homo ergaster* to modern humans occurred during the Middle Pleistocene.

It was in this chaotic, rapidly changing world that natural selection reshaped the hominin lineage once again. *Homo ergaster* was transformed into a smarter and

FIGURE 12.20

(a) A reconstruction of biological habitats about 7 kya during the warmest, wettest part of the present interglacial period. Much of Eurasia and Africa were covered with forest and were connected by a broad swath of grassland across northern Africa and southwestern Eurasia. (b) The habitats during the coldest, driest part of the last glacial period, about 20 kya. There was very little forest cover. Grassland and scrub predominated in central Africa and Southeast Asia. Northern Eurasia was covered with cold, dry steppe and desert. Central and southern Africa were separated from Eurasia by a band of extreme desert across northern Africa, the Arabian Peninsula, and central Asia.

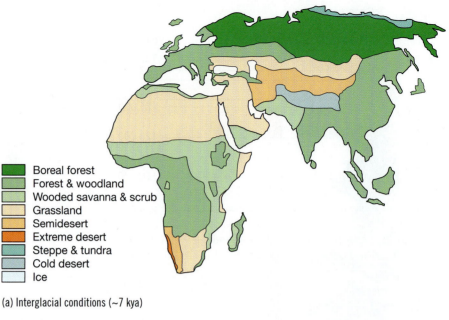

Boreal forest
Forest & woodland
Wooded savanna & scrub
Grassland
Semidesert
Extreme desert
Steppe & tundra
Cold desert
Ice

(a) Interglacial conditions (~7 kya)

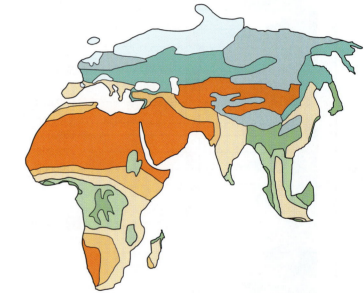

(b) Glacial conditions (~20 kya)

more versatile creature. We will see that hominins were present in Africa and Eurasia for most of the Middle Pleistocene and that hominins living in different parts of the world were morphologically distinct. *H. erectus* lived in eastern Asia until perhaps 30 kya, and a variety of larger-brained forms ranged through Africa and western Eurasia. About 300 kya, hominins in Africa and western Eurasia began to develop more sophisticated technology and behavior. This process of change continued, particularly in Africa, until the behavior and technology of hominins became indistinguishable from those of modern humans.

Although many of these events can be relatively well established in the fossil and archaeological record, there is considerable controversy about the phylogeny of the human lineage during this period. There are fierce debates about how many species of hominins there were during this period and about how different species or forms were related. We will turn to these controversies at the end of the chapter. But first you need to learn something about the hominins of the Middle Pleistocene.

Africa and Western Eurasia: *Homo heidelbergensis*

Sometime during the first half of the Middle Pleistocene (900 to 130 kya), hominins with larger brains and more modern skulls appeared.

Hominins with substantially larger brains and more modern skulls appeared in Africa and western Eurasia during the first half of the Middle Pleistocene. **Figure 12.21** shows two nearly complete crania from this period: the Petralona cranium found in Greece and the Kabwe (or Broken Hill) cranium from Zambia. These individuals had substantially larger brains—between 1,200 and 1,300 cc—in relation to their body size than *Homo ergaster*. The skulls also share a number of derived features with modern humans, including more vertical sides, higher foreheads, and a more rounded back. However, they also retained many primitive features, such as a long, low skull; very thick cranial bones; a large prognathic face; no chin; and very large browridges. Their bodies were still much more robust than modern human bodies. Fossils with similar characteristics have been found at other sites in Africa (including Ndutu in Tanzania

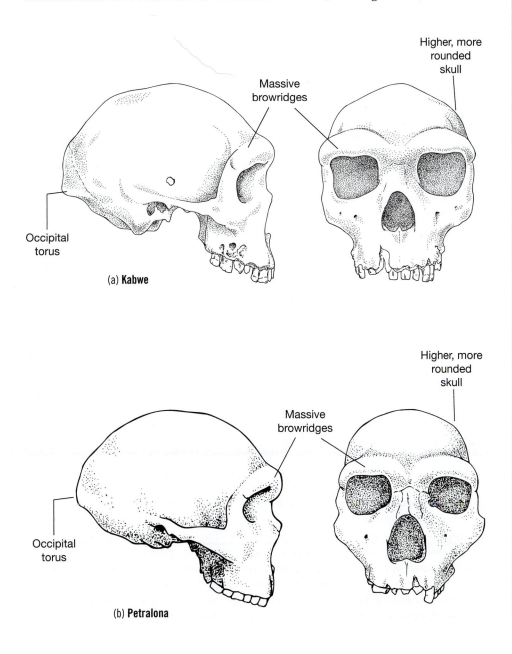

Higher, more rounded skull

Massive browridges

Occipital torus

(a) **Kabwe**

Higher, more rounded skull

Massive browridges

Occipital torus

(b) **Petralona**

FIGURE 12.21

Sometime between 800 and 500 kya, hominins with higher, more rounded crania and larger brains first appear in the fossil record; by 400 kya, *Homo heidelbergensis* was common in Africa and western Eurasia. These *H. heidelbergensis* fossils, from (a) Kabwe (sometimes called Broken Hill) in Zambia and (b) Petralona in Greece, are approximately 400,000 years old.

and Bodo in Ethiopia) and western Eurasia (including Mauer in Germany and Box-grove in England) that date to the same period (see Figure 12.12). There has been no sign of these kinds of fossils in eastern Asia during this period, although they do appear later.

Traditionally, paleoanthropologists have referred to these larger-brained, more modern-looking hominins as **archaic** *Homo sapiens*. As we will explain shortly, however, nowadays only a minority of paleoanthropologists believe that these creatures should be classified as members of *H. sapiens*. There is controversy about whether these hominins belonged to one species or several, and among the anthropologists who believe that there were several species, there is considerable disagreement over which specimens belong to which species. This dispute, which is far from resolved, creates a quandary about what we should call this group of hominins. Here we adopt what is perhaps the most common opinion and use the name ***Homo heidelbergensis*** to refer to all of the Middle Pleistocene hominins of Africa and western Eurasia. (The name *heidelbergensis* is taken from a specimen that was found near the German city of Heidelberg.) Keep in mind, though, that we are not at all sure that this category actually represents a single biological species.

Scientists are uncertain about when or where *H. heidelbergensis* first appeared. One candidate for the oldest *H. heidelbergensis* specimen is the cranium found at Buia in Eritrea. This skull has several derived features that are associated with *H. heilelbergensis* but a small, *H. ergaster*–size braincase. A second possibility is the Kabwe fossil found in Zambia. Although it was originally dated to about 130 kya, more recent work has pushed some estimates of the age of this fossil back to about 800 kya. A third candidate comes from Trinchera Dolina (also called Gran Dolina) in the Sierra de Atapuerca in northern Spain. This site has yielded a number of hominin fossils, including part of an adolescent's lower jaw and most of an adult's face. Although the Trinchera Dolina fossils are too fragmentary to provide an estimate of endocranial volume, they exhibit a number of facial features that are seen in more modern hominins. These fossils have been dated to about 800 kya by means of paleomagnetic methods, but rodent fossils found at the same site indicate a more recent date, perhaps 500 kya. Similar uncertainty afflicts our estimates of the ages of the other early *H. heidelbergensis* fossils, so the best that we can do is to bracket the first appearance of these creatures between 800 and 500 kya.

The tools used by early *Homo heidelbergensis* are similar to those used by *Homo ergaster*. Tool kits are dominated by Acheulean hand axes and other core tools at most sites, but in some cases the hand axes are more finely worked.

There is good evidence that *Homo heidelbergensis* hunted big game.

The first solid evidence for hunting big game comes from this period. On the island of Jersey, off the coast of France, the remains of a large number of fossilized bones from mammoths and woolly rhinoceroses have been found at the base of a cliff. Some of the bones come from adults, which were too big to be vulnerable to most predators. The carcasses clearly have been butchered with stone tools. In some instances, the skull cavity has been opened, presumably to extract the brain tissue. At some places on this site, animal bones have been sorted by body parts (heads here, limbs there, and so on). All this suggests that *H. heidelbergensis* drove the animals over the headland, butchered the carcasses, and ate the meat.

More evidence for hunting comes from three wooden spears that were found in an open-pit coal mine in Schoningen, Germany. This site is dated to about 400 kya. Some anthropologists think that these were throwing spears because they closely resemble modern javelins. They are about 2 m (6 ft.) long and, like modern throwing spears, are thickest and heaviest near the pointed end, gradually tapering to the other end. Some modern people use similar spears for hunting, and it seems plausible that *H. heidelbergensis* used them in the same way. However, the spears are much larger and heavier than modern javelins, and it is possible that they were used for thrusting rather than throwing. The hypothesis that they were used for hunting is strengthened by the fact that anthropologists found the bones of hundreds of horses along with the spears, and many of the bones show signs of having been processed with stone tools.

Homo heidelbergensis used a variety of plant resources and animal resources.

We saw in Chapter 11 that modern human foragers typically dine on many different kinds of foods and that they use complex processing techniques to acquire and process these foods. The site of Gesher Benot Ya'aqov in northern Israel provides the first evidence of such behavior in earlier hominins. This site, now in the dry Dead Sea valley, was on the shore of a lake when hominins lived there 790 kya. Nira Alperson-Afil and colleagues from Bar Ilan University in Israel have found evidence that the hominins who lived there (probably *H. ergaster* or *H. heidelberensis*) used a variety of plant foods, including oak acorns, water lily seeds, and water chestnuts. Modern foragers roast these starchy nuts to make it easier to peel away the inedible shell and reduce the tannin content, and it is plausible that the hominins of Gesher Benot Ya'aqov did the same. Archaeologists have also found the remains of a number of different species of freshwater fish, a species of crab, and turtles, indicating that aquatic resources were also important for subsistence at this site. There are also remains of larger mammals like elephants and fallow deer.

Hominins of the Later Pleistocene (300 to 50 kya)

About 300 kya, and then slightly later in western Eurasia, hominins in Africa shifted to a new stone tool kit.

Beginning about 300 kya, hand axes became much less common and were replaced by tools that were manufactured by the production of sizable flakes, which were then further shaped or retouched. Unlike the small, irregular Oldowan flakes that had been struck from cobble cores, these tools were made from large, symmetrical, regular flakes via complicated techniques. One method, called the **Levallois technique** (after the Parisian suburb where such tools were first identified), involves three steps. First, the knapper prepares a core with one precisely shaped convex surface. Then, the knapper makes a striking platform at one end of the core. Finally, the knapper hits the striking platform, knocking off a flake, the shape of which is determined by the original shape of the core (**Figure 12.22**). A skilled knapper can produce a variety of different kinds of tools by modifying the shape of the original core. Such prepared core tools are classified as **Mode 3** technology.

Microscopic analyses of the wear patterns on Mode 3 tools made during this period suggest that some tools were **hafted** (attached to a handle). Hafting is an extremely important innovation because it greatly increases the efficiency with which humans can apply force to stone tools. (Try using a hammer without a handle.) *Homo heidelbergensis* probably hafted pointed flakes onto wooden handles to make stone-tipped spears, a major innovation for a big-game hunter.

Flake the margin of the core.

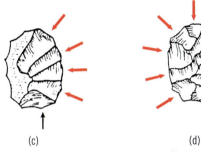

(a)

(b)

Prepare the surface of the core.

(c)

(d)

Remove Levallois flake.

Core   Flake

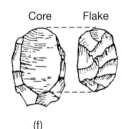

(e)

(f)

FIGURE 12.22

The process of making a Levallois tool. (a) The knapper chooses an appropriate stone to use as a core. The side and top views of the unflaked core are shown. (b) Flakes are removed from the periphery of the core. (c) Flakes are removed radially from the surface of the core, with the flake scars on the periphery being used as striking platforms. Each of the red arrows represents one blow of the hammer stone. (d) The knapper continues to remove radial flakes until the entire surface of the core has been flaked. (e) Finally, a blow is struck (*red arrow*) to free one large flake (outlined in *red*). This flake will be used as a tool. (f) At the end, the knapper is left with the remains of the core (left) and the tool (right).

FIGURE 12.23

Locations of later Pleistocene fossil and archaeological sites mentioned in the text. *Homo erectus* and *H. heidelbergensis* are found in east Asia, Neanderthals in Europe, and both *H. heidelbergensis* and *H. sapiens* in Africa.

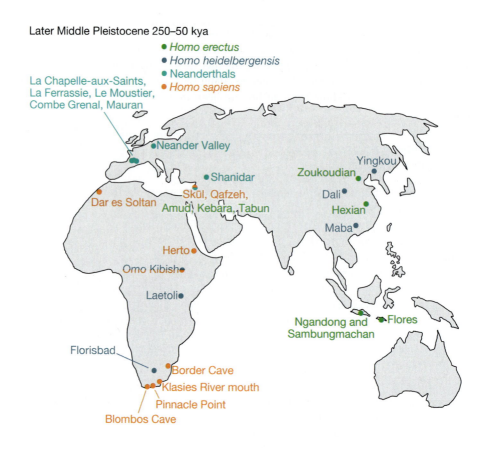

Later Middle Pleistocene 250–50 kya

- • *Homo erectus*
- • *Homo heidelbergensis*
- • Neanderthals
- • *Homo sapiens*

La Chapelle-aux-Saints, La Ferrassie, Le Moustier, Combe Grenal, Mauran

Neander Valley

Shanidar

Skūl, Qafzeh, Amud, Kebara, Tabun

Dar es Soltan

Herto

Omo Kibish

Laetoli

Zoukoudian   Yingkou

Dali

Hexian

Maba

Ngandong and Sambungmachan   Flores

Florisbad

Border Cave

Klasies River mouth

Pinnacle Point

Blombos Cave

Eastern Eurasia: *Homo erectus* and *Homo heidelbergensis*

During the second half of the Middle Pleistocene, *Homo heidelbergensis* appeared in eastern Asia, where it may have co-existed with *Homo erectus*.

FIGURE 12.24

Hominins with the characteristics of *Homo heidelbergensis* appeared in east Asia later than in western Eurasia. The specimen illustrated here, which is from Yingkou in northern China, is approximately 200,000 years old.

Hominins with larger brains and more rounded skulls have been found at several sites in China that date to approximately 200 kya. The most complete and most securely dated fossil is from the Jinniushan site, Yingkou, in northern China (**Figure 12.23**). This specimen (**Figure 12.24**), which consists of a cranium and associated postcranial bones, is similar to early *Homo heidelbergensis* fossils from Africa and Europe. Like the crania found at Kabwe and Petralona, it shares with modern humans a larger braincase (about 1,300 cc) and more rounded skull, but it also has massive browridges and other primitive features. Similar fossils have been found in Dali in northern China and Maba in southern China, and they are probably somewhat younger than the Yingkou specimen. These fossils are associated with Oldowan-type tools. It is unclear whether these hominins were immigrants from the west or the result of convergent evolution in eastern Asia.

Such large-brained hominins may have co-existed with *Homo erectus* in east Asia during this period. Fossils of *H. erectus* that are between 200,000 and 300,000 years old have been found at Hexian (also called He Xian), in

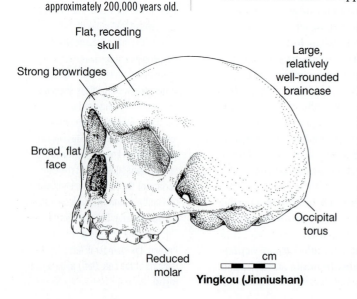

Flat, receding skull

Strong browridges

Broad, flat face

Reduced molar

Large, relatively well-rounded braincase

Occipital torus

cm

Yingkou (Jinniushan)

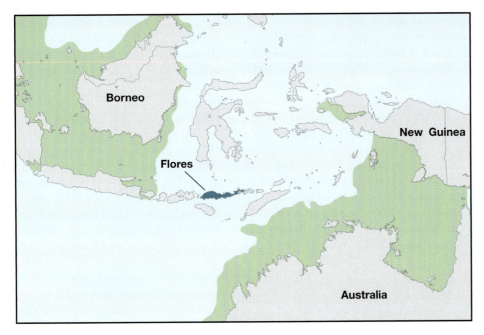

FIGURE 12.25

Fossils of *Homo floresiensis* were discovered on the island of Flores in eastern Indonesia. The shaded green areas are now underwater but were then dry land, showing that Flores was isolated from both Asia and Australia even when sea levels were at their lowest levels. As a result, Flores was home to an odd mix of creatures, including a dwarf elephant, huge monitor lizards, and 1-m-tall hominins.

southern China. The fossils of other animals found in association with *H. erectus* fossils at two sites in Java (Ngandong and Sambungmachan) are consistent with an age of 250,000 to 300,000 years. However, the teeth of bovids (buffalo and antelope) associated with the hominin fossils at these sites have been dated to about 27 kya by means of electron-spin-resonance techniques.

A tiny, small-brained hominin called *Homo floresiensis* lived on the Indonesian island of Flores during the upper Pleistocene.

In the fall of 2004, a team of Indonesian and Australian researchers published what has been dubbed "the most surprising fossil hominin found in the last 50 years." Working at a cave site called Liang Bua on the Indonesian island of Flores (**Figure 12.25**), these researchers uncovered the remains of between nine and fourteen individuals. The fossil specimens included a complete skull (**Figure 12.26**) and much of the rest of the skeleton (**Figure 12.27**). The first surprise about these creatures, named *Homo floresiensis,* was their size. They were slightly more than 1 m tall (about 3 ft.), much smaller than any other member of the genus *Homo*. Their brains were also very small (385 to 417 cc)—so small, in fact, that they may have been less encephalized than *Homo erectus*. The second surprising thing about these creatures is their age. Most of the *H. floresiensis* fossils date to between 16 and 18 kya, when the environment surrounding the cave was a dry grassland. However, a minority date to a second period, 74 to 61 kya, when the environment was humid forest. A number of flake tools were found at Liang Bua, together with the charred remains of many species of animals, including tortoises, lizards, rodents, bats, and numerous specimens of a species of dwarf elephant. Because these materials have dates that overlap those of

FIGURE 12.26

Side view of the skull of one of the *Homo floresiensis* specimens (LB1). The skull is very small but shares a number of derived features with early *Homo*. The creature's brain was about the same size as the brain of australopiths.

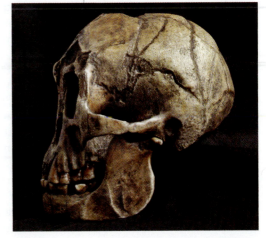

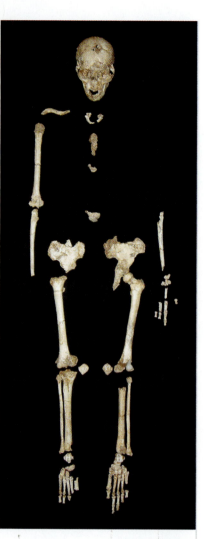

FIGURE 12.27

The skeleton of the *Homo floresiensis* specimen (LB1). This individual would have been about 1 m in height. The skeleton shows a number of features similar to early *Homo*, including the morphology of the wrists, pelvis, and feet.

the hominin fossils and because there is no evidence of other hominins in the cave, the excavation team argues that *Homo floresiensis* was able to hunt large game and make the kinds of tools that are usually associated with *Homo sapiens.* Others have argued that these tools could not have been made by the tiny-brained *H. floresiensis,* because they are much more sophisticated than those associated with *H. erectus.*

The discovery of *Homo floresiensis* stimulated a flurry of public interest in the "hobbits," speculation about their origins, and controversy about their place in the human lineage. Many researchers are convinced that these petite hominins are descendants of an early occupation by either *H. habilis* or *H. ergaster* who became isolated on the island of Flores. They point to the fact that the Flores hominins share a number of primitive characters with early *Homo.* The arms of *H. floresiensis* are long compared to its legs, and its feet are very large and lack the arch that is characteristic of modern humans. Its shoulder, wrists, and pelvises also show a number of primitive features similar to early *Homo* or even the australopiths. In addition, simple Mode 1 tools like those associated with early *Homo* have been found on Flores and are dated to 800 kya.

The small size of the Flores hominins is thought to be an example of evolutionary dwarfism, which occurs when animal populations are confined on islands. Flores and the islands around it have always been isolated from both Asia and Australia by wide stretches of ocean. As a result, only a few species of large animals ever reached these islands, producing a strange impoverished fauna that included Komodo dragons and an even larger species of monitor lizard, a species of dwarf elephant, and, of course, a dwarf hominin. Biologists think that natural selection favors smaller body size on small islands because such islands typically have less predation and more limited food supplies. If islands are isolated, there will be little gene flow from continental populations, and the animals will adapt to local conditions. On Flores, this process may have produced pint-size hominins and tiny elephants.

This interpretation was challenged by other experts who were convinced that the occupants of Ling Bua were members of a modern human population with small stature, and that the tiny crania from Ling Bua belonged to individuals who were afflicted with a pathology that led to small bodies and very small brains. For example, Laron syndrome results from a mutation to a gene that reduces sensitivity to growth hormone and is associated with very small body size. However, careful comparison of the Flores material with modern individuals with this and other known disorders does not support this hypothesis, and most investigators now agree that *H. floresiensis* is a distinctive hominin species.

Western Eurasia: The Neanderthals

During the Middle Pleistocene, the morphology of *Homo heidelbergensis* in Europe diverged from the morphology of its contemporaries in Africa and Asia.

A large sample of fossils from a site in Spain provides evidence that *Homo heidelbergensis* in Europe had begun to diverge from other hominin populations during the Middle Pleistocene. This site, which is called Sima de los Huesos ("Pit of Bones") is located in the Sierra de Atapuerca only a few kilometers from Trinchera Dolina. There, paleoanthropologists excavated a small cave 13 m (43 ft.) below the surface and found 2,000 bones from at least 24 different individuals. These bones, which date to between 600 and 530 kya, include several nearly complete crania as well as many bones from other parts of the body. **Figure 12.28** shows one of the crania, labeled SH 5. Like other fossils of *H. heidelbergensis*, these skulls mix derived features of modern humans and primitive features associated with *H. ergaster.* However, the crania from Sima de los Huesos also share a number of derived characteristics not seen in hominins living at

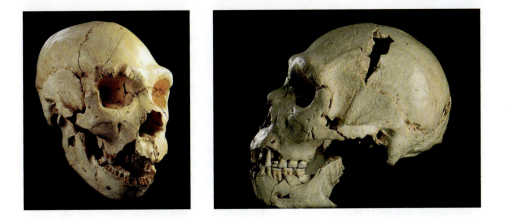

FIGURE 12.28

The many hominin fossils found at Sima de los Huesos in Spain provide evidence that hominins in Europe began to evolve a distinctive cranial morphology at least 300 kya. The features—which include rounded browridges, a large pushed-out face, a skull with a rounded back, and a large brain—are important because they are shared with the Neanderthals, the hominins who dominate the European fossil record during the Upper Pleistocene.

the same time in Africa. Their faces bulge out in the middle and have double-arched browridges, and the backs of some of the skulls are rounded. The fossils from Sima de los Huesos also have relatively large cranial capacities, in one specimen reaching 1,390 cc, close to the average value for modern humans. These characteristics are significant because they are shared by **Neanderthals**, the hominins who dominate the European fossil record from 127 to 30 kya.

Not all of the Sima de los Huesos crania express all the Neanderthal features to the same degree, and this variability has helped settle an important question about hominin evolution in Europe. Before the Sima de los Huesos fossils were discovered, paleoanthropologists had been perplexed by the pattern of variation in Middle Pleistocene hominins in Europe. Fossils from some European sites resemble Neanderthals; fossils from other European sites that date to the same time period do not resemble Neanderthals. It was not clear whether these differences reflected variability within a single population of hominins or whether more than one type of hominin was present in Europe during the Middle Pleistocene. The large and variable sample of individuals at Sima de los Huesos has resolved this issue. These individuals, who likely belonged to a single population, vary in their expression of Neanderthal traits, and this variation mirrors the kind of variation seen at different sites in Europe. However, as we will see later in this chapter, genetic data seem to indicate that the Sima de los Huesos people were not ancestors of the Neanderthals but instead were more closely related to a second hominid lineage, the Denisovans, who are known only from a site in Siberia.

The Neanderthals appeared in western Eurasia about 130 kya.

The Neanderthals were an enigmatic group of hominins who lived in Europe and western Asia from about 127 to 30 kya. These creatures were among the first fossil hominins discovered, and they are still the best known. Their distinctive morphology (large browridges, short muscular bodies, and low foreheads) has become the archetypical image of "early man" for the general public. However, there is now good evidence that the Neanderthals became isolated from the lineage that led to modern humans and eventually disappeared. Molecular analyses of Neanderthal fossils and modern peoples provide strong evidence that modern peoples are mainly descended from African populations living about the same time as the Neanderthals. These modern peoples moved out of Africa about 50 kya, and as they expanded into Europe, some of them mated with Neanderthals. As a result, a small percentage of the genes in modern populations outside of Africa come from Neanderthals.

Although the Neanderthals are for the most part a dead-end branch of the human family tree, we know more about them than we do about any other extinct hominin species. The reason for this is simple: Neanderthals lived in Europe, and paleontologists

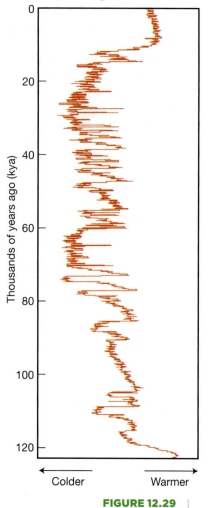

Increasing amounts of ^{18}O

Thousands of years ago (kya)

Colder   Warmer

FIGURE 12.29

Fluctuations in the ratios of ^{18}O to ^{16}O over the last 123,000 years taken from an ice core drilled in northern Greenland. These data indicate that between 120 and 80 kya, the world's climate got colder and less stable. In ice cores like this one, a higher ratio of ^{18}O to ^{16}O indicates higher temperatures. (In deep-sea cores, more ^{18}O relative to ^{16}O indicates lower temperatures.)

have studied Europe much more thoroughly than they have studied Africa or Asia. The upshot is that we know much more about the Neanderthals than we do about their contemporaries in other parts of the world.

The last warm interglacial period lasted from about 130 kya to about 75 kya. For most of the time since then, the global climate has been colder—sometimes much colder.

The data in **Figure 12.29** give a detailed picture of global temperatures over the last 123,000 years. These data are based on the ^{18}O to ^{16}O ratios of different layers of cores taken from deep inside the Greenland ice cap. Because snow accumulates at a higher rate than sediments on the ocean bottom do, ice cores provide more detailed information on past climates than do ocean cores like those used to construct the graph in Figure 12.3. You can see from Figure 12.29 that the end of the last warm interglacial period was marked by a relatively slow decline in temperature beginning about 120 kya. During this interglacial period, the world generally was substantially warmer than it is today. During this warm interglacial period, plants and animals were distributed quite differently from the way they are now. Plankton species currently living in subtropical waters (like those off the coast of Florida) extended their range as far as the North Sea during the last interglacial period. Animals now restricted to the tropics had much wider ranges. Thus the remains of a hippopotamus have been found under Trafalgar Square, in the center of London. In Africa, rain forests extended far beyond their present boundaries; and in temperate areas, broadleaf deciduous forests extended farther north than they do today.

As the last glacial period began, sometime between 100 and 75 kya, the world slowly cooled. In Europe, temperate forests shrank, and grasslands expanded. The glaciers grew, and the world became colder and colder—not steadily, but with wide fluctuations from cold to warm. When the glaciation was at its greatest extent (about 20 kya), huge continental glaciers covered most of Canada and much of northern Europe. Sea levels dropped so low that the outlines of the continents were altered substantially: Asia and North America were connected by a land bridge that spanned the Bering Sea; the islands of Indonesia joined Southeast Asia in a landmass called Sundaland; and Tasmania, New Guinea, and Australia formed a single continent called Sahul. Eurasia south of the glaciers was a vast, frigid grassland, punctuated by dunes of loess (fine dust produced by glaciers) and teeming with animals—woolly mammoths, woolly rhinoceroses, reindeer, aurochs (the giant wild oxen that are ancestral to modern cattle), musk oxen, and horses.

Sometime during the last interglacial period, Neanderthals came to dominate Europe and the Near East.

In 1856, workers at a quarry in the Neander Valley in western Germany found some unusual fossil bones. The bones found their way to a noted German anatomist, Hermann Schaafhausen, who declared them to be the remains of a race of humans who had lived in Europe before the Celts. Many experts examined these curious finds and drew different conclusions. Thomas Henry Huxley, one of Darwin's staunchest supporters, suggested that they belonged to a primitive, extinct kind of human. The Prussian pathologist Rudolf Virchow, on the other hand, proclaimed them to be the bones of a modern person suffering from a serious disease that had distorted the skeleton. Initially, Virchow's view held sway, but as more fossils were discovered with the same features, researchers became convinced that the remains belonged to a distinctive, extinct kind of human. The Germans called this extinct group of people *Neanderthaler*, meaning "people of the Neander Valley" (*Thal*, now spelled *tal*, is German for "valley"). We call them the Neanderthals, and they were characterized by several distinctive, derived features:

- *Large brains.* The Neanderthal braincase is much larger than that of *Homo heidelbergensis*, ranging from 1,245 to 1,740 cc, with an average size of about 1,520 cc. In fact, Neanderthals had larger brains than modern humans, whose brains average about 1,400 cc. It is unclear why the brains of Neanderthals were so large. Some anthropologists point out that the Neanderthals' bodies were much more robust and heavily muscled than those of modern humans, and they suggest that the large brains of Neanderthals reflect the fact that larger animals usually have bigger brains than smaller animals.

- *More rounded crania* (**Figure 12.30**). The Neanderthal skull is long and low, much like the skulls of *H. heidelbergensis,* but relatively thin walled. The back of the skull has a characteristic rounded bulge or bun and does not come to a point at the back like an *H. erectus* skull does. There are also detailed differences in the back of the cranium.

- *Big faces.* Like *Homo erectus* and *Homo heidelbergensis,* the skulls of Neanderthals have large browridges, but they are larger and rounder and they stick out less to the sides. Moreover, the browridges of *H. erectus* are mainly solid bone, while those of Neanderthals are lightened with many air spaces. The function of these massive browridges is not clear. The face, and particularly the nose, is enormous: every Neanderthal was a Cyrano, or perhaps a Jimmy Durante.

- *Small back teeth and large, heavily worn front teeth.* Neanderthal molars are smaller than those of *Homo ergaster*. They had distinctive **taurodont roots** in which the pulp cavity expanded so that the roots merged, partially or completely, to form a single broad root (**Figure 12.31**). Neanderthal incisors are relatively large and show very heavy wear. Careful study of these wear patterns indicates that Neanderthals may have pulled meat or hides through their clenched front teeth. There are also microscopic, unidirectional scratches on the front of the incisors, suggesting that these hominins held meat in their teeth while cutting it with a stone tool. It is interesting that the direction of the scratches suggests that most Neanderthals were right-handed, just as the Oldowan toolmakers were.

- *Robust, heavily muscled bodies.* Like *Homo ergaster, H. erectus,* and *H. heidelbergensis,* Neanderthals were extremely robust, heavily muscled people (**Figure 12.32**). Their leg bones were much thicker than ours, the load-bearing joints (knees and hips) were larger, the **scapulae** (shoulder blades; singular *scapula*) had more extensive muscular attachments, and the rib cage was larger and more barrel shaped. All these skeletal features indicate that Neanderthals were very sturdy and strong, weighing about 30% more than contemporary humans of the same height. A comparison with data on Olympic athletes suggests that Neanderthals most closely resembled hammer, javelin, and discus throwers and shot-putters. They were a few inches shorter, on average, than modern Europeans and had larger torsos and shorter arms and legs.

This distinctive Neanderthal body shape may have been an adaptation to conserve heat in a very cold environment. In cold climates, animals tend to be larger and have shorter and thicker limbs than do members of the same species in warmer environments. This is because the rate of heat loss for any body is proportional to its surface area, so any change that reduces the amount of surface area for a given volume will conserve heat. The ratio of surface area to volume in animals can be reduced in two ways: by increasing overall body size or by reducing the size of the limbs. In contemporary human populations there is a consistent relationship between climate and body proportions. One way to compare body proportions is to calculate the **crural index**, which is the ratio of the length of the shinbone (tibia) to the length of the thighbone (femur).

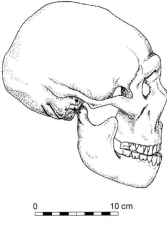

FIGURE 12.30

The skulls of Neanderthals, like this one from Shanidar Cave, Iraq, are large and long, with large browridges and a massive face.

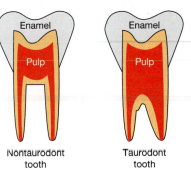

FIGURE 12.31

In Neanderthal molars, the roots often fuse together partially or completely to form a single massive taurodont root. The third root is not shown.

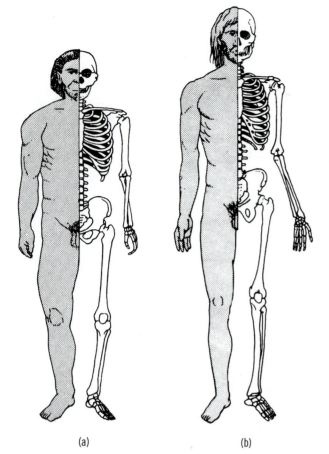

FIGURE 12.32

The Neanderthals were very robust people. Contrast the bones of (a) a Neanderthal with those of (b) a modern human.

As **Figure 12.33** shows, people in warm climates tend to have relatively long limbs in proportion to their height. Neanderthals resemble modern peoples living above the Arctic Circle.

Some authorities believe that Neanderthals lacked modern language.

The larynx (or voice box) of modern humans is much lower than in other primates—an arrangement that allows us to produce the full range of vowels used in modern human languages. On the basis of reconstructions of the Neanderthal vocal tract, Jeffrey Laitman, an anatomist at the Mount Sinai School of Medicine in New York City, argues that the Neanderthals had vocal tracts much like those of other primates and could not have produced the full range of sounds necessary for modern speech. Laitman and his colleagues recorded the positions of several anatomical landmarks on the **basicrania** (singular *basicranium*; "bottom of the skull") of humans and several other primates. In infant humans, this basicranial hump is gentle, like those of other primates; but as humans mature, the bottom of the cranium develops a pronounced upward indentation. Laitman believes that this relatively high hump helps make room for the elongated human vocal tract. Australopithecine adults have apelike basicrania, but the basicranium in *Homo ergaster* is intermediate between those in apes and modern humans. Laitman argues that the initial shift in *H. ergaster* may have facilitated breathing through the mouth during heavy aerobic exercise. The basicrania in Neanderthals show a less humped profile than those of *H. ergaster*, suggesting that the Neanderthals' capacity for language was more restricted than the language capacities of even their own ancestors.

It is also possible that Laitman's reconstructions are correct but that grammatically complex language still appeared long before modern humans evolved. It is possible for a creature with a high larynx to make all of the vowel sounds by using the nasal cavity. In modern humans, such nasalized vowels take longer to produce and are harder to understand. Thus the lowering of the larynx might have served merely to decrease the error rate of understanding a language that was otherwise very modern. Moreover, as Harvard University linguist Steven Pinker points out in his book *The Language Instinct*, "E lengeege weth e smell nember ef vewels cen remeen quete expresseve." So, even if Laitman is correct, early hominins could have had fancy languages.

There is a lot of evidence that Neanderthals made Mode 3 tools and hunted large game.

Although Neanderthals are popularly pictured as brutish dimwits, this is an unfair characterization. As we noted earlier, their brains were larger than ours. And the archaeological evidence suggests that they were skilled toolmakers and proficient big-game hunters. The Neanderthal's stone tool kit is dominated by Mode 3 tools, which are characterized by flakes struck from prepared cores. Their stone tool industry is called the **Mousterian industry** by archaeologists. Neanderthal sites are littered with stone tools and the bones of red deer (called elk in North America), fallow deer, bison, aurochs, wild sheep, wild goats, and horses (**Figure 12.34**). Archaeologists find few bones of very large animals, like hippopotamuses, rhinoceroses, and elephants, even though they were plentiful in Europe at that time.

Again, the conjunction of animal bones and stone tools does not necessarily mean that Neanderthals hunted large game, and there is a reprise of the same debate we

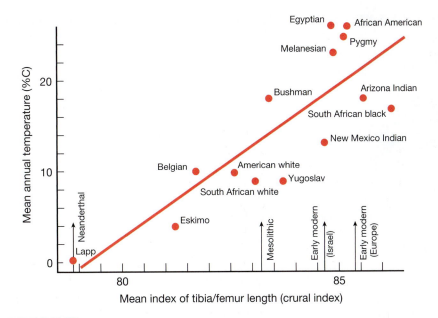

FIGURE 12.33

People have proportionally longer arms and legs in warm climates than in cold climates. Local temperature is plotted on the vertical axis; crural index is plotted on the horizontal axis. Smaller values of the crural index are associated with shorter limbs relative to body size. Populations in warm climates tend to have high crural index values, and vice versa. Neanderthals had a crural index similar to those of present-day Lapps, who live above the Arctic Circle.

have discussed several times before. Some archaeologists, such as the late Lewis Binford, believe that Neanderthals never hunted anything larger than small antelope, and even those prey were taken opportunistically. These researchers claim that the bones of larger animals found at these sites were acquired by scavenging. Binford believed that the hominins of this period did not have the cognitive skills necessary to plan and organize the cooperative hunts necessary to bring down large prey.

However, this position seems hard to sustain in the face of the archaeological evidence. Richard Klein, a Stanford archaeologist, contends that Neanderthals were proficient hunters who regularly killed large animals. He points out that animal remains at sites from this period are often dominated by the bones of only one or two prey species. At Mauran, a site in the French Pyrenees, for example, over 90% of the assemblage is from bison and aurochs. The same pattern occurs at other sites scattered across Europe. It is hard to see how an opportunistic scavenger would acquire such a nonrandom sample of the local fauna. Moreover, the age distribution of prey animals does not fit the pattern for modern scavengers like hyenas, which prey mainly on the most vulnerable members of prey populations: sick or wounded animals, the old, and the very young (**Figure 12.35**). At these European sites, the bones of apparently healthy, prime-age adults are well represented. The distribution of animal bones is what we would expect to see at sites of catastrophic events in which whole herds of animals are killed. For example, several sites are located at the bottoms of cliffs. There are huge jumbles of bones and tools at these sites, suggesting that Neanderthals drove game over the cliffs and butchered the carcasses where they fell. At several sites, such as Combe Grenal in France, the bones from the meatiest parts of prey animals are overrepresented, and the cut marks on these bones suggest that Neanderthals stripped off the fresh flesh. (Remember that hunters often haul away the meatiest bones to eat in peace.) Taken together, these data suggest that Neanderthals were big-game hunters, not opportunistic scavengers.

(a)

(b)

FIGURE 12.34

Neanderthals and their contemporaries are believed to have hunted large and dangerous game, such as (a) red deer and (b) bison.

FIGURE 12.35

Hyenas frequently scavenge kills, and they prey mainly on very young and very old individuals.

There is little evidence for shelters or even organized camps at Neanderthal sites.

There are many Neanderthal sites, some very well preserved, where archaeologists have found concentrations of tools, abundant evidence of toolmaking, many animal remains, and concentrations of ash. Most of these sites are in caves or **rock shelters**, places protected by overhanging cliffs. This doesn't necessarily mean that Neanderthals preferred these kinds of sites. Cave sites are more likely to be found by researchers because they are protected from erosion, and they are relatively easy to locate because the openings to many caves from this period are still visible. Most archaeologists believe that cave sites represent home bases, semipermanent encampments from which Neanderthals sallied out to hunt and to forage.

The archaeological record suggests that Neanderthals did not build shelters. Most Neanderthal sites lack evidence of postholes and hearths, two features generally associated with simple shelters. The few exceptions to this rule occur near the end of the period. For example, hearths were built at Vilas Ruivas, a site in Portugal dated to about 60 kya.

Neanderthals probably buried their dead.

The abundance of complete Neanderthal skeletons suggests that, unlike their hominin predecessors, Neanderthals frequently buried their dead. Burial protects the corpse from dismemberment by scavengers and preserves the skeleton intact. Detailed study of the geological context at sites like La Chapelle-aux-Saints, Le Moustier, and La Ferrassie in southern France also supports the conclusion that Neanderthal burials were common.

It is not clear whether these burials had a religious nature or if Neanderthals buried their dead just to dispose of the decaying bodies. Anthropologists used to interpret some sites as ceremonial burials in which Neanderthals were interred along with symbolic materials. In recent years, however, skeptics have cast serious doubt on such interpretations. For example, anthropologists used to think that the presence of fossilized pollen in a Neanderthal grave in Shanidar Cave, Iraq, was evidence that the individual had been buried with a garland of flowers. More recent analyses, however, revealed that the grave had been disturbed by burrowing rodents, and it is quite possible that they brought the pollen into the grave.

FIGURE 12.36

Two perforated mollusk shells from Cueva de los Aviones in Spain. This site dates to about 50 kya and is associated with Middle Paleolithic tools. The perforations may have allowed the shells to be strung on a cord for use as ornamentation.

Neanderthals may have used painted seashells as personal ornaments.

Humans devote substantial creativity and lots of resources to personal adornment. In the modern world, huge amounts of money are spent on clothes, jewelry, and makeup, and both history and anthropology suggest that personal adornment is a universal human trait. As we will see in the next chapter, there is good evidence that the earliest modern humans also decorated themselves with pigments and jewelry. Thus it is clearly of interest to know whether earlier hominins shared this aspect of our psychology, but until recently the evidence was equivocal. Beautiful personal ornaments were found in association with Neanderthal fossils at a site in France called Arcy sur Cure, but the dates for this site vary wildly, and it seems possible that ornaments made by later, modern human occupants got mixed with Neanderthal layers, perhaps when the moderns dug postholes.

FIGURE 12.37

The perforated scallop shell found at Cueva Antón. The left image shows the naturally red inside of the shell. The right shows the naturally white outside of the shell, which has been stained with the orange mineral pigments goethite and hematite.

However, a recent discovery suggests that Neanderthals used seashells as adornments. A number of pierced shells have been found at Cueva Ánton and Cueva de los Aviones, two sites in southeastern Spain. These shells have holes that could have been used to string them on a leather thong (**Figure 12.36**). They also have been treated with orange mineral pigments (**Figure 12.37**). It seems likely that this was decorative because these pigments come from at least 5 km away and appear only on the shells, not on other artifacts found at the site. Similar shell ornaments have been found at contemporaneous African sites occupied by modern humans.

Neanderthals seem to have lived short, difficult lives.

Careful study of Neanderthal skeletons indicates that Neanderthals didn't live very long. The human skeleton changes throughout the life cycle in characteristic ways, and these changes can be used to estimate the age at which fossil hominins died. For example, human skulls are made up of separate bones that fit together in a three-dimensional jigsaw puzzle. When children are first born, these bones are still separate, but later they fuse together, forming tight, wavy joints called **sutures**. As people age, these sutures are slowly obliterated by bone growth. By assessing the degree to which the sutures of fossil hominins have been obliterated, anthropologists can estimate how old the individual was at death. Several other skeletal features can be used in similar ways. All of these features tell the same story: Neanderthals died young. Few lived beyond the age of 40 to 45 years.

FIGURE 12.38

Many Neanderthal skeletons show signs of injury or illness. The orbit of the left eye of this individual was crushed, the right arm was withered, and the right ankle was arthritic.

FIGURE 12.39

At Gombe, a male chimpanzee named Faben contracted polio, which left one arm completely paralyzed. After the paralysis, Faben received no day-to-day help from other group members, but he was able to survive for many years. Here, Faben climbs a tree one-handed.

Many of the older Neanderthals suffered disabling disease or injury. For example, the skeleton of a Neanderthal man from La Chapelle-aux-Saints shows symptoms of severe arthritis that probably affected his jaw, back, and hip. By the time this fellow died, around the age of 45, he had also lost most of his teeth to gum disease. Another individual, Shanidar 1 (from the Shanidar site in Iraq), suffered a blow to his left temple that crushed the orbit (**Figure 12.38**). Anthropologists believe that his head injury probably caused partial paralysis of the right side of his body, and this in turn caused his right arm to wither and his right ankle to become arthritic. Other Neanderthal specimens display bone fractures, stab wounds, gum disease, withered limbs, lesions, and deformities.

In some cases, Neanderthals survived for extended periods after injury or sickness. For example, Shanidar 1 lived long enough for the bone surrounding his injury to heal. Some anthropologists have proposed that these Neanderthals would have been unable to survive their physical impairments—to provide themselves with food or to keep up with the group—had they not received care from others. Some researchers argue further that these fossils are evidence of the origins of caretaking and compassion in our lineage.

There are reasons to be cautious of such claims. In some contemporary societies, disabled individuals are able to support themselves, and they do not necessarily receive compassionate treatment from others. In addition, nonhuman primates sometimes survive despite permanent disabilities. At Gombe Stream National Park, a male chimpanzee named Faben contracted polio, which left him completely paralyzed in one arm. Despite this impairment, he managed to feed himself, traverse the steep slopes of the community's home range, keep up with his companions, and even climb trees (**Figure 12.39**).

Africa: The Road to *Homo sapiens*?

Hominins living in Africa during the later Middle Pleistocene were more similar to modern humans than were Neanderthals.

The fossil record in Africa indicates fairly clearly that African humans of this period were not like the Neanderthals, although it is not entirely clear what they were like, because the fossil record for this time in Africa is not nearly as good as it is in Europe. A number of fossils dated to later in the Middle Pleistocene (300 to 200 kya) have robust features similar to those of *Homo heidelbergensis*. Examples include the Florisbad cranium found in South Africa (**Figure 12.40**) and the Ngaloba cranium (LH 18) from Laetoli, Tanzania. Like the Neanderthals, these African hominins show large cranial volumes ranging from 1,370 to 1,510 cc. However, none of the African fossils shows the complex of specialized features that are diagnostic of the European Neanderthals. Although these fossils are variable and some are quite robust, many researchers believe that they are more like modern humans than are the Neanderthals or earlier African hominins.

About 190 kya, hominins belonging to our own species began to appear in Africa, although some of the evidence is problematic. The oldest fossils classified as *Homo sapiens* were excavated in 1963 at a site in southern Ethiopia called Omo Kibish, where paleoanthropologists found most of two fossil skulls and a number of other bone fragments. These skulls are quite robust, with prominent browridges and large faces. However, one of them has a number of modern features—most notably a high, rounded braincase (**Figure 12.41**). These specimens have been dated to about 190 kya by new radiometric methods. Several similar skulls were uncovered at Herto, another site in Ethiopia, and are dated to 160 kya. Other more fragmentary fossil materials from other sites in Africa also suggest that more modern hominins were present in Africa between 200 and 100 kya. The archaeological record indicates that Africans during this period developed more sophisticated technology and social behavior than did their contemporaries in Europe or Asia—a pattern that is consistent with the idea that this period saw the gradual accumulation of the cognitive and behavioral characteristics that make modern humans so different from other hominins. We turn to this evidence in the next chapter.

FIGURE 12.40

This cranium found at Florisbad in South Africa shows a mixture of features of *Homo heidelbergensis* and modern *H. sapiens*. Although still quite robust, it has reduced browridges and a more rounded shape. It dates to between 300 and 200 kya.

The Sources of Change

Europe may have been invaded repeatedly by hominins from Africa during the Middle Pleistocene.

The changes in hominin morphology and technology that we have described in this chapter may be the product of a number of different kinds of processes. It is possible that the changes we see reflect adaptive modifications in tool technology in particular regions of the world. Thus it is likely that Africa has been occupied continuously by members of the genus *Homo*, which first appeared 1.8 mya. This means that the makers of Mode 1 tools evolved slowly into the makers of Mode 2 tools, and the makers of Mode 2 tools evolved into the makers of Mode 3 tools.

However, it is also possible that some of the changes in the fossil record are the product of the replacement of one population of hominins by another. Marta Lahr and Robert Foley, anthropologists at the University of Cambridge, have suggested that Europe and western Eurasia were subjected to repeated invasions by hominins from Africa. They argue that the technological shifts seen in Eurasia were associated with the migration of hominins from Africa during interglacial periods. Remember that during glacial periods, Africa and Eurasia were separated by a formidable desert barrier (see Figure 12.20b), and Eurasia was a cold, dry, and inhospitable habitat for primates. During these glacial periods, hominin populations in western Eurasia may have shrunk or disappeared altogether. When the glacial periods ended and the world became warmer, there was substantial movement of animal species from Africa into Eurasia. It is possible that hominins staged repeated invasions of Eurasia during each of these warm interglacial periods, bringing new technologies along with them.

Lahr and Foley's argument is buttressed by archaeological evidence. Remember that the earliest evidence for hominins in Europe dates to about 800 kya. Up until about 500 kya, only Mode 1 tools are found in Europe. Then Mode 2 technologies appear in Europe and persist until about 250 kya, when they are replaced by Mode 3 technologies. In each case, the new technology appears first in Africa and then in Europe and (sometimes) in Asia (**Figure 12.42**). The appearance of new tool technologies at 500 kya and 250 kya coincides neatly with the timing of interglacial periods, consistent with the repeated replacement of Eurasian populations by African populations.

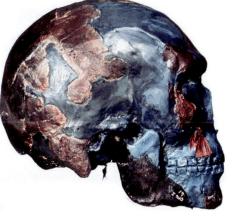

FIGURE 12.41

This fossil skull, called Omo Kibish 1, found in southern Ethiopia in 1963, was dated to 190 kya. It lacks the distinctive features of Neanderthals: The face does not protrude and the braincase is higher and shorter than that of Neanderthals.

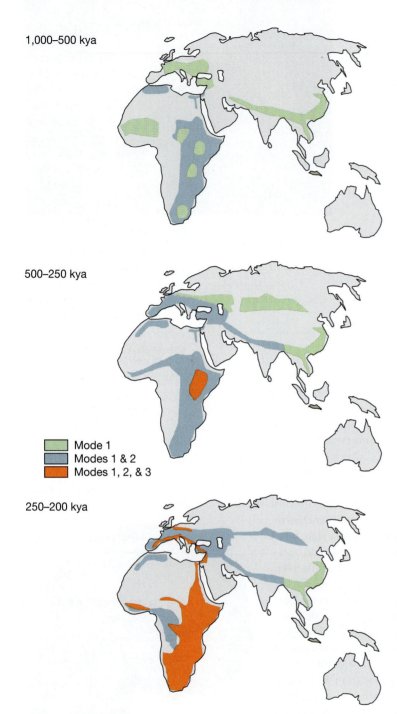

1,000–500 kya

500–250 kya

Mode 1
Modes 1 & 2
Modes 1, 2, & 3

250–200 kya

FIGURE 12.42

The geography of tool technologies through time suggests that Eurasia was subjected to repeated invasions of hominins from Africa. Between 1 mya and 500 kya, Mode 2 technologies were confined to Africa, and hominins in Eurasia were restricted to Mode 1 tools. Beginning about 500 kya, Mode 2 technologies appeared in Eurasia. The introduction of Mode 2 coincided with a relatively warm, moist period, which could have facilitated the movement of hominins from Africa to Eurasia. About 300 kya, elements of Mode 3 technology appeared in East Africa; and by about 250 kya, Mode 3 technology had spread throughout Africa and southern Europe. Once again, this spread coincided with a period of warmer climate.

The Muddle in the Middle

Anthropologists strongly disagree about how to classify Middle Pleistocene hominins.

You will notice that we avoided assigning a species name to the Neanderthals. This is partly because there is a lot of disagreement about how to classify Middle Pleistocene hominins. The disagreement stems from different ideas about the processes that shape human evolution during this period. One school of thought, most closely associated with the University of Michigan anthropologist Milford Wolpoff, contends that hominins in Africa and Eurasia formed a single interbreeding population throughout the Pleistocene. The size of Africa and Eurasia limited gene flow and allowed regional differences to evolve, but there was always enough interbreeding to guarantee that all hominins belonged to a single species during this entire period. Thus Wolpoff and others prefer to include all hominins who lived during the Middle Pleistocene in a single species, *Homo sapiens,* as shown in **Figure 12.43a.** As we will show in the next chapter, this point of view has become increasingly difficult to sustain in the face of information that has become available from molecular genetic studies in the last few years.

Other anthropologists believe that hominins split into several new species as they migrated out of Africa and into Eurasia, although there are disagreements about the details of phylogenetic history. **Figures 12.43b** and **12.43c** illustrate two current hypotheses. According to G. Philip Rightmire of Harvard University, the specimens that we have identified as *Homo ergaster* and *Homo erectus* are members of a single species (which would be called *Homo erectus* because that was the name first used). However, he draws a distinction between early Middle Pleistocene hominins in Europe and Africa and those who came later. He groups all of the early Middle Pleistocene hominins in Europe and Africa into one species, which he labels *H. heidelbergensis,* and he lumps the hominins of the later Middle Pleistocene in Europe and the Neanderthals into one species, *H. neanderthalensis.* Although it may seem peculiar to include specimens without the distinctive Neanderthal features in the species *H. neanderthalensis,* this name is used because it has historical priority.

Richard Klein believes that hominin populations in Africa, western Eurasia, and eastern Eurasia were genetically isolated from each other during most of the Pleistocene and represent three distinct species (Figure 12.43c). In Africa, *Homo ergaster* gradually

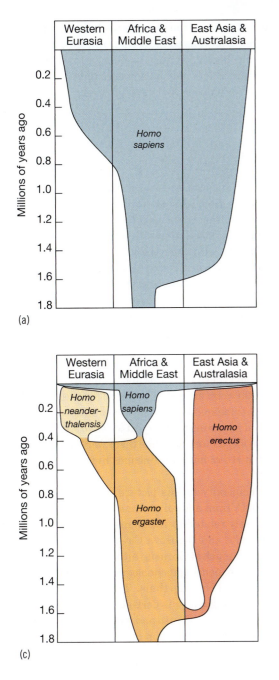

(a)

(c)

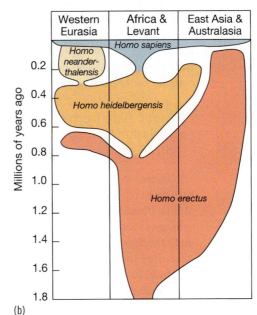

(b)

FIGURE 12.43

Numerous phylogenies have been proposed to account for the temporal and geographic patterns in hominin evolution during the Pleistocene. Three such proposals are present here. (a) Milford Wolpoff holds that beginning about 1.8 mya, there was only one human species. Because there have been no speciation events since that time, all human fossils should be classified as *H. sapiens*. (b) G. Philip Rightmire believes that both African and Asian specimens of *H. erectus* should be classified as a single species. Approximately 800 kya, a larger-brained species, *H. heidelbergensis*, evolved in Africa and eventually spread to Europe and perhaps east Asia. In Europe, *H. heidelbergensis* gave rise to the Neanderthals; in Africa, it gave rise to *H. sapiens*. (c) Richard Klein argues that *H. ergaster* evolved in Africa about 1.8 mya and soon spread to Asia, where it differentiated to become a second species, *H. erectus*. About 500 kya, *H. ergaster* spread to western Eurasia, where it evolved into *H. neanderthalensis*. In Africa, *H. ergaster* evolved into *H. sapiens* at about the same time.

evolved into *H. sapiens* about 500 kya. Isolated in Asia, *H. ergaster* evolved into *H. erectus* early in the Pleistocene. Klein considers the development of larger brains and more modern-looking skulls in the eastern Eurasia fossils, like those found at Yingkou, to be the result of convergent evolution and includes them in *H. erectus*. Once hominins reached Europe about 500 kya, they became isolated from African and east Asian populations and diverged to become *H. neanderthalensis*.

This kind of disagreement is to be expected because the timescales of change become short as we come closer to the present. Instead of being interested in events that took place over millions of years, we are now interested in events that took place in just a hundred thousand years. But this may be roughly how long it took for two species to diverge during the process of allopatric speciation (see Chapter 4). Thus as hominins spread out across the globe and encountered new habitats, regional populations may have become isolated and experienced selection—conditions that would eventually lead to speciation. The rapidly fluctuating climates of the Pleistocene, however, caused the ranges of hominins and other creatures to shift as well. As their ranges expanded and contracted, some populations may have become extinct, some may have become fully isolated and even more specialized, and others may have merged together. This complex set of possibilities is very difficult for paleontologists to unravel.

Genetic data from fossils found at Denisova Cave indicate that the population history of Middle Pleistocene hominins was more complex than previously realized.

Recent discoveries by Svante Pääbo and his colleagues at the Max Planck Institute for Evolutionary Anthropology in Leipzig, Germany, underlines the complexity of Middle Pleistocene hominin evolution. As we will see in the next chapter, Pääbo and his colleagues recovered DNA from a number of Neanderthal fossils and were able to estimate the date of the last common ancestor of these Neanderthals and modern humans. According to their analyses, this was a creature who lived between 550 and 775 kya.

In 2010, Pääbo's team announced that they had extracted DNA from a finger bone and a molar found in Denisova Cave in the Altai Mountains in southern Siberia. These fossils date to over 50,000 years ago. The molar is huge—similar to early *Homo* and much larger than the molars of other Asian fossils—and lacks a number of derived features found in those species. The genetic data indicate that the tooth and finger bone came from different individuals who were members of a single population. What is amazing is that the last common ancestor of these creatures and Neanderthals lived about 450 kya, between 100,000 and 200,000 years after the estimated divergence date for Neanderthals and modern humans. This means the Denisova hominins are likely to be the descendants of a different group of hominins that migrated out of Africa from the groups that led to Neanderthals and modern humans. Thus there were at least two migrations out of Africa and at least two distinct hominin lineages living in Eurasia during the last 500,000 years.

Recent discoveries add even more complexity to this picture. First, Pääbo and his colleagues extracted mitochondrial DNA from a fossil at Sima de los Huesos and found that these hominins were more closely related to the Denisovans than to the Neanderthals. The distance between this site and Denisova Cave suggests that the Denisovans and Neanderthals both occupied much of Eurasia, although they may not have overlapped in time. Second, progress in sequencing technology has provided much higher resolution sequences for Denisovans and Neanderthals. These new data indicate that between 0.5 and 8% of the Denisovan genome is derived from an unknown hominin. The last common ancestor of this mystery hominin and modern humans lived 1–4 mya and so might have been part of an Asian population of *H. erectus*.

Key Terms

occipital torus	sagittal keel	taurodont roots
biface	archaic *Homo sapiens*	scapulae
hand ax	*Homo heidelbergensis*	crural index
cleaver	Levallois technique	basicrania
pick	Mode 3	Mousterian industry
Mode 2	hafted	rock shelters
Acheulean industry	Neanderthals	sutures

Study Questions

1. Which derived features are shared by modern humans and *Homo ergaster*? Which derived features are unique to *H. ergaster*?

2. What does the specimen KNM-WT 15000 tell us about *H. ergaster*?

3. What is a hand ax, and what did *H. ergaster* use it for? How do we know?

4. What evidence suggests that *H. ergaster* controlled fire?

5. What evidence suggests that *H. ergaster* ate significant amounts of meat? Is the evidence for *H. ergaster* carnivory better than that for the Oldowan hominins? Explain.

6. What are the main differences between *H. ergaster* and *H. erectus*? How would you explain the evolution of these differences?

7. Using present-day examples, describe the variation in climate during the Middle Pleistocene. Why is this variation important for understanding human evolution?

8. How is *H. heidelbergensis* different from *H. erectus*?

9. What important technological transition occurred about 300 kya? Why was it important?

10. Explain why the fossils found at Sima de los Huesos are significant.

11. What is the crural index? What does it measure? How does the crural index of the Neanderthals differ from that of modern tropical peoples?

12. How did the Neanderthals differ from their contemporaries in Africa and eastern Asia?

13. What evidence suggests that western Eurasia was subjected to repeated invasions from Africa during the Middle Pleistocene?

Further Reading

Conroy, G. 2005. *Reconstructing Human Origins: A Modern Synthesis*. 2nd ed. New York: Norton.

Hublin, J. J. 2009. "The Origin of the Neandertals." *Proceedings of the National Academy of Sciences U. S. A.* 106: 16022–16027.

Klein, R. G. 2008. *The Human Career: Human Biological and Cultural Origins*. 3rd ed. Chicago: University of Chicago Press.

McBrearty, S. and A. S. Brooks. 2000. "The Revolution That Wasn't: A New Interpretation of the Origin of Modern Human Behavior." *Journal of Human Evolution* 39: 453–563.

Rightmire, G. P. 2008. "*Homo* in the Middle Pleistocene: Hypodigms, Variation, and Species Recognition." *Evolutionary Anthropology* 17: 8–21.

Walker, A. and P. Shipman. 1996. *The Wisdom of the Bones: In Search of Human Origins*. New York: Knopf.

CHAPTER OBJECTIVES

By the end of this chapter you should be able to

- Describe how modern humans differ morphologically from earlier hominins.

- Explain how genetic data allow us to reconstruct the expansion of modern humans out of Africa.

- Understand how genetic data indicate that modern humans interbred with earlier hominins.

- Discuss how we know that modern human behavior emerged in Africa by 100 kya.

- Explain how humans spread across the globe beginning 60 kya.

HOMO SAPIENS AND THE EVOLUTION OF MODERN HUMAN BEHAVIOR

Fossils Classified as Modern *Homo sapiens*

The Origin and Spread of Modern Humans

The African Archaeological Record for the Later Pleistocene

The Archaeological Record Outside of Africa after 60 kya

Beginning about 50 kya (thousand years ago), the fossil record outside Africa documents a striking change: The Neanderthals and other robust hominids disappeared and were replaced by essentially modern people. These people looked much like people in the world today, with high foreheads, sharp chins, and less robust physiques. The archaeological record suggests that they also behaved like modern people, using sophisticated tools, trading over long distances, and making jewelry and art. Anatomically and behaviorally similar people appeared in previously unoccupied Australia around the same time and reached North and South America about 12 kya.

In this chapter, we describe what the fossil and archaeological records and the genetic data tell us about these early modern people. You will see that evidence from the fossil record and molecular genetic studies make it clear that anatomically modern humans evolved in Africa between 200 and 100 kya, then migrated from Africa about 60 kya, and eventually spread throughout the world. The archaeological evidence indicates that the components of modern human behavior and technology evolved in Africa along with modern human morphology over a period of about 200,000 years and that fully modern people were living on the southern coast of Africa by 70 kya. Then, about 50 kya these behaviors abruptly appear outside of Africa, as modern people spread to the rest of the Old World.

Fossils Classified as Modern *Homo sapiens*

Fossils classified as anatomically modern *Homo sapiens* share a number of important derived features with contemporary humans (**Figure 13.1**):

- *Small, flat face with protruding chin.* These people had smaller faces and smaller teeth than earlier hominins had. The face is flat and is tucked under the braincase. The lower jaw had a jutting chin for the first time (**Figure 13.2**). Some anthropologists believe that the smaller face and teeth were favored by natural selection because these people did not use their teeth as tools as much as earlier people had. There is no agreement about the functional significance of the chin.

- *Rounded skull.* Like modern people, these people had high foreheads, a distinctive rounded back of the cranium, and greatly reduced browridges (see Figure 13.2).

- *Cranial capacity of at least 1,350 cc.* Cranial capacity varies to some extent across populations but is generally at least 1,350 cc. This value is smaller than the value for Neanderthals but greater than the value for other hominins in the late Middle Pleistocene.

- *Less robust postcranial skeleton.* The skeleton of these people was much less robust than Neanderthal skeletons. These people had longer limbs with thinner-walled bones; longer, more lightly built hands; shorter, thicker pubic bones; and distinctive shoulder blades. Although these people were less robust than Neanderthals, they were still more heavily built than any contemporary human population. Erik Trinkaus of Washington University in St. Louis suggests that these people relied less on body strength and more on elaborate tools and other technological innovations to do their work.

- *Relatively long limbs and short trunks.* The body proportions of these creatures were similar to those of peoples who live in warm climates and may reflect the African origins of these people.

FIGURE 13.1

The skulls of modern humans have higher, rounder crania and smaller faces than earlier hominins, as illustrated by this skull from a man who lived about 25 kya near the Don River in Russia.

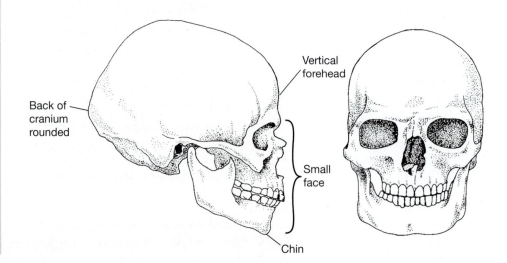

Vertical forehead

Back of cranium rounded

Small face

Chin

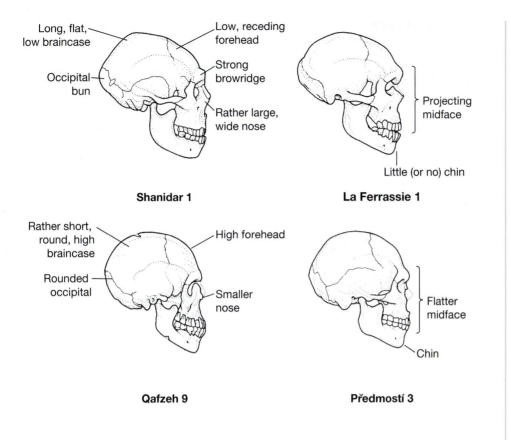

Shanidar 1

Long, flat, low braincase
Occipital bun
Low, receding forehead
Strong browridge
Rather large, wide nose

La Ferrassie 1

Projecting midface
Little (or no) chin

Qafzeh 9

Rather short, round, high braincase
Rounded occipital
High forehead
Smaller nose

Předmostí 3

Flatter midface
Chin

FIGURE 13.2

Neanderthals, represented here by Shanidar 1 from Iraq and La Ferrassie 1 from France, differ from modern *Homo sapiens*, like Qafzeh 9 from Israel and Předmostí 3 from the Czech Republic. Modern humans had higher foreheads, smaller browridges, smaller noses, more rounded skulls, and more prominent chins than Neanderthals.

The Origin and Spread of Modern Humans

A dramatic shift in hominin morphology occurred during the last glacial epoch. About 100 kya, the world was inhabited by a morphologically heterogeneous collection of hominins: Neanderthals in Europe, other robust hominins in east Asia, and more modern humans in the Middle East and Africa. By about 30 kya, most of this morphological diversity had disappeared; and modern humans occupied all of the Old World. How did this transition occur?

Forty years ago most paleoanthropologists would have given the same answer: The robust hominins of the late Middle Pleistocene formed a single morphologically variable species—archaic *Homo sapiens*—from which a more modern morphology gradually evolved throughout the world. More recent evidence, however, both from the fossil record and from molecular genetics, has convinced most paleoanthropologists that this hypothesis is wrong. This evidence indicates that most of the genes that gave rise to modern human morphology and behavior evolved in an African population sometime between 200 and 90 kya. People carrying these genes subsequently spread throughout Africa and differentiated into a number of morphologically modern but genetically variable populations. Then about 60 kya, people from one of these regional populations left Africa and spread across the world, replacing other hominin populations with a modest amount of gene flow between them.

In this chapter, we describe the paleontological, archaeological, and genetic evidence related to the origin and spread of modern humans. As you will see, researchers working in a diverse set of academic disciplines have brought a wide range of methods to bear on this problem.

Genetic Data

Patterns of genetic variation provide information about the origin of modern humans.

The patterns of genetic variation within living people and genetic material extracted from fossils tell us a lot about the history of human populations. The genetic data tell us that

1. modern humans evolved in Africa between 200 and 90 kya,

2. modern humans outside of Africa are all descended from a small population that left Africa about 60 kya, and

3. there was a small amount of interbreeding between the expanding modern human populations and the hominins already living in Eurasia including the Neanderthals and the Denisovans.

Some of the information about genetic variation comes from genes carried on the Y chromosome and in our mitochondria.

Up until this point, we have focused on plain vanilla genes carried on regular chromosomes in the nucleus. However, important information about human evolution has come from more exotic genes carried on the Y chromosome and in our mitochondria.

The X and Y chromosomes determine sex in humans—females carry two X chromosomes, and males carry one X and one Y chromosome. The X is a fairly normal chromosome, but the Y is weird. It is inherited by males from their fathers and carries very few genes. It mostly consists of long stretches of simple repeated sequences, and 95% of the material on the Y chromosome does not recombine with material on the X chromosome.

Mitochondrial genes are even weirder—they are not carried on chromosomes. Instead, they are carried on organelles called **mitochondria** (singular *mitochondrion*), which are responsible for the basic energy processing that goes on inside cells. Mitochondria contain small amounts of DNA (about 0.05% of the DNA contained in chromosomes) called **mitochondrial DNA (mtDNA)**. In humans and other primates, mtDNA codes for 13 proteins used in the mitochondria, for some of the RNA that makes up the structure of ribosomes, and for several kinds of transfer RNA. There are also two major noncoding regions. Both males and females get their mitochondria from their mother's egg cell. The mitochondria present in sperm are not transferred to the fertilized ovum. Therefore, there is no recombination in mtDNA. This means that a child has exactly the same mitochondrial genes as its mother, unless the child's mitochondria carry a novel mutation.

All the copies of any extant DNA sequence that is transmitted without recombination can be traced back to a single copy in an individual who lived in the past.

To make this idea a bit more concrete, let's begin by talking about the nonrecombining part of the Y chromosomes (NRY). The NRYs are just like surnames in the United States. Traditionally, each man transmits his surname to his sons and daughters. The names transmitted to daughters are lost when they marry; but the sons carry the name, as do their grandsons, and so on. It's the same with Y chromosomes because there is no recombination. Fathers transmit their Y chromosome to their sons, who transmit it to their grandsons, and so on.

Now suppose that in each generation some men leave no male descendants; their surnames are lost. Once again, the same goes for Y chromosomes. As the generations pass, more and more names and Y chromosomes are lost until eventually every man carries the name and the Y chromosome of a single man—**the most recent common ancestor (TMRCA)** for the Y chromosome. The same process applies to the mitochondria and to any segment of DNA carried on ordinary chromosomes that is short enough to avoid recombination—all are copies of the DNA segment carried by a single individual sometime in the past.

The number of generations that have passed since TMRCA lived depends on the size of the population. This is because the larger the population, the larger the number of generations, on average, you have to go back to reach TMRCA. To see why, pick a Y chromosome from the present generation at random. If mating takes place at random, the probability that a second randomly chosen Y chromosome derives from the same father is equal to one divided by the population size. If population size is constant from one generation to the next, then if one man has two offspring, another man must have none. Thus the rate at which a population loses lineages declines as population size increases.

It is important to understand that each bit of nonrecombining genetic material that we carry has its own ancestry. The most recent common ancestor of our mitochondria is sometimes given the colorful but misleading name "Eve." But she is not the mother of us all, only the mother of our mitochondria. The most recent common ancestor of our NRY, was not Eve's mate; in fact, he lived tens of thousands of years after Eve. The most recent common ancestors of each of the other genes were different people, who lived at very different times as well.

The accumulation of mutations allows us to derive the phylogenetic history of nonrecombining sections of DNA.

Even though the Y chromosomes of all living people are replicas of a single Y chromosome, they are not identical because mutation occasionally introduces new genetic variants. Because there is no recombination, once a mutation occurs in a particular man, it is carried by all of his descendants (unless they have a mutation themselves). The same goes for the mitochondrial DNA and nonrecombining bits of autosomal genes. Mutation has two important consequences. First, we can use the methods of phylogenetic reconstruction discussed in Chapter 4 to reconstruct a tree of descent based on derived similarities. To make such reconstructions (sometimes called **gene trees**) feasible, mutations must occur frequently enough to allow the branches of the gene tree to be distinguished. Mutation also makes it possible to estimate the time that has passed since TMRCA of that gene lived, using the genetic-distance measures that we discussed in Chapter 4. Because there is a known relationship between population size and the age of the most recent common ancestor, knowing the age of the TMRCA allows biologists to estimate population sizes in the past. Because we can repeat this for every gene, and there are many genes, this method provides a powerful tool for reconstructing human demography.

Gene trees support an African origin for modern humans.

Geneticists have constructed gene trees for the mitochondria, the nonrecombining portion of the Y chromosome, and many of the genes carried on other chromosomes. **Figure 13.3** shows the gene tree based on the entire DNA sequences of the mitochondria of several hundred people. Each branch represents a single individual. The length of the branches is proportional to the number of mutations accumulated along that branch. This means that the mtDNA of two individuals linked by short branches has a more recent common ancestor than the mtDNA of two individuals separated by long branches. A node that links branches represents the common ancestor of those individuals. The deepest and oldest nodes are labeled according to a convention adopted by geneticists and will be useful to refer to when we interpret the tree.

FIGURE 13.3

This gene tree for the complete mitochondrial genomes of 277 people from all over the world indicates that all modern humans are descended from an African population. Each branch represents the mtDNA sequence of a single individual, and the length of the branch represents the number of mutations along that branch. Thus the longer branches for Africans reflect the greater genetic variation on that continent. Almost all non-Africans are descended from a single node in the tree and from a more recent common ancestor than many Africans.

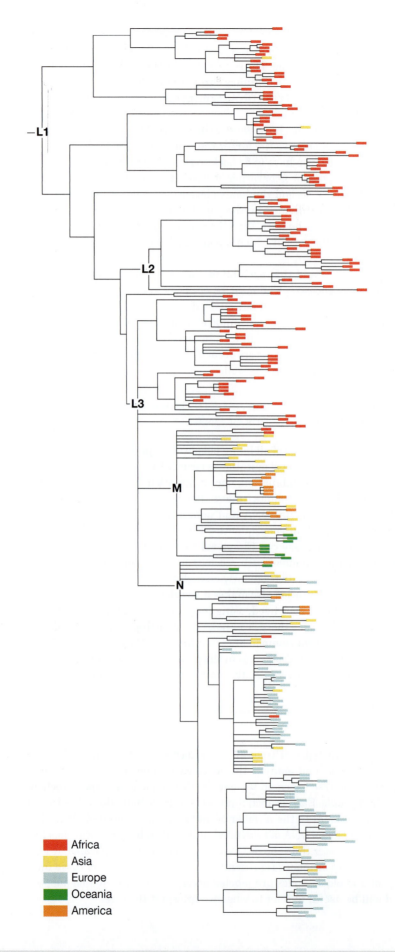

Africa
Asia
Europe
Oceania
America

This tree supports the idea that modern humans originated in Africa and then migrated out of Africa and spread across the rest of the world. Notice that all Africans in the sample are descended from nodes L1, L2, and L3, and are connected by the longest branches in the tree. What is not evident from this tree is that although direct descendants of L1 are found throughout Africa, they are relatively rare; more than two-thirds of modern Africans carry mtDNA descended from L2 and L3. All non-Africans are descendants of two nodes, M and N, that are connected to L3 by very short branches. The branches linking non-Africans are much shorter than branches linking many Africans. This strongly suggests that the population containing the last common ancestor, L1, came from Africa. The genetic distance along branches indicates that this individual lived about 130 kya. Later, perhaps 90 to 60 kya, L2 and L3 arose in Africa and spread through the continent. A population containing M and N left Africa around 60 kya and spread across the rest of the world over the next 50 kya (**Figure 13.4**). The Y chromosome tree and most trees based on other genes tell the same story.

FIGURE 13.4

An illustration of why the current geographical distribution of mitochondrial DNA halotypes is consistent with an initial spread of anatomically modern peoples out of Africa and along the southern coasts of Asia, and then north into Asia and Europe.

150 kya: Modern humans evolve somewhere in Africa and L1 lineage spreads

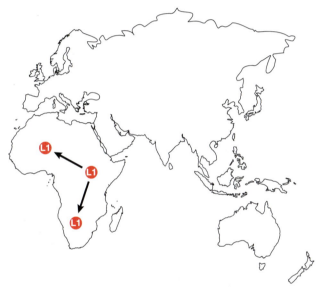

60–80 kya: New expansion spreads L2 and L3 lineages. L1 reduced to a minority.

50–60 kya: L3 gives rise to M and N lineages, which spread across southern Asia

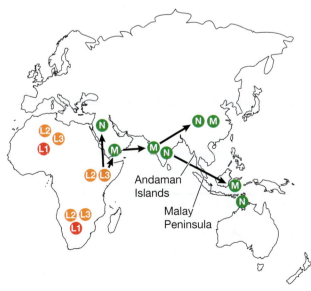

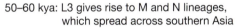

30–50 kya: M and N lineages give rise to main geographical haplotypes in Eurasia

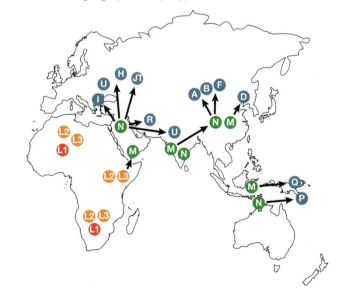

Biologists have devised a number of ways to measure the amount of genetic variation within a population. For example, one important measure of genetic variation is the average number of genetic differences per base pair (nucleotide) in a DNA sequence. To compute this measure, geneticists collect tissue samples from members of a population and assess the same part of the DNA sequence of each individual's mitochondria. Then for each pair of individuals in the sample, they check to see whether DNA at each position is the same or different. They repeat this for all pairs of individuals in the sample and then compute the average number of differences per nucleotide across the sample. As populations become more diverse genetically, the average number of genetic differences per nucleotide increases.

Humans are considerably less variable genetically than chimpanzees. **Figure 13.5** plots the amount of mtDNA genetic variation within and between three geographically separated human populations—Africans, Asians, and Europeans—and the amount of genetic variation within and between chimpanzee populations in eastern, central, and western Africa. The bars on the diagonal (*red*) show that the amount of variation within each of these human populations is much lower than that within any of the chimpanzee populations. These data tell us that any two humans taken at random from a single population are much more similar to one another than are any two chimpanzees taken at random from a single population. The off-diagonal bars (*blue*) plot the average differences among human populations and among chimpanzee populations. Genes on chromosomes paint the same picture.

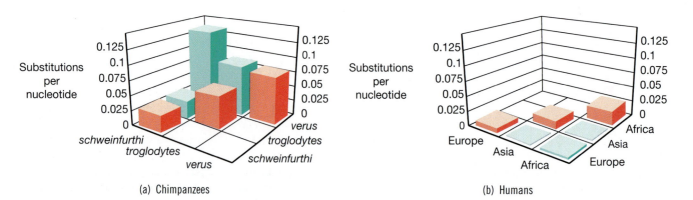

(a) Chimpanzees   (b) Humans

FIGURE 13.5

Humans are less genetically variable than chimpanzees. (a) The mean number of differences per nucleotide in one region of mtDNA for three geographically separated chimpanzee populations: *Pan troglodytes schweinfurthi* (from East Africa), *P. t. troglodytes* (from central Africa), and *P. t. verus* (from West Africa). (b) The same data for three geographically separated human populations (in Asia, Europe, and Africa). In both graphs, each red bar at the intersection of a row and a column gives data for comparing the population(s) identified at the ends of that row and column. Thus the height of each red bar represents the mean number of differences between pairs of individuals drawn from the same population. For example, each pair of chimpanzees belonging to the *verus* population differs at about 7.5% of the nucleotides sampled. Each pair of individuals drawn from the most variable human population, Africans, differs at only about 2.5% of the nucleotides assessed. The height of the blue bars represents the mean number of differences between pairs of populations. On average, an individual drawn from the *verus* population differs from an individual drawn from the *schweinfurthi* population at about 13% of the nucleotides, while Africans and Europeans, the most different pair of human populations, differ at less than 0.3% of the nucleotides. Thus the two graphs show that there is more variation within each of the chimpanzee populations than within any of the human populations, and human populations on the average are more similar to one another than chimpanzee populations are to each other.

Genetic data indicate that all modern humans are descended from a population of about 12,000 reproducing adults.

The data on genetic distance suggest that much of the human genome evolved mainly under the influence of drift and mutation. Remember that mutation introduces new genes at a very low rate and that genetic drift eliminates genetic variation at a rate that depends on the size of the population. In large populations, drift removes genetic variants slowly, but in small populations, drift eliminates variation more quickly. The effects of mutation and genetic drift will eventually balance (**Figure 13.6**) as the amount of variation reaches an equilibrium. The amount of variation at equilibrium depends on the size of the population. For a given mutation rate, bigger populations will have larger amounts of genetic variation at equilibrium. You can combine the observed amount of genetic variation and estimates of the mutation rate to calculate population size. When we do this for humans, the result is about 12,000 people of reproductive age—the existing amount of genetic variation within human populations today is consistent with the drift–mutation equilibrium value for a population of about 12,000 people. (The actual number of people in the population including children and old people would have been two or three times larger.) Data on variation in other genes yield similar estimates, as do calculations based on the age of TMRCA for the very large number of genes that have been sequenced.

This means that we are all descended from a population of about 12,000 reproducing adults. Obviously, this value is far lower than the size of the human population today or even in the recent past. How can that be? The answer is that a small human population expanded very rapidly sometime in the past. When a population grows, the equilibrium amount of genetic variation also grows because genetic drift removes variation more slowly in large populations than it does in smaller ones. If the population expands rapidly, however, it may take a long time to reach a new equilibrium level because mutation adds variation very slowly. Thus the low levels of genetic variation in contemporary human populations may be the result of a rapid expansion from a small population sometime in the past.

Geneticists have sequenced DNA from Neanderthal and Denisovan fossils.

In the film *Jurassic Park*, scientists extract dinosaur DNA from the bodies of bloodsucking insects trapped in amber and use the DNA to clone living dinosaurs. The gap between science fiction and science has narrowed in the laboratory of Svante Pääbo at the Max Planck Institute for Evolutionary Anthropology in Leipzig, Germany. Pääbo and his colleagues have now extracted and sequenced the complete nuclear and mtDNA sequences from a number of Neanderthal fossils.

It is extraordinarily difficult to obtain any genetic material from fossils because only minute amounts of this material remain in the fossilized bones. It is more difficult to get nuclear DNA out of fossils than mtDNA because there are hundreds of mitochondria in each cell, but only two copies of each nuclear gene. Nonetheless, in 2010, Pääbo and his colleagues reported sequencing the complete genome from three Neanderthal fossils found in Vindija Cave in Croatia that date from 38 to 44 kya. They took extraordinary measures to prevent contamination by modern human

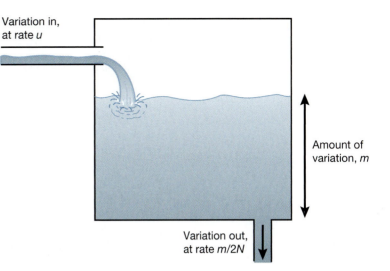

FIGURE 13.6

A physical analogy for the mutation–drift equilibrium can help explain why large populations have more genetic variation at equilibrium than small ones do. Mutation introduces new genetic variants at a constant rate (u) much like a stream of water entering a tank. Genetic drift removes variants, like a drain at the bottom of the tank. The amount of variation (m) is analogous to the volume of water in the tank: as the level of water in the tank rises, the pressure increases and the water drains out more rapidly. Eventually, the rate of outflow equals the rate of inflow, and the depth of the water remains constant. In the same way, as the amount of variation in a population increases, drift removes variation faster; eventually, a steady state is reached at which the amount of variation is constant. To calculate the equilibrium amount of variation, set the rate of inflow (u) equal to the rate of outflow ($m/2N$), and solve for m.

DNA and estimate that less than 1% of the sequence is due to contamination. This sequence is a rough draft, meaning that each nucleotide has been read 1.3 times on average. Then in 2012 as we mentioned in Chapter 12, Pääbo and colleagues used DNA taken from a finger bone and a molar found at Denisova Cave in southern Siberia to sequence the complete genome. Exceptional preservation of the DNA in the finger bone and significant technical advances allowed the researchers to create a sequence in which each nucleotide had been read more than 30 times—equivalent to the resolution achieved using samples from living people. Finally, in early 2014, Pääbo and his colleagues published a complete sequence from a Neanderthal toe bone also found at Denisova Cave. To minimize confusion this fossil is named the Altai Neanderthal. The dates of the two fossils uncovered at Denisova Cave are uncertain, but it seems very likely that the Altai Neanderthal lived earlier than the Denisova individual. The Leipzig researchers also reported a low resolution sequence from a fifth Neanderthal found at Mezmaiskaya in the foothills of the Caucasus Mountains in southern Russia. The human and Neanderthal genomes are very similar, indicating that the last common ancestor of Neanderthals and modern humans lived between 550 and 765 kya.

The sequencing of human and chimpanzee genomes tells us that there are 9,555 human protein coding genes that have a different DNA sequence from the homologous gene in chimpanzees. Neanderthals have the same genetic variant as humans for about 8,600 of these genes (90%). In contrast, Neanderthals have the same genetic variant as chimpanzees for only 78 of these genes (< 1%). Of these 78, only 5 in humans have more than one substitution that affects the primary structure of the protein. The story is similar for other kinds of genes. There are about 300 differences between humans and chimpanzees that might affect regulatory sequences, and less than 5% of the highly accelerated regions differ between humans and Neanderthals.

Genes that affect energy metabolism, cognitive development, and skeletal development have been subject to natural selection in human populations since the split with Neanderthals. We are able to say this with some confidence because, as you will see in the next chapter, long segments of DNA that are widely shared by members of a population are signals of recent directional selection. If we find long segments of DNA that are widely shared among humans, but not found in Neanderthals, then we can conclude that these genes have been subject to selection since human and Neanderthal populations separated. This method indicates that one gene, THADA, which affects non-insulin-dependent diabetes, has been subject to strong directional selection, as have genes associated with autism and schizophrenia. Another gene that affects skeletal development, RUNX2, has also been subject to strong selection.

Neanderthal and Denisova genomes are more similar to each other than to modern humans but also indicate that these two hominins had different evolutionary histories.

Pääbo and his colleagues compared the genomes of modern humans, Neanderthals, and the Denisova fossil. The results of this analysis are summarized by the genetic distance tree shown in **Figure 13.7**. The Neanderthal genomes and the Denisova genome are a bit more similar to each other than either is to the genome of modern humans. The several Neanderthal fossils are much more similar to each other than any are to the Denisova fossil. This suggests that the last common ancestor of Neanderthals and Denisovans and modern humans lived 550–765 kya and that Neanderthals and Denisovans were descended from a common ancestor who lived somewhat more recently, about 450 kya. Neanderthals are very similar to each other, although they come from widely dispersed sites in Germany, Spain, Croatia, and Russia, which encompass most of the Neanderthal geographical range. This suggests that all Neanderthals shared a common ancestor about 140,000 kya, well after the Neanderthal lineage split from the lineage leading to the Denisovans. The most likely explanation for the low genetic variation across the Neanderthal range is that Neanderthal populations suffered a severe population bottleneck after they diverged from the Denisovans.

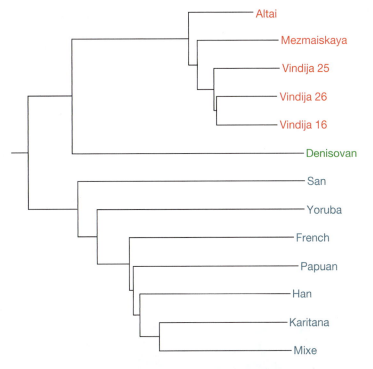

These ancient genomes indicate that there was a modest amount of interbreeding between Neanderthals and Denisovans and the ancestors of modern humans in Eurasia, but not Africa.

As they left Africa and spread into Eurasia, modern humans encountered Neanderthal and Denisovan populations. Thus if there was interbreeding between members of the two older populations and moderns, this should have affected human populations outside Africa to a greater extent than human populations in Africa. As a result, contemporary Europeans and Asians should be more similar to Neanderthals or Denisovans than are Africans.

To test this idea, Pääbo and his colleagues compared the Neanderthal and Denisovan genomes to the genomes of a number of modern humans, two from Africa, one each from Europe, East Asia, and Papua New Guinea, and a much larger sample from Southeast Asia and the Pacific. They estimated the amount of gene flow between these populations using a variety of methods. Africans do not harbor any genes from Neanderthals, while the genomes found in all Eurasian and Pacific populations contain about 2% Neanderthal DNA. In contrast, African and European populations don't carry any Denisovan genes, east Asian populations carry a small amount (less than 0.5%), and Papuans and other Pacific peoples carry between 3% and 6% Denisovan DNA. The simplest explanation for these facts is that there was interbreeding between Neanderthals and early modern humans in Southwest Asia before the modern human population split to colonize Europe, the eastern parts of Asia, and the Pacific. After this split, members of the expanding modern human population, who eventually settled in New Guinea and the Pacific, met and interbred with relatives of the Denisovans, perhaps in Southeast Asia. The small amount of Denisovan DNA found in east Asians could be the result of very low levels of interbreeding between Denisovans and the ancestors of east Asians or it could be the consequence of later interbreeding between east Asian and Pacific peoples.

FIGURE 13.7

A tree giving the overall genetic distance between the genomes of five Neanderthal fossils (*red*), the Denisova fossil (*green*), and seven living people (*blue*) from different parts of the globe. The length of the lines is proportional to the genetic distance. The simplest interpretation of these data is that Neanderthals and Denisovans share a more recent common ancestor with each other than with modern humans but that Denisovans were genetically distinct from Neanderthals.

Genetic variation decreases with the distance from Africa consistent with expansion of human populations out of Africa.

When human populations expanded out of Africa, they didn't intend to colonize Asia. They just moved next door, and next door happened to be a nearby continent. After that population expanded, things got crowded, and another group of emigrants moved again—not back to Africa because it was already occupied, but farther into Eurasia. In this way, modern human populations spread across Eurasia bit by bit. This kind of process could have led to a very rapid geographic expansion, even if no single person moved very far in his or her own lifetime. For example, suppose individuals moved only 25 km (about 15 miles) in their lifetime. Assuming 25-year generations and no movement backward, this would mean that populations would spread 100 km (about 60 miles) a century, fast enough to reach Australia from Africa in about 10,000 years.

This kind of stepwise expansion leaves a distinctive genetic signature because each time emigrants leave their natal population, they carry with them a subset of the genes present in that population. This means that the amount of genetic variation within populations decreases as distance from Africa increases. **Figure 13.8** illustrates how this works. Initially, there are four sites, and only site 1 is inhabited. There are 32 individuals with four different genotypes represented by the colors blue, red, light blue, and green. Initially, there are eight of each genotype. Then eight individuals from site 1 move to neighboring site 2. By chance, the blue and green genotypes are over-represented among the emigrants. This population grows to fill the site, and because the genes are assumed to be neutral, their frequencies are the same as among the founders. Then the process is repeated. Eight emigrants colonize site 3. By chance no red genotypes made the trip. Then that population grows, and then site 4 is colonized. At each step, the emigrants carry only a fraction of the genetic variation present in their natal home. As a result, the amount of variation decreases as they move farther and farther from their site of origin.

This is exactly what we see in modern human populations. Two groups of geneticists, one led by Sohini Ramachandran of Brown University and a second by Franck Prugnolle of the University of Montpellier, independently computed the genetic variation in 51 populations from around the globe using data on a large sample of

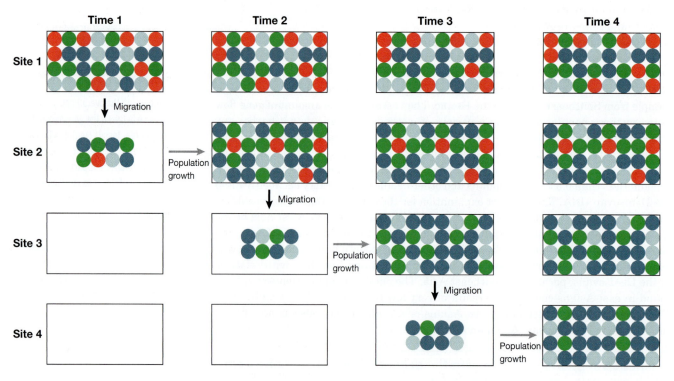

FIGURE 13.8

An illustration of why spreading across Eurasia and the Americas through a series of expansions is expected to lead to reduced genetic variation. At time 1, a population of 32 individuals occupies site 1. There are four genotypes: red, blue, light blue, and green. Sites 2 through 4 are unoccupied. A subset of the population colonizes site 2, and because the number of emigrants is small, the blue and green genotypes are overrepresented by chance. By time 2, these colonists have reproduced, and site 2 has become saturated. Because the genes are not subject to natural selection, they exist in the same frequency as the colonists—blue and green are more common, and red and light blue are less common than in the original population. A subset drawn from site 2 then colonizes site 3. Again, chance affects the genotypes present among the colonists, and the red genotype is lost, and blue is even more common. Once again, the population grows and sends off new emigrants to site 4. As the spread proceeds, variation is lost because at each stage, chance causes some genotypes to be overrepresented and others to be underrepresented. Eventually, this leads to the loss of genotypes.

microsatellite loci collected as part of the Human Genome Diversity Project. **Microsatellite loci** are noncoding, repetitive, and highly variable DNA sequences, often used in criminal investigations for individual identification. The researchers also computed the distance of each population from East Africa along the most likely migration route from Africa. As you can see in **Figure 13.9**, human genetic variation decreases with distance from East Africa.

Interestingly, the same seems to be true for phenotypic variation. The Cambridge group collaborated with Tsunehiko Hanihara, now at the Kitasato University Medical School in Japan, who had compiled 37 different measurements on each of 4,666 human skulls drawn from 105 populations around the world. For each measurement, they calculated a measure of phenotypic variation in each population. The amount of phenotypic variation decreases with geographical distance from Africa, but the relationship is not as strong as the relationship between genetic variation and geographical distance from Africa. This makes sense because the genes that affect variation in skull morphology should be subject to the same sampling processes that affect the microsatellite loci. However, because the genes that affect morphology are expressed in the phenotype, they are subject to natural selection. Local conditions favor different skull shapes, and this partially masks the effects of the original settlement of the world.

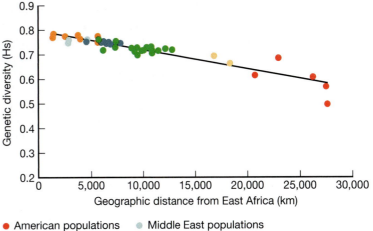

American populations
Asian populations
European populations
Middle East populations
Oceanian populations
African populations

FIGURE 13.9

This figure plots the amount of genetic variation of a number of human populations from a large sample of microsatellite loci against distance from East Africa along the likely path of human expansion through the world. The fact that the amount of genetic variation declines supports the hypothesis that humans emerged from Africa and spread along the hypothesized path.

Genetic data give hints about the route and timing of the human expansion out of Africa.

A team of Cambridge University scientists led by Anders Eriksson and Andrea Manica used the same Human Genome Diversity Project data set to infer the timing of human expansions. They computed the age of the most recent common ancestor for each of the 51 populations in the data set. As we learned earlier in this chapter, the TMRCA depends on population size, which in turn depends on patterns of migration and population growth. This allowed the team to construct a computer model to describe how human populations spread across the globe and generate estimated values of the age of TMRCA in the 51 populations. Eriksson and Manica found the population size and rates of migration that produced results to best fit the observed TMRCA data. **Figure 13.10** shows the estimated pattern and timing of human population expansion. According to the model, modern humans had spread throughout most of Africa by 80 kya, reached southwest Asia by 65 kya, and spread to most of the rest of Eurasia and Australia by 40 kya.

Another recent analysis by Morten Rasmussen of the Natural History Museum of Denmark suggests that there were at least two separate migrations, one along the southern coast of Eurasia and a second one farther north (**Figure 13.11**). This inference was based on the sequencing of the complete genome from DNA extracted from a 100-year-old hair from an Australian aborigine. The Australian genome is closer to the African genome and the European genome is closer to genomes of people in China, suggesting two migrations, first out of Africa to Australia and later out of Africa to northern Asia and Europe. However, the Australian genome is closer to the Chinese genome than the European genome, suggesting that there was gene flow between the ancestors of Australians and Chinese after their split with the ancestors of Europeans. The Australian genome shows evidence of low levels of interbreeding with both Denisovans and Neanderthals.

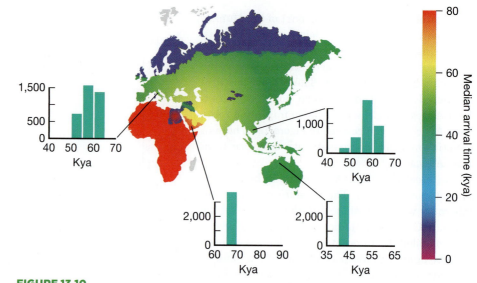

FIGURE 13.10

The median arrival times of modern humans in different parts of the Old World derived by fitting a detailed model of human expansion to the Human Genome Diversity Project data set. The histograms give the range of arrival times for particular locations. This model indicates that modern humans had spread throughout most of Africa by 80 kya. They reached southwest Asia by 65 kya and spread to most of the rest of Eurasia and Australia by 40 kya.

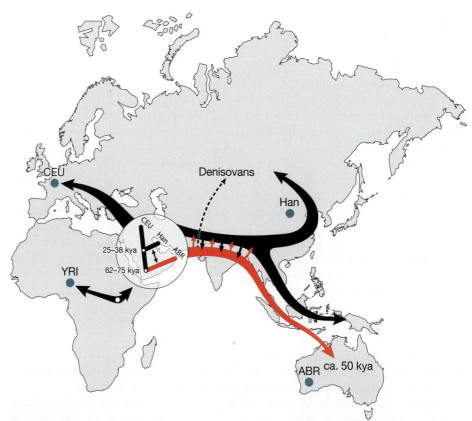

FIGURE 13.11

The pattern of migration inferred from sequencing genomes from four populations: African (YRI), European (CEU), Chinese (HAN), and Australian aboriginal (ABR). The Australian genome is closer to the African genome, and the European genome is closer to that of Chinese, suggesting two migrations. However, the Australian genome is closer to the Chinese than the European, suggesting that there was gene flow between the ancestors of Australians and Chinese after their split with the ancestors of Europeans.

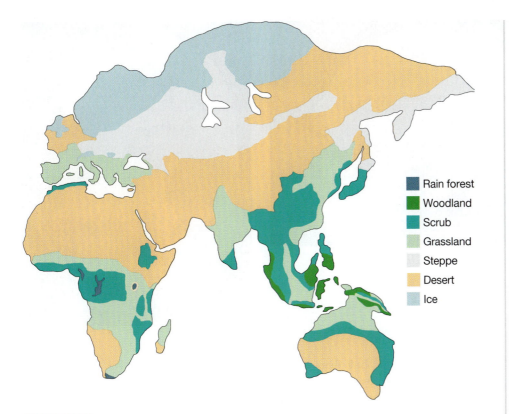

■	Rain forest
■	Woodland
■	Scrub
■	Grassland
■	Steppe
■	Desert
■	Ice

FIGURE 13.12

A reconstruction of the distribution of habitats when humans left Africa (72–60 kya). The world was colder and drier than it is now so sea levels were lower. Sri Lanka was connected to the Eurasian continent, and what are now the islands of southeastern Asia were part of a large peninsula called Sunda. Australia and New Guinea were linked in an isolated continent called Sahul. Forests were much less widespread, mainly limited to central Africa, Sunda, and Sahul. Much of Asia was covered with desert or steppe tundra.

The two-migration scenario fits with what is known about climate and ecology during this period. From 72 to 60 kya the world was in a cold period. Forests and grassland were limited to central and southern Africa; southern Eurasia; and Sahul, the continent made up of present-day New Guinea and Australia (**Figure 13.12**). The rest of the world was very dry and cold. After about 50 kya there was a warmer period that may have made it possible for humans to move to higher latitudes.

Evidence from Fossils

The genetic data are consistent with the fossil evidence for the appearance of anatomically modern *Homo sapiens*.

The oldest modern human fossils were unearthed in 1963 at Omo Kibish, in southern Ethiopia. One of the two skulls found there was relatively modern, while the other was more similar to *Homo heidelbergensis*. Originally, the dates for this site were uncertain, but new methods now indicate a date of 190 kya. More recently, a number of fossils were uncovered at Herto, in Ethiopia. A team led by Tim White, a paleoanthropologist at the University of California, Berkeley, found the fossilized crania of two adults and one immature individual along with a number of other fragments. These skulls are intermediate between those of modern humans and older African hominins classified as *Homo heidelbergensis*. The skulls are longer and more robust than those of most living people. They have prominent browridges, pointed occipital bones, and

FIGURE 13.13

Side and front views of one of the hominin crania found at Herto, Ethiopia. This specimen (BOU-VP-16/1) is intermediate between *Homo heidelbergensis* and modern *Homo sapiens,* displaying prominent browridges but a high, rounded braincase.

other features that link them to earlier African hominins. However, they also have some very modern features—most notably, a high, rounded braincase (**Figure 13.13**). Argon–argon dating was used to date these fossils to about 160 kya.

In those days, the Herto site was on the shores of a lake, and there is good evidence that hominins butchered hippopotamuses. The stone tools found at the site are much like those found in association with earlier African *Homo heidelbergensis.* Multiple unambiguous cut marks indicate that the skulls were defleshed by stone tools, and polished surfaces are consistent with repeated handling by hominins. White and his co-workers point out that the mortuary practices used by some contemporary peoples in New Guinea leave a similar combination of marks on skulls, and they suggest that the Herto fossils may provide early evidence of similar types of ritual behavior.

There is evidence that modern humans also lived in other parts of Africa around the same time. The most extensive finds come from Klasies River sites in South Africa. Excavations at these sites have yielded five lower jaws, one upper jaw, part of a forehead, and numerous smaller skeletal fragments. A variety of dating techniques suggest the Klasies sequence dates between 110 and 50 kya, while most of the human remains are found in sediments estimated to date between 100 and 90 kya. Although one of the lower jaws clearly has a modern jutting chin and the forehead has modern-looking browridges, the fragmentary nature of the fossils makes it difficult to be sure that these are modern humans.

Even more modern fossils have been found at the Qafzeh and caves in Israel. Thermoluminescence and electron-spin-resonance dating techniques have shown that these fossils are 115,000 years old. This was during a relatively warm, wet period, when animals would have been able to move from Africa to the Middle East. This inference is supported by the climate records from caves and the fact that other fossilized animals found at these sites are primarily African species. Thus, although these sites are outside of Africa geographically, they were ecologically African during this period.

Neanderthal fossils also have been found at three other sites located quite close to Qafzeh and Skhūl: Kebara, Tabun, and Amud. For many years there were no reliable absolute dates for any of these sites, and most anthropologists assumed that the Neanderthals came first and were succeeded by the modern hominins at Qafzeh and Skhūl. When the sites were dated by thermoluminescence and electron-spin-resonance methods, the results were a big surprise. The age of Tabun is uncertain, but the Neanderthals at Kebara and Amud lived 60 to 55 kya.

Anatomically modern fossils are found throughout the rest of the world, but none appears outside of Africa until after 60 kya. In Asia, a partial cranium and some postcranial material, probably from the same person, were found at Niah Cave in Borneo. These materials date from 46 to 34 kya. At Tianyuan Cave near Beijing, paleontologists found a modern human mandible and femur dated from 42 to 39 kya. DNA recovered from these fossils indicates that, like contemporary populations from East Asia, these people had a small amount of Neanderthal ancestry but no Denisovan ancestry. In Australia, a cranium and partial skeleton dating from 38 to 42 kya were found at Lake Mungo. Interestingly, this fossil is the oldest that shows evidence of cremation. The oldest modern human fossils in Europe were found in Romania and date to about 34 kya. However, beginning about 30 kya there is a wealth of fossil material from across Europe.

The African Archaeological Record for the Later Pleistocene

Modern human behavior is much more complex and much more variable than the behavior of earlier hominins.

Remember that *Homo ergaster* and *Homo heidelbergensis* used Acheulean tools throughout Africa and western Eurasia for more than a million years. Thus the same tools, and presumably more or less the same adaptive strategies, were used over a wide range of habitats for a very long period of time. In contrast, present-day foragers use a vast range of different, highly specialized tools and techniques to adapt to a very large range of environments. They also engage in elaborate and varied symbolic, artistic, and religious behavior that is unparalleled among other creatures. The extraordinary geographic range and sophistication of modern humans is due partly to our cognitive abilities. Individuals can solve problems that would completely stump other creatures (see Chapter 8). However, being smarter than the average bear (or primate) is only part of our secret. Our other trick is having the ability to accumulate and transmit complex adaptive and symbolic behavior over successive generations. People rarely solve difficult problems entirely on their own. Even the most brilliant of us couldn't construct a seaworthy kayak or invent perspective drawing from scratch. Instead, we gain skills, knowledge, and techniques from being instructed by and watching others. The variety and sophistication of modern human behavior is a product of our ability to acquire information in this way (see Chapter 15).

Archaeological evidence suggests that early modern humans living in Africa were able to accumulate complex adaptive and symbolic behavior.

From about 250 to 40 kya, the African archaeological record is dominated by a variety of stone tool kits that, for the most part, emphasize Mode 3 tools. These industries are collectively labeled the **Middle Stone Age (MSA)**. Until recently, most archaeologists thought that the MSA in Africa was qualitatively similar to the much better-known Mousterian tool industries associated with Neanderthals in Europe. Signatures of modern human behavior, such as more complex tools, long-distance exchange networks, art and ritual, which are well documented in Europe by 30 kya,

FIGURE 13.14

Bifacial Still Bay points found at Blombos Cave that date to about 70 kya. Similar points have been found at several other sites on the coast of South Africa that date to about the same age. These points were likely produced using a sophisticated technique called pressure flaking, which allows great control over the shape of the edge. Previously, the earliest examples of this technique were tools found in southern France that date to about 20 kya.

(a)

(b)

FIGURE 13.15

(a) Microlith found at Pinnacle Point on the coast of South Arica. Many such microliths have been found in layers that date from 72 to 60 kya. (b) A complete arrow found at a site in Europe that dates to about 8 kya. Note how the microlith was hafted to make a composite tool.

were thought to be largely absent in Africa. However, this view has been challenged by a number of twenty-first-century discoveries.

In 2000, archaeologists Sally McBrearty at the University of Connecticut and Alison Brooks at the George Washington University published a paper in which they argued that the MSA is not qualitatively similar to the Mousterian in Europe and that most of the signatures of modern human behavior developed in Africa between 250 and 60 kya. Their point of view has subsequently been strengthened by a number of remarkable archaeological discoveries mainly on the coast of South Africa, and it now seems likely people living in Africa achieved this kind of complex and varied behavior by 70 kya.

- *Technology.* They used highly sophisticated methods to fabricate complex adaptive tools from stone and bone.

- *Social organization.* They lived at higher population densities and were better able to adapt to difficult environments. They also used raw materials that came from sources hundreds of kilometers away for toolmaking, suggesting that they had long-distance exchange networks.

- *Symbolic expression.* They used ornamentation, performed ritual burials, and practiced other forms of symbolic behavior.

Complex adaptive technologies appear in association with MSA archaeological sites.

Blades are long, thin stone tools that are characteristic of modern humans living in Europe after 40 kya. They were long thought to be a signature of modern human behavior. However, at the Kapthurin Formation in Kenya, roughly 25% of the tools are blades. Archaeologists can show that the knappers at this site were highly skilled at blade production, making few mistakes and wasting little raw material. This site has been dated to between 280 and 240 kya by the argon–argon technique. Blades, which are designated as **Mode 4** tools, have also been found at a number of other MSA sites that date between 250 and 60 kya.

Around 70 kya two sophisticated types of stone tools appear in southern Africa. The symmetrical, leaf-shaped Still Bay points are finely made (**Figure 13.14**). Modern experiments suggest that the final phase of shaping involved a technique called **pressure flaking**. Instead of using a hammer stone to shape points, the knapper uses a hard, pointed tool and applies pressure to remove small flakes. This technique allows great control over the flaking process and was used to make beautiful Soultrean points found in southern France (dated to 20 kya) and Clovis points made by early Native Americans (dated to 12 kya). The second new tool type is made up of very small stone tools called **microliths**. These have a sharp edge on one side and a carefully flattened surface on the other side (**Figure 13.15a**). Archaeologists classify these as **Mode 5** tools. Similar tools were made throughout the world over the next 50,000 years and were used either as arrow points (**Figure 13.15b**) or to tip light spears thrown with an atlatl. An atlatl is a notched throwing stick (**Figure 13.16**) that increases the length of the arm and greatly increases the distance a spear can be thrown. The use of bows or atlatls represents a significant increase in technological complexity compared to earlier peoples.

To make these tools, people had to use complex techniques. Tools at this site were manufactured from silcrete, a kind of stone that is usually very difficult to flake. Kyle Brown of the University of Cape Town and his colleagues have shown that these early

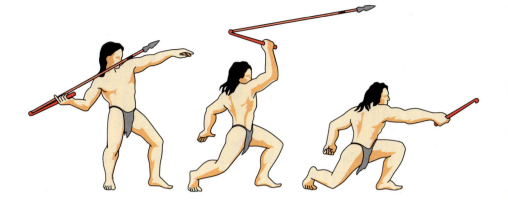

FIGURE 13.16

An atlatl is a tool that lengthens the arm. This allows a light spear to be thrown with much greater velocity than a spear thrown without an atlatl.

humans were able to make the refined Still Bay points and microliths because they heat-treated the silcrete, gradually raising its temperature to around 350°C, probably by burying it in sand under a campfire, transforming it into a much harder, easily flaked material. Heat treating first appears around 164 kya and predominated in southern Africa at 72 kya.

The use of bone is another signature of modern human sites, and bone tools also occur at several MSA sites. Alison Brooks and her co-workers recovered a number of exquisite bone points, some of them elaborately barbed, from Katanda, a site on the northeastern border of the Democratic Republic of the Congo (**Figure 13.17**). The MSA layer containing the points has been dated to between 90 and 60 kya. At Blombos Cave in South Africa, a number of polished bone points have been found that date to about 72 kya.

There is also evidence for shelters and hearths in the MSA. At several sites, MSA peoples built shelters. At the Mumbwa Caves in Zambia, there are three arcs of stone blocks that probably served as windbreaks. Elaborate stone hearths were constructed inside these structures. There are many more MSA sites at which people seem to have constructed hearths and built huts, but for each of these it is impossible to rule out the possibility that natural processes produced the features that archaeologists have documented.

Later people in southern Africa were likely more adaptable than earlier peoples. About 190 kya the world experienced a sharp drop in temperature that lasted for about 60,000 years. Archaeological sites dating to this period are rare, suggesting that the human population in Africa contracted sharply. Then around 130 kya, as the world warmed and became wetter, the population expanded. When the world climate cooled again about 70 kya there was no population contraction; instead there was a period of cultural efflorescence with new tool types and, as we shall see, more symbolic behavior.

MSA people probably had large social networks.

MSA peoples sometimes transported raw material great distances. Most of the stone used to make tools at MSA sites comes from a short distance away. At several MSA sites, however, small amounts of raw materials were transported much farther. At several sites in East Africa, for example, tools were made from obsidian carried 140 to 240 km (about 90 to 150 miles). The long-distance movements of these resources may mean that Upper Paleolithic peoples ranged over long distances or that they participated in long-distance trade networks.

FIGURE 13.17

Beautiful bone points like this one found at Katanda in the Democratic Republic of the Congo have been dated to between 174 and 82 kya. If these dates are correct, then Middle Stone Age peoples were capable of producing bone tools that rival the best of the European Upper Paleolithic tools.

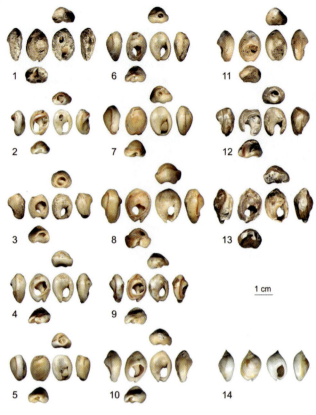

FIGURE 13.18

These shells come from a site in Morocco dated to 82 kya. The shells were gathered and brought to the site, perforated, and covered in red ocher. They may have been strung on a cord.

1 cm

FIGURE 13.19

These are small pieces of ostrich eggshell found at Diepkloopf Rock Shelter in South Africa. They are about 2.5 cm across and date to about 60 kya. They are decorated with a distinctive cross-hatched pattern also found on many such fragments at this site. Modern southern African foragers use ostrich eggs as containers for liquids, usually water.

Modern people in Africa made decorative carvings and beads and used pigment.

In 2007, a team led by Abdeljalil Bouzouggar of the Institut National des Sciences de l'Archéologie et du Patrimoine of Morocco announced the discovery of 41 perforated shell beads from the site of Grotte de Pigeons, which is dated to 82 kya (**Figure 13.18**). The shells are all punctured in a similar way, and some have been painted with ocher. The surfaces of the shells are worn in a way that suggests they may have been strung on a cord or sewn onto clothing. The shells were brought to the site from the coast, which was at least 40 km away. Similar perforated shells have been found at three other sites in northern Africa.

There is also evidence of ornaments and decorative carving at the other end of Africa. A team led by Christopher Henshilwood of the University of Bergen discovered a cache of shell beads at Blombos Cave that are dated to 76 kya. The shells come from a site 20 km away.

Even more striking, Pierre-Jean Texier of the Université Bordeaux and colleagues have found a large number of engraved fragments of ostrich eggshell at Diepkloof Rock Shelter in South Africa (**Figure 13.19**). Modern foragers in southern Africa often use ostrich eggshells as containers—they hold about a liter of water. At Diepkloof, the shells have been engraved with complex geometric patterns, which Texier and colleagues believe symbolized group identity in the same way that pottery and basket decoration do today. These artifacts date to about 60 kya and are associated with the more advanced Howieson's Port stone tools that are found at some South African sites.

There is good evidence for the use of red ocher at a number of sites. The earliest evidence comes from the Kapthurin Formation, which dates between 280 and 240 kya. Two elaborately engraved pieces of red ocher have been found at Blombos Cave, the same site that produced the shell beads (**Figure 13.20**). Many present-day African peoples use red ocher to decorate themselves and for symbolic purposes, but some archaeologists have argued that red ocher might also be used for utilitarian purposes, such as tanning hides. Few images are associated with MSA sites, but the lack of artwork is likely due to the fact that rock surfaces there are constantly peeling away.

FIGURE 13.20

One of two engraved pieces of red ocher found at Blombos Cave in South Africa. The artifact is dated to 77 kya and is associated with MSA tools. The engravings are similar to cave art found in other parts of the world.

Modern human behavior may have been caused by either increased cognitive ability or cultural innovations.

Remember that the first anatomically modern humans appear in the fossil record about 200 kya. This means that the first evidence of complex behaviors associated with modern people occurred well after the first appearance of people who *look* fully modern. However, we need to remember that morphology and behavior can be decoupled. People who look fully modern could have evolved new cognitive abilities that were not reflected in their skeletal anatomy. For example, Richard Klein has suggested that the human revolution may have been caused by a mutation that allowed fully modern speech. It could be that linguistic ability evolved late in the human lineage and gave rise to the technological sophistication and symbolic behavior of the Upper Paleolithic peoples. It seems more likely, however, that cognitive innovations like those that support language evolved gradually through the accumulation of small changes. Such a process requires no special macromutations or unlikely chance events. As we explained in Chapters 7 and 8, behavior is subject to the same kinds of evolutionary forces that shape morphology and physiology.

Alternatively the striking changes in human behavior may have resulted from cultural, not genetic, changes. We know that something like this happened later in human history. About 10 kya, an equally profound transformation was associated with the adoption of agriculture. Agriculture led to sedentary villages, social inequality, large-scale societies, monumental architecture, writing, and many other innovations that we see in the archaeological record. The transition we see in the archaeological record in the MSA could have been caused by a similar kind of technological innovation that allowed for much more efficient food acquisition, which in turn led to a greater economic surplus, more economic specialization, and greater symbolic and ritual activity.

The Archaeological Record Outside of Africa after 60 kya

Archaeological data suggest modern humans first entered southern Asia by 45 kya and brought along microliths similar to those used in southern Africa.

At Mehtakheri, a site in the Narmada Valley of northwestern India, archaeologists have recovered microliths in sediments that date to 45–50 kya. These backed, crescent-shaped tools are strikingly similar to those found on the coast of southern

FIGURE 13.21

Tools, beads, and decorated ostrich eggshells found at African (left) and Indian (right) sites that date to 40–35 kya.

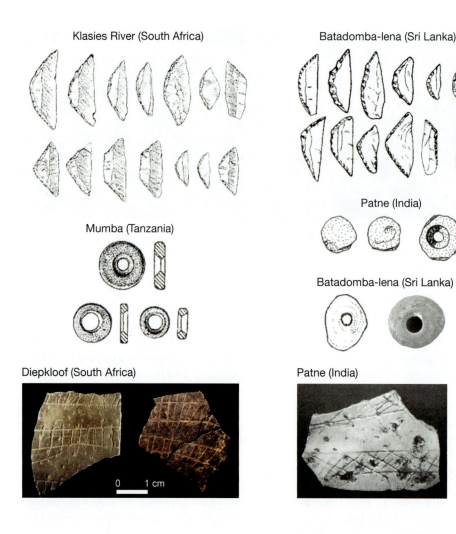

Klasies River (South Africa)

Batadomba-lena (Sri Lanka)

Mumba (Tanzania)

Patne (India)

Batadomba-lena (Sri Lanka)

Diepkloof (South Africa)

Patne (India)

0   1 cm

Africa. Although India is rather poorly explored archaeologically during this period, there are several other sites that date to 35–40 kya with tools like those found in Africa (**Figure 13.21**). These sites also contain beads and decorated ostrich eggshells, which are very similar to those found in Africa.

Modern humans first entered Australia at least 40 kya, bringing sophisticated technology.

The fossil and archaeological record in Australia is quite good. Numerous well-dated archaeological sites indicate that modern *Homo sapiens* entered Australia at least 40 kya, and perhaps as early as 50 kya, and occupied the entire continent by 30 kya. The most complete early site is in southeastern Australia at Lake Mungo. The finds here include three hominin skulls, hearths, and ovens that have been dated to 32 kya using carbon-14 dating. The skull specimens are fully modern and well within the range of variation of contemporary Australian aborigines.

The earliest Australians made sophisticated tools, and there is evidence of symbolic behavior. Some of the tools found at these early sites were made from bone, there are cave paintings dated to 17 kya, and there is evidence of both ceremonial burials and cremation. About 15 kya, Australians seem to have been the first people to have used polished stone tools, which are made by grinding rather than flaking. In other parts of the world, polished stone tools do not appear in the record until agriculture is introduced, about 7 kya.

The fact that people got to Australia at all is evidence of their technological sophistication. Much of the world's water was tied up in continental glaciers 40 kya, so New Guinea, Australia, and Tasmania formed a single continent, named Sahul (see Figure 13.12). However, there was still at least 100 km (62 miles) of open ocean lying between Asia and Sahul. This gap was wide enough to prevent nearly all movement of terrestrial mammals across it and thus to preserve the unique, largely marsupial fauna of Australia and New Guinea. The colonization of Sahul cannot be dismissed as a single lucky event, because people also crossed another 100 km of ocean to reach the nearby islands of New Britain and New Ireland at about the same time.

The people who first settled these islands were able to build seaworthy boats. There is a cave site at Jerimalai on the eastern tip of the island of Timor that dates to 42 kya. At this site, archaeologists have found numerous stone tools and the bones of many species of fish. About half of the fish bones are from pelagic species, mainly tuna, that are found well away from shore. This suggests that the people who lived there had water craft that allowed them to engage in offshore fishing.

More sophisticated stone tools appeared in eastern Asia around the same time.

Modern humans must have come to Australia by way of southern Asia, but signs of modern humans in southern Asia are scarce. Only one site in southern Asia contains the kind of sophisticated artifacts seen in Upper Paleolithic Europe. The Batadomba-lena Cave, in Sri Lanka, is dated to about 28 kya, and it has yielded modern human remains, elaborate stone tools, and tools made from bone.

Upper Paleolithic tools have been found at a number of sites in northern China, Mongolia, and Siberia. Especially notable is Berelekh, a site 500 km (about 300 miles) north of the Arctic Circle where the Yana River empties into the Arctic Ocean. Here, archaeologists have recovered sophisticated stone tools and a number of artifacts made from bone, ivory, and horn (**Figure 13.22**). Radiocarbon methods indicate that these tools were made about 30 kya. Pollen data tell us that this area then had a cool, dry climate in which grasslands were mixed with stands of larch and birch trees. Numerous processed bones of horse, musk ox, bison, and mammoth indicate that big game was plentiful. Nonetheless, life at this site must have been challenging for a recent African emigrant. Today, the winters are long and dark, and January temperatures average −37°C (about −34°F)—a bracing thought, given that the world was much colder 30,000 years ago than it is today.

There is a very rich record of modern human settlement in western Eurasia.

The archaeological record for western Eurasia is exceptionally rich and detailed, and we know much more about the expansion of modern humans in this part of the world than we do in other areas. In the remainder of this chapter we exploit this rich record to give a more detailed picture of the lifeways of the earliest modern humans.

The first modern humans in western Eurasia created a number of different tool industries in different areas. Archaeologists refer to these tool industries collectively as **Upper Paleolithic** industries to distinguish them from the earlier tool industries associated with Neanderthals and other earlier hominins. The earliest Upper Paleolithic tools appear in the Near East about 45 kya, and they disappear from the archaeological record about 10 kya. Archaeologists refer to this period in western Eurasia as the Upper Paleolithic period and the people who made the tools as Upper Paleolithic peoples.

Upper Paleolithic industries varied in time and space.

The first Upper Paleolithic industry in Europe, the Aurignacian, was widespread in Europe by 41 kya (**Figure 13.23**). It is characterized by certain types of large

FIGURE 13.22

Spear foreshafts found at Yana, a site 500 km (about 300 miles) north of the Arctic Circle in eastern Siberia. These rhino horn foreshafts were fitted to the front end of the spear. If a hunter struck an animal without killing it, he could remove his spear, fit a second foreshaft to the spear, and reuse it.

FIGURE 13.23

The earliest Upper Paleolithic industry, the Aurignacian, is found throughout Europe; three industries intermediate between the Mousterian and the Aurignacian (the Châtelperronian, the Uluzzian, and the Szeletian) are found in localized areas. Because each of these transitional industries is distinctive, some scientists believe it unlikely that the Aurignacian evolved from one of them.

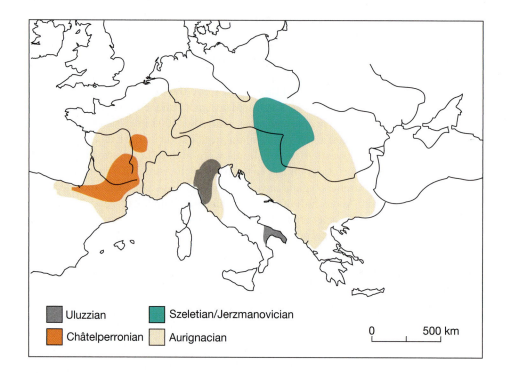

Uluzzian
Châtelperronian
Szeletian/Jerzmanovician
Aurignacian
0   500 km

blades, burins, and bone points. In most areas, it appears that anatomically modern humans and Neanderthals overlapped for only about 1,000 years. This brief overlap suggests that the modern humans using Aurignacian tools appeared and rapidly replaced Neanderthals. However, in southern France, the transition between the Mousterian and the Aurignacian is marked by the presence of a third, intermediate industry—the **Châtelperronian**. Many anthropologists believe that the Châtelperronian is the result of Neanderthals' borrowing ideas and technology from modern humans. Paul Mellars, an archaeologist at the University of Cambridge, argues that three kinds of evidence support this view. First, Châtelperronian tools are associated with Neanderthal fossils at Saint-Césaire and Arcy-sur-Cure in France. Second, archaeological data indicate that the Châtelperronian and Aurignacian industries co-existed in southern France for hundreds of years. Finally, other transitional tool kits have been found. As **Figure 13.24** shows, each of these transitional industries is localized: the Châtelperronian in southern France, the Uluzzian in northern Italy, and the Szeletian in central Europe. Mellars points out that each of these transitional industries is quite distinctive, and he argues that it is not likely that the very widespread Aurignacian industry evolved from several distinctive localized transitional industries.

About 30 kya, the Aurignacian was replaced in southern France by a new tool kit, the Gravettian, in which small, parallel-sided blades predominated and bone points were replaced by bone awls. Then about 21 kya, the Solutrean, with its beautiful leaf-shaped points, developed in the region. And 16 kya, the Solutrean gave way to the Magdalenian, a tool kit dominated by carved, decorated bone and antler points together with many microliths. Other parts of Europe are characterized by different sequences of tool complexes; so after the Aurignacian, each region typically has a distinctive material culture.

Over roughly 25,000 years of the Upper Paleolithic in Europe, there were dozens of distinctive tool kits emphasizing Mode 4 tools. This diversity stands in striking contrast

FIGURE 13.24

Long, thin, delicate points characterized the Solutrean tool tradition.

to the Acheulean tool kit, which remained unchanged throughout more than half of the Old World for over a million years.

Upper Paleolithic peoples manufactured blade tools, which made efficient use of stone resources.

As we noted earlier, blades are stone flakes that look like modern knife blades: they are long, thin, and flat, and have a sharp edge. Blades have a longer cutting edge than flakes do, so blade technology made more efficient use of raw materials than older tool technologies did. However, there was a cost: Although blades made more efficient use of materials, they also took more time to manufacture, requiring more preparation and more finishing strokes.

The Upper Paleolithic tool kit includes a large number of distinctive, standardized tool types.

Upper Paleolithic peoples made many more kinds of tools than earlier hominins had made. Tools thought to be used as chisels, various types of scrapers, a number of different kinds of points, knives, burins (pointed tools used for engraving), drills, borers, and throwing sticks are just some of the items from the Upper Paleolithic tool kit.

Even more striking, the different tool types have distinctive, stereotyped shapes. It is as if the Upper Paleolithic toolmakers had a sheaf of engineering drawings on which they recorded their plans for various tools. When the toolmaker needed a new 10-cm (4-in.) burin, for example, she would consult the plan and produce one just like all the other 10-cm burins. Of course, these toolmakers didn't really use drawings as modern engineers do, but the fact that we find standardized tools suggests that they carried these plans in their minds. The final shape of Upper Paleolithic tools was not determined by the shape of the raw material; instead, the toolmakers seem to have had a mental model of what the tool was supposed to look like, and they imposed that form on the stone by careful flaking. The craft approach to toolmaking reached a peak in the Solutrean tool tradition, which predominated in southern France between 21 and 16.5 kya (**Figure 13.25**). Solutrean toolmakers crafted exquisite points shaped like laurel leaves that were sometimes 28 cm (about 1 ft.) long, 1 cm (about 0.5 in.) thick, and perfectly symmetrical.

Upper Paleolithic people made tools from bones, antlers, and teeth. Earlier hominins had made limited use of bone, but Upper Paleolithic people transformed bone, ivory, and antler into barbed spear points, awls, sewing needles, and beads.

Stones and other raw materials for toolmaking were often transported hundreds of kilometers from their place of origin.

At Bacho Kiro, a 46,000-year-old Aurignacian site in Bulgaria, more than half of the flint used to make blades was brought from a source 120 km (about 75 miles) away. Distinctive, high-quality flint quarried in Poland has been found in archaeological sites more than 400 km (about 250 miles) away. Seashells, ivory, soapstone, and amber used in ornaments were especially likely to be transported long distances. By comparison, most of the stone used at a Mousterian site in France was transported less than 5 km (3 miles).

Modern humans exploited a wider range of prey species than did the Neanderthals, but the subsistence economies of the two populations were similar.

The Upper Paleolithic spanned the depths of the last ice age. The area in Europe that contains the richest archaeological sites was a cold, dry grassland that supported

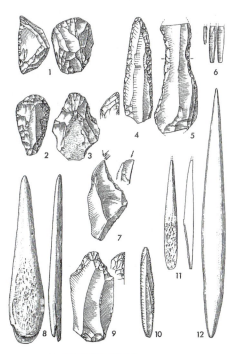

FIGURE 13.25

The Aurignacian tool kit, the earliest of several tool industries in the Upper Paleolithic of Europe, contains a wide variety of standardized tool types: 1, 2, 3, 9 = scrapers; 4, 5 = edged, retouched blades; 6, 10 = bladelets; 7 = a burin (a tool now used for engraving); 8, 11, 12 = bone points.

large populations of a diverse assemblage of large herbivores, including reindeer (called caribou in North America), horse, mammoth, bison, woolly rhinoceros, and a variety of predators, such as cave bears and wolves.

Bones found at Upper Paleolithic sites indicate that large herbivores played an important role in the diets of Upper Paleolithic peoples. Everywhere, Upper Paleolithic peoples hunted herbivores living in large herds, fished, and hunted birds. In some places, they concentrated on a single species—reindeer in France, red deer in Spain (**Figure 13.26**), bison in southern Russia, and mammoths farther north and east. In some areas, such as the southern coast of France, rich salmon runs may have been an important source of food. There are also places where these peoples harvested several different kinds of animals.

Modern humans probably made extensive use of plant foods, but few sites preserve the remains from vegetation.

All modern foraging peoples rely on plant foods that they gather as well as animals that they hunt. It is likely that earlier hominins made use of plant foods as well, but the remains of these foods have not been preserved. Unusual preservation conditions at several sites provide glimpses into this part of the subsistence economy of Upper Paleolithic peoples. Dani Nadel of the University of Haifa and his colleagues have excavated a site on the shores of the Sea of Galilee that is dated to 19 kya. This site, which is called Ohalo II, contains more than 90,000 specimens of plants from 142 different plant taxa. These include wild varieties of barley, wheat, acorns, pistachios, olives, raspberries, figs, and grapes. Starch grains from barley have been found on a grinding stone, indicating that wild cereal grains were processed to make food.

The peoples of the Upper Paleolithic developed more complex forms of shelter and clothing than the Neanderthals.

In what is now western and central Europe, Russia, and Ukraine, the remains of small villages have been found. Living on a frigid, treeless plain, Upper Paleolithic

FIGURE 13.26

The bones of red deer dominate the assemblage at Altamira in northern Spain, as illustrated by these data, which come from a Magdalenian site dated to 15 to 13 kya.

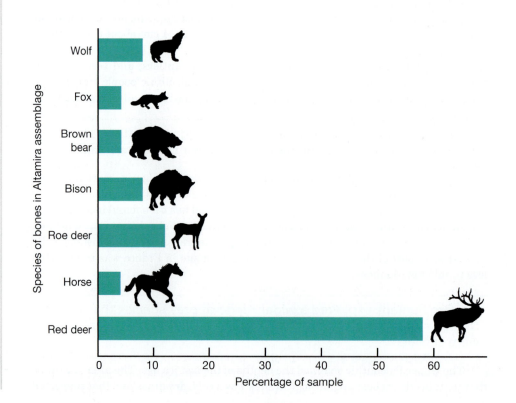

CHAPTER 13: *HOMO SAPIENS* AND THE EVOLUTION OF MODERN HUMAN BEHAVIOR

peoples either hunted or scavenged mammoth and used the hairy beasts for food, shelter, and warmth. At the site of Předmostí in the Czech Republic, the remains of almost 100,000 mammoths have been discovered. The people who lived there constructed huts by arranging mammoth bones in an interlocking pattern and then draping them with skins. (Temperatures of about −45°C [−50°F] outside provided a strong incentive for chinking the cracks!) Huge quantities of bone ash found at these sites indicate that the mammoth bones were also used for fuel. A site about 470 km (about 300 miles) southeast of Moscow contains the remains of even larger shelters. They were built around a pit about a meter deep and were covered with hides supported by mammoth bones. Some of these huts had many hearths, suggesting that a number of families may have lived together (**Figure 13.27**).

Modern foragers living in warm places often construct simple brush huts, using large branches to support the roof and smaller twigs and grasses to form the walls and cover the roof. Grasses may be gathered and spread on the floor and used as bedding. At the Ohalo II site, Nadel and his colleagues found kidney-shaped depressions that are about 5 m by 13 m (16 ft. by 43 ft.) in area. These depressions contain substantial pieces of tree branches that might have held up the roof of a hut as well as smaller twigs and stems that might have been part of the roof of the shelter. In one of the depressions, archaeologists found grass stems that were loosely woven together around a mass of ash. It looks like the grasses may have formed a mat around a fire that people sat on as they cooked and slept on at night. If this interpretation is correct, then this site represents the oldest evidence for the construction brush huts.

Several lines of evidence indicate that Upper Paleolithic peoples living in glacial Europe manufactured fur clothing. When modern hunters skin a fur-bearing animal, they usually leave the feet attached to the pelt and discard the rest of the carcass. Numerous skeletons of foxes and wolves that are complete except for their feet have been found at several Upper Paleolithic sites in Russia and Ukraine, suggesting that early modern humans kept warm in sumptuous fur coats. Bone awls and bone needles are also common at Upper Paleolithic sites, so sewing may have been a common activity. Finally, three individuals at a burial site in Russia seem to have been buried in caps, shirts, pants, and shoes lavishly decorated with beads.

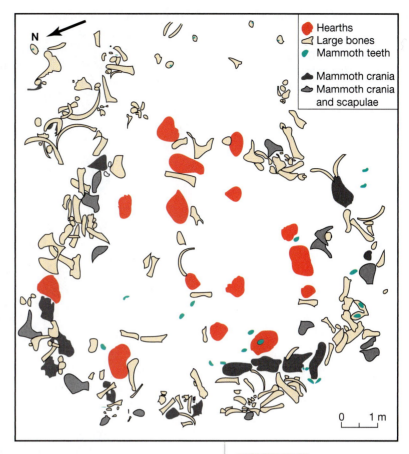

Hearths
Large bones
Mammoth teeth

Mammoth crania
Mammoth crania and scapulae

0   1 m

FIGURE 13.27

On the Russian plain, early humans had to cope with harsh climatic conditions. They may have used mammoth bones to construct shelters. Mammoth bones and teeth litter this Upper Paleolithic site of Moldova. The presence of multiple hearths suggests that the site may have been occupied by several families.

Upper Paleolithic peoples were better able to cope with their environment than the Neanderthals were.

The richness of the fossil and archaeological record in Europe provides a detailed comparison of Neanderthal and Upper Paleolithic peoples. Three kinds of data suggest that Upper Paleolithic peoples were better adapted to their environment than Neanderthals:

1. Upper Paleolithic peoples lived at higher population densities in Europe than did Neanderthals. Archaeologists estimate the relative population size of vanished peoples by comparing the density of archaeological sites per unit of time. Thus if

FIGURE 13.28

A child's grave from the Upper Paleolithic illustrating the rich collection of goods frequently included in Upper Paleolithic burials.

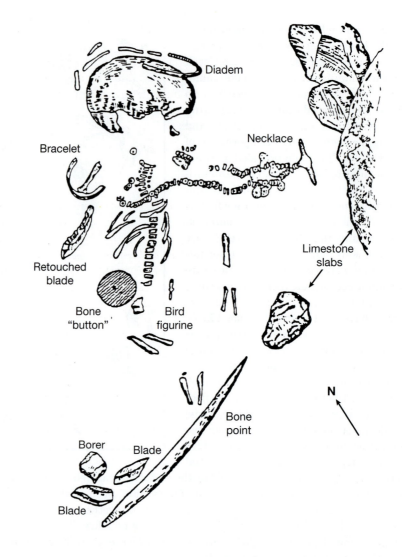

one group of people occupied a particular valley for 10,000 years and left 10 sites, and a second group occupied the same valley for 1,000 years and left 5 sites, then archaeologists would estimate that the second group had 5 times as many people. (In using this method, it is important to be sure that the sites were occupied for approximately the same lengths of time.) By these criteria, Upper Paleolithic peoples had far higher population densities in Europe than the Neanderthals.

2. Upper Paleolithic peoples lived longer than Neanderthals. Anthropologists Rachel Caspari of Central Michigan University and Sang-Hee Lee of the University of California, Riverside, have estimated that Upper Paleolithic peoples lived much longer than the Neanderthals. About a third of their sample of 113 Neanderthals reached twice the age of first reproduction, which is about 30 years of age in modern hunter-gatherer populations. In contrast, two-thirds of a sample of 74 Upper Paleolithic fossil individuals reached that age. The fact that Upper Paleolithic populations included a substantial fraction of older individuals, while Neanderthals were dominated by the young, may have allowed Upper Paleolithic peoples to retain and transmit more complex cultural knowledge than Neanderthals could.

3. Upper Paleolithic peoples were less likely to suffer serious injury or disease than were Neanderthals. In sharp contrast to the Neanderthals, the skeletons of Upper Paleolithic people rarely show evidence of injury or disease. Among the few injuries that do show up in the fossil record, there is a child buried with a stone projectile point embedded in its spine, and a young man with a projectile point in his

abdomen and a healed bone fracture on his right forearm. Evidence of disease is slightly more prevalent than evidence of injury among the remains of Upper Paleolithic peoples; affected specimens include a young woman who probably died as the result of an abscessed tooth, and a child whose skull seems to have been deformed by hydrocephaly (a condition in which fluid accumulates in the cranial cavity and the brain atrophies). Nonetheless, there is still less evidence for disease among these peoples than among Neanderthals.

There is good evidence for ritual burials during the Upper Paleolithic period.

Like the Neanderthals, Upper Paleolithic peoples buried their dead. Upper Paleolithic sites provide the first unambiguous evidence of both multiple burials and burials outside of caves. Unlike the Neanderthals, Upper Paleolithic burials appear to have been accompanied by ritual. Upper Paleolithic burials are often associated with tools, ornaments, and other objects that suggest they had some concept of life after death. **Figure 13.28** shows the diagram of the grave of a child who died about 15 kya at the Siberian site of Mal'ta. The child was buried with a number of items, including a necklace, a crown (diadem), a figurine of a bird, a bone point, and a number of stone tools.

Upper Paleolithic peoples were skilled artisans, sculpting statues of animals and humans and creating sophisticated cave paintings.

It is their art that distinguishes Upper Paleolithic peoples most dramatically from the hominins who preceded them. They engraved decorations on their bone and antler tools and weapons, and they sculpted statues of animals and female figures (**Figure 13.29**). The female statues are generally believed to be fertility figures because

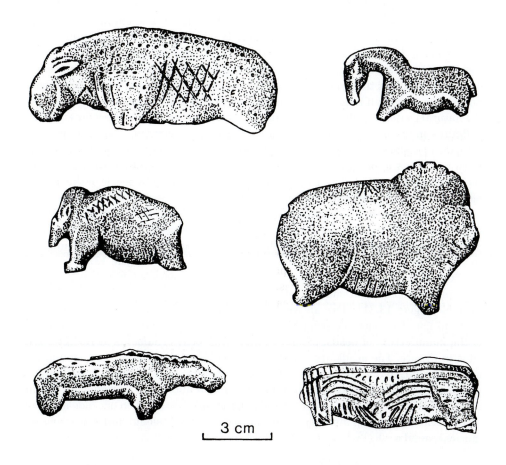

FIGURE 13.29

Small animal figures were carved from mammoth tusks during the Aurignacian period.

3 cm

FIGURE 13.30

This image from Le Chauvet in France was created about 30 kya. At the upper left, several lions are depicted. To the right are a number of rhinoceroses. At the top right, the multiple outlines suggest a rhinoceros in motion.

FIGURE 13.31

This ivory figure depicts a human body with a lion's head. It comes from an Aurignacian site in southern Germany and is 32,000 years old.

they usually emphasize female sexual characteristics. Upper Paleolithic peoples also adorned themselves with beads, necklaces, pendants, and bracelets and may have decorated their clothing with beads.

All of these artistic efforts are remarkable, but it is their cave art that seems most amazing now. Upper Paleolithic peoples painted, sculpted, and engraved the walls of caves with a variety of animal and human figures. They used natural substances that included iron oxides and manganese to create a variety of paint colors. They used their fingers, horsehair, and sticks to apply the paint. Their cave paintings frequently depict animals that they must have hunted: reindeer, mammoths, horses, and bison. Some figures are half human and half animal. Sometimes the creators incorporated the natural contours of the cave walls in their work, and sometimes they drew one set of figures on top of others. Some of their work is spectacular: the perspective is accurate, the characterization of behavior is lifelike, and the scenes are complex. We don't know precisely why or under what circumstances these cave paintings were made, but they represent a remarkable cultural achievement that sets the people of this period apart from earlier hominins.

Techniques for dating pigments have allowed scientists to determine the age of the Upper Paleolithic cave paintings. Many of the famous caves, such as Lascaux, are dated to the end of the Upper Paleolithic, about 17 kya, but spectacular paintings in the Le Chauvet Cave in France are about 36,000 years old (**Figure 13.30**). Most of the famous carved figurines are also less than 20,000 years old, but there are good examples of representational sculpture that date to the earliest Aurignacian. For example, **Figure 13.31** shows an ivory figure with a human body and a lion's head that was found at a site in Germany dated to 32 kya. There is also abundant evidence of the manufacture of beads, pendants, and other body ornaments at Aurignacian sites in France. The beads are standardized and often manufactured from materials that had been transported hundreds of kilometers. Archaeologists have found a well-preserved musical instrument that looks like a flute at an Aurignacian site in southwestern France. It is 10 cm (4 in.) long and has four holes on one side and two on the other. When this instrument was played by a professional flutist, it produced musical sounds.

Key Terms

mitochondria
mitochondrial DNA (mtDNA)
the most recent common ancestor (TMRCA)
gene trees
microsatellite loci
Middle Stone Age (MSA)
blades

Mode 4
pressure flaking
microliths
Mode 5
Upper Paleolithic
Châtelperronian

Study Questions

1. What derived anatomical features distinguish modern humans from other hominins?

2. Explain why it is possible to make phylogenetic trees for mitochondrial DNA and the Y chromosome but not for other chromosomes. Why is it possible to make phylogenetic trees for individual genes on other chromosomes?

3. Explain why the mitochondrial DNA and Y chromosome trees are consistent with the hypothesis that modern humans evolved in Africa and then later spread across the rest of the globe.

4. Suppose you were able to choose three fossils to extract DNA from and that your goal was to test the hypothesis that humans evolved in Africa. Which three would you pick? Explain why.

5. What does the sequencing of Neanderthal and Denisovan genomes tell us that we could not learn from the study of fossils or the genomes of living peoples?

6. How do worldwide patterns of genetic variation support the idea that humans spread from Africa across Eurasia and Australia?

7. Describe what the archaeological record tells us about the pattern of human behavior across the world between 100 and 30 kya. What facts are widely accepted? Which are in dispute?

8. Describe the main differences between the tools of Upper Paleolithic peoples and those of their predecessors.

9. What evidence suggests that Upper Paleolithic peoples were better able to cope with their environments?

Further Reading

Bahn, P. G. 1998. "Neanderthals emancipated." *Nature* 394: 719–721.

Carrol, S. B. 2003. "Genetics and the Making of *Homo sapiens*." *Nature* 422: 849–857.

Garrigan, D., and M. F. Hammer. 2006. "Reconstructing Human Origins in the Genomic Era." *Nature Reviews Genetics* 7: 669–680.

Jobling, M. A., M. E. Hurles, and C. Tyler-Smith. 2004. *Human Evolutionary Genetics.* New York: Garland.

Klein, R. G. 2008. *The Human Career.* 3rd ed. Chicago: University of Chicago Press.

McBrearty, S., and A. Brooks. 2000. "The Revolution That Wasn't: A New Interpretation of the Origin of Modern Human Behavior." *Journal of Human Evolution* 39: 453–563.

O'Bleness, M., V. B. Searles, A. Varki, P. Gagneux, and J. M. Sikelal. 2013. "Evolution of Genetic and Genomic Features Unique to the Human Lineage." *Nature Reviews Genetics* 13: 853–866.

4

PART FOUR

Evolution and Modern Humans

14

CHAPTER OBJECTIVES

By the end of this chapter you should be able to

- Describe how humans differ genetically from other apes.

- Explain why variation in traits influenced by single genes is different from variation in traits affected by many genes.

- Describe how mutation and natural selection maintain differences at single genetic loci between people in the same population.

- Explain how genetic drift and natural selection create variation among populations in traits influenced by single genes.

- Describe how to measure genetic variation in complex traits.

- Understand why the existence of genetic variation within populations in complex traits does not imply that there is variation among populations.

- Evaluate the argument that folk concepts of race do not correspond to any meaningful biological category.

HUMAN GENETICS

Explaining Genetic Variation

How Humans Are Different from Other Apes

The Dimensions of Human Variation

Variation in Traits Influenced by Single Genes

Variation in Complex Phenotypic Traits

The Race Concept

Explaining Genetic Variation

Human beings vary in myriad ways. In any sizable group of people, there are differences in height, weight, hair color, eye color, food preferences, hobbies, musical tastes, skills, interests, and so on. Some people you know are tall enough to dunk a basketball, some have to roll up the hems of their pants; some have blue eyes and freckle in the sun, others have dark eyes and can get a terrific tan; some people have perfect pitch, others can't tell a flat from a sharp. Your friends may include heavy drinkers and teetotalers, great cooks and people who can't microwave popcorn, skilled gardeners and some who can't keep a geranium alive, some who play classical music and others who prefer heavy metal.

If we look around the world, we encounter an even wider range of variation. Some of the variation is easy to observe. Language, fashions, customs, religion, technology, architecture, and other aspects of behavior differ among societies. People in different parts of the world also look very different. For example, most of the people in northern Europe have blond hair and pale skin, and most of the people in southern Asia have dark hair and dark skin. As we described in Chapter 12, Arctic peoples are generally shorter and stockier than people who live in the savannas of East Africa. Groups also differ in ways that cannot be detected so readily. For instance, the peoples of the world vary in blood type and the incidence of many genetically transmitted diseases. For example, Tay-Sachs disease, a recessive genetic disorder which usually kills children before the age of four, is nearly 10 times more common among Ashkenazi Jews in New York than among other New Yorkers.

If you peer even farther out in the natural world, it is easy to see that humans are different from other primates. We are hairless, walk bipedally, live in large cooperative societies, cook our food, depend on complex tools, and occupy every part of the globe. Our closest relatives do none of these things.

In this chapter, we consider how genetic differences lead to phenotypic differences among humans and between humans and other primates. We begin by discussing the genetic differences between humans and other primates. The sequencing of the great ape genomes over the last decade has revealed much about this variation, and we are beginning to understand how apes and humans differ genetically. We then turn to the question of how people vary genetically within and among societies and the processes that create and sustain this variation. We begin by describing the nature of differences between people that are influenced by single genes with large effects and then consider variation in traits that are influenced by many genes. As you will see, the methods used to assess variation in traits caused by single genes and multiple genes are quite different. In both cases, we consider the processes that give rise to variation within and among populations. Finally, we will use our understanding of human genetic diversity to explore the significance and meaning of a concept that plays an important, albeit often negative, role in modern society: race. We argue that a clear understanding of the nature and source of human genetic variation demonstrates that race is not a valid scientific construct.

How Humans Are Different from Other Apes

Sequencing the genomes of humans and other mammals provides new information about genetic differences between modern humans and other primates. In the past, humans were distinguished from other species mainly on the basis of morphology, and fossils were our only source of information about human evolutionary change. But today, molecular genetics provides us with another source of information about our evolutionary history. In this section, we summarize what is known about how modern humans differ genetically from our closest relatives, chimpanzees, bonobos, and gorillas.

For many years, our knowledge of the genome was indirect: We could study the protein products of genes, and we could use specialized molecular techniques to identify particular DNA segments called genetic markers. Lately, however, it has become possible to sequence large chunks of the genome. In 2002, a first cut at sequencing the entire human genome was announced with great fanfare. By 2013, the cost of sequencing had fallen by a factor of 100,000, and thousands of complete genomes had been sequenced, with varying degrees of accuracy. A project is now under way to create very accurate sequences of 2,500 people from 25 populations around the world. More quietly, geneticists have worked on sequencing the genomes of many other organisms, including yeast, fruit flies, mice, cats, dogs, and rhesus macaques. Of particular interest to us are the genomes of our closest relatives, chimpanzees, bonobos, and gorillas. These vast troves of genetic information, all published since 2006, give us new insights about the kinds of evolutionary changes that have occurred in the human lineage.

Human and chimpanzee genomes are very similar.

By aligning the human, chimpanzee, bonobo, and gorilla genomes and comparing the sequences nucleotide by nucleotide, geneticists have been able to measure the magnitude of the genetic differences between us and them. Humans and chimpanzees differ by about 1.3%. This means that in 1.3% of the nucleotides, all chimpanzees have one nucleotide and all humans have a different nucleotide. The difference between humans and bonobos is also about 1.3%, and difference between humans and gorillas is 1.75%. These sound like minuscule differences, but remember that there are 3 billion bases in the human genome. A 1% difference represents differences in about 30 million nucleotides. There have also been approximately 5 million insertions and deletions of bits of DNA in or out of the human genome or the chimpanzee genome. Most of these insertions and deletions involve a small number of nucleotides, and most involve repetitive sequences or **transposable elements**, copies of DNA segments from one part of a genome that have been inserted somewhere else. Insertions and deletions contribute roughly another 3% to the overall difference between the genomes of humans and the three great apes.

A majority of protein coding genes differ between humans and chimpanzees.

Many people are puzzled by the small genetic difference between humans and chimpanzees. How could such a puny genetic difference produce the sizable phenotypic differences between humans and chimpanzees? The answer is that small differences in the sequence of nucleotides can lead to big differences in the phenotype because the percentage of DNA that differs is not the same as the percentage of genes that differ. To understand why this is true, consider two extreme possibilities. If DNA differences were distributed evenly across all of the genes in the genome, then even a 1% difference between two species would cause every gene in the two species to differ. On the other hand, if the differences were clustered in certain parts of the genome, then a smaller proportion of the genes would differ. So clearly it is important to know something about the pattern of differences between chimpanzees and humans as well as the overall magnitude of differences.

This is where we benefit from having sequenced the complete genomes of humans and other ape species. Protein coding genes (DNA sequences that code for proteins) can be identified in a DNA sequence by the "start" and "stop" codons that mark the beginning and end of each coding sequence. For example, using this approach, geneticists identified 13,454 homologous protein coding genes in chimpanzees and in humans. Only 29% of these genes have exactly the same amino acid sequences. Among those that differ, the median number of base substitutions is two. Thus, even though the DNA sequences of chimpanzees and humans differ by only a small percentage, 71% of the proteins produced by their genes differ.

Only a small fraction of protein coding genes shows evidence of selection since the divergence of human and chimpanzee/bonobo lineages.

It seems plausible that many of the differences in morphology and behavior between humans and chimpanzees are the result of natural selection, which favored particular traits in each lineage. However, mutation and genetic drift could also create differences between the DNA sequences of humans and chimpanzees. Are the differences in the protein coding genes of humans and chimpanzees due to natural selection or to nonadaptive processes, like mutation and genetic drift? To try to answer this question, geneticists make use of the fact that the DNA code is redundant (see Chapter 2). This redundancy means that some nucleotide substitutions (**synonymous substitutions**) do not produce any change in the amino acid sequence of the protein that results from the gene. By contrast, **nonsynonymous substitutions** alter the amino acid sequence of proteins. Directional selection typically favors a particular protein that produces a particular phenotype. Thus structural genes that have been subjected to selection are expected to show fewer nonsynonymous substitutions than synonymous ones, while nonadaptive processes like genetic drift are expected to affect synonymous and nonsynonymous substitutions to the same extent.

Once such **positively selected** genes have been identified, we want to determine when the change occurred. To do this, geneticists compare the sequences of humans and chimpanzees to a more distantly related species, called the out-group. Some studies use the mouse as an out-group, while others use the macaque. When the out-group and the chimpanzee are the same and humans differ, it is likely that out-group and chimpanzees share the ancestral DNA sequence and that humans have the derived one. Similarly, when the out-group and humans are the same and chimpanzees differ, then we assume that the chimpanzee sequence is derived.

A number of research groups have used this technique to determine which of the protein coding genes that differ between humans and chimpanzees have been subject to positive selection in one of the two lineages. Although results of these studies vary in detail, they all conclude that the percentage of positively selected genes is quite small. For example, the consortium of scientists that was responsible for sequencing the chimpanzee genome estimated that about 4.4% of the genes showed signs of positive selection. A more recent study by another research group places the estimate at 2.7%. These estimates represent upper bounds on the actual percentage of positively selected genes because a substantial number of cases would be expected to occur by chance alone. Thus, even though most coding sequences differ, only a small fraction of these differences seem to be functional. Again, this result is surprising given the magnitude of the phenotypic differences between humans and chimpanzees.

How can the apparent lack of genetic change be reconciled with the substantial amount of phenotypic change? One possibility is that measuring selection by comparing synonymous and nonsynonymous changes underestimates the amount of change due to selection. This method assumes that the amount of evolution of a protein coding gene is proportional to the number of nonsynonymous DNA bases that differ between two species. However, sometimes the change of one or two base pairs in a DNA sequence can strongly affect phenotype. For example, we will see later in this chapter that the FOXP2 gene in humans has a major impact on speech, even though the human and chimpanzee versions differ by only two substitutions. Such small sequence changes are not usually detected by counting synonymous and nonsynonymous substitutions (and the FOXP2 gene was not identified as a positively selected gene).

Second, many of the big differences in phenotype may involve traits that are affected by genes at many loci. We will see later in this chapter that human height is affected by genes at hundreds of loci, each with a small effect, and that differences in height between human populations are due to small changes in frequency at many loci. This means that selection generating these changes at any particular locus is very weak and leaves little trace in the structure of the genome. It may be that other important differences between humans and chimpanzees are also the result of evolution at many loci.

A final possibility is that most of the evolutionary changes are not the result of changes in protein coding genes but changes in regulatory genes. Unfortunately, we are not yet able to identify regulatory genes from DNA sequence data alone, so geneticists can't study the changes in regulatory genes in the same way that they study changes in structural genes. However, evidence from gene expression suggests that regulatory changes may play a big role in shaping the differences between humans and other apes. Scientists at the Partner Institute for Computational Biology, established by the Chinese Academy of Sciences and the Max Planck Society, studied a group of 184 genes that are expressed at the same time in the prefrontal cortex, the part of the brain involved in reasoning and decision making. As is shown in **Figure 14.1**, these genes are expressed at earlier ages in chimpanzees and macaques than in

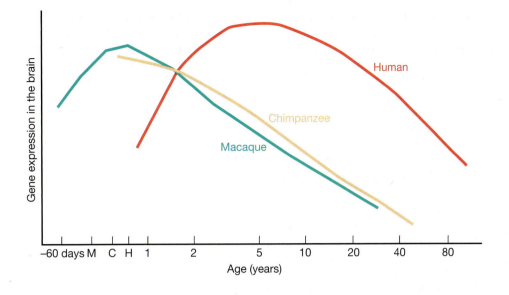

FIGURE 14.1

The level of expression of 184 genes in the prefrontal cortex at different ages for macaques, chimpanzees, and humans. Genes that are rarely expressed in adult macaques or chimpanzees are expressed in adult humans. M, C, and H = age of birth of individuals belonging to the three species; −60 d = time of conception.

humans. This pattern of delayed maturation, called **neoteny**, is seen in many aspects of human development. It means that humans are, in a sense, apes who retain juvenile characteristics into adulthood. In the case of brains, this means that we retain neural plasticity longer, which is consistent with our greater behavioral plasticity. Such a coordinated shift in the expression of many genes is what would be expected to result from a shift in a regulatory cascade (see Chapter 2).

Noncoding sequences show evidence of positive selection since the human–chimpanzee split.

A team led by Katherine Pollard of the University of California, San Francisco, used a different method to identify regions that have experienced significant positive selection after human and chimpanzee lineages diverged. They searched the genomes of the mouse, rat, and chimpanzee to find DNA sequences that were at least 100 base pairs long and were at least 96% identical in all three taxa. Because the two rodent species are separated from chimpanzees by about 70 million years of independent evolution, Pollard and her colleagues reasoned that these sequences must be subject to strong **negative selection**—selection that favored the observed stable sequence over mutants that arose during these millions of years. They found about 35,000 negatively selected sequences. Then, for each of these regions, they compared the rate of change in the human lineage with the average rates of change in 12 other vertebrate species (not including the chimpanzee, rat, or mouse). The rates of change were significantly greater in the human lineage than in other lineages in 202 of these regions. The investigators ranked the regions by the rate of change and then assigned each region a label based on the ranking. Thus HAR1 was the fastest of the fast, and HAR202 was the slowest of the fast; *HAR* stands for "highly accelerated region." Almost all of these HAR segments are in noncoding regions. Even though these segments do not encode the structure of proteins, and for the most part, we don't know what they do, we do know that they have evolved very rapidly during human evolution. This suggests that they have been shaped by natural selection, not genetic drift.

The fastest-changing region, HAR1, provides one example of how this might work. HAR1 is a 118–base pair sequence on chromosome 20. In other vertebrates, HAR1 is extremely conservative, showing only 2 base pair changes between the chicken and the chimpanzee. If this rate of change had been continued in the human lineage, there would be only a 25% chance of having even one difference between the sequence in chimpanzees and modern humans. However, there have been 18 base pair changes, nearly an 80-fold increase in the rate of evolution. The HAR1 segment codes for an lncRNA molecule that folds itself into a stable structure. These kinds of RNA molecules often work with proteins to regulate gene expression, and it seems likely that this is what HAR1 does. Studies by Pollard and her co-workers have shown that HAR1 is expressed exclusively in the brain, especially during development. There, it is associated with the protein reelin, which is linked to the development of the layered structure that is characteristic of human brains but is not seen in other species. Thus it seems likely that the rapid change in HAR1 during human evolution is related to the rapid evolution of the larger and more complex human brain.

The Dimensions of Human Variation

Scientists distinguish two sources of human variation: genetic and environmental.

Scientists conventionally divide the causes of human variation into two categories. **Genetic variation** refers to differences between individuals that are caused by the genes that they inherited from their parents. Environmental variation refers to differences between individuals caused by environmental factors (such as climate, habitat, and competing species) on the organisms' phenotypes. For humans, culture is an important source of environmental variation.

A practical example—variation in body weight—will clarify this distinction. Many environmental factors affect body weight. Some factors, such as the availability of food, have an obvious and direct impact on body weight. The majority of people living under siege in Sarajevo in the mid-1990s were undoubtedly leaner than they were a decade earlier, when Sarajevo was a rich, cosmopolitan city. Other environmental effects are more subtle. For example, culture can affect body weight because it influences our ideas about what constitutes an appropriate diet and shapes our standards of physical beauty. In the United States, many young women adopt strict diets and rigorous exercise regimens to maintain a slim figure because thinness is considered desirable. But in a number of West African societies, young women are secluded and force-fed large meals several times a day for the express purpose of causing them to gain weight and become fat. In these societies, obesity is extremely desirable, and fat women are thought to be very beautiful. Body weight also appears to have an important genetic component. Recent research has shown that individuals with some genotypes are predisposed to be heavier than others, even when diet and levels of activity are controlled.

Genetic and environmental causes of variation may also interact in complicated ways. Consider, for example, two people who have inherited quite different genes affecting body weight. One is easily sated, while the other craves food constantly. Both individuals may be thin if they have to subsist on one cup of porridge a day, but only the one who craves food will gain weight when Big Macs and fries are readily available.

It is difficult to determine the relative importance of genetic and environmental influences for particular phenotypic traits.

It is often difficult to separate the genetic and environmental causes of human variation in real situations. The problem is that both genetic transmission and shared environments cause parents and offspring to be similar. For example, suppose we were to measure the weights of parents and offspring in a series of families living in a range of environments. It is likely that the weight of parents and offspring (corrected for age) would be closely related. However, we would not know whether the association was due to the fact that they share genes or live in the same environment. Children might resemble their parents because they inherited genes that affect fat metabolism or because they learned eating habits and acquired food preferences from their parents.

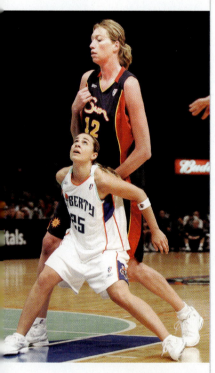

FIGURE 14.2

Variation in stature within the WNBA is illustrated by the difference in height between Margo Dydek (2.2m, or 7 ft. 2 in.) and Becky Hammon (1.7 m, or 5 ft. 6 in.).

Quite different processes create and maintain genetic and environmental variation among groups, and identifying the source of human differences will help us understand why people are the way they are. Genetic variation is governed by the processes of organic evolution: mutation, drift, recombination, and selection. Biologists and anthropologists know a great deal about how the various processes work to shape the living world and how evolutionary processes explain genetic differences among contemporary humans in particular cases.

It is important to distinguish variation within human groups from variation among human groups.

Variation within groups refers to differences between individuals within a given group of people. In the Women's National Basketball Association (WNBA), for example, Becky Hammon, 1.7 m (5 ft. 6 in.), competed against much taller players, like Margo Dydek 2.2 m (7 ft. 2 in.; **Figure 14.2**). **Variation among groups** refers to differences between entire groups of people. For instance, as seen in **Figure 14.3**, the average height of Olympic volley players (exemplified by Ekatarina Gamova, 2.0 m [6 ft. 8 in.]) is much greater than the average height of Olympic gymnasts (exemplified by Gabrielle Douglas, 1.5 m [4 ft. 11 in.]). It is important to distinguish these two levels of variation because, as we will see, the causes of the variation within groups can be very different from the causes of variation among groups.

Variation in Traits Influenced by Single Genes

By establishing the connection between particular DNA sequences and specific traits, scientists have shown that variation in some traits is genetic.

Although it is often difficult to establish the source of variation in human traits, in some cases we can be certain that variation arises from genetic differences between individuals. For example, recall from Chapter 2 that many people in West Africa suffer from sickle-cell anemia, a disease that causes their red blood cells to have a sickle shape instead of the more typical rounded shape. People with this debilitating disease are homozygous for a gene that codes for one variant of hemoglobin, the protein that transports oxygen molecules in red blood cells. Hemoglobin is made up of two different protein subunits, labeled α (the Greek letter alpha) and β (the Greek letter beta). The DNA sequence of the most common hemoglobin allele, hemoglobin A, specifies the amino acid glutamic acid in the sixth position of the protein chain of the β subunit. But there is another hemoglobin allele, hemoglobin S, which specifies the amino acid valine at this position. People who suffer from sickle-cell anemia are homozygous for the hemoglobin S allele.

FIGURE 14.3

Variation in stature between Olympic volleyball players and Olympic gymnasts is illustrated here by the difference in height between Ekatarina Gamova (2.0 m, or 6 ft. 8in.) and Gabrielle Douglas (1.50 m, or 4 ft. 11 in.).

We can prove that traits are controlled by genes at a single genetic locus by showing that their patterns of inheritance conform to Mendel's principles.

We can sometimes make the distinction between genetic and environmental sources of variation when traits are affected by genes at a single genetic locus. In such cases, Mendel's laws make detailed predictions about the patterns of inheritance (see Chapter 2). If scientists suspect that a trait is controlled by genes at a single genetic locus, they can test this idea by collecting data on the occurrence of the trait in families. If the pattern of inheritance shows a close fit to the pattern predicted by

Mendel's principles (conventionally called laws), then we can be confident that the trait is affected by a single genetic locus.

Research on the genetic basis of a language disorder called **specific language impairment (SLI)** illustrates the strengths and weaknesses of this approach. Children with SLI have difficulty learning to speak, and in some cases they have small vocabularies and make frequent grammatical errors as adults. SLI is known to run in families, but the genetic basis of the condition is unclear in most cases.

The pattern of inheritance of SLI in one family suggests that at least some cases of SLI are caused by a dominant allele at a single genetic locus. A group of researchers at the Wellcome Trust Centre for Human Genetics in Oxford, England, studied the expression of SLI in three generations of one family (known as the KE family; **Figure 14.4**). The members of this family who suffer from SLI have severe problems learning grammatical rules; they also have difficulty with fine-motor control of the tongue and jaws. The grandmother (shown as a blue circle at the top of the figure) had SLI, but her husband (shown as an orange triangle) did not. Four of her five children and 11 of her 24 grandchildren also had SLI. Suppose that SLI is caused by a dominant gene. Then because SLI is rare in the population as a whole, the Hardy–Weinberg equations tell us that almost all SLI sufferers will be heterozygotes. Of course, anyone without SLI must be a homozygote for the normal allele at this locus. From Mendel's laws, on average half of the offspring of a mating between a person with SLI and one without the disorder will have SLI and half will have normal linguistic skills. The KE family fits this prediction very well. Both of the children of the son without SLI are normal, and the rest of the matings produced approximately equal numbers of normal and language-impaired children.

Although the pattern in the KE family is consistent with the idea that SLI is caused by a single dominant gene, it is possible that an environmental factor causes SLI to run in families and that the observed pattern arose by chance. Scientists search for two kinds of data to clinch the case. First, they collect data on more families. The larger the number of families that fit the pattern associated with the inheritance of a single-locus dominant gene, the more confident researchers can be that this pattern did not occur by chance. Second, researchers search for genetic markers (genes whose location in the genome is known) that show the same pattern of inheritance. Thus if every individual who has SLI also has a specific marker on a particular chromosome, we can be confident that the gene that causes SLI lies close to that genetic marker.

In 1998, the Wellcome Trust researchers demonstrated that SLI in the KE family is closely linked to a genetic marker on chromosome 7, and so it seems likely that SLI in this family is controlled by a gene closely linked to this marker. The subsequent discovery of an unrelated person with the same symptoms allowed the researchers to

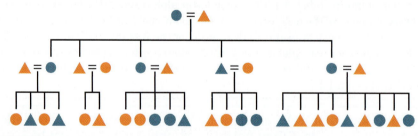

FIGURE 14.4

The pattern of specific language impairment (SLI) in the KE family tree suggests that some cases of SLI are caused by a single dominant gene. Circles represent women, triangles represent men, and blue represents people with SLI. If SLI is caused by a dominant gene, then, because SLI is rare in the population as a whole, we know from the Hardy–Weinberg equations that almost all people with SLI will be heterozygotes. Thus Mendel's principles tell us that, on average, half of the offspring of a mating between a person with SLI and a person without it will have SLI, and half of the offspring will have normal linguistic skills. Notice how well the family shown in this tree fits this prediction.

identify the specific gene that causes the disorder in the KE family. The same allele of this gene, named FOXP2, was found in all affected members of the KE family and not in 364 unrelated people without SLI. It differs from the normal allele by a single nucleotide substitution.

Interestingly, molecular evidence suggests that the FOXP2 gene has undergone strong directional selection since the divergence of humans and chimpanzees. Different alleles of the FOXP2 gene are found in many animal species. The versions found in mice and humans differ by three amino acid substitutions, and the version found in chimpanzees differs from mice by only one of these substitutions. Because the last common ancestor of humans and mice lived more than 65 mya and the last common ancestor of humans and chimps lived only 6 mya, this suggests that there has been rapid change in the FOXP2 gene during human evolution. Moreover, studies of variation in introns of the FOXP2 gene and surrounding noncoding sequences suggest that the normal version of the gene spread throughout human populations less than 200 kya, about the same time as the origin of *Homo sapiens*.

The fact that SLI can be caused by a single gene does not mean that the gene is responsible for all of the psychological machinery in the human brain that gives rise to language. It means only that damage to the FOXP2 gene prevents the normal development of some of the psychological machinery necessary for language. To understand this idea, think about a simple analogy. If you cut the wire connecting the hard disk to the power supply in your computer, the hard disk will stop working, but that does not mean the wire contains all of the machinery necessary for operation of the hard disk. This argument is supported by the fact that the FOXP2 gene codes for a transcription factor belonging to a family of genes that play an important role in regulating gene expression during development. FOXP2 itself is strongly expressed in the brains of developing fetuses. By the same reasoning, SLI in other families may be caused by other genes whose expression is necessary for normal brain development, and geneticists subsequently discovered three other genes that lead to SLI. Just as there are many ways to wreck your hard disk, there are likely many mutants at many loci that damage the parts of the brain necessary for language.

Causes of Genetic Variation within Groups

Mutation can maintain deleterious genes in populations but only at a low frequency.

Many diseases are caused by recessive genes. For example, only people who are homozygous for hemoglobin S are afflicted with sickle-cell anemia. Other diseases caused by recessive alleles include phenylketonuria (PKU), Tay-Sachs disease, and cystic fibrosis. All of these diseases are caused by mutant genes that code for proteins that do not serve their normal function, and all produce severe symptoms and sometimes death. Why haven't such deleterious genes been eliminated by natural selection?

One answer to this question is that natural selection steadily removes such genes, but mutation constantly reintroduces them. Very low rates of mutation can maintain recessive deleterious genes because most individuals who carry the gene are heterozygotes and do not suffer the consequences of having two copies of the deleterious gene. The observed frequency of many deleterious recessive genes is about 1 in 1,000. According to the Hardy–Weinberg equations, the frequency of newborns homozygous for the recessive allele will be $0.001 \times 0.001 = 0.000001$! Thus only 1 in 1 million babies will carry the disease. This means that even if the disease is fatal, selection will remove only two copies of the deleterious gene for every 1 million people born. Because mutation rates for such deleterious genes are estimated to be a few mutations per million gametes produced, mutation will introduce enough new mutants to maintain a constant frequency of the gene. When this is true, we say that there is **selection–mutation balance**.

Selection can maintain variation within populations if heterozygotes have higher fitness than either of the two homozygotes.

Some lethal genes are too common to be the result of selection–mutation balance. In West African populations, for example, the frequency of the hemoglobin S allele is typically about 1 in 10. How can we account for this? The answer in the case of hemoglobin S is that this allele increases the fitness of heterozygotes. It turns out that individuals who carry one copy of the sickling allele, *S,* and one copy of the normal allele, *A,* are partially protected against the most dangerous form of malaria, called **falciparum malaria** (**Figure 14.5**). As a consequence, where falciparum malaria is prevalent, heterozygous *AS* newborns are about 15% more likely to reach adulthood than are *AA* infants.

When heterozygotes have a higher fitness than either homozygote, natural selection maintains a **balanced polymorphism**, a steady state in which both alleles persist in the population. To see why balanced polymorphisms exist, consider what happens when the *S* allele is first introduced into a population and is very rare. Suppose that its initial frequency is 0.001. The frequency of *SS* individuals will be 0.001 × 0.001, or about 1 in 1 million, and the frequency of *AS* individuals will be 2 × 0.001 × 0.999, or about 2 in 1,000. This means that for every individual who suffers the debilitating effects of sickle-cell anemia, there will be about 2,000 heterozygotes who are partially immune to malaria. Thus when the *S* allele is rare, most *S* alleles will occur in heterozygotes, and the *S* allele will increase in frequency. However, this trend will not lead to the elimination of the *A* allele. To see why, let's consider what happens when the *S* allele is common and the *A* allele is rare. Now almost all of the *A* alleles will occur in *AS* heterozygotes, making those individuals partially resistant to malaria. But almost all of the *S* alleles will occur in *SS* homozygotes, and those individuals will suffer debilitating anemia. The *A* allele has higher fitness than the *S* allele when the *S* allele is common (Closer Look 14.1). The balance between these two processes depends on the fitness advantage of the heterozygotes and the disadvantage of the homozygotes. In this case, the equilibrium frequency for the hemoglobin S allele is about 0.1, approximately the frequency actually observed in West Africa.

Scientists suspect that the relatively high frequencies of genes that cause a number of other genetic diseases may also be the result of heterozygote advantage. For example, the gene that causes Tay-Sachs disease has a frequency as high as 0.05 in some Eastern European Jewish populations. Children who are homozygous for this gene seem normal for about the first six months of life. Then, over the next few years a gradual deterioration takes place, leading to blindness, convulsions, and finally death, usually by age four. There is some evidence that individuals who are heterozygous for the Tay-Sachs allele are partially resistant to tuberculosis. Jared Diamond of the University of California, Los Angeles, points out that tuberculosis was much more prevalent in cities than in rural areas of Europe over the last 400 years. Confined to the crowded urban

FIGURE 14.5

(a) Sufferers of sickle-cell anemia have abnormal red blood cells with a sickle shape. (b) Normal red blood cells are round. The sickling allele partially protects against falciparum malaria.

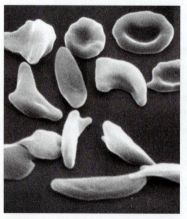
(a)

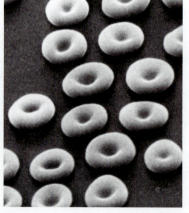
(b)

14.1 Calculating Gene Frequencies for a Balanced Polymorphism

It is easy to calculate the frequency of hemoglobin S when selection has reached a stable, balanced polymorphism. Suppose the fitness of AA homozygotes is 1.0, the fitness of AS heterozygotes is 1.15, and the fitness of SS homozygotes is 0, and let p be the equilibrium frequency of the allele S. If individuals mate at random, a fraction p of the S alleles will unite with another S allele to form an SS homozygote, and a fraction $1 - p$ will unite with an A allele to form an AS heterozygote. Thus the average fitness of the S allele will be

$$0p + 1.15(1 - p)$$

By the same reasoning, the average fitness of the A allele will be

$$1.15p + 1(1 - p)$$

The relationship between the average fitness of each allele and the frequency of hemoglobin S, shown in **Figure 14.6**, confirms the reasoning given in the text. When the S allele is common so that p is close to 1, the average fitness of the S allele is close to 0; but when S is rare, its average fitness is almost 1.15. If one gene has a higher fitness than the other, natural selection will increase the frequency of that gene. Thus a steady state will occur when the average fitnesses of the two alleles are equal—that is, when

$$1.15(1 - p) = 1.15p + (1 - p)$$

If you solve for p, you will find that

$$= \frac{1.15 - 1.10}{1.15 + 1.15 - 1.0}$$
$$= \frac{0.15}{1.30} \approx 0.1$$

which is about the observed frequency of the sickle-cell allele in West Africa.

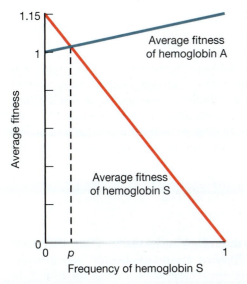

1.15

1

Average fitness of hemoglobin A

Average fitness

Average fitness of hemoglobin S

0

0   p 1

Frequency of hemoglobin S

FIGURE 14.6

The average fitness of the S allele of hemoglobin S declines as the frequency of S increases because more and more S alleles are found in SS homozygotes. Similarly, the average fitness of the A allele of hemoglobin A increases as the frequency of S increases because more and more A alleles are found in AS heterozygotes. A balanced polymorphism occurs when the average fitness of the two alleles is equal.

ghettos of Eastern Europe, Jews may have benefited more from increased resistance to tuberculosis than did other Europeans, most of whom lived in rural settings.

Variation may exist because environments have recently changed and genes that were previously beneficial have not yet been eliminated.

Some genetic diseases may be common because the symptoms they create have not always been deleterious. One form of diabetes, **non-insulin-dependent diabetes (NIDD)**, may be an example of such a disease. **Insulin** is a protein that controls the uptake of blood sugar by cells. In NIDD sufferers, blood-sugar levels rise above normal levels because the cells of the body do not respond properly to insulin in the blood. High blood-sugar levels cause a number of problems, including heart disease, kidney damage, and impaired vision. NIDD is also known to have a genetic basis. (The other form of diabetes, insulin-dependent diabetes, occurs because the insulin-producing cells in the pancreas have been destroyed by the body's own immune system. It is unlikely that insulin-dependent diabetes was ever adaptive.)

In some contemporary populations, the occurrence of NIDD is very high. On the Micronesian island of Nauru, for example, more than 30% of people over 15 years old now have the disease. Such high rates of NIDD are a recent phenomenon, although the genes that cause the disease are not new. The late human geneticist James V. Neel suggested that the genes now leading to NIDD were beneficial in the past because they caused a rapid buildup of fat reserves during periods of plenty—fat reserves that would help people survive periods of famine in harsh environments. Traditionally, life on Nauru was very difficult. The inhabitants subsisted by fishing and farming. The islands of the Pacific are strongly affected by typhoons and volcanic activity; famine was common. NIDD was virtually unknown during this period. However, Nauru was colonized by Britain, Australia, and New Zealand in more recent times, and these influxes brought many changes in the residents' lives. They obtained access to Western food, and prosperity derived from the island's phosphate deposits allowed them to adopt a sedentary lifestyle. NIDD became very common. Genes that formerly conferred an advantage on the residents of Nauru now lead to NIDD.

Causes of Genetic Variation among Groups

There are many genetic differences between groups of people living in different parts of the world. The existence of genetic variation among groups is intriguing because we know that all living people are members of a single species, and as we saw in Chapter 4, gene flow between different populations within a single species tends to make them genetically uniform. In this section we consider several processes that oppose the homogenizing effects of such gene flow, thereby creating and maintaining genetic variation among human populations.

Selection that favors different genes in different environments creates and maintains variation among groups.

The human species inhabits a wider range of environments than any other mammal. We know that natural selection in different environments may favor different genes and that natural selection can maintain genetic differences in the face of the homogenizing influence of gene flow if selection is strong enough. Variation in the distribution of hemoglobin genes provides a good example of this process. Hemoglobin S is most common in tropical Africa, around the Mediterranean Sea, and in southern India (**Figure 14.7a**). Elsewhere it is almost unknown. Generally, hemoglobin S is prevalent where falciparum malaria is common, and hemoglobin A is prevalent where this form of malaria is absent (**Figure 14.7b**). Southeast Asia represents an exception

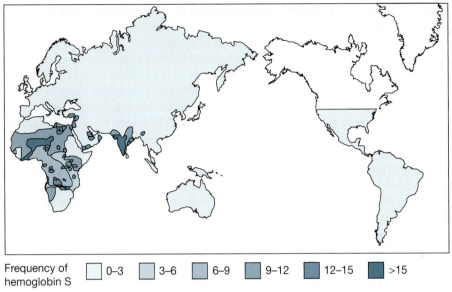

Frequency of
hemoglobin S   □ 0–3 ▨ 3–6 ▨ 6–9 ▨ 9–12 ▨ 12–15 ▨ >15

(a)

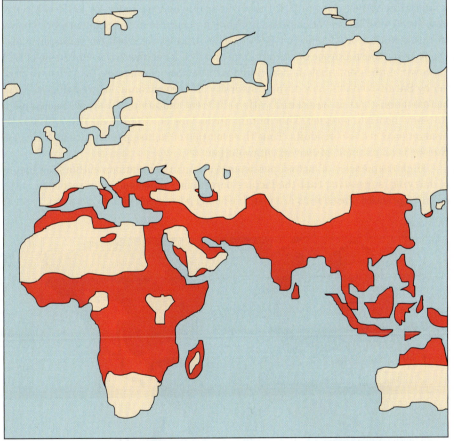

(b)

FIGURE 14.7

Hemoglobin S is common only in areas of the world in which falciparum malaria is prevalent. (a) The colors show the frequency of hemoglobin S throughout the world. (b) The regions of the Old World in which falciparum malaria is prevalent are in red.

to this pattern, and it is possible that hemoglobin E, a variant that is common in that region, also provides resistance to malaria.

The digestion of **lactose**, a sugar found in mammalian milk, provides another interesting example of genetic variation maintained by natural selection. Lactose is synthesized in the mammary glands and occurs in large amounts only in mammalian milk. Most mammals can digest lactose as infants but lose this ability after they are weaned. The majority of humans follow the mammalian pattern, and synthesis of the necessary enzyme, **lactase-phlorizin hydrolase (LHP)**, ends after weaning. Such people are said to lack lactase persistence. When people who lack lactase persistence drink substantial amounts of fresh milk at one sitting, they suffer gastric distress that ranges from mild discomfort to severe pain. However, most northern Europeans and members of a number of North African, Arabian, and South Asian populations retain the ability to digest lactose as adults and are said to have **lactase persistence** (**Figure 14.8**). Evidence from family studies indicates that the ability to digest lactose as an adult is controlled by a single dominant gene. People who have one copy of the dominant allele are lactase persistent; those who are homozygous for the alternative recessive allele are not.

Molecular studies indicate that lactase persistence evolved independently in Africa and in Europe. In 2002, Nabil Enattah and a group of researchers from the University of Helsinki in Finland showed that the mutation of a single nucleotide from C to T in a noncoding region close to **LCT**, the structural gene that codes for LHP, is strongly associated with lactose persistence in Finnish populations. Subsequent work showed that this mutant allele, labeled *T-13910*, is associated with lactase persistence elsewhere in northern Europe and South Asia and that it regulates the expression of LCT. However, a different allele is associated with lactose persistence in Africa. A group led by Sarah Tishkoff, now of the University of Pennsylvania, showed that in Africa lactase persistence is associated with a different mutation of a single nucleotide in the same noncoding region. This mutant allele, labeled *C-14010*, also upregulates the production of lactase in adults. Thus the evolution of lactase persistence in Africa and Europe is an example of convergent evolution.

High frequencies of lactase persistence occur in populations with a long history of dairying, suggesting that the lactase-persistence gene evolved in response to this cultural practice. **Pastoralists** are people who keep livestock and do not farm. It seems

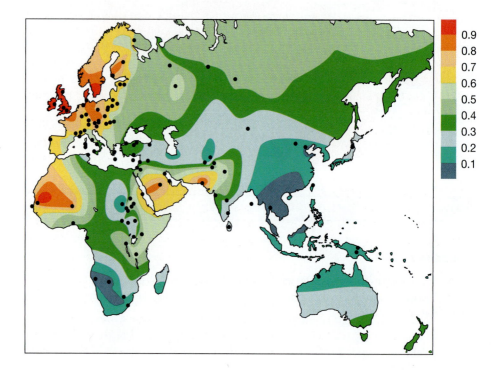

FIGURE 14.8

The distribution of lactase persistence in the Old World interpolated from data given by the black dots.

likely that the ability to digest fresh milk is advantageous for pastoralists. This is clearly the case among desert pastoralists today. Gebhard Flatz of the Medizinische Hochschule Hannover, Germany, studied the Beja, a people who wander with their herds of camels and goats in the desert lands between the Nile and the Red Sea (**Figure 14.9**). During the nine-month dry season, the Beja rely almost entirely on milk from their camels and goats. They drink about 3 liters of fresh milk a day, and they obtain virtually all of their energy, protein, and water from milk.

Several lines of evidence suggest that in northern Europe people adopted pastoralism, and then lactase persistence evolved in response to this new ecological environment. Archaeological sites rich in the bones of domesticated cows, sheep, and goats indicate that pastoralism reached northern Europe about 6 kya. Pottery that dates to this period contains minute residues of chemical compounds found only in milk, suggesting that milk production played a significant role in these early pastoral economies. These data do not prove that lactase persistence evolved in response to milk consumption. It could be that lactase persistence was already common by chance and that these peoples adopted dairying because they could drink milk, rather than the reverse. However, a group led by Joachim Burger of the Johannes Gutenberg University of Mainz, Germany, was able to extract DNA from eight fossil humans from this period, and none of these individuals carried the European lactase-persistence allele *C-13910*. Therefore, it seems unlikely that lactase persistence was already common among these early European pastoralists. Archaeological evidence indicates that pastoralism arose in South Asia after the *C-13910* allele had already begun spreading in Europe. The DNA sequence surrounding the South Asian and European versions of the allele are identical for thousands of bases, so it is likely that this allele spread to South Asia from Europe or Southwest Asia.

FIGURE 14.9

Pastoralists in northern Africa, such as the Beja, herd camels, and during some parts of the year they obtain virtually all of their nourishment from fresh milk. A high proportion of the Beja are able to digest lactose as adults.

The sequencing of the human genome makes it possible to detect selection from DNA sequences.

Until recently, the only way to determine which human genes have been subject to selection was to guess which genetic loci might have been subject to natural selection and then to determine whether this is the case. For example, the relationship between the sickle-cell trait and malaria was initially detected by the correlation between the high frequency of the sickle-cell allele and the prevalence of falciparum malaria. As of 2006, about 90 genes have been shown to be subject to recent positive selection using this "candidate gene" approach.

As we saw earlier, the availability of complete DNA sequences has allowed scientists to detect selection directly, without any information about the function of the gene or its prevalence in different populations. This is possible because positive selection leaves detectable patterns in the genome. Here we focus on one of these patterns, which is called a **selective sweep**. A selective sweep occurs when a beneficial mutation arises and then both the mutation and DNA linked to the mutation on the same chromosome spread through the population. This means that selection leading to the spread of a favorable mutation can be detected by looking at regions of the genome in which identical long DNA sequences are common.

To understand why such sequences provide evidence for positive selection, assume for a moment that there is no crossing over and, therefore, no recombination of genes carried on the same chromosome. Now suppose a favorable mutation arises in the population. Individuals carrying that mutation have higher fitness, and the mutation increases in frequency. But if there were no recombination, all of the DNA on the chromosome that contained the mutant would also spread, and this, in turn, would

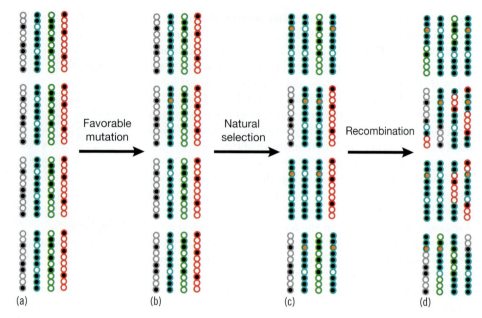

(a)   Favorable   (b)   Natural   (c)   Recombination   (d)

FIGURE 14.10

Why do selective sweeps lead to long haplotypes? (a) There are 16 chromosomes, each with 10 genetic loci. There are two alleles at each locus, black and white, and each has a frequency of 0.5. There are four different kinds of chromosome, each with a different pattern of black and white alleles. These haplotypes are outlined in gray, blue, green, and purple. (b) A favorable mutation, colored red, arises at the third locus on one of the blue chromosomes. Notice that, by chance, this haplotype carries more black alleles than white. (c) Individuals carrying the mutation have higher fitness; thus chromosomes with the mutation increase in frequency. We assume that this happens so fast that there hasn't been any recombination. As a result, a majority of the chromosomes have the same sequence of alleles as the blue haplotype on which the mutation initially occurred. By searching DNA sequences for long common sequences of this type, geneticists can locate beneficial mutations that have recently spread. (d) Eventually, recombination shuffles genes between chromosomes, and, as a result, the blue haplotype is no longer common. However, notice that black alleles have become more common in the population because they have hitchhiked on the beneficial mutant. This means that at all of these loci there is one common allele, the black one, and a rare allele, the white one. We initially assumed that all of the alleles were of equal frequency because they were not subject to selection. Such neutral alleles tend to occur with similar frequencies. Thus by searching for chromosomal regions in which there is one very common allele at each locus, geneticists can find loci that have been subject to selection. The first test is useful for finding very recent selective events, typically less than 10,000 years old, whereas the second method works for somewhat older events, typically less than 50,000 years old.

increase the frequency of all of the alleles that have the good luck to be linked to the beneficial mutant. Eventually, the whole population would carry this particular sequence of genes. Of course, this does not really happen because crossing over occurs and this shuffles the alleles at other loci. However, as we learned in Chapter 2, the rate at which this happens depends on how closely linked the loci are—the closer they are to the beneficial mutant the less likely it is that recombination will separate the mutant from the allele that it was originally linked to. This means that when a new favorable mutant initially spreads, it tends to be surrounded by a long chunk of DNA with the same sequence. Sequences at adjacent loci on a chromosome that are inherited together are called **haplotypes**. Eventually, recombination breaks up the sequence, shortening the haplotype shared by the carriers of the beneficial allele, but this takes about 10,000 years. So genes that have been subject to recent selection are surrounded by a long haplotype, unlike alternative alleles that are not subject to selection. The European version of the lactase-persistence allele lies in the middle of a haplotype that is about 1 million base pairs long, suggesting that it has been subject to recent selection. Using this procedure, geneticists can identify sequences that have recently been subject to strong natural selection. **Figure 14.10** provides a simple example of this process.

Benjamin Voight and his colleagues at the University of Chicago used this technique to scan three different human populations for signs of recent natural selection. They used DNA sequence data on 209 people: 89 from Tokyo and Beijing; 60 Yoruba-speaking individuals from Ibadan, Nigeria; and 60 people of northern and western European origin. These data, collected by a large consortium called the International HapMap Project, include about 800,000 polymorphic **single nucleotide polymorphisms (SNPs)**. A SNP (pronounced *snip*) is a location in the DNA sequence where individuals differ by a single base. In each population for each of these SNPs, researchers calculated the ratio of the length of the haplotype containing the more common allele and the length of the haplotype containing the less common allele. Large values of the index indicate a recent selective sweep. Using this approach Voight and his colleagues identified 579 regions in which a sweep is likely to have occurred. Three-quarters of these sweeps occurred in only one of the three populations. This makes sense because most of the changes detected by this method occurred in the last 10,000 years, long after the populations of Asia, Africa, and Europe split. The coding genes in these regions fall into several categories:

- *Reproductive system*. This includes genes affecting the protein structure of sperm, sperm motility, gamete viability, and the female immune response to sperm. Genes in this category also show rapid evolution during the divergence of humans and chimpanzees and may reflect ongoing male–female conflict or selection for disease resistance.

- *Morphology*. Genes affecting skin color show evidence of strong selection among Europeans, and genes affecting bone development also show rapid evolution. This is consistent with the large amount of phenotypic variation seen in contemporary humans.

- *Digestion*. This includes genes affecting the metabolism of alcohol, carbohydrates, and fatty acids. These genetic changes may be due to changes in diet that followed the adoption of agriculture.

Many people think of evolution by natural selection as a glacially slow process that acts over millions of years. However, the length of the haplotypes surrounding these alleles suggests that they are only 6,000 to 9,000 years old. We don't need to imagine that selection has huge effects on fitness in order to account for such rapid evolution. **Figure 14.11** shows how fast the frequency of a new mutation would increase if it increased fitness by just 3%. As you can see, even this relatively small benefit could easily explain the spread of a new allele in less than 10,000 years.

Genetic drift creates variation among isolated populations.

In Chapter 3, we saw that genetic drift causes random changes in gene frequencies. This means that if two populations become isolated, both will change randomly and, over time, the two populations will become genetically distinct. Because drift occurs more rapidly in small populations than in large ones, small populations will diverge from one another faster than large ones will. Genetic drift caused by the expansion of a small founding population is sometimes called the **founder effect**.

Genetic differences among members of three religious communities in North America demonstrate how this process can create variation among human groups.

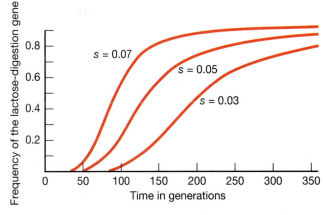

FIGURE 14.11

If the ability to digest lactose as an adult leads to even as little as a 3% increase in fitness (*s*), then it is possible that the gene allowing the digestion of lactose has spread in the 7,000 years (300 to 350 generations) since the origin of dairying.

FIGURE 14.12

The Old Order Amish were founded by a group of 200 people. These Amish dress plainly and shun most forms of modern technology, including motor vehicles.

Two of these groups are Anabaptist sects—the Old Order Amish (**Figure 14.12**) and Hutterites—and the third group is the Utah Mormons. Each of these groups forms a well-defined population. About 2,000 Mormons first arrived in the area of what is now Salt Lake City in 1847, and members of the church continued to arrive until 1890. Virtually all of the immigrants were of northern European descent. At the turn of the twentieth century, there were about 250,000 people in this area, and about 70% of them belonged to the Mormon church. In contrast, the two Anabaptist groups were much smaller. The founding population of the Old Order Amish was only 200 people, and gene flow from outside the group has been very limited. Contemporary Hutterites are all descended from a population of only 443 people and, like the Amish, have been almost completely closed to immigration.

Researchers studying the genetic composition of each of these populations have found that Mormons are genetically similar to other European populations. Thus, even though Mormon populations have been partly isolated from other European populations for over 150 years, genetic drift has led to very little change. This is just what we would expect, given the size of the Mormon population. In contrast, the two Anabaptist populations are quite distinct from other European populations. Because their founding populations were small and the communities were genetically isolated, drift has created substantial genetic changes in the same period of time.

Genetic drift can also explain why certain genetic diseases are common in some populations but not in others. For example, Afrikaners in what is now the Republic of South Africa are the descendants of Dutch immigrants who arrived in the seventeenth century. By chance, this small group of immigrants carried a number of rare genetic diseases, and these genes occurred at much higher frequency among members of the colonizing population than in the Dutch populations from which the immigrants were originally drawn. The Afrikaner population grew very rapidly and preserved these initially high frequencies, causing these genes to occur in higher frequencies among modern Afrikaners than in other populations. For example, sufferers of the genetic disease **porphyria variegata** develop a severe reaction to certain anesthetics. About 30,000 Afrikaners now carry the dominant gene that causes this disease, and every one of them is descended from a single couple who arrived from Holland in the 1680s.

Overall patterns of genetic variation mainly reflect the history of migration and population growth in the human species.

Much of the genetic variation among human groups reflects the history of the peoples of the earth. In Chapter 13 we explained that the geographical patterns of genetic variation indicate that the human species underwent a population expansion first in Africa about 130 kya and then throughout the world about 60 kya. There have been several subsequent population expansions. The invention of agriculture led to expansions of farming peoples from the Middle East into Europe, from Southeast Asia into **Oceania** (the Pacific island groups of Polynesia, Melanesia, and Micronesia), and from west-central Africa to most of the rest of the continent between 4,000 and 1,000 years ago. The domestication of the horse and associated military innovations led to several expansions of peoples living in the steppes of central Asia between 3,000 and 500 years ago, and improvements in ships, navigation, and military organization led to the expansion of European populations during the last 500 years.

As we saw in Chapter 13, worldwide patterns of genetic variation preserve a record of these expansions. As human populations expand, local populations become genetically isolated from one another and begin to accumulate genetic differences. Expanding local populations exchange genes with their neighbors and with other populations they

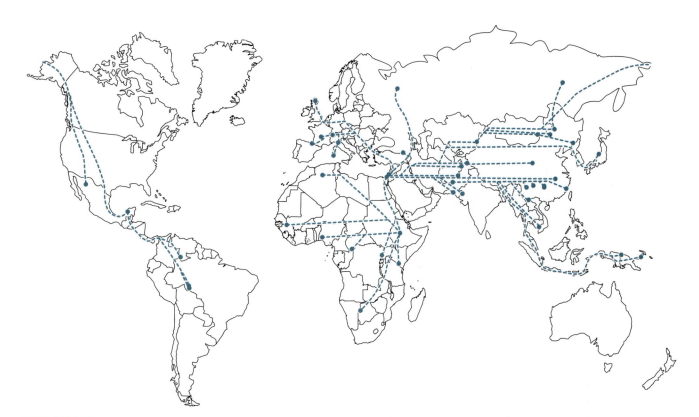

FIGURE 14.13

The location of the 51 populations in the Human Genome Diversity Project (*blue circles*) and the paths used to calculate distances in the Cambridge study (see Chapter 13). The Stanford study used similar paths.

encounter as they expand. This gene flow tends to blur the effects of the expansion. However, if there is not too much gene flow, the present patterns of genetic variation will reflect the pattern of past migrations.

This hypothesis is consistent with a variety of different kinds of genetic data. For example, we have already seen how patterns of variation in Y chromosomes and mtDNA haplotypes can be used to infer the human expansions out of Africa. We have seen that genetic variation decreases along the likely path of human expansion from East Africa about 60 kya to the current location of contemporary population (**Figure 14.13**). If contemporary patterns of human variation are due to the initial expansion of humans out of Africa, genetic distance should also be correlated with these distances, and that is exactly what the data show. Geographical distance is a very good predictor of genetic distance between human populations (**Figure 14.14**).

Variation in Complex Phenotypic Traits

As we saw in Chapter 3, the majority of human traits are influenced by many genes, most having a relatively small effect. Until recently it was impossible to detect the effects of single genes for such traits. Instead, geneticists developed statistical methods that enabled them to estimate the relative importance of genetic and environmental components of variation within groups. Because the relative importance of genetic variation and environmental variation will affect the resemblance between parents and offspring, the measure that computes the proportion of variation due to the effects of genes is referred to as the **heritability** of phenotypic traits. Technological advances are rapidly altering our understanding of the genetic basis of many traits.

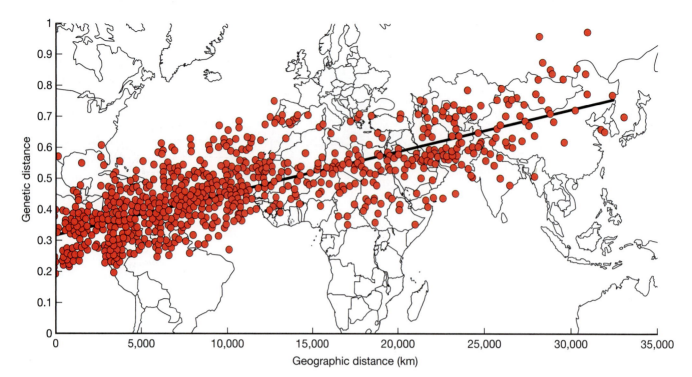

FIGURE 14.14

The genetic distance between each pair of populations plotted against the distance between the populations along the likely pathway of expansion of humans out of Africa. The two distances are strongly correlated, suggesting that the original expansion out of Africa accounts for much of the genetic variation among different human populations.

This material will be easier to understand if we have a concrete example in mind. Height is an ideal trait: It is quite easy to measure, it is quite variable within and between populations, it is relatively stable once individuals reach adulthood, and there is a wealth of data on height of individuals in different populations. In any moderately large sample of people, there will be a wide range of variation in height. For example, the data in **Figure 14.15** are taken from men who joined the British Army in 1939. Some of these young recruits were more than 2 m (around 7 ft.) tall; others were less than 1.5 m (5 ft.) tall.

Genetic Variation within Groups

Under certain conditions, measuring the phenotypic similarities among relatives, particularly twins, allows us to estimate the fraction of the variation within the population that is due to genes.

In Part One, we saw that the transmission of genes from parents to offspring causes children and parents to be phenotypically similar. If parents who are taller than average tend to have offspring who are taller than average, and parents who are shorter than average tend to have children who are shorter than average, you might think that height is determined by genes. In contrast, if parents and offspring are no more similar to each other than to other individuals in the population, you might think that genes have little effect on height. The problem with this reasoning is that nongenetic factors may also cause parents and offspring to be similar. It is known that many environmental factors, such as nutritional levels and the prevalence of infectious diseases,

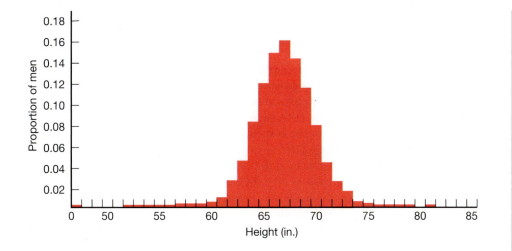

FIGURE 14.15

The heights of men joining the British Army in 1939 varied considerably, illustrating the range of variation in morphological characters within populations. The tallest men joining the army were more than 2 m (around 84 in., or 7 ft.) tall, and others were less than 1.5 m (60 in., or 5 ft.) tall.

affect height. Human parents directly affect their offspring's environment in many ways: They provide food and shelter, arrange for their children to be inoculated against diseases, and shape their children's beliefs about nutrition. Similarity between the environments of parents and their offspring is called **environmental covariation** and is a serious complication in computing heritability.

Data from studies of twins are particularly useful for separating the effects of genetic transmission from environmental covariation. The technique involves comparing the similarity between monozygotic and dizygotic twins. **Monozygotic** (identical) **twins** begin life when the union of a sperm and an egg produces a single zygote. Then, very early in development, this embryo divides to form two separate, genetically identical individuals. **Dizygotic** (fraternal) **twins** begin life when two different eggs are fertilized by two different sperm to form two independent zygotes. Dizygotic twins are just like other pairs of full siblings except that they were conceived at the same time. Like other pairs of full siblings, they share approximately one half of their genes. Both monozygotic and dizygotic twins share a womb and experience the same intrauterine environment. After they are born, most twins grow up together in the same family. Thus if most of the variation in stature has a genetic origin, monozygotic twins are likely to be more similar to one another than dizygotic twins because monozygotic twins are genetically identical. On the other hand, if most of the variation is due to the environment, and the similarity between parents and offspring is due to having a common family environment, then monozygotic and dizygotic twins will be equally similar. Population genetic theory provides a way to use comparisons of the similarity among dizygotic and monozygotic twins to adjust estimates of heritability for the effects of correlated environments.

Twin studies are useful in trying to estimate the relative magnitude of the effects of genetic variation and environmental variation on phenotypic characters, but the data may be biased in certain ways. For example, twin studies will overestimate heritability if the environments of monozygotic twins are more similar than the environments of dizygotic twins. There are several reasons why this may be the case. In the uterus, some monozygotic twins are more intimately associated than dizygotic twins are. Monozygotic twins are always the same sex. After they are born, monozygotic twins may be treated differently by their parents, family, teachers, and friends than dizygotic twins. It is not uncommon to see monozygotic twins dressed in identical outfits or given rhyming names, and it is inevitable that their physical similarities to one another will be pointed out to them over and over (**Figure 14.16**).

Studies of monozygotic and dizygotic twins suggest that about 80% of the variation in height in European populations is due to genetic similarities between parents and their children. The heritability of height in Africa and India is somewhat lower, around 0.6.

FIGURE 14.16

Identical, or monozygotic, twins are produced when an embryo splits at an early stage and produces two genetically identical individuals.

Genomewide association studies confirm that height is affected by many genes, each with a small effect.

Drops in the cost of assessing an individual's genotype at a large number of loci has allowed geneticists to conduct **genomewide association studies**. These studies make use of what are called SNP chips to examine the genetic basis of complex characters. Hundreds of thousands of short DNA segments are bound to each silicon SNP chip. Each of these segments matches the sequence surrounding one allele of a known SNP. Then a sample of an individual's DNA is chemically chopped up into small pieces and applied to the chip; the DNA bits bind to the matching segments on the chip. In this way molecular biologists can assess an individual's genotype at a half a million SNPs at the same time. Because the cost is low, researchers can afford to evaluate the genotypes of large numbers of individuals.

Genomewide association studies use these data to study the genetic basis of complex characters. The basic procedure is very simple. To determine which genes affect height, sample a large number of individuals. Measure the height of each individual and assess his or her genotype for a large number of SNPs. Then determine which SNPs are most often found in tall people and which are more often found in short people. These SNPs are either part of the DNA sequence of a gene that affects height or closely linked to such a gene. Thus, by studying the DNA sequence surrounding the SNPs, geneticists can identify genes that influence height.

Since 2007 there have been a number of studies just like this one, and they have identified about 180 genes that affect height. None of the genes has a large effect—the gene with the biggest effect leads to only a 4 mm (0.16 in.) increase in height, on average. Interestingly, these 180 genes account for only about 10% of the variation in height. We know that about 80% of the variation in height is genetic so this means that most of the genes affecting height have not yet been identified. This is consistent with the fact that the power of genomewide association studies to identify genes with small effects is limited by the size of the sample. Existing studies using sample sizes of more than 10,000 subjects can barely detect genes that affect height by a few millimeters. Much larger samples would be necessary to identify genes with even smaller effects. Thus it seems likely that height is affected by thousands of genes that each have very, very small effects.

Genetic Variation among Groups

Stature varies among human populations.

Just as people within groups vary, groups of people collectively vary in certain characteristics. For example, there is a considerable amount of variation in average height among populations. People from northwestern Europe are tall, averaging about 1.75 m (5 ft. 9 in.). People in Italy and other parts of southern Europe are about 12 cm (5 in.) shorter on average. African populations include very tall peoples like the Nuer and the Maasai and very short peoples like the !Kung. Within the Western Hemisphere, Native Americans living on the Great Plains of North America and in Patagonia are relatively tall, and peoples in tropical regions of both continents are relatively short.

Some of the variation in body size among human groups appears to be adaptive.

In Chapter 12 we learned that larger body size is favored by natural selection in colder climates. Tall peoples, such as the indigenous peoples of Patagonia in South America and the Great Plains in North America, usually live in relatively cold parts of the world, but shorter peoples typically live in warmer areas, like southern Europe or the New World tropics. This pattern suggests that variation in body size among groups may be adaptive, a conjecture that is borne out by data on the relationship between body size and climate from a large number of human groups (**Figure 14.17**). Thus at least some fraction of the variation in body size among groups is adaptive.

The fact that variation within populations has a genetic component does not mean that differences between groups are caused solely by genetic differences.

We have seen that a significant proportion of the variation in height and body size within some populations reflects genetic variation. We also know that the variation in height and body shape among populations seems to be adaptive. From these two facts, it might seem logical that the variation in body size among populations is genetic and that this variation represents a response to natural selection.

However, this logic is wrong! All of the variation in height within populations could be genetic *and* all of the variation in height among populations could be adaptive, but this would not mean that there is variation among populations in the distribution of genes that influence height. In fact, all of the observed variation in height among groups could be due solely to differences in environmental conditions.

This point is frequently misunderstood, and this misunderstanding leads to serious misconceptions about the nature of genetic variation among human groups. A simple example may help you see why the existence of genetic variation within groups does not imply the existence of genetic variation among groups. Suppose Rob and his neighbor Pete both set out to plant a new lawn. They go to the garden store together, buy a big bag of seed, and divide the contents evenly. Pete, an avid gardener, goes home and plants the seed with great care. He fertilizes, balances the soil acidity, and provides just the right amount of water at just the right times. Rob, who lives next door, scatters the seed in his backyard, waters it infrequently and inadequately, and never even considers fertilizing it. After a few months, the two yards are very different. Pete's lawn is thick, green, and vigorous, but Rob's lawn hardly justifies the name (**Figure 14.18**). We know that the difference between the two lawns cannot be due to the genetic characteristics of the grass seed, because Rob and Pete used

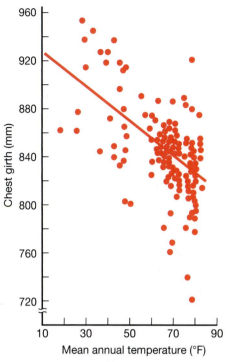

FIGURE 14.17

People living in cold climates have larger bodies than those living in warm climates. The vertical axis plots mean chest girth for numerous human groups, and the horizontal axis plots the mean yearly temperature in the regions in which each group lives. Because chest girth is a measure of overall size, these data show that people living in colder climates have larger bodies.

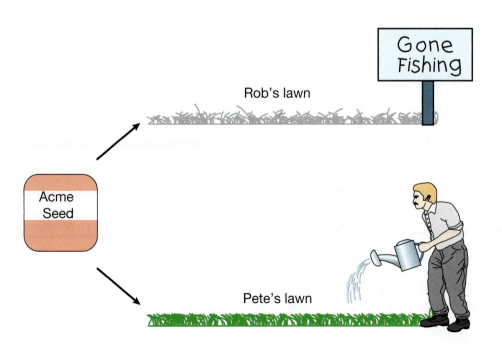

FIGURE 14.18

The differences between two separate lawns planted from the same bag of seed must be environmental. However, if the seed used was genetically variable, the differences within each lawn could be genetic.

seed from the same bag. Nonetheless, variation in the height and greenness of the grass within each lawn might be largely genetic because the seeds within each lawn experience very similar environmental conditions. All of the seeds in Pete's lawn get regular water and fertilizer, while all of the seeds in Rob's lawn are neglected to an equal extent. Thus if the seed company has sold genetically variable seed, differences between individual plants *within* each lawn could be due mainly to genetic differences between the seeds themselves.

The same argument applies to variation in human stature. The fact that much of the variation in stature among Americans has a genetic component does not mean that stature is determined entirely by genes. It means there is genetic variation that affects stature, and these effects are relatively large in comparison with the effects of environmental differences among Americans. But it does not follow that the differences in stature between Americans and other peoples are the result of genetic differences between them. For example, although Americans are taller on average than citizens of Japan, these differences in height are not necessarily genetic. That would be true only if two quite different conditions held. First, there would have to be a difference between Americans and Japanese in the distribution of genes affecting stature. Second, this genetic difference would have to be large compared with the differences in culture and environment between the two groups. The fact that there is genetic variation among Americans does not tell us whether or not Americans are genetically different from Japanese. The relatively small effect of environmental and cultural variation on height among Americans tells us nothing about the average difference in environment between Americans and Japanese.

Genomewide association studies indicate that some of the variation in stature is due to genetic differences.

Earlier we saw that northern Europeans are taller on average than are southern Europeans. A team of geneticists led by Joel N. Hirschhorn of Harvard University showed that this difference is partly due to genetic differences at a large number of loci. Remember that genomewide association studies have identified many loci that affect stature. At each of these loci there are alleles that are more common in taller people and others that are more common in shorter people. Hirschhorn and his colleagues showed that on average "tall" alleles are a little more common in northern European populations and the "short" alleles are a little more common in southern European populations, indicating that the difference in stature between these two populations is in part due to small genetic differences at a large number of loci.

The increase in stature that coincided with modernization is evidence for the influence of environmental variation on stature.

There has been a striking effect of modernization on the average heights of many peoples. For example, **Figure 14.19** plots the heights of several groups of English boys between the ages of 5 and 21 in the nineteenth and twentieth centuries. In 1833, 19-year-old factory workers averaged about 160 cm (about 5 ft. 3 in.). In 1874, laborers of the same age averaged about 167 cm (5 ft. 6 in.). In 1958, the average British 19-year-old stood about 177 cm (5 ft. 9 in.). Similar increases in height over the last hundred years can be seen among Swedish, German, Polish, and North American children. These changes have occurred very rapidly, probably too fast to be due solely to natural selection.

There also have been substantial changes in height among immigrants to the United States in the course of a few generations. During the first part of the twentieth century, when Japan had only begun to modernize, many Japanese came to Hawaii to work as laborers on sugar plantations. The immigrants were considerably shorter than

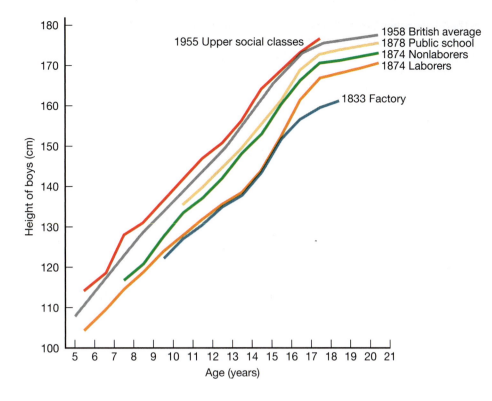

FIGURE 14.19

Height increases with time in English populations, but at any given time richer people are taller. Note that English *public* schools are the equivalent of American *private* schools.

their descendants who were born in Hawaii (**Table 14.1**). This change in height among immigrants and their children was so rapid that it cannot be the result of genetic change. Instead, it must be due to some environmental difference between Japan and Hawaii in the early twentieth century. The underlying cause of this kind of environmental effect is not completely understood. In 1870s England, poverty was involved to some extent because relatively wealthy public-school boys were taller than less affluent nonlaborers, and nonlaborers were taller than poorer laborers. Observations like this have led some anthropologists to hypothesize that increases in the standard of living associated with modernization improve early childhood nutrition and increase children's growth rates. However, this cannot be the full explanation because even the richest people in England 120 years ago were shorter than the average person in England today. Because it seems unlikely that wealthy Britons were malnourished

TABLE 14.1

	Average Height (cm)	Sample Size
Japanese immigrants to Hawaii	158.7	171
People from same regions of Japan who remained in Japan	158.4	178
The immigrants' children born in Hawaii	162.8	188

Japanese men who immigrated to Hawaii during the first part of the twentieth century were shorter than their children who had been born and raised in Hawaii. The immigrants were similar in height to the Japanese who remained in Japan, which indicates that the immigrants were a representative sample of the Japanese populations from which they came. The fact that the children of the immigrants were taller than their parents shows that environmental factors play an important role in creating variation in stature.

in the 1870s, other factors must have contributed to the increase in height during the last 120 years. Some authorities think that the control of childhood diseases may have played an important role in these changes.

The Race Concept

The common view of race is bad biology.

Race is part of everyday life. For better or worse, our race affects how we see the world and how the world sees us; it affects our social relationships, our choice of marriage partners, our educational opportunities, and our employment prospects. We may decry discrimination, but we cannot deny that race plays a major role in many aspects of our lives.

Like any widely used word, *race* means different things to different people. However, the understanding of race held by many North Americans is based on three fundamentally flawed propositions:

1. *The human species can be naturally divided into a small number of distinct races.* According to this view, almost every person is a member of exactly one race; the only exceptions are the offspring of the members of different races. For example, many people in the United States think that people belong to one of three races: descendants of people from Europe, North Africa, and western Asia; descendants of people from sub-Saharan Africa; and descendants of people from eastern Asia.

2. *Members of different races are genetically different in important ways, so knowing a person's race gives you important information about what he or she is like.* For example, biomedical researchers sometimes suggest that race predicts susceptibility to diseases like high blood pressure, heart disease, and infant mortality. Less benignly, some people believe that knowing a person's race reveals something about that person's intelligence or character.

3. *The differences between races are due to biological heritage.* Many people think that members of each race are genetically similar to each other, and genetically different from members of other races. Most Americans view African Americans and European Americans as members of different races because they are marked by genetically transmitted characters like skin color. In contrast, the Serbs and Croats of the former Yugoslavia are seen by most Americans as ethnic groups, rather than racial groups, and they assume that the differences between Serbs and Croats are based on culture rather than genes.

Although many people believe these propositions to be true, they are not consistent with scientific knowledge about human variation. There are genetic differences between groups of people living in different parts of the world, and people from nearby populations are more similar genetically than people from distant populations. However, as we will see, these differences do not mean that the human species can be meaningfully divided into a set of nonoverlapping categories called races. *The common view of race is bad biology.*

Because people vary, it is possible to create classification schemes in which similar peoples are grouped together.

People tend to be more genetically and phenotypically similar to people who live near them than to people who live farther away. As we have seen in this chapter, this is true for many genes. For example, the sickle-cell gene is common in central Africa

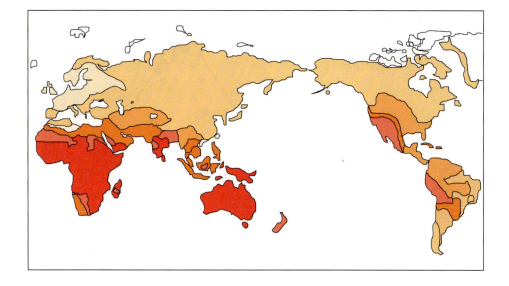

FIGURE 14.20

This map shows contours in skin color. Notice that there are smooth gradients away from the equator.

and in India but rare elsewhere; the lactose-persistence gene, which allows adults to digest lactose, predominates in northern Europe and parts of Africa but is uncommon in the rest of the world. We have also seen that overall genetic similarity is strongly associated with geographic proximity. Morphological similarities also link neighboring peoples. For example, most of the people who live near the equator have dark skin (**Figure 14.20**), and most of the people who live at high latitudes are stocky.

One consequence of these similarities is that it is possible to group people into geographically based categories on the basis of their genetic or phenotypic similarities. However, such classification schemes do not support two properties required by the common concept of race. First, there is no natural classification scheme because genetic variation is continuous, the placement of individuals within any single category is arbitrary, and classifications based on different characters lead to radically different groupings. Second, classification schemes are not very informative. The average difference among groups of people living in different parts of the world is much smaller than the differences among individuals within each group; as a result, knowing an individual's group tells you little about her genotype.

There is no single natural classification of the human species.

In Chapter 4, we argued that species are distinctive entities that can be unambiguously identified in nature. Racial classifications for humans are quite different, and there is no natural classification scheme for categorizing us. To see what is meant by a natural classification scheme, consider the following analogy. Suppose you are a clerk in a hardware store. Your boss gives you the assignment of classifying the contents of two large cabinets. The first cabinet contains power drills made by a number of different manufacturers; there are many drills but only one model per manufacturer. The second cabinet holds various different kinds of screws. The power drills vary in many ways: They have different colors, shapes, weights, and power ratings. The screws also vary: They have different lengths, diameters, pitches, and heads. You will have little trouble sorting the drills into piles according to manufacturer because all the drills made by a single manufacturer are similar in all of their dimensions; they are of the same color, shape, and weight and have the same power rating. Moreover, each model is distinctly different; there are no intermediate types. This is a natural classification system. You will have a much harder time classifying the screws. Using length will produce one set of piles; diameter, a second set of piles; and screw pitch, a third set of piles. Moreover, even a classification based on a single characteristic like length will

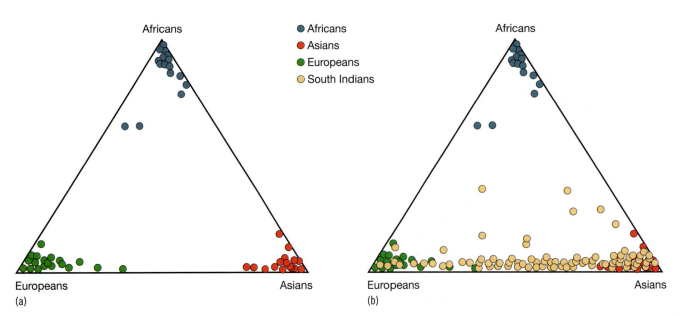

FIGURE 14.21

(a) The proportion of ancestry in three populations for 247 people drawn from western Europe, sub-Saharan Africa, and east Asia based on 100 polymorphic noncoding loci. Every individual is unambiguously classified into one of these three groups. However, this is an artifact caused by sampling distant populations. (b) When data for 263 individuals from south India, a geographically intermediate group, are added, the classification becomes arbitrary.

require arbitrary distinctions: Should there be three or four piles? Should the 1.5-inch screws be put in the pile with the smallest screws or with the next bigger size? There is no natural way to classify the screws.

You might think that the solution to this problem would be to classify people the same way we classify organisms into species categories by using genetic measures of shared descent. However, this strategy fails because human genetic variation changes smoothly from one place to another. Of course, samples taken from widely separate populations are distinct. For example, as shown in **Figure 14.21a**, samples taken from northern Europe, east Asia, and sub-Saharan Africa are completely nonoverlapping and can be easily classified into three distinct groups. However, if geographically intermediate populations—for example, from southern India—are included, this becomes impossible, as shown in **Figure 14.21b.** With this in mind, look again at the plot of genetic distance versus geographic distance and notice that there are no clumps or discontinuities that could form the basis of a natural classification system. The Cambridge scientists tested this statistically and found that after controlling for genetic distance, racial groupings added little additional predictive power.

Racial classification schemes based on different sets of characters don't result in the same groupings for all characters. For example, a classification scheme based on the ability to digest lactose would yield very different groupings from one based on resistance to malaria. A classification based on skin color would produce a different grouping from one based on height. This means that folk classification schemes based on skin color and facial morphology are not reliable predictors of overall genetic similarity. In Brazil, for example, people are classified according to what is called *cor* in Portuguese. Although the literal translation of *cor* is "color," the Brazilians' classification is based on more than skin color; it includes the morphology of the lips and eyes, and hair type. *Cor* plays a role in Brazilian society analogous to race in North America: There is substantial prejudice against those classified as black, and people classified as black earn less money than other Brazilians on average. If the Brazilian folk classification is biologically meaningful, *cor* should be a good predictor of ancestry: Whites should be of mainly European ancestry, and blacks of mainly African ancestry.

To test this idea, Flavia Parra and his colleagues at the Universidade Federal de Minas Gerais in Brazil assembled samples from three populations. They took blood samples from people on São Tomé, an island near the coast of Africa. This is near the area where the ancestors of most African Brazilians lived before being captured and transported to Brazil as slaves. Parra's group also took blood samples from people in Portugal, the area where the ancestors of most European Brazilians came from. It turns out that a small number of genetic loci differ between West African and European populations, and this pattern can be used to compute an index of African ancestry. Finally, these researchers collected two kinds of information from contemporary Brazilians. They assigned each of the individuals to one of three common Brazilian categories—black, white, and intermediate—on the basis of their phenotypes. They also took blood from each individual, extracted DNA, and typed each individual for genetic loci that differentiate West African and European populations. This analysis allowed them to compute the extent of African ancestry for each individual. The results are quite clear: There is very little correlation between phenotype and ancestry (**Figure 14.22**). People classified as black and people classified as white on the basis of their phenotypes have a similar range of genotypes.

Racial classification schemes explain very little of the world's human genetic variation.

Geneticists have tried to account for the patterns of variation across the globe. In these studies the human species was categorized first into local groups of people

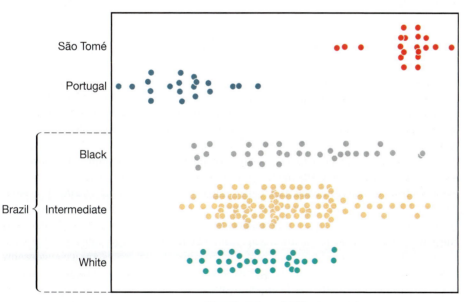

Genetic index of African ancestry

FIGURE 14.22

The genetic index of African ancestry for contemporary Africans living on São Tomé (an island just off the coast of Gabon that served as the entry point for the West African slave trade), contemporary Portuguese, and contemporary Brazilians classified as black, white, and intermediate on the basis of skin color, facial morphology, and hair texture. These data indicate that the Brazilian folk classification system predicts little about overall genetic similarity.

belonging to the same ethnic group, linguistic group, or nationality. Then local groups were collected into larger, geographically based categories that correspond roughly to the usual races. Geneticists computed the amount of variation in these characters within each local group, among groups within each race, and among races. They found that there is much more genetic variation *within* local groups than there is *among* local groups or among races themselves. Differences within local groups account for about 85% of all the variation in the human species. To put this another way, suppose that a malevolent extraterrestrial wiped out the entire human species except for one local group, which it preserved in an extraterrestrial zoo. The alien could pick any local group at random—the Efe, the Inuit, the citizens of Ames, Iowa, or the people of Patagonia—and then wipe out the rest of the humans on the planet. The members of the surviving groups would still contain, on average, 85% of the total amount of genetic variation that exists in the entire human species.

This fact means that knowing somebody's racial classification does not tell you very much about that individual's genotype. For example, Michael Bamshad, now at the University of Washington, and his colleagues classified the 1,064 individuals in the Centre d'Étude du Polymorphisme Humaine (CEPH) data set (the same one used by the Stanford and Cambridge researchers) into the four groups as defined by the U.S. Office of Management and Budget: Europeans (including western Asia), Asians (including Oceania), Africans, and Native Americans. They then calculated the probability that two individuals randomly drawn from the same group are more similar genetically than two individuals drawn randomly from different groups. The answers vary a bit from group to group but cluster around two-thirds. This isn't very good, considering that a flip of a coin would get you this result half of the time. Moreover, the CEPH data omit a number of geographically intermediate populations, like those in northern Africa or India, that would further weaken the predictive power of the four classifications. And this result makes use of all 377 loci in the sample; knowing somebody's racial group would be even less informative about phenotypic characters affected by smaller numbers of genes.

Racial classification schemes don't represent natural biological categories.

The bottom line is that people can be classified, and such classifications are not necessarily arbitrary, but they do not reflect any *natural* subdivision of the human species into biologically distinct groups. Nor does knowing a person's position in a classification reveal very much about what that person is like.

This conclusion is consistent with what we have learned about human evolution. It seems likely that anatomically modern humans are a very recently evolved species; the evidence from genetic analyses and fossils suggests an age of less than 200,000 years. This makes it less likely that natural selection and genetic drift have produced larger genetic differences within the human species than in other, older species. Recall that the genetic differences among different species of chimpanzees are much greater than among different groups of humans, probably because chimpanzees are a considerably older genus. Moreover, we know that gene flow tends to eliminate genetic differences between groups, and there has been extensive gene flow in human history.

Races represent cultural categories that play an important, but unfortunate, role in society.

Many people find the conclusion that races aren't real completely implausible. They "know" from experience that race is real. The late Martin Luther King Jr.'s dream that "my four little children will one day live in a nation where they will not be judged by the color of their skin, but by the content of their character" has not yet been realized. This is because racism is real and remains a pervasive problem in our society and many others. But it's important to separate the reality of racism from the scientific understanding of the concept of race.

Many view the claim that race is not a valid scientific construct as another example of the political correctness that is now common in academia. This view has some support within anthropology. For example, in the November 1994 issue of *Discover* magazine, Alice Brues, an anthropologist at the University of Colorado, stated,

> A popular political statement now is, "There is no such thing as race." I wonder what people think when they hear this. They would have to suppose that the speaker, if he were dropped by parachute into downtown Nairobi, would be unable to tell, by looking around him, whether he was in Nairobi or Stockholm. This could only damage his credibility. The visible differences between different populations tell everyone that *there is something here* (p. 60).

But our intuitions sometimes lead us astray. Our eyes tell us that the earth is flat, but it is really a sphere. Our intuition tells us that a bullet fired horizontally from a rifle will hit the ground long after a bullet dropped from the muzzle at the same instant, yet in reality they will hit the ground at the same time. Our mind tells us that it is impossible for an elephant to have descended from a shrewlike insectivore, even though that is exactly what happened. The intuition that race is real is also an illusion.

Professor Brues is undoubtedly correct that a parachute jumper who landed in Nairobi would be unlikely to think that he was in Stockholm, Tokyo, or Honolulu. But would he be certain that he was in Nairobi and not in Johannesburg or Fiji? Probably not. And what if we imagine an intrepid soul who bicycles from Nairobi to Stockholm? As she pedals from Nairobi through Khartoum, Cairo, Istanbul, and Budapest and finally reaches Stockholm, she would observe that people change in many ways, but the change would always be subtle; there would be no sharp boundaries with one kind of people on one side and a different kind of people on the other side. The cyclist would see that people vary but that this variation does not sort itself out into neat, nonoverlapping categories. Thus our perception of race depends on which of these two metaphors we think captures the essential features of human variation. The scientific evidence conclusively demonstrates that there is considerably more variation within human groups than among them, and this is why our transcontinental bicyclist would not note any sharply defined changes as she made her way slowly north.

In our opinion, race is a culturally constructed category, not a meaningful biological concept. The characters that North Americans conventionally use to sort people into racial categories tend to be biologically transmitted traits, like skin color and facial features. But we could just as well use culturally transmitted traits like religion, dialect, or class. Classifications based on a small set of biologically transmitted traits have no more scientific validity than do classifications based on religion, language, or political affiliation. Although skin color and facial features are salient characteristics in the United States, in some societies other types of characters matter much more. Religion is the basis of bitter animosity in Northern Ireland, although the genetic differences between Protestant and Catholic Irish are even more microscopic than are the genetic differences between African Americans and European Americans. In the ethnic conflicts that have seared the globe in the last 25 years, it is literally a matter of life and death whether you are Sunni or Shia in Baghdad, Tamil or Sinhalese in Sri Lanka, or Serb or Muslim in Kosovo. Yet in each case, people are divided by cultural differences, not genetic ones.

Key Terms

transposable elements
synonymous substitutions
nonsynonymous substitutions
positively selected
neoteny
negative selection
genetic variation
variation within groups
variation among groups
specific language impairment (SLI)
selection–mutation balance
falciparum malaria
balanced polymorphism
non-insulin-dependent diabetes (NIDD)
insulin
lactose
lactase-phlorizin hydrolase (LHP)
lactase persistence
LCT
pastoralists
selective sweep
haplotypes
single nucleotide polymorphisms (SNPs)
founder effect
porphyria variegata
Oceania
heritability
environmental covariation
monozygotic twins
dizygotic twins
genomewide association studies

Study Questions

1. How can we reconcile the fact that humans and other apes differ only by 1% or 2% of their genomes and at the same time there are huge phenotypic differences between humans and apes?

2. What sources of human variation are described in this chapter? Why is it important to distinguish among them?

3. Consider the phenotype of human finger number. Most people have exactly five fingers on each hand, but some people have fewer. What is the source of variation in finger number?

4. How can natural selection maintain genetic variation within human populations?

5. What is the evidence that selection has generated genetic variation between human groups?

6. Why is it hard to determine the source of variation in human phenotypes? Why might it be easier to determine the source of variation for other animals?

7. Explain how studies of human twins allow researchers to estimate the effects of genetic and environmental differences on phenotypic traits.

8. What kind of body size and shape is best in a humid climate? Why?

9. Suppose you are told that differences in IQ scores among white Americans have a genetic basis. What would that tell you about the differences in average scores between white Americans and Americans belonging to other ethnic groups? Why?

10. Explain why race is not a biologically meaningful category of classification.

Further Reading

Bamshad, M., S. Wooding, B. A. Salisbury, and J. C. Stephens. 2004. "Deconstructing the Relationship between Genetics and Race." *Nature Reviews Genetics* 15: 598–609.

Falconer, D. S., and T. F. C. Mackay. 1996. *Introduction to Quantitative Genetics*. 4th ed. Essex, UK: Longman.

Gerbault, P., A. Liebert, Y. Itan, A. Powell, M. Currat, J. Burger, D. M. Swallow, and M. G. Thomas. 2013. "Evolution of Lactase Persistence: An Example of Human Niche Construction." *Philosophical Transactions of the Royal Society* 366: 863–877.

Jobling, M. A., E. Hollox, M. Hurles, T. Kivisild, and C. Tyler-Smith. 2014. *Human Evolutionary Genetics*. 2nd ed. New York: Garland Science.

Mielke, J. H., L. W. Konigsberg, and J. H. Relethford. 2010. *Human Biological Variation*. New York: Oxford University Press.

O'Bleness, M., V. B. Searles, A. Varki, P. Gagneux, and J. M. Sikela. 2012. "Evolution of Genetic and Genomic Features Unique to the Human Lineage." *Nature Reviews Genetics* 13: 853–866.

CHAPTER OBJECTIVES

By the end of this chapter you should be able to

- Evaluate the argument that the application of evolutionary reasoning to understand contemporary human behavior does not entail genetic determinism.

- Understand why evolutionary thinking helps us understand how people learn.

- Discuss reasons why people usually do not mate with close relatives.

- Explain how natural selection helps us understand why men and women both value good character in a marriage partner, and why men usually care more about youth and women more about control of resources.

EVOLUTION AND HUMAN BEHAVIOR

Why Evolution Is Relevant to Human Behavior

Understanding How We Think

Social Consequences of Mate Preferences

Why Evolution Is Relevant to Human Behavior

The application of evolutionary principles to understanding human behavior is controversial. The theory of evolution is at the core of our understanding of the natural world. By studying how natural selection, recombination, mutation, genetic drift, and other evolutionary processes interact to produce evolutionary change, we come to understand why organisms are the way they are. Of course, our understanding of evolution is far from perfect, and other disciplines, most notably chemistry and physics, contribute greatly to our understanding of life. As the great geneticist Theodosius Dobzhansky once said, however, "Nothing in biology makes sense except in the light of evolution."

So far, the way we have applied evolutionary theory in this book is not controversial. We are principally interested in the evolutionary history of our own species, *Homo sapiens*, but we began by using evolutionary theory to understand the behavior of our closest relatives, the nonhuman primates. Forty years ago, when evolutionary theory was new to primatology, this approach generated some controversy, but now most primatologists are committed to evolutionary explanations of behavior. In Part Three, we used evolutionary theory to develop models of the patterns of behavior that might have characterized early hominins. Although some researchers might debate the fine points of this analysis, there is little disagreement about the value of adaptive reasoning in this context. Perhaps this is because the early hominins were simply "bipedal apes," with brains the size of modern chimpanzee brains. Not many people object to evolutionary analyses of physiological traits, such as lactose tolerance, but they may disagree about particular explanations for those traits. Similarly, most people accept evolutionary explanations about why we live so long and mature so slowly. These traits are clearly part of human biology, and there is a broad consensus that evolutionary theory provides an essential key for understanding them.

The consensus evaporates when we enter the domain of contemporary human behavior. Most social scientists acknowledge that evolution has shaped our bodies, our minds, and our behavior to a limited extent. But many have been very critical of attempts to apply evolutionary theory to contemporary human behavior because they think evolutionary analyses imply that behavior is genetically determined. Genetic determinism of behavior in humans seems inconsistent with the fact that so much of our behavior is acquired through learning and that so much of our behavior and many of our beliefs are strongly influenced by our culture and environment. The notion that evolutionary explanations imply genetic determinism is based on a fundamental misunderstanding about how the natural world works.

All phenotypic traits, including behavioral traits, reflect the interactions between genes and the environment.

Many people have the mistaken view that genetic transmission and learning are mutually exclusive. That is, they believe that behaviors are either genetic and thus unchangeable or learned and thus controlled entirely by environmental contingencies. This assumption lies at the heart of the "nature–nurture question," a debate that has plagued the social sciences for many years.

The nature–nurture debate is based on a false dichotomy. It assumes that there is a clear distinction between the effects of genes (nature) and the effects of the environment (nurture). People often think that genes are like engineering drawings for a finished machine and that individuals vary simply because their genes carry different specifications. For example, they imagine that Yao Ming is tall because his genes specified an adult height of 2.3 m (7 ft. 6 in.), and Earl Boykins is short because his genes specified an adult height of 1.65 m (5 ft. 5 in.).

However, genes are not like blueprints that specify phenotype. Every trait results from the *interaction* of a genetic program with the environment. Thus genes are more like recipes in the hands of a creative cook, sets of instructions for the construction of an organism using materials available in the environment. At each step, this very complex process depends on the nature of local conditions. The expression of any genotype always depends on the environment. A person's adult height is shaped by the genes they inherited from their parents, how well nourished they were in childhood, and the nature of the diseases they were exposed to when they were growing up.

The expression of behavioral traits is usually more sensitive to environmental conditions than is the expression of morphological and physiological traits. As we saw in Chapter 3, traits that develop uniformly in a wide range of environments, such as finger number, are said to be canalized. Traits that vary in response to environmental cues, such as subsistence strategies, are said to be plastic. Every trait, however, whether plastic or canalized, results from the unfolding of a developmental program in a particular environment. Even highly canalized characters can be modified by environmental factors, such as fetal exposure to mutagenic agents or accidents.

Natural selection can shape developmental processes so that organisms develop different adaptive behaviors in different environments.

Some people understand that all traits are influenced by a combination of genes and environment, but they reject evolutionary explanations of human behavior because they have fallen prey to a second, more subtle, misunderstanding. Namely, they believe that natural selection cannot create adaptations unless behavioral differences between individuals are caused by genetic differences. If this were true, it would follow that adaptive explanations of human behavior must be invalid because there is no doubt that most of the variation in behavioral traits, such as foraging strategies, marriage practices, and values, is not due to genetic differences but is instead the product of learning and culture.

This belief is false, however, because natural selection shapes learning mechanisms so that organisms adjust their behavior to local conditions in an adaptive way. Recall from Chapter 3 that this is exactly what happens with soapberry bugs. Male soapberry bugs in Oklahoma guard their mates when females are scarce but not when females are abundant. Individual males vary their behavior adaptively in response to the local sex ratio. In order for this kind of flexibility in male behavior to evolve, there had to be small genetic differences in the male propensity to guard a mated female and small genetic differences in how mate guarding is influenced by the local sex ratio. If such variation exists, then natural selection can mold the responses of males so that they are locally adaptive. In any given population, however, most of the observed behavioral variation is due to the fact that individual males respond adaptively to environmental cues.

Behavior in the soapberry bug is relatively simple. Human learning and decision making are immensely more complex and flexible. We know much less about the mechanisms that produce behavioral flexibility in humans than we do about the mechanisms that produce flexibility in mate guarding among soapberry bugs. Nonetheless, such mechanisms must exist, and it is reasonable to assume that they have been shaped by natural selection. (Note that we are not arguing that all behavioral variation in human societies is adaptive. We know that evolution does not produce adaptation in every case, as we discussed in Chapter 3.) The crucial point here is that evolutionary approaches do not imply that differences in behavior among humans are the product of genetic differences between individuals.

In this chapter and the next, we consider how evolutionary theory can be used to understand the minds and behavior of modern humans. As you will see, researchers from different academic disciplines have followed different approaches in their efforts to understand how evolution has shaped human behavior. Some have focused on how natural selection has shaped the design of the human brain and how the reasoning and learning mechanisms created by selection can be used to understand our behavior. Others have tried to understand how the human capacity for culture and the ability to acquire ideas, beliefs, and values from other group members have influenced the evolution of human behavior. In the remainder of this chapter we focus how the first of these approaches can be used to gain insights about the behavior of contemporary humans. In the next chapter we will see how the two approaches can be combined to understand why humans are so different from all other animals.

Understanding How We Think

Evolutionary analyses provide important insights about how our brains are designed.

The adaptation that most clearly distinguishes humans from other primates is our large and very complex brain. Natural selection hasn't just made our brains big; it has shaped our cognitive abilities in very specific ways and molded the way we think.

FIGURE 15.1

Rats initially sample small amounts of unfamiliar foods, and if they become ill soon after eating something, they will not eat it again.

Even the most flexible strategies are based on special-purpose psychological mechanisms.

Psychologists once thought that people and other animals had a few general-purpose learning mechanisms that allowed them to modify any aspect of their phenotypes adaptively. However, a considerable body of empirical evidence indicates that animals are predisposed to learn some things and not others. For example, rats quickly learn to avoid novel foods that make them ill. Moreover, rats' food aversions are based solely on the taste of a food that has made them sick, not the food's size, shape, or color. This learning rule makes sense because rats live in a very wide range of environments where they frequently encounter new foods, and usually forage at night, when it is dark. To determine whether a new food is edible, they taste a small amount and then wait for several hours. If it is poisonous, they become ill, and they do not eat it again. Rats may pay attention to the taste of foods instead of to other attributes because it is often too dark to see what they are eating (**Figure 15.1**). However, there are limits to the flexibility of this learning mechanism. There are certain items that rats will never sample, and in this way their diet is rigidly controlled by genes. Moreover, the learning process is not affected equally by all environmental contingencies. For example, rats are affected more by the association of novel tastes with gastric distress than they are with other possible associations.

Natural selection determines the kinds of problems that the brains of particular species are good at solving. To understand the psychology of any species, we must know what kinds of problems its members need to solve in nature.

Our brains may be designed to solve the kinds of problems that our ancestors faced when they lived in small foraging bands.

We know that people lived in small-scale foraging societies for the vast majority of human history (**Figure 15.2**); stratified societies with agriculture and high population density have existed for only a few thousand years (**Figure 15.3**). John Tooby and Leda Cosmides of the University of California, Santa Barbara, argue that complex adaptations like the brain evolve slowly, so our brains are designed for life in foraging societies. They use the term **environment of evolutionary adaptedness (EEA)** to refer to the social, technological, and ecological conditions under which human mental abilities evolved. Tooby and Cosmides and their colleagues envision the EEA as being much like the world of contemporary hunter-gatherers.

People living in foraging groups face certain kinds of problems that affect their fitness. For example, food sharing is an essential part of life in modern foraging groups. Although vegetable foods are typically distributed only to family members, meat is nearly always shared more widely. Food sharing is a form of reciprocal altruism. The big problem with reciprocal altruism is that it is costly to interact with individuals who do not reciprocate. Thus Cosmides and Tooby hypothesized that human cognition should be finely tuned to detect cheaters, and they have accumulated a convincing body of experimental data suggesting that people are very attentive to imbalances in social exchange and violations of social contracts.

As we have seen, there is quite a bit of uncertainty about how early humans lived, and this adds ambiguity to predictions about human psychology based on evolutionary reasoning. Some authorities believe that early members of the genus *Homo* were much like contemporary human foragers. That is, they lived in small bands and subsisted by hunting and gathering. They controlled fire, had home bases, and shared food. They could talk, and they shared cultural beliefs, ideas, and traditions. Other authorities think that the lives of the earliest species of *Homo* were completely unlike those of modern hunter-gatherers. They think that these hominins didn't hunt large game, share food, or have home bases. If early hominins lived like contemporary foragers, then it is reasonable to think that the human brain has evolved to solve

FIGURE 15.2

Evolutionary psychologists believe that the human mind has evolved to solve the adaptive challenges that confront food foragers because this is the subsistence strategy that humans have practiced for most of our evolutionary history.

the kinds of problems that confront modern foragers, such as detecting freeloaders in social exchange. On the other hand, if lifeways that characterize contemporary foragers did not emerge until 40 kya, then there might not have been enough time for selection to assemble specialized psychological mechanisms to manage the challenges that foragers face, such as food sharing.

Evolved psychological mechanisms cause human societies to share many universal characteristics.

Much of anthropology (and other social sciences) is based on the assumption that human behavior is not effectively constrained by biology. People have to obtain food, shelter, and other resources necessary for their survival and reproduction. But beyond that, human behavior is unconstrained.

But this assumption is not very plausible from an evolutionary perspective. It is likely that evolved mechanisms in the human brain channel the evolution of human societies and human culture, making some outcomes much more likely than others. So the right question is, What kinds of mental mechanisms do humans have? We are likely to share some mental mechanisms with other animals, but we may also have certain mental mechanisms that differentiate us from other creatures. In the discussion that follows, we examine two examples of cognitive mechanisms that are found in all human societies: inbreeding avoidance and mate preferences.

FIGURE 15.3

Indigenous peoples of the Mississippi Delta constructed these mound structures 2,500 to 1,300 years ago. Monumental architecture like this is based on the ability of one group of people to control the labor of others, a signal of social stratification.

Inbreeding Avoidance

The offspring of genetically related parents have lower fitness than the offspring of unrelated parents do.

Geneticists refer to matings between relatives as **inbred matings** and contrast them with **outbred matings** between unrelated individuals. The offspring of inbred matings are much more likely to be homozygous for deleterious recessive alleles than are the offspring of outbred matings. As a consequence, inbred offspring are less robust and have higher mortality than the offspring of outbred matings. In Chapter 14, we discussed a number of genetic diseases, such as PKU, Tay-Sachs disease, and cystic fibrosis that are caused by a recessive gene. People who are heterozygous for such deleterious recessive alleles are completely unaffected, but people who are homozygous suffer severe, often fatal consequences. Recall that such alleles occur at low frequencies in most human populations. However, there are many loci in the human genome. Thus even though the frequency of deleterious recessives at each locus is very small, geneticists have estimated that each person carries the equivalent of two to five lethal recessives. Mating with close relatives is deleterious because it greatly increases the chance that both partners will carry a deleterious recessive allele at the same locus. If inbreeding is deleterious, then we might expect natural selection to favor behavioral adaptations that reduce the chance of inbreeding.

Mating between close relatives is very rare among nonhuman primates.

Remember from Chapter 6 that in all species of nonhuman primates, members of one or both sexes leave their natal groups near the time of puberty. Adult males do not often remain in groups long enough to be able to mate with their own daughters. It is very likely that dispersal is an adaptation to prevent inbreeding. In principle,

FIGURE 15.4

Female chimpanzees avoid mating with closely related males. Although mothers have close and affectionate relationships with their adult sons, matings between mothers and sons are quite uncommon.

primates could remain in natal groups and simply avoid mating with close kin. However, this would limit the number of potential mates and might be unreliable if there were much uncertainty about paternity.

Natural selection has provided at least some primates with another form of protection against inbreeding: a strong inhibition against mating with close kin. In matrilineal macaque groups, some males acquire high rank and mate with adult females before they emigrate. However, matings among maternal kin are extremely uncommon.

Experimental studies conducted by Wendy Saltzman of the University of California, Riverside, and her colleagues suggest that reproductive inhibition in callitrichids is due partly to inbreeding aversion. Young females housed with their mothers and fathers do not reproduce; but when fathers are replaced with unrelated males, both mothers and daughters breed. Adult female chimpanzees often have opportunities to mate with their fathers (**Figure 15.4**). More than 40 years of research at Gombe Stream National Park indicate that, in fact, they rarely do. Female chimpanzees seem to have a general aversion to mating with males much older than they are, and males seem to be generally uninterested in females much younger than themselves. These mechanisms may protect females from mating with their fathers, and vice versa.

Humans rarely mate with close relatives.

During the first half of the twentieth century, cultural anthropologists fanned out across the world to study the lives of exotic peoples. Their hard and sometimes dangerous work has given us an enormous trove of information about the spectacular variety of human lifeways. They found that domestic arrangements vary greatly across cultures: Some groups are polygynous, some monogamous, and a few polyandrous. Some people reckon descent through the female line and are subject to the authority of their mother's brother. In some societies, married couples live with the husband's kin, in others they live with the wife's kin, and in some they set up their own households. Some people must marry their mother's brothers' children; others are not allowed to do so.

In all of this variety of domestic arrangements, there is not a single ethnographically documented case of a society in which brothers and sisters regularly marry, or one in which parents regularly mate with their own children. The only known case of regular brother–sister mating comes from census data collected by Roman governors of Egypt from 20 to 258 C.E. From the 172 census returns that have survived, it is possible to reconstruct the composition of 113 marriages: 12 were between full siblings and 8 between half siblings. These marriages seem to have been both legal and socially approved, as both prenuptial agreements and wedding invitations survive.

The pattern for more distant kin is much more variable. Some societies permit both sex and marriage with nieces and nephews or between first cousins; other societies prohibit sex and marriage among even distant relatives. Moreover, the pattern of mating prohibitions in many societies does not conform to genetic categories. For example, even distant kin on the father's side may be taboo in a given society, while maternal cousins may be the most desirable marriage partners in that same society. Sometimes the rules about who can have sex are different from the rules governing who can marry.

Adults are not sexually attracted to the people with whom they grew up.

The fact that inbreeding avoidance is very common among primates suggests that our human ancestors probably also had psychological mechanisms preventing them from mating with close kin. These psychological mechanisms would disappear during human evolution only if they were selected against. However, mating with close

CHAPTER 15: EVOLUTION AND HUMAN BEHAVIOR

relatives is highly deleterious in humans, as it is in other primates. Thus both theory and data predict that modern humans will have psychological mechanisms that reduce the chance of close inbreeding, at least in the small-scale societies in which human psychology was shaped.

There is evidence that such psychological mechanisms exist. In the late nineteenth century, the Finnish sociologist Edward Westermarck speculated that childhood propinquity stifles desire. By this he meant that people who live in intimate association as small children do not find each other sexually attractive as adults. A number of lines of evidence provide support for Westermarck's hypothesis:

- *Taiwanese minor marriage.* Until recently, an unusual form of marriage was widespread in China. In **minor marriages**, children were betrothed and the prospective bride was adopted into the family of her future husband during infancy. There, the betrothed couple grew up together like brother and sister. According to Taiwanese informants interviewed by Arthur Wolf, an anthropologist at Stanford University, the partners in minor marriages found each other sexually unexciting. Sexual disinterest was so great that fathers-in-law sometimes had to beat the newlyweds to convince them to consummate their marriage. Wolf's data indicate that minor marriages produced about 30% fewer children than other arranged marriages did (**Figure 15.5a**) and were much more likely to end in separation or divorce (**Figure 15.5b**). Infidelity was also more common in minor marriages. When modernization reduced parental authority, many young men and women who were betrothed in minor marriages broke their engagements and married others.

- *Kibbutz age-mates.* Before World War II, many Jewish immigrants to Israel organized themselves into utopian communities called *kibbutzim* (plural of **kibbutz**). In these communities, children were raised in communal nurseries, and they lived intimately with a small group of unrelated age-mates from infancy to adulthood.

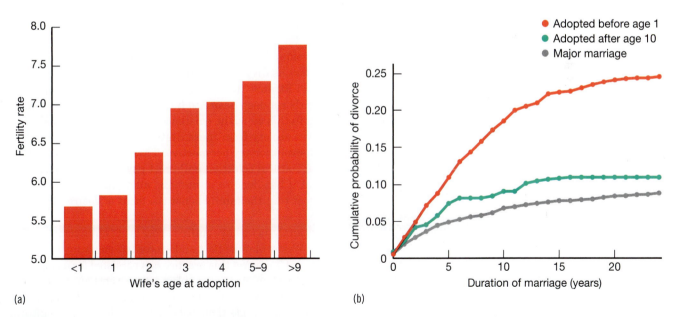

(a)

(b)

FIGURE 15.5

In minor marriages, the age of the wife when she arrives in her future husband's household (age at adoption) affects both fertility and the likelihood of divorce. (a) The fertility of women adopted at young ages is depressed. (b) The younger a woman is when she arrives in her husband's household, the less likely it is that the marriage will survive.

The ideology of the kibbutzim did not discourage sexual experimentation or marriage by children in such peer groups, but neither occurred. The Israeli sociologist Joseph Sepher, himself a kibbutznik, collected data on 2,769 marriages in 211 kibbutzim. Only 14 of them were between members of the same peer group, and in all of these cases one partner joined the peer group after the age of six. From data collected in his own kibbutz, Sepher found no instances of premarital sex among members of the same peer group.

- *Third-party attitudes toward incest.* As you may have realized already, aversions to inbreeding extend beyond our attitudes toward our own mating behavior to include strong beliefs about appropriate mating behavior by other individuals. We are disgusted not only by the idea of having sex with our parents or our own children but also by the idea of other people having sex with their children. Daniel Fessler of the University of California, Los Angeles, and Carlos Navarrete, now at Michigan State University, think that these kinds of third-party aversions are a form of "egocentric empathy." Westermarck hypothesized that co-residence during childhood generates sexual aversions to particular partners. If that is the case, then the extent of exposure to siblings of the opposite sex during childhood might also be linked to the strength of feelings about one's own behavior and the strength of feelings about the behavior of others. These predictions have been tested in experimental studies conducted by Fessler and Navarette and by another team led by Debra Lieberman, now at the University of Miami. Both sets of researchers asked subjects (university undergraduates) to contemplate hypothetical cases of consensual sibling incest involving adults. The results from both studies largely confirmed Westermarck's hypothesis. Those who had grown up with opposite-sex siblings had stronger negative responses to the hypothetical scenario than those who had not. Moreover, women generally had stronger aversive responses to the hypothetical scenario than men did.

Evolutionary interpretations of inbreeding avoidance differ sharply from influential theories about incest and inbreeding avoidance in psychology and cultural anthropology.

Incest and inbreeding avoidance play a central role in many influential theories of human society. Thinkers as diverse as Sigmund Freud (the founder of psychoanalysis) and Claude Lévi-Strauss (the father of structuralist anthropology) have asserted that people harbor a deep desire to have sex with members of their immediate family. According to this view, the existence of culturally imposed rules against incest is all that saves society from these destructive passions. This view is not very plausible from an evolutionary perspective. There are compelling theoretical reasons to expect that natural selection will erect psychological barriers to incest and good evidence that it has done so in humans and other primates. Both theory and observation suggest that the family is not the focus of desire; it's a tiny island of sexual indifference.

However, the evolutionary analysis we have outlined here is not quite complete. For example, we might expect the Westermarck effect and egocentric empathy to produce an aversion to minor marriage in China. Yet this practice has persisted for a long time. It is possible that psychological mechanisms are supplemented or perhaps superseded by conscious reasoning. People in many societies believe that incest leads to sickness and deformity, and their beliefs may guide their behavior and shape their cultural practices. Finally, it seems clear that attitudes about incest are not based solely on the deleterious effects of inbreeding. If they were, then all societies would have the same kinds of rules about who can have sexual relationships. Instead, we find considerable variation. For example, some societies encourage first cousins to marry, while others prohibit them from doing so.

Human Mate Preferences

Marry

Children—(if it Please God)—Constant companion, (& friend in old age) who will feel interested in one,—object *to be* beloved and played with. better than a dog anyhow.—Home, & someone to take care of house—Charms of music & female chit-chat.—These things good for one's health.—*but terrible loss of time.*—

My God, it is intolerable to think of spending one's whole life, like a neuter bee, working, working, & nothing after all.—No, no won't do.—Imagine living all one's day solitary in smoky dirty London house.—Only picture to yourself nice soft wife on a sofa with good fire, & books, & music perhaps—Compare this vision with the dingy reality of Grt. Marlbro St.

Marry—Mary—Marry Q.E.D.

Not Marry

Freedom to go where one liked—choice of Society & *little of it.*—Conversation of clever men at clubs—Not forced to visit relatives, & to bend in every trifle.—to have the expense & anxiety of children—perhaps quarelling—**Loss of time.**—cannot read in the Evenings—fatness & idleness—Anxiety & responsibility—less money for books & c—if many children forced to gain one's bread.—(But then it is very bad for ones health to work too much)

Perhaps my wife wont like London; then the sentence is banishment & degradation into indolent, idle fool (Burkhardt and Smith, 1986, p. 444).

FIGURE 15.6

Charles Darwin courted and married his cousin Emma Wedgwood. This portrait was painted when Emma was 32, just after the birth of her first child.

These are the thoughts of 29-year-old Charles Darwin, recently returned from his five-year voyage on the HMS *Beagle*. Soon after writing these words, Darwin married his cousin Emma, the daughter of Josiah Wedgwood, the progressive and immensely wealthy manufacturer of Wedgwood china (**Figure 15.6**). By all accounts, Charles and Emma were a devoted couple. Emma bore 10 children and nursed Charles through countless bouts of illness. Charles toiled over his work and astutely managed his investments, parlaying his modest inheritance and his wife's more substantial one into a considerable fortune.

Darwin's frank reflections on advantages and disadvantages of marriage were very much those of a conventional, upper-class Victorian gentleman. But people of every culture, class, and gender have faced the problem of choosing mates. Sometimes people choose their own mates, and other times parents arrange their children's marriages. But everywhere, people care about the kind of person they will marry.

Evolutionary theory generates some testable predictions about the psychology of human mate preferences.

For much of their evolutionary history, humans have lived in foraging societies. The adaptive challenges that men and women face in these kinds of societies are likely to have shaped their mating strategies. For women, this might have meant choosing men who would provide them with access to resources. Recall from Chapter 11 that there is considerable interdependence between men and women in foraging societies. Women mainly gather plant foods, and men are mainly responsible for hunting. Women's consumption exceeds their production for much of their reproductive life. Children do not begin to provide substantial amounts of their own food until they reach adolescence. Thus, for women, it might be important to choose a mate who will be a good provider.

Men's reproductive success depends largely on the fertility of their partners, so it is plausible that selection favored men who focused on this attribute. Women's fertility is highest when they are in their 20s and declines to zero when women reach

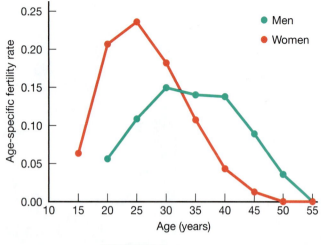

FIGURE 15.7

FIGURE 15.7

Age-specific fertility rates give the probability of producing a child at particular ages. !Kung women have their first child between the ages of 15 and 19, and the highest fertility rate in their 20s. Women's fertility falls to zero by age 50. !Kung men do not begin to reproduce until their early 20s, and their fertility rates are fairly stable in their 30s and 40s, dropping to low levels in their 50s.

menopause, at about 50 years of age (**Figure 15.7**). Thus selection should have favored men who chose young and healthy mates. Because picture IDs were scarce in the Pleistocene, selection may have shaped men's psychology so that they are attracted to cues that reliably predict youth and health, such as smooth skin, good muscle tone, symmetrical features, and shiny hair.

For both men and women, it is important to find mates that they can get along with. Human children depend on their parents for a remarkably long time. During this period, both parents provide food and shelter for their children. Because parental investment lasts for many years, adaptive thinking predicts that both men and women will value traits in their partners that help them sustain their relationships. Both are likely to value personal qualities like compatibility, agreeableness, reliability, and tolerance.

If evolution has shaped the psychology of human mating strategies, then we would expect to find common patterns across societies.

David Buss, a psychologist at the University of Texas at Austin, was among the first to test the evolutionary logic underlying human mating preferences and tactics. Buss enlisted colleagues in 33 countries to administer standardized questionnaires about the qualities of desirable mates to more than 10,000 men and women. Most of the data were collected in Western industrialized nations, and most samples represent university students in urban populations within those countries (**Figure 15.8**). In the questionnaires, people were asked to rate a number of traits of potential mates—good looks, good financial prospects, compatibility, and so on—according to their desirability. Respondents were also asked about their preferred age at marriage and the preferred age difference between themselves and their spouse.

People generally care most about the personal qualities of their mates.

Men and women around the world rate mutual attraction or love above all other traits (**Table 15.1**). The next most highly desired traits for both men and women are

FIGURE 15.8

People in 33 countries (*red*) were surveyed about the qualities of an ideal mate.

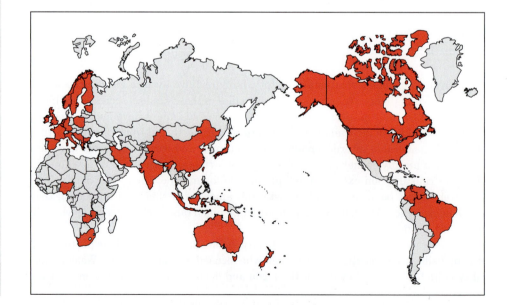

CHAPTER 15: EVOLUTION AND HUMAN BEHAVIOR

TABLE 15.1

Trait	Ranking of Trait by:	
	Males	**Females**
Mutual attraction/love	1	1
Dependable character	2	2
Emotional stability and maturity	3	3
Pleasing disposition	4	4
Good health	5	7
Education and intelligence	6	5
Sociability	7	6
Desire for home and children	8	8
Refinement, neatness	9	10
Good looks	10	13
Ambition and industriousness	11	9
Good cook and housekeeper	12	15
Good financial prospect	13	12
Similar education	14	11
Favorable social status or rating	15	14
Chastity*	16	18
Similar religious background	17	16
Similar political background	18	17

Men and women from more than 33 countries around the world (shown in Figure 15.8) were asked to rate the desirability of a variety of traits in prospective mates. The rankings of the values assigned to each trait, on average, are given here. Subjects were asked to rate each trait from 0 (irrelevant or unimportant) to 3 (indispensable). Thus, high ranks (low numbers) represent traits that were generally thought to be important.

*Chastity was defined in this study as having no sexual experience before marriage.

personal attributes, such as dependability, emotional stability and maturity, and a pleasing disposition. Good health is the fifth most highly rated trait for men and the seventh for women. Good financial prospect is the thirteenth most highly rated trait by men and the twelfth by women. Good looks are rated tenth by men and thirteenth by women. It is interesting, and somewhat surprising, that neither sex seems to value chastity highly. Perhaps this is because people were asked to evaluate the desirability of sexual experience before marriage (that is, virginity), not fidelity during their marriage.

Men and women show the differences in mate preferences predicted by parental investment theory.

Even though the ranking of the scores assigned to these traits is similar for men and women, there are consistent differences between men and women in how desirable they think these traits are. Buss found that people's sex had the greatest effect on their ratings of the following traits: "good financial prospect," "good looks," "good cook and housekeeper," "ambition and industriousness." As the evolutionary model predicts, women value good financial prospects and ambition more than men do, and men value good looks more than women do. Gender has a smaller and somewhat less uniform effect on ratings of chastity. In 23 populations, men value chastity significantly more than women do; in the remaining populations, men and women value chastity equally. There are no populations in which women value chastity significantly more than men do.

Men and women differ about the preferred ages of their partners.

Evolutionary reasoning suggests that men's mate preferences will be strongly influenced by the reproductive potential of prospective mates. Therefore, we would predict men to choose mates with high fertility or high reproductive value. By the same token, we would expect women to be less concerned about their partner's age than about their ability to provide resources for them and their offspring.

A considerable amount of evidence suggests that men consistently seek and marry partners who are younger than they are and that women seek and marry partners somewhat older than themselves. Douglas Kenrick of Arizona State University and Richard Keefe surveyed marriage records in two cities in the United States and in a small Philippine village, as well as personal advertisements in the United States, northern Europe, and India. In all of these cases, they found a similar pattern. As men get older, the age difference between them and their wives increases. Thus young men marry women slightly younger than themselves, and older men marry partners considerably younger than themselves. As women get older, there is little change in the age difference between them and their husbands. Newspaper advertisements in which advertisers specify the range of ages for prospective mates demonstrate a very similar pattern (**Figure 15.9**). Henry Harpending of the University of Utah has found very similar patterns among the Herero, a pastoralist group in the northern Kalahari Desert of Botswana, in which marriages are unstable, divorce is common, and women have a considerable amount of financial independence.

Although men advertise for and marry progressively younger women, the actual age of their partners does not seem to fit the prediction that males will choose fertile mates. Older men seek and marry women who are considerably younger than themselves but not women who are young enough to produce children. Men's choices about who to date and who to marry may be driven by multiple factors, not just women's fertility. Older men may desire younger women, but they may also want to find someone who shares their taste in music, has similar goals in life, and so on. Furthermore, men's preferences and their marriages may reflect their own attractiveness in the mating market. Older men may want young women but know they will have to settle for partners closer to their own age. Together, the data taken from personal advertisements and from marriage records reflect individual desires tempered by pragmatism.

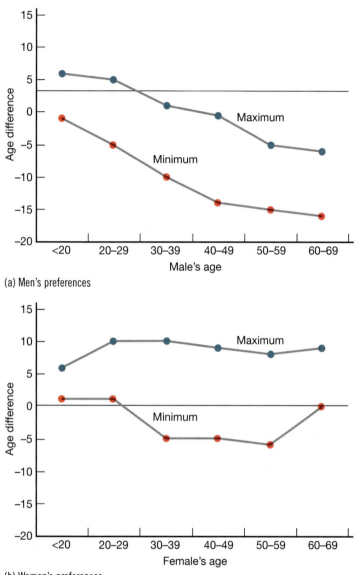

(a) Men's preferences

(b) Women's preferences

FIGURE 15.9

Mate preferences by sex. (a) In personal advertisements, all but the youngest men state preferences for women who are younger than themselves. As men get older, the age difference between themselves and preferred mates increases. (b) Women typically prefer men who are somewhat older than themselves, and these preferences remain the same as women get older.

Men and women vary about the preferred number of partners.

In addition to having different criteria for the ideal mate, men and women may also have different mating tactics. Because women devote nine months to each pregnancy and nurse their children for even longer, selection is likely to have favored a psychology that makes them cautious about involvement in sexual relationships that would expose them to the risks of pregnancy. (Of course, nowadays birth control reduces the risk of pregnancy for women, but effective methods of contraception are a recent innovation. Human mating tactics evolved in a world without such technology.) Women are likely to prefer stable, committed relationships with men who are willing and able to help care for them and their offspring. Because the costs of conception are borne mainly by women, men can afford to be more flexible in their mating tactics, and to have a psychology that makes them more open to mating opportunities that do not involve long-term commitments. However, we would expect men to form committed long-term relationships because children that receive care from both parents are more likely to thrive.

David Schmitt of Bradley University has coordinated a comprehensive cross-cultural study of human sexuality, sampling people, mainly university students, in 62 countries around the world. In this survey, people were asked about the traits that they valued in potential mates and were also asked about various aspects of their mating tactics. For example, they were asked the number of sexual partners they would like to have over various time intervals ranging from 6 months to 30 years. For all time intervals, men reported preferring a larger number of sexual partners than women did (**Figure 15.10**). This difference seems to be common cross-culturally (**Figure 15.11**), although the magnitude of the sex difference and the number of partners desired vary considerably.

Differences in mating tactics may contribute to misunderstandings between men and women.

When you meet someone you're attracted to, you probably feel excitement and some degree of uncertainty. Some of this uncertainty arises because you are not sure whether the other person is as attracted to you as you are to him or her. And some of this uncertainty arises because you don't know what the other person's intentions are. Martie Haselton of the University of California, Los Angeles, and David Buss have pointed out that this uncertainty generates different kinds of problems for men and women. To understand the logic of their argument, let's think about what kinds of mistakes you could make in deciding whether someone was attracted to you. A false positive arises if you think the other person is attracted to you, when in fact that's not

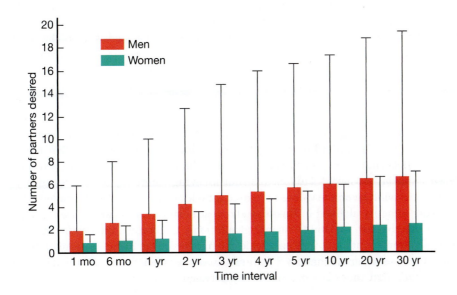

FIGURE 15.10

Men typically prefer a larger number of sexual partners across all time intervals than women do. Note, however, that there is also more variability in men's preferences than in women's preferences. This means that some men prefer large numbers of partners, while others prefer many fewer partners.

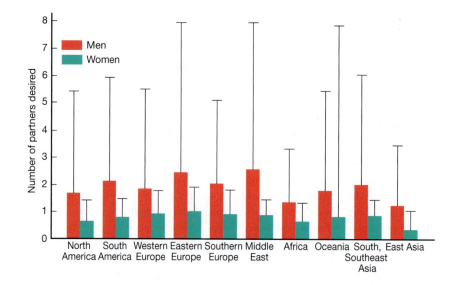

the case. A false negative occurs if you think the other person doesn't like you, when he or she really does. Both kinds of errors are costly: A false positive could lead you to make an overture that would be rejected ("Sorry, I need to wash my hair"); a false negative could prevent you from making any overture at all (and you will have nothing better to do than wash your hair).

Now think about the kinds of errors that can arise when there is uncertainty about the other person's intentions about the relationship. Haselton and Buss hypothesize that natural selection will predispose men and women to bias their judgments about new partners' sexual intentions and commitment in different ways. Women, who could become pregnant, are expected to be cautious about their partner's intentions, and as a result they will make more false negative errors than false positive errors. Put another way, evolutionary reasoning predicts that women are more likely to underestimate men's commitment than to overestimate it. Men, who are interested in pursuing both short-term and long-term relationships, are expected to minimize the chance of missing sexual opportunities, and as a result they will make more false positive errors than false negative errors. That is, they are likely to overestimate women's sexual interest more often than they underestimate it.

Haselton and Buss have conducted a number of different studies on college students in the United States to test this hypothesis. They have asked men and women to evaluate sexual intent and commitment in members of their own sex and the opposite sex, to imagine how they would interpret various kinds of signals directed to themselves (for example, holding hands, declaring love), and to recall instances when their own intentions were misunderstood by members of the opposite sex. The results conform to Haselton and Buss's predictions: Men tend to overestimate women's sexual intent, and women tend to underestimate men's interest in commitment (**Figure 15.12**).

Culture predicts people's mate preferences better than gender does.

Both of the large cross-cultural data sets reveal considerable variation from country to country. Buss and his colleagues found that the country of residence has a greater effect than gender on variation in all of the 18 traits in Table 15.1, except for "good financial prospect." This means that knowing where a person lives tells you more about what he or she values in a mate than knowing the person's gender. Of the 18 traits, chastity (defined in Buss's study as no sexual experience before marriage) shows the greatest variability among populations. In Sweden, men rate chastity at 0.25, and women rate it at 0.28 on a scale of 0 (irrelevant) to 3 (indispensable). In contrast, Chinese men rate chastity 2.54, and Chinese women rate it 2.61 (**Figure 15.13**). This means that there is more similarity between men and women from the same population than there is among members of each sex from different populations.

This result illustrates an important point: evolutionary explanations that invoke an evolved psychology and cultural explanations that are based on the social and cultural milieu are not mutually exclusive. The cross-cultural data suggest there are some uniformities in people's mate preferences that are the result of evolved psychological mechanisms. People everywhere want to marry kind, caring, trustworthy people. Men want to marry young women, and women want to marry prosperous men. But this is not the whole story. The cross-cultural data also suggest that human mate preferences are strongly influenced by the cultural and economic environment in which we live. Ultimately, culture also arises out of our evolved psychology, and the cultural variation in mate preferences that the cross-cultural data reveal must, therefore, also be explicable in evolutionary terms. However, the way our evolved psychology shapes the cultures in which we live is complicated and poorly understood, and many interesting questions remain unresolved. Evolutionary theory does not yet explain, for example, why chastity is considered essential in China but unimportant in Sweden.

Evolutionary analyses of mate choice have generated considerable controversy

As we explained at the beginning of this chapter, evolutionary analyses of human behavior generate considerable controversy. Work on human mate choice is no exception. Many critics have complained that evolutionary analyses simply reflect and reinforce Western cultural values, which celebrate women's youth and beauty and men's wealth and power. They argue that researchers are not studying evolved preferences but rather are learning about cultural values and beliefs. In response, advocates of evolutionary analyses argue that the cross-cultural uniformity of mate preferences and mating tactics reflects evolved psychological predispositions that are modified, but not created, by culture.

Other critics have accepted the general logic of evolutionary reasoning but have questioned the methods used to assess mate preferences and mating tactics. Most of the early work was based on pencil-and-paper tests in which people, often undergraduates, were asked about their preferences and their personal experiences. These kinds of data may be biased in a number of ways. For example, cultural norms may lead men to exaggerate their sexual experience and women to understate their desire for sexual variety, even on anonymous surveys.

Social Consequences of Mate Preferences

You might wonder how people's mate preferences influence their actual decisions and choices about marriage partners. In this section, we describe the findings from one ethnographic study suggesting that these kinds of preferences actually influence people's behavior in social situations and, consequently, shape the societies in which they live.

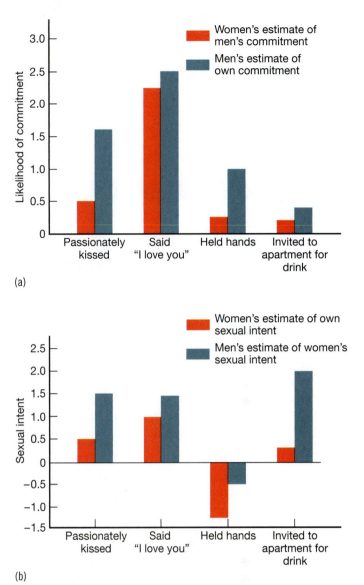

(a)

(b)

FIGURE 15.12

Men and women were asked to estimate how they would interpret particular courtship signals by members of the opposite sex and how they would rate the same signals by members of their own sex, using a scale from +3 (very likely) to −3 (very unlikely). (a) Men and women estimated the extent of commitment implied by a number of different courtship signals. Women tended to underestimate men's interest in commitment relative to men's own estimates of their interest in commitment. (b) Men and women estimated the likelihood of sexual intent implied by the same signals. Men tended to overestimate women's sexual intent relative to women's perceptions of their own intent.

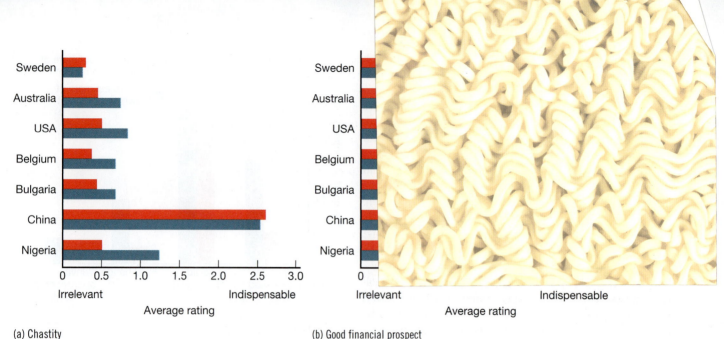

(a) Chastity

Sweden, Australia, USA, Belgium, Bulgaria, China, Nigeria

0   0.5   1.0   1.5   2.0   2.5   3.0
Irrelevant   Indispensable
Average rating

(b) Good financial prospect

Sweden, Australia, USA, Belgium, Bulgaria, China, Nigeria

0
Irrelevant   Indispensable
Average rating

FIGURE 15.13

Culture accounts for substantial variation in mate preferences. The average ratings given by men and women in several countries surveyed are shown for (a) the trait with the highest interpopulation variability ("chastity") and (b) the trait with the lowest interpopulation variability ("good financial prospect").

FIGURE 15.14

These Kipsigis women are eligible for marriage. Their fathers will negotiate with the fathers of their prospective husbands over bridewealth.

Kipsigis Bridewealth

Evolutionary theory explains marriage patterns among the Kipsigis, a group of East African pastoralists.

Among the Kipsigis, a group of Kalenjin-speaking people who live in the Rift Valley province of Kenya, women usually marry in their late teens (**Figure 15.14**), men usually marry for the first time when they are in their early 20s, and it is common for men to have several wives—a practice called polygyny. As in many other societies, the groom's father makes a **bridewealth** payment to the father of the bride at the time of marriage. The payment, tendered in livestock and cash, compensates the bride's family for the loss of her labor and gives the groom rights to her labor and the children she bears during her marriage. The amount of the payment is settled through protracted negotiations between the father of the groom and the father of the bride. The average bridewealth in the 1980s consisted of six cows, six goats or sheep, and 800 Kenyan shillings. This is about one-third of the average man's cattle holdings, one-half of his goat and sheep herd, and two months' wages for men who hold salaried positions. Because men marry polygynously, there is competition over eligible women. Often the bride's father entertains several competing marriage offers before he chooses a groom for his daughter. The prospective bride and groom have little voice in the decisions their fathers make.

Monique Borgerhoff Mulder, an anthropologist at the University of California, Davis, reasoned that Kipsigis bridewealth payments would provide a concrete index of the qualities that each party values in prospective spouses. The groom's father is likely to prefer a bride who will bear his son many healthy children. His bridewealth offer is expected to reflect the potential reproductive value of the prospective bride. The groom's father is also expected to prefer that his son marry a woman who will devote her labor to his household. Kipsigis women who remain near their own family's households are likely to be called on to help their mothers with the harvest and to assist their mothers in childbirth. Thus the groom's father may prefer a woman whose natal family is distant from his son's household. The bride's father is likely to have a different perspective on the negotiations. Because wealthy men can provide their wives with larger plots of land to farm and more resources, we would expect the bride's father to prefer that his daughter marry a relatively wealthy man. At the same time, because the bride's family will be deprived of her labor and assistance if she moves far away from their land, the bride's father is likely to prefer a groom who lives nearby. The fathers of the bride and groom are expected to weigh the costs and benefits of prospective unions in their negotiations over bridewealth payments. For example, although the bride's father may prefer a high bridewealth payment, he may settle for a lower payment if the groom is particularly desirable. In order to determine whether these preferences affected bridewealth payments, Borgerhoff Mulder recorded the number of cows, sheep, and goats as well as the amount of money that each groom's family paid to the bride's family.

Plump women whose menarche occurred at an early age fetched the highest bridewealth payments.

Borgerhoff Mulder found that bridewealth increased as the bride's age at the time of **menarche** (her first menstruation) decreased (**Figure 15.15**). That is, the highest bridewealths were paid for the women who were youngest when they first menstruated. Among the Kipsigis, age at menarche is a reliable index of women's reproductive potential. Kipsigis women who reach menarche early have longer reproductive life spans, higher annual fertility, and higher survivorship among their offspring than women who mature at later ages.

Borgerhoff Mulder wondered how a man assessed his prospective bride's reproductive potential because men often do not know their bride's exact age, nor her age at reaching menarche. One way to be sure of a woman's ability to produce children would be to select one who had already demonstrated her fertility by becoming pregnant or producing a child. However, bridewealth payments for such women were typically lower than bridewealth payments for women who had never conceived. Instead, bridewealth payments were associated with the physical attributes of women. Brides who were considered by the Kipsigis to be plump commanded significantly higher bridewealth payments than brides considered to be skinny. The plumpness of prospective brides may be a reliable correlate of the age at menarche because menarcheal age is determined partly by body weight. Plumpness may also be valued because a woman's ability to conceive is related to her nutritional status.

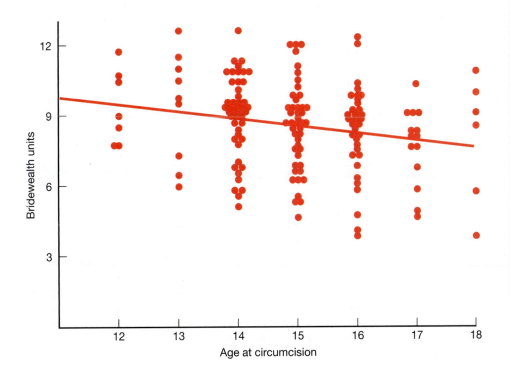

FIGURE 15.15

Kipsigis girls who mature early fetch larger bridewealth payments than older girls do. Among the Kipsigis, girls undergo circumcision (removal of the clitoris) within a year of menarche. The largest bridewealths were paid for the girls who underwent menarche and circumcision at the youngest ages. Bridewealth is transformed into standardized units to account for the fact that the value of livestock varies over time.

Bridewealth payments are also related to the distance between the bride's home and the groom's home; the farther she moves, the less likely she is to provide help to her mother, and the higher the bridewealth payment will be. However, there is no relationship between the wealth of the father of the groom and the bridewealth payment. The bride's father does not lower the bridewealth payment to secure a wealthy husband for his daughter. Although this finding was unexpected, Borgerhoff Mulder suggested that it may be related to the fact that differences in wealth among the Kipsigis are unstable over time. A wealthy man who has large livestock herds may become relatively poor if his herds are raided, decimated by disease, or diverted to pay for another wife. Although land is not subject to these vicissitudes, the Kipsigis traditionally have not held legal title to their lands.

How Much Does Evolution Explain about Human Behavior?

The examples and evidence presented in this chapter demonstrate that evolution can help us understand our minds and behavior. In a way, this should not be very surprising. After all, there is no reason to think that the biological cost of mating with close relatives would be different for us than it is for other primates, so it makes sense that humans would avoid inbreeding just as other primates do. It is somewhat more surprising to find that we seem to share some of the proximate mechanisms that reduce inbreeding, such as a deep-seated aversion to mating with individuals with whom we have had close contact early in life. It seems likely that we inherited these mechanisms from the common ancestor of humans and chimpanzees, and they were preserved in both lineages because they served an important adaptive function. While some societies have elaborated on these shared mechanisms, such as adding rules about which relatives can and cannot marry, none allow matings between very close kin. It is interesting to contemplate how a better understanding of evolution might have altered the thinking of both Sigmund Freud and Claude Lévi-Strauss and influenced the intellectual history of the twentieth century.

Evolutionary theory provides insights about many aspects of our behavior, but it is easy to come up with examples of common behavior that seem to contradict evolutionary logic. What possesses someone to parachute out of a plane or devote their lives to helping others? Critics of evolutionary analyses of human behavior are quick to point to such examples, and use them to bolster the argument that evolution has little relevance to contemporary human behavior. In response to such critics, evolutionary psychologists argue that our minds and behavior are adapted for life in the environment of evolutionary adaptedness, not the present world. Our appetites for salt and sugar fat, for example, were shaped in an environment in which these nutrients were scarce, not one in which it is cheap and easy to "super-size me." Similarity, our capacity for friendship and altruism toward unrelated individuals may have been shaped in an environment in which people routinely lived in small groups composed of close kin, and cooperation was favored by kin selection or reciprocity.

But even people living in foraging societies, whose lives most closely resemble the lives of our ancestors in the EEA, are strikingly different than any other creature on Earth. Foraging peoples occupied virtually every terrestrial habitat on the planet. To survive in such a wide range of habitats they needed well-developed cognitive abilities, the ability to devise new solutions to adaptive challenges, and the capacity to acquire knowledge from others. Foragers are also much more cooperative than any other mammal, even those that live in small, close-knit societies. In the final chapter of the book, we consider how evolutionary processes that shaped human cognition and culture have played a role in making humans such distinctive creatures.

Key Terms

environment of evolutionary adaptedness (EEA)
inbred matings
outbred matings
minor marriages
kibbutz
bridewealth
menarche

Study Questions

1. Much of the behavior of all primates is learned. Nonetheless, we have suggested many times that primate behavior has been shaped by natural selection. How can natural selection shape behaviors that are learned?

2. Many of the things that we do are consistent with general predictions derived from evolutionary theory. We love our children, help our relatives, and avoid sex with close kin. But there are also many aspects of the behavior of members of our own society that seem unlikely to increase individual fitness. What are some of these behaviors?

3. In some species of primates, there seems to be an aversion to mating with close kin. The aversion seems to be stronger for females than for males. Why do you think this might be the case? Under what conditions would you expect this gender difference to disappear?

4. In Chapter 6, we said that the reproductive success of most male primates depends on the number of females with which they mate. Here we discussed Buss's argument that a man's reproductive success will depend mainly on the health and fertility of his mate. Why are humans different from most primates? Among what other primate species should we expect males to attend to the physical characteristics of females when choosing mates?

5. Why should men value fidelity in prospective mates more than women should?

6. In Buss's cross-cultural survey, what was the most important attribute in a mate for both men and women? Does this result falsify his evolutionary reasoning?

7. Are Borgerhoff Mulder's observations about the Kipsigis consistent with Buss's cross-cultural results? Explain why or why not.

Further Reading

Barkow, J. H., L. Cosmides, and J. Tooby, eds. 1995. *The Adapted Mind: Evolutionary Psychology and the Generation of Culture.* New York: Oxford University Press.

Barrett, L., Robin Dunbar, and J. Lycett. 2002. *Human Evolutionary Psychology.* Princeton, NJ: Princeton University Press.

Buss, D. 2011. *Evolutionary Psychology: The New Science of the Mind.* 4th ed. London: Pearson.

16

CHAPTER OBJECTIVES

By the end of this chapter you should be able to

- Describe how cumulative cultural adaptation allows humans to evolve more rapidly to a wider range of habitats than other mammal species.

- Understand that different learning mechanisms can sustain cultural traditions.

- Discuss the fact that cultural traditions are common in other species but that cumulative cultural adaptation is very rare.

- Discuss why adaptive modes of cultural learning can lead to maladaptive behavior.

- Compare the pattern and scope of cooperation in humans to that of other mammal species.

- Explain why the pattern and scale of human cooperation are puzzling from an evolutionary perspective.

CULTURE, COOPERATION, AND HUMAN UNIQUENESS

Evolution and Human Culture

Cooperation

Is Human Evolution Over?

As we conclude this book, we turn to a final question: What has made humans a unique species? Some readers will think that this is a trivial question; others, a controversial one. It may seem trivial because every species is unique, just as every snowflake is different from every other snowflake. But others may think the question is controversial because humans are products of the same evolutionary processes that have shaped all other forms of life on the planet. As we have emphasized throughout this book, each one of us is descended from a tiny shrewlike insectivore that lived among the dinosaurs more than a hundred million years ago. That small creature was gradually transformed by natural selection into a monkey-like animal clambering through the Oligocene forests of Africa, then to one of the many Miocene apes, then to a bipedal australopithecine in the woodlands of East Africa 2 mya, and then to the genus *Homo*, which was the first of our ancestors to venture out of Africa, and finally to *Homo sapiens*, the brainy tool-addicted creature that now lives in practically every part of the world. We share approximately 96% of our genome with chimpanzees and bonobos, our physiology and morphology are only slightly modified versions of the standard primate model, and much of our behavior and psychology can be understood in the same terms as the behavior and psychology of other animals. Many would argue that the claim that humans are unique denies our knowledge of our evolutionary origins and obscures our place in nature.

But humans are an outlier in the natural world. Contemporary human biomass (the sum of all our weights) is eight times the biomass of all other wild terrestrial vertebrates combined and equals the biomass of all the more than 14,000 species of ants. This is not just a consequence of agricultural and modern industrial technology. Human hunter-gatherers were outliers in the natural world even before the origin of agriculture. As we learned in Chapter 13, modern humans left Africa about 60,000 years ago and by 12,000 years ago they occupied every terrestrial habitat on Earth except Antarctica and a few remote islands. Their geographical and ecological range was larger than any other creature. As we have seen, most primates are limited to a narrow range of habitats on a single continent. We find chimpanzees in central African forests, baboons in African woodlands and savannas, and capuchins in the forests of Central and South America. The animals with the largest ranges are big predators like wolves and lions, but their ranges are still much smaller than the range of human foragers 12,000 years ago. Foragers were able to accomplish this because they were better at rapidly adapting to a wide range of environments than any other creatures.

Our goal in this chapter is to explain how and why this happened.

One reason humans have become so successful is that we are smarter than other animals. Over the last 2 million years human brains have become about three times the size of chimpanzee brains, and as we saw in Chapter 8, larger brains seem to lead to more complex cognition. We are better at causal reasoning, theory of mind, and other reasoning tasks that help us learn how to solve novel problems. And this would have helped humans make a living in novel environments. However, we want to convince you that while we are smart, we are not nearly smart enough to solve the problems humans need to solve to survive and thrive in such a wide range of habitats. Two more ingredients are essential parts of the human recipe. The first is culture. Unlike other creatures, people can learn from one another in a way that leads to the accumulation of locally adaptive knowledge, tools, and social institutions, and this allows humans to solve adaptive problems that are too hard for individuals to solve on their own. The second ingredient is cooperation. People cooperate far more than any other mammal. This allows for specialization, exchange, and division of labor, which in turn vastly amplify the ability of people to extract resources from their environments. The three Cs—cognition, culture, and cooperation—have made humans a runaway ecological success.

Evolution and Human Culture

Foraging populations solve problems that are beyond the inventive capacity of individuals.

You learned in Chapter 13 that modern people were living on cold grasslands near what is now Moscow by 40 kya, and by 30 kya they were living above the Arctic Circle near the mouth of the Yana River. The people who left Africa 60 kya were tropical foragers living in a hot, dry coastal environment. To adapt to the high Arctic they had to create an entirely new way of life. We don't know very much about the Yana River people, but we do know a lot about the Central Inuit, foragers who lived at about the same latitude in the Canadian Arctic.

The Central Inuit lived in small groups and made a living mainly by hunting and fishing. They depended on a tool kit crammed with complex, highly refined, and well-designed implements. Winter temperatures average about −25°C (−13°F), so survival required warm clothes. The Central Inuit made cleverly designed clothes, mainly from caribou skins, that were both light and warm. To make these kinds of clothes, you need a host of complex skills; you must know how to cure and soften hides, spin thread, carve needles from bone, and cut and stitch well-fitting garments. Even the best clothing is not enough during winter storms; shelter is mandatory. The Central Inuit made snow houses that were so well designed that interior temperatures were about 10°C (50°F).

There is no wood in these environments, so people carved soapstone lamps and filled them with rendered seal fat to light their homes, cook their food, and melt ice for drinking water. During the winter, the Central Inuit hunted seals with multipiece toggle harpoons, mainly by ambushing them at their breathing holes, and moved their camps using dogsleds. During the summer, they used the leister—a three-pronged spear with a sharp central spike and two hinged, backward-facing points—to harvest Arctic char caught in stone weirs (**Figure 16.1**). They also hunted seals and walrus in open water from kayaks. Later in summer and into the fall, the Central Inuit shifted to caribou, which they hunted with sophisticated composite bows made from driftwood and sinew. And these items and technologies are only part of the Central Inuit tool kits.

Having an extensive tool kit, however, is not enough to survive in the Arctic environment; you also need a vast amount of knowledge. You need to know the habits of the animals that you hunt, how to move on ice, how to judge the weather, and where food can be found as the seasons change. You also need social rules and customs that allow groups of people to work together in such difficult conditions.

Do you think that you could acquire all the local knowledge necessary to live in the Arctic on your own? You are smart and probably did well on the SAT. You can probably drive a car, operate a computer, and understand something about physics. So if individual cognition *alone* is the key to the human ability to adapt to a wide range of environments, you should be able to figure out how to survive in the Arctic. This is exactly the way that other animals learn about their environments—they rely mainly on information encoded in their genes and personal experience to figure out how to find food, make shelter, and in some cases make tools.

We're pretty sure you'd fail because this experiment has been repeated many times, and the outcome is almost always the same. We think of it as "the lost European explorer experiment." Over the last couple of centuries, various European explorers have become stranded in unfamiliar habitats. Despite desperate efforts and ample learning time, these hardy men and women suffered or died because they could not figure out how to adapt to the habitat they found themselves in. The Franklin Expedition of 1846 illustrates this point. Sir John Franklin, a Fellow of the Royal Society and an experienced Arctic traveler, set out to find the Northwest Passage and spent two ice-bound winters in the Arctic. Everyone on his team eventually perished from starvation and scurvy (**Figure 16.2**). Their fate was tragic but also instructive. Members of the expedition spent their second winter on King William Island. The Central Inuit have lived around King William Island for at least 700 years, and this area is rich in animal resources. But the British explorers starved because they did not have the necessary local knowledge to make a living. Even though they had the same basic cognitive abilities as the Inuit and they had two years to use those abilities to figure out how to survive, they failed to acquire the skills necessary to subsist in the northern habitat.

Results from this version of the lost European explorer experiment and many others suggest that the technologies of foragers and other relatively "simple" societies are way beyond the inventive capacity of individuals. It's not hard to see why. Kayaks, bows, and dogsleds are complicated artifacts with multiple interacting parts made of many different materials. Working out the best design, or even a workable design, for something like this from scratch is very hard to do. The Inuit could make the tools that they needed and master all of the tasks that they needed to stay alive in the Arctic because they could draw on a vast pool of information that was known by other people in their population. They could gain access to this information by watching them,

FIGURE 16.1

The Inuit used many specialized tools to make a living in the Arctic. Here a man holds a leister, a specialized fishing spear.

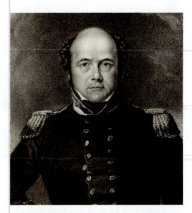

FIGURE 16.2

Sir John Franklin, member of the Royal Society and leader of an expedition lost in the northern reaches of North America.

asking questions, or being taught. That is, unlike other organisms, humans rely on culturally acquired information, and it is the ability to make use of culturally acquired information that has made our species such a spectacular evolutionary success.

Humans rely on the accumulation of culturally acquired information to survive.

For many anthropologists, culture is what makes us human. Each of us is immersed in a cultural milieu that influences the way we see the world, shapes our beliefs about right and wrong, and endows us with the knowledge and technical skills to get along in our environment. Despite the central importance of culture in anthropology, there is little consensus about how or why culture arose in the evolution of the human lineage. In the discussion that follows, we present a view of the evolution of human culture developed by one of us (R. B.) with Peter Richerson at the University of California, Davis. Although we believe strongly in this approach to understanding the evolution of culture, there is not a broad consensus among anthropologists that this or any other particular view of the origins of culture is correct.

There are many different definitions of **culture**. When thinking about the role of culture in human evolution, we think it is useful to define culture as *information acquired by individuals through some form of social learning*. For example, a child may learn that it is important to defer to her elders from watching her parents interact with her grandparents. She may also be corrected if she fails to behave appropriately. When individuals acquire different behaviors as a result of some form of social learning, then we observe cultural variation. The properties of culture are sometimes quite different from the properties of other forms of environmental variation. If people acquire behavior from others through teaching or imitation, then different populations living in similar ecological environments may behave very differently because they acquire different behaviors from members of the previous generation.

Culture is common among other animals but cumulative cultural evolution is rare.

FIGURE 16.3

Capuchin monkeys display a variety of behaviors that seem to vary from group to group. Here, a capuchin monkey at Lomas de Barbudal Biological Reserve in Costa Rica sniffs the hands of its partner.

Over the last few decades, primatologists have documented a range of behavioral variation across groups in a range of species, most notably chimpanzees, orangutans, and capuchins. For example, chimpanzees living on the western shores of Lake Tanganyika raise their arms and clasp hands while they groom, but chimpanzees living on the eastern shore of the lake don't do this. Orangutans in some areas use sticks to pry seeds out of fruits, but orangutans at other sites have not mastered this technique and are unable to extract the seeds. Capuchins show considerable variation in foraging techniques and social conventions. For example, capuchins at some sites participate in long bouts of mutual hand sniffing (**Figure 16.3**), but capuchins at other sites never display this behavior. In some cases, scientists have documented the appearance, diffusion and eventual extinction of behavioral variants. There are also examples of cultural traditions in a wide range of species outside of the primates, such as fish, birds, cetaceans, meerkats, and rodents. These traditions encompass a wide range of ecologically significant behaviors, including food preferences, foraging techniques, and alarm calls.

In human populations, culturally transmitted adaptations can gradually accumulate over many generations (**Figures 16.4** and **16.5**), resulting in complex behaviors that no individual could invent on his or her own. In other animals, there are very few examples of this kind of cumulative cultural evolution. The best-documented case of

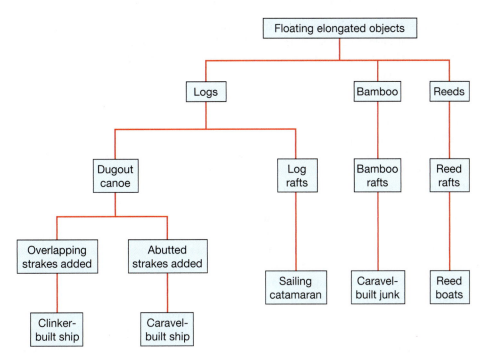

FIGURE 16.4

We can trace the development of certain technological innovations through time. In China, the first boats were elongated structures that floated on the water. Some were made of logs, others of bamboo or reeds. Floating logs were transformed into canoes with the addition of a keel. Other types of ships, including Chinese junks, have a square hull and no keel.

(a)

(b)

FIGURE 16.5

Bamboo rafts (a) may have been the precursors of the great Chinese junks (b).

cumulative cultural evolution comes from studies of song dialects in song birds, such as cowbirds. Cowbirds lay their eggs in the nests of other bird species (a good trick in itself), so chicks don't hear the songs of their own parents when they are growing up. Once they leave the nests of their foster parents, young birds begin to imitate the songs of cowbirds in the neighboring area. The form of the song in each local population changes gradually over time, and dialect variation among populations can be used to create song trees just as genetic variation can be used to construct gene trees. The songs of whales and other cetaceans seem to evolve in the same way as bird song. This is impressive, but in these cases, cumulative cultural evolution is limited to a single domain, song dialect, and other behaviors are not culturally transmitted. Humans are an outlier in the extent of cumulative cultural evolution.

It is not clear why culture in other species does not accumulate.

Social learning creates traditions because experienced individuals do something (perform a behavior, make a tool, vocalize), and this makes it more likely that naive individuals will do something similar. There are a variety of social learning mechanisms that lead to traditions, and it is useful to think of these as ranging along a continuum. At one end of the continuum there are mechanisms that do not preserve innovations and therefore cannot lead to cumulative cultural evolution. For example, **social facilitation** occurs when the activity of one animal increases the chance that other animals will learn the behavior on their own. Social facilitation could account for the persistence of tool use in the following scenario: Young chimpanzees accompany their mothers while they are foraging. In populations in which females use stones to break open nuts, infants and juveniles spend a lot of time around nuts and hammer stones. Young chimpanzees fool around with stone hammers and anvils until they master the skill of opening the nuts. They do not learn the skill by watching their mothers. This means that if a talented (or lucky) individual finds a way to improve nut cracking, the innovation will not spread to other members of the group.

At the other end of the continuum there are mechanisms that preserve innovations. For example **observational learning** (sometimes called imitation) occurs when naive animals learn how to perform an action by watching the behavior of experienced, skilled animals. If a chimpanzee female invents a new nut-cracking technique, then the innovation will be preserved if her offspring imitate it. Imitation allows innovations to persist because unskilled individuals can acquire novel improved techniques by observing the actions of others. Cumulative cultural evolution may occur if a series of innovations arise, get copied, and spread through the group.

In between social facilitation and observational learning, there are other mechanisms, such as **emulation**. Emulation occurs when naive individuals learn the end state of the behavior (a cracked nut) but not the behavior that generated that end state (pounding with hammer stone). This can lead to the spread of innovations when individuals can learn on their own how to produce the end state, but not if the end state is difficult to achieve. For example, suppose one chimpanzee absconds with a can of tuna from the storage tent at the research camp and manages to open the can using the same hammer-and-anvil technique that she uses to crack open nuts. The innovation (opening tuna cans) could spread once chimpanzees learn the goal (tuna) because the chimpanzees already know how to pound open nuts. However, if a new technique is needed to open the can, say prying open the lid with a sharp stone, then emulation would not preserve the innovation.

Several recent studies suggest that monkeys and apes are capable of a form of observational learning. For example, chimpanzees at Gombe strip the leaves from slender twigs and use the twigs as probes to fish for termites. Elizabeth Lonsdorf, of Franklin and Marshall College, and her colleagues videotaped young chimpanzees while their mothers were fishing for termites. She found that young females watched their mothers carefully as they fished for termites, but young males were considerably less attentive (**Figure 16.6**). Lonsdorf also discovered that not all females used the same

FIGURE 16.6

Young female chimpanzees carefully watch their mothers fish for termites, and they tend to acquire the same kinds of techniques that their mothers use. Males are much less attentive to their mothers and do not match their mother's techniques.

fishing techniques; some females consistently used longer twigs than others. Young females tended to use the same kinds of tools that their mothers used, but young males did not adopt the techniques that their mothers used.

White-faced capuchins also seem to learn some foraging techniques by observation. The monkeys feed on seeds of *Luhea* fruits, which they obtain by pounding the fruits against a hard surface or scrubbing the fruit along a rough surface. The two techniques seem to be equally effective, but adults tend to use one technique or the other, not both. Susan Perry of the University of California, Los Angeles, monitored the development of *Luhea* processing techniques among immature monkeys. She found that the juveniles try out both techniques when they are young but eventually settle on only one. Those that associate most often with pounders tend to adopt the pounding technique and those that associate most with scrubbers tend to adopt the scrubbing technique. Thus capuchins seem to learn *Luhea* foraging techniques through observation.

More evidence of observational learning comes from a set of experiments on captive chimpanzees conducted by Andrew Whiten of the University of St. Andrews and his colleagues. In these experiments, the animals are presented with a task, such as extracting a reward from a box that can be opened in two different ways. Naive chimpanzees in one group observe the behavior of a group member that has been trained to open the box one way; naive chimpanzees in a second group learn a different technique (**Figure 16.7**). Chimpanzees tend to use the technique that they have seen demonstrated, suggesting that they must have learned the technique through imitation. Similar types of experiments provide evidence of social learning in vervet monkeys, capuchin monkeys, and lemurs.

FIGURE 16.7

A young chimpanzee trying to open a box in one of Whiten's experiments.

So why don't chimpanzees make stone tools, bows and arrows, or build canopies over their nests to shelter them from the rain? We are not sure, but there are several possibilities. First, while the naturalistic data and experiments show that chimpanzees and capuchins can learn by observing others, the process is not very accurate. Most copy the behavior of demonstrators, but some don't. Repeated over generations, inaccurate social learning would rapidly degrade the innovations. Second, once chimpanzees have learned one way of getting inside the box, they are not inclined to learn another way, even if it is more efficient. Similarly, capuchins seem to settle on one technique for extracting seeds from *Luhea* fruits. This limits their ability to acquire progressively better skills and technology.

The third factor that may limit the development of complex culture repertoires in chimpanzees and by extension other primates is that chimpanzees do not blindly copy all of the details of behaviors that they observe. Oddly enough, blind copying may be an important requirement for cumulative cultural evolution. In one set of experiments chimpanzees observed human experimenters open the boxes in a way that included irrelevant, nonfunctional behaviors along with those required to get inside the box. Chimpanzees tend to acquire only behaviors necessary to actually open the box. In a parallel experiment conducted with people, the subjects faithfully copy all of the irrelevant behaviors as well as the relevant ones. Faithful copying may be important for cumulative cultural evolution because many of the things that we learn are complicated and difficult to understand. (Why do you need to beat the eggs before adding them to the flour when you make a cake?) If people, like chimpanzees, copied only what they could understand, complicated tools and behavioral routines could not evolve. Doing something because you have seen others do it, even if you don't understand why they did it, may be important. But clearly, this could lead to unfortunate consequences.

Suppose that you are trying to learn how to fletch an arrow. Your mentor stops to scratch an itch or swat away a fly. The learner has to separate these irrelevant actions from the relevant ones. Psychologists George Gergely and Gergely Csibra of the Central European University think that learners can solve this problem only if demonstrators provide cues about which components of the behavior are important and which are not. This need not involve overt verbal instruction; instead demonstrators can use subtle cues like the direction of their gaze, pointing, and so on.

Culture Is an Adaptation

Cumulative cultural adaptation is not a byproduct of intelligence and social life.

Chimpanzees and capuchins are among the world's cleverest creatures. In nature, they use tools and perform many complex behaviors; in captivity, they can be taught very complicated tasks. Chimpanzees and capuchins live in social groups and have ample opportunity to observe the behavior of other individuals, and yet the best evidence suggests that neither chimpanzees nor capuchins make much use of observational learning in their daily lives. Thus the learning mechanisms that allow cumulative cultural adaptation, whatever they are, may not simply be a byproduct of intelligence and opportunities for observing others.

This conclusion suggests, in turn, that the psychological mechanisms that enable humans to learn in a way that gives rise to cumulative cultural evolution are adaptations that have been shaped by natural selection because culture is beneficial (**Figure 16.8**). Of course, this need not be the case. These mechanisms may be byproducts of some other adaptation that is unique to humans, such as language. But given the great importance of culture in human societies, it is important to think about the possible adaptive advantages of culture.

Culture allows humans to exploit a wide range of environments using a universal set of mental mechanisms.

Humans can live in a wider range of environments than other primates because culture allows us to accumulate better strategies for exploiting local environments much more rapidly than genetic inheritance can produce adaptive modifications. Animals like baboons adapt to different environments using various learning mechanisms.

FIGURE 16.8

Infants are prone to spontaneous imitation of the behaviors they observe. Here, a 13-month-old infant flosses her two teeth.

For example, they learn how to acquire and process the food they eat. Baboons in the lush wetlands of the Okavango Delta of Botswana learn how to harvest roots of water plants and how to hunt young antelope. Baboons living in the harsh desert of nearby Namibia must learn how to find water and process desert foods. All such learning mechanisms require prior knowledge about the environment: where to search for food, what strategies can be used to process the food, which flavors are reinforcing, and so on. More detailed and more accurate knowledge allows more accurate adaptation because it allows animals to avoid errors and acquire a more specialized set of behaviors.

In most animals, this knowledge is stored in the genes. Imagine that you captured a group of baboons from the Okavango Delta and moved them to the Namibian desert. It's a very good bet that the first few months would be tough for the baboons, but after a relatively short time, the transplanted group of baboons would probably be hard to tell from their neighbors. They would eat the same foods, have the same activity patterns, and have the same kinds of grooming relationships. The transplanted baboons would become similar to the local baboons because they acquire a great deal of information about how to be a baboon genetically; it is hardwired. Of course, the transplanted baboons would have to learn where to find water, where to sleep, which foods are edible, and which foods are toxic, but they would be able to do this without contact with local baboons because they have a built-in ability to learn these kinds of things on their own.

Human culture allows accurate adaptation to a wider range of environments because *cumulative* cultural adaptation provides more accurate and more detailed information about the local environment than genetic inheritance systems can provide. The Inuit could make kayaks and do all the other things they needed to do to stay alive in the harsh environment of the Arctic because they could make use of a vast pool of useful information stored in the minds of other people in their population. The information contained in this pool is accurate and adaptive because the combination of individual learning and human social learning leads to rapid, cumulative adaptation. Even if most individuals blindly imitate the behavior of others, some individuals may occasionally come up with a better idea, and this will nudge traditions in an adaptive direction. Observational learning preserves the many small nudges and exposes the modified traditions to another round of nudging. This process generates adaptation more quickly than genetic inheritance does. The complexity of cultural tradition can explode to the limits of our capacity to learn them.

Culture can lead to evolutionary outcomes not predicted by ordinary evolutionary theory.

The importance of culture in human affairs has led many anthropologists to conclude that evolutionary thinking has little to contribute to understanding human behavior. They argue that evolution shapes genetically determined behaviors but not behaviors that are learned, and so culture is independent of biology. This argument is a manifestation of the nature–nurture controversy, and we explained at the beginning of the last chapter why this reasoning is flawed. Although many anthropologists have rejected evolutionary thinking about culture, many evolutionists have made the opposite mistake. They reject the idea that culture makes any *fundamental* difference in the way that evolution has shaped human behavior and psychology. If natural selection shaped the genes underlying the psychological machinery that gives rise to human behavior, the machinery must have led to fitness-enhancing behavior, at least in ancestral environments. If the adaptation doesn't enhance fitness in modern environments, that's because our evolved psychology is designed for life in a different kind of world.

We think both sides in this argument are wrong. Humans cannot be understood without the complex interplay between biology and culture. This is because cumulative cultural evolution is rooted in a novel evolutionary trade-off between benefits and costs. Human social learning mechanisms are beneficial because they allow humans to accumulate vast reservoirs of adaptive information over many generations, leading to the cumulative cultural evolution of highly adaptive behaviors and technology. Because this process is much faster than genetic evolution, it allows human populations to develop cultural adaptations to local environments: kayaks in the Arctic and blowguns in the Amazon. The ability to adjust rapidly to local conditions was highly adaptive for early humans because the Pleistocene was a time of extremely rapid fluctuations in world climates. However, the psychological mechanisms that create this benefit come with a built-in cost. Remember that the advantage of learning from others is that it avoids the need for everyone to figure out everything for herself. We can just do what others do. But to get the benefits of social learning, people have to be credulous, generally accepting that other people are doing things in a sensible and proper way.

This credulity helps us learn complicated things, but it also makes us vulnerable to the spread of maladaptive beliefs and behaviors. If everyone in our community believes that it's beneficial to bleed sick people or that it's a good idea to treat corn with lime, we believe that, too. This is how we get wondrous adaptations like kayaks and blowguns. But we have little protection against the perpetuation of maladaptions that somehow arise. Even though the capacities that give rise to culture and shape its content must be (or at least must have been) adaptive on average, the behavior observed in any particular society at any particular time may reflect evolved maladaptations. Examples of these sorts of maladaptations are not hard to find.

Maladaptive beliefs can spread because culture is not acquired just from parents.

The logic of natural selection applies to culturally transmitted information in much the same way that it does to genes. Beliefs compete for our memory and our attention, and not all beliefs are equally likely to be learned or remembered. Beliefs are heritable, often passing from one individual to another without major change. As a result, some beliefs spread, and others are lost. However, the rules of cultural transmission are different from the rules of genetic transmission, so the outcome of selection among beliefs can be different from the outcome of selection on genes. The basic rules of genetic transmission are simple. With some exceptions, every gene that an individual carries in his body is equally likely to be incorporated into his gametes, and the only way that those genes can be transmitted is through his offspring. Thus only genes that increase reproductive success will spread. Cultural transmission is much more complicated. Beliefs are acquired and transmitted throughout an individual's life, and they can be acquired from grandparents, siblings, friends, co-workers, teachers, and even completely impersonal sources such as books, television, and now the Internet.

Most important, ideas and beliefs can spread even if they do not enhance reproductive fitness. If ideas about dangerous hobbies like rock climbing or heroin use spread from friend to friend, these ideas can persist even though they reduce survival and individual reproductive success (**Figure 16.9**). Beliefs about heaven and hell can spread from priest to parishioner, even if the priest is celibate and has no offspring of his own to influence. Moreover, cultural variants may accumulate and be transmitted within groups of people who form clans, fraternities, business firms, religious sects, or political parties. This process can generate groups that are defined by cultural values and traditions, not by genetic relatedness.

Culture is part of human biology, but culture makes human evolution qualitatively different from that of other organisms.

The fact that culture can lead to outcomes not predicted by conventional evolutionary theory does not mean that human behavior has somehow transcended biology. The idea that culture is separate from biology is a popular misconception that cannot withstand scrutiny. Culture is generated from organic structures in the brain that were produced by the processes of evolution. However, cultural transmission leads to

FIGURE 16.9

Cultural evolution may permit the spread of ideas and behaviors that do not contribute to reproductive success. Dangerous sports, such as rock climbing, may be examples of such behaviors.

novel evolutionary processes. Thus to understand the whole of human behavior, evolutionary theory must be modified to account for the complexities introduced by these poorly understood processes.

The fact that culture can lead to outcomes that would not be predicted by conventional evolutionary theory does not mean that ordinary evolutionary reasoning is useless. The fact that there are processes that lead to the spread of risky behaviors like rock climbing does not mean that these are the only processes that influence cultural behavior. In the last chapter we saw that it is likely that many aspects of human psychology have been shaped by natural selection so that people learn to behave adaptively. We love our children and feel strong aversions to mating with close relatives. There is every reason to suspect that these predispositions play an important role in shaping human cultures. As long as this is the case, ordinary evolutionary reasoning will be useful for understanding human behavior.

Cooperation

Humans are more cooperative than other mammals.

Most mammals live solitary lives, meeting only to mate and raise their young. Among social species, cooperation is limited to relatives and, perhaps, small groups of reciprocators. After weaning, individuals acquire virtually all of the food that they eat themselves. There is little division of labor, no trade, and no large-scale conflict. The sick, hungry, and disabled must fend for themselves. The strong take from the weak without fear of sanctions by third parties. Seventeenth-century philosopher Thomas Hobbes (**Figure 16.10**) famously described life in the state of nature as "the warre of all against all." Amend Hobbes to account for nepotism, and his picture of the state of nature is not so far off for most mammals.

In stark contrast, cooperation is an essential component of the economies of all foraging societies. Arizona State University anthropologist Kim Hill illustrates the difference with the following anecdote. Human hunter-gatherers and nonhuman primates both forage for fruit in trees. When a party of chimpanzees comes upon a fruiting tree, they all climb the tree and gather as much fruit as they can. Human hunter-gatherers send a couple of young guys up into the tree to shake the branches so that the fruit falls to the ground where everybody can easily harvest it. The young men are willing to go up into the tree because they know there will be fruit waiting for them when they get down, and this cooperative arrangement allows people to harvest the fruit more efficiently.

This kind of cooperative activity pervades human hunter-gatherer societies. Hill has studied the Aché, a hunter-gatherer group living in the forests of Paraguay for more than 20 years (**Figure 16.11**). Here is a list of the cooperative foraging behaviors he recorded:

> Cuts a trail for others to follow; makes a bridge for others to cross a river; carries another's child; climbs a tree to flush a monkey for another hunter; allows another to shoot at prey when ego has first (best) shot; allows another to dig out an armadillo or extract honey or larva when ego encountered it; yells whereabouts of escaping prey; calls the location of a resource for another individual to exploit while ego continues searching; calls another to come to a pursuit of a peccary, paca, monkey, or coati; waits for others to join a pursuit, thus lowering own return rate; tracks peccaries when ego has no arrows (for other men to kill); carries game shot by another hunter; climbs fruit trees to knock down fruit for others to collect; cuts down palms (for others to take heart or fiber); opens a "window" in a tree to test for palm starch (for others

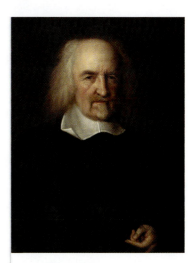

FIGURE 16.10

The English political philosopher Thomas Hobbes.

FIGURE 16.11

The Ache are a group living in Paraguay who lived solely by hunting and gathering until the 1970s and still acquire much of their food by foraging. Here, two Ache women cooperate to extract starch from a palm tree.

to come take); carries the palm fiber others have collected; cuts down fruit trees for others to collect the fruit; brings a bow, arrow, ax, or other tool to another in a pursuit; spends time instructing another on how to acquire a resource; lends bow or ax to another when it could be used by ego; helps to look for another's arrows; prepares or repairs another man's bow and arrows in the middle of a pursuit; goes back on trail to warn others of wasp nest; walks toward other hunters to warn of fresh jaguar tracks or poisonous snakes; removes dangerous obstacles from the trail before others arrive (Hill, 2002, pp. 113–114).

In each case, one individual helps another individual and incurs some cost in doing so. Such helping behavior is not structured by kinship among the Aché. Only a very small percentage of helping behavior is directed toward kin. Men help unrelated men, and women tend to help their husbands. Food produced by cooperative foraging is shared throughout the band.

Human cooperation increases our ability to adapt.

While the members of other mammal species don't engage in the division of labor, trade, mutual aid, and the construction of large-scale capital facilities, there are animals that do all of these things, and they have been spectacular ecological successes and have radiated into a vast range of habitats. Multicellular organisms arose when groups of single-celled creatures evolved specialization and exchange, and multicellular organisms have been able to occupy a dramatically large number of niches. Their success indicates that the benefits of cooperation among cells were present in niches as different as those occupied by plants and animals; ecologies as different as aquatic, terrestrial, and subterranean habitats; and climates ranging from tropical to tundra. Similarly, eusocial insects have a very wide range of lifeways—some ant species herd aphid "cows," protect their herds from predators, and subsist on sweet "honeydew" produced by their carefully tended domesticates. Others are like farmers, carefully tending and fertilizing fungus gardens. Army ants, which have several castes of workers specialized for different tasks, are able to work together to build bridges, defend the colony, and manage traffic. Like humans, the eusocial insects have been a spectacular ecological success. Ants, for example, make up 2% of insect species but more than a third of insect biomass; in tropical forests, ants outweigh all vertebrates combined.

We believe that cooperation has played a similar role in the human expansion across the globe. Specialization is beneficial because it is efficient to subdivide labor among individuals who specialize in one or a few specific tasks. Exchange allows the output of efficient production to be shared. If one individual specializes in building houses, a second in farming, and a third in making music, and they trade their products, all three will typically enjoy better housing, food, and music than if they tried to produce everything themselves. The same goes for mutual aid. When an individual is sick and cannot forage, others can greatly improve her fitness by providing food at relatively small cost to themselves. Cooperative child care can greatly increase the ability of parents to produce food and other resources.

Humans cooperate in large groups of unrelated individuals.

One of the most striking differences between people and other social mammals is the scale on which humans cooperate. In most other mammals, cooperation is limited to small groups of kin and reciprocators. The most striking exception is a spectacularly homely subterranean African rodent called the naked mole rat, which lives in underground colonies numbering about 80 individuals (**Figure 16.12**). Naked mole rat colonies work much like the colonies of ants or termites. There is a single reproducing

FIGURE 16.12

The naked mole rat is a subterranean rodent that lives in large cooperative colonies with a single reproducing female. Individuals within a colony are closely related.

female, and colony members forage cooperatively, maintain the burrow, and defend the colony. The members of a colony are closely related to one another. Other mammals that cooperate in sizable groups, like African wild dogs, are also closely related. Human societies differ from other cooperative species because they are able to mobilize large numbers of *unrelated* individuals for collective enterprises. This is obviously true of modern societies in which government institutions like courts and police regulate behavior. But, it turns out, societies without such institutions can also mobilize large numbers of cooperators.

The joint production of capital facilities, such as roads and bridges, relies on large-scale cooperative behavior. Each worker invests time and labor, but all members of the community will travel on the road or use the bridge to cross the river. In modern societies, contracts enforced by governments mean that workers are guaranteed to be compensated directly. But in small-scale societies, in which workers don't receive wages for their labor or sign legally binding contracts, communities can also organize large-scale construction projects. For example, before the twentieth century, there were massive runs of salmon up the Trinity, Klamath, and other western coastal rivers. The Native American groups living along these rivers constructed large weirs, which act like fences, across the rivers to harvest the salmon as they swam upstream to spawn (**Figure 16.13**). The Yurok constructed a weir across the Klamath River at Kepel. Cutting the wood for this weir required the labor of hundreds of men from several different villages, and the construction involved 70 workers over an extended period. During the 10 days of the salmon run huge amounts of salmon were collected, dried, and shared among members of the tribe.

Warfare is a particularly interesting case of large-scale cooperation for two reasons. First, warfare has played an undeniably important role in human history. Second, our ability to wage war is remarkable because war creates an especially high-stakes collective action problem. Individual warriors risk injury or death, while victorious military actions provide benefits to all group members. People engage in armed conflict with neighboring groups in almost all human societies. In foraging societies, the size of warring groups is typically small, but societies that do not have any formal

FIGURE 16.13

A salmon weir built across the Trinity River in northern California by members of the Hupa tribe in the early part of the twentieth century. The weir remained in place for a short period during the early summer run of king salmon. By blocking the path of the migrating salmon, it allowed the Native Americans to harvest large numbers of salmon using nets. Many people cooperated in constructing the weir and harvesting the salmon.

FIGURE 16.14

The Turkana are a group of nomadic herders who live in northern Kenya.

FIGURE 16.15

The distribution of the size of raiding parties among the Turkana. The horizontal axis gives the number of warriors participating in a raid, and the height of the vertical bars gives the fraction of the sample of raids that had that number of warriors. The average size was about 300 fighters and the largest parties consisted of more than 1,000 individuals. This means that a single individual has only a small effect on the success of the raid.

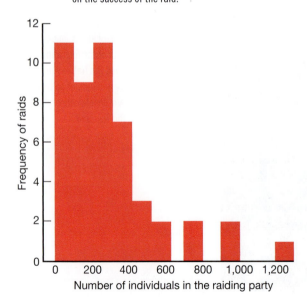

institutions can mobilize sizable war parties under the right circumstances. A recent study of warfare among the Turkana, an African pastoralist society, conducted by Sarah Mathew of Arizona State University, provides a good example.

The Turkana herd cows and sheep in the arid savanna of northwest Kenya (**Figure 16.14**). They live in mobile settlements numbering a few hundred people. The Turkana are divided into approximately 20 territorial sections—geographic regions within which herdsmen from each territory are free to graze. Men also belong to age groups, which are composed of similar-aged men who tend to herd and fight together. There is no recognized political or military authority; no elected officials, official police, or fighting forces. The Turkana frequently engage in armed combat with members of other ethnic groups that live just outside the border of Turkana territory. Victors may acquire livestock to supplement their herds and new grazing land, and they may also deter attacks by other groups. However, going to war has sizable costs for individuals; Mathew's data indicate that warriors have a 1% chance of dying each time they go on a raid. The Turkana cooperate in large numbers; on average 300 warriors are mobilized for each raid (**Figure 16.15**), and the warriors come from several different settlements, several different territorial sections, and several different age groups (**Figure 16.16**). This means that most of the men in these large raiding parties are unrelated to one another and many members of the war party barely know one another.

Notice that cooperation does not always produce nice or socially desirable outcomes. When the Yurok construct a weir, they catch more salmon, and everyone in the group gets more food. When other group members give food to a woman too sick to forage, she and her children are better off. When the Turkana go off on a raid, some are wounded, suffer, and may die; the threat of attacks and counter-attacks forces everyone to put effort into guarding herds, wasting resources that could be used for more productive purposes.

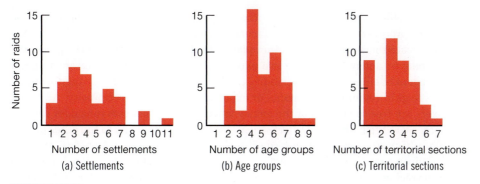

FIGURE 16.16

Membership in Turkana raiding parties is drawn from a number of different settlements, age groups, and territorial sections. This means that warriors fight with many individuals they do not know well, suggesting that cooperation is not maintained by reciprocity.

Human cooperation is regulated through prosocial sentiments and culturally transmitted norms enforced by rewards and punishments.

People are much more cooperative than other mammals, but they are not angels. Like other organisms, people are motivated by their own well-being and the welfare of their kin. The effect of each individual's contribution to large-scale collective enterprises is small. Selfish motives will tempt people to free ride; that is, to hide behind a tree when the shooting starts or feign illness when it is time to cut timber for the weir. If people succumb to these motives, there will be no cooperation. So what prevents free riding and sustains cooperation?

For most animals the answer is some combination of kinship and reciprocity. When individuals cooperate with kin, free riding can reduce their inclusive fitness. A naked mole rat who shirks its duties reduces the fitness of kin, and because relatedness is high, this effect can be sufficient to prevent free riding. In some primates, reciprocity plays an important role. Here, free riders are punished by retaliation by injured parties. A baboon who fails to reciprocate grooming may not get groomed by its partner next time.

While similar motives undoubtedly play a role in human cooperation, especially on smaller scales, they are not the whole story. Prosocial sentiments and the enforcement of culturally evolved moral norms by third parties play a crucial role in sustaining human cooperation.

Humans are not just exceptionally clever and cooperative creatures; we are also unusually nice ones. We make donations to charity, give blood, return lost wallets, and give directions to bewildered tourists. As we noted earlier, individuals go to war, risking their lives to gain rewards that will mainly benefit others. Empathy motivates us to feel compassion for others, even people that we don't know and will never meet. We have prosocial sentiments, such as generosity and a sense of fairness, and feel concern for the welfare of others. Such sentiments may motivate us to perform altruistic acts. As Abraham Lincoln once said, "When I do good, I feel good. When I do bad, I feel bad. That's my religion."

However, some researchers believe that people perform these kinds of acts for largely selfish reasons. They point out that heroes get to ride in parades, crusaders for justice become famous, and generous donors get their names on brass plaques. And, in some cases, we may expect recipients to reciprocate in the future. In an effort to get at the nature of peoples' social preferences, behavioral economists have designed a set of simple games in which individuals are faced with decisions that will affect their own welfare and the welfare of others. For example, in the dictator game, one player (the proposer) is given a sum of money. The proposer can keep all of the money or can allocate some amount to another player. In the standard form of the game, the offer is relayed anonymously; the two players never meet and never interact again. This is meant to eliminate the possibility that proposers will take advantage of opportunities to gain reputational benefits or expectations based on reciprocity. Although proposers are free to keep all of the money for themselves, not everyone does this. In fact, proposers typically allocate 20% to 30% of their endowments to the other player.

The ultimatum game adds a second step to the dictator game. As before, the proposer is given a monetary endowment and makes an anonymous allocation. But in this game the recipient decides whether to accept or reject the proposer's offer. If the recipient accepts the offer, each player gets the designated amount; if the recipient rejects the offer, neither one gets any money. A recipient who rejects an offer above zero will actually lose money. Nonetheless, recipients typically reject offers of less than 20%. This is striking because recipients incur a cost when they reject a low offer, and they seem willing to punish proposers who make low offers, even though they are strangers and will not interact again.

You might think that these results reflect some peculiarity of industrialized societies or college students, who are usually the subjects of these kinds of experiments. But the ultimatum game has now been played by thousands of people in dozens of countries all over the world. Joseph Henrich, now at the University of British Columbia, coordinated a project in which the ultimatum game was played in a dozen small-scale societies around the world (**Figure 16.17**). Henrich and his colleagues found considerable variation across societies in the size of offers and the likelihood that low offers would be rejected (**Figure 16.18**). However, in all societies, the more unequal an offer was, the more likely it was that it would be rejected.

Third-party enforcement of culturally evolved moral norms sustains human cooperation.

In the ultimatum game, recipients are often willing to punish proposers who make low offers even when they don't know their identity and won't interact again. They seem to be motivated by a sense of what constitutes an acceptable offer and what is simply unfair. Their behavior represents one example of what behavioral economists refer to as third-party enforcement of culturally evolved moral norms. Third-party enforcement of moral norms plays an important role in sustaining cooperation. To see

FIGURE 16.17

Populations in which the ultimatum game experiments were performed.

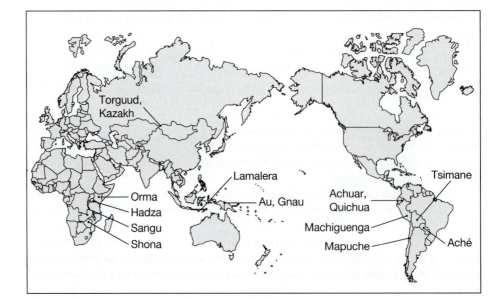

how this works, let's revisit Turkana warfare. Warriors have many opportunities to free ride. They can desert before the battle begins. During the battle they can lag behind, hide, or otherwise reduce their own risk of getting killed. After the battle they can make off with more than their share of the cows. Moreover, some free riding occurs in about 50% of raids. Why doesn't free riding spread? The answer is that cowards and other free riders are punished. Mathew's research indicates that punishment takes two forms. First, there is direct punishment, usually by members of the free rider's age group. The first violation usually results in verbal sanctions; the free rider is ridiculed and told not to do it again. Subsequent violations elicit corporal punishment and fines—the violator's age mates tie him to a tree and beat him, and then slaughter one of his cows for a feast. Free riders lose various kinds of social support. They are less attractive as mates and less likely to get help from others when they need it. For example, a Turkana man traveling away from his settlement can count on getting shelter and food from other Turkana because they are obliged to provide such hospitality. However, there is no obligation to provide hospitality to a man who has a reputation for cowardice.

Norms enforced by third-party sanctions regulate a wide range of behaviors in even the simplest foraging societies. Anthropologist Kim Hill surveyed the ethnographic literature and compiled a long list of norms that regulate behavior:

- *Marriage.* Who you can marry based on age, kin relationship, or ritual group membership and whether it is permissible to have more than wife or husband.

- *Food production.* What land is yours to exploit, what kinds of plants and animals you may harvest, and what economic activities are permissible.

- *Food sharing.* Who you must share with, how much they receive, and who receives which cuts of meat.

- *Food consumption.* What kinds of food you may eat based on your age, sex, reproductive status, and ritual group membership.

- *Display rights.* What kinds of rituals you may participate in.

- *Residence.* Where you may live and with which people, again based on your sex, age, reproductive status, and ritual group membership.

- *Politics.* Who has political power and who can be a leader based on kinship, ritual membership, sex, age, and other factors.

- *Conflict.* Who is a legitimate opponent in ritual dueling and divining, what kinds of conflict are just and what kinds are not, and whether you are obligated to participate in conflicts with other groups.

- *Life history.* When you can have sex and who must invest in children.

- *Pollution.* Where and when you can relieve yourself, dispose of waste, and other potentially polluting activities.

Notice that some norms regulate victimless crimes. For example, it is very common for norms to prohibit sex among siblings or parents and offspring. These behaviors don't injure third parties, yet third parties sometimes go to great efforts to suppress these kinds of behaviors.

It seems likely that third-party enforcement of norms makes it easier to maintain cooperation than simple reciprocity for several reasons. First, it can increase the magnitude of penalties imposed on free riders. With reciprocation, a man who cheats his partner will lose the benefits of that relationship. With community enforced norms, the violator may face more severe punishment and the loss of social support from nearly everyone in the community. Second, third-party norm enforcement can increase the chance that violators are detected. Without community monitoring and enforcement,

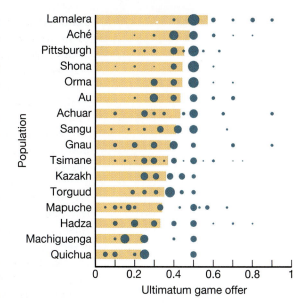

FIGURE 16.18

Results from cross-cultural ultimatum game experiments. The horizontal axis gives the fraction of the total monetary endowment offered by the proposer. The yellow bar gives the mean offer in each society, and the diameter of the blue circles gives the fraction of proposers who offered that fraction of the endowment. So, for example, most Lamalera participants offered half of the endowment, and the mean offer was slightly greater than a half. Among the Quichua, the most common offer was about 25% of the endowment, and the mean offer was about the same.

a child who tells her mother she is too sick to gather firewood or mind the goats can go out and play with her friends when her mother is out of camp. With community monitoring and enforcement the cost of malingering will be much greater—she can't play when anyone is around the camp.

The extent of human cooperation is an evolutionary puzzle.

All of the available evidence suggests that the societies of our Pliocene ancestors were like those of other social primates. Sometime over the last several million years, important changes occurred in human psychology that support larger, more cooperative societies. Given the magnitude and complexity of the changes in human societies, the most plausible hypothesis is that they were the product of natural selection. However, the standard theory of the evolution of social behavior is consistent with Hobbes's vision of "the warre of all against all" tempered by a bit of nepotism, not observed human behavior. Apes fill the bill, but not humans.

Scientists have advanced two different kinds of explanations for the high level of human cooperation. The **mismatch hypothesis** holds that the psychological machinery that supports human cooperation evolved in small hunter-gatherer societies in which genetic relatedness was high (**Figure 16.19**). While high relatedness does not lead to very much cooperation in other primates, some special ecological situation may have favored it in early hominin populations. For example, a shift to hunting and the production of highly dependent infants may have favored male parental investment, food sharing, and cooperative hunting. In this kind of social environment, natural selection may have favored a psychology that made people more cooperative. Prosocial emotions, such as shame and guilt, may have been favored by selection because it motivated people to follow cooperative social norms. Because groups were small and made up of relatives, selection may have favored cooperation and psychological mechanisms that promote cooperation. Our evolved psychology misfires in contemporary societies in which most people live in groups with much lower degrees of relatedness.

The mismatch hypothesis has several weaknesses. First, surveys by Kim Hill and his colleagues indicate that the members of contemporary hunter-gatherer bands are not very closely related. People frequently move from one band to another so that the social world of modern hunter-gatherers typically encompasses about 500 people who

FIGURE 16.19

Hunter-gatherers often live in small, nomadic groups.

all speak the same language. So the mismatch hypothesis is plausible only if ancestral hunter-gatherers lived in small, closed groups like other primates, not in the kinds of groups that characterize modern foragers. Second, the mismatch hypothesis cannot easily explain the scale of cooperation observed in contemporary societies. People, even people in small-scale societies, cooperate in large groups with people they do not know. The simplest version of the mismatch hypothesis suggests that people should be acutely sensitive to cues of kinship and reciprocity. They should be motivated to cooperate with relatives and people they know, and suspicious of strangers.

The **cultural group selection** hypothesis holds that extensive human cooperation is a side effect of rapid cultural adaptation. Systems of rewards and punishments can stabilize a vast range of moral norms, including noncooperative ones, on a wide range of scales. As long as the cost of being punished exceeds the cost of following the norm, obeying the norm will be advantageous for individuals. It doesn't matter what the norm requires. Mutually enforced sanctions could maintain cooperative or noncooperative norms: "You may steal your neighbor's cows to feed your family," or "You may not steal your neighbor's cows to feed your family." Similarly, punishment can maintain norms at different scales. "Do not steal a clan member's cattle, but the cattle of other clans are for brave men to steal," or "Do not steal the cattle of someone from your tribe, but the cattle of other tribes are for brave men to steal." These are both group-beneficial norms, but one benefits clans, the other benefits tribes. The list of possible variations is nearly endless. As a result, different groups may tend to evolve toward different equilibria—one set of norms is enforced in one group, a different set in another group, a third set in a third group, and so on. This tendency will be opposed by migration and other kinds of social contact. Cultural adaptation is more rapid than genetic adaptation. Indeed, if we are correct, this is the reason we have culture—to allow different groups to accumulate different adaptations to a wide range of environments. As a result we expect that as culture became more important in the human lineage, behavioral differences between groups increased.

In Chapter 1 we saw that three conditions are necessary for adaptation by natural selection: First, there must be a struggle for existence so that not all individuals survive and reproduce. Second, there must be variation so that some types are more likely to survive and reproduce than others, and finally, variation must be heritable so that the offspring of survivors resemble their parents. We argued that selection typically occurs at the levels of individuals because these three conditions don't hold for groups. Groups may compete with one another and groups may vary in their ability to survive and grow, but the factors that lead to group-level variation in competitive ability are not transmitted from one generation to another, so there is no cumulative adaptation at the level of groups. The cultural evolution group selection hypothesis emphasizes that once rapid cultural adaptation in human societies gave rise to stable (heritable), between-group differences, the stage was set for a variety of selective processes to generate adaptations at the group level.

Different human groups have different norms and values, and the cultural transmission of these traits can cause differences that can persist for long periods of time. The norms and values that predominate in a group may well affect the probability that the group survives, whether it is economically successful, whether it expands, and whether it is imitated by its neighbors (**Figure 16.20**). For example, suppose that groups with norms that promote military success are more likely to survive than groups lacking this sentiment. This creates a selective process that leads to the spread of such norms.

These two hypotheses are not mutually exclusive. It could easily be that some of the psychological machinery necessary to create and enforce norms evolved in small groups of related individuals, and then these mechanisms made possible the norms that enforced more extensive and larger-scale cooperation. However, we would argue that the mismatch hypothesis alone is not sufficient to understand the profound differences that have evolved between humans and other primates or to understand how humans have achieved such high levels of cooperation.

FIGURE 16.20

The Nuer and Dinka are two groups who live in the Southern Sudan. Each of these groups includes a number of separate tribes that compete for grazing land. During the nineteenth century the Nuer expanded at the expense of the Dinka because all of the Nuer tribes shared norms about tribal membership and obligations that allowed them to organize war parties that were much larger than those organized by the Dinka.

Is Human Evolution Over?

Students in our courses often wonder whether human evolution is over, and it seems a sensible question to consider as we come to the end of the story of human evolution. As we have seen, modern humans are the product of millions of years of evolutionary change. But so are cockroaches, peacocks, and orchids. All of the organisms that we see around us, including people, are the products of evolution, but they are not finished products. They are simply works in progress.

In one sense, however, human evolution is over. Because cultural change is much faster than genetic change, most of the changes in human societies since the origin of agriculture, almost 10 kya, and perhaps even before this point, have been the result of cultural, not genetic, evolution. Most of the evolution of human behavior and human societies is not driven by natural selection and the other processes of organic evolution; rather, it is driven by learning and other psychological mechanisms that shape cultural evolution. However, this fact does not mean that evolutionary theory or human evolutionary history is irrelevant to understanding contemporary human behavior. Natural selection has shaped the physiological mechanisms and psychological machinery that govern learning and other mechanisms of cultural change, and an understanding of human evolution can provide important insights into human nature and the behavior of modern peoples.

Key Terms

culture
social facilitation
observational learning
emulation
mismatch hypothesis
cultural group selection

Study Questions

1. The verb *to ape* means "to copy or imitate." Is its meaning consistent with what we now know about the learning processes of other primates?

2. Why is cumulative cultural change likely to require emulation or observational learning?

3. Primatologists have documented many examples of behaviors that vary across populations, and some have concluded that this variation is a form of culture. Explain why this is or is not a reasonable conclusion.

4. Some things that we do seem to be maladaptive (think about skydiving, drug abuse, and collecting classic cars). Some people would argue that these behaviors provide evidence that natural selection has no important impact on modern humans. Is this a reasonable argument? Why or why not?

5. How do the dictator and ultimatum games provide evidence of prosocial sentiments? How crucial are anonymity and cross-cultural results for the conclusion that people are prosocial?

6. What is the evidence that people cooperate in large, weakly related groups? Why is this a puzzle from an evolutionary perspective?

Further Reading

Boyd, R., and P. J. Richerson. 2009. "Culture and the Evolution of Human Cooperation." *Philosophical Transactions of the Royal Society (B)* 364: 3281–3288.

Cronk, L., and B. Leech. 2013. *Meeting at Grand Central: Understanding the Social and Evolutionary Roots of Cooperation.* Princeton, NJ: Princeton University Press.

Hill, K., M. Barton, and M. Hurtado. 2009. "The Emergence of Human Uniqueness: Behavioral Characters underlying Behavioral Modernity." *Evolutionary Anthropology* 18: 187–200.

Mesoudi, A. 2010. *Cultural Evolution.* Chicago: University of Chicago Press.

Richerson, P. J., and R. Boyd. 2005. *Not by Genes Alone: How Culture Transformed Human Evolution.* Chicago: University of Chicago Press.

EPILOGUE

There is Grandeur in This View of Life...

Here we end our account of how humans evolved. As we promised in the Prologue, the story has not been a simple one. We began, in Part One, by explaining how evolution works: how evolutionary processes create the exquisite complexity of organic design, and how these processes give rise to the stunning diversity of life. Next we used these ideas in Part Two to understand the ecology and behavior of nonhuman primates: why they live in groups, why the behavior of males and females differs, why animals compete and cooperate, and why primates are so smart compared with other kinds of animals. Then, in Part Three, we combined our understanding of how evolution works and our knowledge of the behavior of other primates with information gleaned from the fossil record to reconstruct the history of the human lineage. We traced each step in the transformation from a shrewlike insectivore living at the time of dinosaurs; to a monkeylike creature inhabiting the Oligocene swamps of northern Africa; to an apelike creature living in the canopy of the Miocene forests; to the small-brained, bipedal hominins who ranged over Pliocene woodlands and savannas; to the large-brained and technically more skilled early members of the genus Homo, who migrated to most of the Old World; and, finally, to creatures much like ourselves who created spectacular art, constructed simple structures, and hunted large and dangerous game just 100 kya. Finally, in Part Four, we turned to look at ourselves—to assess the magnitude and significance of genetic variation in the human species, Evolutionary analyses of human behavior

are not always well received. In Darwin's day, many were deeply troubled by the implications of his theory. One Victorian matron, informed that Darwin believed humans to be descended from apes, is reported to have said, "Let us hope that it is not true, and if it is true, that it does not become widely known." Darwin's theory profoundly changed the way we see ourselves. Before Darwin, most people believed that humans were fundamentally different from other animals. Human uniqueness and human superiority were unquestioned. But we now know that all aspects of the human phenotype are products of organic evolution—exactly the same processes that create the diversity of life around us. Nonetheless, many people still feel that we diminish ourselves by explaining human behavior in the same terms that we use to explain the behavior of chimpanzees or soaperry bugs or finches.

In contrast, we think the story of human evolution is breathtaking in its grandeur. With a few simple processes, we can explain how we arose, why we are the way we are, and how we relate to the rest of the universe. It is an amazing story. But perhaps Darwin himself (**Figure 1**) put it best in the final passage of *On the Origin of Species:*

> It is interesting to contemplate an entangled bank, clothed with many plants of many kinds, with birds singing on the bushes, with various insects flitting about, and with worms crawling through the damp earth, and to reflect that these elaborately constructed forms, so different from each other, and dependent on each other in so complex a manner, have all been produced by laws acting around us. These laws, taken in the largest sense, being Growth with Reproduction; Inheritance which is almost implied by reproduction; Variability from the indirect and direct action of the external conditions of life, and from use and disuse; a Ratio of Increase so high as to lead to a Struggle for Life, and as a consequence, Natural Selection, entailing Divergence of Character and the Extinction of less-improved forms. Thus, from the war of nature, from famine and death, the most exalted object which we are capable of conceiving, namely, the production of the higher animals, directly follows. There is grandeur in this view of life, with it several powers having been originally breathed into a few forms or only one; and that, whilst this planet has gone cycling on according to the fixed law of gravity, from so simple a beginning endless forms most beautiful and most wonderful have been, and are being evolved. [From C. Darwin, 1859, 1964, *On the Origin of Species,* facs. of 1st ed. (Cambridge, Mass.: Harvard University Press), p. 490.]

The Skeletal Anatomy of Primates

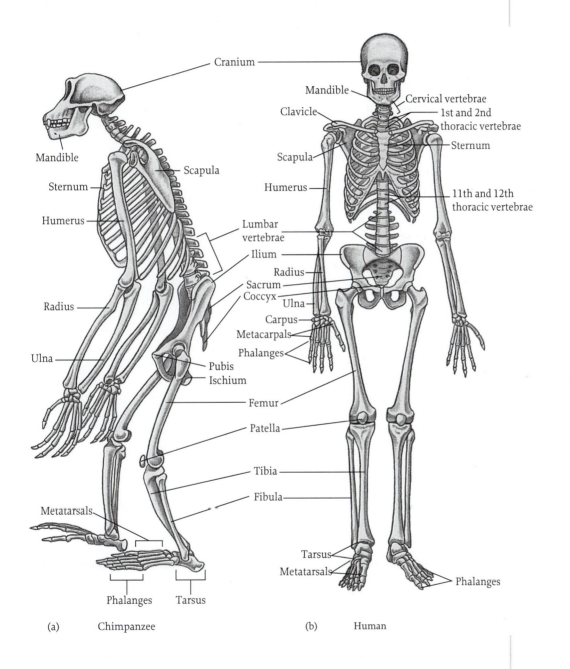

(a)   Chimpanzee

(b)   Human

GLOSSARY

abductor A muscle whose contraction moves a limb away from the midline of the body. The abductors that connect the pelvis to the femur act to keep the body upright during bipedal walking.

Acheulean A Mode 2 tool industry found at sites dated at 1.6 to 0.3 mya and associated with *Homo ergaster* and some archaic *Homo sapiens*. Named after the French village of Saint-Acheul, where it was first discovered, the Acheulean industry is dominated by teardrop-shaped hand axes and blunt cleavers.

activator A protein that increases transcription of a regulated gene. Compare *repressor*.

adaptation A feature of an organism created by the process of natural selection.

adaptive radiation The process in which a single lineage diversifies into a number of species, each characterized by distinctive adaptations. The diversification of the mammals at the beginning of the Cenozoic era is an example of an adaptive radiation.

adenine One of the four bases of the DNA molecule. The complementary base of adenine is thymine.

affiliative Friendly.

alkaloids Secondary compounds produced and kept in plant tissues to make the plant distasteful or even poisonous to herbivores.

allele One of two or more alternative forms of a gene. For example, the *A* and *S* alleles are two forms of the gene controlling the amino acid sequence of one of the subunits of hemoglobin.

alliance An interaction in which two or more animals jointly initiate aggression against, or respond to aggression from, one or more other animals. Also called *coalition*.

allopatric speciation Speciation that occurs when two or more populations of a single species are geographically isolated from each other and then diverge to form two or more new species. Compare *parapatric speciation* and *sympatric speciation*.

altruism (altruistic, adj.) Behavior that reduces the fitness of the individual performing the behavior (the actor) but increases the fitness of the individual affected by the behavior (the recipient). Compare *mutualism*. See also *selfish* and *spiteful*.

amino acids Molecules that are linked in a chain to form proteins. There are 20 different amino acids, all of which share the same molecular backbone but have a different side chain.

analogy (analogous, adj.) Similarity between traits that is due to convergent evolution, not common descent. For example, the fact that humans and

kangaroos are both bipedal is an analogy. Compare *homology*.

ancestral trait A trait that appears earlier in the evolution of a lineage or clade. Ancestral traits are contrasted with *derived traits*, which appear later in the evolution of a lineage or clade. For example, the presence of a tail is ancestral in the primate lineage, and the absence of a tail is derived. Systematists must avoid using ancestral similarities when constructing phylogenies.

angiosperms The flowering plants. The radiation of the angiosperms during the Cretaceous period may have played an important role in the evolution of the primates.

anticodon The sequence of bases on a transfer RNA molecule that binds complementarily to a particular *codon*. For example, for the codon ATC the corresponding anticodon is TAG because A binds to T, and G to C.

apatite crystal A crystalline material found in tooth enamel.

arboreal Active predominantly in trees. Compare *terrestrial*.

archaic *Homo sapiens* An older term for hominins with larger brains and more modern crania that appear in the fossil record about 500 kya in Africa and Europe, and somewhat later in eastern Asia.

argon–argon dating A sophisticated variant of the potassium–argon dating method that allows very small samples to be dated accurately.

bachelor male A male that has not been able to establish residence in a bisexual group. Bachelor males may live alone or reside in all-male groups.

balanced polymorphism A steady state in which two or more alleles coexist in a population. This state occurs when heterozygotes have a higher fitness than any homozygote.

basal metabolic rate The rate of energy use required to maintain life when an animal is at rest.

base One of four molecules—adenine, guanine, cytosine, and thymine—that are bound to the DNA backbone. Different sequences of bases encode the information necessary for protein synthesis.

basicranium (basicrania, pl.) The base or underside of the cranium.

biface A flat stone tool made by working both sides of a core until there is an edge along the entire circumference. See also *hand ax*.

bilaterally symmetrical Describing an animal whose morphology on one side of the midline is a mirror image of the morphology on the other side.

binocular vision Vision in which both eyes can focus together on a distant object to produce three-dimensional images. See also *stereoscopic vision*.

biochemical pathway Any of the chains of chemical reactions by which organisms regulate their structure and chemistry.

biological species concept The concept that species are defined as a group of organisms that cannot interbreed in nature. Adherents of the biological species concept believe that the resulting lack of gene flow is necessary to maintain differences between closely related species. Compare *ecological species concept*.

bipedal Describing locomotion in which the animal walks upright on two (hind) legs.

blade A stone tool, made from a flake, that is at least twice as long as it is wide. Blades dominate the tool traditions of the Upper Paleolithic.

blending inheritance A model of inheritance, widely accepted during the nineteenth century, in which the hereditary material of the mother and father was thought to combine irreversibly in the offspring.

bridewealth The collection of valuable items that is transferred from the groom's family to the bride's family at the time of marriage.

camera-type eye An eye in which light passes through a transparent opening and is then focused by a lens on photosensitive tissue. Camera-type eyes are found in vertebrates, mollusks, and some arthropods.

canalized Describing traits that are very insensitive to environmental conditions during development, resulting in similar phenotypes in a wide range of environments. Compare *plastic*.

canine The sharp, pointed tooth that lies between the incisors and the premolars in primates.

carbohydrates Certain organic molecules with the formula $C_nH_{2n}O_n$, including common sugars and starches.

carbon-14 dating A dating method based on an unstable isotope of carbon with atomic weight of 14. Carbon-14 is produced in the atmosphere by cosmic radiation and is taken up by living organisms. After organisms die, the carbon-14 present in their bodies decays to a stable isotope (nitrogen-14) at a constant rate. By measuring the ratio of carbon-14 to the stable isotope of carbon (carbon-12) in organic remains, scientists can estimate the length of time that has passed since the organism died. The carbon-14 method is useful for dating specimens that are younger than about 40,000 years old. Also called *radiocarbon dating*.

character A trait or attribute of the phenotype of an organism.

character displacement The result of competition between two species that causes the members of different species to become morphologically or behaviorally more different from each other.

Châtelperronian An Upper Paleolithic tool industry found in France and Spain that dates from 36 to 32 kya and is associated with Neanderthal fossil remains.

chimera A combination of more than one genetic lineage within a single individual.

chorion The outer membrane that surrounds the fetus in utero and gives rise to the placenta.

chromosome A linear body in the cell nucleus that carries genes and appears during cell division. Staining cells with dyes reveals that different chromosomes are marked by different banding patterns.

cladistic taxonomy A system for classifying organisms in which patterns of descent are the only criteria used. Compare *evolutionary taxonomy*.

cleaver A biface stone tool with a broad, flat edge. Cleavers are common at Acheulean sites.

coalition See *alliance*.

codon A sequence of three DNA bases on a DNA molecule that constitutes one "word" in the message used to create a specific protein. There are 64 different codons. Compare *anticodon*.

coefficient of relatedness (*r*) An index measuring the degree of genetic closeness between two individuals. The index ranges from 0 (for no relation) to 1 (which occurs only between an individual and itself, or between identical twins). For example, the coefficient of relatedness between an individual and its parents or its siblings is 0.5.

collected food Type of food resource, such as a leaf or fruit, that can be gathered and eaten directly.

combinatorial control The control of gene expression in which more than one regulatory protein is used and expression is allowed only in a specific combination of conditions.

comparative method A method for establishing the function of a phenotypic trait by comparing different species.

compound eye An eye in which the image is formed by a large number of discrete photoreceptors. Compound eyes are found in insects and other arthropods.

conspecifics Members of the same species.

continental drift The movement over the surface of the globe of the immense plates of relatively light material that make up the continents.

continuous variation Phenotypic variation in which there is a continuum of types. Height in humans is an example of continuous variation. Compare *discontinuous variation*.

convergence The evolution of similar adaptations in unrelated species. The evolution of camera-type eyes in both vertebrates and mollusks is an example of convergence. See also *analogy*.

core A piece of stone from which smaller flakes are removed. Cores and/or flakes may themselves be useful tools.

correlated response An evolutionary change in one character caused by selection on a second, correlated character. For example, selection favoring only long legs will also increase arm length if arm length and leg length are positively correlated.

cortex The original, unmodified surface of a stone used to make stone tools.

cross In genetics, a mating between chosen parents.

crossing over The exchange of genetic material between homologous chromosomes during meiosis. Crossing over causes recombination of genes carried on the same chromosome.

crural index The ratio of the length of the shin bone (tibia) to the length of the thigh bone (femur).

cultural group selection A process in which competition between culturally different groups leads to the spread of cultural practices prevalent in the successful groups.

culture Information stored in human brains that is acquired by imitation, teaching, or some other form of social learning and that is capable of affecting behavior or some other aspect of the individual's phenotype.

cytosine One of the four bases of the DNA molecule. The complementary base of cytosine is guanine.

dental formula The number of incisors, canines, premolars, and molars in the upper and lower jaws.

deoxyribonucleic acid See *DNA*.

derived trait A trait that appears later in the evolution of a lineage or clade. Derived traits are contrasted with *ancestral traits*, which appear earlier in the evolution of a lineage or clade. For example, the absence of a tail is derived in the hominin lineage, and the presence of a tail is ancestral. Systematists seek to use derived similarities when constructing phylogenies.

development All of the processes by which the single-celled zygote is transformed into a multicellular adult.

diastema (diastemata, pl.) A gap between adjacent teeth.

diploid Referring to cells containing pairs of homologous chromosomes, in which one chromosome of each pair is inherited from each parent. Also referring to organisms whose somatic (body) cells are diploid; all primates are diploid. Compare *haploid*.

discontinuous variation Phenotypic variation in which there is a discrete number of phenotypes with no intermediate types. Pea color in Mendel's experiments is an example of discontinuous variation. Compare *continuous variation*.

diurnal Active only during the day. Compare *nocturnal*. See also *cathemeral*.

dizygotic twins Twins that result from the fertilization of two separate eggs by two separate sperm. Dizygotic twins are no more closely related than other full siblings. Compare *monozygotic twins*.

DNA Deoxyribonucleic acid, the molecule that carries hereditary information in almost all living organisms. DNA consists of two very long sugar-phosphate backbones (called "strands") to which the bases adenine, cytosine, guanine, and thymine are bound. Hydrogen bonds between the bases bind the two strands together.

dominance The ability of one individual to intimidate or defeat another individual in a pairwise (dyadic) encounter. In some cases, dominance is assessed from the outcome of aggressive encounters; in other cases, dominance is assessed from the outcome of competitive encounters.

dominance matrix A square table constructed to keep track of dominance interactions among a group of individuals. Usually winners are listed down the left side and losers are listed across the top, and the number of times each individual defeats another is entered in the cells of the matrix. Individuals are ordered in the matrix so as to minimize the number of entries below the diagonal. This ordering is then used to construct the dominance hierarchy.

dominant Describing an allele that results in the same phenotype whether in the homozygous or the heterozygous state. Compare *recessive*.

ecological species concept The concept that natural selection plays an important role in maintaining the differences between species, and that the absence of interbreeding between two populations is not a necessary condition for defining them as separate species. Compare *biological species concept*.

EEA See *environment of evolutionary adaptedness*.

electron-spin-resonance dating A technique used to date fossil teeth by measuring the density of electrons trapped in apatite crystals in teeth.

emulation A form of social learning in which naïve individuals acquire information about the end state of behavior, but do not acquire information about the process required to generate the end state.

endocranial volume The volume inside the braincase.

environment of evolutionary adaptedness (EEA) The past environment(s) in which currently observed adaptations were shaped. For example, the psychological mechanisms that cause contemporary humans to overeat were likely shaped in an environment of evolutionary adaptedness in which overeating was rarely a problem.

environmental covariation The effect on phenotypes that occurs when the environments of parents and offspring are similar. Because environmental covariation causes the phenotypes of parents and offspring to be similar, it can falsely increase estimates of heritability.

environmental variation Phenotypic differences between individuals that exist because those individuals developed in different environments. Compare *genetic variation*.

enzyme A protein that serves as a catalyst, increasing the rate at which particular chemical reactions occur at a given temperature. Enzymes can control the chemical composition of cells by causing some chemical reactions to occur much faster than others.

equilibrium A steady state in which the composition of the population does not change.

estrus A period during the reproductive cycle of most mammals (and most primates) when the female is receptive to mating and is capable of conceiving.

eukaryotes Organisms whose cells have cellular organelles, cell nuclei, and chromosomes. All plants and animals are eukaryotes. Compare *prokaryotes*.

evolutionary taxonomy A system for classifying organisms that uses both patterns of descent and patterns of overall similarity. Compare *cladistic taxonomy*.

exon A segment of the DNA in eukaryotes that is translated into protein. Compare *intron*.

extracted food Food that is embedded in a matrix, encased in a hard shell, or otherwise difficult to extract. Extracted foods require complicated, carefully coordinated techniques to process.

F$_0$, F$_1$, and F$_2$ generations A system for keeping track of generations in breeding experiments. The initial generation is called the F$_0$ generation, the offspring of the F$_0$ generation constitute the F$_1$ generation, and the offspring of the F$_1$ generation constitute the F$_2$ generation.

falciparum malaria A severe form of malaria. The sickle-cell allele for hemoglobin is common in West Africa because it confers resistance to falciparum malaria in the heterozygous state.

family A taxonomic level above genus but below order. A family may contain several genera, and an order may contain several families. Humans belong to the family Hominidae, and the other great apes belong to the family Pongidae.

fecundity The biological capacity to reproduce. In humans, fecundity may be greater than fertility (the actual number of children produced) when people limit family size.

femur The thigh bone.

fixation A state that occurs when all of the individuals in a population are homozygous for the same allele at a particular locus.

flake A small chip of stone knocked from a larger stone core.

folivore (folivorous, adj.) An animal whose diet consists mostly of leaves.

foramen magnum The large hole in the bottom of the cranium through which the spinal cord passes.

fossil A trace of life more than 10,000 years old preserved in rock. Fossils can be mineralized bones, plant parts, impressions of soft body parts, or tracks.

founder effect A form of genetic drift that occurs when a small population colonizes a new habitat and subsequently greatly increases in number. Random genetic changes due to the small size of the initial population are amplified by subsequent population growth.

frugivore (frugivorous, adj.) An animal whose diet consists mostly of fruit.

gametes In animals, eggs and sperm.

gene A segment of the chromosome that produces a recognizable effect on phenotype and segregates as a unit during gamete formation.

gene flow The movement of genes from one population to another, or from one part of a population to another, as the result of interbreeding.

gene frequency The fraction of the genes at a genetic locus that are a particular allele (therefore also called *allele frequency*). For example, a population that contains 250 *AA* individuals, 200 *AS* individuals, and 50 *SS* individuals has 700 copies of the *A* allele and 300 copies of the *S* allele; therefore the frequency of the *S* allele is 0.3.

gene tree A phylogenetic tree tracing the pattern of descent for a particular gene.

genetic distance A measure of the overall genetic similarity of individuals or species. The best estimates of genetic distance utilize large numbers of genes.

genetic drift Random change in gene frequencies due to sampling variation that occurs in any finite population. Genetic drift is more rapid in small populations than in large populations.

genetic variation Phenotypic differences between individuals that result from the fact that those individuals have inherited different genes from their parents. Compare *environmental variation*.

genome All of the genetic information carried by an organism.

genomewide association studies Look for statistical associations between phenotypic traits (e.g., stature) and a very large number of genetic markers located throughout the genome. An association between a particular marker and a phenotypic trait indicates that a gene near that marker affects the trait.

genotype The combination of alleles that characterizes an individual at some set of genetic loci. For example, in populations with only the *A* and *S* alleles at the hemoglobin locus, that locus has only three possible genotypes: *AA*, *AS*, and *SS*. (*SA* is the same as *AS*.) Compare *phenotype*.

genotypic frequency The fraction of individuals in a population that have a particular genotype.

genus (genera, pl.) A taxonomic category below family and above species. There may be several species in a genus, and several genera in a family.

Gondwanaland The more southerly of the two supercontinents that existed from about 100 mya to roughly 120 mya. Gondwanaland included the continental plates that now make up Africa, South America, Antarctica, Australia, New Guinea, Madagascar, and the Indian subcontinent.

grooming The process of picking through hair to remove dirt, dead skin, ectoparasites, and other material. Grooming is a common form of affiliative behavior among primates.

guanine One of the four bases of the DNA molecule. The complementary base of guanine is cytosine.

gum A sticky carbohydrate produced by some trees in response to physical damage. Gum is an important food for many primates.

gummivore (gummivorous, adj.) An animal whose diet consists mostly of gum.

gymnosperms A group of plants that reproduce without flowering. Modern gymnosperms include pines, redwoods, and firs.

haft To attach a spear point, ax head, or similar implement to a handle. Hafting greatly increases the force that can be applied to the tool.

Hamilton's rule A rule predicting that altruistic behavior among relatives will be favored by natural selection if $rb > c$, where r is the *coefficient of relatedness* between actor and recipient, b is the sum of the benefits of performing the behavior on the fitness of the recipient(s), and c is the cost, in decreased fitness of the donor, of performing the behavior. See also *kin selection*.

hand ax The most common type of biface stone tool found in Acheulean sites. It is flat and teardrop-shaped, with a sharp point at the narrow end.

haploid A cell with only one copy of each chromosome. Gametes are haploid, as are the cells of some asexual organisms. Compare *diploid*.

haplorrhine Any member of the group containing tarsiers and anthropoid primates. The system that classifies primates into haplorrhines and strepsirrhines is a cladistic alternative to the evolutionary systematic taxonomy, in which primates are divided into prosimians and anthropoids, and tarsiers are grouped with prosimians. Compare *strepsirrhine*.

haplotype A particular set of alleles at some number of genetic loci that are transmitted together on the same chromosome.

Hardy–Weinberg equilibrium The unchanging frequency of genotypes that results from sexual reproduction and occurs in the absence of other evolutionary forces such as natural selection, mutation, or genetic drift.

hemoglobin A protein in blood that carries oxygen, including two α (alpha) and two β (beta) subunits.

heritability The fraction of the phenotypic variation in the population that is the result of genetic variation.

heterozygous Referring to a diploid organism whose cells carry two different alleles for a particular genetic locus. Organisms that are heterozygous are called "heterozygotes." Compare *homozygous*.

hind-limb dominated A form of locomotion which depends mainly on the hind legs for power and propulsion.

home base A temporary camp that members of a group return to each day. At the home base, food is shared, processed, cooked, and eaten; subsistence tools are manufactured and repaired; and social life is conducted.

hominin Any member of the family Hominidae, including all species of *Australopithecus* and *Homo*.

hominoid Any member of the superfamily Hominoidea, which includes humans, all the living apes, and numerous extinct apelike and human-like species from the Miocene, Pliocene, and Pleistocene epochs.

Homo heidelbergensis Middle Pleistocene hominins from Africa and western Eurasia. These hominins had large brains and very robust skulls and postcrania.

homologous pair See *homologous chromosomes*.

homology (homologous, adj.) Similarity between traits that is due to common ancestry, not convergence. For example, the reason that gorillas and baboons are both quadrupedal is that they are both descended from a quadrupedal ancestor. Compare *analogy*.

homozygous Referring to a diploid organism whose chromosomes carry two copies of the same allele at a single genetic locus. Organisms that are homozygous are called "homozygotes." Compare *heterozygous*.

humerus The bone in the upper part of the forelimb (arm).

hunted food Live animal prey captured by human foragers or nonhuman primates.

hybrid zone A geographic region where two or more populations of the same species or two different species overlap and interbreed. Hybrid zones usually occur at the habitat margins of the respective populations.

ilium (ilia, pl.) One of the three bones in the pelvis.

inbred mating Mating between closely related individuals. Also called *inbreeding*. Compare *outbred mating*.

inbreeding See *inbred mating*.

incisors The front teeth in mammals. In anthropoid primates, incisors are used for cutting, and there are two on each side of the upper and lower jaw.

independent assortment The principle, discovered by Mendel, that each of the genes at a single locus on a pair of homologous chromosomes is equally likely to be transmitted when gametes (eggs and sperm) are formed. This happens because during meiosis the probability that a particular chromosome will enter a gamete is 0.5 and is independent of whether other nonhomologous chromosomes enter the same gamete. Thus, knowing that an individual received a particular chromosome from its mother (and thus a particular allele) tells you nothing about the probability that it received other, nonhomologous chromosomes from its mother.

infraorder The taxonomic level between order and superfamily. An order may contain several infraorders, and an infraorder may contain several superfamilies.

insectivore (insectivorous, adj.) An animal whose diet consists mostly of insects.

insulin A protein that is created by the pancreas and is involved in the regulation of blood sugar.

intersexual selection A form of sexual selection in which females choose who they mate with. The result is that traits making males more attractive to females are selected for. Compare *intrasexual selection*.

intrasexual selection A form of sexual selection in which males compete with other males for access to females. The result is that traits making males more successful in such competition, like large body size or large canines, are selected for. Compare *intersexual selection*.

intron A segment of the DNA in eukaryotes that is not translated into protein. Compare *exon*.

isotope A chemical element with the same atomic number as another element but having a different atomic weight. Unstable isotopes spontaneously change into more stable isotopes.

kibbutz (kibbutzim, pl.) An agricultural settlement in Israel, usually organized according to collectivist principles.

kin selection A theory stating that altruistic acts will be favored by selection if the product of the benefit to the recipient and the degree of relatedness (*r*) between the actor and recipient exceeds the cost to the actor. See also *Hamilton's rule*.

knapping The process of manufacturing stone tools.

knuckle walking A form of quadrupedal locomotion in which, in the forelimbs, weight is supported by the knuckles, rather than by the palm or outstretched fingers. Chimpanzees and gorillas are knuckle walkers.

lactase persistence Retention of the capacity to synthesize the enzyme lactase, which is necessary to digest the main carbohydrates in fresh milk after weaning.

lactase-phlorizin hydrolase (LHP) An enzyme produced in the small intestine that breaks down lactose in milk. The term is frequently shortened to lactase.

lactation (lactate, v.) Production of milk by the mammary glands in females; also, the period during which milk is produced for nursing offspring. Lactation is a characteristic feature of mammals.

lactose A sugar present in mammalian milk. Most mammals—including most humans—lose the ability to digest lactose as adults.

Laurasia The more northerly of the two supercontinents that existed from roughly 150 mya to 120 mya. Laurasia included what is now North America, Greenland, Europe, and parts of Asia.

LCT The structural gene that codes for lactase-phlorizin hydrolase (lactase).

Levallois technique A three-step toolmaking method used by Neanderthals. The knapper first makes a core having a precisely shaped convex surface, then makes a striking platform at one end of the core, and finally knocks a flake off the striking platform.

linked Referring to genes located on the same chromosome. The closer together two loci are, the more likely they are to be linked. Compare *unlinked*.

locus (loci, pl.) The position on a chromosome that is occupied by a particular gene.

long noncoding RNA (lncRNA) RNA molecules longer than 200 nucleotides. LncRNA has many functions including gene regulation.

macroevolution Evolution of new species, families, and higher taxa. Compare *microevolution*.

maladaptive Detrimental to fitness.

mandible The lower jaw. Compare *maxilla*.

marsupial A mammal that gives birth to live young that continue their development in a pouch equipped with mammary glands. Marsupials include kangaroos and opossums.

mate guarding A behavior in which the male defends his mate after copulation to prevent other males from mating with her.

mating system The form of courtship, mating, and parenting behavior that characterizes a particular species or population. An example is polygyny.

matrilineage Individuals related through the maternal line.

maxilla The upper jaw. Compare *mandible*.

meiosis The process of cell division in which haploid gametes (eggs and sperm) are created. Compare *mitosis*.

menarche First menstruation.

messenger RNA (mRNA) A form of RNA that carries specifications for protein synthesis from DNA to the ribosomes.

microevolution Evolution of populations within a species. Compare *macroevolution*.

microlith A very small stone flake. Typical of African Later Stone Age industries, microliths were probably hafted onto wood handles to make spears and axes.

microRNA (miRNA) Short segments of RNA that are involved in the translation of mRNA into protein and gene expression. Some are involved in regulating development and cell differentiation in complex organisms.

microsatellite loci Regions within DNA sequences in which short sequences of DNA are repeated multiple times—GTGTGT or ACTACTACT. They are also known as short tandem repeats.

Middle Stone Age (MSA) The stone tool industries of sub-Saharan Africa and southern and eastern Asia that existed 250 to 40 kya. The MSA is the counterpart of the Middle Paleolithic (Mousterian) in Europe. The MSA industries varied, but flake tools were manufactured in all of them.

mineralization (mineralized, adj.) The process by which organic material in the bones of dead animals is replaced by minerals from the surrounding rock, creating fossils.

minor marriage A form of marriage, formerly widespread in China, in which children were betrothed in infancy and then raised together in the household of the prospective groom.

mismatch hypothesis The idea that human minds are adapted to life in small-scale foraging societies, and that this causes maladaptive behavior in complex, urban societies.

mitochondrial DNA (mtDNA) DNA in the mitochondria that is particularly useful for evolutionary analyses, for two reasons: (1) mitochondria are inherited only from the mother, and thus there is no recombination, and (2) mtDNA accumulates mutations at relatively high rates, thus serving as a more accurate molecular clock for changes in the last few million years.

mitochondrion (mitochondria, pl.) A cellular organelle that is involved in basic energy processing.

mitosis The process of division of somatic (normal body) cells through which new diploid cells are created. Compare *meiosis*.

Mode 1 A category of simple stone tools made by removing flakes from cores without any systematic shaping of the core. Both the flakes and the cores were probably used as tools themselves. Tools in the Oldowan industry are Mode 1 tools.

Mode 2 A category of stone tools in which cores are shaped into symmetrical bifaces by the removal of flakes. The Acheulean industry is typified by Mode 2 tools.

Mode 3 A category of stone tools made by striking large symmetrical flakes from carefully prepared stone cores using the Levallois technique. The Mousterian industry in Europe and the Middle Stone Age industries in Africa are typified by Mode 3 tools.

Mode 4 A category of stone tools in which blades are common. Mode 4 tools are found in some Middle Stone Age industries in Africa, and they predominate in the Upper Paleolithic industries of Europe.

Mode 5 A category of stone tools in which microliths are common. The African Later Stone Age industries are typified by Mode 5 tools.

modern synthesis An explanation for the evolution of continuously varying traits that combines the theory and empirical evidence of both Mendelian genetics and Darwinism.

molars The broad, square back teeth that are generally adapted for crushing and grinding in primates. Anthropoid primates have three molars on each side of the upper and lower jaw.

molecular clock The hypothesis that genetic change occurs at a constant rate and thus can be used to measure the time elapsed since two species shared a common ancestor. The molecular clock is based on observed regularities in the rate of genetic change along different phylogenetic lines.

monozygotic twins Twins that result from the fertilization of one egg by a single sperm. Early in development the fertilized egg splits to create two zygotes. Compare *dizygotic twins*.

morphology The form and structure of an organism; also a field of study that focuses on the form and structure of organisms.

Mousterian A stone tool industry characterized by points, side scrapers, and denticulates (tools with small toothlike notches on the working edge), but an absence of hand axes. The Mousterian is generally associated with Neanderthals in Europe.

mRNA See *messenger RNA*.

MSA See *Middle Stone Age*.

mtDNA See *mitochondrial DNA*.

mutation A spontaneous change in the chemical structure of DNA.

natural selection The process that produces adaptation. Natural selection is based on three postulates: (1) the availability of resources is limited; (2) organisms vary in the ability to survive and reproduce; and (3) traits that influence survival and reproduction are transmitted from parents to offspring. When these three postulates hold, natural selection produces adaptation.

Neanderthal A form of archaic *Homo sapiens* found in western Eurasia from about 127 kya to about 30 kya. Neanderthals had large brains and elongated skulls with very large faces. They were also characterized by very robust bodies.

negative selection Selection against novel mutants that preserves the existing genotype.

negatively correlated Describing a statistical relationship between two variables in which larger values of one variable tend to co-occur with smaller values of the other variable. For example, the size and number of seeds produced by an individual plant are negatively correlated in some plant populations. Compare *positively correlated*.

neocortex Part of the cerebral cortex; generally thought to be most closely associated with problem solving and behavioral flexibility. In mammals, the neocortex covers virtually the entire surface of the forebrain.

neocortex ratio The size of the neocortex in relation to the rest of the brain.

neotony The retention of juvenile traits into later stages of life.

neutral theory A theory postulating that genetic change is caused only by mutation and drift.

niche The way of life, or "trade," of a particular species—what foods it eats and how the food is acquired.

NIDD See *non-insulin-dependent diabetes*.

nocturnal Active only during the night. Compare *diurnal*. See also *cathemeral*.

noncoding RNA Molecules of RNA that do not code for proteins, including transfer RNA, ribosomal RNA, and microRNAs.

non-insulin-dependent diabetes (NIDD) A form of diabetes in which cells of the body do not respond properly to levels of insulin in the blood. NIDD is known to have a genetic basis.

nonsynonymous substitution Substitution of one nucleotide for another in a DNA sequence that changes the amino acid coded for.

nucleus (nuclei, pl.) The distinct part of the cell that contains the chromosomes. Eukaryotes (fungi, protozoans, plants, and animals) all have nucleated cells; prokaryotes (bacteria) do not.

observational learning A form of learning in which animals observe the behavior of other individuals and thereby learn to perform a new behavior. Compare *social facilitation*.

occipital torus A horizontal ridge at the back of the skull in *Homo ergaster, Homo erectus,* and archaic *Homo sapiens*.

Oceania A region of the South Pacific that includes Polynesia, Melanesia, and Micronesia.

Oldowan A set of simple stone tools made by removing flakes from cores without any systematic shaping of the core. Both the flakes and the cores were probably used as tools. This industry is found in Africa at sites that date from about 2.5 mya.

olfaction (olfactory, adj.) The sense of smell.

opposable Most primates, including humans have an opposable thumb, which means that they touch all of their other fingers on the same hand with the thumb. Most primates, but not humans also have an opposable big toe, and can bend their big toe to touch the other toes on the same foot.

organelle A portion of the cell that is enclosed in a membrane and has a specific function; examples are mitochondria and the nucleus.

out-group A taxonomic group that is related to a group of interest and can be used to determine which traits are ancestral and which are derived.

outbred mating Mating between unrelated individuals. Compare *inbred mating*.

pair bonding A mating system in which a male and female form an exclusive mating relationship. Most primates that live in pairs mate mainly with one another, but may sometimes mate with outsiders. Thus, most pair-living primates are not strictly monogamous.

paleontologist A scientist who studies fossilized remains of plant and animal species.

palimpsests Term used to describe archaeological sites that accumulate artifacts from use or settlement across time.

Pangaea The massive single continent that contained all of the Earth's dry land until about 120 mya.

parapatric speciation A two-step process of speciation in which (1) selection causes the differentiation of geographically separate, partially isolated populations of a species and (2) subsequently the populations become reproductively isolated as a result of reinforcement. Compare *allopatric speciation* and *sympatric speciation*.

parent–offspring conflict Conflict that arises between parents and their offspring over how much the parents will invest in the offspring. These conflicts stem from the opposing genetic interests of parents and offspring.

pastoralists People who make a living herding livestock.

phenotype The observable characteristics of organisms. Individuals with the same phenotype may have different genotypes. Compare *genotype*.

phenotypic matching A mechanism for kin recognition in which animals assess similarities between themselves and others.

phylogeny The evolutionary relationships among a group of species, usually diagrammed as a "family tree."

pick A triangular-shaped biface stone tool found in Acheulean sites.

placental mammal A mammal that gives birth to live young that developed for a period of time in the uterus and were nourished by blood delivered to a placenta.

plastic Describing traits that are very sensitive to environmental conditions during development, resulting in different phenotypes in different environments. Compare *canalized*.

pleiotropic effects Phenotypic effects created by genes that influence multiple characters. See also *correlated characters*.

plesiadapiform Any member of a group of primatelike mammals that lived during the Paleocene (65 to 55 mya). Although many paleontologists do not consider them to have been primates, the plesiadapiforms probably were similar to the earliest primates, who lived around the same time.

polyandry A mating system in which a single female forms a stable pair-bond with two different males at the same time. Polyandry is generally rare among mammals, but it is thought to occur in some species of marmosets and tamarins. Compare *polygyny*.

polygyny A mating system in which a single male mates with many females. Polygyny is the most common mating system among primate species. Compare *polyandry*.

population genetics The branch of biology dealing with the processes that change the genetic composition of populations through time.

porphyria variegata A genetic disease caused by a dominant gene in which carriers of the gene develop a severe reaction to certain anesthetics.

positive selection Selection that favors novel genotypes and thus leads to genetic change.

positively correlated Describing a statistical relationship between two variables in which larger values of one variable tend to co-occur with larger values of the other variable. For example, the height and weight of individuals are positively correlated in human populations. Compare *negatively correlated*.

postcranium (postcrania, pl.; postcranial, adj.) The skeleton excluding the skull.

potassium–argon dating A radiometric method of dating the age of a rock or mineral by measuring the rate at which potassium-40, an unstable isotope of potassium, is transformed into argon. This method

can be used to date volcanic rocks that are at least 500,000 years old.

prehensile Describing the ability of hands, feet, or tails to grasp objects, such as food items or branches.

premolars The teeth that lie between the canines and molars.

pressure flaking A method for finishing stone tools. The tool maker presses the edge of the tool with a sharp item, such as a piece of bone or antler, to remove small flakes.

primary structure The sequence of amino acids that make up a protein.

primiparous Refers to a female who has given birth for the first time.

proconsulid Any member of a group of early-Miocene hominoids that includes the genus *Proconsul*.

prokaryotes Organisms that lack a cell nucleus or separate chromosomes. Bacteria are prokaryotes. Compare *eukaryotes*.

protein A large molecule that consists of a long chain of amino acids. Many proteins are enzyme catalysts; others perform structural functions.

protein coding genes Genes that encode instructions for making proteins.

Punnett square A diagram that uses gene (or allele) frequencies to calculate the genotypic frequencies for the next generation.

quadrupedal Describing locomotion in which the animal moves on all four limbs. Compare *bipedal*.

radioactive decay Spontaneous change from one isotope of an element to another isotope of the same element or to an entirely different element. Radioactive decay occurs at a constant rate that can be measured precisely in the laboratory.

radiocarbon dating See *carbon-14 dating*.

radiometric method Any dating method that takes advantage of the fact that isotopes of certain elements change spontaneously from one isotope to another at a constant rate.

rain shadow An area of reduced rainfall found on the lee (downwind) side of large mountains and mountain ranges.

recessive Describing an allele that is expressed in the phenotype only when it is in the homozygous state. Compare *dominant*.

reciprocal altruism A theory that altruism can evolve if pairs of individuals take turns giving and receiving altruism over the course of many encounters.

recombination The creation of novel genotypes as a result of the random segregation of chromosomes and of crossing over.

redirected aggression A behavior in which the recipient of aggression threatens or attacks a previously uninvolved party. For instance, if A attacks

B and B then attacks C, B's attacks are an example of redirected aggression.

regulatory gene A DNA sequence that regulates the expression of a structural gene often by binding to an activator or repressor.

reinforcement The process in which selection acts against the likelihood of hybrids occurring between members of two phenotypically distinctive populations, leading to the evolution of mechanisms that prevent interbreeding.

repressor A protein that decreases transcription of a regulated gene. Compare *activator*.

reproductive isolation A relationship between two populations in which there is no gene flow between them.

ribonucleic acid See *RNA*.

ribosome A small organelle composed of protein and nucleic acid that temporarily holds together the messenger RNA and transfer RNAs during protein synthesis.

RNA Ribonucleic acid, a long molecule that plays several different important roles in protein synthesis. RNA differs from DNA in that it has a slightly different chemical backbone and it contains the base uracil instead of thymine.

rock shelter A site sheltered by an overhang of rock.

sagittal crest A sharp fin of bone that runs along the midline of the skull that increases the area available for the attachment of chewing muscles.

sagittal keel A feature running along the midline of the skull shaped like a shallow, upside-down *V*. The sagittal keel is a derived characteristic of *Homo erectus*.

sampling variation The variation in the composition of small samples drawn from a large population.

scapula (scapulae, pl.) Shoulder blade.

secondary compounds Toxic (poisonous) chemical compounds produced by plants and concentrated in plant tissues to prevent animals from eating the plant.

selection–mutation balance An equilibrium that occurs when the rate at which selection removes a deleterious gene is balanced by the rate at which mutation introduces that gene. The frequency of genes at selection–mutation balance is typically quite low.

selective sweep A process in which one allele increases in a population due to positive selection.

sex ratio The number of individuals of one sex in relation to the number of the opposite sex. By convention, sex ratios are generally expressed as the number of males to the number of females.

sexual dimorphism Differences between sexually mature males and females in body size or morphology.

sexual selection A form of natural selection that results from differential mating success in one gender.

In mammals, sexual selection usually occurs in males and may be due to male–male competition.

sexual selection infanticide hypothesis A hypothesis postulating that infanticide has been favored by sexual selection because males who kill unweaned infants are able to enhance their own reproductive prospects if they (1) kill infants whose deaths hasten their mothers' resumption of cycling, (2) do not kill their own infants, and (3) are able to mate with the mothers of the infants that they kill.

sickle-cell anemia A severe form of anemia that afflicts people who are homozygous for the sickle-cell gene.

single nucleotide polymorphism (SNP, pronounced "snip") Occurs when members of a population differ at a particular necleotide position in the genome.

SLI See *specific language impairment*.

SNP See *single nucleotide polymorphism*.

social facilitation The situation that occurs when the performance of a behavior by older individuals increases the probability that younger individuals will acquire that behavior on their own. Social facilitation does not mean that young individuals copy the behavior of older individuals. For example, the feeding behavior of older individuals may bring younger individuals in contact with the foods that adults are eating and, therefore, increase the chance that they acquire a preference for those foods. Compare *observational learning*.

social intelligence hypothesis The hypothesis that the relatively sophisticated cognitive abilities of higher primates are the outcome of selective pressures that favored intelligence as a means to gain advantages in social groups.

social organization The size, age-sex composition, and degree of cohesiveness of primate social groups.

solitary A term used for animals that do not live in social groups and do not form regular associations with conspecifics.

species (sing. and pl.) A group of organisms classified together at the lowest level of the taxonomic hierarchy. Biologists disagree about how to define a species (see *biological species concept* and *ecological species concept*).

specific language impairment (SLI) A family of language disorders in which the affected person experiences difficulty using language but is of otherwise normal intelligence. Evidence suggests that at least some cases of SLI are hereditary.

spliceosomes Organelles that splice the mRNA in eukaryotes after the introns have been snipped out.

stabilizing selection Selection pressures that favor average phenotypes. Stabilizing selection reduces the amount of variation in the population but does not alter the mean value of the trait.

stereoscopic vision Vision in which three-dimensional images are produced because each eye sends a signal of the visual image to both hemispheres in the brain. Stereoscopic vision requires binocular vision.

strategy A complex of behaviors deployed in a specific functional context, such as mating, parenting, or foraging.

stratum (strata, pl.) A geological layer.

strepsirrhine Any member of the group containing lemurs and lorises. The system classifying primates into haplorrhines and strepsirrhines is a cladistic alternative to the evolutionary systematic taxonomy, in which primates are divided into prosimians and anthropoids, and tarsiers are grouped with prosimians. Compare *haplorrhine*.

subnasal prognathism The condition in which the part of the face below the nose is pushed out.

superfamily The taxonomic level that lies between infraorder and family. An infraorder may contain several superfamilies, and a superfamily may contain several families. For example, humans are a member of the superfamily Hominoidea, which contains the families Hominidae and Pongidae.

sutures Wavy joints between bones that mesh together and are separated by fibrous tissue.

sympatric speciation A hypothesis that speciation can result from selective pressures favoring different phenotypes within a population, without positing geographic isolation as a factor. Compare *allopatric speciation* and *parapatric speciation*.

synonymous substitution Substitution of one nucleotide for another in a DNA sequence that does not change the amino acid coded for.

systematics A branch of biology that is concerned with the procedures for constructing phylogenies. Compare *taxonomy*.

tapetum (tapeta, pl.) A layer behind the retina that reflects light in some organisms.

taphonomy The study of the processes that affect the state of the remains of an organism from the time the organism dies until it is fossilized.

taurodont root A single broad tooth root in molars, resulting from the fusion of three roots. Taurodont roots were characteristic of Neanderthals.

taxonomy A branch of biology that is concerned with the use of phylogenies for naming and classifying organisms. Compare *systematics*.

temporalis muscle A large muscle involved in chewing. The temporalis muscles attach to the side of the cranium and to the mandible.

terrestrial Active predominantly on the ground. Compare *arboreal*.

territory A fixed area occupied by animals that defend the boundaries against intrusion by other individuals or groups of the same species.

tertiary structure The three-dimensional folded shape of a protein.

testes (testis, sing.) The male organs responsible for sperm production.

the most recent common ancestor (tMRCA) The most immediate ancestor of individuals belonging to two different species or lineages.

theory of mind The capacity to be aware of the thoughts, knowledge, or perceptions of other individuals. A theory of mind may be a prerequisite for deception, imitation, teaching, and empathy. It is generally thought that humans, and possibly chimpanzees, are the only primates to possess a theory of mind.

thermoluminescence dating A technique used to date crystalline materials by measuring the density of trapped electrons in the crystal lattice.

third-party relationships Relationships among other individuals. For example, monkeys and apes are believed to understand something about the nature of kinship relationships among other group members.

thymine One of the four bases of the DNA molecule. The complementary base of thymine is adenine.

tibia The larger of the two long bones in the lower leg.

torque A twisting force that generates rotary motion.

toxin A chemical compound that is poisonous or toxic.

trait A characteristic of an organism.

transfer RNA (tRNA) A form of RNA that facilitates protein synthesis by first binding to amino acids in the cytoplasm and then binding to the appropriate site on the mRNA molecule. There is at least one distinct form of tRNA for each amino acid.

transitive Describing a property of triadic (three-way) relationships in which the relationships between the first and second elements and the second and third elements automatically determine the relationship between the first and third elements. For example, if A is greater than B and B is greater than C, then A is greater than C. In many primate species, dominance relationships are transitive.

transposable elements Segments of DNA that move from one location to another within the genome of a single individual.

tRNA See *transfer RNA*.

unlinked Referring to genes on different chromosomes. Compare *linked*.

Upper Paleolithic The period from about 45 kya to about 10 kya in Europe, North Africa, and parts of Asia. The tool kits from this period are dominated by blades.

uracil One of the four bases of the RNA molecule. Uracil corresponds to the base thymine in DNA; as with thymine, its complementary base is adenine.

uranium–lead dating A method of dating zirconium crystals in igneous rocks that is based on the ratio of uranium to lead. This method can be used to date stalactites, stalagmites, and flow stone formed by precipitation in limestone caves, and has been particularly useful for dating hominin remains found in caves in South Africa.

variant The particular form of a trait. For example, blue eyes, brown eyes, and gray eyes are variants of the trait eye color.

variation among groups Differences in the average phenotype or genotype between groups.

variation within groups Differences in phenotype or genotype between individuals in a group.

viviparity Giving birth to live young.

zygomatic arch A cheekbone.

zygote The cell formed by the union of an egg and a sperm.

CREDITS

(middle-right): Robert Boyd; p. 134 (bottom-all): Robert Boyd; p. 139: Tim Davenport/Wildlife Conservation Society; p. 140: Norman Myers/Bruce Coleman Inc./Photoshot.

CHAPTER 6

Photos: p. 144: Roine Magnusson/age footstock; p. 147 (top): Courtesy of Joan Silk; p. 147 (bottom): Arco Images GmbH/Alamy; p. 148 (top): Courtesy of Kathy West; p. 148 (bottom): Rudie H. Kuiter, OSF/Animals Animals; p. 150 (top): Courtesy of Kathy West; p. 150 (bottom): Ardella Reed Stock Photography; p. 154 (top): © Bazuki Muhammed/Reuters/Corbis; p. 154 (bottom): K. G. Preston-Mafham/Premaphotos Wildlife; p. 156: Photograph courtesy of Carola Borries; p. 157: Arco Images GmbH/Alamy; p. 158 (top): © Art Wolfe/artwolfe.com; p. 158 (bottom): BIOS/Peter Arnold, Inc.; p. 159 (top-left): Peter Arnold Inc.; p. 159 (top-right): Courtesy of Robert Boyd; p. 159 (bottom): Courtesy of Joan Silk; p. 162 (top): Martin Harvey/Peter Arnold Inc.; p. 162 (bottom): Erwin and Peggy Bauer/Wildstock; p. 163: Erwin and Peggy Bauer/Wildstock; p. 164: Courtesy of Joan Silk; p. 166: Ryne A. Palombit, Anthropology Dept., Rutgers University; p. 168: Courtesy of Joan Silk.

Drawn art: Figure 6.5: Figure 10.3 from *The Evolution of Primate Societies* by John C. Mitani, et al. © 2012 by The University of Chicago. Reprinted by permission of the University of Chicago Press. Figure 6.10: Figure 3 from S.C. Alberts, et. al (2013) "Reproductive aging patterns in primates reveal that humans are distinct." *Proceedings of the National Academy of Sciences* 110(33), 13440-1344. Reprinted with permission. Figure 6.19: Figure from L. Barrett & S.P. Henzi (2000). "Are baboon infants Sir Philip Sydney's offspring?" Ethology 106(7), 645-658. Reprinted by permission of John Wiley & Sons. Figure 6.35a: Figure from M. Heistermann, et al. (2001). "Loss of oestrus concealed ovulation and paternity confusion in free-ranging Hanuman langurs." *Proceedings of the Royal Society of London. Series B: Biological Sciences* 268:1484, 2445-2451. Reprinted by permission of the Royal Society. Figure 6.35b: Figure from M. Heistermann, et al. (2001). "Loss of oestrus concealed ovulation and paternity confusion in free-ranging Hanuman langurs." *Proceedings of the Royal Society of London. Series B: Biological Sciences* 268:1484, 2445-2451. Reprinted by permission of the Royal Society. Figure 6.36: Figure 2 from E.K. Roberts, et al. (2012) "A Bruce effect in wild geladas." *Science* 335(6073), 1222-1225. Reprinted with permission from AAAS.

CHAPTER 7

Photos: p. 172: Anup Shah/naturepl.com; p. 174 (top): K. G. Preston-Mafham/Premaphotos Wildlife; p. 174 (bottom): AP Photos; p. 175: Courtesy of Joan Silk; p. 180 (left): Courtesy of Kathy West; p. 180 (right): Courtesy of Joan Silk; p. 181 (top): Courtesy of Joan Silk; p. 181 (bottom): Courtesy of Joan Silk; p. 182: 2013 Kazem, Widdig; p. 183 (top-left): Courtesy of Susan Perry; p. 183 (top-right): Courtesy of Marina Cords; p. 183 (bottom-left): Joan Silk; p. 183 (bottom-right): John Mitani; p. 184: Courtesy of Joan Silk; p. 187 (top): credit N/A; p. 187 (bottom): Terry Whitaker; Frank Lake Picture Agency/Corbis; p. 189 (all): Courtesy of Joan Silk.

Drawn art: Figure 7.11b: Figure from A.J. Kazem & A. Widdig (2013) "Visual phenotype matching: cues to paternity

are present in rhesus macaque faces." *PLOS One*, 8(2), e55846. Reprinted by permission of the Public Library of Science.

CHAPTER 8

Photos: p. 192: Frans Lanting/National Geographic Creative; p. 194: Time Life/Getty Images: Photo:AP Photo; p. 195 (top): W. Perry Conway/Corbis; p. 195 (bottom): Courtesy of Joan Silk; p. 196: Gallo Images/Corbis; p. 197: Frans Lanting/Corbis; p. 198 (top): National Geographic/Getty Images; p. 198 (bottom): Wolfgang Kohler; p. 199 (left): Courtesy of Joan Silk; p. 199 (right): Photograph courtesy of Susan Perry; p. 200 (left): Mary Beth Angelo/Science Source; p. 200 (right): Wolfgang Kohler, The Mentality of Apes. Routledge & Kegan Paul, Ltd., London, 1927. Reproduced with permission from the publisher; p. 201: Robert Boyd & Joan Silk; p. 202: Courtesy of Joan Silk; p. 203 (left): Courtesy of Joan Silk; p. 203 (right): Photograph courtesy of Susan Perry; p. 204: Courtesy E. Menzel; p. 206 (left): Photo courtesy of Cognitive Evolution Group, University of Louisiana at Lafayette; p. 206 (middle & right): Figure 1, in E. Hermann, J. Call, M.V. Hernandez-Lloreda, B. Hare, and M. Tomasello, 2007, "Humans Have Evolved Specialized Skills of Social Cognition."

Drawn art: Figure 8.18a & b: Reprinted from *Current Biology*, Vol. 15, Issue 5, Jonathan I. Flombaum and Laurie R. Santos, "Rhesus Monkeys Attribute Perceptions to Others," pp. 447-452, Copyright © 2005 Elsevier Ltd., with permission from Elsevier. http://www.sciencedirect.com/science/journal/09609822.

Part Three
CHAPTER 9

Photos: p. 210: Magdalena Rehova/Alamy; p. 213: © Art Wolfe/artwolfe.com/artwolfe.com; p. 223: SHAUN CURRY/AFP/Getty Images; p. 231 (top): Christophe Ratier/NHPA.UK; p .231 (bottom): Photograph courtesy Laura MacLatchy; p. 234: Photo courtesy Salvador Moya-Sola. Reproduced with permission of Nature, 379: 156–159.

Drawn art: Figure 9.1a & b: Figure from *Mammal Evolution: An Illustrated Guide* by R.J.G. Savage, pp. 38-39, 1986. Copyright © 1986 by Facts On File, Inc., an imprint of Infobase Publishing. Reprinted with permission of the publisher. Figure 9.2: Figure 5.3 from Robert D. Martin. *Primate Origins and Evolution: A Phylogenetic Reconstruction.* © 1990 R.D. Martin. Reprinted by permission of Princeton University Press. Figure 9.7: Figure from *The Cambridge Encyclopedia of Human Evolution*, edited by Steve Jones, Robert Martin, and David Pilbeam, p. 200. Copyright © Cambridge University Press 1992. Reprinted with the permission of Cambridge University Press. Figure 9.8: Artwork of Carpolestes simpsoni by Doug M. Boyer, from "Paleontology: Primate Origins Nailed" by Eric J. Sargis, *Science* 298, Nov. 22, 2002, p. 1564. Reprinted with permission. Figure 9.10a & b: Figure 3 from Kenneth D. Rose, "The Earliest Primates," *Evolutionary Anthropology*, Vol. 3, Issue 5 (1994): 159-173. Copyright © 1994 Wiley-Liss, Inc., A Wiley Company. Reprinted with permission of Wiley-Liss, Inc., a subsidiary of John Wiley & Sons, Inc. Figure 9.11a & b: This figure was published in *Primate Adaptation and Evolution*, J.G. Fleagle, (Academic Press, 1988). Copyright ©

1988 Elsevier Ltd. Reprinted by permission. Figure 9.23: This figure was published in *Primate Adaptation and Evolution*, J.G. Fleagle, (Academic Press, 1988). Copyright © 1988 Elsevier Ltd. Reprinted by permission. Figure 9.24: Figure 8.21 from *Principles of Human Evolution, 2nd Edition* by Roger Lewin and Robert Foley. © 2004 by Blackwell Science Ltd, a Blackwell Publishing company. Reproduced with permission of Blackwell Publishing Ltd. Figure 9.25: Figure 2.23 from Robert D. Martin. *Primate Origins and Evolution: A Phylogenetic Reconstruction.* © 1990 R.D. Martin. Reprinted by permission of Princeton University Press.

CHAPTER 10

Photos: p. 236: Anup Shah/Animals Animals/age footstock; p. 241 (top): Copyright M.P.F.T. Photograph courtesy of Michael Brunet; p. 241 (bottom): B. Senut et al./C.R. Acad. Sci. Paris, Sciences de la Terre et des planetes/Earth and Planetary Sciences 332 (2001) 141; p. 242: Redrawn from Y. Haile-Selassie, G. Suwa, and T. D. White, 2004, "Late Miocene Teeth from Middle Awash, Ethiopia, and Early Hominid Dental Evolution"; p. 243: Tim D. White/Provided by David Brill; p. 244: © Tim D. White & Gen Suwa/Provided by David Brill; p. 245: C. Owen Lovejoy, Gen Suwa and colleagues/Provided by David Brill; p. 250: National Museum of Kenya; p. 251 (top): Institute of Human Origins/Nanci Kahn; p. 251 (bottom): John Reader/Science Photo Library/Photo Researchers, Inc; p. 252: VILEM BISCHOF/AFP/Getty Images; p. 254 (top): from figure 3a Alemseged et al 2006. "A juvenile early hominin skeleton from Dikika, Ethiopia". Nature 443:296-301; p. 254 (bottom): John Reader/Photo Researchers, Inc.; p. 255: from figure 5 Alemseged et al 2006. "A juvenile early hominin skeleton from Dikika, Ethiopia". Nature 443:296-301; p. 258: Courtesy of Lee R. Berger and The Universtiy of The Witwatersrand; p. 259: DeSilva, J., 2013; p. 260: National Museum of Kenya; p. 261: University of Witswatersrand; p. 262 (top): Wolfgang Kaehler Photography; p. 262 (bottom): Courtesy of Maeve Leakey.

Drawn art: Figure 10.3: Three individual drawings, showing the angles of articulation for the knee, in lateral view: (1.) modern human; (2.) A. afarensis; (3.) ape. From *LUCY: The Beginnings of Humankind* by Donald C. Johanson and Maitland A. Edey. © 1981 Luba Dmytryk Gudz \ Brill Atlanta. Reprinted with permission. Figure 10.20: Figure 4.24 from *The Human Career: Human Biological and Cultural Origins, Second Edition* by Richard G. Klein. © 1989, 1999 by The University of Chicago. Reprinted by permission of the University of Chicago Press. Figure 10.25: A. garhi, BOU-VP-12/130, Bouri, cranial parts, cranium reconstruction. Original housed in National Museum of Ethiopia, Addis Ababa. © 1999 David L. Brill. Reprinted with permission. Figure 10.26: Figure 4.2, © 1999 by Kathryn Cruz-Uribe, from *The Human Career: Human Biological and Cultural Origins, Second Edition* by Richard G. Klein. © 1989, 1999 by The University of Chicago. Reprinted by permission of the University of Chicago Press. Figure 10.29: Figure from P. Schmid, et. al. (2013) "Mosaic Morphology in the Thorax of Australopithecus sediba." Science 340(6129). Reprinted with permission from AAAS.

CHAPTER 11

Photos: p. 266: Peter Bostrom; p. 272: Courtesy of Kim Hill; p. 273: Courtesy of Nicholas Blurton Jones; p. 275: Craig

Stanford; p. 279: Francisco d'Errico; p. 282: National Museum of Natural History, Smithsonian Institution, Washington, D.C. (Rdg. 1–2) Courtesy of Kathy D. Schick and Nicolas Toth, CRAFT Research; p. 283 (top): Art Wolfe/www.artwolfe.com; p. 283 (bottom): Manuel Dominguez-Rodrgigo; p. 284 (top-left & right): Y. Arthus-Bertrand/Peter Arnold, Inc.; p. 284 (middle & bottom): Courtesy of Robert Boyd & Joan Silk; p. 285 (top & bottom): Robert Boyd; p. 286: Courtesy of Robert Bailey.

Drawn art: Figure 11.25: Figure 4.41 from *The Human Career: Human Biological and Cultural Origins, Second Edition* by Richard G. Klein. © 1989, 1999 by The University of Chicago. Reprinted by permission of the University of Chicago Press.

CHAPTER 12

Photos: p. 290: Javier Trueba/MSF/Science Source; p. 292: JAVIER TRUEBA/MSF/SCIENCE PHOTO LIBRARY; p. 293: National Museum of Kenya; p. 297 (top): Alan Walker, Anthro. Dept. Penn State; p. 297 (bottom): Alan Walker, Anthro. Dept. Penn State; p. 300: National Museum of Kenya. Photograph courtesy of Alan Walker; p. 303 (top): www.dmanisi.org.ge/index.html; p. 303 (bottom): David Lordkipanidze, Georgian State Museum, Georgian Academy of Sciences; p. 304 (left): Guram Bumbiashvili/Georgian National Museum; p. 304 (right): A Complete Skull from Dmanisi, Georgia, and the Evolutionary Biology of Early Homo/Jay Matternes; p. 304 (bottom): National Anthropological Archive Negative no. 01019100; p. 306: R. Potts, Smithsonian Institution; p. 313: JAVIER TRUEBA/MSF/SCIENCE PHOTO LIBRARY; p. 314: William Jungers, Stony Brook University; p. 315 (left): JAVIER TRUEBA/MSF/SCIENCE PHOTO LIBRARY; p. 315 (right): JAVIER TRUEBA/MSF/SCIENCE PHOTO LIBRARY; p. 319 (top): BIOS/Peter Arnold, Inc; p. 319 (bottom): Maurizio Lanini/Corbis; p. 320 (top): Len Rue, Jr./Science Source; p. 320 (bottom): Photo from Joao Zilhao; p. 321: Photo from Joao Zilhao; p. 322 (top): Erik Trinkaus; p. 322 (bottom): Courtesy of Joan Silk; p. 323 (top): Eric Delson; p. 323 (bottom): NATURAL HISTORY MUSEUM, LONDON/SCIENCE PHOTO LIBRARY.

Drawn art: Figure 12.5: Figure 5.10, © 1999 by Kathryn Cruz-Uribe from *The Human Career: Human Biological and Cultural Origins, Second Edition* by Richard G. Klein. © 1989, 1999 by The University of Chicago. Reprinted by permission of the University of Chicago Press. Figure 12.6: Figures 4.2 (© 1999 by Kathryn Cruz-Uribe), 4.23, 5.10 (© 1999 by Kathryn Cruz-Uribe), 7.2 from *The Human Career: Human Biological and Cultural Origins, Second Edition* by Richard G. Klein. © 1989, 1999 by The University of Chicago. Reprinted by permission of the University of Chicago Press. Figure 12.18: Figure from *The Cambridge Encyclopedia of Human Evolution*, edited by Steve Jones, Robert Martin, and David Pilbeam, p. 244. Copyright © Cambridge University Press 1992. Reprinted with the permission of Cambridge University Press. Figure 12.22: Figures 5.22, 5.26, © 1999 by Kathryn Cruz-Uribe, from *The Human Career: Human Biological and Cultural Origins, Second Edition* by Richard G. Klein. © 1989, 1999 by The University of Chicago. Reprinted by permission of the University of Chicago Press. Figure 12.23: Figure 6.24 from *The Human Career: Human Biological and Cultural Origins, Second Edition* by Richard G. Klein. © 1989, 1999 by The University of Chicago. Reprinted by permission of the

University of Chicago Press. Figure 12.25: Figure 5.32, © 1999 by Kathryn Cruz-Uribe, from *The Human Career: Human Biological and Cultural Origins, Second Edition* by Richard G. Klein. © 1989, 1999 by The University of Chicago. Reprinted by permission of the University of Chicago Press. Figure 12.31: Figure 6.48, © 1999 by Kathryn Cruz-Uribe, from *The Human Career: Human Biological and Cultural Origins, Second Edition* by Richard G. Klein. © 1989, 1999 by The University of Chicago. Reprinted by permission of the University of Chicago Press.

CHAPTER 13

Photos: p. 328: Javier Trueba/MSF/Science Source; p. 344 (left & right): Housed in National Museum of Ethiopia, Addis Ababa . Photo (c) 2001 David L. Brill \ Brill, Atlanta; p. 346 (top): Image courtesy of Prof Christopher Henshilwood/University of Bergen, Norway; p. 346 (bottom): Curtis Marean/Institute of Human Origins, ASU; p. 347: © Chip Clark: Museum of Natural History, Smithsonian; p. 348 (top): Figure 3 from Bouzouggar, A. et al. 2007 "82,000-year-old shell beads from North Africa and implications for the origins of modern human behavior." PNAS 104:9964-9969; p. 348 (bottom): Pierre-Jean Texier, Diepkloof Project (MAE), CNRS, UMR 5199-PACEA; p. 349: Erlend Eidsvik/Centre for Development Studies/University of Bergen; p. 350 (all): Mellars P (2006) Going east: New genetic and archaeological perspectives on the modern human colonization of Eurasia; p. 351: From V. V. Pitulko et al., 2004, "The Yana RHS Site: Humans in the Arctic before the Last Glacial Maximum," Science 303:52-56; p. 352: © Jean-Michel Labat/AUSCAPE All rights reserved; p. 358 (top): © Jean Clottes/DRAC Rhône-Alpes; p. 358 (bottom): Ulmer Museum, Ulm, Germany.

Drawn art: Figure 13.1: Figure 7.2 from *The Human Career: Human Biological and Cultural Origins, Second Edition* by Richard G. Klein. © 1989, 1999 by The University of Chicago. Reprinted by permission of the University of Chicago Press. Figure 13.11: Figure from M. Rasmussen et al. (2011) "An Aboriginal Australian Genome Reveals Separate Human Dispersals into Asia," Science 334(97). Reprinted with permission from AAAS. Figure 13.16: Drawing: "An atlatl is a tool that lengthens the arm," from The Testimony of Hands: Atlatls (http://hands.unm.edu/atlatls.html). Reprinted by permission of James Dixon. Figure 13.21: Figure from P. Mellars (2006) "Going East: New genetic and archaeological perspectives on the modern human colonization of Eurasia." Science 313(5788), 796-800. Reprinted with permission from AAAS. Figure 13.27: Figure 34.8 from Soffer, Olga, "The Middle to Upper Patheolithic Transition on the Russian Plain," from Mellars, Paul; *The Human Revolution.* © 1989 Edinburgh University Press. Reprinted by permission of Edinburgh University Press and Princeton University Press. Figure 13.28: Figure 7.22 from *The Human Career: Human Biological and Cultural Origins, Second Edition* by Richard G. Klein. © 1989, 1999 by The University of Chicago. Reprinted by permission of the University of Chicago Press. Figure 13.29: Figure 13.4 from Paul Mellars. *The Neanderthal Legacy: An Archaeological Perspective from Western Europe.* © 1996 Princeton University Press. Reproduced by permission of Princeton University Press.

Part Four
CHAPTER 14

Photos: p. 362: Mira/Alamy; p. 368: AP Photo/Gregory Bull; p. 369 (top): AP Photo/Chris O'Meara; p. 369 (bottom): Al Tielemans/Sports Illustrated/Getty Images; p. 372 (all): Courtesy of Marion I. Barnhart, Wayne State University Medical School, Detroit, Michigan; p. 377: Sarah Errington/Panos Pictures; p. 380: Jean Higgins/Unicorn Stock; p. 383: Jan Halaska/Science Source.

Drawn art: Figure 14.1: Figure from Jobling et al. (2014) *Human Evolutionary Genetics*, p. 274. Reprinted by permission of Taylor & Francis. Figure 14.8: Figure from Pascale Gerbault, et al. (2011). "Evolution of lactase persistence: an example of human niche construction." *Philosophical Transactions of the Royal Society (B)* 366, 863-877. Reprinted by permission of the Royal Society. Figure 14.13: This figure was published in *Current Biology*, Vol. 5, Issue 15, F. Prugnolle, et al., "Geography predicts neutral genetic diversity of human populations," pp. R159-R160. Copyright © 2005 Elsevier Ltd. All rights reserved. Reprinted by permission. Figure 14.14: With kind permission from Springer Science+Business Media: Figure 2 from Andrea Manica, et al., "Geography is a better determinant of human genetic differentiation than ethnicity," *Human Genetics*, Vol. 118, Number 3 & 4, December 2005. Copyright © 2005, Springer Berlin/Heidelberg. Figure 14.21a & b: Reprinted by permission from Macmillan Publishers Ltd: Figure 1 a-b from Michael Bamshad, Stephen Wooding, Benjamin A. Salisbury, and J. Claiborne Stephens, "Deconstructing the Relationship Between Genetics and Race," *Nature Reviews Genetics*, Volume 5, August 2004: 598-609. Copyright © 2004, Nature Publishing Group.

CHAPTER 15

Photos: p. 396: Jodi Cobb/National Geographic Creative; p. 400 (top): Tom McHugh/Science Source; p. 400 (bottom): Joe Cavanaugh/DDB Stock Photo; p. 401: Oil painting by Martin Pate. Courtesy Cultural Resources, National Park Service; p. 402: Anup Shah/naturepl.com; p. 405: English Heritage Photo Library/G. P. Darwin on behalf of Darwin Heirlooms Trust; p. 412: Courtesy of Monique Borgerhoff Mulder.

CHAPTER 16

Photos: p. 416: O. Cochran/Arcticphoto; p. 419 (top): B&C Alexander/Arcticphoto; p. 419 (bottom): Classic Image/Alamy; p. 420: Courtesy of Susan Perry; p. 423 (top): Anup Shah/naturepl.com, p. 423 (bottom): Reprinted by permission from Macmillan Publishers Ltd: Nature 437:52-55, copyright 2005; p. 424: Robert Boyd; p. 426: Kennan Harvey Photography, Durango, CO; p. 427 (top): National Portrait Gallery London; p. 427 (bottom): Kim Hill and Magdalena Hurtado; p. 428: Raymond Mendez/Animals Animals/Earth Scenes; p. 429: Charles Deering McCormick Library of Special Collections, Northwestern University Library; p. 430: Sarah Mathew; p. 434: Alan Compton/Jon Arnold Images Ltd/Alamy; p. 435 (top): Copyright Pitt Rivers Museum, University of Oxford. Accession Number: 1998.355.395.2; p. 435 (bottom): Copyright Pitt Rivers Museum, University of Oxford. Accession Number: 2005.51.87.1.

INDEX

Page numbers in *italics* refer to illustrations, tables, and figures.

flakes (tool), 268, *269,* 270, 271, *271,* 278, 279, 287, 298, 299, 311, 313, 318, 346
    cortex of, 270, *271*
Flatz, Gebhard, 377
Flores, Indonesia, 313, *313*
Florisbad cranium, 322, *323*
Foley, Robert, 323
folivores, *116,* 128, 129, 130, 146, 222, 225
    dentition and digestive tracts of, 116, *116*
folk classification schemes, 390, 391
"follower" males, 163, 164
F$_1$ generation, 26, 31, 32, 33, 34, 57
food, distribution of, *126,* 126–30
food resources, categories of, 271
food sharing, 400, 401, 433
    among chimpanzees, 275, *275*
    meat eating and, 274
    by modern humans, 273, 275–76, 286
    sexual dimorphism and, 278
foragers, technologies of, 419, *419*
foraging:
    by apes, 200, 272
    brain size and, 276–77
    capuchin monkeys and, 420
    by chimpanzees, 82, 272, *272*
    home bases and, 286
    by modern humans, 270, 272, *272,* 273, *273,* 354, 355, 400, *400,* 414
    by Oldowan toolmakers, 278–88
    ranging patterns and, 129–30
    by rats, 400, *400*
    self-sufficiency and, 275–76, *276*
    sexual division of labor and, 273, 286
    slow maturation and, 276–77
foraging societies:
    human mating strategies and, 405
    warfare and, 429, 430, *431,* 433, *433*
foramen magnum, 241
forebrain, *199*
fossas, 134
Fossey, Dian, 124
fossil record, 17–20, 101, 215
    anatomically modern humans in, 329, 330, 343–45, *344,* 349
    ancestral characters in, 101
    climate change in, 213, 215, 306–7
    continental drift in, 213
    dating methods and, 215, 217–18
    footprints in, 254, *254*
    H. erectus in, 305
    H. ergaster in, 294–95, 301
    H. heidelbergensis in, *309,* 309–10
    on Haplorrhini evolution, 223–24, 226–28
    hominins in, 238, 248, *249,* 264
    incompleteness of, 224, 227, *228*
    missing links in, 223, 224, 227, *228,* 229–30, *230, 231*
    Neanderthals in, 315, 344
    New World fossil evidence, *227*
    Old World monkeys in, 234
    P. boisei in, 262
    primates in, 224, 225, *225*
    teeth in, 225
    tools in, *269*
founder effect, 379
FOXP2 gene, 366, 371
France, 310, *331,* 352, 353, 354
Franklin, John, 419, *419*
free riders, 431, 433
Freud, Sigmund, 404, 414
frugivores, 115, *116,* 128, 129, 130, 197, 220, 223, 225, 231, 247, *247*
    dentition and digestive tracts of, 116, *116*
fruit flies *(Drosphila),* 29, 49, 50
F$_2$ generation, 26, 31, 32, *32, 33, 36,* 57
F$_0$ generation, 26

Gabunia, Leo, 302
galagos, *115,* 118, *119,* 127
Galápagos Islands, 6, *6,* 7, 10, 17, 20, 62, 69, 86–88, 90, 91
Galdikas, Biruté, 123
Game of Thrones, The, 12
gametes, 26, 55, 56, *72,* 73, 187
    haploid, 29, *29,* 32
    meiosis and, 29, *29,* 32
Gamova, Ekatarina, 369, *369*
Garber, Paul, 162
Gebo, Daniel, 231
gelada baboons, *112,* 137, 138, 163, *163,* 167, 168, *168, 198*
gene flow, 82–83
    character displacement and, 88
    between Darwin's finches, 83, *83,* 84, *84,* 84–86, *85*
    in human history, 392
    migration patterns and, 324, 339, *381*
    reinforcement and, 88
gene frequency:
    calculating, 55, *56, 57,* 373, *373*
    evolution and, 60, 62
    genetic drift and, 71–74
    Hardy-Weinberg equilibrium and, 57–58
    natural selection and, 59–60
    random mating and, 55, 57, 59
    sexual reproduction and, 55–58
    stability reached by, 57
genes, 26, 50, 426
    on chromosomes, 27–28, 36
    combinatorial control and, 48–49
    crossing over, 34, *35*
    DNA in, 38–41
    FOXP2, 366
    mutation of, 54
    natural selection and, 54
    phenotypic traits and interactions between environment and, 398
    pleiotropic effects of, 69
    in populations, 54–55
    positively selected, 366
    recessive, 371
    regulatory, 366
    senescence and, 195
genetic determinism, 398
genetic distance, 335
    among humans and three great ape species, 101, 102, *102*

psychoanalysis, 404
psychological mechanisms, special-purpose, 400, 401
psychology, evolutionary, 411
    in inbreeding avoidance, 401–4, *402,* 414
    learning predisposition and, 400, *400*
    mate preferences and, 405–6
    mismatch hypothesis and, 434–35
    personal qualities of ideal mates, 406, *407*
    reasoning ability and, 400–401
    reciprocity and, 400
pubis, 245
Punnett square, 33, *33,* 34, *35, 36, 58*
Pusey, Anne, 155, 158
pygmy chimpanzees, *see* bonobos
pythons, 133, *134*

Qafzeh, Israel, *331,* 344
quadrupedal locomotion, 94, 212, 219, 223, 246, 247, *247*
Quichua, *433*

race concept:
    classification schemes for, 388–92, *389, 390, 391*
    culture and, 392–93
    as flawed, 388
racism, race concept and, 393
radioactive decay, 217
radiocarbon (carbon-14) dating, 217
radiometric dating methods, 215, 217–18
rain shadow, 228
Ramachandran, Sohini, 340
random mating, genotypic frequencies and, 55–58, *58,* 59
raptors, 133, 134, 135
Rasmussen, Tab, 220
rats, 204, 400, *400*
Reader, Simon, 198, 200
reasoning:
    by analogy, 110
    by homology, 109
recessive alleles, 31
reciprocal altruism, 188–90, *189,* 400, 414, 431
reciprocity, cooperation and, 431
recombinant DNA technology, 46
recombination, 33–37, 397
reconciliatory behavior, in primates, 184–85, *185*
red deer (elk), 17–18, 158, *158,* 318, *319*
red howler monkeys, 163, 167, 186
redirected aggression, 202
red ocher, 348
reelin, 368
regulatory genes, 41, 46–49
Reichard, Ulrich, 161
reindeer, 316, 354, 358
reinforcement, 88
relative dating methods, 218
repressor protein, 47
reproductive effort, energy requirement and, 126
reproductive isolation, 82, 83, *85,* 86
reproductive strategies, evolution of, 147–49
resource defense territoriality, 132, 133
resting, 130, *131*

Reznick, David, 19
rheas, 148
rhesus macaques, 183, 205
rhinoceros, 279, 318
ribonucleic acid, *see* RNA
ribosomes, 44, 49
Richerson, Peter, 420
Rieseberg, Loren, 85
Rift Valley, Kenya, 234
Rightmire, G. Philip, 324, *325*
ring-tailed lemurs, 111, *112, 119,* 163
RNA (ribonucleic acid), 41, 44, 332
    messenger, 44, *45, 47*
Robbins, Martha, 155
Roberts, Eila, 168
rock climbing, 426, *426,* 427
rock shelters, 320
rodents, 226, 313, 420
Romania, 345
Ross, Corinna, 187
Rungwecebus primates, 140
RUNX2, 338
Russia, *330,* 338, 354, 355
Rwanda, 141, 167

saber-toothed cat, 16, 287
sagittal crest, 256, *256,* 260, 305
sagittal keel, 305, *305*
Sahara Desert, 306
Sahelanthropus tchadensis, 241, *241,* 243, 245
Sahul, 316, 343, *343,* 351
Saint-Césaire, France, 352
saki monkeys, 121, 226
salmon, 194, 354, 429, *429,* 430
Saltzman, Wendy, 402
Sambungmachan, Java, 313
Samburupithecus kiptalami, 234
sampling variation, *71,* 71–72, *72*
sandpipers, spotted, 148
Santos, Laurie, 205, 206
scapulae, 255, *255,* 317
scavenging, hunting and, 283–85
Schaafhausen, Hermann, 316
Schick, Kathy, 270, 278, 299
schizophrenia, 368
Schmitt, Daniel, 246
Schmitt, David, 409
Schöningen, Germany, 310
sciatic notch, 246
sea horses, 148, *148,* 158
seashells, as personal adornment, 321, *321*
secondary compounds, 127, 129
selection:
    artificial, 18, *19, 21*
    correlated response to, 69, *70*
    detecting from DNA sequences, 377–79
    group selection, 176, 177
    individual, 10–11
    intersexual, 158
    intrasexual, 158, 159–61
    life history and, 196

of Upper Paleolithic, *351,* 351–53, *352, 353*
   wear patterns on, 278–79, *279, 282*
toothcomb, 222
torque, 239, *240*
tortoises, 313
Toth, Nicholas, 270, 278, 299
toxins, 126, 127
tradeoffs, life history theory and, 194–97
traditions, social learning and, 422
traits, *see* characters
transfer RNA (tRNA), 44, 332
transposable elements, 365
Tree of Life, 91–93
tree shrews, Belanger's, *213*
Triassic period, 211
Trinchera Dolina, Spain, 310, 314
Trivers, Robert, 174, 188
tropical forests, 129
   destruction of, *123,* 140, *140*
tryptophan, *42*
Tschermak, Erich, 27
tuberculosis, 372, 374
tubers, *279,* 298, 302
Tugen Hills, Kenya, *249*
turban shell, *15*
Turkana (nomadic herders), 430, *430, 431,* 433
Turkanapithecus, 232
turtles, 311
Tutin, Caroline, 268
Tuttle, Russell, 254
twins, *150,* 162, 382–83, *383*
   chimerism and, 187

uakari monkeys, 121
Uganda, 231
   Kibale Forest, 125, *130,* 134, 189
Ukraine, 354
ultimatum game, 432, *432,* 433
Uluzzian tool industry, 352, *352*
ungulates, 226
unlinked loci, 37
Upper Paleolithic people, 349
   burials of, *356*
   cave painting of, 357, 358, *358*
   clothing for, 355, 358
   diets of, 354
   injury and disease in, 356–57
   life expectancy of, 356
   Neanderthals compared with, 355–57
   population density of, 356
   ritual burials and, 357
   subsistence economy of, 354
   toolmaking of, *351,* 351–53, *352, 353*
uracil, 44
uranium-lead dating, 217

valine, *42,* 43
van Noordwijk, Maria, 154
van Schaik, Carel, 154, 167, 197
variants, 25

variation, 47
   in adaptation, 12–17
   in anatomically modern humans, 332, *334,* 336
   behavioral plasticity and, 66–68
   in chimpanzees, 336, *336*
   in complex phenotypic traits, 381–88
   continuous, 12, 13, 21, 60–62
   Darwin on, 20–22
   discontinuous, 12, 21, 22
   environmental, 62, 368, 369, 381
   expressed, *64*
   genetic drift and, 337, *337*
   geographic patterns of, *335,* 336, *336,* 339–41, *340, 341*
   hidden, *64,* 64–65
   human, dimensions of, 368–69
   loci and, 60–62
   maintenance of, 63–65
   mutations and, 63–64, 337
   recombination and, 33
   sampling, *71,* 71–72, *72*
   sexual reproduction and, 64
   see also genetic diversity; genetic variation
Venezuela, 163, 167, 186, 273
vertebrates, 49, 74, *92,* 367
vervet monkeys, 122, *130,* 134, 135, 186, 201, 202, 204
   alarm calls of, 135
   coalition formation and, 190
   mating system of, 163
   reciprocal altruism and, 189
   social learning in, 423
Vilas Ruivas, Portugal, 320
Vindaja Cave, Croatia, 337
Virchow, Rudolf, 316
Virginia opossum *(Didelphis virginiana),* 195
Virunga Mountains, *124,* 167
vitamins, 127, *128*
viviparity, 109
Voight, Benjamin, 379
vultures, *285*

Walker, Alan, 260, 297, 299–300
wallabies, 246
Ward, Carol, 234
warfare, as large-scale cooperation, 429–30
warthogs, 299, 301
water, 127, *128*
waterbirds, 224
Watson, James, 37
Watts, David, 189
weathering, 287, *287*
Wedgwood, Josiah, II, 5, 405
Weinberg, Wilhelm, 57
Westermarck, Edward, 403, 404
whales, 211, 422
Wheeler, Peter, 247
White, Tim, 242, 243, 246, 250, 251, 255, 292, 343, 344
Whiten, Andrew, 154, 423
Widdig, Anja, 181
wild dogs, 284
wildebeests, 279, *283*